Contents

1. Introduction to Economics 1

Microeconomics

How do sellers price their goods for their buyers?

2. The Consumer 11
3. Introduction to Demand 22
4. Introduction to Supply 42
5. Equilibrium 58
6. Elasticity of Demand and Supply 69

How much does it cost to be in business?

7. Costs of Production 91

Who else is in your market?

8. Perfect Competition 116
9. Imperfect Competition 129
10. Monopoly 140
11. Price Discrimination 151
12. Oligopoly 158

How do products actually get to the shelf ... and why does anybody put them there?

13. Introduction to the Factor Markets 168
14. Land 180
15. Labour 189
16. Capital 205
17. Enterprise and Profit 221

Macroeconomics

"Money makes the world go round..."

18. Money and Banking 229

"What impact has the economy on you, your C.V. and your pocket?"

19. Measuring National Income 254
20. The Determination of National Income 271

"Can you afford your weekly shopping basket?"

21. Inflation 293
22. Employment 308

Where does the government get and spend its money?

23. Government Budget and Finances 324
24. The Role of Government: Economic Aims and Policies 355
25. Economic Development and Growth 380

The economic world around us...

26. Economics of Population 395
27. International Trade 418
28. Balance of Payments and Foreign Exchange 444
29. The Global Economic System 465

Rolling back the years...

30. Schools of Economic Thought 482

Preparation for YOUR Leaving Cert Exam

31. Exam Technique and Preparation 492

Glossary of Economic Terms and Definitions 496
Index 511

POSITIVE ECONOMICS
LEAVING CERTIFICATE

SUSAN HAYES, TRUDIE MURRAY, BRIAN O'CONNOR

Edco

First published 2012
The Educational Company of Ireland
Ballymount Road
Walkinstown
Dublin 12

A member of Smurfit Kappa Group plc

© Susan Hayes, Trudie Murray, Brian O'Connor, 2012
ISBN 978-184536-471-7

Editor: Kristin Jensen
Design: Outburst Design
Layout: Compuscript Ltd.
Cover Design: Graham Thew Design
Illustrations: Derry Dillon
Photographs: iStock photos, Shutterstock, Getty Images, Photocall Ireland, Alamy and as referenced on individual pages.
1 2 3 4 5 6 7 8 9

The publishers have made every effort to trace and correctly acknowledge copyright holders. If, however, they have inadvertently overlooked any, they will be pleased to make the necessary arrangements at the first opportunity. The publishers and authors would like to acknowledge the assistance of the Central Statistics Office, Central Bank of Ireland, International Monetary Fund, European Union, United Nations, Fine Gael, Fianna Fáil, nationmaster.com, The Competition Authority and Eurostat.

All rights reserved. No part of this publication may be reproduced, stored in a retrieval system, or transmitted in any form or by any means, electronic, mechanical, photocopying, recording or otherwise, without either the prior permission of the Publisher or a licence permitting restricted copying in Ireland issued by the Irish Copyright Licensing Agency, 25 Denzille Lane, Dublin 2.

Web references in this book are intended as a guide for teachers. At the time of going to press, all web addresses were active and contained information relevant to the topics in this book. However, The Educational Company of Ireland and the authors do not accept responsibility for the views or information contained on these websites. Content and addresses may change beyond our control and pupils should be supervised when investigating websites.

ACKNOWLEDGEMENTS
We would like to say a heartfelt thanks to Eoghan O'Leary & Ted O'Sullivan for your valuable, insightful and helpful feedback as we went through the process.

We would dearly like to thank our loved ones, Ciarán Keohane, Kate and Caoimhe O'Connor, and Ardle Culleton. You have all stuck with us throughout the months of work that went into this creation! For your patience, encouragement, perseverance, despite being authors, we don't think there really are any words. This book is for you.

05M18

Foreword

You are at an exciting stage where the study you do now will have an impact on the rest of your life. Economics is a subject that will give you a different perspective on how you view the world. After all, economics forms the basis for governments to make decisions, companies to employ people and for people to spend or not to spend. It affects how much VAT you pay on a bag of crisps, how easy it is for you to get a summer job and also the points you will need to get your course in college.

We wrote this book with your needs as a student very much in mind. We understand that economics is a dynamic subject, constantly changing, and that it can be difficult to keep up, especially when you are busy juggling lots of other subjects. That's why this book bulges with suggestions of how you can stay up to date. We have minimised the time that you and your teachers need to spend finding the right sources of information by detailing everything you need to know and directing you to where you can find it. While we three authors come from different backgrounds, we were all once economics students ourselves which is why we all agreed that we wanted each and every key concept to be illustrated by an example. We know that economics can be quite a theoretical subject, but its practical implications are what really affect our lives. We wanted to reflect that so each colourful chapter is packed full of vibrant examples, complete with handy 'remember' boxes, case studies and a detailed glossary of economic terms and definitions.

Finally, we understand that your ultimate goal is to achieve the best possible mark in your Leaving Certificate exam and that there is one key way to do that – maximise your performance. As a result, every chapter is exam focused: we have exam-style examples throughout and past exam questions at the end of each chapter. We have structured the chapters so that your learning and revision are as seamless as possible. In fact, you can visit www.edcoexamcentre.ie, and use the free online test facility, to access multiple choice quizzes and activities to test your knowledge of the course. These tests are an easy and quick way for you to revise and will ensure that your 'economic muscles' are well exercised and fighting fit.

Economists are often expected to predict the future. We don't expect you to do that, but in terms of Leaving Certificate Economics we have given you all the tools that you need to create your own future.

The Authors:

Trudie M. Murray, B.Sc, M.Sc, MA, M.Phil, P.G.D.E, MMII

Trudie Murray teaches Economics and Business at St Patrick's College, Cork City. She has previously tutored at UCC and has worked on a number of occasions with the School of Entrepreneurship in the Faculty of Business at Dublin Institute of Technology. Trudie was an Assistant Advising Examiner in Higher Level Leaving Certificate Economics for a number of years and has presented the Marking Scheme Conference to Cork teachers and members of the BSTAI (Business Studies Teachers' Association of Ireland) in the Cork Education Centre on a number of occasions. For the past three years she has co-presented the BSTAI Student Revision Conference on Economics in UCC. Trudie is also secretary of the Cork Branch of the BSTAI.

Brian O'Connor, B.Comm., B.A., M.Sc., H.Dip. in Ed.

Brian O'Connor enjoys teaching Economics and Accounting at Douglas Community School, Cork City, and has over 30 years' experience. Brian was an Assistant Advising Examiner in Higher Level Leaving Certificate Economics and has reviewed the Economics Leaving Certificate Exam papers for a number of years on behalf of the BSTAI. For the past four years he has co-presented the BSTAI Student Revision Conference on Economics in UCC.

Susan Hayes B.Sc.

Susan Hayes is Managing Director of Hayes Culleton – an international financial training and educational consultancy company, specialising in E-Learning. She has a B.Sc. in Financial Maths & Economics and is a regular contributor to the Professional Development Services for Teachers. She regularly contributes to RTÉ, Newstalk, Today FM and other national and international media outlets, speaking on matters relating to economics, the stock market, banking, entrepreneurship and finance.

Online Teacher's Resources

With this edition of *Positive Economics*, we provide an online teacher's e-book version of the text. Embedded in this e-book is a range of additional resources designed to support your work in the classroom.

edco DIGITAL

Online Teacher's Resources

Gain access to *Positive Economics* **Interactive Textbook** online, a comprehensive set of free eLearning materials to aid lesson plans, revision and exam preparation:

- Weblinks
- Solutions by chapter
- Powerpoints
- Podcasts
- Scenario analysis

Resources are **embedded in the Interactive Textbook** helping you to deliver stimulating lessons in your classroom, in an **easy-to-use, hassle-free way.**

Register Now!
www.edcodigital.ie

You can find all resources on **www.edcodigital.ie**, our online teacher centre, which hosts a wide range of our textbooks, additional resources and partner resources for onscreen use by teachers.

Edco Resources

Here are some of the features included with the online e-book:

 Allows you to view the entire textbook page by page, skip to a certain page or use the contents to jump to a chapter.

Toolbar: The moveable onscreen toolbar contains tools to write, zoom, add text, create links, add notes and lots more.

Your Resources: You can upload documents, images and weblinks, which are stored in the easily searched file manager, unique to each e-book. Other tools like the blank page, save and bookmark tool allow teachers to tailor each book to suit their own needs. These resources will help you to build a bank of your own personal resources, to support your lessons.

www.edcodigital.ie

Chapter 1 | Introduction to Economics

Specific Learning Outcomes

At the end of this chapter, students should be able to:

- [ ] Understand the scope, purpose and limitations of economics as a science.

- [ ] Understand economic concepts such as wealth, income, welfare, scarcity, choice, wants, needs, opportunity cost and factors of production.

- [ ] Explain how economists draw up theories by using the Inductive and Deductive methods.

- [ ] Differentiate between economic laws and absolute truths.

- [ ] Identify the differences between factor, intermediate and final markets and give examples.

- [ ] Differentiate between microeconomics and macroeconomics.

- [ ] Differentiate between economic systems.

Introduction

- What would happen if none of the ATMs had any cash?

- Should we save our money under the mattress or in a bank?

- How can €100 be turned into €1,000 ... for real?

- Mobile phone charges to halve – government opens up the market to competition.

- If 1,000 extra places (supply) were made available to study medicine (demand) in each university, would the points required fall?

- In 2010, the value of US foreign direct investment in Ireland stood at US$235 billion, more than the US total for China, India, Russia and Brazil (the BRIC countries) combined. As a result of our connections with the US, many American companies choose to base their European headquarters here. Could one of them be your first employer?

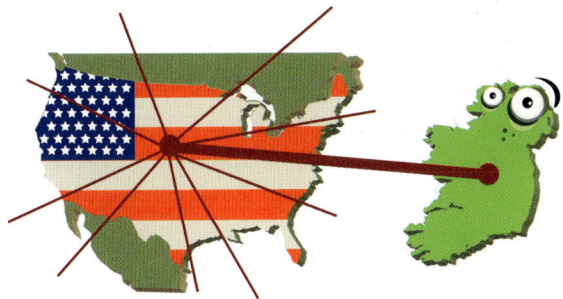

- Why do shops offer student discounts?

Economics is a fascinating subject that can answer all of the above questions and many, many more. All of the above statements relate to particular areas of the syllabus that will be studied throughout the course of this book.

Did you know that economics is actually a science? But what is a science? A science can be described as a body of knowledge on a certain topic. This store of knowledge grows as new research is undertaken and new theories are formulated.

Positive Economics

Economics is actually a social science because it studies some aspect of human behaviour. We usually associate science with things like the law of gravity, the respiratory system and chemical reactions. In each of these cases, the same outcome is guaranteed. For example, because of the law of gravity, if your pen falls off the desk, it will always hit the ground. We can be less definite in our study of human behaviour because humans don't always behave in the same way.

Normally, if the price of something falls, more people will buy it because it's cheaper. For example, if the price of a can of cola falls from €0.80 to €0.60 in your school shop, some students might consume more in a week. However, people who prefer an orange mineral wouldn't drink more cola even if the price halved. Therefore, we can be less definite about how humans will behave when circumstances change, and that's why economics is called a social science.

We are now going to develop a toolkit of ideas to study economics.

Needs and Wants

A **NEED** is immediate, e.g. food and shelter, which we *need* to survive.

Consumers distinguish between needs and wants. We make a living by working. We work because there are lots of things we desire, e.g. clothes, a new car and holidays. We can earn money by working and then pay for things that we would like to have. We can divide these desires into needs and wants.

A **WANT** is anything in excess of needs which is not necessary for our survival, e.g. a foreign holiday or a new car.

OPPORTUNITY COST is the cost of foregone alternatives (choice).

Do you have enough money to buy all the things you want? Probably not! We all have a limited income (scarce resources) and don't have enough money to buy everything we desire. Since our income is scarce, we must make a choice between which goods and services we buy. For example, it's a warm summer day and you're hot and thirsty. You have €1 in your pocket. Do you buy a drink or an ice cream? You don't have enough for both products. Therefore, you must choose. In economics, we refer to the product that you **don't buy** as the opportunity cost.

Opportunity cost is central to our study of economics because it involves making a **choice** on **scarce resources**.

Alfred Marshall (an economist we will study in Chapter 13) defined economics as 'the study of man in the ordinary business of life'.

A more formal definition is:

ECONOMICS is a social science which studies the allocation of scarce resources which have alternative uses.

Examples of opportunity cost:
- Do you buy the drink or the ice cream?
- Do your parents decide to go on holiday or upgrade the car?
- Does the government decide to build a new hospital or a new school?
- Does the Minister for Finance decide to increase income tax or reduce government spending?

How Does Economics Work?

Sciences always have theories. A theory is drawn up after analysis of the facts relating to a particular problem. For example, many economies at some stage may experience unemployment. Economists investigate why and might conclude that people lose their jobs when wages get too high. This is a theory.

How Do Economists Draw Up These Theories?

A problem is identified and existing information is examined, e.g. unemployment of 25%. An economist must decide to use the **deductive** or the **inductive** method of research.

Deductive
- Step 1: Start with statements (hypotheses) that we believe are true.
- Step 2: Apply this statement to a situation.
- Step 3: Arrive at a conclusion. This conclusion will be accurate assuming the original statement is accurate.

Positive Economics

> **Example**
>
> - Step 1: All animals will die.
> - Step 2: A rabbit is an animal.
> - Step 3: Therefore, all rabbits will die.
>
>
>
> An application to economics would be:
>
> - Step 1: If the price of a product increases, fewer people will buy it.
> - Step 2: A can of cola is a product.
> - Step 3: If the price of the cola increases, fewer people will buy it.
>
> Clearly, we can see a movement from a **general** statement (if the prices of products increase, the quantity sold will fall) to a **particular** situation (if the price of the cola increases, the quantity sold will fall).

Inductive

In inductive reasoning, we examine real-life situations and come up with generalisations.

- Step 1: The researcher collects data.
- Step 2: The researcher looks for a pattern.
- Step 3: From this pattern, a conclusion is drawn, which then becomes an economic law.

> **Example**
>
> - Step 1: A researcher examines attendance at 40 football grounds.
> - Step 2: The researcher spots the pattern that there was a 50% drop in attendance when games were played on Tuesdays.
> - Step 3: This leads to a general principle that in terms of gate receipts, Tuesdays are bad for football matches.
>
> Clearly, we can see a movement from **particular** cases (gate receipts from football grounds on Tuesdays) to the **general** statement (Tuesdays are not good for football games).

Economic Laws

Economic laws are constructed from deductive and inductive theories. These laws are statements that under certain conditions, certain people will behave in certain ways. Economic laws do not apply to **everybody**. They are not absolute truths, but rather are general statements about human behaviour, e.g. not everyone will buy more cola if the price falls because they might prefer orange minerals. However, **in general**, those who do like cola will buy more of it as the price decreases. We will study this in more detail in Chapter 3.

The Four Factors of Production

To produce any good, we need lots of inputs, e.g. a ham and cheese roll sold in Pat's Deli. Can you think of the inputs that would go into making a ham and cheese roll?

- The ingredients, including ham and cheese, which originate from farm animals.
- The deli assistant needs to butter the bread, put the ham and cheese into the roll, wrap it up and process the transaction.
- Before the shop opens, the ingredients need to be stored in the fridge.
- Pat, the entrepreneur who owns the deli, decided to open a local shop selling food products. If this decision wasn't taken, people would need to go elsewhere to get their sandwich for lunch.

Can you think of any more inputs?

It is much easier to classify the inputs into production under four main headings. These are called the factors of production: land, labour, capital and enterprise.

- **Land: Anything provided by nature that helps in the production of wealth**, e.g. the farm animals in the above example. Other examples include the sea, fields, air and climate.
- **Labour: The human effort involved in creating wealth**, e.g. the deli assistant, a plumber, a teacher.
- **Capital: Anything man-made that assists in the production of wealth**, e.g. a fridge, machinery, computers and vehicles.
- **Enterprise: The factor of production which takes the initiative and bears the risk involved in setting up a business to produce goods**, e.g. Pat in Pat's Deli.

A further detailed examination of each factor of production will be covered in Chapters 14 to 17.

Markets

A market is where buyers and sellers meet. It can be a physical place like a car boot sale in your local area or it can be virtual, like eBay. Markets answer the following questions:

- What is to be produced?
- How is it to be produced?
- For whom is it to be produced?

The following are the main types of markets.

Factor Markets

Factor markets are markets in which the factors of production are bought and sold. Each individual product starts off its life requiring land, labour, capital and enterprise. An entrepreneur or manager buys these factors to begin the process of making the good.

> **Example**
>
> A group of young people are employed to pick oranges off trees in Portugal and are paid 5c per orange.

Intermediate Markets

Intermediate markets deal with partly finished goods. People either buy goods on this market to sell them on to somebody else at a small profit, who will then make them ready for sale, or they can add value themselves to sell at a greater price.

> **Example**
>
> The business owner who employed the young people to pick the oranges sells the oranges to a large juicing company at 10c per orange.

Final Markets

The buying and selling of finished goods takes place in final markets.

> **Example**
>
> The juicing company compresses the orange juice into cartons and sells it for €1.50 per litre in its own shop.

Factor market   *Intermediate market*   *Final market*

Economic Systems

Earlier in the chapter we stated that making a choice is one of the main elements in economics. We have to choose what types of goods we produce because resources are scarce. These decisions can be made:

- Entirely by private individuals (a free enterprise economy).
- Entirely by the government (a centrally planned economy).
- A combination of both (a mixed economy).

Free Enterprise
A **free enterprise economy** is where private businesspeople make the decisions on the goods and services to be produced, e.g. the US. (This is sometimes known as a capitalist system.)

The US is a free enterprise economy

Command/Centrally Planned Economy
A **command/centrally planned economy** is where the government makes the decisions on the goods and services to be produced, e.g. Cuba and North Korea. (This is sometimes known as a communist/socialist system).

Cuba has a centrally planned economy

Mixed Economy
A **mixed economy** is one that incorporates elements of both central planning (government involvement) and private enterprise in its economic system, e.g. in Ireland, RTÉ is government owned and Dunnes Stores is privately owned.

Ireland has a mixed economy

Other Economic Concepts

In economics, there are other basic concepts that assist in our understanding of the subject.

- **Income:** People work so that they earn an income. This **income is a flow of wealth because it is received regularly for providing a factor of production**, e.g. a waitress receives an hourly wage for providing labour.
- **Wealth: Wealth is the total value of all assets owned by an individual or group of people**. It includes intangible (e.g. musical talent) and tangible (e.g. car) assets.

- **Welfare**: **Welfare is the overall condition of well-being of an individual or group of people.** It includes both a person's material well-being and psychological and moral happiness/comfort.

Branches of Economics

Microeconomics studies how an individual producer (one firm) and a consumer make decisions and attempt to solve their economic problems. For example, a microeconomist examines how a student spends their income from a part-time job and how a company reduces costs to increase profits.

Macroeconomics deals with aggregates (totals) in an economy. For example, a macroeconomist analyses the *rate* of employment, the *rate* of inflation, the *amount* of exports and the *rate* of immigration in an economy.

Economic Statements

Economists appear regularly in the media making statements about various aspects of the economy. There are two types of these statements:

- When **factual** statements are made, e.g. unemployment of 10%, these are known as **positive** statements because they state what is or was and can be confirmed or denied by the analysis of the facts.

- **Normative** statements go beyond the facts and state what ought to happen (**value judgements**), e.g. the government should spend more money and increase the national debt to create employment. Here, the economist is giving us an opinion on their beliefs.

Questions

Short Questions

1. Define opportunity cost.
2. Define economics.
3. Define a mixed economy. State two examples of economic activity which support the view that Ireland is a mixed economy.
4. Differentiate between deductive and inductive theories and give an example of each.
5. List the four factors of production.
6. Identify the factors of production in a hotel.
7. Define and give examples of factor, intermediate and final markets.
8. Differentiate between microeconomics and macroeconomics.
9. Define the following: wealth, income and welfare.
10. Give three examples of positive and normative statements.
11. Define a free enterprise system and give one economic advantage of this system.

Chapter 2 | The Consumer

Specific Learning Outcomes

At the end of this chapter, students should be able to:

- ☐ Define economic goods.

- ☐ Explain the characteristics of economic goods.

- ☐ Explain and evaluate the assumptions underlying consumer behaviour.

- ☐ Explain and illustrate the concept of utility.

- ☐ Explain the concept of marginal utility.

- ☐ Define and illustrate the law of diminishing marginal utility.

- ☐ Explain and evaluate the assumptions underlying the law of diminishing marginal utility.

- ☐ Define and illustrate the principle of equi-marginal utility.

Positive Economics

Introduction

A **CONSUMER** is an individual who makes the decision whether to buy goods or services.

We will start our analysis of microeconomics with an examination of the factors that affect the purchasing of goods by the household. The household is any group of individuals whose purchasing decisions are made by one person. We refer to this person as the consumer.

UTILITY is the amount of benefit or satisfaction derived from the consumption of a good or service.

Assumptions Concerning Consumer Behaviour

In economics, we make certain assumptions about consumer behaviour.

- **It is assumed that consumers have limited incomes:** The consumer's income is not large enough to satisfy all their needs and wants. Therefore, the consumer must choose between those goods they wish to buy.

- **It is assumed that consumers seek to get maximum utility (satisfaction) from that income/obey the equi-marginal principle of consumer behaviour:** Consumers will spend their limited incomes in such a way that they will try to achieve the most satisfaction (utility) from the goods and services they purchase and receive the best value for money.

CASE STUDY: Drinking Tea!

Linda likes to drink tea. On a cold day after a brisk walk from work, the first cup of tea gives Linda maximum utility. However, the second cup of tea doesn't give as much utility as the first and the third gives even less. As she drinks more tea, the extra utility she receives from that extra cup of tea eventually begins to fall.

- **It is assumed that consumers will act rationally:** The consumer acts in a manner consistent with their preferences, e.g. if the person sees an identical commodity priced differently in two shops, they will buy the good at the lower price.

- **It is assumed that consumers are subject to the law of diminishing marginal utility.**

Characteristics of Economic Goods

To be considered an economic good, a commodity or service must have the following characteristics:

An **ECONOMIC GOOD** is a product or service which commands a price, derives utility and is transferable.

- **Price – it must command a price:** The good must be scarce in relation to the demand for it, i.e. there is not enough of it to satisfy the demand of all those who want it. For example, fresh air is not scarce – it is plentiful in supply – so people are not prepared to pay for it. It does not command a price.

- **Utility: The good must provide the consumer with some feeling of satisfaction** (e.g. chocolate bars). Consumers will not demand something that does not provide satisfaction, i.e. anything that is a nuisance or irritant, such as weeds in the garden.

- **Transferable: Ownership or benefit must be capable of being given from one person to another**. For example, you could buy a chocolate bar and give it to somebody. However, beauty or good health are not capable of being sold – they are not transferable.

A tennis raquet is an economic good

A talent at playing tennis is not an economic good

MARGINAL UTILITY (MU) is the addition to total utility (TU) brought about by the extra utility received caused by the consumption of one extra unit of a good. In other words, marginal utility refers to the extra satisfaction a consumer gets from consuming an extra unit of the good.

The Law of Diminishing Marginal Utility

Schedule of the Law of Diminishing Marginal Utility

From the table below, it is clear that in a given span of time, the first glass of water gives 20 units of utility to a thirsty athlete. A util is one unit of satisfaction. The marginal utility decreases to 12 utils when the athlete drinks a second glass of water. The marginal utility drops down to 2 utils when the athlete consumes a fourth glass of water.

Units of water	Total utility	Marginal utility
1st glass	20	0
2nd glass	32	12
3rd glass	40	8
4th glass	42	2

THE LAW OF DIMINISHING MARGINAL UTILITY states that as more units of a good are consumed, a point will be reached where marginal (extra) utility *eventually* begins to decline.

Assumptions Underlying the Law of Diminishing Marginal Utility

- **It applies only after a certain minimum (the origin) has been consumed:** The origin is the minimum quantity of the commodity that must be consumed and marginal utility begins to diminish only when this stage has been reached. For example, it's not the first segment of an orange, it must be the full orange that is consumed for utility to decline.

- **Sufficient time has not elapsed for circumstances to change:** The circumstances that could change include changes in tastes, the nature of the product and no gap in time between the consumption of successive units. For example, if a person eats four cream cakes in a row, each additional cream cake consumed will eventually give diminished marginal utility. However, if a person eats one on Monday, one on Thursday and one on Sunday, because of the time that has elapsed between the consumption of each extra cream cake, marginal utility may not diminish.

- **It assumes that income doesn't change:** If income rises, then the combination of goods purchased may change, affecting the marginal utility derived from the good.

- **It does not apply to addictive goods/medicines:** In the case of goods to which one becomes addicted, the law of diminishing marginal utility does not apply. The consumer may gain increasing marginal utility by consuming each additional unit.

Commodities that do not comply with the law of diminishing marginal utility:

- **Medicine:** Every dose may be just as important as the initial one and marginal utility does not decline.

- **Addictive goods**, e.g. alcohol or cigarettes: The consumer's marginal utility will not decline because each extra unit consumed brings the consumer constant/increasing marginal utility.

Example — The table below illustrates the law of diminishing marginal utility.

Number of goods consumed	1	2	3	4	5	6	7	8
Total utility in units	10	25	45	70	90	105	120	125
Marginal utility in units	0	15	20	25	20	15	15	5

Question: At what point does diminishing marginal utility set in?

Answer: When the fifth good is consumed/after the consumption of the fourth good.

Reason: This is because the marginal utility of the fifth good consumed declined by 5 units (25 – 20) compared to the fourth good consumed.

2: The Consumer

Example The table below illustrates the law of diminishing marginal utility.

Number of goods consumed	1	2	3	4	5	6
Total utility in units	30	65	85	100	110	115
Marginal utility in units	0					

Question: Complete the table and state the point after which diminishing marginal utility sets in.

Number of goods consumed	1	2	3	4	5	6
Total utility in units	30	65	85	100	110	115
Marginal utility in units	0	**35**	**20**	**15**	**10**	**5**

Answer: When the third good is consumed/after the consumption of the second good.

Reason: This is because the marginal utility of the third good consumed declined by 15 units (35 – 20) compared to the second good consumed.

Consumer Equilibrium

The consumer is in equilibrium when they follow the equi-marginal principle, i.e. to obtain maximum utility. A consumer must spend their income in such a way that the ratio of marginal utility to price is the same for all the commodities which they buy. Maximum utility is achieved when the consumer is obtaining the same utility from the last cent spent on each good.

EQUILIBRIUM is the condition where there is no tendency to change.

The Equi-marginal Principle/Law of Equi-marginal Returns

How does a consumer allocate their income? The equi-marginal principle illustrates how consumers allocate their income in such a way that the last cent spent on each good will bring the same marginal utility (consumer equilibrium).

The EQUI-MARGINAL UTILITY PRINCIPLE explains the behaviour of a consumer in distributing their limited income among various goods and services.

Positive Economics

Util = 1 unit of satisfaction

Formula: $MU_x / P_x = MU_y / P_y \ldots\ldots MU_n / P_n$

If Px (price of Good X) falls, then MUx/Px > MUy/Py, therefore consumers buy more of Good X. But as QD (quantity demanded) increases, MUx decreases. We will also see in Chapter 3 that this is why a demand curve slopes downwards – as price falls, more is bought as utility per penny increases.

Example Suppose a person has €5 to spend on two goods: tea and biscuits, both costing €1 each. The marginal utility derived from both of these goods is as shown in the table below.

Units of goods	MU of tea	MU of biscuits
1	10	12
2	8	10
3	6	8
4	4	6
5	1	3
	Total utility = 29 utils	Total utility = 39 utils

A rational consumer would like to get maximum satisfaction from €5. They can spend their money in three ways:

- €5 may be spent on tea only.
- €5 may be spent on biscuits only.
- Some may be spent on tea and some on biscuits.

$$\frac{\text{Marginal utility of tea}}{\text{Price of tea}} = \frac{\text{Marginal utility biscuits}}{\text{Price of biscuits}}$$

$$\frac{8}{1} = \frac{8}{1}$$

Therefore, the consumer obeys the equi-marginal principle. If the prudent consumer spends €5 on the purchase of tea, they get 29 utils. If they spend €5 on the purchase of biscuits, the total utility derived is 39 utils, which is higher than tea. In order to make the best of the limited resources, they adjust their expenditure.

- By spending €4 on tea and €1 on biscuits, they get 40 utils (10 + 8 + 6 + 4 + 12 = 40).
- By spending €3 on tea and €2 on biscuits, they derive 46 utils (10 + 8 + 6 + 12 + 10 = 46).
- By spending €2 on tea and €3 on biscuits, they get 48 utils (10 + 8 + 12 + 10 + 8 = 48).
- By spending €1 on tea and €4 on biscuits, they get 46 utils (10 + 12 + 10 + 8 + 6 = 46).

The rational consumer will spend €2 on tea and €3 on biscuits and will get maximum utility.

When they spend €2 on tea and €3 on biscuits, the marginal utilities derived from both of these goods is equal to 8.

Example

Let's suppose a person still has €5 to spend on two goods, tea and biscuits, but in this case, the price of tea is €1 and the price of biscuits is €2. The marginal utility derived from both of these commodities is as follows.

Units of goods	MU of tea	MUt/P	MU of biscuits	MUb/P
1	10	$\frac{10}{1} = 10$	12	$\frac{12}{2} = 6$
2	8	$\frac{8}{1} = 8$	10	$\frac{10}{2} = 5$
3	6	$\frac{6}{1} = 6$	8	$\frac{8}{2} = 4$
4	4	$\frac{4}{1} = 4$	6	$\frac{6}{2} = 3$
5	1	$\frac{1}{1} = 1$	3	$\frac{3}{2} = 1.5$

A rational consumer would like to get maximum satisfaction from €5. They should obey the equi-marginal principle and spend their money in the following way:

- The first item they would buy would be tea (10 utils per penny).
- The second item bought would be tea (8 utils per penny).
- The third item bought would be either tea or biscuits (6 utils per penny).
- To get maximum satisfaction, they buy 3 units of tea and 1 unit of biscuits with the budgetary constraint of €5.

$$\frac{\text{MU of tea}}{\text{Price of tea}} = \frac{\text{MU of biscuits}}{\text{Price of biscuits}}$$

$$\frac{6}{€1} = \frac{12}{€2}$$

Positive Economics

Question 4 (short), 2005 (16 marks)

A consumer in equilibrium buys 10 cups of coffee at €2 each and 10 phone cards at €6 each. The marginal utility of the cups of coffee is 5 utils. What is the marginal utility of phone cards? Show your workings.

Solution

$$\frac{\text{Marginal utility of coffee}}{\text{Price of coffee}} = \frac{\text{Marginal utility of phone cards}}{\text{Price of phone cards}}$$

$$\frac{5}{€2} = \frac{MUpc}{€6}$$

Therefore, MUpc (marginal utility of phone cards) = **15 utils**

Question 1(c), 2011 (25 marks)

The law of diminishing marginal utility states that as more of a product is consumed, eventually each additional unit of the good provides less additional utility (marginal utility).

(i) Explain **two** assumptions underlying the law of diminishing marginal utility.
(ii) A consumer in equilibrium buys 6 health bars at €0.80 each and 9 cartons of juice at €1.50 each. The marginal utility of the 6th health bar is 40 utils. Using the **equi-marginal principle of consumer behaviour**, calculate the marginal utility of the **ninth** carton of juice (show all your workings).

Solution

(i) Assumptions underlying the law of diminishing marginal utility:

- **It applies only after a certain minimum (the origin) has been consumed:** The origin is the minimum quantity of the commodity that must be consumed and marginal utility begins to diminish only when this stage has been reached. For example, it's not the first segment of an orange, it must be the full orange that is consumed for utility to decline.

- **Sufficient time has not elapsed for circumstances to change:** The circumstances that could change include changes in tastes, the nature of the product and no gap in time between the consumption of successive units. For example, if a person eats four cream cakes in a row, each additional cream cake consumed will eventually give diminished marginal utility. However, if a person eats one on Monday, one on Thursday and one on Sunday, because of the time that has elapsed between the consumption of each extra cream cake, marginal utility may not diminish.

- **It assumes that income doesn't change:** If income rises, then the combination of goods purchased may change, affecting the marginal utility derived from the good.

- **It does not apply to addictive goods/medicines:** In the case of goods to which one becomes addicted, the law of diminishing marginal utility does not apply. The consumer may gain increasing marginal utility by consuming each additional unit.

(ii) $$\frac{\text{Marginal utility of health bars}}{\text{Price of health bars}} = \frac{\text{Marginal utility of cartons of juice}}{\text{Price of cartons of juice}}$$

$$\frac{40}{€0.80} = \frac{MU_j}{€1.50}$$

Therefore, MU_j (marginal utility of juice) = **75 utils**

Question 1(c), 2005 (20 marks)

Assume that the average spending on energy by a low-income family is €40 weekly. The price of energy rises by 20% so that the same consumption by a low-income family would now cost €48 weekly.

The government is considering introducing one of the following policy measures to assist low-income families:

- Giving low-income families an increased allowance of €8 weekly (income supplement).
- Subsidising the producers of energy so that energy can continue to be sold at the initial price (price subsidy).

Which policy measure would you advise the government to take? Explain the economic reasons for your answer.

Solution

Giving low-income families an increased allowance of €8 weekly (income supplement)

1. **Cost efficient:** As the income supplement specifically targets low-income families, it is cost efficient and cheaper for the government than the price subsidy.

2. **Purchasing power maintained/no change to standard of living:** Low-income families will now receive an additional €8 weekly income. The family now has a choice in deciding how to allocate this. It can maintain existing energy consumption or economise on the use of energy and use the €8 in some alternative way.

3. **Efficient use of state scarce resources:** As government revenue is limited and there are many demands on it, the specific targeting of low-income families could lead to more efficient use of these scarce revenues.

4. **Efficient use of scarce resources by consumers:** As the price of energy rises, consumers seeing this may economise on energy use, thus saving scare resources.

OR

Subsidising the producers of energy so that energy can continue to be sold at the initial price (price subsidy)

1. **Protecting employment:** By using a price subsidy, the demand for energy will remain unchanged, so employment is protected.

2. **Prevent an increase in inflation/maintain competitiveness:** The government may use the price subsidy so that energy prices remain unchanged, hence maintaining price stability and ensuring that our competitiveness is not affected, subject to EU rules.

3. **Pressure on employees for greater cost efficiencies/maintain partnership agreements:** The government may use this price subsidy as leverage for achieving cost reductions within the industry. This could involve encouraging employees to face cutbacks/rationalisation or encouraging employees and trade unions to continue with partnership agreements in return for maintaining price stability.

Question 1(a)(ii), 1999 (12 marks)

Give **two** examples of commodities which would not be considered as economic goods. Justify each choice with a brief explanation.

Solution

- **Fresh air:** Is plentiful in supply/not scarce, therefore it doesn't command a price.

- **Weeds:** Weeds don't provide you with utility and you are not prepared to pay a price for them.

- **Beauty/good health:** These are not transferable.

Questions

Short Questions

1. Define an economic good.
2. Define utility.
3. Define marginal utility.
4. Define the law of diminishing marginal utility.

Long Questions

1. Explain the characteristics that identify economic goods.
2. Evaluate the assumptions concerning consumer behaviour.
3. Outline the assumptions of the law of diminishing marginal utility.
4. Explain the equi-marginal principle.
5. The table below illustrates the law of diminishing marginal utility. Complete the table and state the point after which diminishing marginal utility sets in and explain your reasoning.

Number of units consumed	1	2	3	4	5	6
Total utility in units	20	45	65	80	90	95
Marginal utility in units	0					

6. The table below illustrates the law of diminishing marginal utility. Complete the table and state the point after which diminishing marginal utility sets in and explain your reasoning.

Number of goods consumed	1	2	3	4	5	6
Total utility in units	10	40	64	82	96	106
Marginal utility in units	0					

7. The table below illustrates the law of diminishing marginal utility. Complete the table and state the point after which diminishing marginal utility sets in and explain your reasoning.

Number of goods consumed	1	2	3	4	5	6
Total utility in units	5	28	45	58	68	74
Marginal utility in units	0					

8. In equilibrium a consumer buys 6 packets of biscuits at €1 each and 9 cakes at €2 each. The marginal utility of the 6 packets of biscuits is 8 utils. What is the marginal utility of cakes? Show your workings.
9. In equilibrium a consumer buys 5 cups of coffee at €2 each and 8 bagels at €3 each. The marginal utility of the 5 cups of coffee is 10 utils. What is the marginal utility of bagels? Show your workings.
10. In equilibrium a consumer spends all their income on two goods. They buy 7 units of Good A at €5 each and 20 units of Good B at €3 each. The marginal utility of the 7 units of Good A is 25 utils. What is the marginal utility of Good B? Show your workings.
11. In equilibrium a consumer purchases 10 units of Product X and 10 units of Product Y. The price of each unit of X is €10. The marginal utility of the tenth unit of X is 50 units and the marginal utility of the tenth unit of Y is 200 units. What is the price of each unit of Y?
12. In equilibrium a consumer purchases 5 units of Product A and 5 units of Product B. The price of each unit of A is €15. The marginal utility of the fifth unit of A is 60 units and the marginal utility of the fifth unit of B is 180 units. What is the price of each unit of Y?

Chapter 3: Introduction to Demand

Specific Learning Outcomes

At the end of this chapter, students should be able to:

- Distinguish between individual demand and market/aggregate demand.

- List and explain the determinants and influences of demand.

- Explain a demand schedule and illustrate by means of a demand curve.

- Demonstrate a change in any of the determinants of demand and interpret the outcomes using diagrams.

3: Introduction to Demand

Introduction

Consumers demand goods and services to satisfy their needs (e.g. food and clothing) and wants (e.g. cars and jewellery). Utility (satisfaction) is the basis of all demand. We will now take a further look at this concept of demand.

> **DEMAND** is the number of units of goods a consumer will buy at various prices.

The Law of Demand

> The **LAW OF DEMAND** states that an increase in price leads to a decrease in quantity demanded (P↑Q↓) or a decrease in price leads to an increase in quantity demanded (P↓Q↑). If the price of a bar of chocolate increased by €0.20 per bar, then the quantity demanded of chocolate bars purchased would fall (all else being equal).

> **CONSUMER SURPLUS** The benefit to consumers due to the difference between what consumers actually pay to consume a good and what they would have been willing to pay rather than go without the good. For example, if you want to purchase a house and have a budget of €300,000 and you manage to buy it for €280,000, you have a consumer surplus of €20,000.

> **INDIVIDUAL DEMAND:** Individual demand studies the quantities of a good that an individual consumer is prepared to buy at each price.
>
> **MARKET DEMAND/AGGREGATE DEMAND:** Aggregate demand shows the different quantities of a good that all consumers in the market are prepared to buy at each price. It is derived by adding together all the individual quantities demanded for the good.
>
> **DEMAND SCHEDULE:** A demand schedule is a table that shows the different quantities demanded for a good at various market prices at any given time.
>
> **INDIVIDUAL DEMAND SCHEDULE:** Lists the different quantities of a good that an individual consumer is prepared to buy at each price.
>
> **MARKET/AGGREGATE DEMAND SCHEDULE:** Lists the different quantities of a good that all consumers in the market are prepared to buy at each price. It is derived by adding together all the individual demand schedules for the good.

Positive Economics

Let's assume there are two consumers in the world, Chris and David. The table below illustrates the quantities of coffee they demand at various prices. For example, Chris is willing to pay 40c for 20 g of coffee, whereas David is willing to purchase 30 g at the same price. Their combined demand schedules make up the market aggregate demand schedule, e.g. at 40c the aggregate demand for coffee is 50 g.

Demand schedule for coffee			
Price (cent per g)	Chris's demand (g)	David's demand (g)	Total market demand (g)
20	25	40	65
40	20	30	50
60	15	25	40
80	10	20	30
100	5	15	20

A **DEMAND CURVE** is a graph illustrating the demand for a good at various prices at any given time.

- At higher prices, consumers are generally willing to purchase less than at lower prices.
- The demand curve is said to have a negative slope (downward sloping from left to right).

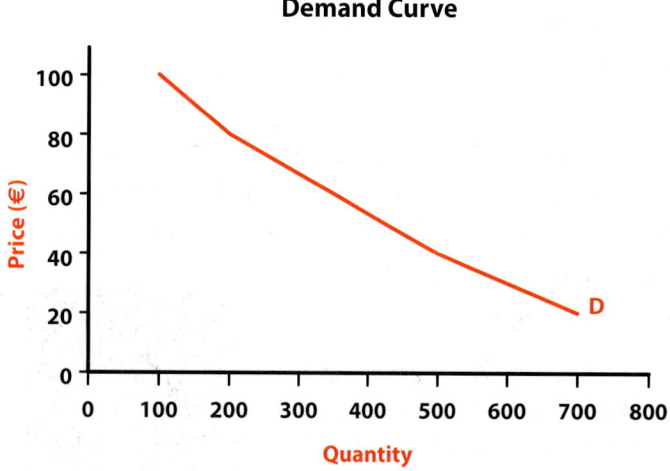

Demand Curve

Looking at the diagram, at €80, the quantity demanded of Good X is 200 units, while at €40 the quantity demanded of Good X is 500 units. This illustrates the law of demand – as prices increase, less quantity is demanded. On the other hand, the lower the price, the greater the quantity consumers are willing to purchase.

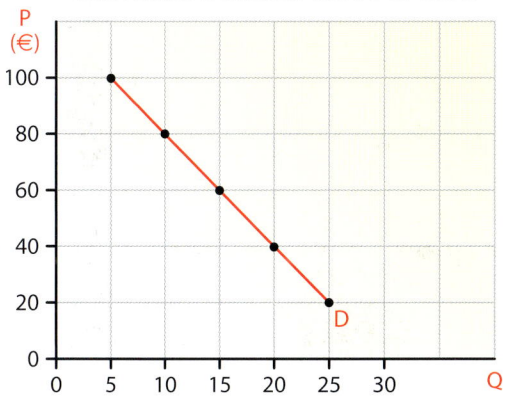
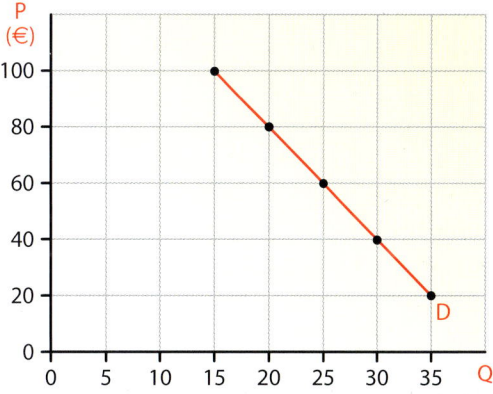
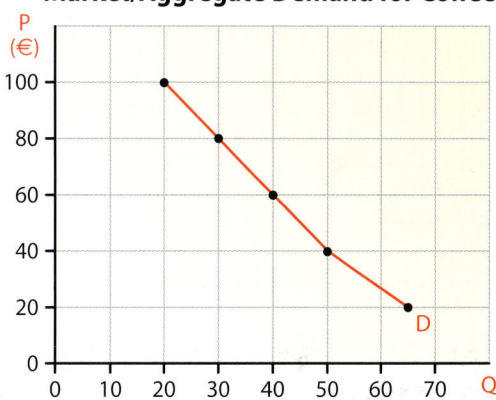

> **Note:**
> Make sure the diagrams of a demand curve are labelled (P, Q and D) and that they are graduated.

The above diagrams illustrate the individual demand curve for both Chris and David and the market/aggregate demand curve, calculated by adding all the individual demand curves together.

Other Types of Demand

- **Effective demand:** Consumers must be willing to buy *and* be capable of paying the price set by the supplier. It is demand backed by the necessary purchasing power (i.e. money).

- **Derived demand:** Derived demand occurs when one commodity is an essential part of another commodity and it is demanded not for its own sake but because it is required to manufacture another good. Examples include timber and furniture, steel and cars.

- **Composite demand:** Composite demand occurs when a commodity is required for a number of different uses, e.g. sugar.

- **Joint demand:** Joint demand occurs when the demand for one commodity is joined with the demand for another. Ordinarily, the commodities involved cannot be separated and in fact form a single good or can also be called complementary goods. Examples include cars and petrol, cameras and memory sticks, golf clubs and golf balls.

Positive Economics

Why Does the Demand Curve Slope Downwards from Left to Right?

It is because there is a negative (inverse) relationship between price and quantity demanded. As the price of a good falls, the consumer buys more of this cheaper good. This is because the marginal utility per penny spent on this good increases as price decreases and the consumer aims to maximise their total utility (satisfaction). The example below illustrates this concept.

Recall that a consumer is in equilibrium when they are following the law of equi-marginal returns/equi-marginal principle:

$$\frac{MU_x}{P_x} = \frac{MU_y}{P_y}$$

Example

The consumer buys two goods: X (Mu = 20 utils and P = €10) and Y (MU = 40 utils and P = €20).

$$\begin{array}{ccc} X & & Y \\ \frac{20}{10} & = & \frac{40}{20} \\ 2 & = & 2 \end{array}$$

Let's suppose the price of X falls to €5. Now what happens to the quantity demanded of X? The equi-marginal principle needs to be recalculated as:

$$\frac{MU_x}{P_x} > \frac{MU_y}{P_y}$$

$$\frac{20}{5} \neq \frac{40}{20}$$

$$4 \neq 2$$

Therefore, to restore equilibrium the consumer should buy more of the cheaper good (i.e. Good X), as they are receiving more utility per penny spent on X rather than Y. This explains the inverse (negative) relationship between price and quantity demanded and tells us why the demand curve slopes downwards from left to right.

3: Introduction to Demand

There Can Be Movement Along or a Shift in the Demand Curve

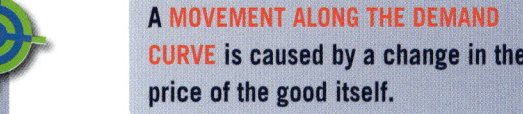

A **SHIFT IN THE DEMAND CURVE** is caused by a change in any non-price determinant of demand, e.g. a change in consumers' income.

A **MOVEMENT ALONG THE DEMAND CURVE** is caused by a change in the price of the good itself.

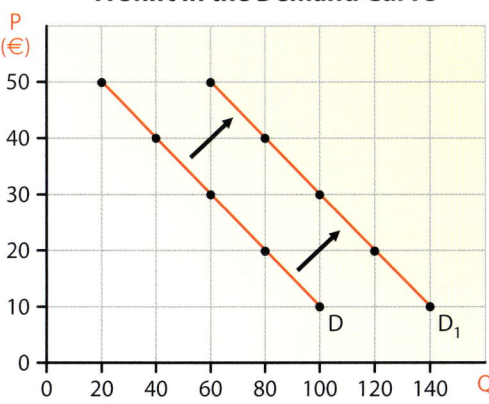

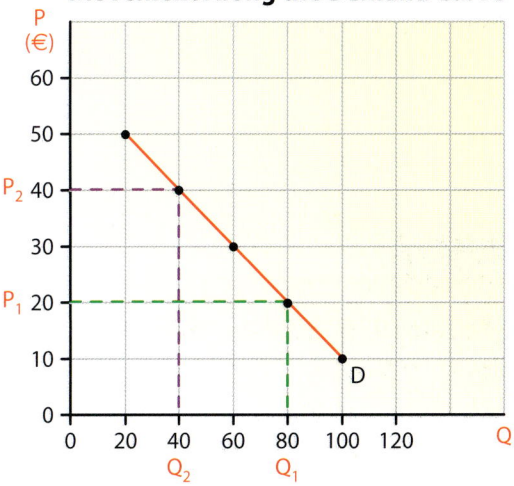

A shift shows the different quantities demanded at the same price. (These will be discussed later on in the chapter.) The curve can shift to the right or left. A rightward shift represents an increase in the quantity demanded (at all prices), while a leftward shift represents a decrease in the quantity demanded (at all prices).

A Rightward Shift

If there is an increase in quantity demanded for a good, the demand curve will **shift** to the **right** from D_1 to D_2, as seen in the graph below.

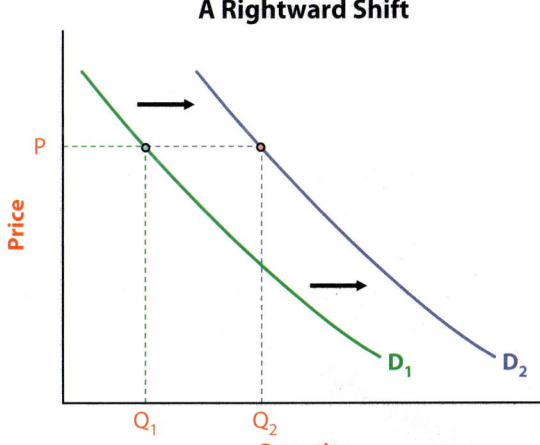

Positive Economics

A Leftward Shift

If there is a decrease in the quantity demanded for a good, the demand curve will **shift** to the **left** from D₁ to D₂, as seen in the graph below.

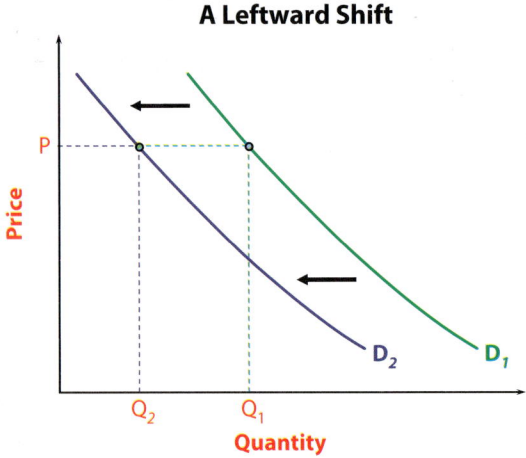

A Leftward Shift

Factors Affecting the Demand for a Good

Demand for a Good Depends on Its Own Price

If the price of a good rises, then the quantity demanded of that good falls. (If P ↑ then Q_D↓.) If the price of a normal good falls, then the quantity demanded rises. (If P ↓ then Q_D↑.)

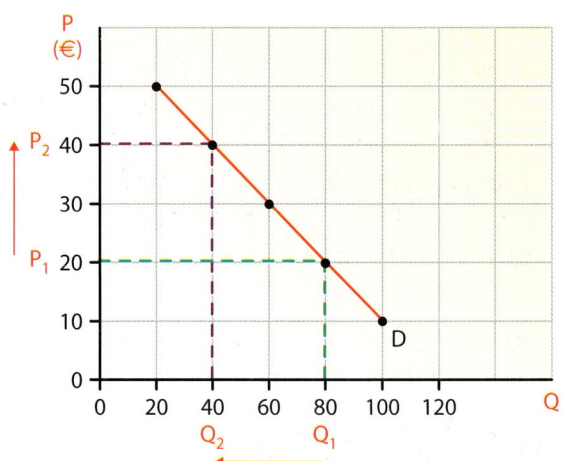

The Demand Function

$$D_x = f(P_x, P_{og}, Y, E, T, U, G)$$

P_x = the price of the good itself
P_{og} = price of other goods (price of complementary and substitute goods)
Y = income of the consumer
E = consumers' expectations concerning future prices
T = consumer tastes or preferences
U = unplanned factors
G = government regulations

From the diagram above you can see that at €20, there are 80 units of Good X demanded, but as the price increases to €40, the quantity demanded falls to 40 units.

3: Introduction to Demand

Demand for a Good Depends on the Price of Other Goods

COMPLEMENTARY GOODS

Complementary goods must be purchased together to satisfy a need or want and achieve maximum utility from the purchase. If the price of a complementary good rises, then the quantity demanded for this good falls.

> **COMPLEMENTARY GOODS** are goods that are used jointly. The use of one involves the use of the other, e.g. bread and butter, cars and petrol, cameras and memory cards.

Complementary Goods

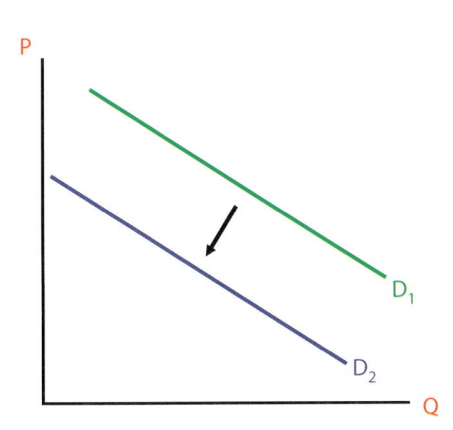

An increase in price of a complementary good causes the quantity demanded for Good X to fall

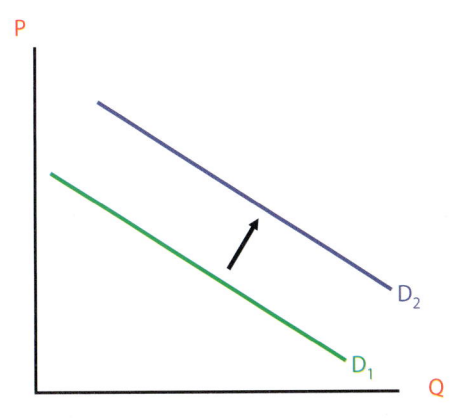

A fall in price of a complementary good causes the quantity demanded for Good X to rise

For example, an increase in the price of petrol will result in a decrease in the quantity demanded for high-powered cars. Since they are complementary goods, the price change of one will affect the demand for both.

SUBSTITUTE GOODS

If an increase in the price of one good leads to an increase in the quantity demanded for another good as an alternative, then the two goods are said to be substitutes. For example, an increase in the price of Berrys Tea will result in an increase in the demand for Lions Tea. As they are substitute goods, a price increase in one good will lead to an increase in the quantity demanded of its substitute.

> **SUBSTITUTE GOODS** are goods that satisfy the same needs and thus can be considered as alternatives to each other. Examples of substitute goods include butter and low-fat spread and different brands of tea, coffee, milk and breakfast cereals.

Positive Economics

Substitute Goods

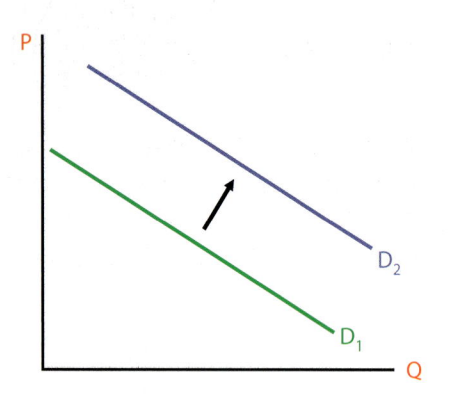

An increase in price of a substitute good causes the quantity demanded for Good X to rise

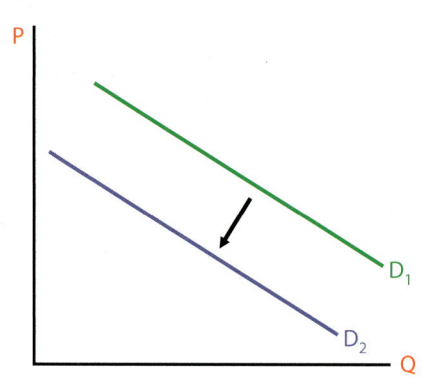

A fall in price of a substitute good causes the quantity demanded for Good X to fall

Demand for a Good Depends on Level of Income

As consumers' income rises, the quantity demanded of normal goods increases. As incomes fall, the quantity demanded for normal goods falls (positive income effect).

NORMAL GOODS

A rise in income causes more of these goods to be demanded, while a fall in income leads to a lower quantity of these goods being purchased.

> A **NORMAL GOOD** is a good that obeys the law of demand and which has a positive income effect.

Normal Goods

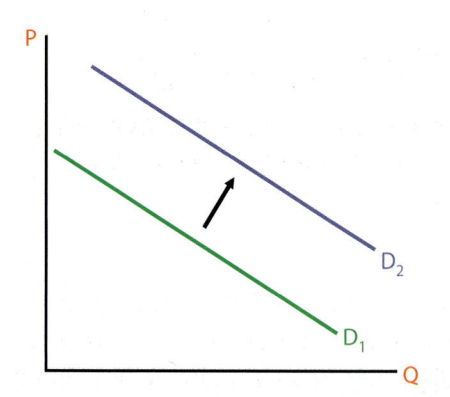

A rise in income causes the quantity demanded for a normal good to increase from D_1 to D_2

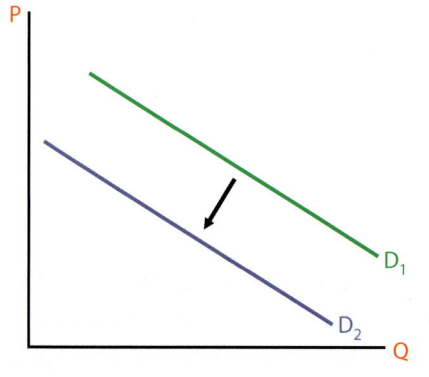

A fall in income causes the quantity demanded for a normal good to fall from D_1 to D_2

Inferior Goods

A rise in income causes less of these goods to be demanded, while a fall in income causes more of these goods to be demanded (negative income effect). Inferior goods are a minority of goods that are not necessarily of inferior quality. These goods are less attractive at high incomes and tend to be replaced by more expensive substitutes. For example, you might be shopping for a new dress and your income significantly increased. As a result, you may replace the department store dress (the inferior good) with a designer dress instead (its more expensive substitute).

> An **INFERIOR GOOD** is a good with a negative income effect.

Income effect: Positive for normal goods and negative for inferior goods.

Inferior Goods

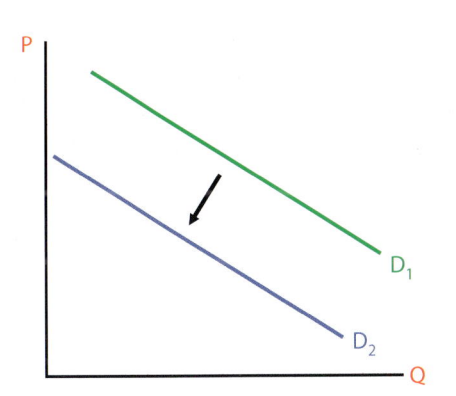

An increase in income causes the quantity demanded for an inferior good to fall from D_1 to D_2

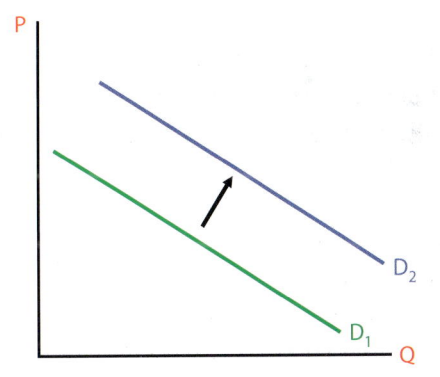

A decrease in income causes the quantity demanded for an inferior good to rise from D_1 to D_2

Demand for a Good Depends on Consumer Expectations

Consumers' expectations about the price or availability of the good at some stage in the future can affect the quantity demanded for a good. If a consumer expects that future prices are likely to be greater than they are at present, then there may be an increase in the quantity demanded for the good at each price, e.g. the price of oil, share prices in the stock market, the price of gold. The explanation below illustrates the factors that will cause a shift in the demand curve and will result in either an increase or decrease in the quantity demanded.

The quantity demanded for a good will increase and the demand curve will shift to the right if consumers expect:

1. The price of Good X to be higher in the future, e.g. stocks and shares.
2. A scarcity of Good X in the future, e.g. oil.

The quantity demanded for a good will decrease and the demand curve will shift to the left if consumers expect:

1. The price of Good X to be lower in the future, e.g. property prices in a recession.
2. A plentiful supply of Good X in the future, e.g. fruit after a good harvest.

Consumer Expectations

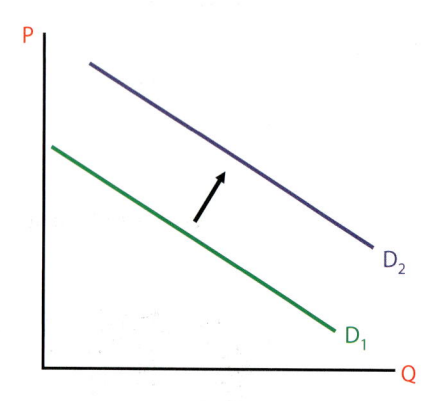

Quantity demanded for Good X will rise if consumers expect higher future prices, scarcity or higher future incomes

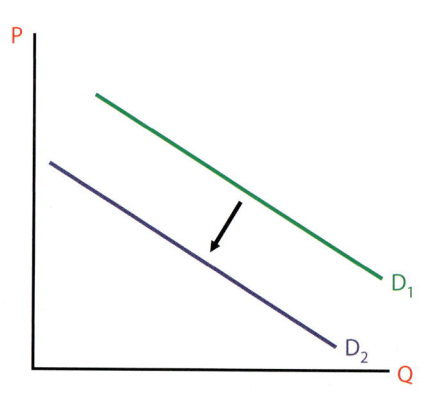

Quantity demanded for Good X will fall if consumers expect lower future prices, abundance or lower future incomes

Demand Depends on Consumer Tastes

Goods may become less or more appealing to consumers with the passing of time, as a person's taste is constantly changing. Some goods that were very much in demand in the past have now gone out of fashion completely, e.g. black and white televisions and certain types of clothes. If there is a change in taste or preferences in favour of the good, it causes an increase in the quantity demanded, which shifts the demand curve to the right. If there is a change in taste or preferences against the good, it causes a fall in quantity demanded, which shifts the demand curve to the left. Advertising attempts to influence taste in favour of the good.

Examples

- An advertising campaign for a diet cola which shows the low calorie content may cause a shift in the demand curve and increase the quantity demanded.
- If a celebrity endorses a new product, this may increase the quantity demanded for that good.
- If a new health study is published reporting that a product is bad for your health, this may decrease the quantity demanded for the product.

3: Introduction to Demand

Change in Taste

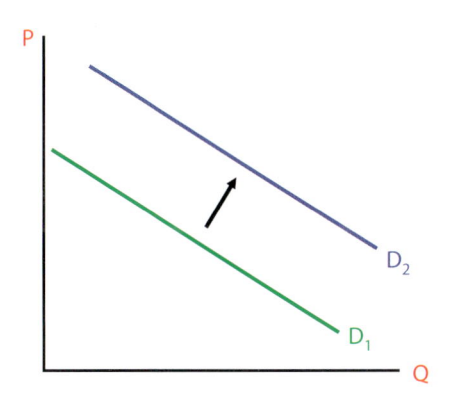

A change in taste in favour of a good causes quantity demanded to increase

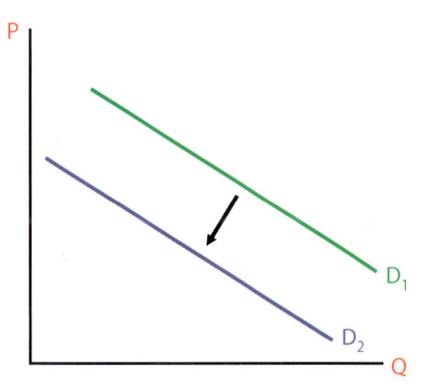

A change in taste against a good causes quantity demanded to fall

Demand for a Good Depends on Unplanned Factors

Occasionally there are circumstances where the change in the quantity demanded for a product cannot be anticipated.

- If there is a sudden heat wave, which would be an unplanned factor, there would be an increase in the quantity demanded for sunscreen and a decrease in the quantity demanded for home heating oil.

- If flash floods occur across the country, which would be an unplanned factor, there would be an increase in the quantity demanded for Wellingtons and flood gates.

Unplanned Factors

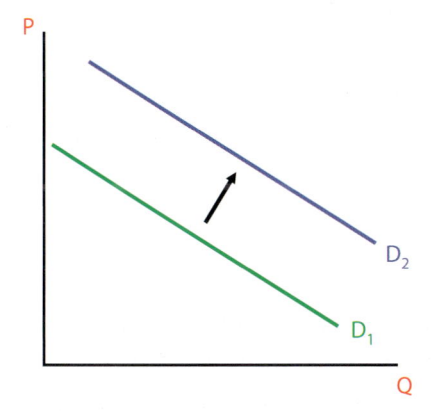

Factors such as weather can affect the demand for goods, e.g. a sudden heat wave would increase the quantity demanded for sunscreen

Positive Economics

Demand for a Good Depends on Government Regulations

The government can introduce new legislation that will affect consumer demand for goods and services. These laws can cause either an increase or a decrease in the quantity demanded.

- If the government initiates a programme that is aimed at increasing the consumption of a particular product, then the quantity demanded for this good will be affected and will increase.

- If the government implements a programme that is aimed at reducing the consumption of a particular product, then the quantity demanded for this good will decrease. Examples:
  - The smoking ban is aimed at curtailing tobacco consumption.
  - The plastic bag levy is aimed at reducing the consumption of plastic bags.

Government Regulations
Example: The smoking ban

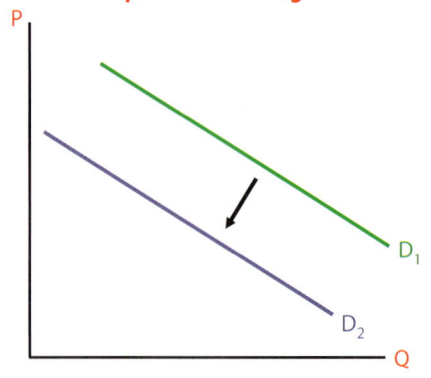

If the government implements a policy to reduce consumption, quantity demanded for Good X may fall

EXAM ✓ Question 1(c), 2010   (15 marks)

Many health advisors wish to reduce the consumption of soft drinks. Advise the Minister for Health and Children on possible economic actions that the Government could take to reduce the consumption of soft drinks.

Solution

- **Taxation: Increase taxes on soft drinks** – by increasing indirect taxes (e.g. VAT), the price will increase, which may cause demand to fall.

- **Education: Education/awareness campaign** – the government could increase spending on advertising campaigns to raise awareness of the problems that may result from the consumption of soft drinks. It could insist on more stringent product labelling.

- **Legislation: Introduce legislative changes** – it could ban the sale of soft drinks in schools and colleges as well as their sale in vending machines. It could place a quota on imports of such drinks.

- **Subsidisation: Subsidise the price of substitute goods/reduce VAT rates on substitute goods** – by doing this, the prices of substitute goods may be more attractive and this may lead to a drop in the demand for soft drinks, e.g. the subsidisation of milk in schools.

3: Introduction to Demand

Exceptions to the Law of Demand

Giffen Goods

For certain necessities, a rise in price causes an increase in quantity demanded, while a fall in price causes a fall in quantity demanded. Goods of lower quality make up a large part of the expenditure of low-income families, e.g. bread, rice and potatoes. As the price falls, real incomes (the amount of goods and services you can buy with your money) increase and families buy less of these lower-quality goods and increase their purchase of better-quality goods. As the price rises, they have less income to spend on other types of goods (i.e. the better-quality food), so they tend to increase their demand for Giffen goods (lower-quality goods) instead.

> **GIFFEN GOODS** are goods with a positive price effect, i.e. more is bought as the price rises and less is bought as the price falls.

Even if the price of bread (a Giffen good) is increased, people on low incomes would probably continue to buy the quantity they require even after the price increase. They would get the extra money by cutting back on something else that is less of a necessity.

Status Symbols/Snob Items/Ostentatious Goods/Goods of Conspicuous Consumption

Some commodities are attractive to some buyers because of their exclusiveness or high price. A rise in price makes them more exclusive and therefore more attractive to those with the income to purchase them. If the price of these items was reduced by a small amount, it is unlikely that many additional people would be able to afford them. On the other hand, they would become less expensive, perhaps less exclusive and therefore less desirable to those wealthy people considering buying them (i.e demand would fall). Examples include yachts, sports cars and designer clothes.

Goods Influenced by Consumer Expectations/Speculative Goods

If prospective buyers think that prices are likely to be higher in the future in comparison to current prices, the current level of quantity demanded may not fall even if prices increase slightly. For example, if a person is considering buying stocks and shares, the possibility that prices are likely to be even higher in the future will stimulate and probably increase quantity demanded at current prices. On the other hand, the quantity demanded of property could decrease, even as prices fall, because consumers may expect further price decreases.

Goods of an Addictive Nature

In the case of goods to which a person becomes addicted, e.g. drugs, they no longer act rationally. They become so addicted to the drug that in order to get the same satisfaction from their consumption of the drug, even when the price of the commodity increases, they will continue to purchase these goods and their demand for the commodity may actually also increase because of their addiction.

Positive Economics

An increase in quantity demanded is caused by:	In the case of Chris & David, our two coffee drinkers, an increase in quantity demanded will result if:
A decrease in the price of the good itself.	The price of coffee falls.
An increase in the price of a substitute good.	The price of tea increases.
A fall in the price of a complementary good.	The price of the chocolate croissant they buy with their coffee falls.
An increase in income (if the good is normal).	They get a pay rise.
Expectations of higher prices in the future or scarcity.	Their favourite coffee shop is going to move to another city.
A change in taste in favour of the good.	Most of their friends invite them to go for coffee, as it's a more fashionable thing to do.
Favourable unplanned factors.	Their accountant prefers to meet them in their local coffee shop rather than their office – an unplanned development.
Government legislation influencing an increase in consumption.	The government launches a campaign encouraging people to drink coffee rather than alcohol.

> **EXAM ✓**
>
> ### Reasons for shifts in the demand curve – shift to the right
>
> #### Points to note when answering a question:
>
> - You *must* state that there has been a shift to the right, which indicates an increase in quantity demanded of the product, e.g. coffee.
> - Not all factors affecting the quantity demanded for a good will apply – you must use the *most relevant*, e.g. government policy may not be relevant.
> - Each point *must relate* to the product specifically, e.g. coffee.

The Price Effect

The Price Effect = Substitution + Income Effects

If the price of a good changes, it gives rise to both a substitution effect, i.e. more of the cheaper good will always be bought, and an income effect, i.e. because of the increased real income, the demand for both goods can change.

3: Introduction to Demand

Substitution Effect

As the price of a good decreases, people are likely to purchase more of this good if they are to follow the equi-marginal principle. This is because they are now getting more marginal utility per penny spent on the good.

If the price of a good decreases, it becomes a cheaper option relative to the similar goods that have remained at the same price. The substitution effect is always positive for the relatively cheaper good, i.e. a greater quantity of it will be bought.

Income Effect

The **income effect** refers to the effect on the quantity demanded for a good arising from a change in the consumer's real income as a result of a change in the price of a good. If the price of a good falls, it means that the consumer's purchasing power has increased.

Substitution + Income Effect in Action

Case	ΔP =	Substitution + Income = Overall ΔQuantity demanded
Case A (normal good)	Price falls	Quantity demanded for A rises by 10 units **(positive substitution effect)** + quantity demanded for A increases by 10 units **(income effect)** = quantity demanded increases by 20 units

The good is normal with respect to both price and income.

Case B (inferior goods)	Price falls	Quantity demanded for B rises by 10 units **(positive substitution effect)** + quantity demanded for B decreases by 4 units **(negative income effect)** = quantity demanded for B increases by 6 units

While this good is inferior with regard to income, overall it's a normal good with respect to price changes.

Case C (Giffen goods)	Price falls	Quantity demanded for C rises by 6 units **(positive substitution effect)** + quantity demanded for C decreases by 8 units **(negative income effect)** = quantity demanded for C decreases by 2 units

This is a Giffen good and also an inferior good. The negative income effect is greater than the positive substitution effect.

> A Giffen good must be inferior, but an inferior good can be Giffen or normal.

Can a Normal Good Be a Giffen Good?

For a normal good, the substitution effect is always positive. The income effect will also be positive. For a Giffen good, however, the income effect is negative as it's an inferior good. Hence, a normal good cannot be a Giffen good.

Positive Economics

Question 3(c), 2003 — EXAM ✓ (25 marks)

A consumer spends all their income on two goods, Good A and Good B. Both goods are normal goods but they are not complementary goods. The price of Good A is reduced and the price of Good B remains unchanged. The consumer continues to spend all income on the two goods.

Distinguish between the **substitution effect** and the **income effect** of the price reduction in Good A.

Solution

Substitution effect: Quantity Demanded for Good A = Increases
Good A is relatively cheaper; hence the consumer is getting increased marginal utility for their good.

Income effect: Quantity Demanded for Good A = Increases
The consumer has additional real income due to the reduction in price of Good A. As Good A is a normal good, the quantity demanded for this good will increase.

Question 1(b), 2011 — EXAM ✓ (30 marks)

(i) Distinguish between the economic meanings of a 'movement along a demand curve' and a 'shift in a demand curve' for concert tickets.

Illustrate your answer using diagrams.

(ii) State and explain **two** factors that would cause a shift in a demand curve for concert tickets. In **each** case explain how the factor affects the demand curve.

Solution

(i)

Movement along a demand curve
Caused by a change in the selling price of the good itself, *ceteris paribus* (all other things being equal).

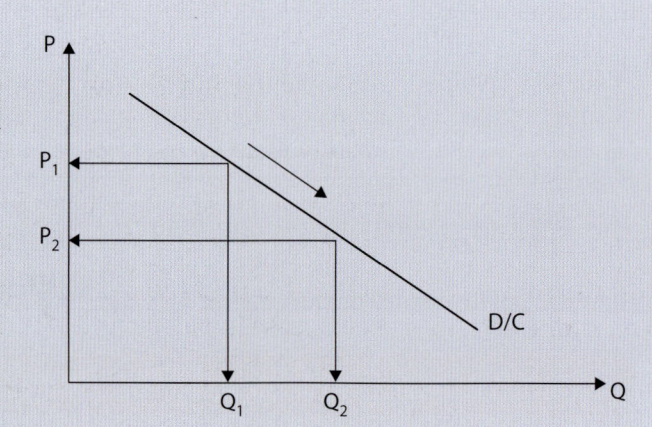

Shift in a demand curve

If any of the factors other than the price of the good itself change, this will result in a shift in the demand curve.

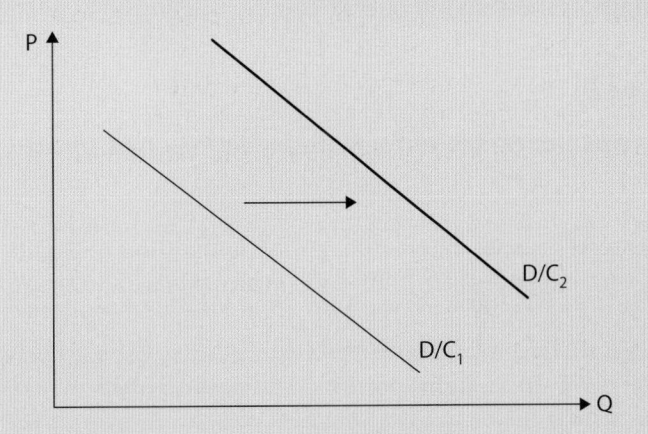

[Diagram: Demand curves shifting right from D/C$_1$ to D/C$_2$ on a P vs Q graph]

(ii)

Two factors that would cause a shift in a demand curve for concert tickets

Factor	How this factor affects the demand curve – the demand curve shifts to the right
Income levels	If income rises, then the quantity demanded for concert tickets will increase, assuming concert tickets are a normal good.
Taste/preference	If the consumer's preference for the artist/event becomes stronger, then the quantity demanded for concert tickets will increase.
Expectations about the future	If consumers expect the concert will not be repeated, this may increase the quantity demanded. If they expect ticket prices to rise in the future, they may buy the ticket now and the quantity demanded will increase.
Unplanned events	Factors such as the weather may influence the current quantity demanded for tickets, e.g. good weather may increase the quantity demanded for an outdoor event.
Change in price of substitute good	If the price of tickets for an alternative concert increased, then the quantity demanded for tickets for this concert may increase.
Change in price of complementary good	If the price of hotel accommodation near the concert venue decreased, then the quantity demanded for the concert tickets may increase.

Positive Economics

Sample Exam Question (12 marks)

What are the reasons for an increase in demand for the latest laptop and a shift to the right in the demand curve?

Solution

- **Increase in consumers' incomes:** With higher incomes, people can afford to buy luxuries such as the latest laptop and will increase their spending on such goods.

- **Change in tastes:** Consumers are constantly demanding new and improved services and products that improve their lifestyle. Consumers like to keep up to date.

- **More convenient than available substitute goods:** People prefer the convenience of laptops. They are small, light, portable and easy to use.

Questions

Short Questions

1. Define market price.
2. Define demand in economic terms.
3. Explain, with the aid of an example, the law of demand.
4. Define individual demand and market demand.
5. Explain, with the aid of labelled diagrams, the relationship between individual demand and market demand.
6. Distinguish between a demand schedule and a demand curve.
7. Explain the economic rationale for assuming that a person's demand curve for a good slopes downwards.
8. List the elements of the demand function.
9. Distinguish, using examples, between complementary goods and substitute goods.
10. Define, using examples, normal goods, inferior goods and Giffen goods.

Long Questions

1. Illustrate, using an example, the difference between a movement along a demand curve and a shift along a demand curve.
2. Give one reason that will cause a movement along the demand curve and five reasons that will cause a shift in the demand curve.
3. Illustrate, using a diagram, what happens when there is an increase in quantity demanded.
4. Illustrate, using a diagram, what happens when there is a decrease in quantity demanded.
5. Other than price, state and explain five factors affecting the quantity demanded of a good.
6. Explain, using examples, the substitution effect.
7. Explain, using examples, the income effect.
8. State and explain the exceptions to the law of demand.

Long Questions – *continued*

9. Outline the causes of an increase in quantity demanded.
10. Outline the causes of a decrease in quantity demanded.
11. Discuss the factors that influence the consumer's demand for commodities.
12. 'All Giffen goods are inferior goods but not all inferior goods are Giffen goods.' Discuss this statement.
13. State and explain the effect on the demand for Good X in each of the following circumstances. Use a separate diagram for each answer.
    (a) The price of a substitute good increases
    (b) The price of a complementary good increases
    (c) The price of the good itself decreases
    (d) Consumers' tastes change in favour of a product
    (e) Consumers' income decreases
    (f) The consumer expects the price to be higher in the future
    (g) The government implements a regulation discouraging consumption of the product
    (h) There are favourable weather conditions for the product

14. The data in the table represents the demand schedule for laptops. Using the data, draw a diagram showing the demand curve for laptops.
    (a) With reference to your diagram, assume the consumer demand for laptops increases by 20 units at each price listed. Draw the new demand curve.
    (b) Explain two possible reasons for this shift in the demand curve.

Price (€)	Quantity demanded (units)
20	25
40	20
60	15
80	10
100	5

15. The data in the table represents the demand schedule for smartphones. Using the data, draw the diagram showing the demand curve for smartphones.
    (a) With reference to your diagram, assume the consumer demand for smartphones increases by 40 units at each price listed. Draw the new demand curve.
    (b) Explain two possible reasons for this shift in the demand curve.

Price (€)	Quantity demanded (units)
10	250
30	200
50	150
70	100
90	50

16. The data in the table represents the market demand schedule for Good X for two consumers, A and B. Using the data, draw a diagram showing the market demand curve for Good X.

Price (€)	Quantity demanded (units) A	Quantity demanded (units) B
10	100	120
20	80	100
30	60	80
40	40	60
50	20	40

Chapter 4: Introduction to Supply

Specific Learning Outcomes

At the end of this chapter, students should be able to:

- [ ] Distinguish between individual supply and market/aggregate supply.

- [ ] List and explain the determinants and influences of supply.

- [ ] Explain the supply schedule and illustrate by means of a supply curve.

- [ ] Demonstrate a change in any of the determinants of supply and interpret the outcomes using diagrams.

4: Introduction to Supply

Packing material manufacturer → Packaging manufacturer → Packaging filler → Wholesaler → Retailer → Consumer

Introduction to Supply

We examined demand in detail in Chapter 3 and focused on the factors that influence buyers. At the other side of every transaction is a seller. Economists refer to the behaviour of sellers as the market force of supply.

> **SUPPLY** refers to the quantity of a good that firms are willing to make available at various prices over a particular period of time.

The supplier determines the level of output it is willing to supply at the prevailing market price. Just as utility was the basis of demand, costs (the focus of Chapter 7) are the basis of supply.

> **INDIVIDUAL SUPPLY** refers to the quantity of a good supplied by an individual firm at different prices.
>
> **MARKET/AGGREGATE SUPPLY** refers to the quantity of a good supplied by all the firms in the market at different prices.
>
> A **SUPPLY SCHEDULE** is a table illustrating the different quantities of a good made available for sale at various market prices at any given time.
>
> An **INDIVIDUAL SUPPLY SCHEDULE** is a table illustrating the different quantities of a good made available for sale by an individual firm at various market prices at any given time.
>
> A **MARKET/AGGREGATE SUPPLY SCHEDULE** is a table illustrating the total quantities of a good that all the firms in the market are willing to make available for sale at various prices at any given time.

Positive Economics

Supply of coffee beans			
Price (€)	Firm A (individual supply)	Firm B (individual supply)	Market (Firm A and Firm B) (aggregate supply)
€20	200	400	600
€40	400	600	1,000
€60	600	800	1,400
€80	1,000	1,000	2,000

From the above table you can see that Firm A is willing to supply 1,000 units of coffee beans when the price is €80 and only 200 units when the price is €20. At €20 Firm B is actually willing to supply 400 units. The aggregate supply at €20 is 600 units.

A **SUPPLY CURVE** is a graph illustrating the number of units of a good made available for sale at various market prices at any given time. There is a positive relationship between price and quantity supplied. The supply curve is usually upward sloping from left to right.

An **INDIVIDUAL SUPPLY CURVE** is a graph illustrating the different quantities of a good made available for sale by an individual firm at various market prices at any given time.

A **MARKET/AGGREGATE SUPPLY CURVE** is a graph illustrating the total quantities of a good all the firms in the market are willing to make available for sale at various prices at any given time.

Note:
As the price increases, quantity supplied increases.

Note:
To derive the market supply, we add the quantity supplied by each individual firm at each price to calculate the aggregate quantity supplied to the market at each price.

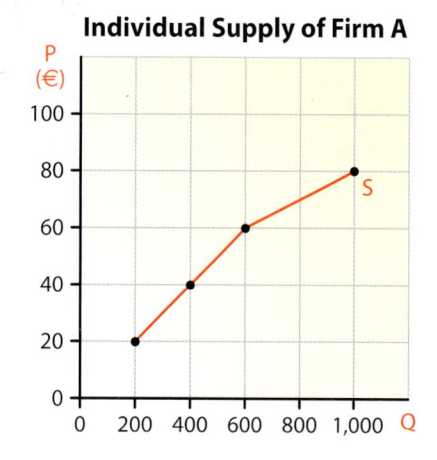

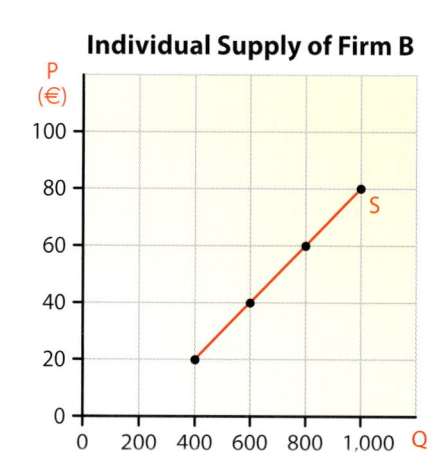

Individual Supply of Firm A

Individual Supply of Firm B

44

4: Introduction to Supply

Market/Aggregate Supply of Coffee Beans

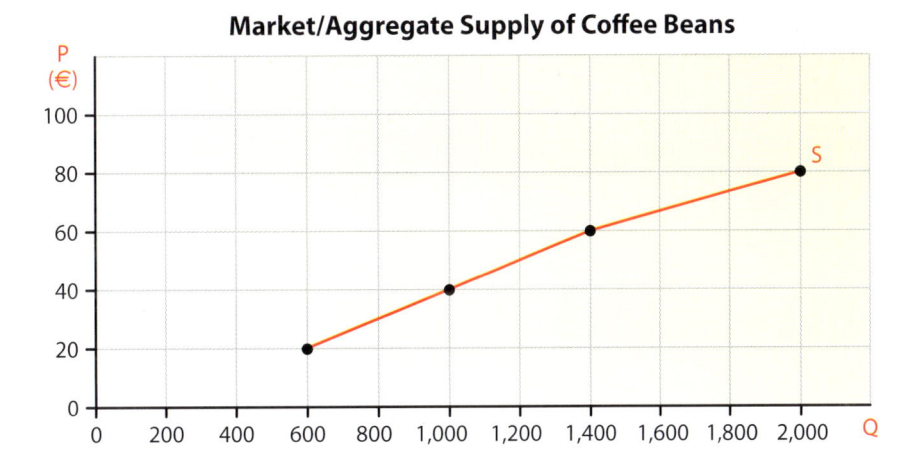

Other Circumstances of Supply

- Supply restricted by a minimum market price.
- Supply restricted by limited capacity.
- Fixed supply.

Supply Restricted by a Minimum Market Price

In order to stay in production in the long term, firms have to cover their costs. Therefore, many goods and services will not be supplied if the market price is below a certain minimum price. Any price below this level would not cover their costs and would result in the firm making a loss. Therefore, no producers would enter into the market until this minimum price has been reached.

For example, let's say that a plant in a gardening centre has the following costs:

- Seeds: 10c
- Pot: 50c
- Wages of staff to sell the plant for 15 minutes: €3
- Plant food and water to grow the plant and have it ready for sale: €1

Total cost = €4.60

€4.60 upwards

Positive Economics

It would not make any sense to sell the plant for less than €4.60 as there isn't any profit whatsoever and it would actually cost the garden centre to be in business!

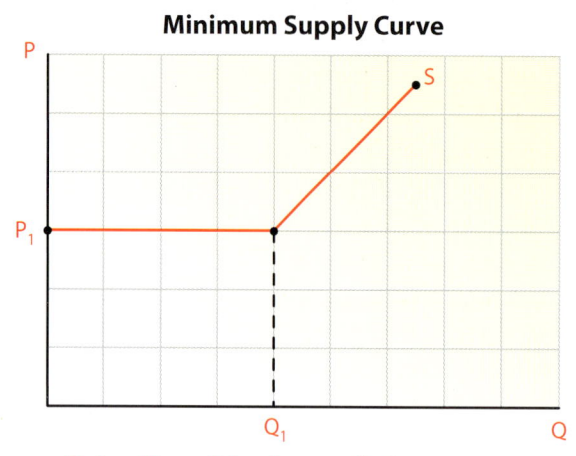

Minimum Supply Curve

- Below P_1 nothing is supplied
- At prices above P_1, quantity supplied increases
- As P increases, quantity supplied increases

Supply Restricted by Limited Capacity

An industry's capacity to supply a good may be limited. This could be due to the plants' productive capacity, a shortage of specialised labour (e.g. only a small number of horticultural graduates are available) or a shortage of raw materials. Once the maximum capacity is reached, the quantity supplied remains the same no matter what the price is.

For example, the garden centre might only be able to stock 10,000 plants, which means that it cannot hold any more goods available for sale. As a result, supply is restricted.

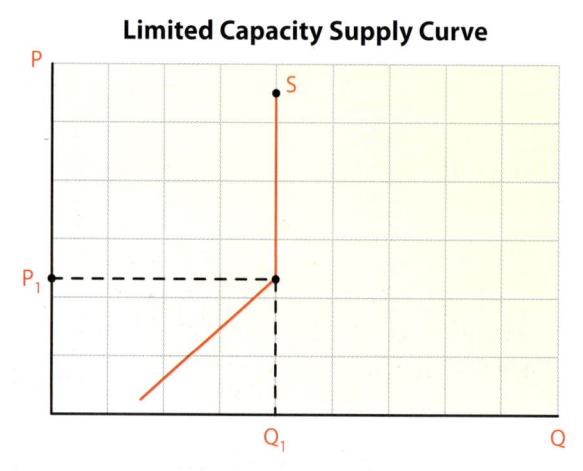

Limited Capacity Supply Curve

- As price increases up to P_1, output increases up to a maximum level of Q_1
- As price increases above P_1, quantity supplied will not increase

Fixed Supply (Perfectly Inelastic Supply)

Fixed supply or perfectly inelastic supply (to be discussed in Chapter 6) occurs when the supply of a product cannot be changed in the short run, no matter what the price is. Examples include perishable goods, e.g. a supply of fish on a given day, the supply of land and seating capacity of a stadium. For example, there are 20,000 tickets for a concert but there is a demand for 60,000. If there are only 20,000 seats in the concert venue, then no matter what price is offered for tickets, the supply of seats is fixed.

Fixed Supply Curve

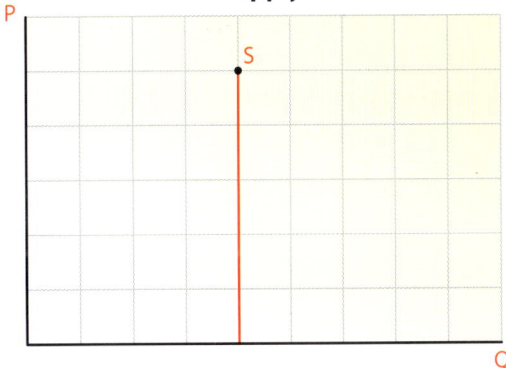

- Any change in price will not bring about change in the quantity supplied
- The entire daily supply must be sold regardless of the prevailing price because the good cannot be held for sale over the following days

There Can Be Movement Along or a Shift in the Supply Curve

A MOVEMENT ALONG THE SUPPLY CURVE is caused by a change in price of the good or service.

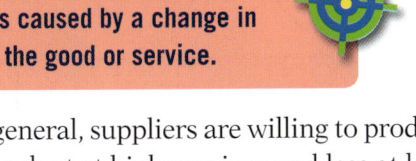

In general, suppliers are willing to produce more of a product at higher prices and less at lower prices. An increase in the price of a good will result in an increase in quantity supplied, whereas a decrease in the price of a good will result in a decrease in the quantity supplied.

Movement Along the Supply Curve

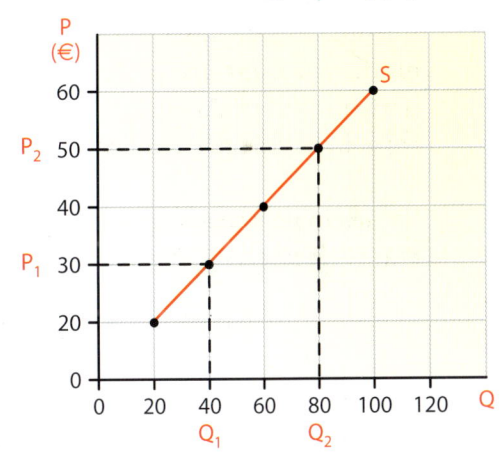

A Shift in the Supply Curve

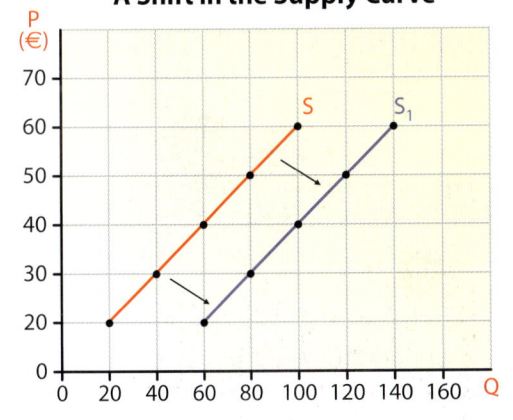

A SHIFT IN THE SUPPLY CURVE is caused by a change in any non-price determinant of supply (any other variable that influences the quantity supplied).

A shift in the supply curve illustrates the different quantities supplied at the same price (these will be discussed later on in the chapter). The curve can shift to the right or left.

Positive Economics

An Increase in Supply
If there is an increase in the quantity supplied of a good, the supply curve will **shift** to the **right** from S_x to S_1, as seen in the graph.

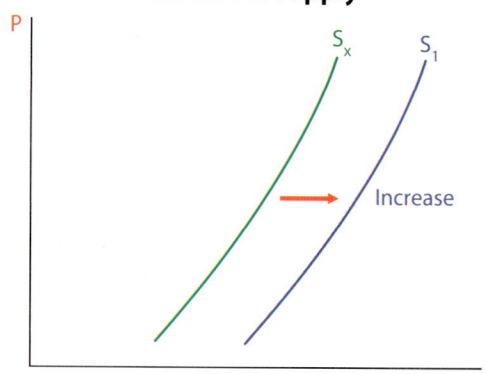

A Decrease in Supply
If there is a decrease in the quantity supplied of a good, the supply curve will **shift** to the **left** from S_x to S_2, as seen in the graph.

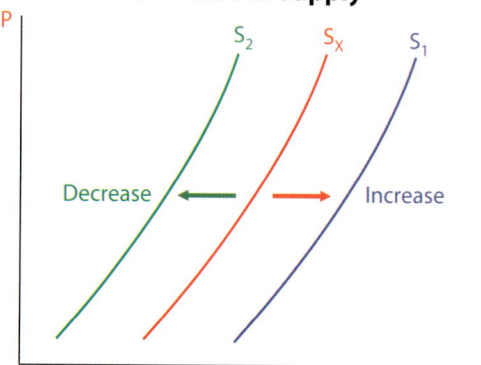

Factors Affecting the Supply of a Good

Supply of a Good Depends on Its Own Price
If there is a rise in the price of the good, the quantity supplied will generally respond and also rise. This is because it becomes more profitable for firms to supply the goods, as the higher the price, the more money they will receive. As a result, many more firms will be attracted into the market and will also start supplying the good. If price decreases, the opposite will take place. Production and supply of the product become less profitable and it acts as a deterrent to new entrants and may even see some existing firms leave the market, i.e. shut down.

The supply function

$$Sy = f(Py, Pr, C, U, Tch, Tx, O, N)$$

- Py = price of Good Y
- Pr = price of related goods
- C = cost of production
- U = factors outside the control of the firm
- Tch = state of technology
- Tx = taxation/subsidy
- O = objectives of the firm
- N = number of firms in the industry

4: Introduction to Supply

The Supply Curve

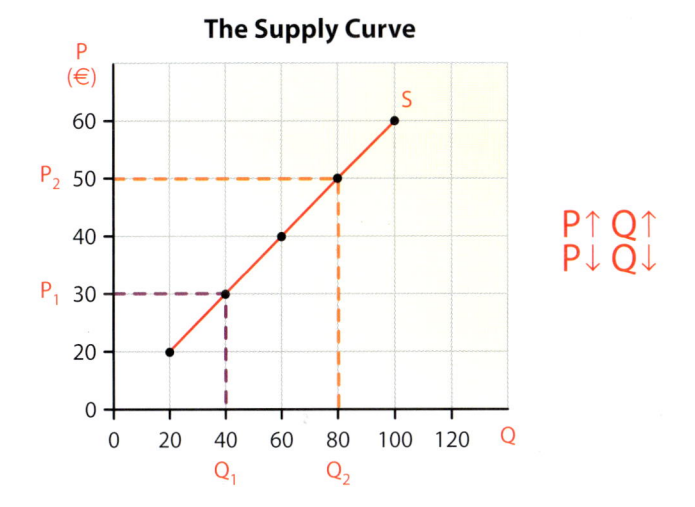

P↑ Q↑
P↓ Q↓

Supply of a Good Depends on Prices of Related Goods

From the aspect of supply, the price of related goods refers to other goods that the supplier could produce as an alternative to those currently being produced.

If the price of a related good rises, irrespective of whether the price of the good the firm is currently producing remains the same or falls, it will become a much more attractive and profitable alternative to switch its resources to the production of the related good.

For example, a computer manufacturing company may find that the price of tablets is increasing while the price of laptop computers remains constant. The increase in the price of tablets makes it a more attractive and profitable product to produce rather than laptops. The computer manufacturing company will therefore switch its resources to the production of tablets and hence will reduce its supply of laptops as a result of this increase in the price of tablets.

Alternatively, a fall in the price of tablets will have the opposite effect and will cause an increase in the supply of laptops.

Supply of a Good Depends on Prices of Related Goods

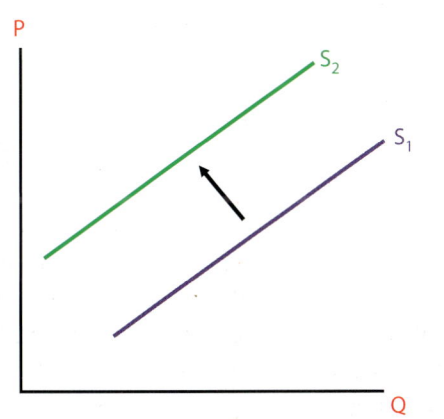

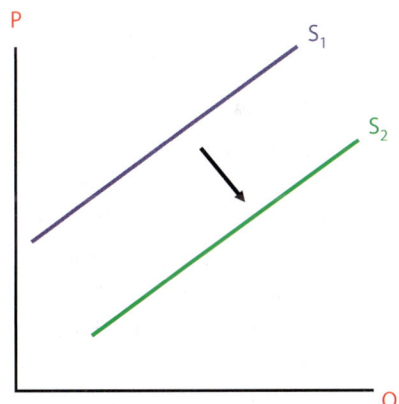

An increase in the price of a related good will cause a fall in the quantity supplied of Good Y

A fall in the price of a related good will cause an increase in the quantity supplied of Good Y

Supply of a Good Depends on the Cost of Production

A supplier combines raw materials, capital and labour to produce the output they supply. These are all costs incurred by the firm. If there is an increase in these costs, then it will be more expensive to manufacture the good. The firm will not continue to supply the same quantity of the good at the old price, so there will be a reduction in the quantity supplied.

Supply of a Good Depends on Cost of Production

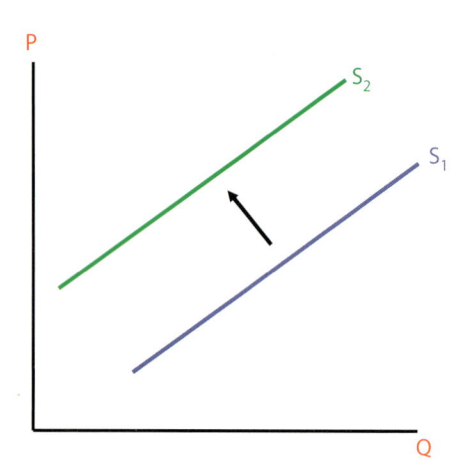

An increase in the cost of production will cause a fall in the quantity supplied of Good Y

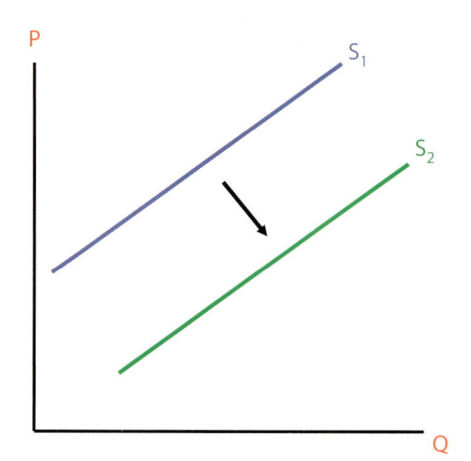

A fall in the cost of production will cause an increase in the quantity supplied of Good Y

Causes of an increase in the cost of production:

- A rise in labour costs.
- A rise in the cost of raw materials.
- An increase in taxes.
- A reduction in subsidies.

Causes of a decrease in the cost of production:

- A fall in labour costs.
- A fall in the cost of raw materials.
- A reduction in taxes.
- An increase in subsidies.

Supply of a Good Depends on Factors Outside the Control of a Firm/Unforeseen Circumstances

There may be changes in the quantity supplied that were never intended by the producer. Favourable or unfavourable unplanned factors cannot be forecasted but can influence supply and can result in either an increase or decrease in the quantity supplied.

For example, each of the following unforeseen circumstances would lower supply in a garden centre:
- Unfavourable weather conditions may result in a lower yield of plants.
- Strikes by workers.
- Shortage of raw materials.
- Transport failures restricting the movement of pots and seeds.

Supply of a Good Depends on Factors Outside the Control of a Firm

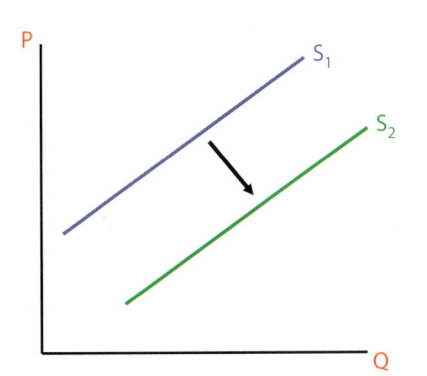

Favourable unplanned factors will cause an increase in quantity supplied and a shift to the right

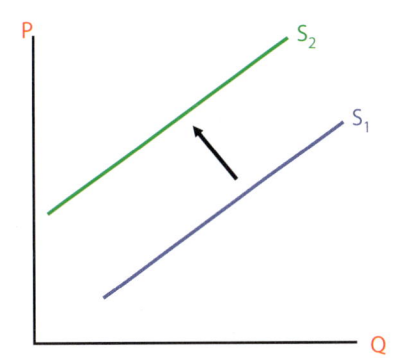

Unfavourable unplanned factors will cause a decrease in quantity supplied and a shift to the left

Supply of a Good Depends on the State of Technology

Technology is a cost-reducing innovation. Technological progress allows firms to produce a given item at a lower cost. Computer prices, for example, have declined radically as technology has improved, lowering their cost of production. Advances in communications technology have lowered telecommunications costs. The advancement of technology will cause an increase in the quantity supplied of Good Y (e.g. computers). We do not generally discuss a 'fall' in technology – we assume any new method of production is an option for a firm, so as technology improves, supply increases.

Supply of a Good Depends on the State of Technology

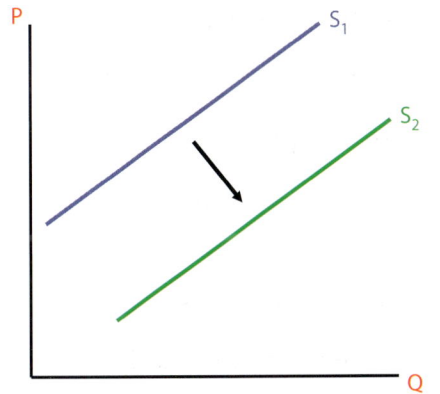

An improvement in the state of technology will cause an increase in the quantity supplied of Good Y

As new machinery is invented and as labour becomes more specialised and efficient, the factors of production become more efficient. It becomes possible to increase the supplier's output even though the payments they receive remain the same. A technological improvement means that the supplier can use inputs more efficiently and the cost of producing a unit of output falls.

Supply of a Good Depends on the Rates of Taxation/Granting of Subsidies

- A reduction in taxes will result in a reduction in the cost of raw materials/production and as a result the quantity supplied will increase. As the level of taxes increases, a firm's profit is reduced. This may force some firms out of production, resulting in a decrease in the quantity supplied to the market.

- An increase in subsidies granted to a firm for raw materials/labour employed will result in a reduction in costs and as a result, the quantity supplied will increase. A decrease in these subsidies will have the opposite effect.

Supply of a Good Depends on the Rates of Taxation/Granting of Subsidies

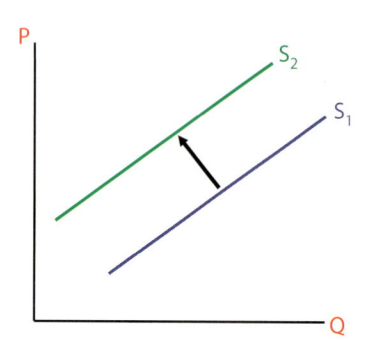

An increase in the level of taxation/decrease in subsidies will cause a fall in the quantity supplied of Good Y

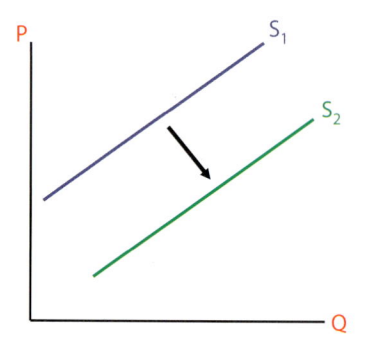

A fall in the level of taxation/increase in subsidies will cause an increase in the quantity supplied of Good Y

Objectives of the Firm

If the objectives of the firm changed from that of profit maximisation to satisfactory profit, then the quantity supplied may fall. For example, a bed & breakfast owner in Killarney is open seven nights a week and has no family time. The owner decides to close on a Saturday at 2 p.m. and not accept guests until the following Tuesday at 2 p.m., giving herself the weekend off and time with her family. Clearly, profit maximisation is not the objective of this B&B, as weekends would be the busiest nights. Her objective is to earn satisfactory profit levels but also have family time.

Objectives of the Firm

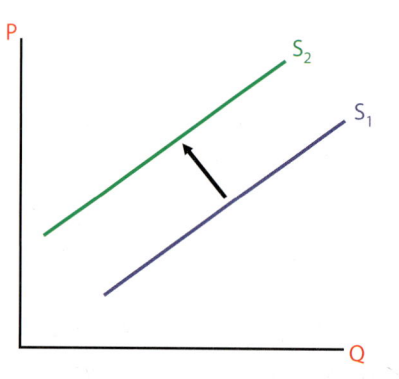

A deliberate reduction in output will cause a fall in the quantity supplied of Good Y

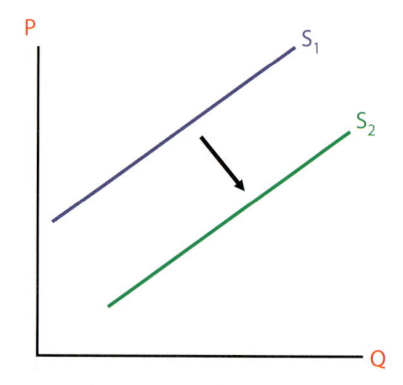

A deliberate increase in output will cause a rise in the quantity supplied of Good Y

4: Introduction to Supply

Number of Sellers in the Industry

If the number of sellers in the industry decreased (e.g. due to a recession), then the overall quantity supplied to the market would decrease. In contrast to this, if the number of sellers in the industry increased due to an increase in quantity demanded, then the overall quantity supplied to the market would increase.

Supply of a Good Depends on the Number of Sellers in the Industry

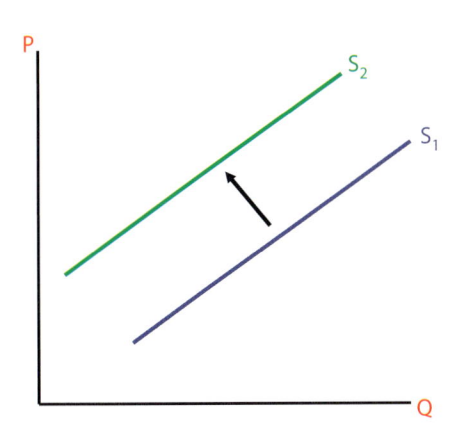

A decrease in the number of sellers in industry will cause a fall in the quantity supplied of Good Y

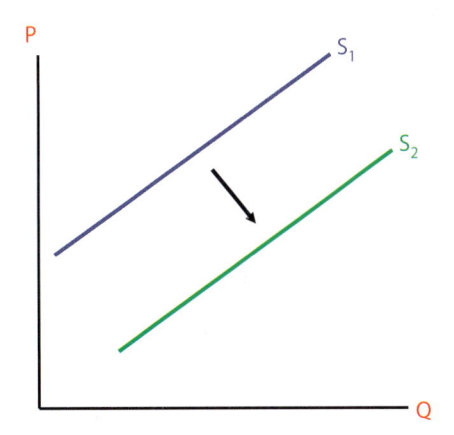

An increase in the number of sellers in industry will cause a rise in the quantity supplied of Good Y

An increase in quantity supplied is caused by:	The Economist's Garden Centre would increase its level of supply if:
A fall in price of a related good.	The cost of compost fell. Since it would cost less to maintain a garden, more people would need more plants.
A fall in the cost of production.	The cost of wages fell or the cost of pots, plants, food for the coffee shop and packaging fell.
Favourable unplanned factors.	There was an unexpected surge in tourists to Ireland this year and they had many more visitors than planned.
An improvement in technology.	They bought new irrigation systems that watered the plants twice as fast so that they could conserve water and bring down costs.
A reduction in taxation/ granting of a subsidy.	VAT and corporation tax fell. They received employment subsidies as well as 'green grants'.
A deliberate increase in output.	They decided to expand and increase the amount of stock they could offer and sell.
An increase in the number of sellers in the industry.	If a new garden centre opened in their vicinity, the aggregate amount of plants and trees available for sale would increase.

Positive Economics

Producer Surplus

Producer surplus is the difference between the lowest price a supplier is willing to accept for a good and the price they actually receive.

PROFILE: Jean Baptise Say (1767–1832)

Jean Baptise Say, a French economist, was a dedicated disciple of the classical economic doctrines of Adam Smith. His most famous contribution was his theory of markets, called Say's Law, outlined in his book, *A Treatise on Political Economy*, published in 1803.

Say's Law – 'Supply Creates Its Own Demand'
Say maintained that economic crises and overproduction could not exist. This was because all production created demand. A person produced goods so that they could exchange them for other goods. Therefore, total production was matched by total demand and overproduction could not exist.

- **People work to acquire needs/wants:** People do not work for its own sake, but only to obtain goods and services that they need and desire.

- **Specialisation of labour:** In an economy that practises division of labour and exchange, each individual person does not attempt to supply all their needs directly. Rather, each person produces those goods at which they are most efficient and exchanges their surplus goods for the surplus goods of others.

- **Production creates demand:** The very act of production constitutes the demand for other goods. Thus, there can never be overproduction of goods. Each individual's production (supply) constitutes their demand for other goods, so aggregate demand must equal aggregate supply.

- **Savings decrease interest rates:** The accumulation of savings would lead to a drop in interest rates simply because of the increase in the supply of loanable funds. This would lead to a rise in demand for capital goods while at the same time discourage savings.

- **Self-adjusting system:** As a result of the above, Say believed that the economic system was self-adjusting and that full employment would be maintained.

Say's analysis obviously failed to explain how a deficiency in aggregate demand could cause unemployment. The role of savings in regulating demand was not satisfactorily explained until Keynes's writings in the 1930s.

4: Introduction to Supply

> **EXAM** ✓ **Question 6, Section A, 2008** (17 marks)
>
> China will host the Beijing Olympic Games in August 2008 and 7 million tickets are available for the event. On the diagram, draw the supply curve for the tickets and explain the reason for its shape.
>
> ### Solution
>
> **Explanation:** The supply of tickets available for the Olympics is fixed at 7 million. Regardless of price, this capacity will remain unchanged.

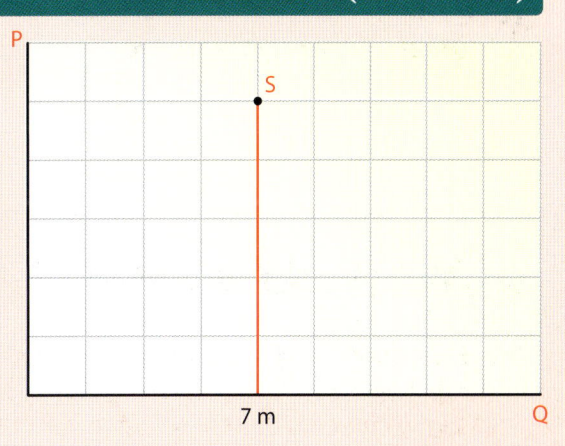

Questions

Short Questions

1. Define supply in economic terms.
2. Define individual supply and market supply.
3. Explain, with the aid of labelled diagrams, the relationship between individual supply and market supply.
4. Distinguish between a supply schedule and a supply graph.
5. Explain the economic rationale for assuming that a firm's supply curve for a good slopes upwards.
6. List the elements of the supply function.

Long Questions

1. Illustrate, using an example, the difference between a movement along a supply curve and a shift in a supply curve.
2. Give one reason that would cause a movement along the supply curve and five reasons that would cause a shift in the supply curve.
3. Illustrate, using a diagram, what happens when there is an increase in the quantity supplied.
4. Illustrate, using a diagram, what happens when there is a decrease in the quantity supplied.
5. Other than price, state and explain five factors affecting the quantity supplied of a good.

Long Questions – *continued*

6. Explain, with the aid of a labelled diagram, the supply curve of an individual firm in each of the following circumstances. State an example of each case.
   (a) A firm is willing to increase supply as price rises, but there is a minimum price below which the firm will not supply at all
   (b) A firm can supply only up to a maximum production capacity
   (c) The product is fixed in supply (e.g. perishable goods)
7. Outline four factors, other than price, that affect the supply curve of an individual firm. In each case, explain how the factor affects the supply curve.
8. Outline the causes of an increase in supply.
9. Outline the causes of a decrease in supply.
10. State and explain, with the aid of diagrams, the factors that influence a firm's supply of commodities.
11. State and explain the effect on the supply of Good X in each of the following circumstances. Use a separate diagram for each answer.
    (a) The price of a related good decreases
    (b) The cost of production increases
    (c) There is an increase in corporation tax
    (d) 50% of the production line is replaced with new, modern machinery
    (e) The government introduces a new subsidy
    (f) There are transport problems due to a strike at the airport in Paris
    (g) The stock ordering system becomes computerised
    (h) The government implements an educational campaign encouraging consumption of the product
    (i) There is a significant decrease in labour costs
    (j) There is a shortage of raw materials
    (k) There is a three-week strike at the plant
    (l) 50 new sellers join the industry
    (m) The objective of the firm's owner is to attract new investors
12. (a) The data to the right represents the market supply schedule for Good X. Using the data, draw the diagram showing the market supply curve for Good X.
    (b) With reference to your diagram, assume the firm's supply of Good X decreases by 50 units at each market price listed. Draw the new supply curve.
    (c) Explain two possible reasons for this shift in the supply curve.

Price (€)	Quantity supplied (units)
20	200
40	400
60	600
80	800
100	1,000

Long Questions – *continued*

13. **(a)** The data to the right represents the market supply schedule for computer chips. Using the data, draw the diagram showing the market supply curve for computer chips.
    (b) With reference to your diagram, assume the firm's supply of computer chips increases by 100 units at each market price listed. Draw the new supply curve.
    (c) Explain two possible reasons for this shift in the supply curve.

Price (€)	Quantity supplied (units)
20	50
40	100
60	150
80	200
100	250

14. **(a)** The data to the right represents the market supply schedule for cars. Using the data, draw the diagram showing the market supply curve for cars.
    (b) With reference to your diagram, assume the firm's supply of cars increases by 40 units at each market price listed. Draw the new supply curve.
    (c) Explain two possible reasons for this shift in the supply curve.

Price (€)	Quantity supplied (units)
20	20
40	40
60	60
80	80
100	100

Chapter 5 | Equilibrium

Specific Learning Outcomes

At the end of this chapter, students should be able to:

☐ Explain and illustrate, by means of a diagram, equilibrium price and equilibrium quantity.

☐ Apply the tools of demand and supply analysis to price and quantity changes in markets.

5: Equilibrium

Introduction

If no interference in the market occurs (by the government or other agency), price will eventually settle at the level where quantity demanded equals quantity supplied. This position where there is no tendency for prices to change is called the **MARKET EQUILIBRIUM**.

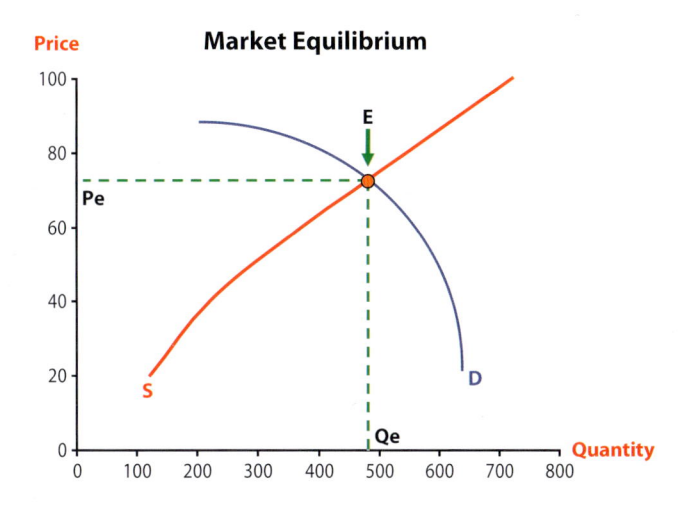

At equilibrium, the allocation of goods is at its most efficient because the amount of goods being supplied is exactly the same as the amount of goods being demanded. Thus, everyone (individuals, firms or countries) is satisfied. At the given price, suppliers are selling all the goods that they have produced and consumers are getting all the goods that they are demanding.

As you can see on the diagram, equilibrium occurs at the intersection of the demand and supply curves. At this point, the equilibrium price of the goods will be at Pe and the equilibrium quantity will be at Qe. In the real marketplace, equilibrium can only ever be reached in theory, so the prices of goods and services are constantly changing in relation to fluctuations in demand and supply.

Market Equilibrium and Price

- **Scenario 1:** If the quantity supplied exceeds the quantity demanded, producers will lower the price to get rid of surplus stock: P↓.

- **Scenario 2:** If the quantity demanded exceeds the quantity supplied, scarcity would exist and price would increase: P↑.

The diagram below illustrates the market demand and supply for a product and the equilibrium price and quantity in this market is shown.

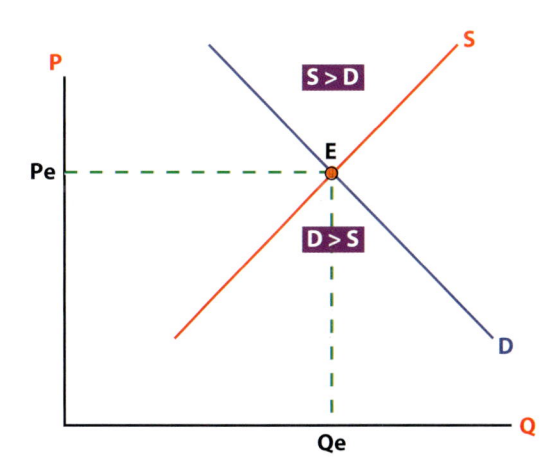

Positive Economics

EXAM ✓ Question 1(a), 2010 (30 marks)

The data below represents the market demand and market supply schedules for the soft drink Quencher.

Price (€)	Quantity demanded ('000 units)	Quantity supplied ('000 units)
2.00	40	5
2.25	30	10
2.50	20	20
2.75	10	30
3.00	5	40

(i) Using the above data, draw the diagram showing the market demand and the market supply for the soft drink Quencher. Clearly mark the **point of equilibrium** and the **equilibrium price and quantity**.

(ii) Explain what it means for the market **to be in equilibrium**.

(iii) Assume costs of production fell, resulting in an extra 20,000 units applied at each of the above listed prices. With reference to your diagram in 1 (a)(i) above and assuming that demand remains unchanged, draw the **new** supply curve. Clearly indicate the **new** point of equilibrium and the new equilibrium price and quantity.

Solution

(a) (i)

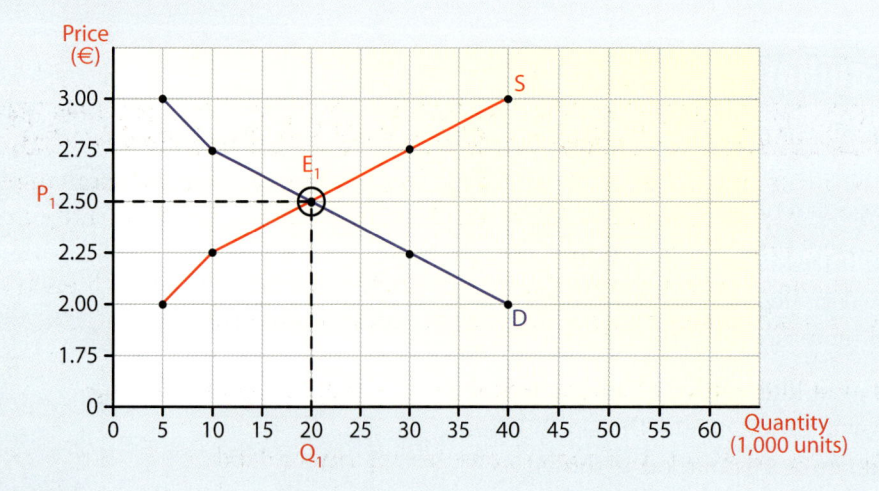

[Diagram: Price (€) on y-axis from 0 to 3.00, Quantity (1,000 units) on x-axis from 0 to 60. Supply curve S slopes upward, Demand curve D slopes downward, intersecting at E₁ where P₁ = 2.50 and Q₁ = 20.]

(a) (ii)

To be in equilibrium means where the quantity demanded meets/equals the quantity supplied and there is no tendency for prices to change.

(a) (iii)

Price (€)	Quantity demanded ('000 units)	Quantity supplied ('000 units)	New quantity supplied (extra 20,000 units supplied)
2.00	40	5	25 (5 + 20,000)
2.25	30	10	30 (10 + 20,000)
2.50	20	20	40 (20 + 20,000)
2.75	10	30	50 (30 + 20,000)
3.00	5	40	60 (40 + 20,000)

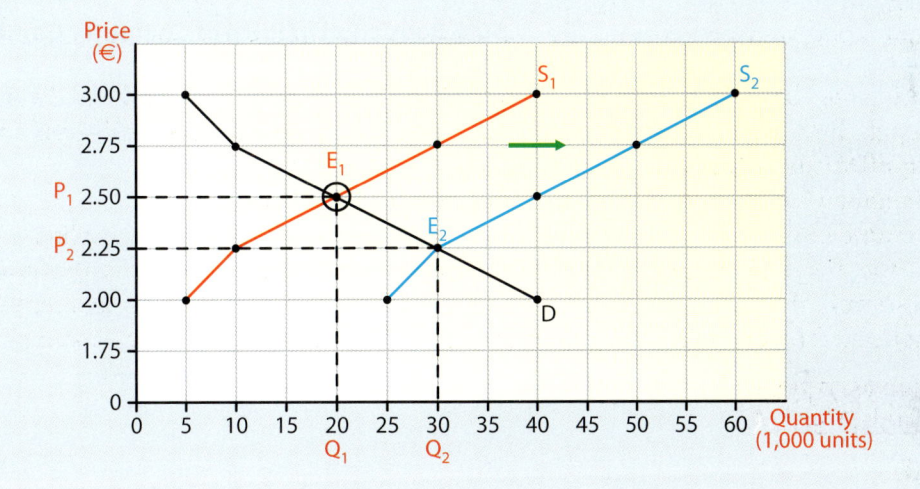

EXAM ✓ Question 1(a), 2009 (30 marks)

(i) Show, by means of a labelled diagram, the market demand and supply for games consoles, e.g. Xbox, PlayStation or Nintendo DS. Identify and explain the market equilibrium position.

(ii) Explain, with the aid of a separate diagram in **each** case, the effects which **each** of the following is most likely to have on the above equilibrium position:

- 50% reduction in the price of computer games used with the games console.

- Quota placed on the quantity of games consoles entering Ireland.

- Government introduce a 2% levy (tax) on all income earned.

Positive Economics

Solution

(a) (i)

The firm is in equilibrium where the market demand curve equals the market supply curve and there is no tendency for the price to change.

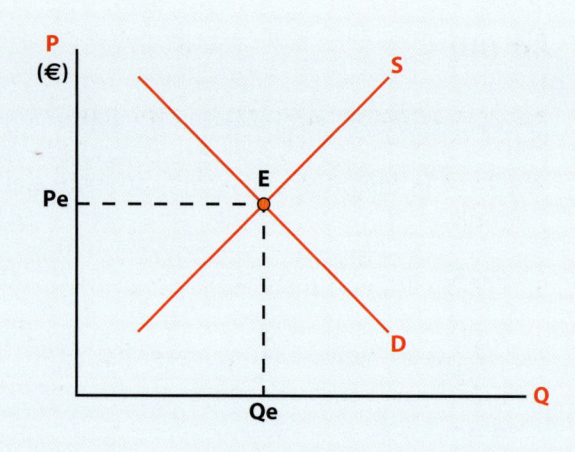

(a) (ii)

50% reduction:

- Demand curve shifts to the right (D_2).

- This is because the complementary good is now cheaper, resulting in an increase in demand.

- There is a new higher price (P_2).

- There is a new higher quantity (Q_2).

Quota:

- The supply curve shifts to the left (S_2).

- This is because fewer consoles can now be imported.

- There is a new higher price (P_2).

- There is a new lower quantity (Q_2).

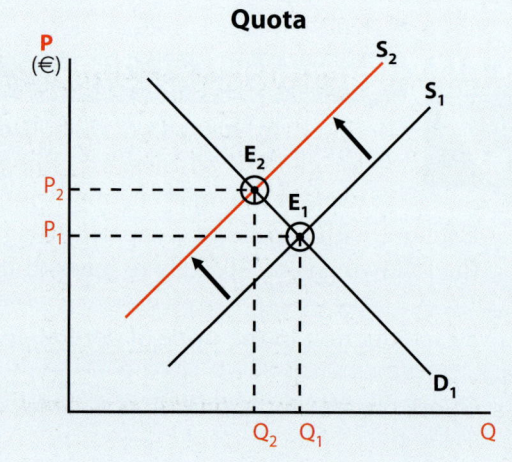

50% Reduction in Price of Computer Games

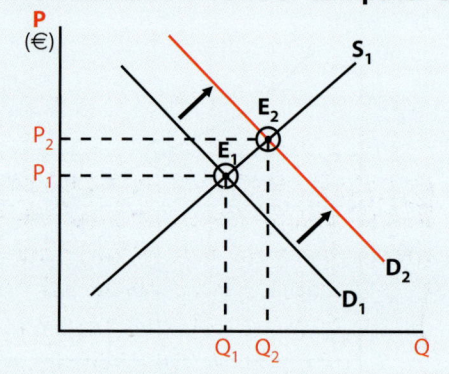

Quota

Levy:

- The demand curve shifts to the left (D_2).

- This is because consumer income has fallen.

- There is a new lower price (P_2).

- There is a new lower quantity (Q_2).

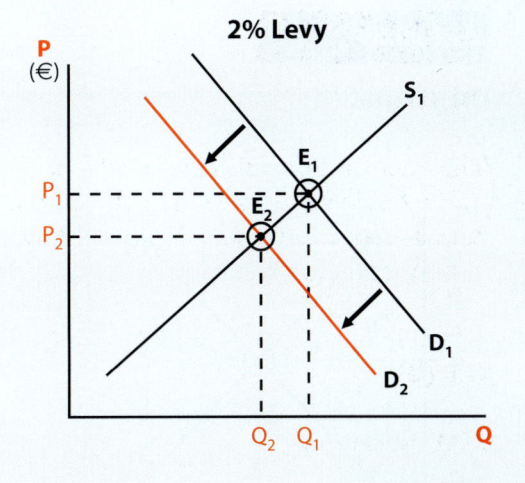

EXAM Question 1(b) and (c), 2008 (32 marks)

(b) (i) Using the data below, draw the diagram showing the market demand and supply curves for MP3 players.

(ii) Show on your diagram the price and quantity of MP3 players at which this market is in equilibrium.

(c) (i) With reference to your diagram in 1(b)(i), assume that consumer demand for MP3 players increases by 40 units at each price listed, while supply remains unchanged. Draw the **new** demand curve for this situation and show the new equilibrium price and quantity.

Price (€)	Quantity demanded (units)	Quantity supplied (units)
20	100	20
30	80	40
40	60	60
50	40	80
60	20	100

Positive Economics

Solution

(b) (i) and (ii)

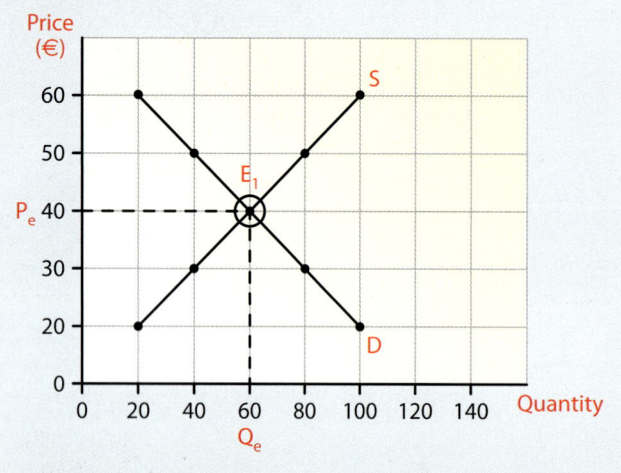

[Supply and demand diagram: Price (€) on y-axis from 0 to 60, Quantity on x-axis from 0 to 140. Supply curve S rises from (20, 20) to (100, 60); Demand curve D falls from (20, 60) to (100, 20). Equilibrium E_1 at $P_e = 40$, $Q_e = 60$.]

(c) (i)

Price (€)	Quantity demanded (units)	Quantity supplied (units)	New quantity demanded
20	100	20	140
30	80	40	120
40	60	60	100
50	40	80	80
60	20	100	60

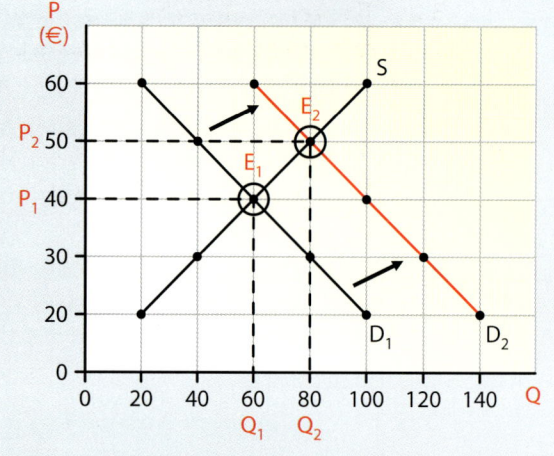

[Diagram showing demand curve shifting right from D_1 to D_2. New equilibrium E_2 at $P_2 = 50$, $Q_2 = 80$; original E_1 at $P_1 = 40$, $Q_1 = 60$.]

EXAM ✓ Question 1(b)(ii), 2005 (15 marks)

Explain, with the aid of a separate diagram in each case, the effects which **each** of the following may have on the equilibrium position:

- A successful advertising campaign in favour of the product is introduced.

- A tariff on imports of the product is removed.

Solution

A successful advertising campaign in favour of the product is introduced

- **Effect:** The **demand curve** will shift to the right.

- **Why:** Consumers are persuaded to buy more due to the successful advertising campaign.

- **Equilibrium:** Both price and quantity increase. The new equilibrium position is P_2 and Q_2.

A tariff on imports of the product is removed

- **Effect:** The **supply curve** will shift to the right.

- **Why:** The removal of the tariff will result in an increase in the quantity of imports into the market, resulting in an increase in supply.

- **Equilibrium:** Price falls and quantity increases. The new equilibrium position is P_2 and Q_2.

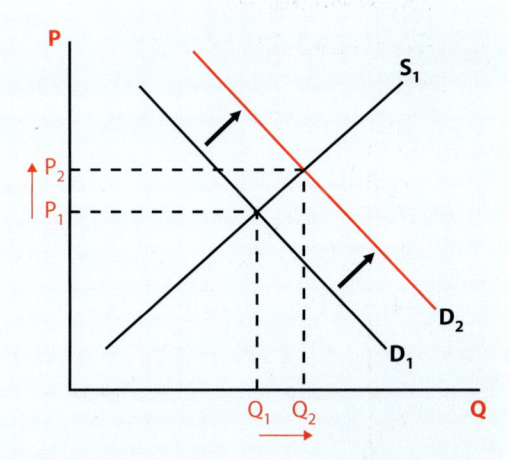

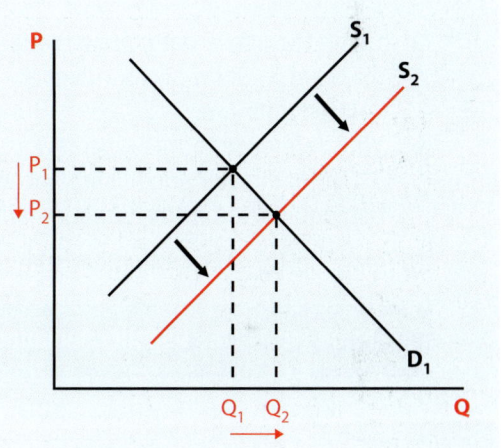

Questions

Short Questions

1. Define equilibrium.
2. Illustrate, using a labelled graph, your understanding of equilibrium.
3. What is meant by equilibrium price?
4. What is meant by equilibrium quantity?
5. Using a labelled diagram, show the equilibrium price and quantity.

Positive Economics

Long Questions

1. The data below represents the market demand and supply schedules for Good X.

Price (€)	Quantity demanded (units)	Quantity supplied (units)
10	25	5
20	20	10
30	15	15
40	10	20
50	5	25

   (a) Using the above data, draw the diagram showing the market demand and supply curve for Good X. Show on your diagram the price and quantity of Good X at which this market is in equilibrium.
   (b) With reference to this diagram, assume the consumer demand for Good X increases by 15 units at each price listed above, while supply remains unchanged. Draw the new demand curve for this situation and show the new equilibrium price and quantity.

2. The data below represents the market demand and supply schedules for Good B.

Price (€)	Quantity demanded (units)	Quantity supplied (units)
20	500	100
40	400	200
60	300	300
80	200	400
100	100	500

   (a) Using the above data, draw the diagram showing the market demand and supply curve for Good B. Show on your diagram the price and quantity of Good B at which this market is in equilibrium.
   (b) With reference to this diagram, assume the firm's supply for Good B decreases by 50 units at each price listed above, while demand remains unchanged. Draw the new supply curve for this situation and show the new equilibrium price and quantity.

Long Questions – *continued*

3. The data below represents the market demand and supply schedules for Good Y.

Price (€)	Quantity demanded (units)	Quantity supplied (units)
20	250	50
40	200	100
60	150	150
80	100	200
100	50	250

(a) Using the above data, draw the diagram showing the market demand and supply curve for Good Y. Show on your diagram the price and quantity of Good Y at which this market is in equilibrium.

(b) With reference to this diagram, assume the consumer demand for Good Y decreases by 20 units at each price listed above, while supply remains unchanged. Draw the new demand curve for this situation and show the new equilibrium price and quantity.

4. The data below represents the market demand and supply schedules for Good A.

Price (€)	Quantity demanded (units)	Quantity supplied (units)
15	200	40
30	160	80
45	120	120
60	80	160
75	40	200

(a) Using the above data, draw the diagram showing the market demand and supply curve for Good A. Show on your diagram the price and quantity of Good A at which this market is in equilibrium.

(b) With reference to this diagram, assume the firm's supply for Good A increases by 30 units at each price listed above, while demand remains unchanged. Draw the new supply curve for this situation and show the new equilibrium price and quantity.

Long Questions – *continued*

5. Explain, with the aid of a labelled diagram, the effect of each of the following on the equilibrium quantity and equilibrium price of a good.
    (a) A rise in the price of a complementary good
    (b) A fall in the price of a complementary good
    (c) A rise in the price of a substitute good
    (d) A fall in the price of a substitute good
    (e) A rise in income if the good is a normal good
    (f) A fall in income if the good is a normal good
    (g) A rise in income if the good is an inferior good
    (h) A fall in income if the good is an inferior good
    (i) An improvement in technology
    (j) An expectation of a rise in prices in the future
    (k) An expectation of a fall in prices in the future
    (l) A rise in the price of a related good
    (m) A fall in the price of a related good
    (n) A rise in the cost of production
    (o) A fall in the cost of production
    (p) An increase in corporation tax
    (q) A decrease in PAYE
    (r) A subsidy is provided by the European Union
    (s) A subsidy provided to a producer is withdrawn by the government
    (t) An industrial strike prevents production and the supply of products
    (u) A transport strike prevents the supply of raw materials

Chapter 6: Elasticity of Demand and Supply

Specific Learning Outcomes

At the end of this chapter, students should be able to:

- Explain the concept of elasticity.
- Explain price elasticity of demand (PED).
- Calculate PED from given data using the supplied formula and interpret values for PED.
- Understand the usefulness of a knowledge of PED to the consumer, producer and government.
- Explain the factors that determine the PED of a good.
- Apply a knowledge of price elasticity to determine the effect of a change in price on a firm's revenue and profits.
- Explain cross elasticity of demand (CED).
- Calculate CED from given data using the supplied formula and interpret values for CED (substitute goods and complementary goods).
- Understand the significance of a knowledge of CED to a firm.
- Explain income elasticity of demand (YED).
- Calculate YED from given data using the supplied formula and interpret values for YED (normal goods and inferior goods).
- Apply a knowledge of income elasticity to determine the effect of a change in income on a firm's sales.
- Explain price elasticity of supply (PES).
- Calculate PES from given data using the supplied formula and interpret values for PES.
- Explain the factors that affect the PES of a good.

Introduction

We know from the law of demand that if the price of a good rises, the quantity demanded falls and if the price of a good falls, the quantity demanded rises. However, this economic law does not tell us the extent of the increases or decreases in quantity demanded. It is not much use from a businessperson's point of view to be told that if they increase their prices by €0.10, quantity demanded will drop – they want to know the **extent** of the drop. It may mean the difference between surviving or closing down.

What the shopkeeper really needs to know is the **elasticity** of their good. Let's now define elasticity of demand.

> **ELASTICITY** is a measure of responsiveness (sensitivity) of the quantity demanded of a good to a change in some variable.

These variables can be:

- The price of the good.
- The price of some other good.
- The consumer's income.

€1 — *Price of the good*

€2 — *Price of some other good*

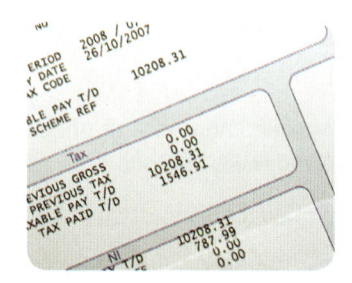

Consumer's income

For example, consider what happens to attendance at the cinema when:

- The price of cinema tickets rises.
- The price of rental DVDs falls.
- The consumer's income increases.

This means we have three types of elasticity to measure:

- **Price elasticity:** This is the change in quantity demanded of a good caused by the change in the price of a good itself.

6: Elasticity of Demand and Supply

- **Income elasticity:** This is the change in quantity demanded of a good caused by a change in the consumer's income.
- **Cross elasticity:** This is the change in quantity demanded of a good caused by a change in the price of a substitute/complementary good.

Price Elasticity of Demand (PED)

PRICE ELASTICITY OF DEMAND (PED) measures the percentage/proportionate change in the quantity demanded for a good caused by the percentage/proportionate change in the price of the good itself.

In essence, price elasticity of demand measures the responsiveness of the quantity demanded of a good to changes in the price charged for the good itself. This allows the producer to make feasible predictions regarding the outcome of price changes. For example, take your local chipper. The chip shop owner must be aware of the effect on quantity demanded if they increase the price of chips. It helps them to plan and predict sales revenue, which makes the purchase of raw materials, e.g. potatoes, more efficient.

If the coefficient of elasticity is:	The demand for a good is:	
Greater than 1 (>) (in absolute terms)	Elastic	−7, +3.3
Less than 1 (<) (in absolute terms)	Inelastic	+0.6, −0.1
Equal to 1 (=)	Unit elastic/unitary	+1, −1
Zero (0)	Perfectly inelastic	
Infinity (∞)	Perfectly elastic	

Degree of Elasticity

Elasticity varies among products as some products may be more essential to the consumer. Products that are necessities are more insensitive to price changes because consumers would continue buying these products despite price increases. Equally, a price increase of a luxury good or service may discourage consumers from purchasing it.

Elastic

A GOOD IS RELATIVELY ELASTIC when the proportionate/percentage change in quantity demanded of a good is *greater* than the proportionate/percentage change in the price of the good itself.

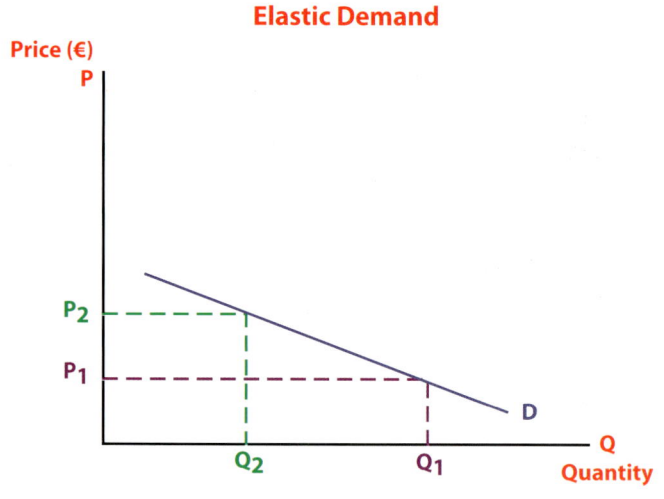

- These items often tend to be considered as luxury goods and are items of discretionary expenditure. We tend to cut back on purchasing these goods if price increases, e.g. we may replace an expensive brand of biscuits with an own brand.

- Goods such as consumer durables (goods that do not have to be purchased frequently), e.g. home appliances, home and office furniture and garden equipment, and goods with many substitutes, e.g. bottled water and shampoo, also tend to be **elastic**.

- Example: If price goes up by 10%, quantity demanded falls by 25%.

- When the formula is applied and the result is greater than 1 in absolute terms (ignoring the sign) (PED > 1), the good is said to be **elastic**.

- The larger the value, the greater the elasticity, i.e. the more sensitive it is to a change in the price of the good itself, e.g. +2.5, –2.5, +1.4, –1.4; each of these numbers has a **PED > 1**.

PERFECTLY ELASTIC

- Perfect elasticity implies that individual producers can sell all they want at a given price, e.g. €2 per unit. However, if any producer tries to increase that price, even by one cent more, quantity demanded would be zero as no consumer would buy their product. Instead, consumers would prefer to buy from another producer who sells the same good at the prevailing market price of €2 per unit.

> **A GOOD IS PERFECTLY ELASTIC** when any increase in the price of that good results in its quantity falling to zero.

- A good is perfectly elastic if it has a price elasticity that is infinite (PED = ∞).

- Perfectly elastic goods are sold by firms that operate in the perfect competition market structure, which we will examine in Chapter 8.

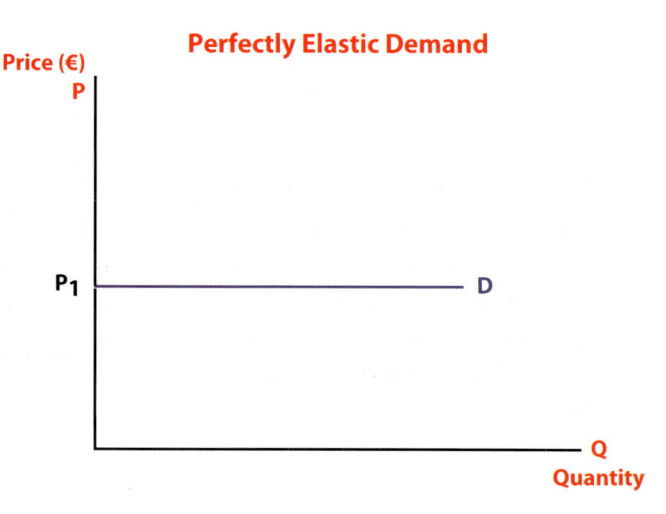

6: Elasticity of Demand and Supply

EQUAL TO UNITY/UNITARY

A GOOD IS SAID TO BE UNITARY ELASTIC when the proportionate/percentage change in the quantity demanded of a good is equal to the proportionate/percentage change in the price of that good.

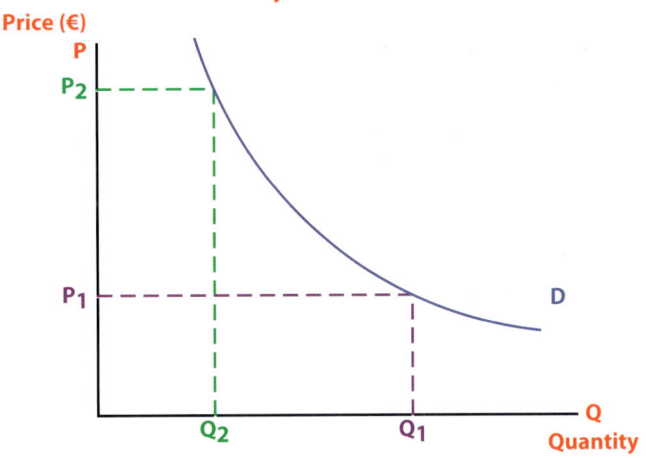

Unitary Elastic Demand

- For example, a 30% decrease in the price of the good itself leads to a 30% increase in the quantity demanded of the good: $\frac{30\%}{30\%} = 1$.
- PED = +/− 1.

INELASTIC

A GOOD IS RELATIVELY INELASTIC if the proportionate/percentage change in quantity demanded of a good is less than the proportionate/percentage change in price of that good.

- Goods considered to be inelastic are typically goods people consider necessities in our daily life. It is difficult to cut back our expenditure on these goods, e.g. food and petrol.
- It also applies to addictive goods such as cigarettes and alcohol.
- For example, a 10% increase in price leads to a 3% fall in the quantity demanded of a good.
- When the formula is applied, the result is less than 1 in absolute terms and a good is said to be inelastic (PED < 1), e.g. +0.7, −0.7, +0.04, −0.04; each of these numbers has a **PED < 1**.

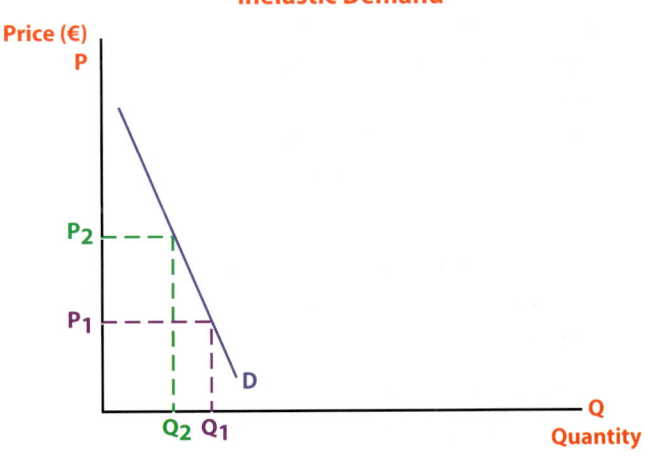

Inelastic Demand

Positive Economics

PERFECTLY INELASTIC

A GOOD IS PERFECTLY INELASTIC if the proportionate/percentage change in the price of a good causes no change in the quantity demanded of that good.

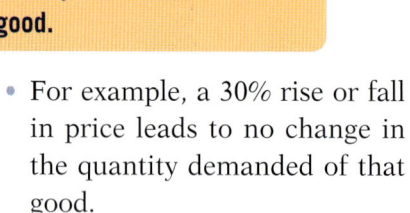

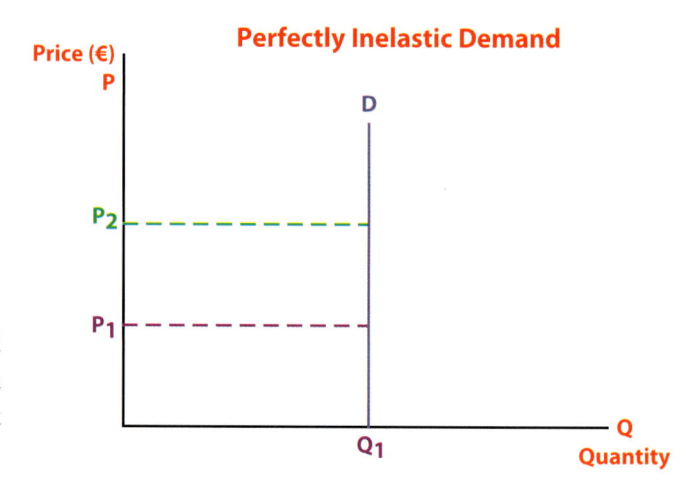

- For example, a 30% rise or fall in price leads to no change in the quantity demanded of that good.
- Examples of such goods are life-saving medicines such as insulin for a diabetic or medical equipment.

As such, PED measures the extent of movement along the demand curve.

- If elasticity is greater than 1, demand is said to be elastic.
- If elasticity is between zero and one, demand is inelastic.
- If elasticity equals one, demand is unitary elastic.

Examples

Elastic = +1.5, −1.2   PED > +/−1 = elastic

Inelastic = −0.4, +0.6   PED < +/−1 = inelastic

Unitary = −1, +1   PED = 1 = unitary elastic

PED and Total Revenue

When examining elasticity, it is important to consider its relationship with the revenue of a firm, i.e. income from sales. The following table is a useful summary.

Elasticity	Total revenue (TR)
If the good is elastic	TR will move in the opposite direction to the price change
If the good is unitary elastic	TR will not change no matter what direction the price change
If the good is inelastic	TR will move in the same direction as the price change

6: Elasticity of Demand and Supply

Inelastic Demand Curve

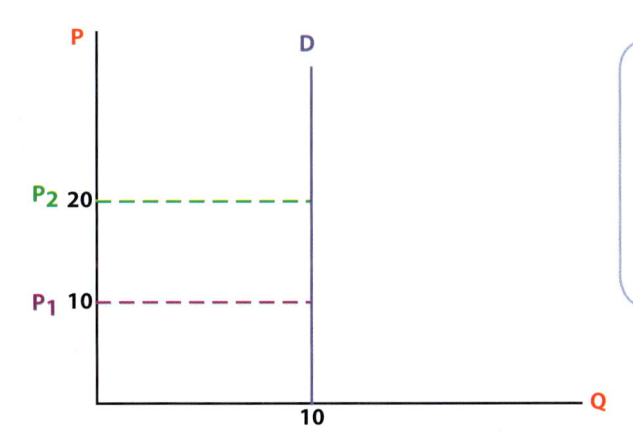

P × Q = TR
10 × 10 = 100
20 × 10 = 200
If P↑ and TR↑, price and total revenue move in the same direction

Note:

When we discuss elasticity it is possible for us to examine only the effect of price change on revenue. We do not know if profits will maximise if revenue increases, as elasticity does not take into consideration the costs involved in production. We have no knowledge of costs and therefore are unable to determine profit.

Summary of Price Elasticity of Demand = Change in Quantity Demanded

Type of elasticity	Elastic	Unitary	Inelastic
Elasticity value	PED > 1	PED = 1	PED < 1
Comparison	The % change in quantity demanded is > the % change in price **OR** The % change in price is < the % change in quantity demanded	The % change in quantity demanded = the % change in price	The % change in quantity demanded is < the % change in price **OR** The % change in price is > the % change in quantity demanded
Effect on total revenue	Revenue increases if price decreases and decreases if price increases P↑, TR↓ or P↓, TR↑	Remains constant as any price increase will be offset exactly by a decrease in the quantity demanded, e.g. P↑ 10% ⇒ Qd↓ 10%	Revenue decreases if price decreases and increases if price increases P↑, TR↑ or P↓, TR↓

Positive Economics

Elasticity formulae are on p. 28 of your log tables.

Formula:

$$\frac{\Delta Q}{\Delta P} \times \frac{P_1 + P_2}{Q_1 + Q_2}$$

P_1 = original price
P_2 = new price
ΔP = change in price
Q_1 = original quantity
Q_2 = new quantity
ΔQ = change in quantity

For normal goods, PED is usually negative (−), i.e. as price increases (+), quantity demanded falls (−) and vice versa.

For Giffen goods, PED is positive (+). This is because price and demand travel in the same direction, i.e. if price increases, the quantity demanded also increases and vice versa.

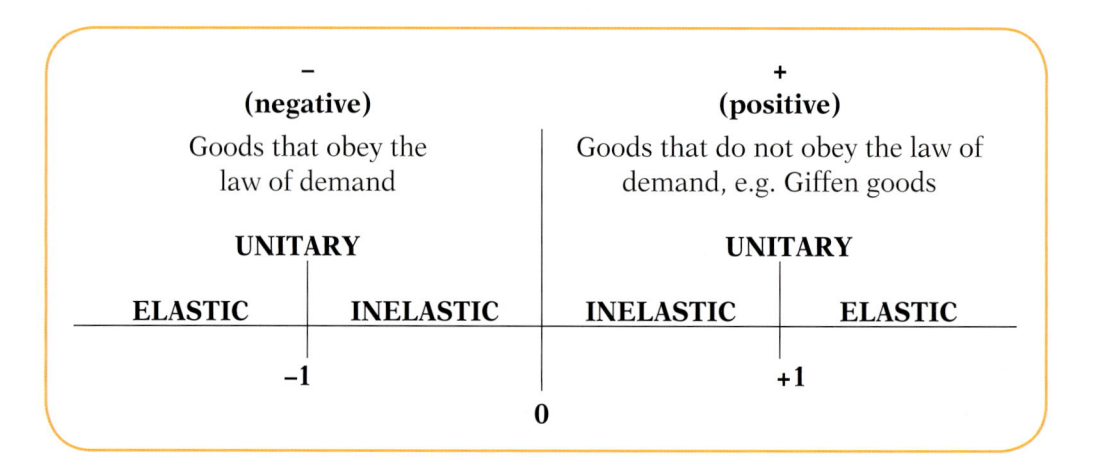

−	+
(negative)	(positive)
Goods that obey the law of demand	Goods that do not obey the law of demand, e.g. Giffen goods

```
              UNITARY                    UNITARY
  ELASTIC   |   INELASTIC    INELASTIC   |   ELASTIC
            |                            |
           −1              0            +1
```

Example
A consumer buys 120 units of a product when the price is €1. When the price is increased to €1.25, the consumer buys 100 units.

(a) Calculate the price elasticity of demand for the consumer.
(b) Is the demand for this good elastic, inelastic or unitary elastic?

Solution
Quantity fell from 120 units to 100 units:
Q_1 = 120
Q_2 = 100
ΔQ = −20 (**minus** because it has **decreased** by 20)

Price increased from €1 to €1.25:
P_1 = €1
P_2 = €1.25
ΔP = +0.25 (**positive** because it has **increased** by 0.25 cent)

Formula: $\dfrac{\Delta Q}{\Delta P} \times \dfrac{P_1 + P_2}{Q_1 + Q_2} = \dfrac{-20 \times 1 + 1.25}{+0.25 \times 120 + 100} = -0.8$ **(rounded)**

Explanation:
- Demand for the good is **inelastic** as the **PED < 1**.
- The result shows a negative sign so we assume it is a **normal** good.

EXAM Question 3, Section A, 2007 (16 marks)

Consumers buy 50 units of a product when the price is €1.50. When the price is reduced to €1 consumers will buy 90 units. Using an appropriate formula, calculate the consumers' **price elasticity of demand**. Show your workings and explain your answer.

Solution

Quantity increased from 50 units to 90 units:
Q_1 = 50
Q_2 = 90
ΔQ = +40 (**plus** because it has **increased** by 40)

Price decreased from €1.50 to €1:
P_1 = €1.50
P_2 = €1
ΔP = −0.50 (**negative** because it has **decreased** by 0.50 cent)

Formula

$\dfrac{\Delta Q}{\Delta P} \times \dfrac{P_1 + P_2}{Q_1 + Q_2} = \dfrac{+40}{-0.50} \times \dfrac{1.50 + 1}{50 + 90} = -1.4$

Explanation

- Demand for the good is **elastic** as the **PED > 1**.

- The result shows a negative sign so we assume it is a **normal** good.

Positive Economics

Example — If a consumer spends €30 per week on bottled water when its price is 50 cent per litre and continues to spend €30 per week on it when its price increases to 52 cent, what is the consumer's price elasticity of demand for bottled water?

Solution

$Q_1 = 30/0.50 = 60$ litres
$Q_2 = 30/0.52 = 57.69$ litres
$\Delta Q = -2.31$ (**minus** because it has **decreased** by 2.31 litres)

Price increased from €0.50 to €0.52:
$P_1 = 0.50$
$P_2 = 0.52$
$\Delta P = +0.02$ (**positive** because it has **increased** by 0.02 cent)

Formula

$$\frac{\Delta Q}{\Delta P} \times \frac{P_1 + P_2}{Q_1 + Q_2} = \frac{-2.31}{+0.02} \times \frac{0.50 + 0.52}{60 + 57.69} = -1$$

Explanation
- Demand for the good is **unitary elastic** as the **PED = 1**.
- The result shows a negative number so we assume that it is a **normal** good.

EXAM — Question 1(b), 2006 (30 marks)

A manufacturer of three different products calculates the price elasticity of demand for each product as follows:

Product X: –1.5   Product Y: –1.0   Product Z: –0.3

The company wishes to maximise its revenues. Explain in respect of **each** of these products, what change, if any, the company should make in the prices currently being charged to enable it to achieve its aim.

Solution

	Product X: –1.5	Product Y: –1.0	Product Z: –0.3
Type of elasticity	Elastic	Unitary	Inelastic
Elasticity value	PED > 1	PED = 1	PED < 1
Comparison	The % change in quantity demanded is > the % change in price	The % change in quantity demanded = the % change in price	The % change in price is > the % change in quantity demanded
Effect on total revenue	Revenue increases if price decreases	Remains constant	Revenue increases if price increases

Factors That Affect Price Elasticity of Demand (PED)

The Availability of Close Substitutes

- This is probably the most important factor influencing the elasticity of a good or service. In general, **the more substitutes that are available, the more elastic the demand** tends to be. For example, if the price of Berrys Tea went up by €0.25, consumers may switch to Lions Tea.

- The closer the substitutability between goods, the more consumers will tend to switch from one substitute brand to another and thus the greater the PED will be.

> **REMEMBER!**
> In Chapter 3 we learned that substitute goods are goods that satisfy the same need and so can be considered alternatives to each other.

Complementary Goods

- If the good in question is **the cheaper of two goods which are in joint demand, then the demand for it is likely to be relatively inelastic** in response to changes in its own price. For example, if shoelaces are cheaper than shoes, then any change in the price of shoelaces will have very little effect on the demand for shoes.

> **REMEMBER!**
> In Chapter 3 we learned that complementary goods are goods that are used jointly. The use of one good involves the use of another good.

Is the Commodity a Luxury or Necessity?

- As consumers, it is not essential that we should possess luxuries. These are wants and are a discretionary expenditure. Therefore, PED for **luxury goods will be relatively elastic**.

- Necessities, however, are essential in our everyday lives – people have no choice but to buy them even when their price is increased. Therefore, PED for **necessities will be relatively inelastic**.

The Proportion of Income That Is Spent on the Commodity
- This factor affecting elasticity of demand refers to the total income a person can spend on a particular good or service. In general, as income increases, so does the quantity demanded of goods.

- In general, **the greater the proportion of income that is spent on a good, the more elastic** the demand for it is likely to be in response to a change in its own price. A rise of 50% in the price of a bag of sugar is unlikely to have a significant effect on demand.

The Durability of the Commodity
- **The more durable the commodity, the more elastic** the demand for it is likely to be in response to a change in its own price.

- If products such as motor vehicles increase in price, it is likely that the public will extend the life of their existing model and postpone the purchase of a replacement.

Expectations as to Future Changes in Price
- If, in the face of a price reduction, the public considers that **prices are likely to fall even further**, they may wait for the further reduction in price, in which case demand may **not be very elastic** on the initial price reduction.

The Length of Time Allowed for Adjustment to Price Changes
- **In the long run, demand is more elastic** as consumers have time to adjust to a change in price.

- If the price of electricity rose by 80%, a consumer may economise on the use of various appliances in the short term. In the long term the consumer will have to consider substituting other forms of energy. The demand will be highly inelastic at first, but as time goes on will become more elastic.

- If the price of cigarettes goes up by €2 per pack, a smoker with very few available substitutes will most likely continue buying their daily cigarettes. This means that tobacco is inelastic because the change in price will not have a significant influence on the quantity demanded. However, if that smoker finds that they cannot afford to spend the extra €2 per day and begins to quit smoking over a period of time, the price elasticity of cigarettes for that consumer becomes elastic in the long run.

Consumer Purchase Habits/Brand Loyalty/Advertising Effectiveness
- A consumer may become strongly attached to a particular product through **habit or loyalty to that brand**. An increase in price for that good will not cause them to consume less of the product or switch to cheaper substitutes. The demand for such goods will therefore be **price inelastic**.

6: Elasticity of Demand and Supply

Number of Alternative Uses the Good Has

- **A commodity that has a large number of uses will usually have a relatively elastic demand.** For example, sugar is used in direct consumption, sweetening purposes, baking, food processing, etc. Any increase in the price of sugar may only result in a small fall in its demand in each of these markets, but the total drop overall may be significant.

Importance of Understanding Elasticity

Importance in Taxation Policy/Minister for Finance

The concept of elasticity has huge relevance to the government and its financial planning. When a Finance Minister levies a tax on a certain commodity, he has to see whether the demand for that commodity is elastic or inelastic. If the demand is inelastic, he can increase the tax and thus can collect more revenue. But if the demand for a commodity is elastic, he is unlikely to increase the rate of that tax. If he does so, the demand for that commodity will decrease and therefore total revenue will be reduced.

Importance to Businesspeople

The concept of elasticity is of great importance to businesspeople. When demand for a good is elastic, lowering the price of a good will increase sales and increase total revenue (monopolists will do exactly the same thing). In the case where demand is inelastic, they are then likely to charge a higher price for a commodity and increase total revenue (e.g. in monopoly; see Chapter 10).

Use in International Trade

If €1 = £1 and the value of the euro falls against sterling, how will this affect our imports and exports? Exports become relatively cheaper and imports become more expensive. The effects of devaluation depend on elasticities of demand of exports and imports. Devaluation in the euro will improve our balance of payments if the sum of the elasticities of demand for a country's exports and its elasticity of demand for a country's imports are greater than 1 in absolute terms (the Marshall-Lerner Law) (see Chapter 28).

Cross Elasticity of Demand (CED)

Formula:

PB_1 = original price
PB_2 = new price
ΔPB = change in price
QA_1 = original quantity
QA_2 = new quantity
ΔQA = change in quantity

$$\frac{\Delta QA}{\Delta PB} \times \frac{PB_1 + PB_2}{QA_1 + QA_2}$$

CED measures the proportionate/percentage change in the quantity demanded for one good caused by the proportionate/percentage change in the price of another good.

Positive Economics

Substitute Goods
Substitute goods are goods that satisfy the same needs and act as alternatives to each other, e.g. Berrys Tea and Lions Tea.

- A change in the price of Berrys will have an effect on the quantity demanded of Lions.

- If the price of Berrys increases, the quantity demanded of Lions will increase as consumers will stop purchasing Berrys and switch to its cheaper alternative, Lions.

- A **positive** result from the cross elasticity formula indicates a **substitute good**, as we can see from the above that there is a positive relationship between the price of Berrys and the quantity demanded of Lions $(Q_L\uparrow^+)$ $(P_B\uparrow^+)$.

- The bigger the value from the formula, the closer the substitute.

Complementary Goods
Complementary goods are goods that are interrelated and should be used in conjunction with each other, e.g. high-performance cars and petrol, golf clubs and golf balls, cameras and memory cards.

- A change in the price of petrol will have an effect on the quantity demanded of high-performance cars.

- If the price of petrol increases, the quantity demanded of high-performance cars will decrease in the long run as consumers will reduce their spending on petrol and therefore also reduce spending on its complement, high-performance cars.

- A **negative** answer from the cross elasticity formula indicates that the goods are **complementary**. The petrol $(P_p\uparrow^+)$ and the quantity demanded of high-performance cars $(Q_h\downarrow^-)$.

- The bigger the value from the formula, the more complementary the goods.

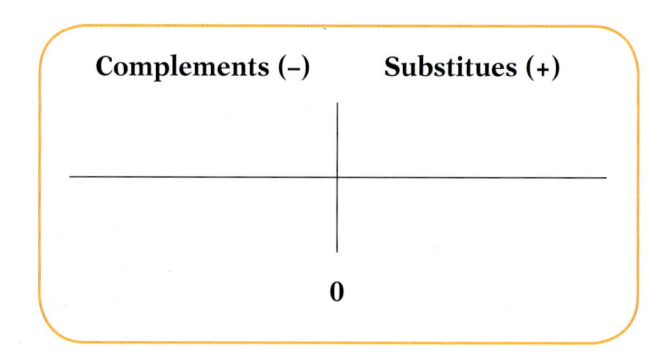

```
    Complements (–)    Substitues (+)
                  |
    _____|_____
                  |
                  0
```

6: Elasticity of Demand and Supply

EXAM ✓ Question 1(c), 2006 (30 marks)

A consumer buys 10 units of Good A when the price of Good B is €5. When the price of Good B rises to €6 (the price of Good A remaining unchanged), the consumer buys 14 units of Good A.

(i) Define **cross elasticity of demand**.
(ii) Using on appropriate formula, calculate this consumer's cross elasticity of demand for Good A. Show your workings.
(iii) Is Good A a substitute for, or a complement to, Good B? Explain your reasoning.

Solution

(i) Cross elasticity measures the proportionate/percentage change in the quantity demanded for one good caused by the proportionate/percentage change in the price of other goods.

(ii) $QA_1 = 10$ (original quantity)
$QA_2 = 14$ (new quantity)
$\Delta QA = +4$ (**positive** because there is an increase of 4 units)
$PB_1 = 5$ (original price)
$PB_2 = 6$ (new price)
$\Delta PB = +1$ (**positive** as there is an **increase** of €1)

$$\frac{\Delta QA}{\Delta PB} \times \frac{P_1B + P_2B}{Q_1A + Q_2A} \quad \frac{+4}{+1} \times \frac{5+6}{10+14} = \mathbf{+1.83}$$

(iii) Good A is a **substitute good** because it has a **+** sign. This means that as the price of Good B increased, the consumer switched from consuming Good B to the cheaper alternative, Good A.

EXAM ✓ Question 4(b), 1999 (25 marks)

Cross Elasticity of Demand between Good A and Good B = +2.5
Cross Elasticity of Demand between Good A and Good C = –0.3
Cross Elasticity of Demand between Good A and Good D = +0.3
Cross Elasticity of Demand between Good A and Good E = –1.4

Which of these goods are complements to Good A? Explain your answer.

Which of these goods is the closest substitute for Good A? Explain your answer.

Solution

Good C and Good E are complements to Good A as they have negative signs, which indicates a negative relationship between the quantity demanded of Good A and the prices of Good C and Good E, i.e. if the price of Good C and Good E increases (+), the quantity demanded of Good A decreases (–). Good E is the closest complement to Good A.

Positive Economics

The closest substitute is Good B. A positive sign indicates that Good B is a substitute good for Good A. This means there is a positive relationship between Good A and Good B. If the price of Good A increases (+), the quantity demanded of Good B also increases (+), as the consumer will switch to the cheaper alternative, Good B. The bigger the number, the closer the substitute.

Income Elasticity of Demand (YED)

Formula:
$$\frac{\Delta Q}{\Delta Y} \times \frac{Y_1 + Y_2}{Q_1 + Q_2}$$

Y_1 = original income
Y_2 = new income
ΔY = change in income
Q_1 = original quantity
Q_2 = new quantity
ΔQ = change in quantity

YED measures the proportionate/percentage change in the quantity demanded for a good caused by the proportionate/percentage change in the income (Y) of consumers.

REMEMBER!
In Chapter 3 we learned that a normal good is a good with a positive income effect. A rise in income causes more of it to be demanded, while a fall in income causes less of it to be demanded.

REMEMBER!
In Chapter 3 we learned that an inferior good is a good with a negative income effect. A rise in income causes less of it to be demanded, while a fall in income causes more of it to be demanded.

Normal Goods = A Positive Result

- In general, an increase (+) in income (Y) results in an increase (+) in the quantity demanded of goods. These goods would be classified as normal goods as they have a positive income effect.

- If the YED > 1, the good is a normal necessity (inelastic).

- If the YED < 1, the good is a luxury necessity (inelastic).

- An increased proportion of income is spent on goods such as luxuries when income increases. For example, demand for consumer durables have a high YED, e.g. dishwashers.

- Conversely, in a recession or economic slowdown, these items of discretionary spending might be the first victims of decisions by consumers to rein in their spending and rebuild savings and household finances, e.g. foreign holidays.

- In contrast, demand for food items or other necessities, e.g. toothpaste, does not increase very rapidly as income increases.

Inferior Goods = A Negative Result

- With some goods and services, we may actually notice a decrease in demand as income increases. These are goods and services that will be replaced by a consumer when income increases.

- If the answer is negative it indicates that the good is an inferior good. There is a negative relationship between the quantity demanded and income.

- An example of this is when a consumer's income increases there may be an increase in the demand for tailor-made suits as opposed to off-the-rack suits. There may be an increase in the demand for organic food as opposed to own-brand food.

- Inferior goods have a negative income elasticity of demand. Fewer goods are bought as income rises. In a recession the demand for inferior products might actually grow (depending on the severity of the change in income).

- Products for which the demand decreases as income increases have an income elasticity of less than zero.

Income Elasticity of Demand

Inferior goods (–)		Normal goods (+)	
←		Necessity	Luxury
	0		1

Goods with Zero Income Elasticity of Demand

Goods that have a zero income elasticity of demand are goods that people purchase when their income is low. They do not purchase additional quantities of these goods when their income increases, e.g. salt.

Note:
A positive YED always implies a normal good. A negative YED implies an inferior good. If YED > 1, the good is elastic and a luxury. If YED < 1, it is inelastic and a necessity.

EXAM ✓ Question 1(b) and (c), 2009 (30 marks)

(b) Which figure stated below is most likely to represent each of the following?

- **Income** elasticity of demand for low-price cuts of meat.

- **Income** elasticity of demand for Apple iPhones.

- **Price** elasticity of demand for petrol.

    –1.6   –0.1   +4.3

Give reasons for your choice in **each** case.

Positive Economics

(c) Assume **income** elasticity of demand for games consoles is **+2.5** and total sales in 2008 were 100,000 units. Calculate the expected total sales for the year if consumers' incomes are expected to fall by 8% in 2009. Show your workings.

Solution

(b)

YED for low-price cuts of meat **= −1.6**.

- Low-price cuts of meat are inferior goods and so have a negative YED.

- Low-price cuts of meat are not a necessity so it is income elastic (YED > 1).

YED for Apple iPhones **= +4.3**.

- Apple iPhones are a normal good so they have a positive YED.

- Apple iPhones are a luxury so they are income elastic (YED >1).

PED for petrol **= −0.1**.

- Petrol is a normal good so it has a negative PED.

- Petrol is a necessity so it is price inelastic (PED < 1).

(c)

- If income decreases by 8% then sales will decrease by (8% × 2.5) = 20%.

- Sales will fall by 20% of 100,000 units = 20,000 units.

- Sales in 2009 will equal 100,000 − 20,000 = 80,000 units.

Price Elasticity of Supply (PES)

Formula:
$$\frac{\Delta Qs}{\Delta P} \times \frac{P_1 + P_2}{Qs_1 + Qs_2}$$

PES measures the relationship between proportionate/percentage change in quantity supplied and a proportionate/percentage change in price.

PES measures the responsiveness of supply to price changes in the market. The greater the price elasticity, the more responsive and sensitive producers are to changes in price. High price elasticity suggests that as price increases there will be an increase in the quantity supplied and vice versa. A very low price elasticity implies that changes in price have little influence on quantity supplied.

6: Elasticity of Demand and Supply

> **PES** is usually positive, as an increase in its own price (+) will normally lead to an increase in the quantity supplied (+).

- If **PES** > 1 = elastic supply (supply is responsive/sensitive to changes in price).
- If **PES** = 1 = unitary supply.
- If **PES** < 1 = inelastic supply (supply is unresponsive to changes in price).

Degree of Elasticity of Supply

Elastic Supply

> **A GOOD IS ELASTIC** when the proportionate change in quantity supplied is greater than the proportionate change in price.

Elastic Supply

The percentage change in supply is greater than the percentage change in price.

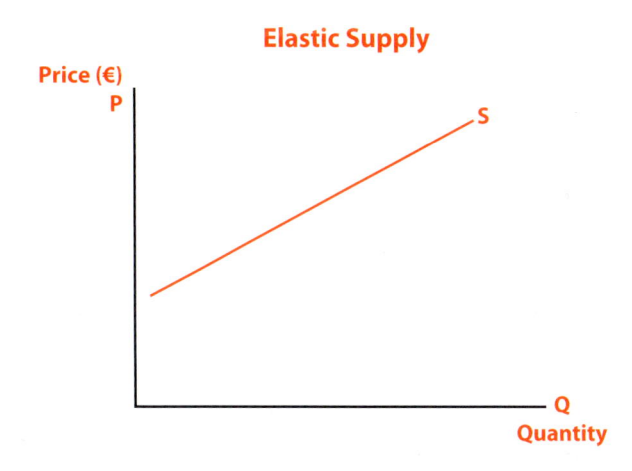

Inelastic Supply

> **A GOOD IS SAID TO BE INELASTIC** when a change in the price of the good causes less than a proportionate change in the quantity supplied of a good.

Inelastic Supply

The percentage change in quantity supplied is less than the percentage change in price.

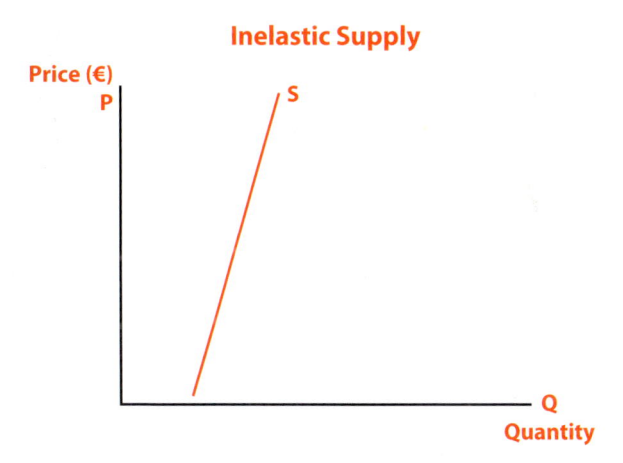

Zero Elasticity of Supply

Zero elasticity of supply (perfectly inelastic supply) would indicate that an increase in the selling price of the good does not result in any increase in the quantity supplied, e.g. the supply of fish on market day is fixed.

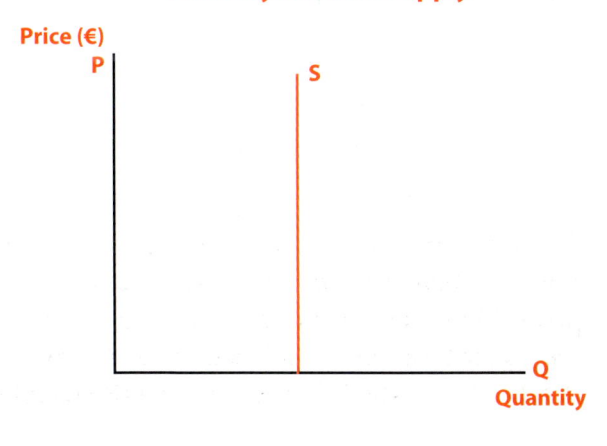

Perfectly Inelastic Supply

Factors That Affect Elasticity of Supply

- **Firm's capacity:** If the firm is operating with plenty of capacity, it should be able to increase production output more quickly without any great increase in costs. The firm is therefore more able to respond to price and hence supply will be elastic. On the other hand, if the firm is operating close to its maximum level of output, it will be less able to respond to changes in price, resulting in more inelastic supply.

- **Mobility of the factors of production:** The greater the ease of the mobility from one type of production to another, the more responsive the producer will be to a change in supply. If the production process is flexible, producers can respond by increasing the supply of goods, e.g. switching production of Cork jerseys to Manchester United jerseys. Supply will tend to be more elastic. The firm will allocate more resources to the production of the goods for which there is an increase in demand.

- **Time period:** Supply is likely to be inelastic in the short run as the firm has to adjust its production. For example, the supply of fish and seasonal vegetables on market day is fixed. An increase in price cannot bring about an immediate increase in the quantity supplied.

- **Nature of the product:** Perishable products are likely to be inelastic in supply. A fall in the price of fish will not result in a proportionate change in the quantity supplied on the day. On the other hand, any increase in the price of cars will lead to more than a proportionate change in the supply of the commodity, indicating elastic supply.

- **Storage costs:** If storage costs are low, producers may increase supply (i.e. supply is elastic).

- **Cost conditions:** If additional output can be supplied at a constant or reduced unit cost, the supply will be responsive to an increase in the selling price (i.e. elastic supply) and vice versa.

- **Products in joint supply:** When a good is the less important of two goods that are in joint supply, then quantity supplied of this less important good will be relatively inelastic in response to changes in its own price. For example, supply would be less elastic for memory cards than cameras.

- **Stock:** If stocks of raw materials and finished products are high, then the firm is able to quickly respond to changes in quantity demanded and is able to supply these stocks to the market more quickly. As a result, supply will be elastic.

6: Elasticity of Demand and Supply

Questions

Short Questions

1. Define price elasticity of demand (PED).
2. What is the formula for PED?
3. Define cross elasticity of demand (CED).
4. What is the formula for CED?
5. Define income elasticity of demand (YED).
6. What is the formula for YED?
7. Define price elasticity of supply (PES).
8. What is the formula for PES?
9. What is the significance of a + or – sign in price elasticity of demand?
10. What is the significance of a + or – sign in cross elasticity of demand?
11. What is meant by the statement 'the PED of a good is elastic'?
12. What is meant by the statement 'the PED of a good is inelastic'?

Long Questions

1. Discuss the factors that determine price elasticity of demand.
2. Discuss the importance of elasticity to the Minister for Finance.
3. Discuss the factors that determine price elasticity of supply.
4. A consumer buys 140 units of a product when the price is €1.20. When the price is increased to €1.45, the consumer buys 120 units.
   (a) Calculate the price elasticity of demand for the consumer.
   (b) Is the demand for this good elastic, inelastic or unitary elastic?
5. A consumer buys 150 units of a product when the price is €1.50. When the price is increased to €1.70, the consumer buys 120 units.
   (a) Calculate the price elasticity of demand for the consumer.
   (b) Is the demand for this good elastic, inelastic or unitary elastic?
6. A consumer buys 100 units of a product when the price is €1. When the price is increased to €1.10, the consumer buys 80 units.
   (a) Calculate the price elasticity of demand for the consumer.
   (b) Is the demand for this good elastic, inelastic or unitary elastic?
7. The PED values of three different goods are as follows:
   A = –2.5   B = –1.0   C = –0.5
   If a company wishes to maximise revenue for the above products, what changes, if any, should the firm make in the prices presently being charged?

Positive Economics

Long Questions – *continued*

8. The PED values of three different goods are as follows:
   A = –1.7   **B = –1**   **C = 0.8**
   If a company wishes to maximise revenue for the above products, what changes, if any, should the firm make in the prices presently being charged?

9. The PED values of three different goods are as follows:
   A = +1.8   **B = –0.4**   **C = –1.9**
   If a company wishes to maximise revenue for the above products, what changes, if any, should the firm make in the prices presently being charged?

10. CED between Good A and Good B = +1.7
    CED between Good A and Good C = –0.6
    CED between Good A and Good D = +0.9
    CED between Good A and Good E = –2.4
    (a) Which of these goods are complements to Good A? Explain your answer.
    (b) Which of these goods is the closest substitute for Good A? Explain your answer.

11. CED between Good A and Good B = +2.5
    CED between Good A and Good C = –0.1
    CED between Good A and Good D = +0.3
    CED between Good A and Good E = –1.2
    (a) Which of these goods are complements to Good A? Explain your answer.
    (b) Which of these goods is the closest substitute for Good A? Explain your answer.

12. Which figure stated below is most likely to represent each of the following?
    (a) Income elasticity of demand for off-the-rack suits
    (b) Income elasticity of demand for a cruise to the Caribbean
    (c) Price elasticity of demand for toothpaste
       –1.4   –0.1   +5.2

Chapter 7 | Costs of Production

Specific Learning Outcomes

At the end of this chapter, students should be able to:

- Explain the short run period.
- Explain the long run period.
- Define implicit, explicit and opportunity cost.
- Define, apply and interpret the law of diminishing returns.
- Explain, calculate and illustrate average fixed cost, average variable cost and average total cost.
- Explain, calculate and illustrate total, average and marginal revenue and marginal cost.
- Define and illustrate total profit and normal profit.
- Derive and illustrate the SRAC (or SAC) and account for its shape.
- Define and identify the point of optimum production.
- Derive and illustrate the LRAC and account for its shape.
- Analyse the reasons why businesses grow (economies of scale) and the constraints on growth (diseconomies of scale).
- Examine the economic reasons for the survival of small firms in the Irish economy.
- Explain social costs and benefits.
- Analyse the short and long run profit-maximising conditions of a firm.

Positive Economics

Introduction

In previous chapters we looked at demand and supply and concluded that price is the main factor determining both. We referred to the point where demand and supply curves meet as equilibrium – a situation where there is no tendency to change. We also noted that utility (satisfaction) is the basis of demand and cost of production is the basis of supply. It is these costs – money that must be paid for inputs (factors of production) to produce output – that we will study in this chapter.

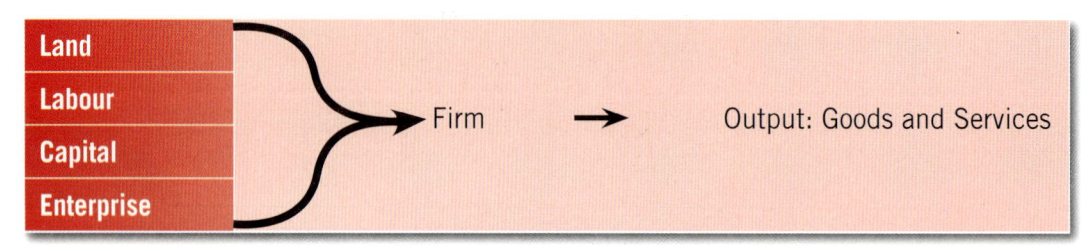

| Land / Labour / Capital / Enterprise | → Firm → | Output: Goods and Services |

Time Periods

SHORT RUN: A period of time during which at least one factor of production is fixed in supply.

LONG RUN: A period of time during which all the factors of production are variable in quantity.

Before we start our analysis, it is important that we understand that a firm operates in either the short run or the long run period.

The time periods involved in each of the above can vary in terms of months or years from industry to industry, e.g. a popular deli that uses capital and labour (the building/equipment and staff) and is constantly busy will not be able to expand its premises immediately in response to an increase in demand. Instead, an application for planning, negotiating with contractors and building the extension all take time. Here, the premises (capital) is fixed in supply and the only method available to increase output in the interim is to hire more staff (labour) – the variable factor.

Short run

In the long run, both the size of the deli and the number of staff are all variable, i.e. in the long run all factors are variable. The time period for the deli to increase in size could be one year – this is its short run time period. Contrast this to a car manufacturer where the corresponding time period might be several years.

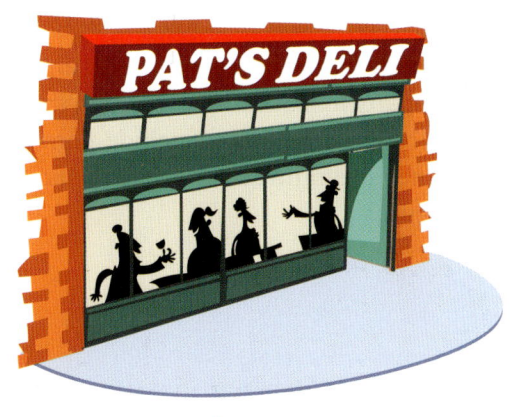

Long run

An Overview of Costs

In the short run, producers have some fixed costs: in the long run, all costs are variable.

In our study of costs we shall look at implicit and explicit costs. **Explicit costs are costs incurred by a firm when it pays an amount of money for something**, e.g. when a firm pays its electricity bill of €500, this €500 is considered an explicit cost.

Implicit costs, on the other hand, do not involve the paying out of money but should still be considered in our analysis. For example, Pat invested €200,000 in a business and didn't charge the company any interest on this sum. However, if Pat deposited the money in the bank and received interest of 3%, then there is an implicit cost of €6,000 by investing in his own business. Similarly, when the enterprise is first set up, Pat might take a lower wage than what would be paid to other employees.

Allied to this is the concept of **opportunity cost,** which is simply **the cost of foregone alternatives**.

> **Example**
>
> Opportunity cost is central to our study because it looks at the allocation of resources that have alternative uses, e.g. a restaurateur using a premises they fully own sacrifices the money they could get if they sold the premises and invested the money or rented out the building and earned an income.

Positive Economics

Fixed and Variable Costs

As output is increased, total costs of production increase. These total costs are composed of two parts: fixed costs and variable costs.

> **FIXED COSTS** are costs that don't change as output changes.

Fixed costs will be incurred even when output is zero, e.g. rent of premises. If a contract has been entered into by a company to lease premises, then even if nothing is produced, rent will still have to be paid. Other examples include commercial rates, salaries of administrative staff or insurance premiums. As output is increased, these costs won't vary over a wide range of output.

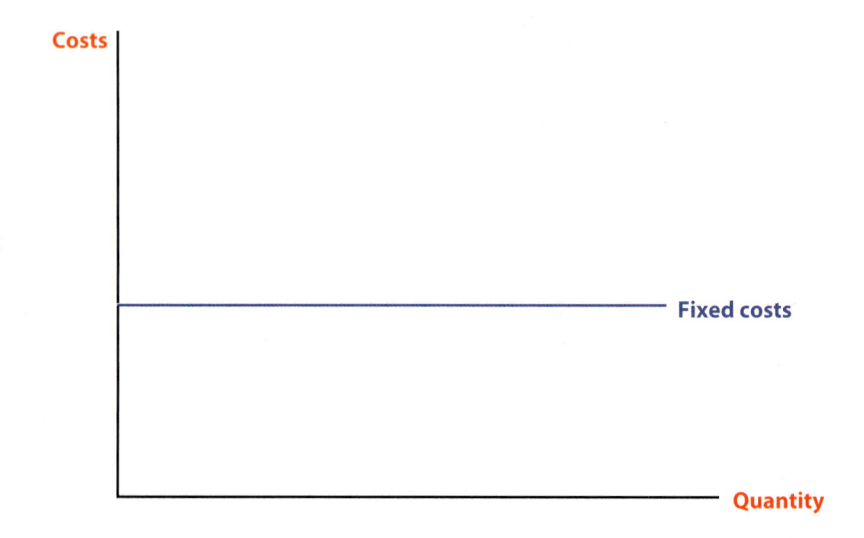

As the level of output increases, variable costs increase. Similarly, when the level of output decreases, variable costs fall, e.g. raw materials, wages, electricity.

> **VARIABLE COSTS** are costs that vary as output changes.

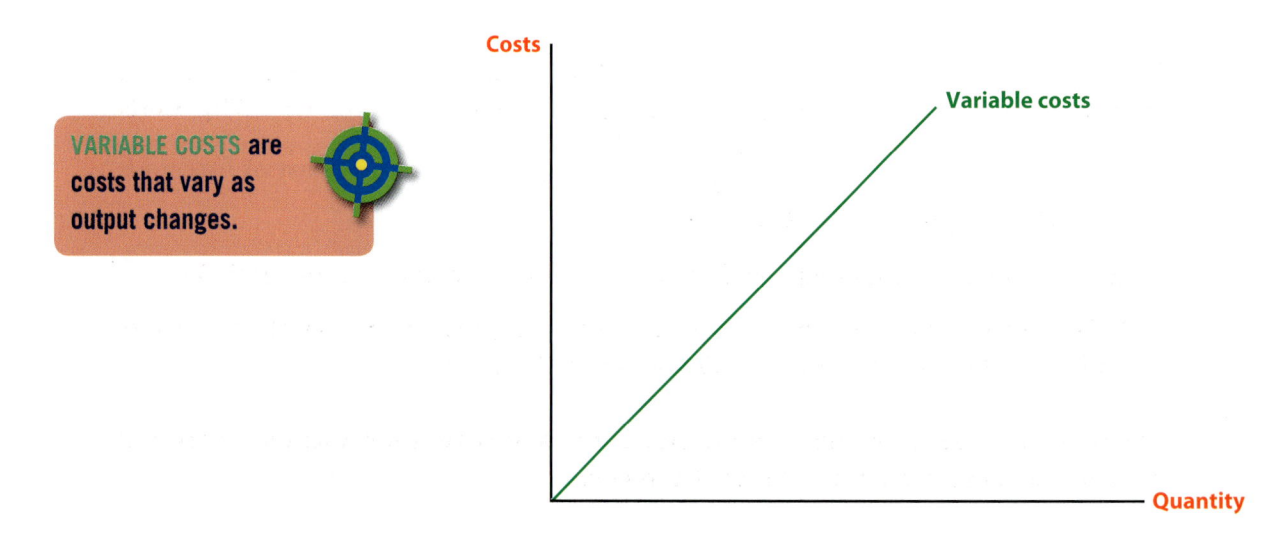

Total cost is both fixed and variable costs added together, giving us the total cost of production.

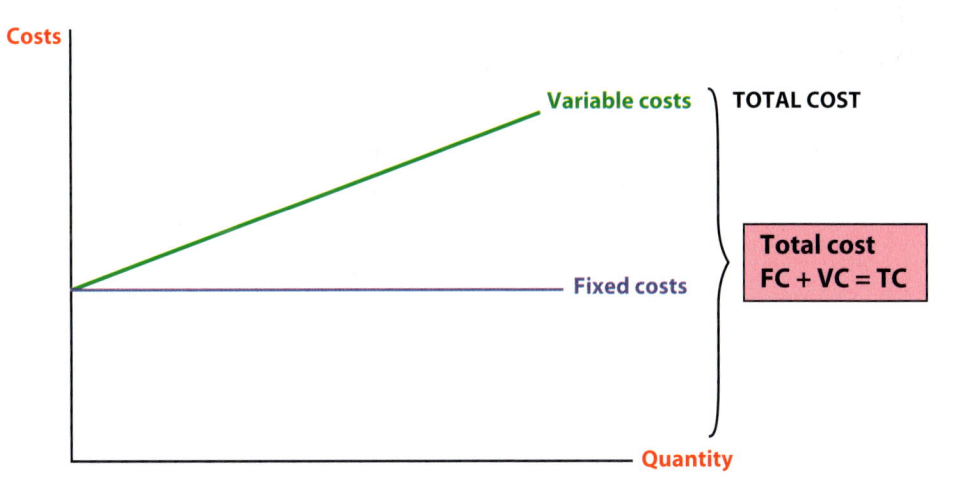

$$FC + VC = TC$$

What Is a Company's Shut Down Point in the Short Run?

In the short run, a company may make a loss. Does that mean it should shut down? Let's take the following firms and see if they should stay in production in the short run.

Pat's Deli	€	Chris's Deli	€
Fixed costs (rent)	500	Fixed costs (rent)	500
Variable costs (wages/supplies)	1,000	Variable costs (wages/supplies)	1,000
Total cost	1,500	Total cost	1,500
Total revenue	1,250	Total revenue	900

While both companies are making a loss (and this could not be sustained in the long run), Pat should stay in business and Chris should close the business down. Why? Chris doesn't cover variable cost, while Pat does. Since both delis have the same fixed cost (e.g. rent) and assuming that they are in a timed lease agreement, *they both will incur a loss of €500 if no production takes place.*

- Pat's loss is €250 if the company produces, which is preferable to a loss of €500.
- Chris's loss is €600 if the company produces and if no production takes place – the loss would be €500, as fixed costs of €500 would still be incurred.

The maxim for all companies in the short run is to cover their variable costs and contribute to the reduction of their fixed costs.

Positive Economics

Law of Diminishing Marginal Returns

As more and more of a variable factor is added to a fixed factor, at some stage the increase in output caused by the last unit of the variable factor will begin to decline.

Let's look at an example (Pat's Deli) to understand this economic law. Suppose that Pat is the sole employee in the deli. Pat is responsible for ordering supplies, making the produce, serving customers and ensuring the premises is clean. Regardless of how hard Pat works, it doesn't take long to realise that extra help would be beneficial and profitable.

An assistant is employed and production in the deli rises. Consequently, a second and a third worker join the team and production continues to increase. Each new employee specialises in one particular task and becomes efficient at this job: one serving hot food, one making the rolls and the third handling money. However, at some stage the extra (marginal) output per worker will eventually decline as more and more workers are employed – imagine 10 or 15 workers in the deli! They would begin to get in each other's way and hinder each other's work as the premises becomes overcrowded.

Look at the following example.

A	B	C	D
Number of workers	Total output	Marginal (extra) output (Δ total output)	Average output per worker $\left(\frac{\text{column B}}{\text{column A}}\right)$
1	10	–	10
2	25	15	12
3	42	17	14
4	60	18	15
5	70	10	14
6	78	8	13
7	85	7	12

* Numbers in the table have been rounded to the nearest whole number.

From the above analysis we can say that:

- **Total output** increases as an extra worker is employed. For example, the total output of seven workers is greater than that of four.

- However, the fifth worker's extra contribution (e.g. marginal output) is 10 rolls, a fall from the fourth worker's extra contribution of 18. Diminishing returns has set in after the fourth worker/on employing the fifth.
- The average output per worker begins to fall, as the average output of the sixth worker is lower than that of the fourth. As a result, there is an increase in the amount of workers used per unit produced, therefore increasing average cost.

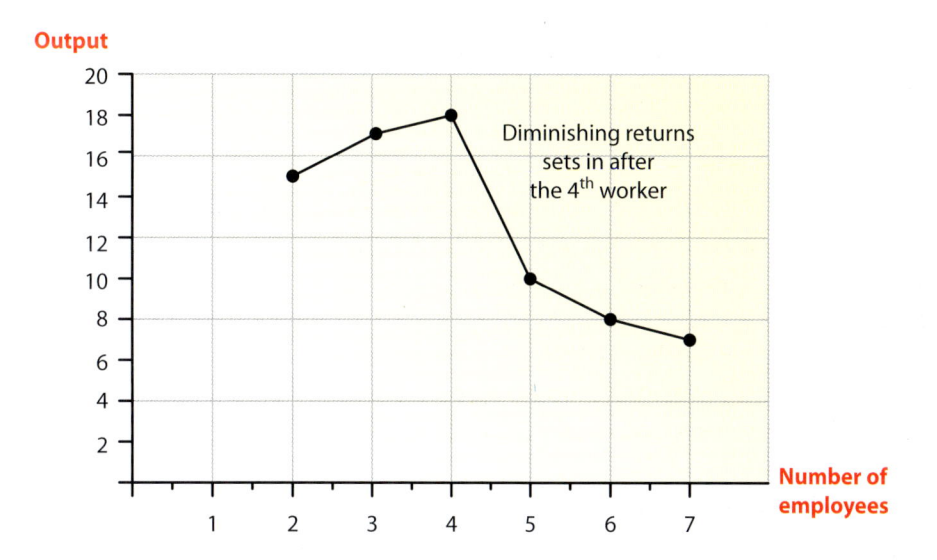

Average Costs (ATC or AC)

In our study of economics we are much more interested in costs per unit than total costs. For example, Pat's Deli needs to calculate the cost of making one ham and cheese roll (to come to a conclusion on the price to be charged to consumers). This is known as **average cost and it's calculated by dividing total cost by quantity.**

> **Average cost = (TC/Q) or (AFC + AVC)**

Likewise, FC/Q gives us average fixed cost and VC/Q gives average variable cost.

It is important to note at this stage that **average cost also includes normal profit**.

> **NORMAL PROFIT** is the return that sufficiently rewards the risk-taking of an entrepreneur and it must be earned to stay in business.

An example will illustrate these costs.

Pat's Gourmet Deli – short run production costs							
1	2	3	4	5	6	7	8
Quantity	Fixed costs	Variable costs	Total costs (FC + VC)	Average fixed costs (FC/Q)	Average variable costs (VC/Q)	Average total costs (TC/Q) or (AFC + AVC)	Marginal costs (change in TC)
0	20	–	20	–	–	–	
1	20	10	30	20	10	30	–
2	20	14	34	10	7	17	4
3	20	20	40	6.6	6.7	13.3	6
4	20	28	48	5	7	12	8
5	20	40	60	4	8	12	12
6	20	55	75	3.3	9.2	12.5	15
7	20	83	103	2.85	11.85	14.7	28
8	20	135	155	2.5	16.8	19.3	52

From the above table we can see that:
- Average fixed cost (AFC) is calculated by dividing fixed costs by quantity.
- Average variable cost (AVC) is arrived at by dividing variable cost by quantity.
- Average total cost (ATC) is derived by either adding AFC and AVC or dividing total cost (TC) by quantity (Q).
- The marginal costs are the costs of producing an extra unit of a good. It is arrived at by calculating the change in total cost.
- If the marginal cost of making an extra unit of a good is increasing (MC is rising), then we can say that the average cost of producing the good is increasing.

Explanation of Table

Column 1: The **quantity** of items produced (zero to eight units).

Column 2: Fixed costs don't change as output changes in the short run, e.g. rent of the premises.

7: Costs of Production

Column 3: Variable costs rise as output is increased. As diminishing returns set in, there is an increase in workers required to produce a unit and hence costs rise at a quicker rate.

Column 4: Total cost is arrived at by adding Column 2 + Column 3.

Column 5: Fixed costs divided by quantity produced leads to fixed cost per unit. AFC declines rapidly at the beginning and then gently falls as a fixed number is divided by an ever-increasing number, i.e. fixed costs are spread out over a greater number of units produced.

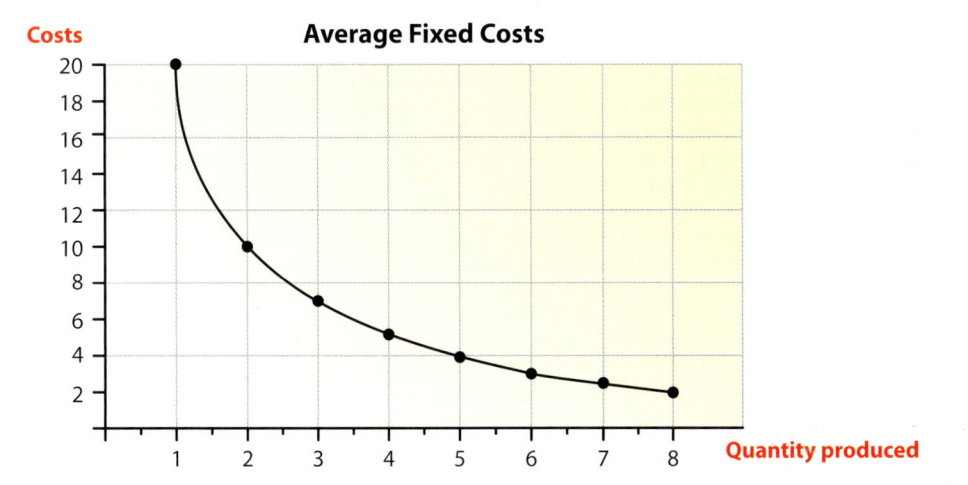

Average Fixed Costs

Column 6: Variable cost divided by the quantity produced leads to variable cost per unit. These costs fall as workers specialise. Variable costs per unit begin to rise when diminishing returns set in.

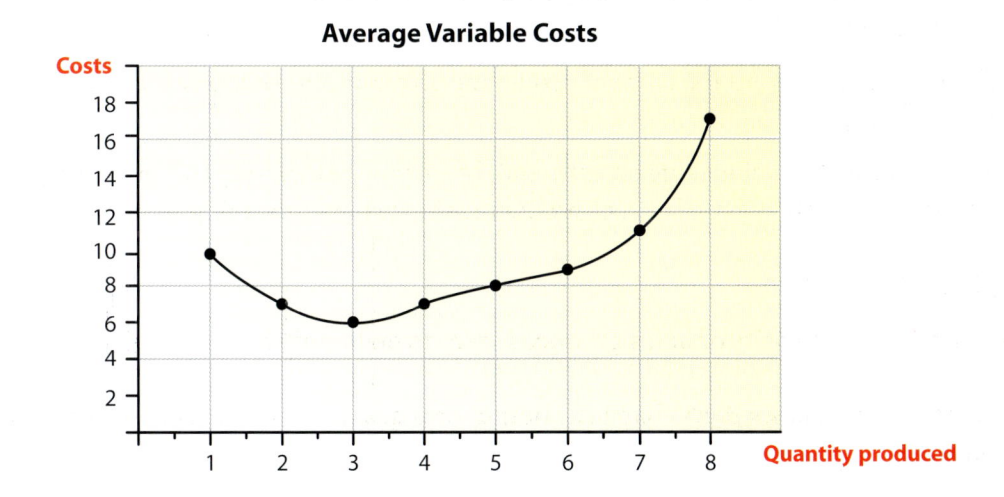

Average Variable Costs

Positive Economics

Column 7: This is usually called average cost and is arrived at by adding AFC and AVC, i.e. the cost of making each good. Its shape is determined by its two components. Initially, AC falls as fixed costs are spread over a bigger output and specialisation of workers occurs. This eventually rises due to the law of diminishing marginal returns. Thus the average cost curve (AC) has a U shape.

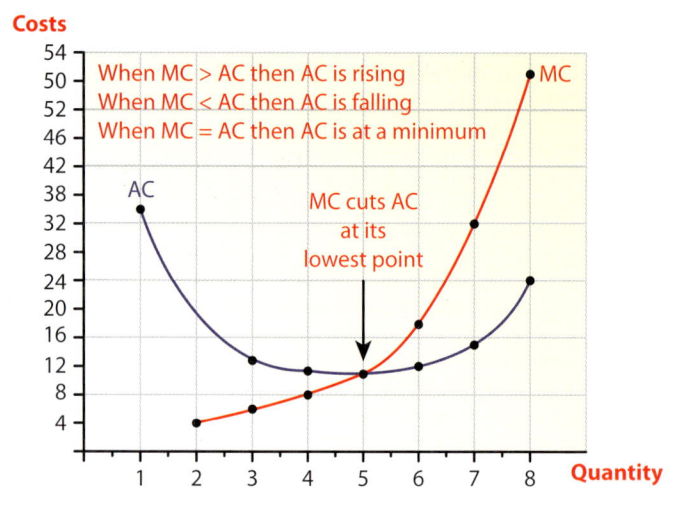

When MC > AC then AC is rising
When MC < AC then AC is falling
When MC = AC then AC is at a minimum

MC cuts AC at its lowest point

Column 8: The marginal cost is the increase in total cost when one more unit is produced. The relationship between MC and AC is noteworthy. If MC is lower than AC it pulls AC down and if MC is higher than AC it brings AC upwards. When MC = AC then AC is at its minimum (see the diagram above). This relationship can also be explained mathematically as follows:

- A student scores 70% in three economics tests and their average clearly is 70%. On their fourth test they score 90%.
- Their average now for the four tests is (70% + 70% + 70% + 90%)/4 = 75%.
- Their average has increased when the marginal (fourth test) was higher than the previous average results.
- Likewise, if they scored 50% in their fourth test, their average would fall to 65%. (Their marginal result is less than the average result, thereby bringing the average result down.)
- If their result in test four was 70% again, then their average would stay the same. (If their marginal result equals average result, then their average result remains unchanged.)

Application of MC

If a company wishes to increase the number of employees from 15 to 16 it has to increase the weekly wage from €200 to €210. What's the marginal cost of labour?

Total cost of 15 employees: 15 × €200 = €3,000

Total cost of 16 employees: 16 × €210 = €3,360

The MC of the 16th worker = €360

7: Costs of Production

Shape of Short Run Average Cost (SAC) Curve

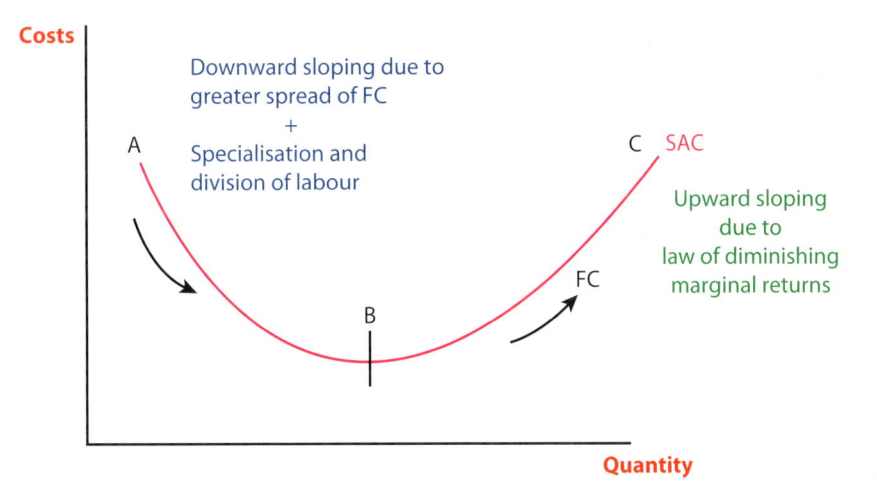

Graph showing a U-shaped SAC curve. Y-axis: Costs. X-axis: Quantity. Point A at top left, point B at the bottom, point C at top right. Labels: "Downward sloping due to greater spread of FC + Specialisation and division of labour" on the left side; "Upward sloping due to law of diminishing marginal returns" on the right side; "FC" label near the upward-sloping section.

The SAC curve is generally U-shaped and slopes downwards from A to B due to the following.

1. **Specialisation/division of labour:** This can occur if production increases and the firm decides to employ specialists **or** if existing workers concentrate on a smaller number of tasks. This can lead to greater efficiency (constant repetition of a small number of jobs) and thereby lowers unit costs. For example, one worker makes sandwiches and another serves hot food.

2. **Greater spread of fixed costs:** As a company expands, its fixed costs won't increase directly as more is produced. Fixed costs are static over a range of output and behave in a step-like fashion. Therefore, fixed costs are spread over an increasing number of units and as production increases, the fixed cost per unit falls.

The SAC slopes upwards from B to C due to the law of diminishing marginal returns.

THE LAW OF DIMINISHING MARGINAL RETURNS
To produce more in the short run, a company requires increasing quantities of the variable factor (labour) per unit produced to increase output, i.e. it takes

> **REMEMBER!**
> In Pat's Deli, he had fixed costs of €20. If he was producing one unit, the fixed cost per unit was €20. If he was producing eight units, the fixed cost per unit was €2.50.

101

more workers to produce a given quantity of output than it did when production first commenced. This is due to the law of diminishing marginal returns and this, in turn, results in higher unit costs and causes the SAC to slope upwards.

For example, a firm operates in the short run and this corresponds to a certain factory size. It is only when a company is in business for a while that it may contemplate expanding. It has to be sure that there is increased demand for its product. Increased capital costs will be involved; it may move into a bigger premises and buy additional equipment. A company will only consider these new costs if there is additional demand for its output. As the company plans for the future, it constructs a new SAC curve where all factors of production are variable. Consider the diagram below.

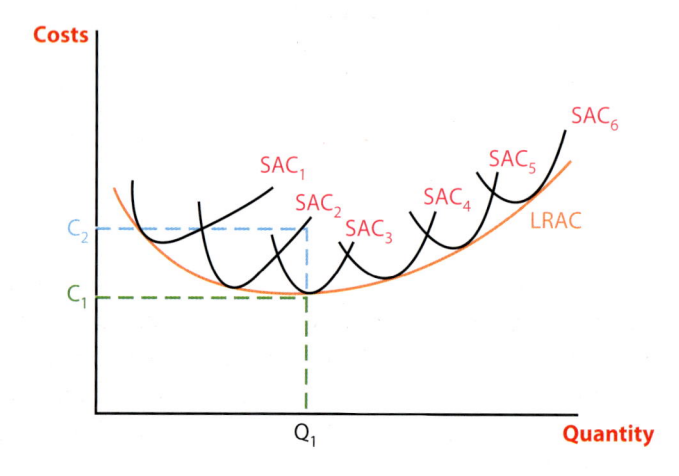

Each SAC curve represents a new factory size with an optimum production quantity.

The minimum point of each SAC will give us the quantity that a company can produce at the lowest possible cost.

The diagram above shows six SAC curves all representing different factory sizes. The lowest cost of production for that quantity is at the minimum point of each SAC curve, e.g. Q_1 could be produced in factories 2 and 3 but clearly diminishing returns have begun in SAC_2 and so the firm opts for SAC_3 with the lowest cost of production, C_1.

The minimum point of each SAC curve when joined together gives us the long run average cost (LRAC) curve.

The Long Run

In the long run, all factors of production (land, labour, capital and enterprise) are variable and the company may use the exact amount of each factor to achieve maximum efficiency. Just like the short run, the long run does not refer to any set period of time. It may be one month, if that's the length of time that a shop renews its rental contract for its premises. It could also be a few years, as in the case of building a new car production plant.

In effect, the long run is a series of short runs into the future. Likewise, **the long run average cost curve is made up of the minimum point of many SAC curves**, each representing a different factory size.

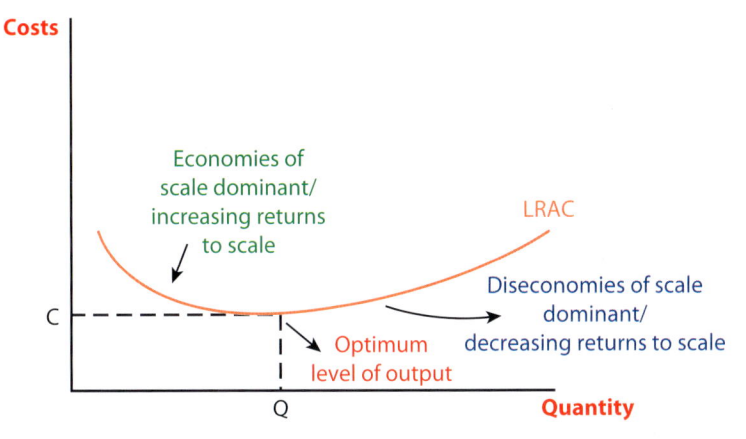

What Determines the Shape of the LRAC Curve?

The LRAC curve is generally shown as saucer shaped (see the diagram). As the firm grows in size it experiences cost savings called economies of scale. These savings cause the LRAC to slope downwards and average costs decrease. The upward part of the LRAC is due to diseconomies of scale and average costs begin to increase.

It is important to note that both economies and diseconomies of scale are present at all levels of output. It is when economies are dominant that the curve slopes downwards; when diseconomies are more prevalent, the curve slopes back upwards. The minimum point shown on the LRAC above is referred to as the optimum level of output. If a firm operates at this point, society benefits as the firm is operating efficiently and making the best use of all its resources.

Economies of Scale

Economies of Scale/Savings Due to Size

These savings can be both internal and external.

INTERNAL ECONOMIES OF SCALE

- **Increased use of machinery:** As a company grows in size it will be able to buy more specialised equipment/machinery. It might also be able to use bigger and more economical machines that would not have been suitable in a smaller unit.

- **Specialisation/division of labour:** Dividing a job into many individual parts allows greater efficiency and thereby reduces costs.

- **Construction savings:** The cost of building a 50,000 square metre factory is not five times more expensive than building a 10,000 square metre factory, i.e. larger plants cost less per square metre than smaller ones.

> **INTERNAL ECONOMIES OF SCALE** are forces within a firm that cause the average/unit cost of that firm to decline as it grows in size.

Positive Economics

- **Purchasing economies:** A company that buys in large quantities can get bigger discounts from its suppliers than companies with smaller orders.

- **Economies in distribution:** As a company gets bigger it may be able to organise deliveries to certain areas on set days rather than trying to deliver to all areas every day.

- **Financial economies:** Larger established companies may be able to negotiate lower interest rates than smaller companies because they may be viewed as being safer.

- **Marketing economies:** Larger companies may be able to avail of savings in advertising and be able to afford bigger advertising campaigns achieving lower advertising cost per unit.

- **Management economies:** As a company expands it will be able to employ specialised management to look after certain tasks, e.g. human resource functions.

- **Problem of indivisibility reduced:** Larger companies may be able to maintain 24-hour production shifts and thus avoid closing down machines and the costly start-ups of these machines each day.

External Economies of Scale

- **Better infrastructure:** As roads and communications systems improve, all firms in the industry will benefit.

- **Specialist firms established:** As an industry gets bigger, it will attract specialist firms to set up and perform jobs that can be contracted out, e.g. payroll functions.

- **Development of separate research and development units:** As an industry grows, research and development companies may set up to provide facilities for individual firms. Companies may also share the cost of research.

- **Subsidiary trades may set up:** As an industry grows, subsidiary trades may develop to meet the needs of the expanding industry, e.g. petrol stations or hotels located near airports, and time and money are not wasted on needless commuting.

- **Availability of training courses:** Expanding industries may have training courses provided by private colleges or public bodies (SOLAS), e.g. FETAC Care Skills course for the residential care industry.

I'm interested in giving you a BIG contract. What discount can you offer me?

> **EXTERNAL ECONOMIES OF SCALE** are forces outside a firm that cause the average/unit cost of that firm to decline as the industry grows in size.

- **Supports from public bodies:** Government bodies may assist certain industries, e.g. Fáilte Ireland supports the tourist industry, BIM helps the fishing sector.

Diseconomies of Scale/Disadvantages Due to Size

These can be both internal and external. These factors may hinder rather than help further growth and are likely to reduce the company's efficiency.

INTERNAL DISECONOMIES OF SCALE

- **Poor decision-making:** As the company gets bigger, the lines of authority may be less clearly defined. As a result, decision-making may take longer and be less effective than in the past.

> **INTERNAL DISECONOMIES OF SCALE** are forces within a firm that cause the average/unit cost of that firm to increase as it grows in size.

- **Fall in staff morale:** Due to increased specialisation and the repetitive nature of some tasks, workers may experience frustration and boredom, leading to absenteeism, high labour turnover and lower productivity.

- **Communication problems:** As a firm grows in size, effective communication may become more difficult. This can be caused by management and workers growing apart due to increased layers in the company hierarchy.

- **Control problems:** As a company expands, it becomes more difficult to control the amount of waste, stock breakages, stolen items, etc. than in the past.

- **Increase in administrative overheads:** The ratio of office staff often increases relative to the production staff, thereby increasing unit costs as a company grows. Likewise, legal, accounting and office costs tend to proportionately increase more than production costs.

EXTERNAL DISECONOMIES OF SCALE

- **Shortages of factors of production:** As the industry expands, demand for qualified labour increases. This can lead to staff shortages consequently causing an increase in their price/wage rate. Sometimes unqualified/less efficient workers may need to be hired, leading to increased unit cost of production.

> *You need to send an e-mail to get an appointment to make a call with the boss's personal assistant to see if there is a spot in her diary next week to think about whether you can take an hour off tomorrow.*

> **EXTERNAL DISECONOMIES OF SCALE** are forces outside a firm that cause the average/unit cost of that firm to increase as the industry grows in size.

- **Raw material shortage:** Pressure will be put on the supply of raw materials with increased demand and a possible shortage may arise.
- **Infrastructural problems:** As an industry expands, its demand for infrastructure (public transport, telecommunications, etc.) may not easily be met, leading to increased costs.

What Effect Do Returns to Scale Have on Costs?

- **Returns to scale** refers to changing all factors, for example doubling all factors of production and the consequent effect on output.
  - **Increasing returns to scale** refers to doubling inputs with output more than doubling. This would cause the LRAC to slope downwards, e.g. one worker produces 5 units and when a second worker is employed total output rises to 12 units.
  - **Decreasing returns to scale** refers to doubling inputs with output less than doubling. It would cause the LRAC to slope upwards.
  - **Constant returns to scale** refers to output changing at exactly the same rate as factors. This results in the LRAC being horizontal.

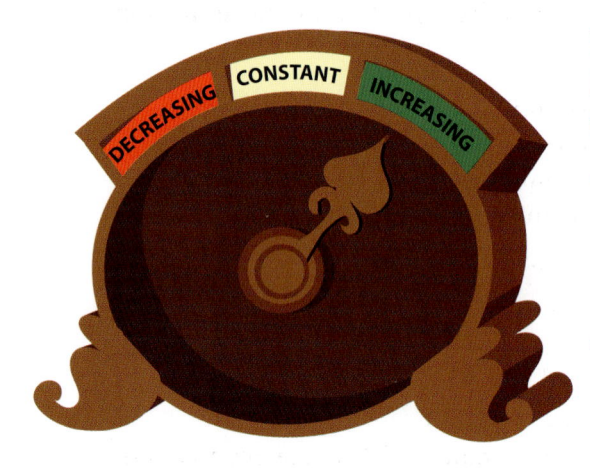

Why Do Small Firms Survive in the Irish Market Even Though They Don't Benefit from Economies of Scale?

- **Small size of the market:** The small size of the local market may not allow a large-scale business to survive, e.g. a small guesthouse may be viable whereas a large hotel may not.
- **Consumer loyalty:** A small business in existence for a number of years may have built up a reputation and a loyal customer base that makes it difficult for a new firm to enter the market.
- **Personal services:** A small business may be the only one able to provide the personal attention that consumers desire, e.g. handcrafted individual jewellery.
- **Traditional markets:** A small firm may find it easier to locate near the market whereas a bigger one may not be able to, e.g. street hawkers can locate in different markets on different days of the week.
- **Nature of the good:** Heavy commodities that are costly to transport may be made locally on a small scale to supply local markets, e.g. the manufacture of concrete blocks.
- **Membership of voluntary groups:** Some companies operating on a small scale may decide to join other similar companies and subscribe to a joint marketing/purchasing strategy in order to be able to compete with large-scale operators, e.g. sole owner grocery shops.

7: Costs of Production

Benefits of Small-scale Enterprises

As suggested above, some small operations may be better suited to the production of certain goods and services and achieving economies of scale may not be important. Indeed, there are many County Enterprise Boards around the country giving start-up grants in order to encourage individuals to establish small firms that may give gainful employment.

So what are the advantages of a small enterprise?

- **Quick response time:** Smaller companies may be able to respond quickly to changing economic circumstances. Less staff need to be consulted, and often employees can see the need for change and can adapt rapidly to downturns in economic activity.

- **Decision-making:** A sole owner won't need to consult or negotiate with others, thereby facilitating quick and easy decision-making.

- **High output per head:** A small workforce may have high productivity with staff multitasking, thereby reducing the monotony associated with the repetition of single tasks in larger companies.

- **Fewer HR problems:** In smaller companies staff often have a greater say in the day-to-day running of a business, making decisions and feeling empowered, resulting in fewer conflicts between management and staff.

- **Lower overheads:** Small firms can operate out of small plants with fewer overheads.

Social Costs and Benefits

Examples of social costs include traffic congestion, air/water pollution, global warming and the disfigurement of the landscape due to the construction of roads.

If goods are produced by a company, there may be external effects of their actions, which can be both of benefit and cost to society.

> A SOCIAL COST is a cost to society of an action or output OR the cost or price that society has to pay for the existence of a particular product OR the price that society has to pay as a result of the production/consumption of a community.

> A SOCIAL BENEFIT is the benefit/advantage that accrues to society as a whole as a result of an individual firm consuming/producing a commodity that is not measured by the price system.

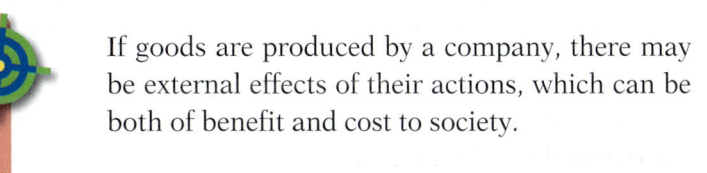

Positive Economics

If an action is taken by an individual, there may be external effects, again with both benefits and costs to society.

EXTERNAL DISECONOMIES OF CONSUMPTION occur when an action is taken by a consumer and this imposes a cost on third parties for which they are not compensated, e.g. a drummer practises in a loud fashion and disturbs the neighbours.

EXTERNAL ECONOMIES OF CONSUMPTION occur when a consumer undertakes an action and it benefits third parties for which the consumer is not compensated, e.g. a person volunteers the management skills they learned at work to co-ordinate a local youth club.

EXTERNAL DISECONOMIES OF PRODUCTION occur when a *producer* carries out an activity and imposes a cost on third parties for which they are not compensated, e.g. a manufacturing plant causing air or noise pollution.

EXTERNAL ECONOMIES OF PRODUCTION happen when actions taken by *producers* result in benefits to third parties for which the producer is not compensated, e.g. a company training staff who later leave and work for other firms.

All of the above refer to actions affecting third parties – these are collectively known as **externalities, i.e. unintended costs or benefits to third parties.**

The *private cost* of a good or service is the *cost to the firm* of making the good or providing the service.

Revenue

Total Revenue, Average Revenue and Marginal Revenue

Up to now in our analysis we have concentrated on costs of production in both the short and long run. We will now turn our attention to revenue and explore how a firm can maximise its profits. **Revenue** is the money received from sales, and as sales increase, so does total revenue.

We calculate total revenue by multiplying price by the quantity sold, i.e. P × Q.

AVERAGE REVENUE (AR) is calculated by dividing total revenue by quantity, i.e. TR/Q. This is also known as the price of the good. The AR curve is the demand curve.

MARGINAL REVENUE is the change in total revenue when an extra unit of output is sold.

7: Costs of Production

Example

Quantity	Price (€)	TR (P × Q)	AR (TR/Q)	MR (change in TR)
1	20	20	20	–
2	18	36	18	16
3	16	48	16	12
4	14	56	14	8
5	12	60	12	4

The above table shows that:

- Average revenue is the same as price.
- MR and AR relate in the same way as MC and AC, i.e. when marginal revenue is less than average revenue, average revenue is falling. A company facing a downward sloping demand curve for its goods needs to reduce its price to sell more, hence marginal revenue will be less than price (AR).

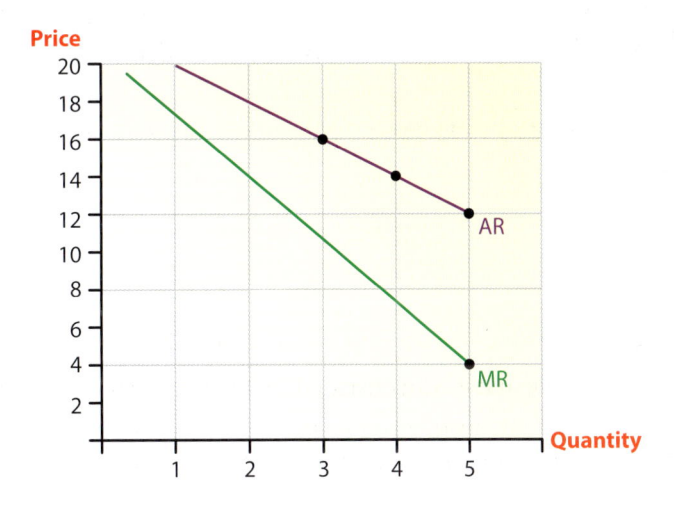

We will now look at a business where AR (price charged for the good) is fixed (we will also study this situation in Chapter 8).

Quantity	Price (€)	TR (P × Q)	AR (TR/Q)	MR (change in TR)
1	10	10	10	–
2	10	20	10	10
3	10	30	10	10
4	10	40	10	10
5	10	50	10	10

Positive Economics

From the above table we can see that AR = MR (remember, this is also the demand curve). We can use this data to find the profit-maximising position of a company.

How Are Profits Calculated?

A firm will make a profit if its total revenue (TR) exceeds its total costs (TC). As already stated, included in these costs is normal profit, i.e. the return that sufficiently rewards the risk taken by the entrepreneur/the minimum that must be earned to stay in business.

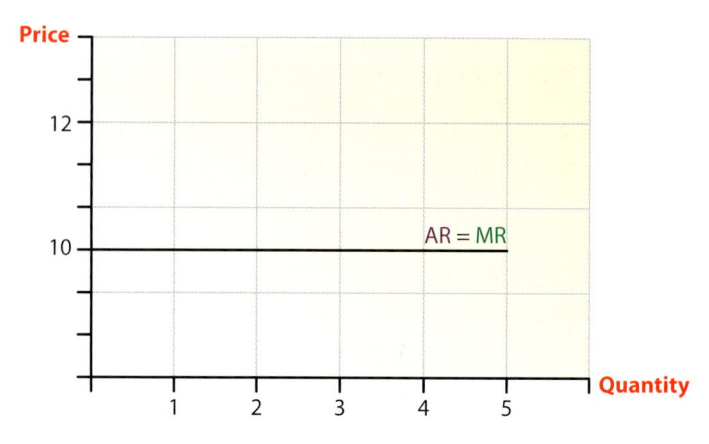

A company seeking to maximise profit will produce an extra unit of output if its total profit is increased by making this unit. This occurs if the marginal revenue received from producing the good is greater than the marginal cost of producing it, i.e. MR > MC.

Quantity	Price	Total cost	Marginal cost	Total revenue	Marginal revenue	Profit
1	15	19	–	15	–	–4
2	15	34	15	30	15	–4
3	15	37	3	45	15	8
4	15	42	5	60	15	18
5	15	48	6	75	15	27
6	15	59	11	90	15	31
7	15	74	15	105	15	31
8	15	90	18	120	15	30

In the table above we can see that:

- If the firm produces the sixth item (marginal revenue is 15 and its marginal cost is 11), it adds 4 to the total profit (31 – 27 = 4).
- Clearly, the company should produce this unit and continue to do so until the marginal cost equals marginal revenue.
- This occurs when the seventh unit is produced, where the marginal cost of 15 equals the marginal revenue of 15.

7: Costs of Production

- In fact, the company does not necessarily have to produce the seventh unit since it adds €15 to total revenue and €15 to total cost.
- But it gets too awkward to say 'produce just before where MC = MR'. Instead, we use the phrase 'produce where MC = MR'.

Any goods produced after the seventh unit will lead to a fall in profits. If the company produces the eighth unit, its MC (18) will exceed its MR (15) and profits fall. The company doesn't incur losses by selling the eighth unit, it's just that the profit at eight units is lower than the level of profits at seven units because the marginal cost of the eighth unit is greater than the marginal revenue. Therefore, the company should not produce this unit.

We can now state our first profit-maximising condition:

> **A company should produce where MC = MR.**

A further examination of the table will show that:

- MC equals MR at two points: at unit 2 and unit 7.
- If the company produces two units (MC = MR) it would make a loss of 4.
- Profit is being earned between units 3 and 7.
- At an output of 7 units, MC cuts MR where MC is increasing at a faster rate than MR (MC cuts MR from below). This is where profit is maximised (as can be seen in the diagram below).

We can now state our second profit-maximising condition:

> **MC cuts MR from below/MC is increasing at a faster rate than MR.**

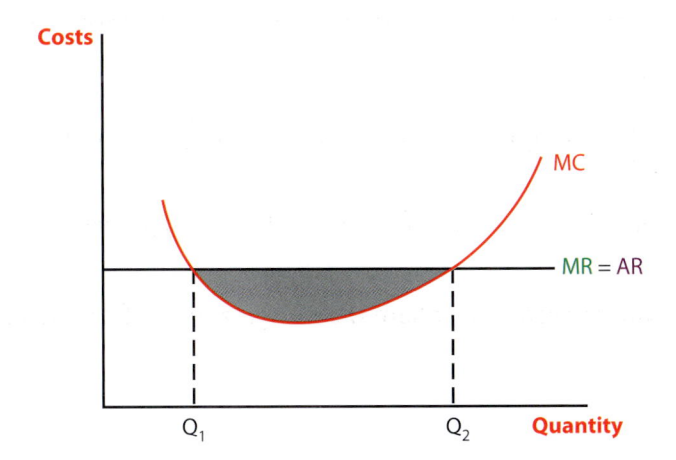

REMEMBER!

We have already stated that a company should produce in the short run if it covers its variable costs and contributes towards fixed cost reduction. (Refer to Pat and Chris in the earlier part of the chapter.)

Positive Economics

In the long run, *all costs* must be covered (AFC, AVC and normal profit), otherwise a business could not pay its bills and would have to cease operating.

We can now state our third profit-maximising condition:

> If a firm is to continue trading in the long run, **AR must be at least equal to AC**.

Summary of Profit-maximising Conditions

Short run	Long run
MC = MR	MC = MR
MC cuts MR from below	MC cuts MR from below
AVC covered	AC covered

EXAM Question 1 (75 marks)

(a) Assuming a competitive market, under what conditions would a profit-maximising firm be at (1) long run equilibrium and (2) short run equilibrium?

(b) Max Flow Ltd incurred the following costs in producing their maximum output of two units per week:

- Rent €2,500 (per week). The lease has two years to run.
- Normal profit €400 (€200 per unit).
- Labour €500 (hired on a weekly basis).
- Raw materials €600 (€300 per unit).

What is the minimum price at which each unit can be sold if production is to continue:

(i) In the short run?

(ii) In the long run?

Explain your answer.

7: Costs of Production

Solution

(a)

1. A profit-maximising firm would be at long run equilibrium when:

- MC = MR.
- MC cuts MR from below or MC is rising faster than MR.
- Price/average revenue must cover all costs, both fixed and variable, otherwise the firm will close down.

2. The firm will be in equilibrium in the short run when:

- MC = MR.
- MC cuts MR from below.
- Price/average revenue must cover variable costs and contribute to the reduction of fixed costs.

(b)

Suppose FC = €100 and VC = €150 and the firm sells at €151. If the firm produced nothing it would lose €100, but if it produces one unit and gets €151 it covers variable costs and there is €1 remaining to put towards FC. This means a loss of only €99, which is preferable.

(i) In the short run the firm needs to cover only variable costs:

	€
Labour	500
Raw materials	600
Total	1,100

Normal profit does not have to be in the short run because price need only cover variable costs. As €1,100 is the amount of variable cost, then €550 is the minimum price a unit can be sold at.

(ii) In the long run a firm has to cover all costs or it will be forced to close.

	€
Rent	2,500
Labour	500
Raw materials	600
Normal profit	400
Total	4,000

€4,000 is the cost of two units, so €2,000 is the total cost of one. Normal profit has to be included, as without it the entrepreneur would not produce. Therefore, in the long run the firm must get a minimum price of €2,000, otherwise it will have to close.

Positive Economics

Questions

Short Questions

1. Define both the short run and long run periods.
2. Distinguish between implicit and explicit costs.
3. Why is opportunity cost central to our study in economics?
4. Distinguish between fixed and variable costs, giving examples of each.
5. How is AC calculated?

Long Questions

1. Explain, with an example, a company's shut down point in the short run.
2. Explain, with an example, the law of diminishing marginal returns. Why does average output per worker fall?
3. Explain, with examples, how AFC and AVC are calculated.
4. Illustrate and explain the relationship between MC and AC.
5. Draw the SAC and explain its shape.
6. Derive the LRAC curve.
7. What influences the shape of the LRAC curve?
8. State and explain three internal economies and diseconomies of scale.
9. State and explain three external economies and diseconomies of scale.
10. What are the advantages of small-scale production?
11. Complete the following table and draw the AFC, AVC and MC curves.

1	2	3	4	5	6	7	8
Quantity	Fixed costs	Variable costs	Total costs (FC + VC)	Average fixed costs (FC/Q)	Average variable costs (VC/Q)	Average total costs (TC/Q) or (AFC + AVC)	Marginal costs (change in TC)
0	25	–					
1	25	20					-
2	25	27					
3	25	35					
4	25	45					
5	25	60					
6	25	80					
7	25	105					
8	25	145					

Long Questions – continued

12. Complete the following table and draw the MC and AC curves.

1	2	3	4	5	6	7	8
Quantity	Fixed costs	Variable costs	Total costs (FC + VC)	Average fixed costs (FC/Q)	Average variable costs (VC/Q)	Average total costs (TC/Q) or (AFC + AVC)	Marginal costs (change in TC)
0	36	–	36	–	–	–	
1			44				–
2			48				
3			51				
4			56				
5			63				
6			72				
7			82				
8			101				
9			126				
10			166				

13. Explain, with an example, the difference between social and private cost.
14. Explain the relationship between AR, TR and MR.
15. State and explain the profit-maximising conditions of a firm in the short and long run.

Chapter 8: Perfect Competition

Specific Learning Outcomes

At the end of this chapter, students should be able to:

- Explain, with examples, the theory of perfect competition.
- Describe and assess the assumptions underlying perfect competition.
- Illustrate, explain and interpret a firm's demand curve.
- Describe the equilibrium for a perfectly competitive firm in the short run.
- Define and illustrate supernormal profits.
- Discuss why new firms enter the industry.
- Critically analyse the effects on equilibrium of new entrants.
- Describe, with the aid of a diagram, the equilibrium for a perfectly competitive firm in the long run.
- Derive the supply curve for a perfectly competitive firm.
- Analyse perfect competition as a market from the point of view of consumers, producers and the use of scarce resources.
- Assess the usefulness of the perfectly competitive model in understanding market structures.

8: Perfect Competition

Introduction

A market is a place where buyers and sellers meet. This could be a physical location like a shopping centre, the buy and sell section of a newspaper or using the internet to book a flight.

> An **INDUSTRY** is all the firms in the marketplace selling the same product or service, e.g. all the fast food outlets, all the book publishers, all hotels. Industries operate in different market structures.

We will now study all of these various **market structures**, ranging from perfect competition, where there are many sellers, each of whom has a very small and insignificant part of the total market, to monopoly, where there is a single seller of a good. In between these two extremes lies imperfect competition and oligopoly.

Adam Smith, a classical economist, wrote about 'pure competition' and said that it provided 'an efficient resource allocation system'. It is rare that we see this form of competition in reality, but it is a good starting point for our study of markets. We can evaluate other market structures against the advantages of this form of competition. It's also the ideal market from consumers' and society's point of view, as the lowest price will be charged for the goods (benefiting consumers) and scarce resources are used efficiently (benefiting society).

Market Structures

PERFECT COMPETITION
Many sellers of an identical product
Example: Strawberry sellers on the side of the road

IMPERFECT COMPETITION
Many sellers of a similar product
Example: Different restaurants

OLIGOPOLY
Few sellers
Example: Banks in Ireland

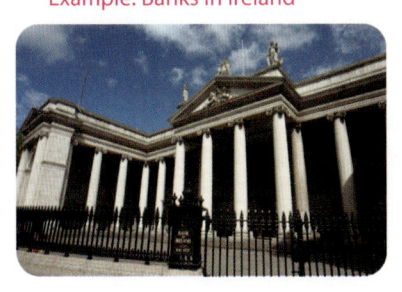

MONOPOLY
Sole supplier
Example: Iarnród Éireann

Assumptions/Characteristics of Perfect Competition

There are Many Buyers in the Market

No one buyer, by their own actions, can influence the market price of the goods. They accept the market price, i.e. they are a price taker and each buyer acts independently.

CASE STUDY: Moore Street Markets

Moore Street is a place in Dublin famous for its outdoor market that stocks meat, fish, fruit and vegetables. There are various different stalls all along the street and this represents a perfectly competitive market because of all of the assumptions of perfect competition.

©Alamy

> Each firm is a price taker, i.e. it accepts the price as it is set on the market. Each firm supplies such a small fraction of the market that it cannot influence the market price.

There Are Many Competitive Sellers in the Market

No one seller by their actions can influence the market price of the goods. Since there are so many sellers, each seller's contribution is insignificant in the context of the total market, i.e. if production is increased by one seller, then they won't have to lower their price to sell this extra output. Likewise, if one firm was to stop producing, the selling price of the good would not increase.

The Goods Are Homogenous

The goods supplied by each firm are exactly the same (identical). They are perfect substitutes for each other. Consumers are indifferent as to whether milk is produced by farmer A or farmer B. This means that advertising is pointless.

There Is Freedom of Entry to and Exit from the Industry/No Barriers to Entry or Exit within the Industry

It's possible for firms to enter or leave the industry as they wish. Companies already in the industry cannot prevent new firms from entering and likewise existing firms can close down if they wish.

Perfect Knowledge Exists as to Prices and Profits

Each firm is fully aware of the profits made by other firms. Similarly, consumers are fully aware of the prices being charged for the products.

Each Firm Seeks to Maximise Profits

The sole objective of each firm is to maximise profits. To achieve this, they produce the quantity where MC = MR.

No Collusion Exists on the Market
No collusion exists between buyers or sellers of the good. Buyers don't group together with other buyers and sellers do not group together with other sellers (to restrict quantity) in order to influence the price at which the good is sold. This is because there are so many small firms that it is very difficult for them to collude.

Firms Face a Perfectly Elastic Supply of Factors of Production
If a firm wants to increase output, it can do so and acquire the necessary factors of production at the existing price, i.e. a scarcity of factors of production will not arise, thereby pushing up price. The unit cost of each of the factors of production is the same for all firms.

Implications of the Assumptions
Markets characterised by the above assumptions are infrequently seen in their purist form. Information is rarely perfect in the markets at the same time. However, some of the best examples include:

- Organised commodity markets (tea, coffee, etc.).
- The market in stocks and shares (homogenous products).
- The market for agricultural produce (many buyers and sellers/identical products).
- The vast market in global currencies.
- Fruit and vegetable vendors in local markets, e.g. English Market in Cork and Moore Street in Dublin.

Why Don't Firms in Perfect Competition Engage in Advertising?

Homogenous Goods
Because the goods are identical and no differences exist, an individual producer cannot differentiate their product, therefore there is no point in advertising.

Increased Cost and No Additional Revenue
If a firm advertises, it would increase its own costs and decrease its profits, thereby not gaining any additional revenue for itself.

Benefits the Entire Industry
Advertising by a single firm would benefit the entire industry and not just the firm undertaking the advertising, which incurs the cost.

Positive Economics

Perfectly Elastic Demand

Each firm enjoys a perfectly elastic demand for its product at existing prices so that it does not need to advertise.

> **CASE STUDY: Moore Street Markets**
>
> Could you imagine Joan at Stand No. 4 spending money advertising oranges in Moore Street?
>
> - There wouldn't be anybody who would differentiate between the oranges on Joan's or any other stands because of homogenous goods.
> - It would increase the costs for Joan's particular stand and wouldn't necessarily increase revenue for her.
> - Everybody selling oranges on Moore Street (i.e. the industry) would benefit.
> - Anybody who wants oranges on Moore Street knows where to find them!

Perfect Competition – The Short Run

We have already stated that the individual firm in perfect competition is a price taker. It accepts the price as determined by market demand and supply forces. The individual producer can't, by their own actions, affect this market price since they supply an insignificant part of the total supply.

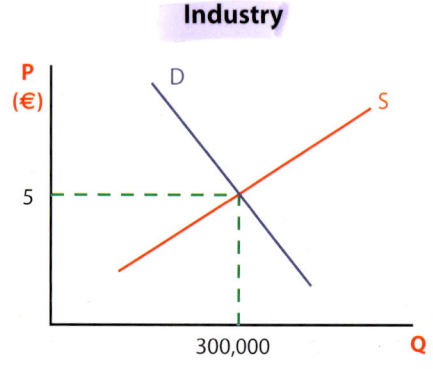

Industry

Market price is determined by market demand and supply curves

Firm Accepts the Market Price

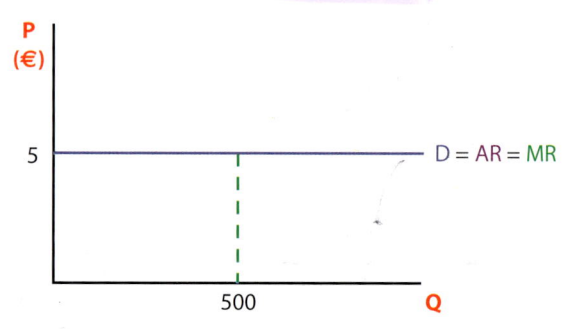

D = AR = MR

Horizontal/perfectly elastic demand curve of an individual firm in perfect competition

We can see from the market situation that equilibrium price and quantity are €5 and 300,000 tonnes per annum, respectively. If one firm who is producing 500 tonnes increases its supply to 1,000 tonnes (this is an increase of 100%), while this is a huge increase for this firm, it still only represents an insignificant .0033% of the total market supply.

- The horizontal demand curve in the diagram above is also called the price line (shows the different quantities bought at different prices).

8: Perfect Competition

- The price of a product is often called the average revenue (remember: TR/Q).
- When average revenue is constant, marginal revenue is equal to average revenue.

Let's look at the following example.

Quantity	Price (€)	Total revenue (P × Q)	Average revenue (TR/Q)	Marginal revenue (change in TR)
1	10	10	10	10
2	10	20	10	10
3	10	30	10	10
4	10	40	10	10
5	10	50	10	10

We can see that average revenue is equal to marginal revenue, which is the same as price. This is the horizontal, perfectly elastic demand curve of a firm in perfect competition.

What Quantity Will the Firm Produce?

Since we know the shape of the firm's demand curve, we now have to find out the quantity it will produce, i.e. its equilibrium point. Now we need to find out its costs of production, i.e. its AC (cost of producing one unit) and its MC (cost of producing an extra unit).

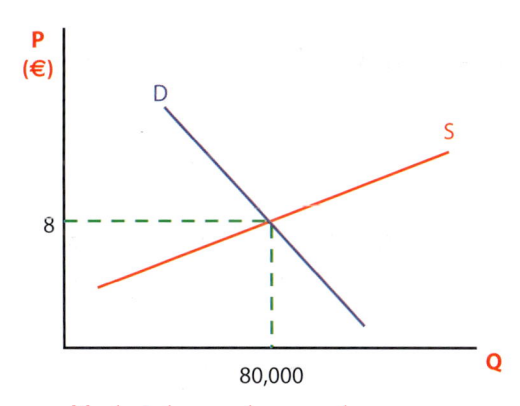

Market demand + supply curves

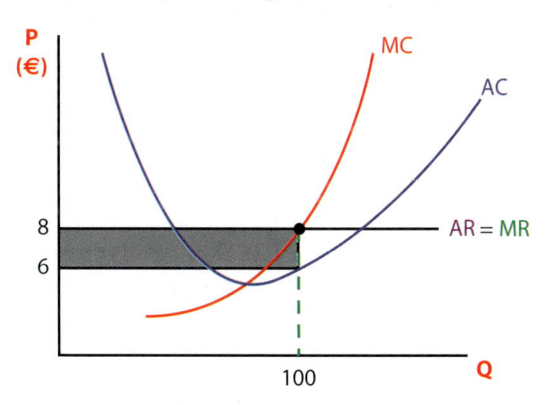

AR > AC, SNP being earned represented by the shaded area

Short Run – AR > AC → SNP Being Earned

Take a look at the diagram above. It shows us the market equilibrium of €8 and 80,000 units.

- The individual firm accepts this price (€8) and produces 100 units. This is the quantity that produces the highest profit. At this point MC = MR.

REMEMBER!
In Chapter 7, we learned that in the *short run* a firm will be in equilibrium when:
- MC = MR.
- MC cuts MR from below.
- AVC is covered.

Positive Economics

- The company covers its variable cost and is making extra profits – supernormal profit. This happens because AR is greater than AC.

- The cost of making one unit is €6. This is found out by looking firstly at the AC curve and then at the price axis. Normal profit is included in this €6. The firm is receiving €8, thereby making supernormal profit of €2 per unit. The area shaded represents total SNP.

SUPERNORMAL PROFIT is defined as profit in excess of normal profit.

REMEMBER!
AC is comprised of AFC, AVC and normal profit.

This situation won't exist for long. The SNP earned in the short run will attract new firms to enter the market. Remember, there is freedom of entry into and exit from this market structure.

As more firms enter the industry the market supply curve will shift to the right (S_1 to S_2), i.e. increasing market supply. Market price will fall from P_1 to P_2. This will eliminate SNP to a point where only normal profit is being earned.

AR will equal AC – remember that AC will include normal profit. See the diagram below.

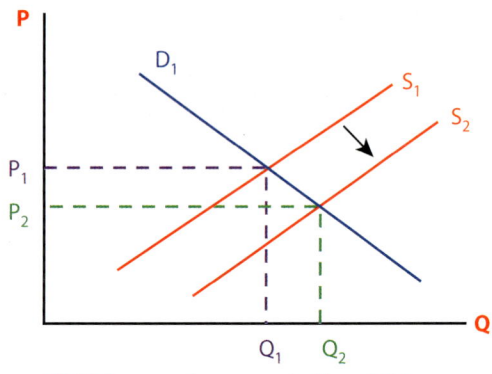

Shift in supply curve to the right. Price falls from P_1 to P_2.

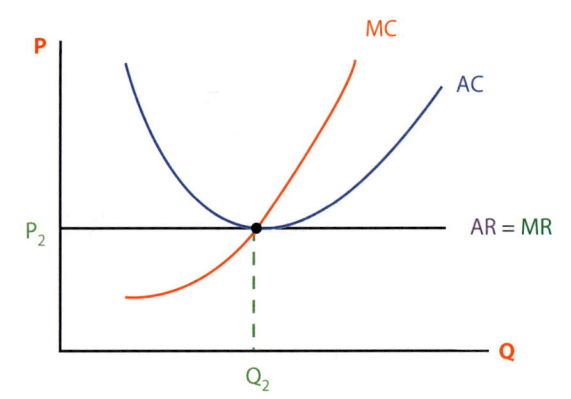

Normal profit being earned. AR = AC where MC cuts MR from below.

Short Run – AC Greater than AR: A Loss-making Situation

At the point of equilibrium in the diagram below, the average cost is higher than average revenue; this indicates that the company is not earning normal profit. If normal profit is not being earned, firms will leave the industry. This will reduce the quantity supplied from S_1 to S_2 and consequently increase market price from P_1 to P_2.

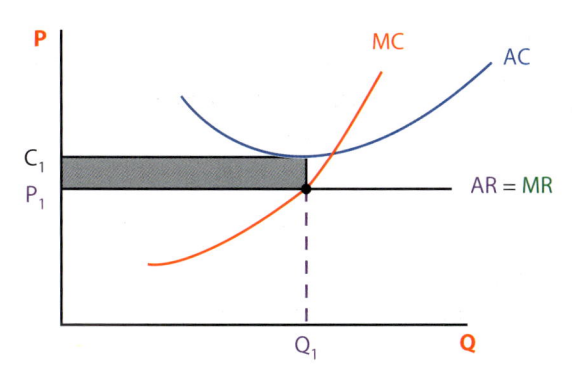

8: Perfect Competition

AC is greater than AR.
This indicates a loss-making situation.
Costs C_1 are greater than price P_1 (AR).
Firms will leave the industry.

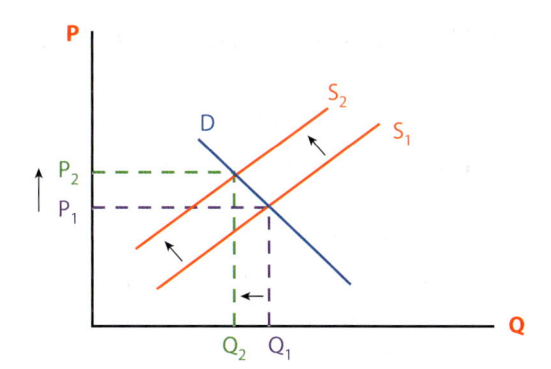

As firms leave the industry there will be a reduction in quantity supplied (Q_1 to Q_2) and consequently price will increase from P_1 to P_2.

Perfect Competition – The Long Run

In the long run there will be sufficient time for new firms to enter or leave the market. New firms will be attracted because of supernormal profits. Existing firms will leave if normal profits are not being earned. Eventually there will be the right number of firms in the industry with each firm in equilibrium where AC = AR, as shown in the diagram below.

The AR curve will be tangent to the AC curve, indicating that all costs are covered and only normal profit is being earned. We also note that **MC = MR** and that the AC curve is at its minimum.

Long Run Equilibrium

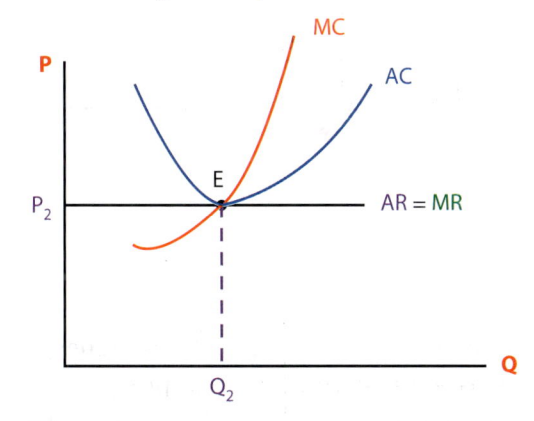

- **S** SNP not earned as AR = AC.
- **P** Price P_2 is the selling price and Q_2 is quantity produced.
- **E** Equilibrium occurs at 'E'. MC = MR [MC is rising at a faster rate than MR].
- **C** Cost of producing is at point 'E' and normal profit is earned.
- **S** Scarce resources are used efficiently as production is at the lowest point of AC.

Short Run Supply Curve in Perfect Competition

The supply curve of a firm is a graph showing the quantity that will be supplied by a firm at each price (see the diagram below).

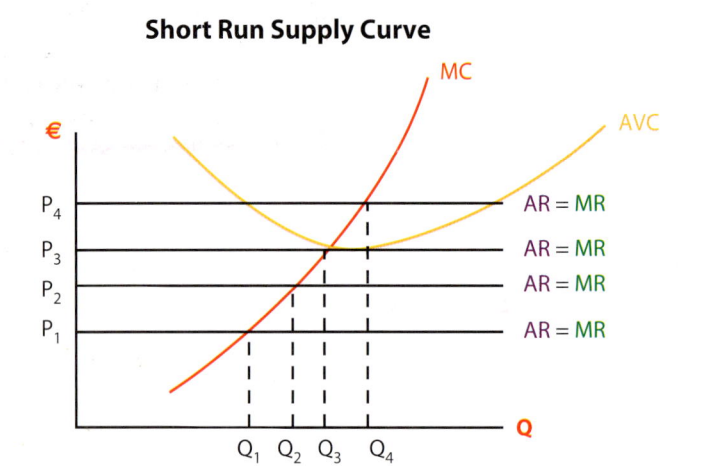

Short Run Supply Curve

A profit-maximising firm will supply output where MC = MR and MC is increasing at a faster rate than MR.

- If price is P_3 then Q_3 will be supplied.
- If price is P_4 then Q_4 will be supplied.
- At price P_1 and P_2 the firm will not produce, as it would not be recouping its variable costs.

> We can now say: **the short run supply curve of a firm in perfect competition is that part of the MC curve that lies above the lowest point of the** *average variable cost curve*.

- Recall that a firm will stay in business in the short run as long as it covers its variable costs and contributes to the reduction of fixed costs.

Long Run Supply Curve in Perfect Competition

Similarly, a profit-maximising firm in the long run will supply output where MC = MR and where MC is increasing at a faster rate than MR (see the diagram below).

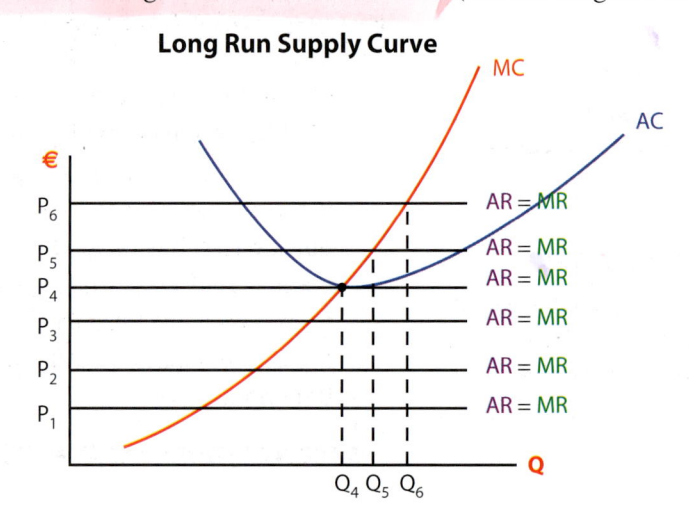

Long Run Supply Curve

8: Perfect Competition

- If the selling price is P_6 then Q_6 will be supplied.
- If the selling price is P_5 then Q_5 will be supplied.
- At any point below P_4 the firm won't supply since in the long run all costs, including normal profit, must be recouped.

> We can now say: **the long run supply curve of a perfectly competitive firm is that portion of its marginal cost curve that lies above the lowest point of its *average cost curve*.**

In Perfect Competition in the Long Run, Marginal Cost is Equal to Price (MC = P). How?

At equilibrium:

- MC = MR.
- MR = AR (AR is price).
- Therefore, MC = price.
- This is unique to perfect competition only.

Benefits of Perfect Competition

Production Occurs at the Point of Lowest Cost

In the long run, market price equals the minimum average cost, i.e. the firm produces at the lowest point on the AC curve. In effect, this means that each unit is made at the lowest possible cost, thereby achieving maximum efficiency.

Market stall

Minimum Prices

The firm only earns normal profit and therefore the consumer is not being exploited as only minimum prices are charged.

No Advertising

Resources will not be wasted through advertising and therefore no additional costs will be passed on to the consumer.

Efficiency Is Encouraged

Competition between firms will act as a spur to increase efficiency, as only those producing at the lowest point of the AC will survive in the long run.

CASE STUDY: Moore Street Markets

Moore Street is a very **efficient** market. Joan in Stall No. 4 knows that if she increases the price of oranges by 50c, there is plenty more on offer in the several other stalls around her and she will quickly lose business. On the other hand, she doesn't pay for advertising, light and heat, etc., so without these bills, all she needs to charge is her cost price plus a small margin to make her time worthwhile.

Disadvantages of Perfect Competition

No Scope for Economies of Scale
Because there are many small firms producing relatively small amounts, no one firm can achieve economies of scale.

Little Choice for Consumers
Undifferentiated products are unattractive and give little choice to consumers, unlike markets such as clothing and footwear.

No Research and Development
Lack of supernormal profits may make investment in R&D unlikely and this is important in industries like pharmaceuticals where research is essential.

No Incentive to Develop New Technology
With perfect knowledge there is little incentive to develop new technology, as it would be shared with other companies.

> **CASE STUDY: Moore Street Markets**
>
> Due to the size of her business, Joan can't negotiate a discounted price from her suppliers. In addition, her produce only stays fresh for a certain length of time and therefore she can't bulk buy. Joan is also unlikely to possess the funds to engage in research and development.

Summary

Short run	Long run
Produces where MC = MR Must cover AVC SNP may be earned (AR > AC)	Produces where MC = MR Must cover all costs, i.e. AC Normal profit earned (AR = AC) Produces where MC = MR = AC = AR

Sample Exam Question (20 marks)

What are the effects of the assumptions underlying the theory of perfect competition in the long run?

Solution

The firm faces a horizontal demand curve because:

- Each producer is selling an identical good.

- Consumers have perfect information as to price and quality.

- There are many sellers, all of whom produce a small quantity relative to the size of the market and therefore can't influence the market price of the good.

The firm produces where MC = MR, where marginal cost is increasing at a faster rate than MR. Normal profit is being earned, as profit maximisation is the goal of the company.

Freedom of entry and exit: Any firm can enter the market if SNP is being earned. Likewise, firms may leave if losses are incurred.

Perfect information: Since there is perfect knowledge as to profits and prices, prospective firms can decide to enter the market if SNP is being earned.

Question 2(a), 2007 (12 marks)

(a) A firm operating under conditions of perfect competition is a **'price taker'**. Explain the concept of being a 'price taker'.

Solution

Each firm is a price taker, i.e. it accepts the price as it is set on the market/each firm supplies such a small fraction of the market it cannot influence the market price.

Question 2(c), 2007 (25 marks)

Explain the effect of product differentiation on the AR and MR curves of a firm that previously operated under conditions of perfect competition.

Solution

Product differentiation is where firms highlight differences between products that are close substitutes through branding, packaging and competitive advertising. As a result of product differentiation:

- A firm's AR will be downward sloping from left to right.

- If it lowers its price, consumers will switch to its products from those of its close competitors and demand will increase.

- If AR is falling, MR will also fall and will lie below AR.

Questions

Short Questions

1. Explain, with examples, two markets you consider to operate under conditions of perfect competition.
2. State and explain the assumptions underlying perfect competition.
3. Draw and explain the demand curve facing an individual firm under perfect competition.
4. Explain and illustrate the term 'price taker'.

Long Questions

1. Explain normal profit and supernormal profit.
2. Illustrate and explain the effect of new entrants into the market that is earning SNP.
3. Illustrate and explain the equilibrium for a perfectly competitive firm in the short run.
4. Explain why the AR and MR curves are the same in perfect competition.
5. Derive the short run and the long run supply curves in perfect competition.
6. What would be the cross elasticity of demand for goods in perfect competition? Explain.
7. Draw and explain the long run equilibrium of a firm in perfect competition.
8. Explain the firm's shut down point in the short run.
9. What are the benefits and disadvantages of perfect competition to the consumer and to society?
10. Explain how MC = P in perfect competition.
11. Why don't firms in perfect competition advertise?

Chapter 9 | Imperfect Competition

Specific Learning Outcomes

At the end of this chapter, students should be able to:

- ☐ Explain, with examples, the theory of imperfect competition.
- ☐ Describe the assumptions underlying imperfect competition.
- ☐ Illustrate and explain the firm's demand curve.
- ☐ Describe the equilibrium for an imperfectly competitive firm in the short run.
- ☐ Define and illustrate supernormal profits.
- ☐ Discuss why new firms may enter the industry.
- ☐ Analyse the effects on equilibrium of new entrants.
- ☐ Describe, with the aid of a diagram, the equilibrium for an imperfectly competitive firm in the long run.
- ☐ Illustrate and explain profit-maximising output/price.
- ☐ Analyse imperfect competition as a market form from the point of view of consumers, producers and the use of scarce resources.
- ☐ Describe, with examples, price competition and non-price competition and analyse which form is better for the consumer.

Introduction

Both perfect competition and monopoly are at opposite ends on our spectrum of market structures. In perfect competition there are many sellers, but in monopoly there is only one supplier.

Imperfect competition is probably the form of market structure that is seen most often in our everyday lives. It occurs in industries such as the restaurant business, hotels and pubs and consumer services such as hairdressing. In the above industries there are many producers supplying close but not perfect substitutes.

In the 1930s a number of economists wondered whether just perfect competition and monopoly accurately described the marketplace they experienced at that time. In 1933 Edward Chamberlain wrote a pioneering book on this subject, *Theory of Monopolistic Competition*, in which he set forth his ideas on what we will now study – imperfect/monopolistic competition.

Assumptions/Characteristics of Imperfect Competition

There Are Many Buyers in the Industry
Each buyer acts independently and no one individual buyer by their own actions can influence the market price of the goods.

There Are a Large Number of Sellers in the Industry
Each seller acts independently but sellers can set their own prices, thus influencing the quantity sold.

Product Differentiation Exists
The goods that the different suppliers bring to the market are not identical. However, they are very close substitutes. Companies try to establish in the minds of consumers that the goods are not perfect substitutes by selling their goods under brand names.

A central feature of imperfect competition is that products are differentiated using some of the following methods.

- **Physical product differentiation**, where firms use size, design, colour, shape, performance and features to make their products different.

- **Marketing differentiation**, where firms try to distinguish their product by distinctive packaging, e.g. breakfast cereals, and other promotional techniques.

- **Human capital differentiation**, where the firm creates differences through the skill of its employees, the level of training received, distinctive uniforms, etc.

- **Differentiation through distribution**, including distribution via mail order or through internet shopping such as Amazon, which differentiates itself by selling online.

There Is Freedom of Entry to and Exit from the Industry
Firms already in the industry cannot prevent new firms, each with their own unique product, from entering the industry. Likewise, firms unable to cover costs can leave the industry as they wish.

Reasonable Knowledge as to Profits Made by Other Firms
In the industry, everyone has reasonable knowledge as to the profits made by other firms. Consumers may not be fully aware of the prices being charged for different products.

Each Firm Tries to Maximise Profits
The sole goal of each firm is to produce that quantity that will maximise its profits in the short run. In so doing, they aim to minimise costs and will produce the quantity where MC = MR.

CASE STUDY: Pat's Deli

Remember Pat's Deli from Chapter 7? There are many people who want to buy goods sold in several hundred delicatessens throughout the country. Pat could have any amount of new competitors, but they would need to find a niche to do well. Indeed, anybody thinking of entering this sector would need to do some market research beforehand and hence would have a reasonable knowledge as to the profits made by Pat and other firms. Like any business, the deli will try to maximise profits. The differentiating factors between Pat's Deli and any other competitor could be any of the following:

- Selling fresh ready-made meals
- Having an in-store coffee shop
- Specialising in wine
- The shopfront

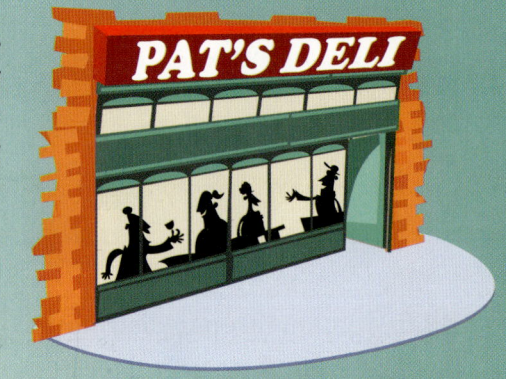

Long run

Demand Curve Facing a Monopolistic/Imperfectly Competitive Firm

Because each firm makes a unique product, it can charge a higher or lower price than its rivals. If the producer increases price, there will be a reduction in demand as some consumers will switch to the rival goods that have become relatively cheaper (due to price elasticity of demand). Likewise, if the firm lowers its price, then its sales will increase, indicating an inverse relationship between price and quantity demanded. This means that each firm faces a downward sloping demand curve (AR curve) and consequently a marginal revenue curve (MR curve) lower than it. However, not all consumers will switch to a competitor's product if price is changed because consumers do not perceive the goods as being perfect substitutes.

Monopolistic firms are *price makers*. The price the company decides to charge for its good is at their own discretion and does not have to be decided by supply and demand (as in perfect competition), even though the industry price may be a good guideline. This also indicates that the demand curve will slope downwards from left to right.

Successful product differentiation means a more inelastic demand curve.

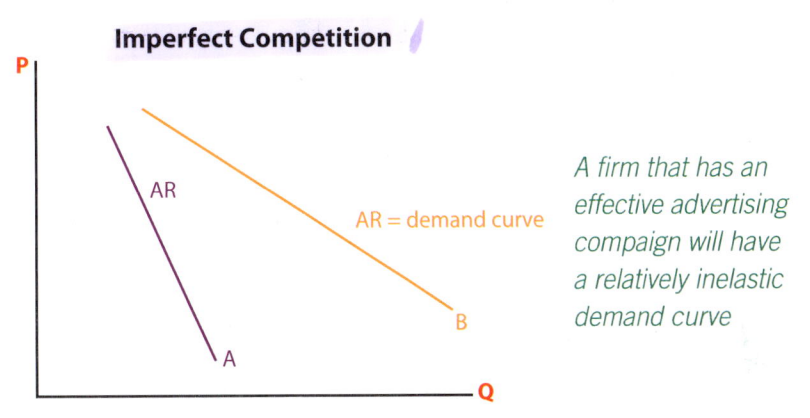

Imperfect Competition

A firm that has an effective advertising compaign will have a relatively inelastic demand curve

Look at the above demand curves for similar products. Both are downward sloping but A is more inelastic, indicating that it is less responsive to a change in its own price. This is because A's product differentiation is more successful in making its good seem important to the consumer. Buyers of this good won't readily switch to competing brands when its price increases.

Equilibrium in Imperfect Competition

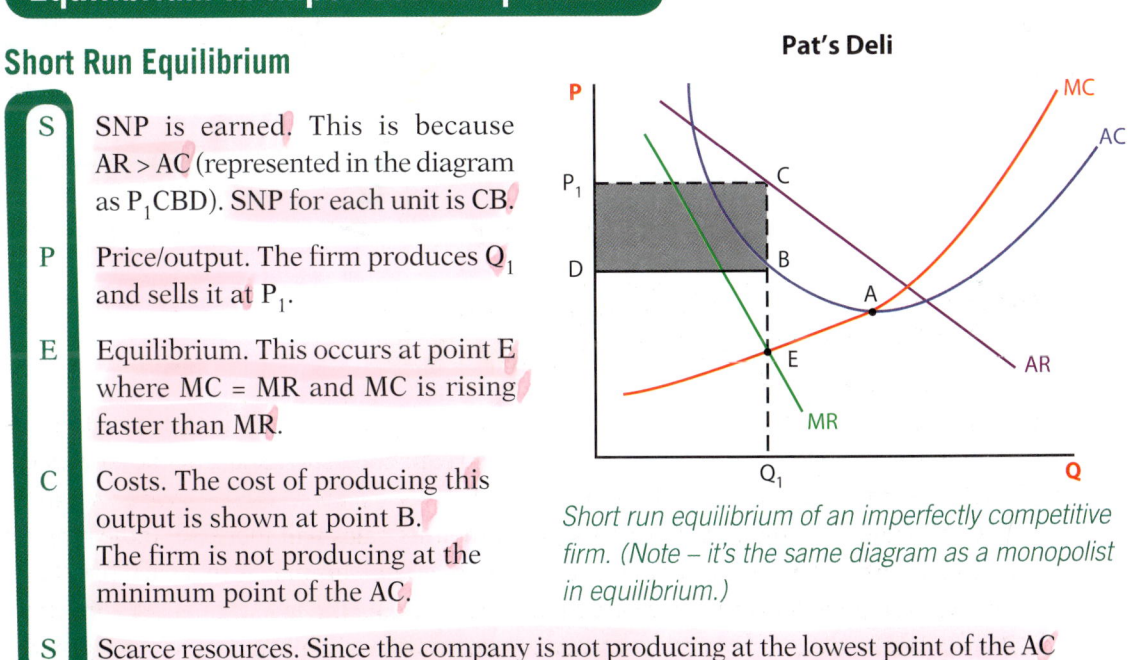

Short Run Equilibrium

S SNP is earned. This is because AR > AC (represented in the diagram as P_1CBD). SNP for each unit is CB.

P Price/output. The firm produces Q_1 and sells it at P_1.

E Equilibrium. This occurs at point E where MC = MR and MC is rising faster than MR.

C Costs. The cost of producing this output is shown at point B. The firm is not producing at the minimum point of the AC.

S Scarce resources. Since the company is not producing at the lowest point of the AC (point A), it is considered to be wasting scarce resources.

Short run equilibrium of an imperfectly competitive firm. (Note – it's the same diagram as a monopolist in equilibrium.)

Positive Economics

The existence of supernormal profits will attract new firms into the market who will make similar but not identical goods. Pat's Deli will now lose customers to the new entrants. However, not all customers will be lost due to effective product differentiation, e.g. brand loyalty, special offers, advertising and satisfaction with the existing product.

Some customers will be lost, causing Pat's demand curve to shift to the left (see the diagram). This will continue until the SNP is eliminated and Pat only earns normal profit. This occurs in the diagram below, where we see the AR curve tangent to the AC curve.

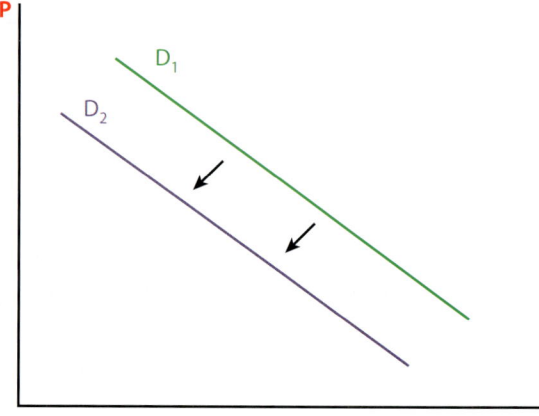

More entrants into the market means demand falls, i.e. a shift in demand curve to the left.

Long Run Equilibrium of an Imperfectly Competitive Firm

S — SNP is not earned. There are low barriers to entry and reasonable knowledge about profits being made. This attracts new firms into the market, eliminating SNP until normal profits, i.e. AR = AC, are being made.

P — Price/output. The firm produces Q_1 and sells it at P_1.

E — Equilibrium. This occurs at point E where MC = MR and MC is rising faster than MR.

C — Costs. The cost of producing this output is shown at point B. The firm is not producing at the minimum point of the AC.

S — Scarce resources. Since the company is not producing at the lowest point of the AC (point A), it is wasting scarce resources.

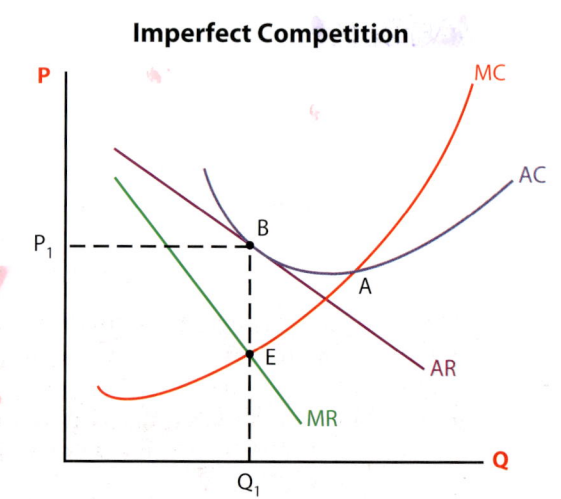

Long run equilibrium of an imperfectly competitive firm

9: Imperfect Competition

> **In monopolistic/imperfect competition, long run equilibrium occurs where MC = MR and AR = AC.**

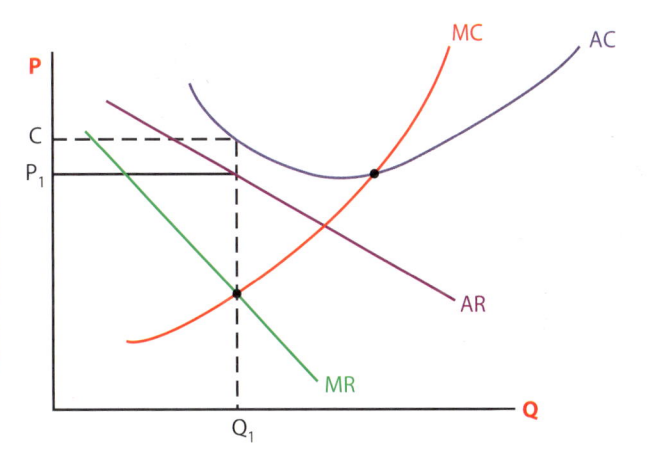

Short run equilibrium: a loss is being earned, AC > AR. This could lead to firms leaving the industry.

In the short run, it is possible that a firm would not earn normal profit, as depicted in the diagram. Here the AC curve lies above the AR curve, indicating that cost is greater than price. Firms would leave the industry and the demand curve facing the remaining firms would shift to the **right**, indicating a greater demand at each price. This situation would continue until long run equilibrium is achieved, as seen in the diagram.

Advantages and Disadvantages of Imperfect Competition

Advantages

- **Contestable markets:** There are few barriers to entry, making markets relatively competitive and thus benefiting consumers in the form of lower prices.
- **Choice of goods:** Differentiation creates diversity of goods for consumers, although this may mean higher prices, compensated by higher perceived value. Consumers like to have a wide variety of goods and services to choose from, e.g. many different restaurants can be found in most towns.

- **Dynamically efficient:** Monopolistic firms are constantly striving to provide a better product or service. They are innovative, developing new production processes or products in order to gain a competitive edge over their rivals, e.g. retailers often have to develop new ways to attract and retain local custom.

- **Normal profit:** In the long run consumers are not being exploited, as the firm is earning normal profit (AC = AR).

- **Access to information:** Consumers have more information available to them because of the extensive competitive advertising used within the industry.

> **CASE STUDY: Pat's Deli**
>
> In Pat's Deli, they don't only offer minced meat, but also ready-made chilli con carne, spaghetti Bolognese, burgers and shepherd's pie. As a result it attracts different customers from its competitor which specialises in pizzas. This is an example of a dynamically efficient market because the customer has lots of choice. In addition, both delis advertise in the local paper and their customers are well aware of their pricing structure.

Disadvantages

- **Production is not at the minimum point of AC:** In equilibrium the firm is not producing at a level where costs are at their lowest, as in perfect competition. This is because money is spent on advertising, differentiated packaging, etc., which increases the cost of production and is inevitably passed on to the consumer.

- **Excess capacity:** Production is not where average costs are at a minimum and this is considered to be wasteful of scarce resources. The firm could produce a greater output than it does, meaning that it has overcapacity. Thus, resources are considered to be wasted.

- **Price is greater than MC:** The price charged by a firm in imperfect competition will exceed marginal cost. In perfect competition, price equals MC.

> **CASE STUDY: Pat's Deli**
>
> Pat has to spend money turning minced meat into different cuisine meals as well as advertising, packaging and brand awareness. This is in contrast to Joan on Stall 4 in Moore Street (see Chapter 8), who does not have any of these costs. As a result, Pat's production is not at the minimum point of the average costs curve.

Imperfect Competition Compared with Perfect Competition

- The firms in both of these markets earn normal profit where AR = AC in the long run.

- The perfectly competitive firm produces at the lowest point of the AC, indicating efficient use of resources. This is not the case in imperfect competition.

9: Imperfect Competition

- Price is equal to MC in perfect competition, which is not the case in imperfect competition. In the latter, price is greater than MC, indicating that more of the good could be produced.
- The perfectly competitive firm faces a horizontal demand curve and the imperfectly competitive firm faces a downward sloping demand curve.

Differences between Price and Non-price Competition

> **PRICE COMPETITION** is where firms compete by changing their prices. **NON-PRICE COMPETITION** is where firms compete using methods other than changing their prices, e.g. giveaways, competitions, club points.

The consumer prefers price competition because:

- The buyer gets the good at a lower price.
- It means the consumer has more disposable income.
- The consumer now has a choice – they can decide what to do with their income, e.g. buy more goods and get greater utility from the same income than previously.

What are the benefits of non-price competition to consumers?

- Prices remain stable rather than increasing and this benefits the consumer.
- There may be better after-sales service.
- Consumer loyalty may be rewarded by getting free gifts/club points, home delivery, 24-hour shopping, internet shopping and innovative use of technology for shoppers, including self-scanning machines, etc.
- Consumers gain as advertising keeps them informed of special offers and new variations available in the product.

CASE STUDY: Pat's Deli

Pat's customers pay more for chili con carne in Pat's Deli than they do if they were to buy the ingredients and make it themselves. However, they value the convenience offered to them and are willing to pay for it. In addition, because Pat engages in advertising, consumers may be enticed into the deli using special offers/loyalty cards, which also benefit them.

Positive Economics

✓ EXAM Question 2(c), 2005 (15 marks)

Consider the retail market for petrol.
Do you believe that this market operates under conditions of imperfect competition? State reasons for your answer.

Solution

Yes, the market for petrol operates under conditions of imperfect competition because:

- There are many sellers of petrol within the market, e.g. Topaz, Statoil, Maxol.

- The products sold are close substitutes. There is competitive advertising and heavy product loyalty promotion. Various gimmicks are used to attract customers. Sellers also use brand names extensively to maintain consumer loyalty.

- Each seller can influence the demand for petrol by altering the price as consumers are becoming far more sensitive to the price differences for petrol.

(Arguments for oligopoly from a national point of view were also accepted.)

✓ EXAM Question 1(b), 2001 (10 marks)

Draw the demand curve which faces a firm in imperfect competition and justify its shape.

Solution

Because there are many goods that are close substitutes, if a firm increases its price, there will be a reduction in demand, as some consumers will switch to the competitive goods that have become relatively cheaper.

If a firm lowers its price it will increase its sales, as some consumers of other substitute goods will switch to this firm's good because it is relatively cheaper.

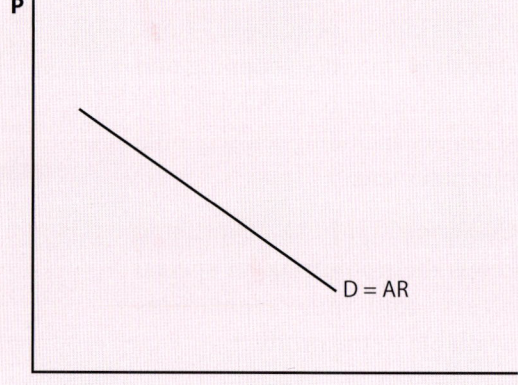

Downward Sloping Demand Curve

(Graph: P on vertical axis, Q on horizontal axis, downward sloping line labelled D = AR)

9: Imperfect Competition

Questions

Short Questions

1. Give three examples of goods/services that you consider to operate in an imperfectly competitive market.
2. State and explain the assumptions underlying the imperfectly competitive market.
3. How does each firm aim to maximise profits?
4. Explain two types of product differentiation.
5. Justify the shape of the demand curve of an imperfectly competitive firm.

Long Questions

1. Firms in long run equilibrium in imperfect competition are not operating at minimum cost. Discuss.
2. Draw and explain the short run equilibrium of an imperfectly competitive firm.
3. How might advertising in imperfect competition act as a form of barrier to entry to new firms?
4. Explain non-price competition.
5. Draw and explain the long run equilibrium of an imperfectly competitive firm.
6. State and explain two advantages and two disadvantages of imperfect competition.
7. Draw and explain the differences between the demand curves of a perfectly competitive firm and that of an imperfectly competitive firm.
8. What is the significance of the equation MC = MR?
9. Compare perfect competition and imperfect competition, stating one similarity and one difference.
10. Do consumers prefer price or non-price competition? Explain your answer.

Chapter 10 | Monopoly

Specific Learning Outcomes

At the end of this chapter, students should be able to:

- [ ] Explain, with examples, the theory of monopoly.

- [ ] Describe and assess the assumptions underlying monopoly.

- [ ] Illustrate and explain the firm's demand curve under monopoly.

- [ ] Describe, with the aid of a diagram, the equilibrium for a monopolist.

- [ ] Define and illustrate supernormal profits.

- [ ] Explain and illustrate profit-maximising output/price.

- [ ] Critically analyse monopoly as a market form from the point of view of consumers, producers and the use of scarce resources.

- [ ] Suggest ways as to how state monopolies could be made more effective.

- [ ] Compare and contrast the long run equilibrium position of perfect competition, monopoly and imperfect competition.

Introduction

Just as perfect competition is one extreme form of competition, so too is monopoly. In perfect competition there are large numbers of buyers and sellers. In contrast, monopoly has only one seller. A pure monopoly exists when there is no competition at all in the sector. In reality this is very rare. For example, rail transport is serviced only by Iarnród Éireann, but there are many other forms of transport available to the public, e.g. car, bus, cycling, flying. However, Iarnród Éireann is the main supplier of rail transport and is therefore the dominant firm in the industry.

Characteristics of Monopoly

Sole Supplier in the Industry

There is only one firm and it supplies the entire output of the industry. Due to this fact, we don't distinguish between the firm and the industry, as in effect, the firm *is* the industry.

Controls Either Price or Quantity Supplied

The firm can control either the price that it charges or the quantity it sells. It cannot control both.

For example, Iarnród Éireann can charge any price it wishes, but it can't control the quantity that the public will buy. Likewise, it may supply a certain quantity but it can't make the public buy this quantity at the price it sets.

Maximises Profit

The firm in monopoly will produce where MC = MR, with MC rising faster than MR. Since the objective of the monopolist is to earn maximum profit, the monopolist may earn supernormal profit.

Barriers to Entry

Since there are no other firms in the industry, it is likely that the monopolist will earn supernormal profits. This situation will occur in both the short and long run due to barriers to entry.

What Are the Sources of Monopoly Power/What Are the Barriers to Entry into the Industry?

Legal/Statutory Monopoly
The government may confer the sole right to produce a good or service to one firm. This is done by passing laws (statutory monopoly) that prohibit any other company from competing with the monopoly firm. The main reason for granting such rights is to avoid any unnecessary waste and duplication of services. For example, could you imagine a second company building an entirely new rail network just so that it could compete with Iarnród Éireann?

Ownership of a Patent/Copyright
If a firm has the sole right to a manufacturing process, then no other company can produce the good until the patent has expired. This encourages firms to invest in research and development and consequently benefit from the rewards of costly research.

Ownership of Raw Materials
A company may have complete control over the source of essential raw materials and hence has monopoly power, e.g. a gas/copper drilling firm.

Economies of Scale/Large Capital Investment
In some areas of production, economies of scale are essential for survival. If an industry requires large capital investment, then it may discourage new entrants because of the high start-up costs. A company is thus prohibited from low unit costs of production and can't compete with the established company.

Cartels/Collusion
Firms may enter into trade agreements with similar companies and divide up the market, thus ensuring no competition exists.

Mergers/Takeovers
A company may gain monopoly power by merging with or taking over a rival company, thus eliminating the competition.

Brand Proliferation
Some firms achieve monopoly power through aggressive advertising/branding and this creates the perception that consumers don't have any alternative.

10: Monopoly

Demand Curve Facing a Monopolist

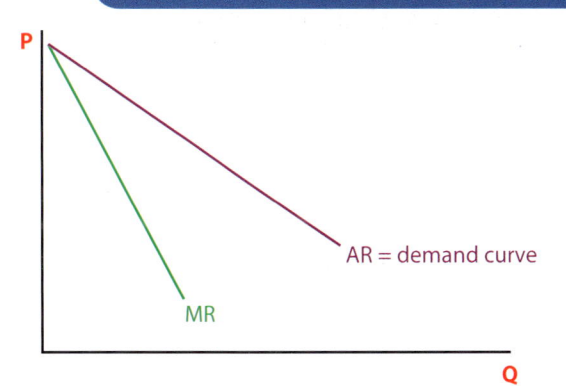

The monopolist faces a normal downward sloping demand curve, indicating an inverse relationship between price and quantity demanded. The demand curve is also known as the average revenue curve. When AR is reduced to sell more output, marginal revenue will be lower than AR.

The figures below show that when AR (price) is dropped, more goods will be sold and MR will be lower than AR.

Price (€)	Quantity	TR	AR (TR/Q)	MR (change in TR)
10	1	10	10	–
9	2	18	9	8
8	3	24	8	6
7	4	28	7	4

Equilibrium of the Monopolist

A profit-maximising monopolist will produce where MC = MR with MC rising faster than MR. As AR will be greater than AC, the firm will earn SNP. Due to the fact that there are barriers to entry, these supernormal profits can exist in the long run. In effect there is no difference between the short and long run, as the equilibrium position remains unchanged.

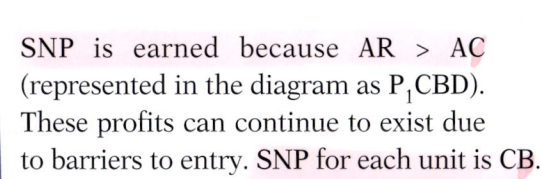

Monopolist – Long Run Equilibrium

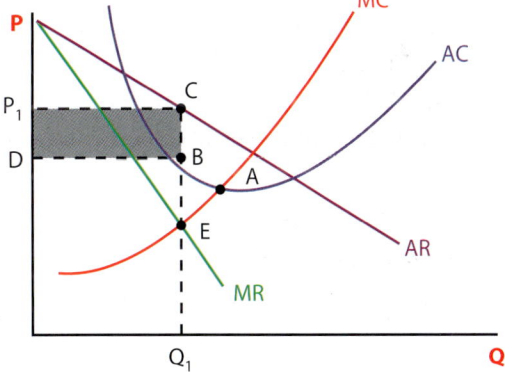

- **S** SNP is earned because AR > AC (represented in the diagram as P_1CBD). These profits can continue to exist due to barriers to entry. SNP for each unit is CB.
- **P** Price/output. The firm produces Q_1 and sells it at P_1.
- **E** Equilibrium. This occurs at point E where MC = MR and MC is rising faster than MR.
- **C** Costs. The cost of producing this output is shown at point B. The firm is not producing at the minimum point of the AC.
- **S** Scarce resources. Since the company is not producing at the lowest point of the AC (point A), it is considered to be wasting scarce resources.

143

Perfect Competition and Monopoly Compared

Efficiency

The monopolist makes inefficient use of society's scarce resources as it does not produce at the minimum point of the average cost curve (C_m), unlike the perfectly competitive firm that does produce at the lowest point of the AC (C_p).

Perfect Competition and Monopoly with Similar Cost Conditions

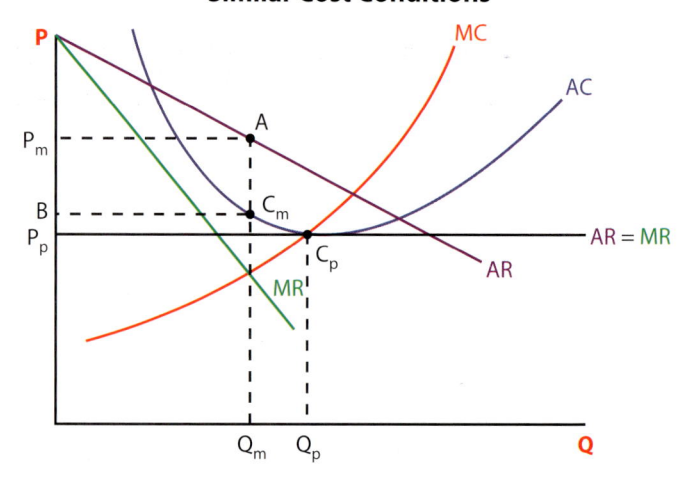

Price

The monopolist charges a higher price (P_m) than the perfectly competitive firm (P_p). In monopoly, price is greater than MC, while price equals MC in perfect competition.

- P_m = price of the monopolist
- P_p = price of the perfectly competitive firm
- Q_m = quantity produced by the monopolist
- Q_p = quantity produced by the perfectly competitive firm

Output

A monopolist produces a smaller output than perfect competition (Q_m and Q_p, respectively).

Profits

SNP is earned by the monopolist, as AR > AC ($P_m AC_m B$), while AR = AC in perfect competition and normal profit is earned (C_p).

Demand Curve

A monopolist faces a downward sloping demand curve, while a perfectly competitive firm faces a horizontal demand curve.

Imperfect Competition and Monopoly

- Neither produces at the lowest point of the AC, indicating a wasteful use of resources.
- Both face a downward sloping demand curve – price must be lowered to increase the quantity demanded.

- In both markets, price is greater than MC, indicating that more of the good could be produced.
- The monopolist earns SNP in both the long and short run. The imperfectly competitive firm earns SNP only in the short run and normal profit in the long run.

Advantages of Monopoly as a Market Structure

Economies of Scale
Production on a large scale allows the firm to benefit from economies of scale and these cost savings may be passed on to the consumer in the form of lower prices.

Guaranteed Supply of Product/Service
In some state monopolies the product/service may be sold at very low profit margins, so consumers benefit. These services may not be provided by private enterprise, e.g. regular bus services to remote/low-density populated areas.

Secure Employment
As there is no competition, employees have greater security of tenure and may have better conditions of employment.

Reduced Use of Scarce Resources
There may be less duplication in the provision of products/services. There may be less need for competitive advertising, so society's resources are not wasted. Some services may be best provided by one provider, e.g. rail networks.

Potential for Innovation/Research and Development
The profits that monopolies make could be used for investment in research and development as well as to fund high-cost capital investment. Successful research can be used as the basis for the development of improved products and lower costs in the long term. Investors also need patent protection, otherwise they may not invest.

Disadvantages of Monopoly as a Market Structure

Exploitation of Consumers
The supernormal profit that monopolists achieve may be due to the exploitation of consumers. As the sole supplier of a good or service, the monopolist may abuse their position by pushing up prices and leaving the consumer with no alternative but to purchase their good or service.

Inefficient Use of Scarce Resources
The monopolist makes inefficient use of society's scarce resources. It does not produce where average cost is at its minimum, but where MC = MR. This is due to a lack of competition and causes a waste of economic resources.

The Production of Fewer Goods at a Higher Price than Perfect Competition

Consider two companies operating in a perfectly competitive market and hence under similar cost conditions. The monopolist will produce a lower quantity at a higher price than the perfectly competitive firms.

Less Efficient/Innovative

It is often argued that monopolies tend to become less efficient and innovative over time. Due to the fact that monopolies have a dominant position, they may not necessarily have to compete in the marketplace and consequently may not engage in R&D or be innovative.

Who Regulates Monopolies?

Competition Act 2002

The Competition Authority is an independent statutory body that enforces Irish and European competition law. It seeks to ensure that competition works for the benefit of all consumers, including businesses, who buy products and services in Ireland. We will briefly look at how their work prevents firms from abusing their monopoly power.

MONOPOLIES DIVISION

The Authority will investigate agreements that have anti-competitive effects but are not considered to be cartels, e.g. agreements between manufacturers and distributors of their products or between distributors and retailers can sometimes be found to be anti-competitive and be in breach of the Competition Act 2002.

They will also investigate where there is an abuse of a dominant position in the market, i.e. exploiting your position to stifle competition or attempting to eliminate your competitors or prevent new competitors from emerging.

CARTELS DIVISION

A cartel is an illegal agreement between two or more competitors not to compete with each other. The sole purpose of cartels, which usually involves a secret conspiracy, is to make more profit at the expense of their customers. Price fixing, market sharing, limiting production and bid rigging are all illegal and the involved parties can be prosecuted.

MERGERS DIVISION

Businesses may join together to restructure in order to compete and prosper. Some mergers may have a negative effect on consumers, e.g. leading to an increase in price or a reduction in output. That is, they lessen competition and consumers suffer. The Authority has the power to clear mergers, clear mergers with conditions, or block mergers where it finds that they will lead to a substantial lessening of competition.

(*Source*: The Competition Authority)

10: Monopoly

Deregulation of Markets

Deregulation could affect consumers and employees in the following ways.

> **DEREGULATION** is the removal of government controls from an industry or sector to allow for a free and efficient market place, e.g. the airline industry, the taxi industry and the supply of electricity.

Consumers

Increased competition may lead to an increase in supply (e.g. taxi industry) and this may cause prices to fall. There may also be improved services with greater efficiency and a wider choice for consumers. On the other hand, non-profit-making services (provided by government companies) that had previously been provided may be discontinued in order to reduce costs.

Employees

Existing companies may lose business due to new, increased competition forcing redundancies. There may also be a renegotiation of working conditions and benefits as the company is now forced to compete. On the other hand, some employees may join the new suppliers and view the change as an opportunity for advancement.

Profits

If existing businesses lose customers, their market share will fall, as will profits. These companies may find it difficult to adapt their business processes to the decrease in revenues and may consequently fail. Conversely, the existing company may be able to compete and expand its business, achieving economies of scale and higher profits.

How Can State Companies Who Are Often Cited as Being Inefficient Achieve Greater Productivity?

- Deregulation of their market would force efficiency, leading to better services and a decrease in operating costs.

- Appointing experienced entrepreneurs with proven business records onto state boards might bring a different attitude that would increase profits and eliminate wasteful practices.

- State trading organisations were not initially set up to maximise profits, so the introduction of a profit motive and performance-related remuneration may lead to better-functioning organisations.

- Allow the companies to form strategic alliances, e.g. Aer Lingus and JetBlue.
- Discontinue unprofitable services (this may be unpopular and difficult to implement).
- Privatise the company – this will encourage efforts towards cost reduction (see below).
- If political appointments are made, they should be based solely on the skills and knowledge that are needed for the industry.
- An absence of government interference in the day-to-day operations and management of the company, as a different skill set needs to be employed in running a business.

Privatisation

Some state-owned monopolies have been sold to the private sector in the last decade. The benefits of these sales mean lower prices and a better service, with the revenue from the sale benefiting government finances. Some disadvantages include the loss of non-profit-making services and the deterioration of standards. Also, overseas buyers may become owners of previously owned national assets and control might go out of the state. The 1990s saw a number of privatisations: Irish Sugar Company to Greencore, B&I Line to Irish Ferries and Telecom Éireann to Eircom.

> **PRIVATISATION** is the sale of a state company to private owners.

> **NATIONALISATION** means taking a company or assets in the private sector into public ownership by a government.

EXAM Question 1(d), 2004 (20 marks)

Irish semi-state transport companies are facing increasing competition. Discuss **one** possible advantage and **one** possible disadvantage of this development for consumers **and** employees of semi-state companies.

Solution

Advantages for consumers:

- **Quality of services:** The competition may force the semi-state companies to improve the quality/efficiency of the service provided.

- **More competitive prices:** Increased competition may force the firm to offer consumers more competitive prices.

- **Increased choice/availability of services:** Consumers may now be able to avail of a wider choice of goods/services.

Disadvantages for consumers:

- **Loss of non-profit-making services:** Non-profit-making services may be discontinued by the semi-state company in an effort to reduce costs.

- **Disruption to supply of service:** Workers' fears about the effects of competition may cause them to engage in industrial disputes, disrupting the service for consumers.

Advantages for employees of semi-state transport companies:

- **More motivated workforce:** Competition may pressurise the workforce to become more innovative in their jobs.

- **Reward/incentive for innovation:** If the semi-state firm can meet the challenges of competition, employees may reap more rewards for their innovation, e.g. bonuses.

- **Provision of extra services:** It may now be possible for the company to aggressively pursue its share of the market without state restrictions, ensuring growth in employment/additional job security.

- **Opportunities for settlement packages:** Workers might take the opportunity to change career or use their settlement packages to invest in or start a business.

Disadvantages for employees of semi-state transport companies:

- **Loss of job/reduced job security:** The biggest risk is the loss of their jobs through rationalisation of services.

- **Change of conditions of employment/loss of benefits:** The firm may change the conditions of employment for its employees, resulting in a worsening of these.

- **Curtailment in pay/pensions:** The firm may limit the pay and pension increases due to its employees.

Questions

Short Questions

1. Define the term 'monopoly', giving an example.
2. State and explain three characteristics of a monopoly.
3. Draw the demand curve of a monopolist. Justify its shape.
4. Justify the shape of the MR curve.
5. Explain the phrase 'the firm *is* the industry' in relation to monopoly.

Long Questions

1. Draw and explain the long run equilibrium of a monopolist.
2. State and explain four barriers to entry into a monopoly market.
3. Compare monopoly and perfect competition on the same diagram, indicating price, quantity, SNP and cost of production.
4. Explain why the short run and long run equilibrium are the same in monopoly.
5. How are monopolies regulated in Ireland?
6. State and explain four advantages of monopoly.
7. State and explain four disadvantages of monopoly.
8. Explain the term 'deregulation'.
9. How does deregulation affect consumers and employees?
10. Suggest two ways state companies can be made more efficient.

Chapter 11 | Price Discrimination

Specific Learning Outcomes

At the end of this chapter, students should be able to:

- Define price discrimination.
- Describe, with the aid of examples, price discrimination.
- Examine the reasons for the existence of price discrimination.
- Describe the conditions necessary for price discrimination.
- Identify the degrees of price discrimination.
- Analyse price discrimination from the point of view of producers and consumers.

Positive Economics

Introduction

Why is it that adults and children are charged different prices at the cinema? Why do doctors charge different prices to different patients? Why are different entrance fees charged to adults and children when attending the same football game?

In economics we refer to this situation as price discrimination. It refers to a situation where different prices are charged for the same good to different consumers. However, we must be careful with our definition. A bag of oranges sold in Donegal may be a little more expensive than the same bag sold in Dublin. This could be due to the extra costs that need to be incurred in order to take them off the boat or plane in Dublin and transport them up to Donegal. Although different prices are charged for the same good, this would not be considered price discrimination as there are different costs involved. So our full definition is:

> **PRICE DISCRIMINATION** is when goods and services are sold to different consumers at varying ratios between marginal cost and price, i.e. P/MC is not constant.

Examples include students and OAPs being charged different prices, doctors charging patients different fees or **selling the same good (or service) to different consumers at different prices, where such price differences are not caused by differences in costs.**

What Are the Conditions Necessary for Price Discrimination to Take Place?

Monopoly Power

A company that price discriminates must have some element of monopoly power. If there was freedom of entry into the industry, competitors would enter this market where the supplier was charging higher prices and earning SNP. This would continue and cause supply to increase, driving down price until only normal profit was being earned. *and PD can't occur*

Separation of Markets

It must be possible to separate the markets so that a good purchased in the low-priced market can't be resold in the higher-priced one. If this was not the case, then goods could be bought in the low-priced market and resold in the higher-priced market and this would continue until no price differential existed.

11: Price Discrimination

It Must Be Possible to Differentiate between Consumers with Different Price Elasticities of Demand

Consumers with high price elasticity of demand will be charged lower prices for their goods, e.g. students are assumed to have lower incomes and so are unable to pay the full price for certain goods and services. Similarly, OAPs who are not in a position to pay the full price are sometimes offered discounted rates to entice them to buy and thus increase sales.

Characteristics of Consumers That May Permit Price Discrimination to Take Place

- **Consumer ignorance:** The consumer paying the higher price may be unaware that the good is available elsewhere at a lower price.

- **Consumer indifference:** The difference in price may be so small that consumers don't care and don't mind paying the higher price.

- **Consumer attitude:** Consumers may be willing to pay a higher price for a good they think is of better quality, is in fashion or that provides status, e.g. branded goods.

Degrees/Types of Price Discrimination

Now that we have an understanding of price discrimination and the conditions necessary for it to take place, we can take a closer look at the different types/degrees of price discrimination.

First Degree

This is sometimes called perfect price discrimination, whereby the seller knows:

- The maximum price each consumer is willing pay rather than do without the good/service and
- Charges that exact price, i.e. eliminates consumer surplus.

This usually works if the seller has a small number of buyers and can predict what each buyer is willing to pay. It can occur in one-to-one confidential relationships where it is possible for the seller to estimate the price elasticity of demand of the buyer, e.g. visiting a member of the legal or medical profession.

Second Degree

This occurs when the seller lowers their price because the purchaser is buying a large quantity. This is not because of any drop in their unit cost due to producing a big quantity, but instead is a recognition of the fact that the consumer would not purchase if they were charged the full amount. This is related to the law of diminishing marginal utility and recognises the fact that the consumer would only be prepared to buy more if unit selling price is reduced, e.g. two for the price of one offers or annual magazine subscriptions (€5 for a weekly magazine or €200 for a yearly subscription – a saving of €60).

CINEMA PRICE LIST

Adults - regular price
Students - 10% discount
Pensioners - 20% discount
Children - half price

Third Degree

This is the one we are most familiar with. It involves dividing up the market on the basis of price elasticity of demand. Consumers with inelastic demand pay a higher price than consumers with elastic demand, e.g. students, OAPs and children are charged lower prices for certain services like going to the cinema.

A Price Discriminating Monopolist Operating in Two Markets

We now turn our attention to markets where the supplier may be both a monopolist and operate as a perfectly competitive firm, albeit in different markets.

For example, take a situation where the seller operates as **a monopolist in the domestic market** and also supplies **the export market, which is perfectly competitive**. Our explanation will be done in two ways. We'll first look at a numerical example and then illustrate the answer by means of a diagram.

Domestic market				Export market			
Quantity	AR	TR	MR	Quantity	AR	TR	MR
1	10	10		1	8.65	8.65	
2	9.70	19.4	**9.40**	2	8.65	17.30	**8.65**
3	9.35	28.05	**8.65**	3	8.65	25.95	8.65
4	8.90	35.60	7.55	4	8.65	34.60	8.65
5	8.40	42.00	6.40	5	8.65	43.25	8.65

The monopolist will sell the quantity on both markets that will ensure that marginal revenues are equal, i.e. the last unit sold brings the same revenue (similar to the law of equi-marginal returns).

Price Discrimination

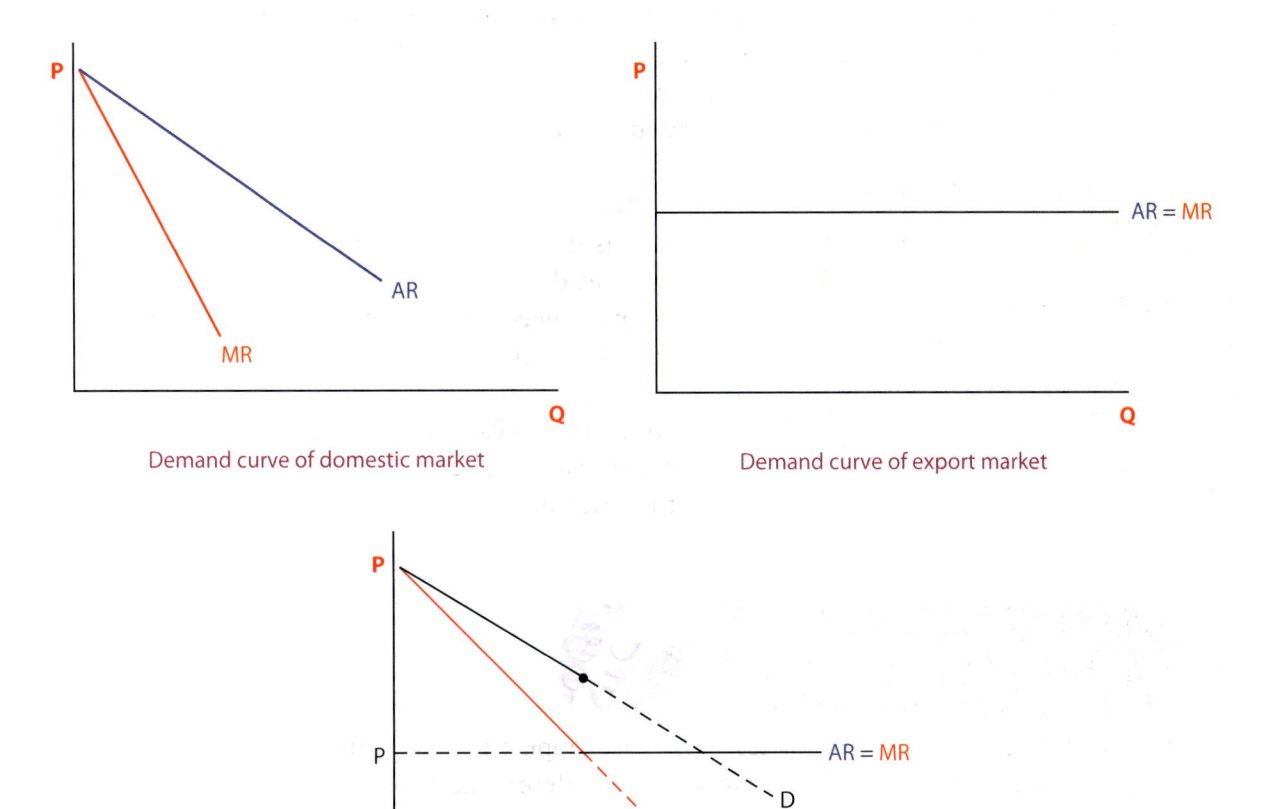

Demand curve of domestic market

Demand curve of export market

Units 1, 2 + 3 supplied on domestic market.
Units 4 + 5 supplied on export market.

If the firm produced just two units, both would be supplied to the domestic market, as MR is greater. After three units the monopolist will supply in the following way:

- Quantities 1, 2 and 3 would be supplied on the home market, as MR is higher.
- Quantities 4 and 5 would be supplied on the export market, as MR is now higher.

In this way, total revenue is maximised, i.e. MR (home market) = MR (export market).

The dotted lines in the figure above show that portion of the demand curves for the individual markets which the producer will *not* be prepared to supply because by doing so they would reduce their revenue.

Where will the price discriminating monopolist earn maximum profits as opposed to maximum revenue? This always occurs where MC = MR.

Positive Economics

We can now say that operating in two distinct markets, the firm will operate where MC = MR on the export market and where MC = MR on the home market, i.e. MC = MR (home market) = MR (export market), as the diagram below illustrates.

Explanation:

- Equilibrium occurs at point X. The firm will produce OB. This is where MC = MR (home market) = MR (export market).

- It will sell OA at home because the MR here is greater than the MR on the export market.

- It will sell AB on the export market because MR here is greater than MR on the home market.

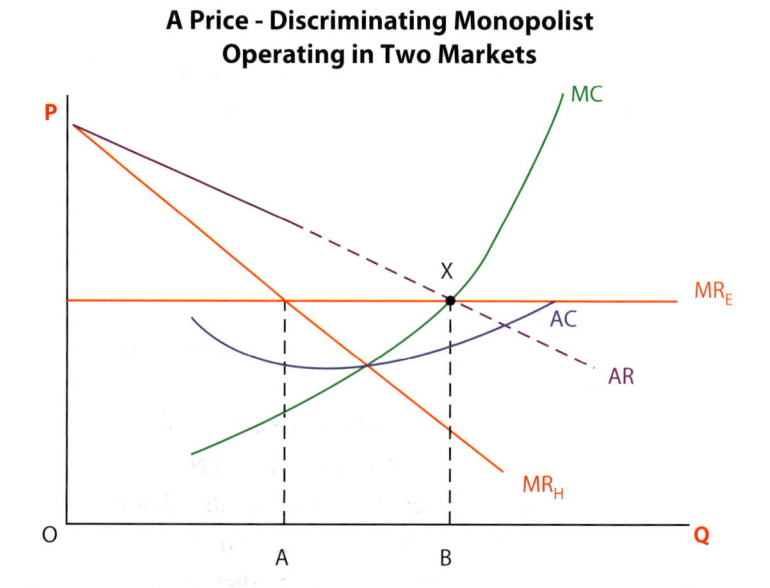

A Price - Discriminating Monopolist Operating in Two Markets

EXAM ✓ Question 2(b), 2008 (20 marks)

Define price discrimination and explain three types of price discrimination, using suitable examples in each case.

Solution

Price discrimination is when the same goods or services are sold to different consumers (in different markets) at varying ratios between marginal cost and price or the price difference is not due to a difference in the cost of production.

- **First degree:** Monopolist attempts to remove consumer surplus. Identifies those who are prepared to pay a higher price and charges them that higher price. It can occur in one-to-one confidential services, e.g. visiting a medical consultant, consulting a solicitor.

- **Second degree:** Monopolist gives discounts for bulk buying, e.g. night saver electricity, magazine subscriptions, three for two offers.

- **Third degree:** Based on the fact that consumers have different price elasticities of demand. Consumers with inelastic demand pay a higher price than consumers with an elastic demand, e.g. business air travel versus leisure air travel, student/OAP rates for the cinema.

11: Price Discrimination

Questions

Short Questions

1. Define price discrimination.
2. Describe second degree price discrimination.
3. Explain third degree price discrimination.

Long Questions

1. Explain why knowledge of price elasticity of demand is useful for a price discriminating monopolist.
2. Explain, with an example, first degree price discrimination.
3. State and explain three conditions necessary for price discrimination to take place.
4. Describe three characteristics of consumers that may make price discrimination possible.
5. Why is it possible for a firm to practise price discrimination?
6. A monopolist who seeks to maximise their profits is at long run equilibrium. If circumstances change so that this firm could engage in price discrimination, would it do so? Explain.
7. A firm is a monopolist in the home market and exports to perfectly competitive markets abroad. It seeks to maximise its profits. Explain, with the aid of a clearly labelled diagram, the long run equilibrium of this price discriminating monopolist.

Chapter 12 | Oligopoly

Specific Learning Outcomes

At the end of this chapter, students should be able to:

- ☐ Explain, with examples, the theory of oligopoly.

- ☐ Describe the assumptions underlying oligopoly.

- ☐ Illustrate and explain the kinked demand curve.

- ☐ Describe the relationship between the demand and marginal revenue curves.

- ☐ Describe the long run equilibrium of an oligopolistic firm.

- ☐ Explain rigidity of prices.

- ☐ Explain the types of collusion that may occur in this market.

- ☐ Explain why firms may pursue goals other than profit maximisation.

- ☐ Explain price and non-price competition.

- ☐ Describe price leadership.

12: Oligopoly

Introduction

The word 'oligopoly' comes from the Greek *oligoi*, meaning 'few', and *polein*, meaning 'to sell'. It is a market form in which the industry is dominated by a few/small number of sellers. Our analysis of markets thus far has concentrated on firms aiming to maximise profits while not taking into consideration the likely reaction of their competitors. Oligopolists, on the other hand, are likely to be aware of the actions of other firms. The decisions of one firm influence, and are influenced by, the decisions of other firms. Strategic planning by oligopolists needs to take into account the likely responses of the other market participants.

Some examples of markets in Ireland that may be considered oligopolies would be mobile phones, retail banking, petrol companies, supermarkets and newspaper industries. In the US, Anheuser-Busch and MillerCoors control about 80% of the beer industry, while Boeing and Airbus have a duopoly (i.e. an oligopoly with just two participants) in supplying the airline industry with airplanes. A small number of firms exist and it is likely that each will contemplate the likely reaction of its rivals before it takes any new action – thus, firms are interdependent.

Characteristics of an Oligopolistic Market

Few Sellers in the Industry

Since there are few sellers in the industry, the companies can influence the price of the commodity or the output sold. They tend to be price setters rather than price takers.

Interdependence between Firms

Firms in oligopoly do not act independently of each other. They will take into account the likely reactions of their competitors, which leads to prices that tend to be rigid.

Oligopoly can be likened to a game of chess where a player must anticipate a whole sequence of moves and countermoves in determining how to achieve their objectives.

A firm considering a price reduction may wish to estimate the likelihood that competing firms would also lower their prices and possibly trigger a price war. Alternatively, if the firm is considering a price increase, it may want to know whether other firms will also increase prices or hold existing prices constant. This high degree of interdependence is not seen in other markets.

Product Differentiation Occurs
The goods that firms sell are close substitutes. Firms will engage in advertising to persuade consumers to buy their product rather than a competitor's product. However, the scope for advertising may be limited where the good being produced is very similar, e.g. petrol.

Barriers to Entry
Barriers to entry are high as existing firms will wish to maintain their share of the market. Barriers include:

- Economies of scale achieved by existing companies means that they have worked to achieve low unit costs of production.
- Access to expensive technology.
- High set-up costs.
- Brand proliferation. Brand proliferation is when a firm puts out new brand names under the same product line.

All of the above are designed to discourage new firms.

Collusion May Occur
Firms within the industry may meet to control the output in the industry and/or control prices. Cartels may be formed, e.g. OPEC, which has a huge influence on the international price of oil. Collusions in most countries, including Ireland, are illegal.

Non-price Competition Is More Common than Price Competition
Oligopolistic firms fear that their competitors will react so they tend not to engage in price competition. Instead, they engage in non-price competition to gain customers, e.g. good after-sales service, promotional gifts/coupons, free car park, late openings and advertising.

- Persuasive advertising tries to persuade people that they can't live without a product, e.g. deodorant.
- Competitive advertising tries to convince customers that one product is better than another, e.g. cars.
- Informative advertising gives factual information about a product, e.g. sale starts tomorrow.

The Kinked Demand Curve

In 1939, Paul Sweezy put forward a theory that explained the reasoning behind the fact that some prices in some markets tend not to change, hence price rigidity. He suggested that firms faced a kinked demand curve, which in reality is two distinct demand curves crossing at the point where price is set (see the diagram).

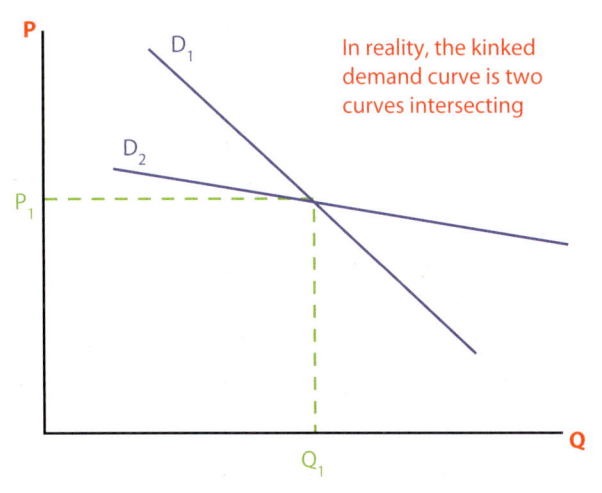

In reality, the kinked demand curve is two curves intersecting

He explained that a firm's competitors would not follow a price increase but would instead increase their market share by selling more at existing prices and thereby gaining extra profit. If price was reduced then all firms would similarly reduce their prices. Thus, firms would end up selling the same amount at lower prices and consequently be less profitable. This accounted for price rigidity – firms would not be willing to alter their prices unless there was a huge cost increase.

Look at the above diagram again. The top of the kinked demand curve is considered to be relatively elastic, while the bottom part is taken to be inelastic.

- In the elastic section, raising prices will dramatically lower demand as competitors will not follow the price increase.

- In the inelastic section, lowering prices will not bring any significant benefit as other firms will follow suit and also lower their prices, thus no extra revenue will be earned.

DI is the inelastic demand curve and DE is the elastic curve. They both intersect at point A and this is the price that will be charged.

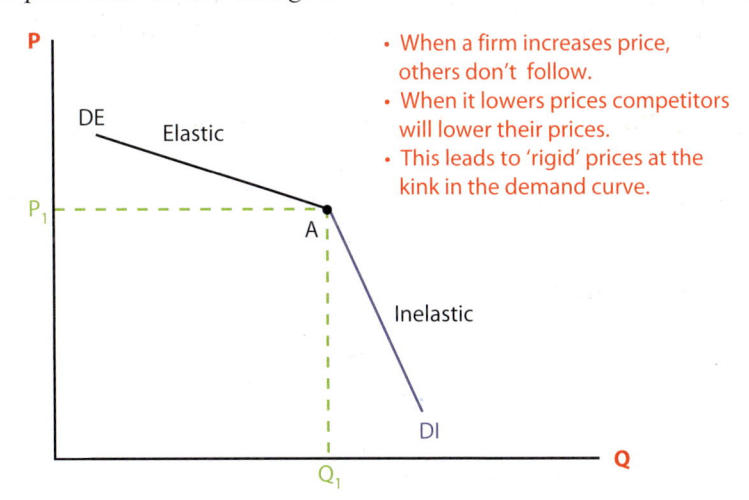

- When a firm increases price, others don't follow.
- When it lowers prices competitors will lower their prices.
- This leads to 'rigid' prices at the kink in the demand curve.

The Kinked Demand Curve: Long Run Equilibrium

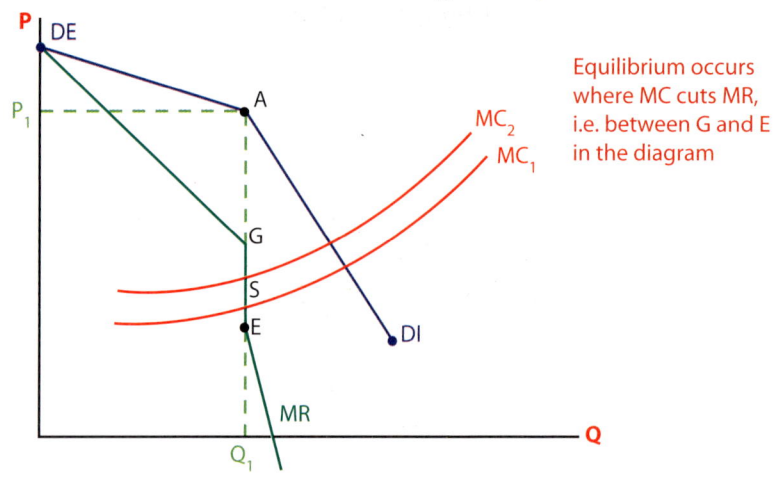

Kinked demand curve – LR equilibrium

Equilibrium occurs where MC cuts MR, i.e. between G and E in the diagram

As with all downward sloping demand curves, the marginal revenue curve will be below the AR curve. In this case, however, there are two AR curves, which means there will be two MR curves. At the point where the demand curves meet (A), there will be a break in the MR curve.

- The two MR curves are associated with the two (elastic and inelastic) AR curves, i.e. because the demand curve is kinked, the firm's MR curve consists of two distinct parts.

- The MC curve cuts the discontinuous part of the MR curve. This represents an equilibrium point.

- If MC_1 were to increase to MC_2, then equilibrium price and output would not change, i.e. marginal cost would still equal marginal revenue.

- While there are two MR curves, they are in essence joined by the vertical section GE so that when the MC curve cuts the gap in the MR, it is considered that (MC = MR) at that point.

The equilibrium position is as follows:

S	SNP	As barriers to entry exist, this firm can earn SNP if AR > AC.
P	Price/output	The firm produces at Q_1 and sells at P_1.
E	Equilibrium	This occurs where MC cuts MR and where MC is rising. Point S in the diagram.
C	Costs	If costs rise between points G and E, then market price tends to remain constant at P_1.

There can be many MC curves cutting the discontinuous part of the MR without affecting price and quantity. This indicates that prices can be constant although costs increase slightly. This is the basis of the term 'price constancy'. Companies tend not to change prices for every slight cost increase, as this would create costs involved in changing catalogues, price lists and advertising material.

12: Oligopoly

Long Run Equilibrium Position of the Oligopolistic Firm

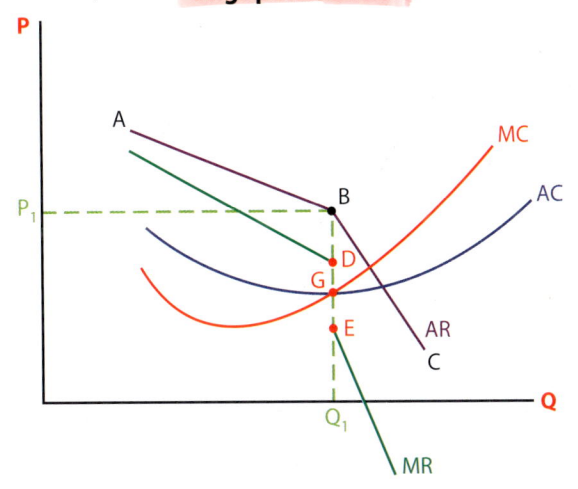

S	The firm is earning SNP because AR > AC or barriers to entry exist.
P	Price will be charged at P_1 and quantity produced will be at Q_1.
E	Equilibrium occurs at point G where MC = MR and MC is rising.
C	Should costs rise between points D and E, then market price tends to remain constant at P_1. The firm's cost of production is shown at point G.
S	The firm is producing at the lowest point of AC, therefore scarce resources are being used efficiently.

Sweezy's model has been criticised because his theory is silent on how price is initially set. It explains why price does not change in response to small cost changes. In response to large shifts in cost, the theory predicts that price should change, although it does not provide any guidelines as to how the new price will be set.

Collusion in Oligopolistic Markets

In an effort to gain extra profits, companies may decide to collude (agree to act together) in restricting price/output. Agreements may often only last for short time periods as some companies may not abide by the original agreement and a lack of trust sets in.

Types of Collusion

Pricing Policy/Limit Pricing
With the tacit agreement of others, one firm could reduce prices, forcing unwanted entrants out of the industry. This can be done as the existing firms in the industry would already be benefiting from economies of scale.

Production/Output Policy
Firms could join together to limit output to certain agreed amounts, e.g. OPEC.

Sales Territories

Firms could divide up the markets between them and agree not to compete in each other's market segments.

Implicit Collusion

Each firm recognises that by behaving as if they were branches of a single firm, their joint profits would be higher. As a result, firms do not provoke their rivals by cutting prices. Instead, they try to increase market share by engaging in non-price competitive measures.

Price Leadership/Dominant Firm Model

In some oligopolistic markets there is a single firm that controls a dominant share of the market due to its economies of scale, financial security, etc. This dominant firm sets prices (price leader) which are simply taken by the smaller firms in determining their profit-maximising level of production. As long as they don't interfere with the market share of the price leader, the larger firm tends to leave them alone.

Pursuing Objectives Other than Profit Maximisation

All of the market structures studied so far have profit maximisation as one of their goals. However, companies may have other objectives.

Government Intervention
Avoid

Some companies that hold dominant positions in the market may decide against earning huge supernormal profits for fear that they may attract government intervention that would restrict their activities.

Managers Not Owners

In some companies where managers are not shareholders (owners), they may not pursue profit maximisation as salaries may be fixed and unrelated to performance. This can be the case in state companies.

Limit Pricing

Existing companies may not wish to encourage new entrants by earning large supernormal profits. Instead, they may set their prices at a level that prevents new entrants from wanting to or being able to gain entry into the market. This limit price can be so low that new firms would find it unattractive to set up business. This means that existing companies sacrifice larger profits, which is a price they are happy to pay for their long-term survival.

Satisfactory Profit Levels

After many years of long hours and immense effort in building up a business, an owner may decide not to aggressively pursue maximum profits. Instead, they may be content with adequate profit levels and enjoy more leisure/family time.

Managers May Pursue Increased Sales

Managers of companies may try maximising sales because:

- Managers' salaries can be correlated to sales rather than profit.
- Banks tend to lend to firms with increasing sales.
- Prestige/status: Increased sales means a larger workforce and more people reporting to the manager.

William Baumol's Model of Sales Maximisation

Baumol presented his theory of non-profit-maximising behaviour in 1959. He stated that managers may be more interested in maximising sales revenue rather than maximising profit. The reason for this is that managers may think that the size of the company is more important to the advancement of their own career rather than maximising profits.

In his theory he states that sales maximisation is the desired goal with a minimum (target) level of profit being earned, i.e. enough profit to pay dividends, satisfy banks and have funds available for reinvestment. However, this target profit level is less than the maximum profits that the firm could earn (see the graph).

In the diagram on the next page, the curve Pr represents profit (TR – TC) that the firm could earn at different levels of output.

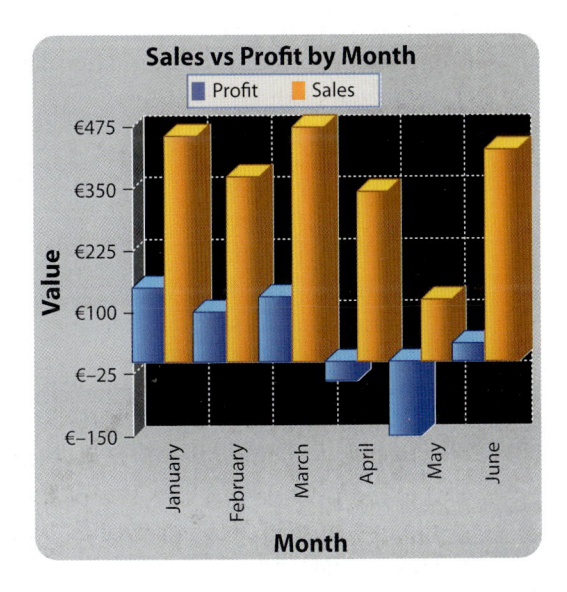

Positive Economics

Target profit is represented by T.

- When Qm is produced, the firm has produced output that will maximise profits.

- When Qf is produced, target profits are earned with the minimum output needed. This may be a business where the owner does not aggressively pursue maximum profits and is content with target profits.

- When Qs is produced, target profit is being earned and sales are maximised.

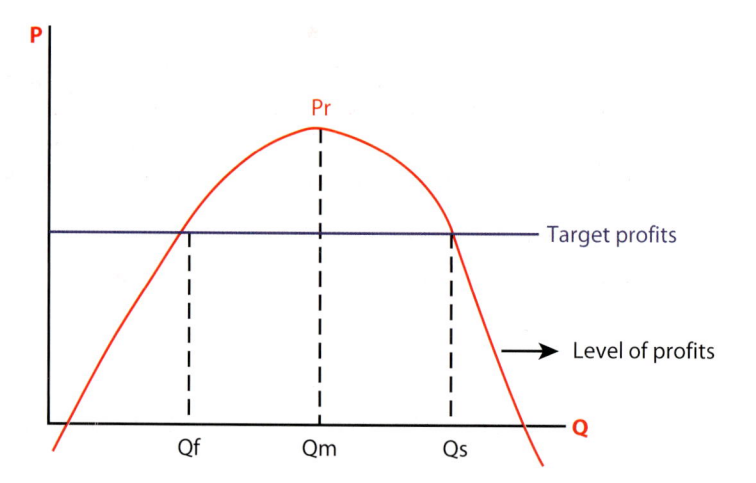

EXAM ✓ Question 2(a)(i), 2006 (10 marks)

Explain, with the aid of a diagram, the shape of the kinked demand curve under oligopoly.

Solution

- If a firm increases its price, other firms leave their prices unchanged – this firm will lose customers.

- The firm faces an elastic demand curve AB.

- If a firm lowers its price, other firms will match this price decrease – the firm will gain few extra customers.

- Hence the firm faces an inelastic demand curve XY.

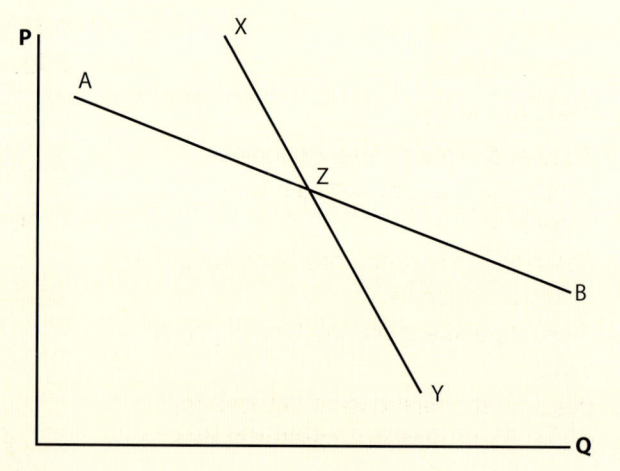

- If the price leader sets the price at point Z, then the firm faces a distinct demand curve **AZY**, kinked at point Z.

12: Oligopoly

EXAM ✓ Question 2(c)(ii), 2006 (15 marks)

Do you believe that the Irish retail market for banking services (e.g. personal currents accounts) operates under oligopolistic conditions? Explain your answer.

Solution

Yes, it does operate under oligopolistic conditions because:

1. **Few sellers:** There are relatively few banks providing personal services within the market, e.g. AIB, Bank of Ireland, Permanent TSB.

2. **Interdependence between firms:** The banks do not act independently of each other. They take into account the likely reactions of their competitors to any changes they may make.

3. **Close substitutes:** The services provided are very close substitutes. There is competitive advertising and heavy product loyalty promotion. Various gimmicks are used to attract customers.

Questions

Short Questions

1. Explain oligopoly.
2. State and explain three examples of markets that you consider to be oligopolistic.
3. Describe the assumptions underlying the theory of oligopoly.
4. Illustrate and explain the kinked demand curve.
5. Describe the relationship between the demand and marginal revenue curves.

Long Questions

1. Draw and explain the long run equilibrium of an oligopolistic firm.
2. Explain rigidity of prices.
3. Distinguish between price constancy and price rigidity.
4. Explain the types of collusion that may occur in an oligopolistic market.
5. Distinguish between price and non-price competition.
6. Why do firms pursue goals other than profit maximisation?
7. Describe how price leadership operates.
8. What is limit pricing?
9. Explain the term 'interdependence of firms' in oligopoly.
10. Can SNP be earned by oligopolists?

Chapter 13: Introduction to the Factor Markets

Specific Learning Outcomes

At the end of this chapter, students should be able to:

- [ ] Define each of the factors of production.

- [ ] Illustrate and explain the concept of derived demand.

- [ ] Understand the concepts of marginal revenue productivity (MRP) and marginal physical productivity (MPP).

- [ ] Examine the factors that affect MRP and MPP.

- [ ] Understand that the demand curve for a factor of production is its MRP curve.

- [ ] Apply MRP theory to both perfect competition and monopoly/imperfect competition.

- [ ] Illustrate the concepts of supply price, economic rent, quasi economic rent and transfer earnings.

13: Introduction to the Factor Markets

Factors of Production

In Chapter 1 we introduced the four factors of production. All businesses require one or a combination of these inputs to operate, as you can see from Pat's Deli in the table below. In the next few chapters we will study the four factors of production and examine how the returns to each of the factors are determined by the price system.

Factor	Definition	Return/payment	Example: Pat's Deli
Land	Anything supplied by *nature* that helps in the production of wealth	Rent	Physical land that the deli is built on
Labour	*Human activity* directed towards the production of wealth	Wages	Staff to cook and serve customers
Capital	Anything *man made* that helps in the production of wealth	Interest	Pat's Deli uses fridges, ovens
Enterprise	A person who *combines the other factors of production*, takes the initiative and risk in setting up a firm	Profit/loss	Pat is the risk-taker

Derived Demand

Derived demand suggests that a factor of production is demanded for its contribution to the production process (i.e. it is demanded because it assists in the attainment of some objective). For example, timber is demanded not in and of itself but because it's used to make furniture. In Pat's Deli, ovens are sought because they are used for cooking. *but not for itself*

Specific Factors and Non-specific Factors

A specific factor of production is one that is so specialised that it doesn't have many different uses, e.g. a milking machine, a lawnmower. On the other hand, non-specific factors of production can have many different uses, e.g. farmland used for growing crops or pasture or a smartphone used as a camera.

Occupational and Geographical Mobility of Factors

- Occupational mobility is the ease with which a factor of production can move from one occupation to another, e.g. how easy is it for a teacher to change jobs and become a doctor?

How easy is it for a teacher to change jobs and become a doctor?

How easy is it for a graphic designer to move from Dublin to London?

- Geographical mobility is the ease with which a factor can move from one area to another, e.g. a graphic designer moving from Dublin to London.

Demand for the Factors of Production

The amount of a factor that will be used will be determined by its contribution to the business and the price that has to be paid for that factor. To assist in our study we need to understand two important concepts at this point: **marginal revenue productivity** and **marginal physical productivity**.

For example, suppose Pat's Deli employs five workers. The total revenue earned is €455.

- If an extra worker is employed, total revenue increases to €470.
- Therefore, the marginal revenue productivity of the sixth worker is €15 (€470 – €455).
- A fourth person adds €50 to total revenue, a fifth adds €25 and so on.

> The **MARGINAL REVENUE PRODUCTIVITY (MRP)** of a factor is the extra revenue earned when an additional unit of a factor of production is employed.

Number of workers	Total revenue (€)	Marginal revenue productivity
1	200	–
2	280	80
3	380	100
4	430	50
5	455	25
6	470	15
7	480	10

If the **wage rate is set at €15 per hour**, then six workers will be employed.

At this wage rate of €15, if four workers were employed the company would not be maximising profit, as the fourth worker adds €50 to total revenue and his wage costs €15. Therefore, he adds €35 to total profit.

13: Introduction to the Factor Markets

Employing a seventh worker would add €10 to total revenue and €15 to total costs, i.e. a loss of €5. This worker would not be employed.

The company maximises profit when the wage rate equals the marginal revenue productivity of labour. In our example, the firm will employ six workers at €15 per hour.

From the graph, we can identify that:

- If the wage rate fell to €10 per hour, then seven workers would be employed.
- If the rate increased to €25, then five workers would be employed.
- At a wage rate of €50, four workers would be employed.

From this analysis, we can conclude that the **MRP curve is the demand curve for labour** (the downward sloping section of the MRP curve). It shows the quantity of labour that will be demanded at each wage rate.

> The downward sloping section of the MRP curve is the demand curve for labour.

The MRP theory of wages states that each worker is paid an amount equal to the additional revenue which is received from the employment of the last worker, i.e. the equivalent of the **value that the last worker contributes**, not the value of their own contribution to production when all other factors are held constant.

In our example, this is the sixth worker, whose MRP is €15, which is also the wage rate. Workers 1 to 5 don't receive their MRP – they receive the MRP of the last worker employed.

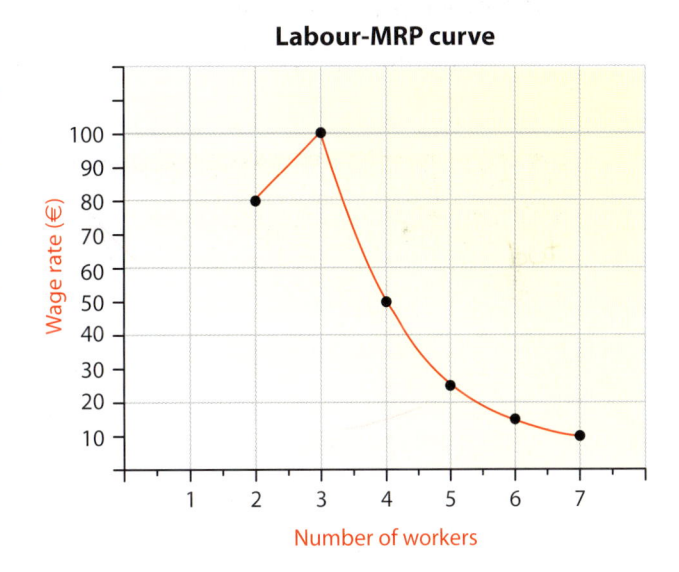

Labour-MRP curve

Labour Hoarding

Sometimes a firm may continue to employ labour even though it is unprofitable to do so. This is called labour hoarding and can occur because:

- Management may feel that demand is likely to improve and more workers would be required in the future.
- Retaining existing workers is easier than retraining new staff.

In the above example we have concentrated on the factor of production labour. However, the analysis could be applied to any of the other factors, which leads us to say: **the MRP curve of any of the four factors of production is its demand curve**.

Positive Economics

Why Does the MRP Curve Slope Downwards from Left to Right?

- **The law of diminishing returns:** As more labour is applied to the production process, at some stage the return from each additional worker will begin to decline, i.e. as more workers are employed, their marginal product will begin to decline. As a result, the MRP of each extra worker is less than the previous employee.

- **The law of demand:** In order to sell a larger amount, a company will have to reduce the price of its product. If a firm produces more and more units, then they can only be sold at lower prices. The revenue earned from each extra unit of output produced declines. Consequently, the MRP of each extra unit of labour decreases.

> **MARGINAL PHYSICAL PRODUCT (MPP) is** the extra output produced when an additional unit of a factor of production is employed.

Marginal Physical Product

Labour	Total output	Marginal physical product
1	20	–
2	45	25
3	75	30
4	90	15
5	100	10

As we can see from the table, the contribution to output of four workers is 90 units, but the fourth worker contributes only 15 units. Likewise, output is 100 when five workers are employed but the fifth worker adds 10 units.

What Factors Influence MPP and MRP?

Marginal Physical Product

QUALITY/SPECIALISED NATURE OF THE FACTORS

If the quality of the factors used improves, then they become more efficient and additional output will be produced, e.g. if a builder using a shovel changes to using a mechanical digger, then output will increase.

TRAINING/EDUCATION PROVIDED FOR THE FACTORS
If the factors are trained, they become more skilled, resulting in increased efficiency and more output. For example, in a hospital, nurses who are trained in the use of specialised equipment can perform their work more efficiently.

EXPERTISE OF THE ENTREPRENEUR
If the entrepreneur is good at organising the production unit, then each factor will be more productive and work to their maximum efficiency. A disorganised business unit with staff who are unsure of their tasks and roles will produce less output and will be of inferior quality.

LAW OF DIMINISHING MARGINAL RETURNS
As each additional unit of a factor is used, a point will be reached where the additional output produced will decline.

Marginal Revenue Productivity

THE PRODUCTIVITY OF THE FACTOR
The more productive each additional factor employed is, the more MRP that factor will earn. In Pat's Deli, trained staff with the correct equipment will produce more than untrained labour with faulty equipment.

THE MR/SELLING PRICE OF THE OUTPUT
If the selling price obtained on the market is rising or constant (and not falling), then that factor's MRP will be higher.

THE LAW OF DEMAND (ELASTIC/INELASTIC DEMAND CURVE)
The law of demand dictates that in order for more to be sold, price must be reduced and hence this affects the MR obtained by the firm. If the firm faces an inelastic demand curve, then price may be readily increased with little fall in demand.

Is MRP (Price of a Factor of Production) Easy to Calculate?

In reality, MRP is quite difficult to measure. How do you value the contribution of a care assistant in a hospital or the contribution of a member of An Garda Síochána?

Positive Economics

What Contribution Is Made by Capital or Labour?
If capital and labour are required to carry out a task, how do you allocate the MRP to either capital or labour? For example, an accountant uses a computer to assist in calculating the payroll of a company. How can MRP be allocated to the computerised package or to the accountant? The same problem arises with a delivery van and driver.

Services Not Sold on the Market
There are some jobs where it is difficult to measure MPP. In the case of a manufacturing company, physical output can be easily measured and hence a wage rate based on MRP is possible. However, in many situations there is no final tangible product that is sold at market prices. For example, should nurses be paid by the number of patients on their ward? Should judges be paid by the number of cases they preside over?

Trying to establish MRP in these situations is very difficult, so we tend to look to equivalent work that is valued in the marketplace to establish some semblance of MRP, e.g. ambulance drivers working for the Department of Health and paramedics working for private companies, to assist in determining wage rates.

Marginal Revenue Product in Perfectly Competitive Markets

REMEMBER! Remember that the firm faces a horizontal (perfectly elastic) demand curve.

In perfect competition, the price for the individual firm's output is constant.

Competition and MRP and MPP					
Number of workers	Total physical output	Average revenue (P)	Total revenue (total physical output × AR)	MPP (Δ physical output)	MRP (MPP × P)
1	40	5	200	—	
2	50	5	250	10	50
3	56	5	280	6	30
4	59	5	295	3	15

MPP	x	AR (P)	=	MRP
10	x	5	=	50
6	x	5	=	30
3	x	5	=	15

> **MPP × P = MRP**
> MPP multiplied by price equals MRP. This is always the case in perfect competition.

Marginal Revenue Productivity: Imperfect Competition and Monopoly

In both imperfect competition and monopoly, the price of goods needs to be lowered in order to sell a higher quantity. Therefore, MPP × AR will not equal MRP. This only applies in markets with fixed prices.

Number of workers	Physical output	Marginal physical output	Price	Total revenue	Marginal revenue	Marginal revenue product
1	24	—	6	144	—	—
2	36	12	5.32	191.52	8.04	96.48
3	44	8	5.06	222.64	3.89	31.12
4	50	6	4.6	230	1.22	7.36

- In the above example, price falls from €6 per unit to €4.60 per unit to sell 26 extra units (50 – 24).
- As the amount of labour is increased, the output of the last unit of labour employed falls.
- The third unit of labour contributes 8 units to output and €31.12 to revenue.
- The fourth worker contributes 6 units to output and €7.36 to revenue.
- With two employees, total revenue is €191.52 and with three workers it is €222.64, so the MRP of the third worker is €31.12.
- However, marginal revenue is only €3.89 for the third worker.
- This is because marginal revenue is the extra revenue generated by a one-unit change in quantity produced. Between the second and third worker, quantity produced increases by 8 units, so the MRP of €31.12 must be divided by 8. This gives a marginal revenue for the third worker of €3.89.
- Consequently, we can conclude that:

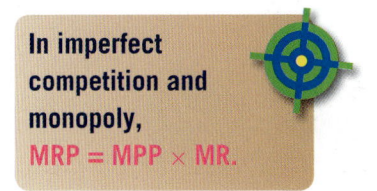

> **In imperfect competition and monopoly,**
> **MRP = MPP × MR.**

Supply Price, Transfer Earnings, Economic Rent, Quasi Economic Rent

To assist in our understanding of the four factors of production, it is necessary to understand some new concepts.

> The **SUPPLY PRICE** of a factor of production is the minimum payment necessary to bring a factor into use and maintain it in that particular use.

Supply Price

Example

A chef in Pat's Deli may have to be paid a minimum of €400 per week to entice him to work there and stay in the job. Therefore, the supply price in this situation is €400. If the amount paid falls below €400, the chef won't make himself available for employment.

Transfer Earnings

> The **EARNINGS OF A FACTOR** is the next best alternative employment or what a factor must receive to keep it in its present use and prevent it from transferring to another use.

Example

If the chef in Pat's Deli could earn €450 per week in another deli, then his transfer earnings would be €450. Transfer earnings can be equal to supply price.

FACTORS AFFECTING TRANSFER EARNINGS

- **Productivity of the factor:** The transfer earnings of a factor can depend on how productive the factor would be in alternative uses. The chef earning €400 per week might have the skill to become a writer of cookbooks and earn €1,000 per week, hence his transfer earnings in this case would be €1,000.

- **Length of time:** The longer the time period under consideration, the greater the transfer earnings of a factor will be. Training can improve adaptability and access to information on alternative uses of the factor. Training can also increase transfer earnings.

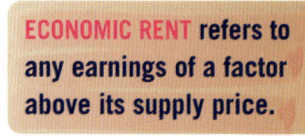

> **ECONOMIC RENT** refers to any earnings of a factor above its supply price.

Economic Rent

Example

If the chef in Pat's Deli earns €600 per week and his supply price is €400 per week, then his economic rent is €200. Economic rent can apply to all the factors of production. The more specific a factor of production, the more likely it is to earn economic rent. This is because the supply is inelastic in relation to price, e.g. if wages offered to brain surgeons increased overnight, there would be very little increase in the number of brain surgeons in the short run.

Quasi Economic Rent

QUASI ECONOMIC RENT refers to economic rent of a temporary nature.

Example

The first computer science graduates earned high salaries because there was a shortage of qualified professionals at that time. However, in the long run, with an increase in the supply of graduates, this temporary rent was eliminated and salaries were reduced.

PROFILE: Alfred Marshall (1842–1924)

A neo-classical economist, Marshall favoured private enterprise with some government interference. His main theories were the utility theory of value, marginal revenue productivity, quasi economic rent and competition regulating economic activity.

Utility Theory

Marshall suggested that demand was determined by the utility a good possessed (this replaced the labour theory of value). He also developed the idea that utility diminished as more was consumed (the law of diminishing marginal utility). He further stated that as utility was the basis of demand, costs were the basis of supply, with both combining like blades of a scissors.

Positive Economics

Marshall developed his theory of utility and applied it to the factors of production. He contended that the returns to a factor were dependent on what the last unit of that factor made, hence his MRP theory.

Quasi Economic Rent
This meant a temporary increase in earnings of existing workers due to a shortage in their supply. In the long run more workers would be trained and the higher earnings would revert back to their normal level.

Power of Competition
Marshall held that intelligent government intervention and some inter-business co-operation could regulate economic activity and enhance economic freedom. Monopolies could be prevented by government regulation, good consumer information and an increase in the number of small investors.

Developed Economic Concepts
- Price elasticity of demand: The sensitivity of quantity demanded by consumers to a change in price.
- Consumer surplus: The surplus value or utility a consumer enjoys.
- Market time periods: Long run and short run time periods.

EXAM Question 3(b), 2008 (15 marks)

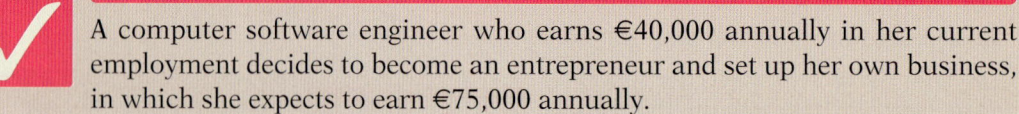

A computer software engineer who earns €40,000 annually in her current employment decides to become an entrepreneur and set up her own business, in which she expects to earn €75,000 annually.
1. What is this entrepreneur's 'supply price'? Explain your answer.
2. If the business performs as expected, will the entrepreneur earn an 'economic rent'? Explain your answer.

Solution

Software Engineer
1. The supply price is €40,000. This is the minimum payment they need to receive as a software engineer.
2. Economic rent is earned because there is a €35,000 payment in excess of supply price.

OR

Entrepreneur
1. The supply price is €75,000. This is the minimum payment they need to receive to become an entrepreneur.
2. No, there is no payment in excess of supply price.

13: Introduction to the Factor Markets

EXAM ✓ Question 4(a), 2003 (20 marks)

Define **each** of the following:

- Supply price of a factor of production.
- Transfer earnings.
- Economic Rent.

Solution

- **Supply price:** The supply price of a factor of production is the minimum payment necessary to bring a factor into use and maintain it in that particular use.

- **Transfer earnings:** Transfer earnings of a factor of production are the earnings in the next best alternative employment.

- **Economic rent:** Economic rent is any earnings of a factor above its supply price.

Questions

Short Questions

1. Define and state the return to each of the four factors of production.
2. The demand for a factor of production is a derived demand. Explain.
3. Compare specific and non-specific factors of production.
4. Distinguish between occupational and geographical mobility of factors of production.
5. Illustrate your understanding of MRP.

Long Questions

1. Explain why the MRP curve of a factor of production is its demand curve.
2. Explain the MRP theory of wages.
3. State and explain two reasons why the MRP curve slopes downwards.
4. Illustrate your understanding of MPP.
5. Explain the relationship between MRP and MPP in perfect competition.
6. All workers should receive their MRP. Discuss.
7. Illustrate your understanding of supply price and transfer earnings.
8. Discuss the factors that influence the value of transfer earnings.
9. Distinguish between economic rent and quasi economic rent.
10. Discuss three factors that influence both MRP and MPP.

Chapter 14 | Land

Specific Learning Outcomes

At the end of this chapter, students should be able to:

- ☐ Define land as a factor of production.

- ☐ Give examples of land and state how they contribute to the production of wealth.

- ☐ Explain the economic characteristics of land.

- ☐ Explain why land is a unique factor of production.

- ☐ Explain why the demand for land is a derived demand.

- ☐ Illustrate and explain the concept of economic rent.

- ☐ Explain the factors that influence the price paid for land.

- ☐ Describe the factors that determine the location of a factory.

- ☐ Explain the factors leading to the price of property increasing/decreasing in Ireland.

14: Land

Introduction

LAND, as a factor of production, is anything provided by nature that helps in the production of output, including goods, services and wealth.

The return to land is rent. Land includes seas, rivers, climate, mineral wealth and land itself. So how do these assist in the production of output?

Seas/rivers	• They are a source of food, i.e. fishing and fish farming. • Hydroelectric power can be produced and a supply of water is needed as a raw material in the production of many goods.
Climate	• Tourism: Sunny or snowy weather can bring tourists to an area, generating wealth. • Favourable weather (adequate rain/sunshine) allows the growth of certain crops, e.g. oranges in hot regions. • The amount of daylight influences the length of the working day and can have an influence on a company's energy costs. • Solar/wind energy is a relatively new source of power that is provided by nature.
Mineral wealth	• Extractive industries: Oil/coal/natural gas are sources of energy and are used in the production of output. • The quantity of the natural resource and the ease with which it can be extracted are factors that will determine whether it is cost efficient to extract.
Physical land	• Land itself is used in food production for growing crops, fruit and vegetables and is used as pasture for animals. It is also used for building offices, retail units, etc. • There are a number of determinants in land's value as well as the contribution it makes to the production of goods and services, i.e. whether land is fertile or mountainous and its proximity to a city or trading centre can determine its value. • We can say that the productivity of land can be influenced by the factors of production labour and capital, e.g. irrigation, use of fertilizers/machinery. Likewise, the yield of land can be reduced, e.g. by over-cropping.

Positive Economics

What Are the Economic Characteristics of Land?

Land Is Fixed in Supply

Nature has provided only a certain amount of land and this cannot easily be increased by people. Reclaiming land from the sea is probably matched by soil erosion. In either case, the net effect on total land supply is probably miniscule.

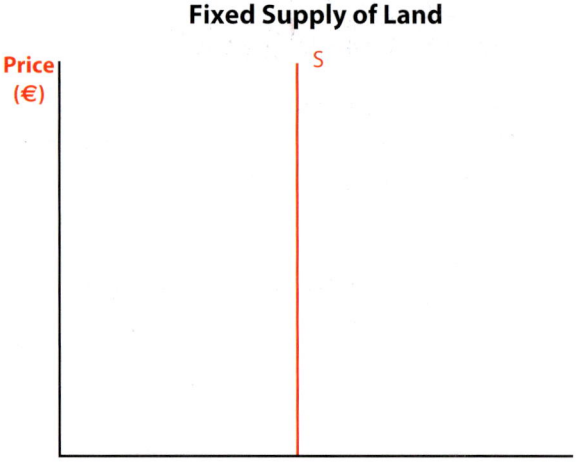

Fixed Supply of Land

(Graph showing a vertical supply curve S, with Price (€) on the y-axis and Quantity on the x-axis.)

Land Doesn't Have Any Cost of Production/The Earnings of Land Are Economic Rent

Economic rent is any payment made for a factor above its supply price. The supply price of land is the price that has to be paid to bring it into use. Land in a global context has no supply price, as it is exclusively supplied by nature. In this case, every penny paid for it is economic rent, since it is above a supply price of zero.

It Is a Non-specific Factor of Production

Land is not confined to one specific use, but rather, its uses can change, e.g. farmland can be used for growing different crops or changed to be used as pasture or for construction.

The Price of Land Does Not Affect the Quantity Available

In the case of labour, an increase in wages may increase the supply. However, an increase in the price of land won't bring about an increase in supply, as the quantity provided by nature is fixed. This is not the case for the other factors of production.

Lack of Mobility

Land can't be shifted from its place to another region. Its geographical mobility is nil but its ownership or value can be transferred.

Why Is Land Considered to Be a Unique Factor of Production?

- **Land is a gift of nature and therefore has no cost of production to society as a whole:** However, there is a cost in bringing it into use. Capital and labour may be required for output to be produced. Likewise, there is a cost to the individual who wishes to use the land. It has to be purchased or rented.

- **It is fixed in supply: the supply of land as a whole of an economy is fixed:** If the price offered for land increases, supply stays constant. It is perfectly inelastic. We can therefore conclude that the price of land is influenced solely by demand.

14: Land

Demand for Land

A Derived Demand

The demand for land is a derived demand, i.e. land itself is not demanded in its own right, but it is sought for the goods it helps to produce. For example, physical land is demanded not for its own sake, but for the crops that it grows or the houses built on it.

The Demand for Land Depends On Its MRP

Land, as we have already stated, is fixed in supply and can't be increased in response to an increase in demand. Instead, the price paid for land will increase.

If demand for land increases and supply is fixed, then price rises

- The rent that will be paid for land depends on its marginal rate of productivity (MRP).

- MRP in return is related to the selling price of the finished good.

- Therefore, we can conclude that the selling price of the good will determine the rent to be paid for land.

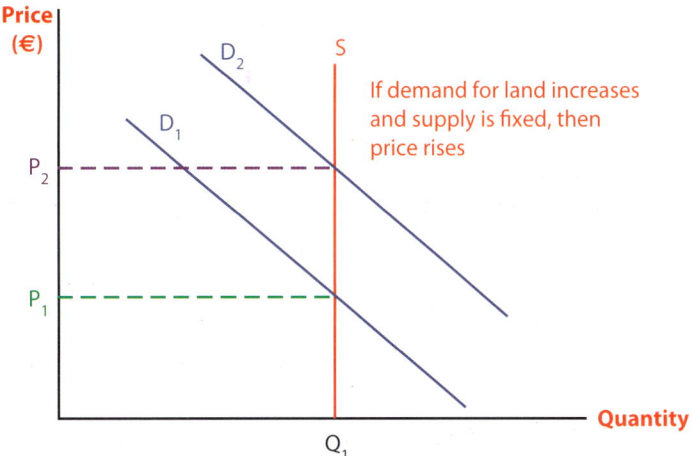

> **Example**
>
> Suppose a plot of land yields one bag of potatoes and this output is fixed. The only way the MRP of land can go up is for the selling price of the potatoes to increase. Thus, the selling price of the potatoes influences the MRP, which in turn determines the rent to be paid for the plot of land.

Stephen's Green Shopping Centre, Dublin

Positive Economics

Land Use Goes to the Highest Bidder

Land in a city can be used in different ways, such as building office blocks, shopping centres, etc. Its use will be determined by its MRP. Competition ensures that land is sold to the highest bidder, who in turn uses the land to earn maximum profit. This is why we see apartment blocks rather than detached houses in city centre locations. Land is put to its most profitable use and goes to the person who pays the highest price.

What Are the Factors That Influence the Price Paid for Land?

- **Demand for private houses:** The building boom during the early 2000s saw the price of land in areas increase to satisfy the demand for houses. On the other hand, the subsequent recession saw a huge fall in demand for housing, and coupled with the chronic oversupply of property, prices collapsed.

- **Road building:** As part of the National Development Plan, major road networks have been built around the country. These wider and better roads use large amounts of land, which in turn pushes up the price of available land even more because of its better access to urban areas.

- **Business demand:** The demand for offices and factory sites has recently pushed up the price of land near urban areas. Upward-only rent reviews allow commercial land prices to hold their prices better than residential housing.

- **Public amenities:** As the number of housing estates in the country increased, so did the demand for public parks, green areas and sporting sites.

Top 10 most expensive pieces of land in the world

1. Monte Carlo, Monaco – $47,578
2. Moscow, Russia – $20,853
3. London, England – $20,756
4. Tokyo, Japan – $17,998
5. Hong Kong – $16,125
6. New York, USA – $14,898
7. Paris, France – $12,122
8. Singapore – $9,701
9. Rome, Italy – $9,166
10. Mumbai, India – $9,163

(Prices are denominated in square metres.)

Source: Global Property Guide.

Government Intervention

The government (local authority) can intervene in the market to regulate the use of land. County and city councils can zone land for particular purposes, such as agricultural, residential, commercial or recreational uses. This is done to ensure that:

- Development is done in an orderly and planned fashion, e.g. to ensure that play areas are included in new housing estates.

- An adequate supply of land is available for commercial and industrial use.
- Historical sites and places of beauty are not demolished in the course of development.
- Green belts, i.e. open space, are preserved, especially in urban areas.

What Factors Need to Be Considered Before Deciding Where to Locate a Factory?

A firm's choice of location is essential in its quest for profit and indeed survival. Any company considering locating in Ireland will look at a number of factors that will determine if it locates here or in lower-cost regions.

Labour and Wage Rates

The availability of a local, suitably qualified labour supply is essential for any new start-up company. Colleges and training centres located in a region can often be a factor in a company deciding to establish in one area over another. The minimum wage rate and wage rates in general can also be a deciding issue that will influence a company's geographical position.

Cost of Land

The cost of land will influence the choice of factory site. It is noteworthy that urban sites generally cost more than agricultural ones.

Nature of the Product Manufactured

- **Weight losing:** Industries where the raw material used is more bulky than the final good will tend to locate close to the source of raw materials, e.g. creameries tend to be located in rural regions and fish processing plants locate near ports.
- **Weight gaining:** These are industries where the finished product is more fragile or perishable than the raw material used in the production process. These companies tend to locate near their market, e.g. bakeries.
- **Footloose:** This is an industry that has relatively low transport costs and therefore does not need to locate near either the market or the source of raw material, e.g. ebooks.

Availability of Infrastructure

Water and power supplies will be required by a business to operate machines as well as provide light and heat, cooling systems and sanitation services. A good road system is needed to transport staff and raw materials to and from the business. The telecommunications network available in the area is also an important factor, particularly the accessibility of high-powered broadband.

Government Influence

The government may provide grants and subsidies for locating in disadvantaged areas, including tax relief on profit earned from exporting, building advance factories and developing infrastructure to encourage new start-ups. In addition, training schemes may be introduced to provide the necessary skill base for a new business.

Positive Economics

PROFILE: David Ricardo (1772–1823)

David Ricardo was an English MP who worked as a stockbroker and earned a large fortune. His main work was *The Principles of Political Economy and Taxation*. An economist of the classical school who strongly believed in the power of competition, he is best known for the theory of rent and the law of comparative advantage.

Theory of Rent
Ricardo maintained that as population increased it was necessary to use inferior land for crop production, as all the fertile land was being used. Using less favourable land incurred extra costs in cultivation and thus the cost of food increased. However, the cost of producing food on fertile land was considerably lower than on second-class land, but both gained from higher food prices. Consequently, food grown on fertile land would yield a surplus over food grown on inferior land. This surplus will lead to a rent being paid for the better land. This, according to Ricardo, was rent.

Law of Comparative Advantage
This law states that if one country is more efficient than another in the production of two goods, it should specialise and produce the good it is relatively more efficient at producing and import its other requirements.

Accepted the Subsistence Wages Theory/Iron Law of Wages
He believed that any increase in wages above the subsistence level would cause an increase in population, which in turn would cause wage levels to fall.

EXAM Question 3(c), 2005 (20 marks)

The price of residential property has increased in Ireland in recent years. Discuss **four** reasons for this development.

Solution

Any four of the examples below would be acceptable.

- **General inflation:** Inflation in Ireland has been rising, which leads to a general increase in prices, including house prices.

- **Lower interest rates/availability of loans:** Interest rates continue to fall, which has led to increases in mortgage lending by financial institutions and to an easing in lending in recent years.

- **Economic growth:** With economic growth and high employment, more people are entering the property market, thereby increasing demand.

- **Increased demand:** An increasing proportion of Ireland's population is within the age group capable of buying property. In addition, if Ireland has many returning emigrants and rising immigration, there would be more people looking for houses, thus increasing demand for accommodation. In particular, since land supply is limited in urban centres, there would be upward pressure on house prices in these areas. Socio-economic factors can also have an impact, e.g. if the number of separations are high, there would be a larger demand for housing given that the former husband and wife would now reside in separate houses.

- **Speculation in housing:** Increased property prices fuels speculative demand, with more people seeking opportunities in property/growth in demand for second houses. Availability of Section 23 incentives and tax-designated zones have attracted investment in certain areas, leading to a demand for holiday homes.

- **Inadequate supply:** Supply side issues include lack of zoned land, hoarding of land, planning difficulties and labour shortages. All these factors limit supply, thereby increasing prices.

- **Government policies:** The lack of affordable housing has forced prices for rental accommodation upwards and this has fuelled speculative demand for property.

Sample Exam Question (15 marks)

Why have house prices fallen in the last couple of years?

Solution

- **Supply exceeding demand:** Due to the construction boom, we now have a supply of property (ghost housing estates) that is greater than demand. This forces prices to fall.

- **Uncertain future:** Young couples who are uncertain of their jobs and future prospects may postpone buying a house until more stability enters the market.

- **Expectations of further fall in prices:** Potential buyers may decide to postpone their purchase in the hope that house prices may continue to fall further, thereby needing a smaller mortgage and consequently lower monthly payments.

- **Lack of speculative demand:** In the recent past, house prices increased in part due to speculators in the market buying and hoping to sell at a higher price. These speculators are not as active in the market at present.

Positive Economics

- **Emigration:** As young people are forced to leave and find employment in other areas, the demand for rental property has fallen. This in turn has led to a fall in the demand for houses.

- **Economic climate:** Unstable government finances (necessitating the introduction of water charges, USC) and a fall in consumer demand due to unemployment have resulted in reduced consumer spending power and hence demand for houses has declined.

- **Banking crisis:** Due to unwise lending practices in the past and current liquidity problems, banks have found themselves in a position where they are unable to issue loans for house purchases in the manner they did in the recent past.

Questions

Short Questions

1. Define land as a factor of production.
2. What is the return on the factor land?
3. Explain the economic characteristics of land.
4. Explain why land is a unique factor of production.
5. Draw the supply curve of land.

Long Questions

1. Explain economic rent.
2. Outline the three different types of industry.
3. The demand for land is a derived demand. Explain.
4. Why are rents in popular areas of cities higher than quieter streets?
5. State and explain the factors that influence the price paid for land.
6. Explain why the government might intervene in the market for land.
7. State and explain the factors that would influence a company's decision to locate in a particular area.
8. Explain the term 'supply price' of a factor of production.
9. Do you consider supernormal profits to be economic rent?
10. Should governments control the price of houses?

Chapter 15 | Labour

Specific Learning Outcomes

At the end of this chapter, students should be able to:

- ☐ Define labour.
- ☐ Illustrate and explain the concept of derived demand.
- ☐ Understand MRP and MPP as they relate to labour.
- ☐ Examine the factors that affect the demand for labour by an individual firm.
- ☐ Illustrate by means of a diagram the relationship between the wage rate and the quantity demanded of labour.
- ☐ Illustrate by means of a diagram the relationship between the wage rate and the quantity supplied of labour.
- ☐ Examine the factors affecting the mobility of labour.
- ☐ Define geographical mobility and occupational mobility of labour.
- ☐ Illustrate and interpret the backward bending supply curve of labour.
- ☐ Illustrate and explain equilibrium wage level.
- ☐ Examine the reasons for differences in wage rates.
- ☐ Examine what factors make labour efficient.

Positive Economics

Introduction

The demand for labour as a factor of production is a derived demand, i.e. labour is demanded for its contribution to the production process or from the demand for the goods it produces.

> **LABOUR** is the human activity directed towards the production of wealth. Its payment is the wage rate.

Demand for Labour

Like all equilibrium rates, the price of labour is determined by demand and supply. In Chapter 12, we saw that the demand curve for any factor of production is its marginal revenue product curve. Therefore, **the demand curve for labour is its MRP curve, which is downward sloping from left to right.**

As you can see from the graph, if the wage rate is €400 per week, then 50 workers will be employed, **as every worker is demanded up to and including the worker whose MRP and wage rate are equal.**

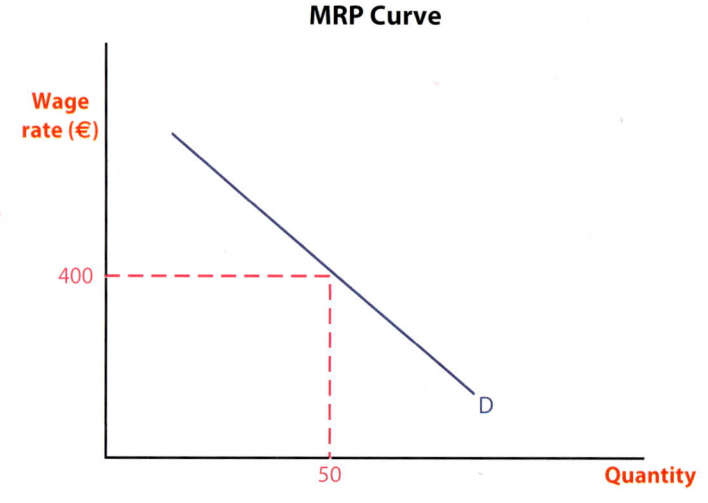

MRP Curve

(Graph: Wage rate (€) on vertical axis, Quantity on horizontal axis, downward sloping demand curve D, with dashed lines showing 400 on wage axis and 50 on quantity axis.)

Factors Affecting an Individual Firm's Demand for Labour

The MRP of the Worker

How much extra revenue does the employee generate compared to their cost?

> **REMEMBER!**
> Remember, a worker will be employed as long as their MRP = **wage rate**.

> **Example**
>
> If an additional sales assistant generated €20 an hour, then this is the maximum that could be paid to all employees. A sales assistant would not be paid €25 per hour if they were generating only €20. (See Chapter 13 for a more detailed illustration.)

If the wage rate that the worker is seeking is higher than the revenue that the worker generates, then the staff member won't be hired.

Wage Rate

The lower the wage rate, the higher the firm's demand for labour.

The Demand for a Firm's Output
If demand is buoyant, a company will hire extra staff. In recessionary times, as the demand for goods and services falls, so too does the demand for labour.

Price of Other Factors of Production
Prior to employing more labour, the firm would compare the cost of the additional labour with that of other factors of production available (e.g. capital) to determine which option is the most competitive and productive.

Government Incentives
Governments offer different incentives to companies to encourage employment of additional staff, e.g. reducing employers' PRSI for lower-paid staff, reduction of travel tax to encourage tourists into the country. As a result of these government initiatives in labour-intensive industries, demand for labour may increase.

Availability of New Technology
The introduction of new technology can often lead to a fall in the demand for labour that it replaces, e.g. self-service checkouts in some supermarkets, online check-in at airports.

Corporation Tax
The competitive corporation tax rate in Ireland has been a big determinant in encouraging foreign multinationals to set up here and thus increases the demand for labour. An increase in this favourable tax rate may have detrimental effects on the demand for labour in this country.

Entrepreneurs' Expectations
If businesspeople's expectations about the future are positive, they may invest in new projects or expand existing firms, thus generating a demand for labour. Factors that influence expectations include the international business climate, current economic growth, tax rates and interest rates.

Supply of Labour

Supply of labour is determined by a number of factors, including the following.

> The **SUPPLY OF LABOUR** in the economy is the total number of hours worked in the economy during a specific period.

Size of Population
The larger a country's population, the greater the labour force that is available for employment. As a country's population increases, so does the number of citizens in the working age bracket.

Wage Levels in the Economy
Higher wage levels act as an incentive for more people to supply their labour. However, a situation can arise when wage levels increase that some workers will substitute leisure time and reduce their supply of labour.

Participation Rate

This is the percentage of the active population in the labour force, i.e. the number of people willing to work. This depends on:

- **Social attitudes:** The age of retirement and the normal school-leaving age. If these change, so will the participation rate, e.g. an increase in the retirement age will cause an increase in the participation rate.

- **Attitudes of homemakers** working full time or part time outside the home.

- **State of the economy:** When the economy is growing and expanding and employment is easier to find, then some groups in society who might otherwise not have sought employment, e.g. older/retired people and students, may now enter into the workforce.

- **Welfare benefits:** If an economy has generous welfare provisions, recipients may be less likely to seek employment.

Levels of Income Tax

If tax rates fall, it may encourage people to join the workforce. Similarly, an increase in marginal rates of income tax may encourage substitution of leisure for labour. A worker who pays high marginal rates of tax on overtime earnings may consider that after tax, the amount received is not worth the effort and inconvenience involved.

Number of Hours Worked

The longer the working week, the greater the supply of labour in an economy.

Labour Mobility

The workforce in Ireland has become more occupationally mobile, i.e. fewer barriers are in place preventing the movement of workers. With EU enlargement, the free movement of labour is increasing.

Government Policies

Any government that eases restrictions on the entry of immigrants into a country and liberalises the entry requirements into certain occupations, e.g. nursing, will increase the supply of labour.

Labour Supply Curve

As with most supply curves, the supply of labour is upward sloping from left to right. In addition, when wages increase, more labour will be supplied, but when the wage rate falls, less labour will be supplied, i.e. there is a positive relationship between labour supply and wage rates.

Supply Curve of Labour

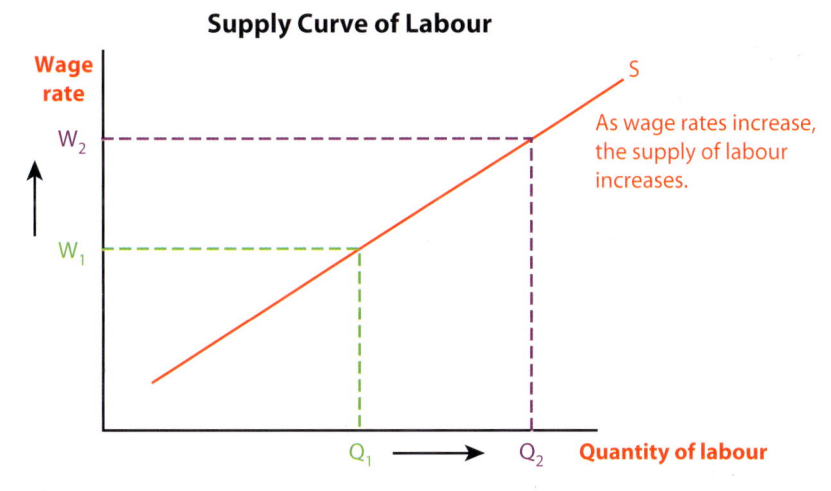

As wage rates increase, the supply of labour increases.

Backward Bending Supply Curve of Labour

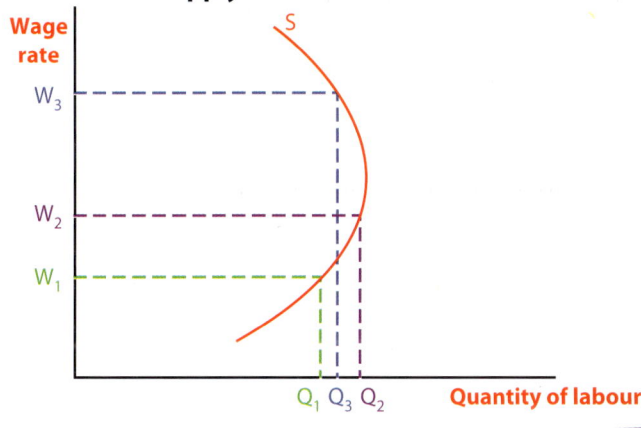

There may be a decline in the supply of labour at higher wage rates as workers substitute leisure for labour. This produces a backward bending supply curve of labour. This can be seen in an economy where there are high marginal rates of tax and workers feel that the after-tax pay is not worth the increased effort and leisure time is preferred.

At wage rate W_1 the quantity of labour supplied is Q_1. As wages increase to W_2 the quantity of labour supplied rises to Q_2. At wage rates above W_2, e.g. W_3, the amount of labour supplied falls back from its previous level.

The Equilibrium Wage Rate

When the demand and supply curves of labour are brought together, we can find the equilibrium wage rate for the economy. The demand curve for labour

Think about it!

Think about a job where you earned thousands and thousands per year but you had to work Monday to Sunday, 6 a.m. to 11:30 p.m. Do you think you would give up €1,000 to do other things rather than work?

- You could buy a sports car, but you wouldn't have the time to drive it.
- You could afford expensive holidays, but you wouldn't have time to go on them.
- You could buy a big house, but all you could do is sleep in it.

will be the MRP of labour and will slope downwards from left to right. The supply curve will be upward sloping, indicating more labour supplied at higher wage rates.

Determination of Equilibrium Wage Rate in a Free Market

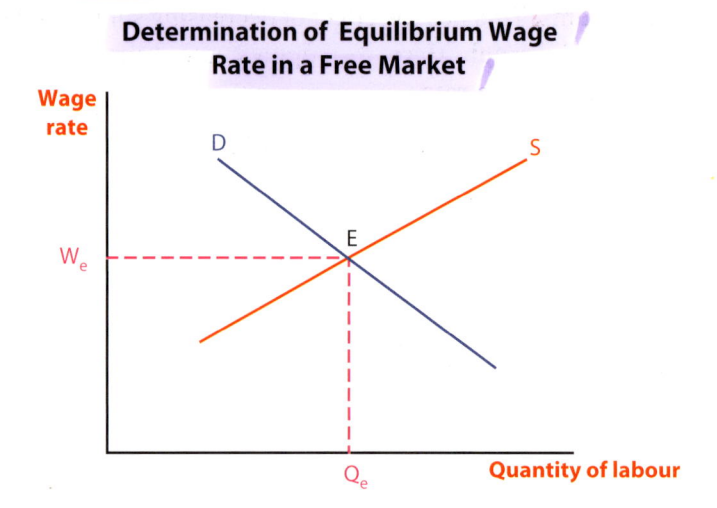

The curves intersect at W_e with quantity Q_e. This point represents the equilibrium wage rate in the economy. If the wage rate was above this level, then excess supply would force the wage rate downwards. Likewise, if the wage rate was below W_e, excess demand would force wages upwards.

This analysis ignores the influence of trade unions, government legislation (minimum wage rate), employment subsidies and rates of taxes in the economy, all of which could influence the equilibrium wage rate.

Horizontal Supply Curve of Labour

In a perfectly competitive market, the individual firm whose demand for labour is so small that it does not influence the wage rate would face a horizontal supply curve of labour. The same situation may operate in a small community where there is a single employer of labour. If workers are considered immobile because they won't leave the area, then the single employer can hire all workers for any wage, as long as it is above the minimum rate, as increasing the wage rate is not necessary to get people willing to work.

Supply Curve of Labour in a Perfectly Competitive Market

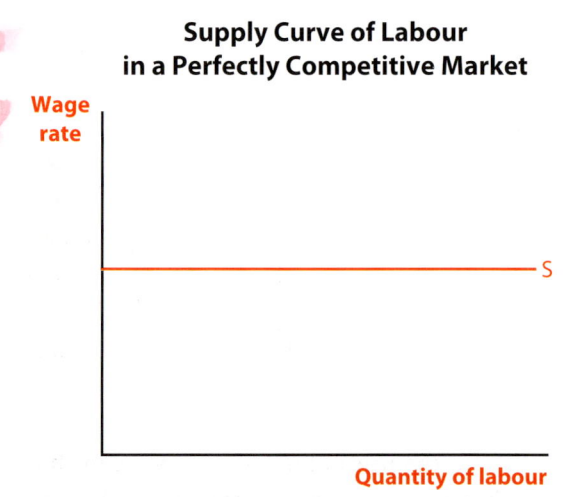

Restricting Entry Into a Profession

Some professions may curtail the admission of newly qualified staff by increasing the standards of entrance exams. This has the effect of decreasing supply and thus increasing the wage rate, as seen in the graph. Here, the supply curve shifts to the left, indicating a lower quantity and a higher wage rate.

Restricting Entry into a Profession

Restricting entry into a profession may shift the supply curve to the left, quantity decreases and wage increases

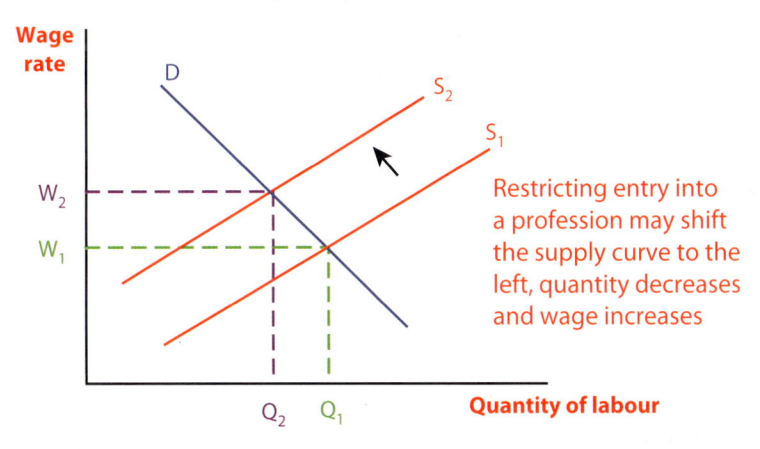

Trade Unions and Wage Rates

Trade unions negotiate a wage rate for their members and they usually ensure that there is no supply of labour below the negotiated rate. In times of high unemployment, wage rates could fall to a very low level as unemployed workers compete for the available jobs. A union-negotiated rate prevents this from happening.

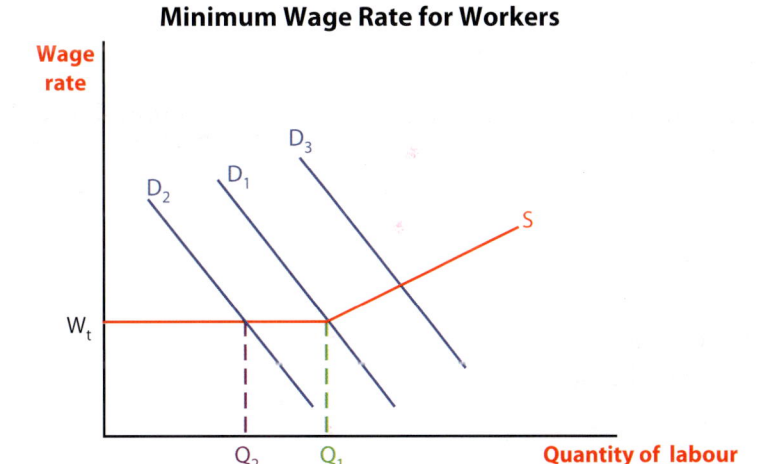

Minimum Wage Rate for Workers

In the diagram above it can be seen that the negotiated wage rate is W_t and no labour will be supplied below this level. Q_1 represents the quantity of workers available at this negotiated rate.

At Q_1, the demand for labour equals the supply at the negotiated rate, i.e. all those available for work at this wage rate are working.

If the demand for labour falls, e.g. during a recession (D_1 shifts to D_2), then at Q_2, some workers who are prepared to work at the union rate (Wt) won't be employed. The union, being a monopoly supplier, decides the price/wage rate, but the market decides the quantity demanded at this price.

Points on the supply curve beyond Q_1 represent the normal supply curve of labour. As wages increase, so does the supply.

Wage Drift
This occurs when wage levels rise above the negotiated levels. This occurs when demand for labour increases beyond the available supply at the negotiated rate.

Ratchet Economy
This is an economy that experiences wage and price increases, usually due to increased demand, but prices and wages do not tend to fall when demand falls.

Mobility of Labour

The ease with which workers can move from one region to another and/or move from one job to another is termed mobility of labour. We will look at two types: geographical and occupational.

Geographical Mobility
A number of factors inhibit this transition, such as:

- Existing social connections in the area where a family lives.

- The disruption that could be caused to children's education due to the move.

- The cost of selling and buying a house elsewhere (especially if a family is moving from a rural area to a large city that has higher house prices).

- A general fear or reluctance to consider a major change in one's life.

GEOGRAPHICAL MOBILITY is the ability/ease of a worker to move from one area to another, e.g. moving from Dublin to Sligo.

What are the economic policies that could increase geographical mobility?

- **Increase housing:** Increase the availability of (affordable) housing in the area where shortages exist.
- **Educational facilities:** Improve the availability of educational facilities to ease the concerns of parents.
- **Social infrastructure:** Improve the social amenities to make areas more appealing for families, e.g. shops, parks and leisure facilities.
- **Government supports:** The government might provide support to entice people to move, e.g. relocation grants.
- **Updated information:** Provide up-to-date and adequate information on the possibilities of moving.

Occupational Mobility

A number of factors can discourage occupational mobility:

- If a worker has a high degree of skill and specific training, then they will not find it as easy to source alternative employment.

> **OCCUPATIONAL MOBILITY** is the ease/ability of a worker to move from one job to another.

- High costs associated with retraining.
- Some professions present barriers to entry in the form of a very high standard of exams.

What are the economic policies that could increase occupational mobility?

- **Education courses:** Provide courses for further educational opportunities and at accessible costs.
- **Training:** Provide opportunities for training/retraining at suitable times and at reasonable costs.
- **Government policies:** Change regulations on work permits and entry into government training schemes.
- **Trade union barriers:** Reduce barriers to entry into occupations, e.g. National Union of Journalists.

Factors That Influence the Elasticity of Demand for Labour

Percentage of Labour Costs to Total Costs

If labour costs are small in relation to overall costs, then an increase in wages won't influence the demand for labour.

Substitutability of Labour
If labour can easily be replaced by machines and if the wage rate increases, then the demand for labour will fall, as it is elastic. On the other hand, if machines can't do the work and if the wages increase, then labour won't be replaced, as it is inelastic.

Elasticity of Demand for the Finished Good
If the product sold on the market is relatively inelastic and wages increase, then the higher costs can be passed on to the consumer and the demand for labour is unaffected.

Productivity of Labour
If the productivity of labour is high, then it is unlikely that it will be replaced by technology.

Factors Affecting the Efficiency of Labour

Can you imagine working in Pat's Deli if the ovens don't heat properly, the coffee machine keeps breaking down, one staff member is always late or the kitchen has little ventilation? Clearly, the efficiency of the staff would be less than it could be!

Amount of Training
The quality/extent of training available to the worker may improve the worker's skill, e.g. a staff member who has undergone several years' training as a chef will have achieved a degree of proficiency.

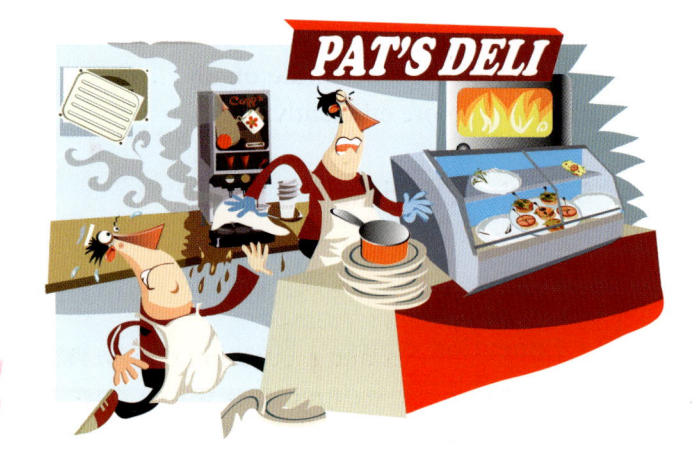

Management Expertise
Good managers organise the workplace, ensure that standards and deadlines are met and can get the best out of their valued staff. They reward efficiency, raise morale and motivate those around them, e.g. Richard Branson.

Level of Education
The level and quality of education attained by the worker can improve efficiency, e.g. someone who has attained a masters degree may be able to undertake a high level of independent research.

15: Labour

Innate Talent
Some people may possess innate talents making them highly efficient, e.g. golf or tennis players.

Quantity/Quality of Other Factors Available
Workers' efficiency will improve if they have a sufficient quantity and quality of other factors of production, e.g. contrast working in a deli with one knife, one chopping board and very little space with a deli that has a plentiful supply of these items.

Living Conditions of the Workforce
If workers are healthy, well nourished and have decent accommodation, then they will work in a more efficient manner.

Degree of Specialisation
When workers concentrate on one task, they become more skilful and can work faster and hence more efficiently.

Climatic Conditions
If a place of work is too hot or too cold, this may affect the workers' effort.

Dedication of the Worker
The commitment and motivation of a worker will affect their efficiency. An interested and enthusiastic staff member who is open to new ideas and who is innovative will be very productive.

How Appropriate Is MRP for Setting Wages in the Public Sector?

Physical Output Is Not Always Produced
Many jobs in the public sector are services, so it is difficult to measure output, thus making it difficult to measure MPP and consequently MRP, e.g. nurses.

Non-market Output
Workers in the public sector who produce physical output that is not sold in the marketplace can't have their output valued and hence have difficulty calculating the marginal revenue for the output produced, e.g. a carpenter in the Office of Public Works.

(MRP)

Capital and Labour Used Together
It is difficult to estimate whether a worker's extra productivity is due to either labour or capital when a combination of both is used, e.g. a civil servant and a computer. It is not possible to allocate MRP to the civil servant alone.

A system of pay comparability with those working in the private sector doing similar work and with similar qualifications could be used to determine public sector wage levels. The government did introduce benchmarking as a method of setting wages in the public sector. The Benchmarking Review Body examined the earnings of similar jobs in the private sector and made recommendations on wage increases.

Why Do Different Categories of Workers Receive Different Wages?

Different Skills
The skills attached to different jobs vary and pay is commensurate with the level of skill involved, e.g. a doctor receives a higher rate of pay than that of a nurse.

Length of Training
Workers who undergo longer periods of training will receive higher pay levels, e.g. a nurse who trains and becomes more specialised will receive higher pay.

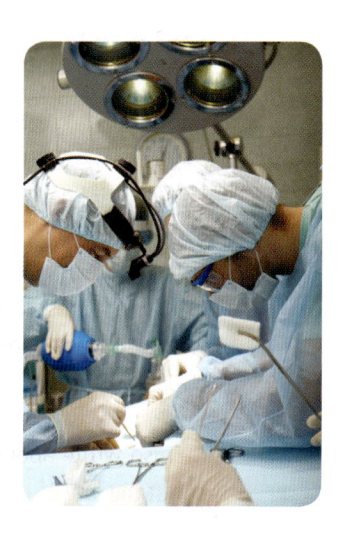

Educational Qualifications
Generally, wage levels recognise the educational qualifications achieved by the worker, e.g. a job that requires a post-graduate qualification will usually command a higher salary than a job that requires no formal standard of education.

Nature and Conditions of the Job
Certain jobs are dangerous, have unsociable hours or are temporary. Workers in these areas usually command higher wages, e.g. miners, steeplejacks, night shift staff.

Possession of Innate Talent
Some people may be born with an innate talent or develop skills during their lives that allow them to earn high incomes, e.g. successful film stars, professional tennis players, golfers and premier football players. They earn amounts in excess of their supply price and hence earn economic rents.

Tradition Attached to Certain Jobs
It has been possible for those involved in the self-governing professions, i.e. those in the legal or accountancy professions, to maintain high pay levels because of the tradition that is attached to such professions.

Non-monetary Benefits
Workers in different jobs may receive non-monetary benefits such as long holidays, low-interest loans, subsidised healthcare, etc. to compensate for relatively lower wage levels.

Negotiating Strength of the Workers' Trade Union
If workers are members of a strong trade union, they may obtain wages in line with their MRP.

PROFILE: John Stuart Mill (1806–73)

John Stuart Mill was an English economist who was also an MP and campaigned for extending the franchise to women. An economist in the classical tradition, he favoured free trade, laissez-faire principles, perfect competition, etc.

He developed his **wage fund theory**. He thought that there was a certain amount of money available for distribution and wages could not be increased unless savings increased. If workers were to receive higher wages, then the wage fund needed to increase. This would cause the population to increase and eventually drag wages back down to subsistence level.

He also wrote about increasing returns to scale and was one of the first economists to write about the law of diminishing returns.

EXAM Question 3(a)(ii), 2007 (10 marks)

Outline **two** developments, other than a fall in MRP, which may result in a firm reducing its number of employees.

Solution

Any two of the following points would be acceptable.

- **Demand for pay increases:** If the workers are successful for such demands, costs of production will increase and profitability will fall. This may result in the firm having to make some workers redundant.

- **Introduction of new technology/mechanisation:** Increased mechanisation of the production process or the introduction of cost-saving technologies will reduce the demand for labour.

- **Fall in demand for the firm's output:** Any factors that cause a drop in the demand for the firm's output, e.g. higher prices for the commodity, may lead to a reduction in demand for workers.

- **Government policies:** If the government pursues policies that make it more expensive to employ workers, e.g. raising the minimum wage, then the employer may reduce the workforce.

- **Increased competition in the market:** If new firms enter the industry, existing firms may suffer a reduction in demand, resulting in a loss of jobs in that particular firm, e.g. new supermarkets opening in many towns around the country.

- **Increases in the costs of production:** Any factor that causes a firm to become less competitive will result in a loss of sales, leading to job losses, e.g. increases in oil prices or increases in employer's PRSI.

EXAM Question 3(b)(ii), 2007 (15 marks)

The demand for labour has increased significantly in certain sectors of the Irish economy in recent years, e.g. construction.

Discuss three economic consequences of this situation.

Solution

Any three of the following points would be acceptable.

- **Pressure on wage levels to rise:** Employers will be forced to increase wage levels in order to attract workers into those areas where shortages are occurring.

- **Deterioration/loss of services:** Where workers are not available, it will result in either a deterioration of services in those areas or a total loss of certain services, e.g. the health sector, education sector.

- **Loss of investment:** Indigenous and foreign entrepreneurs may see such shortages of labour as a deterrent to investing in and starting a business.

- **Inflationary pressures:** If wage levels increase, such increases may be passed on to the final consumer in the form of higher prices.

- **Immigration:** Shortages of labour in the Irish labour market are reported internationally. FÁS has attempted to entice foreign workers to Ireland.

- **Difficulty of attracting/keeping workers in some sectors:** With the current labour shortages and the attractiveness of higher pay in alternative employment, certain sectors find it increasingly difficult to attract workers, e.g. hotel, catering, tourism industries.

- **Inability to maintain development of the state's infrastructure:** Because of the shortage of workers, developing the infrastructure at the pace necessary to sustain economic growth is not possible, which may affect future investment.

EXAM — Sample Short Question (15 marks)

List the consequences of decreased demand for labour due to the economic recession.

Solution

- Emigration might increase.

- Increase in unemployment could decrease living standards.

- The minimum wage may need to be lowered.

- There may be lower inflation rates due to a fall in quantity demanded for goods and services.

- Government finances may disimprove (less direct and indirect taxes and an increase in social welfare payments).

- There may be an increase in the dependency ratio if emigration sees a large section from the working age group going abroad.

- Government services curtailed due to cutbacks in expenditure.

- Imposition of new stealth taxes (water charges/residential property tax).

Questions

Short Questions

1. Define labour as a factor of production and state its return.
2. Why is the demand for labour a derived demand?
3. State and explain four factors that affect a firm's demand for labour.
4. State and explain three factors affecting the supply of labour.
5. Illustrate how the equilibrium wage rate is determined.

Long Questions

1. Illustrate the effect of the government imposing a minimum wage rate in the labour market.
2. Explain the terms 'wage drift' and 'ratchet economy'.
3. Distinguish between occupational and geographical mobility of labour.
4. Describe three factors that would increase occupational and geographical mobility.
5. Why do certain categories of workers receive different rates of pay?
6. Do you think MRP is an appropriate measure for establishing wages in the public sector?
7. State and explain five factors that influence a worker's efficiency.
8. State and explain three factors that influence the elasticity of demand for labour.
9. The demand curve for labour is downward sloping. Explain.
10. What factors affect a worker's MRP?
11. Illustrate how labour could earn economic rent.

Chapter 16 | Capital

Specific Learning Outcomes

At the end of this chapter, students should be able to:

- ☐ Define capital and explain why interest is the return.
- ☐ Examine why capital is needed in an economy.
- ☐ Explain the different types of capital.
- ☐ Illustrate an understanding of marginal efficiency of capital.
- ☐ Explain the factors that influence marginal efficiency of capital.
- ☐ Compare capital widening and capital deepening.
- ☐ Define savings and state those who save in society.
- ☐ Explain the factors that influence the level of savings.
- ☐ Evaluate why savings are important.
- ☐ Define investment.
- ☐ State the factors that influence the level of investment in an economy.
- ☐ Examine why investment is important in an economy.
- ☐ Explain the loanable funds theory of interest rates.
- ☐ Explain the Keynesian theory of interest rates.

Positive Economics

Introduction

Demand for capital is a derived demand, i.e. the demand for capital arises because of the contribution it makes to the production process.

> **CAPITAL** is anything manmade that assists in the production of wealth. Examples of capital are machinery, mobile phones, tractors, buildings and roads, etc.

Interest is the payment for capital.

The production of capital in any society necessitates sacrificing (opportunity cost) current spending so that an economy can be productive in the future. If a country is spending all its resources on consumer goods and not putting resources into the production of capital goods, then a time would come in the future when there would be insufficient amounts of capital (machinery) available to produce goods that are needed, i.e. there will be a shortage of consumer goods. Economic growth would slow down and the standard of living would probably fall.

An economy could prevent this by encouraging savings, which would ultimately lead to an increase in investment (production of capital goods). In Chapter 25 we examine the situation in poorer countries of the world, with lower levels of GDP per capita, where most of the income earned is spent and very little is saved. Consequently, there is little investment as there aren't any funds available. These countries will remain poor if capital goods are not produced to increase productivity and hence improve their standard of living. This cycle can be broken with aid from other countries.

Think about it!

Let's say you get a part-time job for the summer and you spend all your money in the first hour. Instead, you would be well advised to save your earnings and use them over a longer period of time so that you can stretch out your consumption and the utility that you derive from your wages.

We can identify different types of capital in an economy.

> **SOCIAL CAPITAL** refers to the assets/wealth owned by the community or society in general, e.g. hospitals, parks, roads.

> **WORKING CAPITAL** includes all finished goods, work in progress goods and stocks of raw materials.

> **FIXED CAPITAL** is the stock of fixed assets such as plant, equipment and tools.

> **PRIVATE CAPITAL** is assets owned by individuals, e.g. computers, cars.

We must also distinguish between capital and income. Capital is what's owned by a society, i.e. its stock of wealth, whereas income (a flow of wealth) is what's earned or the wealth produced by a society over a period of time.

How Is Interest the Payment for Capital?

We can say that the **RATE OF INTEREST** is the payment to capital, as those who sacrifice present consumption must be rewarded by those who need funds for present use.

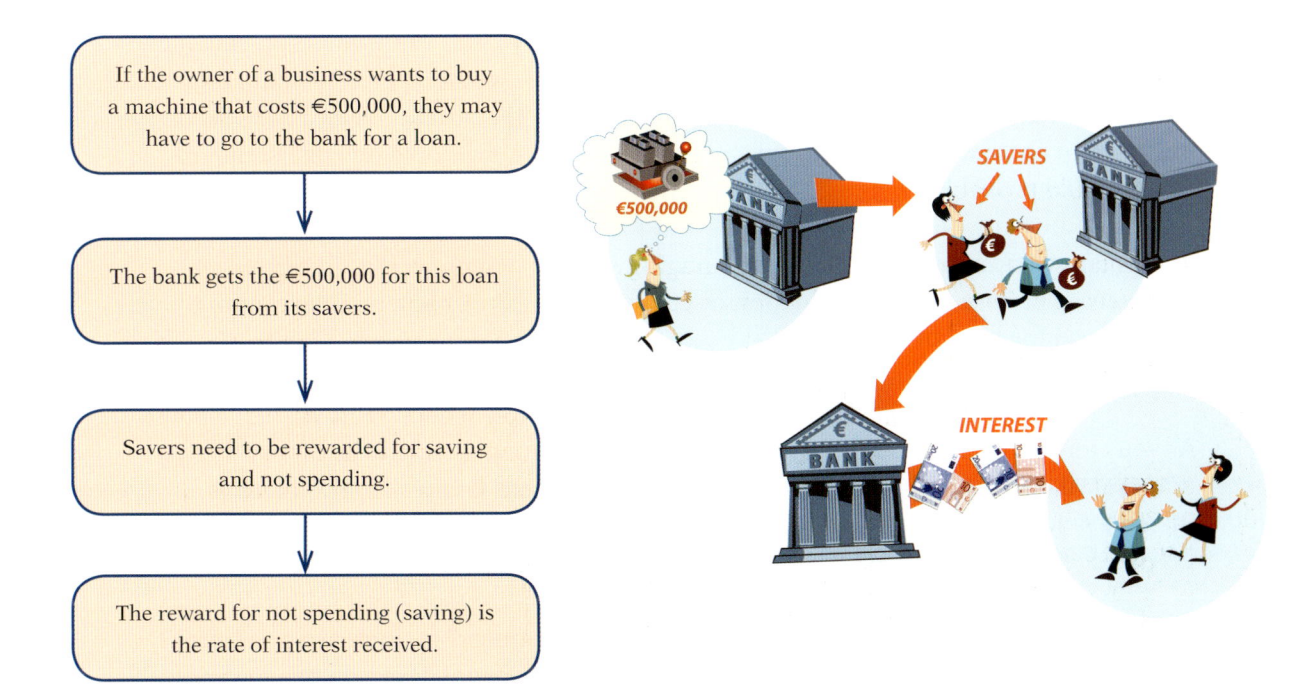

- If the owner of a business wants to buy a machine that costs €500,000, they may have to go to the bank for a loan.
- The bank gets the €500,000 for this loan from its savers.
- Savers need to be rewarded for saving and not spending.
- The reward for not spending (saving) is the rate of interest received.

Capital is necessary if an economy is to be productive both now and in the future. However, capital works in tandem with land and labour. The better capital a worker possesses, the higher the MRP and MPP are likely to be.

Examples

- An accountant preparing a cash flow forecast for Pat's Deli will perform this task much faster with the use of accounting software rather than preparing it manually.
- The use of food processors, mixers, microwaves, etc. increases the productivity of the staff in the deli, i.e. capital makes labour more productive.

Positive Economics

In both cases, less time, money and labour used as well as an ability to create more output leads to an increase in profits.

An entrepreneur will invest in projects where the MEC is highest.

This extra profit earned as a result of employing one extra unit of capital is known as the **MARGINAL EFFICIENCY OF CAPITAL (MEC)**, i.e. the marginal revenue productivity of additional capital goods minus their cost. For example, if an extra oven costs €2,000 and adds €5,000 to total revenue, its MEC is €3,000.

The more expensive the capital (the higher the rate of interest), the lower the demand for capital. Thus, the MEC curve is downward sloping from left to right, indicating an inverse relationship between the rate of interest and the level of investment.

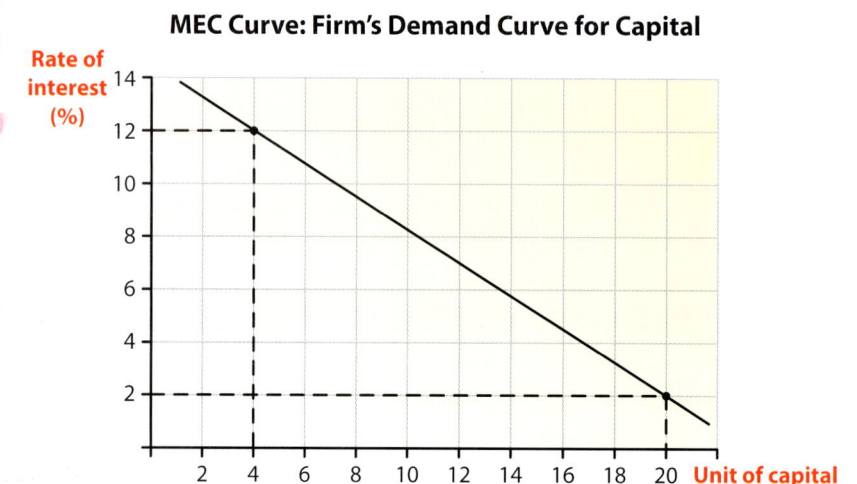

MEC Curve: Firm's Demand Curve for Capital

As you can see from the diagram, if the rate of interest is 12%, only 4 units of capital will be employed. If interest rates fall to 2%, it becomes cheaper to borrow, so 20 units of capital will be sought.

What Factors Influence MEC?

A company may decide to increase or leave unchanged the stock of capital in a company based on the following factors.

Cost of Capital Goods

The higher the cost of capital (e.g. machines), the longer the payback period. As a result, the machine is less profitable as more of the sales revenue is used to repay the loan.

Rate of Interest

If the price of capital (i.e. interest rate) increases, the purchase of capital goods becomes less attractive. For example, if a hotel is considering building an extension and interest rates increase to 18% from 4%, then the payback period increases and the viability of the project is questioned.

Selling Price of the Good Being Sold

If the selling price of the good decreases (because competitors have lowered their prices or there is a fall in demand due to a recession), then total revenue falls. Consequently, the purchase of additional capital goods becomes less attractive and existing capital goods are less profitable. For example, restaurants may have to lower prices and offer deals during lean economic times to stay in business, thereby lowering the return on capital invested.

Fall in Productivity of the Extra Capital Being Used

As existing capital goods get older, their productivity may decrease due to wear and tear and may even become obsolete. For example, a 20-year-old delivery van needs more servicing and parts replaced than a newer model.

Capital Widening and Capital Deepening

As a factor of production, capital generally does not work in isolation from land and labour. Generally, the more capital workers have, the more productive they will be. Two concepts are used to describe the relationship between capital and labour: capital widening and capital deepening.

> **CAPITAL WIDENING** is a scenario whereby the amount of capital per worker remains unchanged. An increase in the capital stock leaves the capital/labour ratio unchanged. For example:
>
> Year 1:   5 machines   and   5 workers
> Year 2:   10 machines   and   10 workers

> **CAPITAL DEEPENING** is a scenario whereby the amount of capital increases, resulting in more capital per worker in the economy. Here, the production process is becoming more capital intensive.
>
> Year 1:   5 machines   and   5 workers
> Year 2:   10 machines   and   5 workers

Savings

> **SAVING** is non-consumption/income not spent.

Savings are good for an individual and for an economy. It is this money which is used for future investment. Individuals may save for different reasons.

> **Example**
>
> €200   –   €160   =   €40
> Income   Spending   Savings

- **Deferred expenditure:** Saving for holidays, furniture or the purchase of a car. These expenses can't usually be met out of weekly income, so people save for future consumption.

- **Unforeseen events:** People save to provide for emergencies such as unexpected medical expenses, house repairs, etc.

- **Speculation:** Saving for an investment opportunity, e.g. the purchase of shares in anticipation of a price rise and hence a profit.

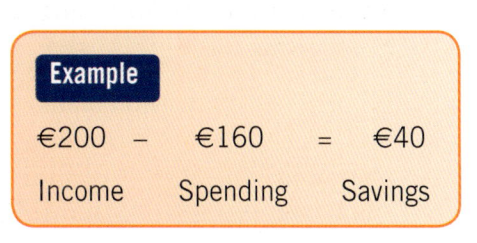

- **Credit rating:** Saving to build up a credit rating with a financial institution for a future loan.
- **Retirement:** Some people engage in private pension schemes so that they will have more money to preserve their lifestyle after they stop working.

Who Saves in Our Economy?

- Individuals save by depositing funds in financial institutions and earning a rate of interest. They also save by paying PRSI, as this is a contribution to a future state pension. Individuals may also contribute to personal pension schemes to provide for their retirement.
- Businesses save by retaining profits and not paying out dividends. These funds can be used for future expansion.
- Government saves if it incurs a budget surplus (government current revenue greater than government current spending).

What Influences the Amount Saved by Individuals?

- **Level of income:** An individual with a small income will be unable to save, as all of their income is needed to provide for current consumption. Those on higher incomes can afford much higher levels of savings.
- **Rate of interest:** If interest rates are high then savings will be high, since interest is the reward for saving and foregoing current consumption.
- **Rate of inflation:** If interest rates are 5% and inflation is 3%, then the real rate of interest is 2%. Savers often look for index-linked saving schemes to maintain the value of their savings. The higher the rate of inflation, the lower the incentive to save.
- **Tax on savings:** If DIRT (Deposit Interest Retention Tax) is high, then savers are less inclined to save, as the net reward has to be high to compensate for non-consumption. Tax relief on pension plans encourages savings.

Investment

The decision to invest is made by producers/firms. They have to pay a level of interest in order to use that capital.

The total production of capital goods in an economy is known as gross investment. These

> **INVESTMENT** involves the production of capital goods or any addition to capital stock in the economy.

capital goods wear out because of use/age (also called depreciation). Net investment is gross expenditure on capital formation less depreciation. It is important that an economy continually replaces old capital to enable continued future production and prevent a running down of the capital stock.

Factors Affecting the Level of Investment in the Economy

The following affect the level of investment in the economy and hence the future productive capacity/economic growth of the country.

Rates of Interest

The higher the rate of interest, the higher the cost of borrowing and the lower the level of investment. A company planning to build an extension will consider the cost of finance before committing. Contrast interest rates of 2% to 12% – during times of low interest rates, investment will tend to be high as the cost of borrowing is lower.

Businesspeople's Expectations of the Future

If businesspeople are optimistic about the economy or their sector, they are more likely to invest in new enterprises or expand old ones. If the future looks bleak, with high unemployment, high inflation and high taxation, then expansion may be postponed.

The Cost of Capital Goods

The greater the cost of capital goods, the lower the profitability of the investment and hence investment will fall. Entrepreneurs considering spending large sums on new capital equipment with high repayments will closely examine the costs and benefits associated with the project.

Government Policy

If government policy is favourable towards investment, then amounts invested will tend to rise. Examples of favourable policies include attractive state grants, reduction in corporation tax, development of infrastructure, etc.

The International Economic Climate

Open economies (i.e. economies that engage in international trade) like Ireland rely on foreign investment. If the international economic climate is optimistic and booming, then this may result in a growth in demand benefitting indigenous companies.

Industrial Relations Climate

Countries that have a relatively peaceful industrial climate will attract investment, since there is an implied guarantee of uninterrupted production. Also, countries that have an educated/skilled workforce will attract high-valued-added types of firms.

Availability of Credit

If banks envisage the potential in a business venture and are willing to offer finance, then the project may go ahead. Banks that are very cautious and unwilling to entertain loan applications stifle potential investment.

The Marginal Efficiency of Capital

The greater the potential MEC for any possible investment project, the more likely that the investment will take place. A business will decide to invest in a new product, extend the premises, etc. if it forecasts that the future income will be greater than costs and thus add to the company's profitability.

The Importance of Investment and Production of Capital Goods in an Economy

Increased Productive Capacity

Greater investment allows a country to produce more output. A greater number of machines, computers, etc. enables a larger amount and a greater selection of goods that can be produced. Investment also replaces worn out capital resources.

Increased Labour Productivity

More investment allows labour to become more efficient. A country that possesses up-to-date and technologically advanced equipment enables workers to be more efficient.

Increased Employment
Extra investment increases aggregate demand, resulting in the demand for more employees to meet this additional demand for goods and services.

Increased GNP
Increased investment leads to a higher gross national product (GNP), greater demand, increased spending and a higher standard of living.

Investment Generates Future Wealth for the Economy
Investment into the economy safeguards the future wealth-creating capacity of the country by ensuring that capital goods exist in the future, e.g. road and hospital infrastructure.

Increased Government Revenue
An increase in investment will increase economic activity. This will generate additional tax revenues for the government to use in the economy. In addition, extra employment implies less expenditure needed for social welfare.

> Return on capital = interest

> **REMEMBER!**
> The wage rate is the return for the factor of production labour and rent is the return to land.

We will now explain how the interest rate, which is the return on capital, is determined. Two theories will be studied.

Loanable Funds Theory of Interest Rates: Classical Theory

This theory contends that:

- The demand for funds was created by people who wanted assets now rather than in the future, i.e. people who wanted to invest.
- The supply of funds was given by people who were prepared to forego present consumption, i.e. willing to save.

The rate of interest brought the demand and supply of loanable funds together. It was the reward for saving and the cost of borrowing.

If the rate of interest was to rise, savings would be encouraged and investment discouraged. This was because as the cost of capital increased, less would be borrowed. If interest rates fell, the opposite would happen. Thus, a typical demand and supply situation would

Positive Economics

Equilibrium Rate of Interest

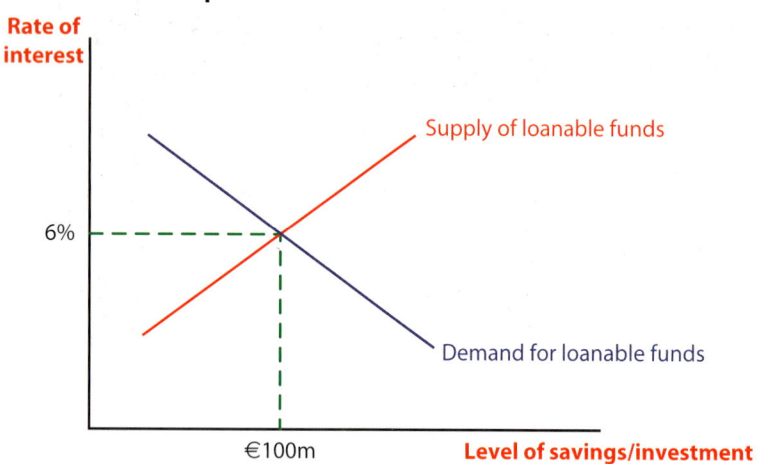

[Graph showing Supply of loanable funds (upward sloping) and Demand for loanable funds (downward sloping) intersecting at 6% and €100m. Axes: Rate of interest (vertical), Level of savings/investment (horizontal).]

manifest itself. Just as price brings demand and supply into equilibrium, so too, the theory stated, the rate of interest brought the supply of and demand for funds into equilibrium. This assumed that the rate of interest would always make savings and investment equal.

A criticism of the theory is that it attributed too much influence to the rate of interest. Experience shows that a fall in interest rates doesn't automatically encourage investment and later writers suggested that factors other than the rate of interest (e.g. businesspeople's expectations of the future) were also important in influencing the level of investment.

The Keynesian Theory: Liquidity Preference Theory

This theory was put forward by the English economist John Maynard Keynes in the 1930s. His theory looked at the demand and supply of money to explain how interest rates were determined. The supply of money was taken as fixed by the Central Bank and did not depend on the rate of interest, as depicted in the diagram below.

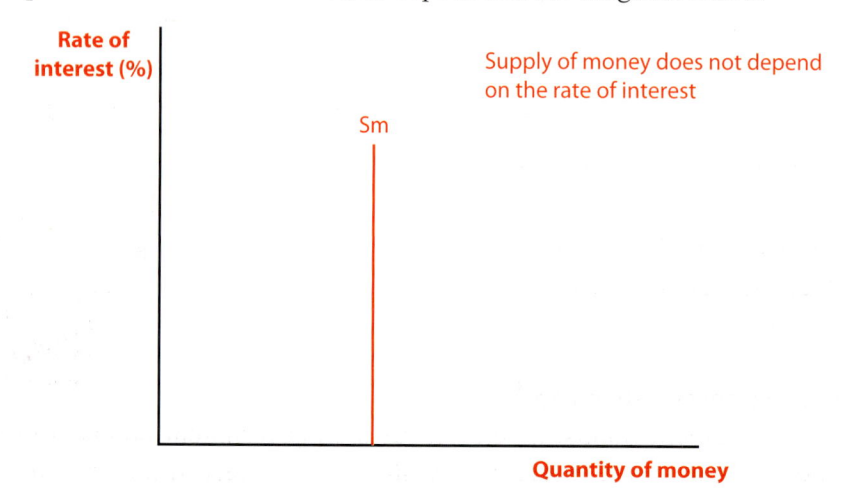

[Graph showing a vertical line labelled Sm. Axes: Rate of interest (%) (vertical), Quantity of money (horizontal). Annotation: "Supply of money does not depend on the rate of interest".]

According to Keynes, people desire money for its own sake and want to hold it in liquid form such as cash and current account bank balances, i.e. in a liquid state, hence the term 'liquidity preference theory'.

Keynes argued that there were three reasons why people wish to hold their wealth in a liquid state: transactions, precautionary and speculative motives.

Transactions Motive

Consumers require money for everyday purchases such as food, bills, petrol, etc. The amount required for this purpose mainly depends on income levels and is unaffected by changes in the rate of interest. If interest rates increase, the amount of money demanded for transactions purposes stays the same. If a person's income increases, then the demand for money for transactions purposes increases as consumption increases.

Precautionary Motive

People hold money in liquid form in case of emergencies, e.g. car repairs or unexpected spending such as a family wedding in Australia. The amount of money held for precautionary purposes mainly depends on income levels and is only slightly influenced by the rate of interest. However, if large changes occur in interest rates, then some of the money held for this purpose may be invested.

Speculative Motive

This is the third motive for keeping money in liquid form and is the most affected by changes in the rate of interest.

- People demand money (wealth in liquid form) because the return from investment (rate of interest) is too low.
- Similarly, if the return from investment is high (high interest rates), then the demand for money will be low.

When individuals invest, they can buy fixed-interest government bonds. If interest rates on government bonds are low, it is likely that they will rise in the future, so investors won't invest. If they did invest, they would be stuck with a fixed low-interest government bond. Instead, they hold their wealth in liquid form, i.e. **with low interest rates there will be a high demand for money**.

If interest rates are high there is a good chance that they will come down so investors will buy fixed bonds and the demand for money will be low, i.e. **with high interest rates the demand for money will be low.**

Positive Economics

> ### Example
>
> Suppose Pat buys a government bond (i.e. gives a loan to the government) for €100 with an interest rate of 5%. This means at some agreed date in the future Pat will receive the original €100 back plus annual interest payments of €5.
>
> In the meantime, interest rates on newer bonds rise to 10% and Pat wishes to sell the bond. Will Pat get €100? The answer is no. Who would be willing to buy a bond with a 5% interest rate when new bonds earn 10%? The value of Pat's bond is calculated as:
>
> $$\frac{\text{Original price of bond} \times \text{rate of interest on original bonds}}{\text{Rate of interest on new bonds}}$$
>
> $$= \frac{€100 \times 5}{10}$$
>
> $$= €50$$
>
> Therefore, when the rate of interest rises, the capital value of bonds falls.
>
> The higher the interest rate (i.e. bond yield), the more likely they are to fall in the future and people will want to hold investment bonds rather than money as there is the prospect of a capital gain. Likewise, when interest rates are low, people will hold money instead of bonds to avoid a capital loss.

We can now summarise the relationship between the demand for money and the rate of interest.

Transactions motive	Unrelated to the rate of interest
Precautionary motive	Slightly (negatively) related to the rate of interest
Speculative motive	Closely (negatively) related to the rate of interest

The demand for money is therefore a combination of the three motives discussed above. The demand for money is inversely related to the rate of interest. If the rate of interest is high, then the demand for money will be low and vice versa. Recall that the rate of interest is determined by the demand for and supply of money. The supply of money is fixed by the Central Bank and is perfectly inelastic and unaffected by the rate of interest. If we combine the demand for and supply of money, we find the equilibrium rate of interest (see Figure 2).

If the money supply was expanded by the Central Bank, then the rate of interest would fall (see Figure 3).

16: Capital

Summary

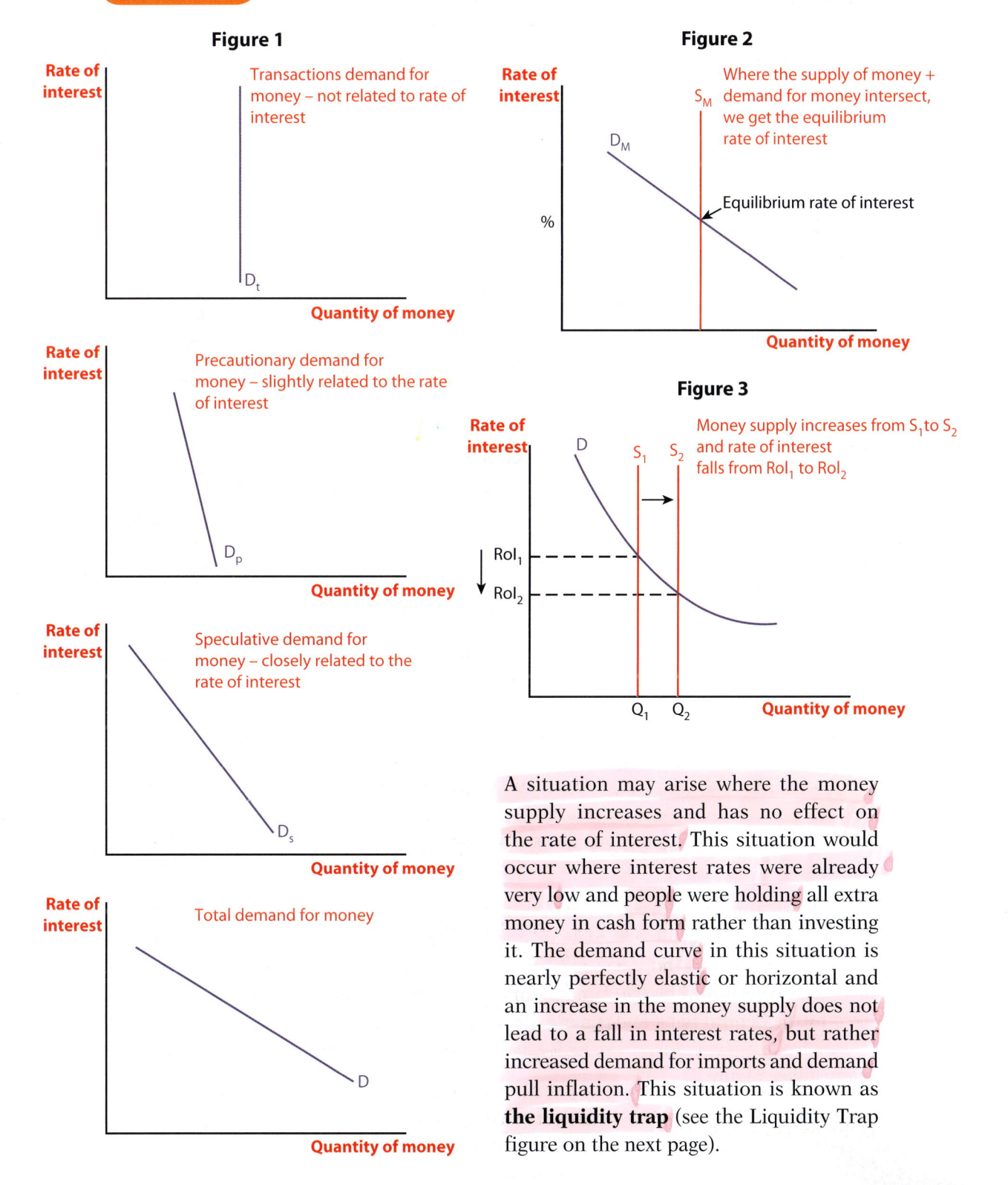

Figure 1

Transactions demand for money – not related to rate of interest

(Rate of interest vs Quantity of money; vertical line D_t)

Precautionary demand for money – slightly related to the rate of interest

(Rate of interest vs Quantity of money; steep downward curve D_p)

Speculative demand for money – closely related to the rate of interest

(Rate of interest vs Quantity of money; downward sloping line D_s)

Total demand for money

(Rate of interest vs Quantity of money; downward sloping line D)

Figure 2

Where the supply of money + demand for money intersect, we get the equilibrium rate of interest

(Rate of interest (%) vs Quantity of money; vertical S_M, downward D_M, intersection marked Equilibrium rate of interest)

Figure 3

Money supply increases from S_1 to S_2 and rate of interest falls from RoI_1 to RoI_2

(Rate of interest vs Quantity of money; demand curve D, vertical S_1 at Q_1 and S_2 at Q_2, with RoI_1 and RoI_2 marked)

A situation may arise where the money supply increases and has no effect on the rate of interest. This situation would occur where interest rates were already very low and people were holding all extra money in cash form rather than investing it. The demand curve in this situation is nearly perfectly elastic or horizontal and an increase in the money supply does not lead to a fall in interest rates, but rather increased demand for imports and demand pull inflation. This situation is known as **the liquidity trap** (see the Liquidity Trap figure on the next page).

Positive Economics

Liquidity Trap

Rate of interest — S_1, S_2

Money supply increases from S_1 to S_2 and equilibrium changes from Q_1 to Q_2 but has no effect on rate of interest

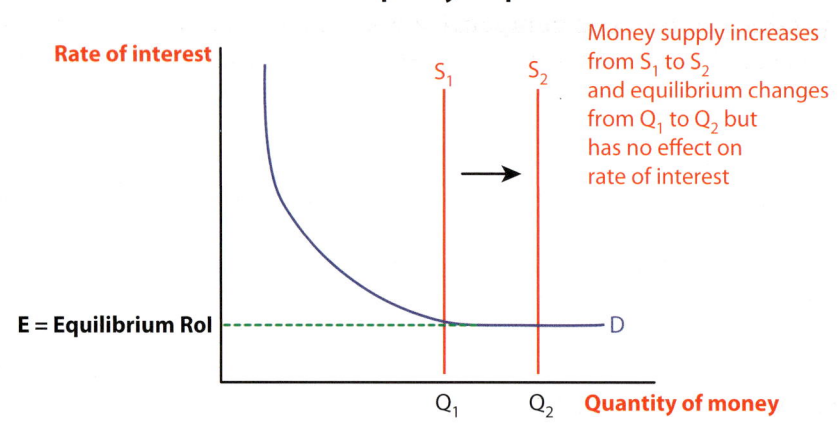

E = Equilibrium RoI — D

Q_1 Q_2 *Quantity of money*

> **Note:**
> A run on a bank is where there is huge demand on the part of depositors for their money back because there has been a collapse in confidence in the bank's ability to make good on its promises to customers. In this extreme circumstance, the European Central Bank as well as Ireland's Central Bank need to supply the banks with emergency money to ensure the financial institutions can give depositors their money. As a result, the supply of money can expand fast and in large amounts if it is called upon. There will be more discussion on this topic in Chapter 18.

EXAM ✓ Question 4(c), 2000 (25 marks)

Discuss the effects that a rise in interest rates may have on the Irish economy.

Solution

- **Borrowing discouraged:** Borrowing is now more expensive, resulting in higher loan repayments. This leads to reduced spending power and a lower standard of living.

- **Savings encouraged:** With higher rates of return, people may find it more attractive to save. This would decrease spending.

- **Value of the currency:** Rising interest rates offer a higher return on savings. As a result, if interest rates increase, this may attract international money into the eurozone, thereby increasing/protecting the value of the euro.

- **Costs of production/reduced competitiveness:** Production costs will increase due to the extra cost of capital, resulting in possible higher prices and/or a reduction in the numbers employed.

- **Disincentive to invest:** The MEC would fall, resulting in lower profits and discouraging investors. It becomes more expensive for businesses to borrow, so they may not invest.

- **Economic growth is hindered:** With possible lower investment, future economic growth in Ireland may be hindered.

- **Revenue received from DIRT:** With additional savings, the government may receive additional revenue through DIRT.

Sample Exam Question (15 marks)

Discuss the effect, if any, a fall in interest rates is generally expected to have on each of the following.

- The demand for money for transactionary motive reasons is not affected by the fall in the rate of interest. Why?

- The demand for money for precautionary reasons is affected slightly (negatively) by the rate of interest. Why?

- The demand for money for speculative reasons is greatly affected (negatively) by the rate of interest. Why?

Solution

- **Transactionary:** People need to have cash for day-to-day spending and this, allied to their level of income, not rates of interest, determines the motive.

- **Precautionary:** As interest rates fall slightly, more money will be held for precautionary purposes due to the opportunity cost of lower rates of interest.

- **Speculative:** As interest rates fall, more money will be held for speculative purposes as people will hold more wealth in cash form to profit from future higher rates of interest.

Questions

Short Questions

1. Define capital as a factor of production.
2. Explain how interest is the return to capital.
3. Define MEC.
4. Define the term 'savings'.
5. Define the term 'investment'.

Long Questions

1. State and explain the factors that influence MEC.
2. Distinguish between capital widening and capital deepening.
3. Discuss the factors that influence the amount saved by individuals in an economy.
4. State and explain five factors that influence the level of investment in an economy.
5. State and explain four reasons why investment is important to an economy.
6. Outline the loanable funds theory of interest rates.
7. Keynes outlined three motives for holding money. Explain these motives.
8. State and explain the effect of an increase in interest rates on the motives for holding money.
9. Explain why the production of capital goods is important for the economy.
10. Distinguish between gross and net investment.

Chapter 17: Enterprise and Profit

Specific Learning Outcomes

At the end of this chapter, students should be able to:

- [ ] Explain profit, supernormal profit, enterprise and entrepreneur.
- [ ] Identify different risk-takers in the economy.
- [ ] Explain why enterprise is a unique factor of production.
- [ ] Understand the role of the profit motive in an economy.
- [ ] Examine the role that entrepreneurs play in an economy.
- [ ] Identify the risks taken by businesses.
- [ ] Apply the concept of economic rent to enterprise.

Positive Economics

Steve Jobs was the co-founder of Apple Inc., which makes iPhones, iPods, iCloud, etc.

© Getty Images

Denis O'Brien set up and chaired the Esat Digifone consortium that won a mobile phone licence in the 1990s. The company was later called O2.

Bill Gates is the co-founder of Microsoft, the software company that developed Windows.

© Kevin Abosch

Moya Doherty is an Irish entrepreneur and the producer and co-founder of Riverdance.

Enterprise

Production will not take place in an economy unless someone takes the risk and the initiative in combining the other factors of production into a unit to produce goods and services. The entrepreneur is the person who undertakes this task.

> **ENTERPRISE** is the factor of production that organises other factors of production in order to produce a good or service and takes all the risk in the hope of making a profit. The return to enterprise is profit or loss.

Who Are the Risk-takers?

In Pat's Deli, where there is one owner, Pat is the risk-taker and bears any losses that may be incurred. In limited liability companies, there are many owners, called shareholders, and these risk-takers bear the loss (i.e. they won't receive dividends) if the firm doesn't perform well. In large state-owned companies, it is the public who are the risk-takers as they have to bear the losses in the form of increased taxation or decreased expenditure.

How Enterprise Differs from the Other Factors of Production

Enterprise differs (is unique) from the other factors of production in a number of ways.

It Can Earn a Loss

It is the only factor of production that can earn a loss. An entrepreneur sets out with the intention of making a profit, but due to a number of factors (e.g. fall in demand for the product or the entry of new competitors), they may sustain a loss. All the other factors of production are guaranteed a return.

Returns Can Vary

The return to enterprise can vary from supernormal profits to losses. This is not the case with the other factors, where a contractual entitlement exists, e.g. a worker receives an agreed wage. If raw material costs increase and sales revenue falls, then profits will be lower and the return to enterprise falls.

Return Is Residual

The return of the other factors of production is usually of a contractual nature, e.g. labour receives an agreed wage or finance is loaned for a specified rate of interest. However, the return to the entrepreneur is residual. Enterprise receives its return *after* all the other factors have received their payments.

Risks Involved in Running a Business

An entrepreneur faces many risks when setting up a business. These risks can be divided into two categories: insurable risks and non-insurable risks.

Insurable Risks

These are risks that can be mathematically estimated and an entrepreneur can insure against occurring. A premium will be paid in return for an insurance policy to provide for compensation in the event of a loss, e.g. theft of stock or cash, fire to premises and damage to stock caused by fire, accidents to members of staff and accidents to members of the public.

Non-insurable Risks

These are risks that the entrepreneur cannot insure against occurring. An insurance policy cannot be purchased to provide compensation and the entrepreneur suffers the entire loss, e.g. loss of profit. Examples of non-insurable risks are bad decision-making, industrial relations disputes, changes in taste or fashion away from the product, entry of competition into the market, changes in competitive conditions such as new legislation.

Positive Economics

CASE STUDY: Pat's Deli

Pat's Deli is not guaranteed to make a profit. If customer service slips or a new competitor enters the market, Pat could end up making a loss. On the other hand, Pat could offer new products and new services that customers love and the deli could make a huge supernormal profit. This illustrates how variable the returns could be. In addition, the rent, interest, wages and sundries need to be paid before Pat makes a (residual) profit. Finally, Pat can insure the building and against the theft of stock. However, there isn't any insurance company that will offer cover for a downturn in business.

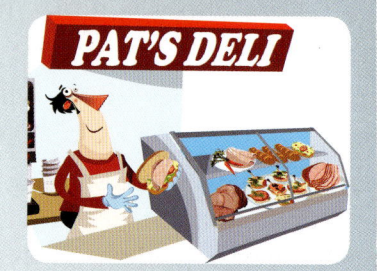

Profits

Normal Profits
Normal profit is the minimum amount of profit an entrepreneur must receive if they are to stay in production in the long run. It is the supply price of the factor of production enterprise.

Supernormal Profits (SNP)
SNP is any profit earned by an entrepreneur in excess of normal profit. If the minimum profit that Pat must earn to stay in business is €50,000 and he earns €60,000, then SNP is €10,000. This is an example of economic rent if it lasts in the long run and an example of a quasi rent if it's earned in the short term.

Implicit and Explicit Costs and Profit
In the first year of trading Pat pays out explicit costs (insurance, wages, light and heat, etc.) of €30,000 and sales revenue amounts to €60,000. An accountant would calculate profit as €30,000.

However, an economist would note that Pat does not take a wage in the first year of trading to keep costs down. Pat could have earned €20,000 elsewhere. This is considered to be an implicit cost. An economist would therefore calculate profit as €30,000 – €20,000 = €10,000.

Why Are Profits Important in a Market Economy?

Nobody would set up a business if they thought they would make a loss and lose their investment. Risk-takers need to think that they will at least earn normal profit before they undertake the task. Consequently, profits are important for a number of reasons.

Encourage Risk-taking
Profits are a prerequisite for encouraging entrepreneurs to undertake the risks inherent in business. Without profits, firms would not supply goods and services.

17: Enterprise and Profit

Indicate the Best Use of Resources/Consumer Demand
Profits are an indication to entrepreneurs as to what goods and services consumers want (demand) and hence indicate the areas that are the most suitable for the use of scarce resources. The absence of normal profits indicates the unpopularity of such goods and leads to the eventual withdrawal from production.

Encourage Investment
If profits are earned, entrepreneurs are encouraged to invest in further ventures. Indeed, if SNP is being earned this could encourage the entry of new firms into the industry and increase the quantity of the good being supplied on the market.

Provide Funds for Expansion
Entrepreneurs may use the profits earned to invest in their existing business and to expand their existing activities and diversify production. The use of internal funds is a cheaper source of finance than bank borrowings.

Continuity of Production
If normal profits are not earned, an entrepreneur will cease trading. Therefore, profits are essential to ensure that production continues. Normal profit is the minimum price that must be paid in order to ensure the entrepreneur continues to operate into the future.

SNP Rewards Innovation
Those entrepreneurs who earn SNP do so because they may be more efficient and innovative, i.e. introducing new commodities and improving existing ones, or because they are minimising their cost of production.

Source of Revenue to the Government
Any profits earned by entrepreneurs are taxed by the government and thus become a source of revenue for the state. These profits can be used by the government for day-to-day spending or to further develop infrastructure and hence increase the growth potential of the economy.

SNPs May Promote Mergers/Takeovers
The existence of SNPs within some industries may entice large multinationals to take over these profitable businesses so that they increase their overall profit or gain a foothold in various markets.

The Importance of Entrepreneurs in an Economy

Entrepreneurs are an important group in an economy for the following reasons:

They Create Employment
Entrepreneurs need workers to produce goods and services. They also take pressure off the government by creating jobs. The creation of a healthy private sector that creates jobs means less social welfare payments by the government.

Positive Economics

They Organise Production
Entrepreneurs organise the other factors of production into production units in the hope of making a profit. They are risk-takers. They also increase the choice of goods and services available to the public.

They Decide What Prices to Be Charged
Entrepreneurs decide what prices to charge for their goods and services, hoping there will be demand at these prices levels. Competition amongst businesses can lead to lower prices and better services.

They Encourage Further Investment
Entrepreneurs put both their money and skills into a business in the hope of making a profit and this may encourage further investment in the economy if successful. These desirable results may encourage others to undertake similar risks and set up businesses.

They Provide an Investment Outlet for Savers' Funds
Entrepreneurs provide an investment outlet for savers' funds, generating a return on savings.

They Generate Revenue for the Government
Entrepreneurs help generate revenue for the government through taxation revenues on profits earned. They also contribute employer's PRSI to the exchequer as well as reduce the government's social welfare bill.

They Create Wealth in the Country
Successful entrepreneurs create wealth (increase in GNP), which helps increase the standard of living in a country.

Do All Entrepreneurs Earn the Same Level of Profit?

Now that we have discussed the importance of entrepreneurs and the role of profits in an economy, we now ask, 'Do all entrepreneurs earn the same level of profit?'

NO.

All entrepreneurs don't earn the same level of profit. They are not an identical group; some are more gifted than others. The more gifted entrepreneurs can earn well in excess of normal profit due to business acumen or superior ability and this

> **RENT OF ABILITY** is the economic rent/SNP earned by an entrepreneur due to their business acumen, innate talent or natural talent, e.g. a Premier football player has superior football skills and talent.

will not be competed away with the entry of new firms. These earnings in excess of normal profit (SNP) are often referred to as 'rent of ability' and are an example of an economic rent earned by the factor of production enterprise. However, entrepreneurs working in a more competitive industry may earn lower profits than other entrepreneurs in a less competitive environment.

17: Enterprise and Profit

How Can Enterprise Be Encouraged?

Enterprise is an important factor in stimulating economic growth, creating jobs and increasing the standard of living in a country. So how can this vital activity be encouraged?

A government can try to create an enterprise culture by giving incentives and tax breaks to new start-up companies. The mass media could highlight successful companies and entrepreneurs, thus creating an optimistic economic outlook. The availability of credit *banks* and low interest repayments would lower the cost of and encourage risk-taking. Some other ideas that would incentivise enterprise include relaxing business regulation and reducing administrative payments. *Low corporation tax*

EXAM ✓ Question 3(a)(iii), 2010 (10 marks)

Do all entrepreneurs earn the same level of profit? Explain your answer.

Solution

No, all entrepreneurs don't earn the same level of profit. This is due to rent of ability. Some are better than others and can earn SNP or an economic rent. Entrepreneurs cannot be replaced easily by another because of talent and business acumen possessed. If the entrepreneur works in a competitive industry, they may earn lower profits than an entrepreneur in a less competitive industry.

EXAM ✓ Question 8, 2010 (17 marks)

Explain, with the aid of an example, the meaning of the term 'rent of ability'.

Solution

Rent of ability is the economic rent/SNP earned by an entrepreneur due to their business acumen, innate talent or natural talent, e.g. a Premier league footballer has superior football skills and talent.

Positive Economics

Questions

Short Questions

1. Explain the term 'entrepreneur'.
2. Define enterprise as a factor of production.
3. What is the price paid for enterprise?
4. Identify three different categories of risk-takers in an economy.
5. Explain the term 'normal profit'.

Long Questions

1. Explain and illustrate how normal profit is the supply price for the factor of production enterprise.
2. Do all entrepreneurs earn the same level of profit? Explain your answer.
3. State and explain the role profits play in a market economy.
4. Entrepreneurs play a vital role the economy. Do you agree? Why or why not?
5. State and explain two examples each of insurable and non-insurable risks that entrepreneurs bear.
6. State and explain how enterprise is a unique factor of production.
7. State and explain how enterprise might be encouraged.
8. Explain how economic rent is applied to the factor of production enterprise.
9. Explain the term 'rent of ability'. Can this be earned in the long run?
10. Distinguish between normal and supernormal profit.

Chapter 18 | Money and Banking

Specific Learning Outcomes

At the end of this chapter, students should be able to:

- Define money and legal tender.
- Analyse the functions that money performs and the properties required to fulfil this role successfully.
- Explain the main forms of money in use in a modern economy.
- Define monetary policy.
- Describe examples of cashless transactions.
- Outline the role of national financial institutions.
- Outline the current role and functions of the Central Bank.
- Outline the current role and functions of the European Central Bank (ECB).
- Evaluate the ECB's policies/actions on the Irish economy.
- Critically analyse the suitability of these policies for the Irish economy.
- Differentiate between the nominal interest rate and the real interest rate.
- Outline the factors that influence the rate of interest and their economic effects.
- Demonstrate how financial institutions can create credit.
- Discuss the limitations on an institution's ability to create credit.
- Analyse the changes in the demand and supply of money.
- Critically analyse the implications of an excess supply of credit on the economy.
- Examine how a financial institution reconciles liquidity with profitability.
- Analyse the need for regulation of the financial sector.

Positive Economics

Introduction

Imagine a bank employee who wants to produce their own car, from scratch, in order to get to work. Many individuals have natural talents as well as skills that have been studied and perfected. If we, as individual consumers, do not wish to produce or supply all that we require, we will often purchase from those who specialise in the particular product/service we need or want.

However, specialisation can't provide us, as consumers, with all our economics needs. In order to obtain additional goods and services that we need and/or want, we can engage in exchange, which is vital in all modern economies. **Money** acts as the connecting link in the exchange process.

A History of Money

During the ninth century AD, the Danes had an expression, 'to pay through the nose'. It comes from the practice of cutting the noses off people who were careless in paying the Danish poll tax.

Bartering and the Commodity System

Before the introduction of money, individuals and businesses directly exchanged goods and services for other goods and services. This is known as the barter system.

Barter is an extremely intricate method of exchange and its disadvantages outweigh its benefits significantly when trading in modern economies. Some form of money had to be introduced for the following reasons.

- **Double coincidence of needs and wants:** If I want to exchange goods, I must find a person who is willing to purchase the good that I have to sell and is also selling the good that I want to purchase. How likely is this to happen?
- **Uncertainty of exchange rate:** For example, I am selling beef and want to purchase potatoes. How many potatoes will I receive in exchange for one side of beef, and do I need or want all the potatoes I will receive in this exchange?
- **Goods are not of uniform quality:** If I accept that one side of beef equals three bags of vegetables, there may well be differences in the quality of vegetables.
- **Problem of divisibility:** Someone with a valuable item to trade, e.g. a bicycle, will encounter great difficulty if they only want a small item.

- **Specialisation and division of labour in the economy are discouraged:** A specialised worker such as a dentist or teacher would find it very difficult to barter their professional services for food, clothing and shelter.

In order to overcome the double coincidence of needs and wants of the barter system, humans developed commodity money, i.e. a basic item used by almost everyone. In addition to acting as a means of exchange, these commodities were also useful due to their own intrinsic value. Some early examples included cattle and seeds in ancient Ireland, whale teeth in Fiji, salt in ancient Rome and cowries (brightly coloured shells) in India. However, using commodities as money had other problems. For example, they may be difficult to store, carry and preserve.

Coinage – The Beginning

Precious metals such as gold and silver had the most desirable characteristics for money. They were easily recognisable, acceptable, durable, scarce and could be subdivided into small units.

Metal was used because it was readily available, easy to work with and could be recycled. Since coins were given a certain value, it became easier to compare the cost of items people wanted.

Banking

People who had accrued large amounts of precious metals such as gold were worried about the safety of such valuable commodities. Merchants stored their gold with goldsmiths who possessed private vaults and charged a fee for that service. In exchange for each deposit of precious metal, the goldsmiths issued receipts certifying the quantity and purity of the metal they held in trust. The depositor expressly allowed the goldsmith to use the money for any purpose, including advances to his customers. Gold deposits were relatively stable, often remaining with the goldsmith for years on end, so there was little risk of default assuming the public had trust in the goldsmith's integrity and financial soundness was maintained.

During the 18th century, goldsmiths found new ways of increasing their profits. It seemed unlikely that all the depositors would wish to withdraw all their gold at the same time. They began to issue receipts to those who did not hold deposits of gold, for a charge, and for amounts in excess of the actual lodgements they held. In doing so, the first system of credit creation began. This was naturally a risky system, but as long as there wasn't any run on the bank by depositors to convert receipts into gold all at the same time, it was a lucrative, successful business and a system that worked smoothly. However, if a large volume of people did demand their gold back, the goldsmith would not have had sufficient amounts to honour all the receipts. People would then lose confidence in goldsmiths' receipts as money and the goldsmiths would be put out of business as bankers.

Positive Economics

Representative Money and Convertible Currencies

Token money may be called representative money in the sense that a piece of paper might represent or be a claim on a commodity as opposed to being intrinsically valuable itself. All token money was initially convertible – it could be exchanged into gold on demand.

A currency where notes are fully backed and redeemable in an equivalent amount of gold is often called THE GOLD STANDARD.

With the outbreak of World War I, Britain was forced to abandon the Gold Standard even for their international transactions. Other nations quickly followed suit.

Fiduciary issue is that proportion of a country's currency that is not backed by gold but by foreign currencies and securities. This is a concept based on trust.

Fiduciary Issue

As time passed the governments began to regulate the issue of notes by the banks, as the value of notes issued exceeded the reserves of gold to back these issues.

After a brief attempt to revive the Gold Standard during the 1920s, it finally collapsed in 1931. However, people continued to accept bank notes and coins because they had confidence in them, as the government declares it to be legal tender.

MONEY is defined as anything that is generally accepted by people in exchange for goods and services or repayment of debt.

Functions of Money

A Medium of Exchange

The primary function of money is to act as a medium of exchange. People who supply labour exchange their work for money. This money is then used to purchase goods and services from retailers. As a medium of exchange, money overcomes the major disadvantage of the barter system (the double coincidence of needs and wants). Trading is made much easier and straightforward by using money.

A Measure of Value/Unit of Account

Money enables us to measure exactly how much something is worth and provides us with a framework whereby we can relate the value of one item to the value of another. Knowing the value or price of a good in terms of money enables both the supplier and the purchaser of the good to make decisions about how much of the good to supply and how much of the good to purchase. This unit of measurement allows for a quick comparison of prices across goods (i.e. relative prices). For example, if Product X costs €10 and Product Y costs €30, this indicates that Product Y is three times more valuable than Product X.

A Standard for Deferred Payments

When debts are denominated in money, the real value of debts may change due to inflation and deflation.

A Store of Value/Wealth

In order to be a medium of exchange, money must hold its value over time. Therefore, money must be a store of value or saving of wealth. A euro today needs to have the power to purchase goods in the future.

As a store of value, money is not unique. Land, houses, jewellery, boats and works of art can provide a better store of value in certain circumstances. People can accumulate wealth knowing that it will be equally acceptable as payment for goods and services at some future date. People can deposit their earnings in bank accounts and financial institutions.

Life using barter vs. money

Question: What is the opportunity cost of a movie in terms of chocolate?

Good	Price in units of another good
Movie	2 six-packs of cola
Can of cola	2 ice cream cones
Ice cream	3 packets of sweets
Sweets	2 bars of chocolate
Chocolate	3 texts on your mobile

In an inflationary period, money loses some of its value when stored or saved during a period of rising prices. For example, €100 buys 100 items today at €1. If the price rises to €1.10 next year, then €100 can only buy 90 whole items. As a result, a store of cash loses some of its value due to inflationary pressures. This may discourage conventional savings and force people to store any excess wealth they possess in appreciating assets such as those listed above. However, money is more liquid than most other stores of value because as a medium of exchange, it is readily accepted everywhere. (Liquidity is simply a measure of how easy it is to turn assets into consumption. Furthermore, money is an easily transported store of value that is available in a number of convenient denominations.) Therefore, although money is not a perfect store of value as it loses buying power over time, its high liquidity can explain why everybody holds some of their assets as money.

Characteristics of Money

Instantly Recognisable as Genuine
People must be in no doubt of the authenticity of the item being used as money. If not, they simply will not accept it and it would no longer be recognised as money. The watermark and metal strip are used in paper currency for this reason. In addition, money must be a specific weight, measure or size to be accountable. For instance, coins are often milled with a reeded edge so that any removal of material from the coin (lowering its commodity value) would be easy to detect. As a result, the production of counterfeit money is made much more difficult.

Generally Acceptable
People using money should feel a sense of security and confidence in it as a medium of exchange, a measure of value, a store of wealth and a standard of deferred payments. If confidence is lost in the commodity, it will no longer be acceptable as a form of exchange for goods and services.

Portable
Money must be easy to carry and light for individuals and customers who are engaging in trade and monetary transactions. It must also be capable of being transported discreetly, safely and in large value if necessary.

Reasonably Durable and Long Lasting
Money must be tough, durable and able to withstand the vast amount of handling it receives. From a practical perspective it also cuts down on the costs of having to replace it. Tissue paper or pieces of chalk would not make very durable forms of money. The Australian dollar is so durable it physically cannot be torn.

Divisible into Units of Small Value
Money must come in different denominations so that the purchase of both large and small items is facilitated. Smaller denominations enable the trade of goods of low value and also enable sellers to give change after the transaction.

Scarce in Relation to the Demand for It
We have already studied this to be a characteristic of any good that has a value. If money is too plentiful, it would quickly lose its value. This is one of the reasons why a government cannot solve a country's financial problems simply by printing infinite amounts of money.

Homogonous and Fungible
One unit must be perceived as equivalent in value to any other. For instance, if one coin contains more silver than another coin then people will place a greater value on the coin with the higher silver content and the exchange process will be disturbed. That is why

diamonds, works of art or real estate are not suitable as money.

Forms of Money

Cash (Notes and Coins)

Cash (i.e. legal tender) is the official currency of a country, which creditors are legally required to accept in payment of debts owed to them. In Ireland, euro notes are legal tender up to unlimited amounts, while the euro coins are legal tender up to specified amounts.

> ### A point to ponder
>
> **Why can't we just print enough money so that everybody in the world has enough?**
>
> If we all had more money than we needed, we wouldn't need to work for more money ... and neither would anybody else! If we wanted a loaf of bread, who would bother to set up an expensive bakery to make it? Who would set up a shop to devote their time to selling bread when they had all the money they wanted? They could go on holidays, but who would bother to make a plane or a car to bring them there? They could read books, but who would write them, publish them and sell them? They could go shopping, but to what shops? In fact, if we just kept printing money, we would probably starve and have nothing to do!

Cheques

As an alternative to money, you could write a cheque to make a payment, although this is not as common as it once was. It must be noted that cheques are *not* money and are *not* legal tender, therefore a creditor is not legally required to accept a cheque in settlement of

> **LEGAL TENDER** is money that must be accepted if offered as payment for a purchase or settlement of a debt.

a debt. A cheque is simply an instruction for a bank to transfer funds from one account holder to another. The actual transfer is the final payment for goods and services.

Electronic Payments/Plastic Money

The fastest-growing form of payments are electronic payments. More and more transactions are becoming electronic because they are easy and because using a paper trail, e.g. cheques, is more costly. The money is automatically withdrawn from your account. Most electronic payments take the form of plastic money (ATM cards, debit cards and credit cards). There is strong evidence to support the benefits of a move to a cashless society.

Automated Teller Machine (ATM) Cards

Cardholders can withdraw cash from or lodge cash to their current account as well as transfer money between accounts. ATMs and cards have been an evolution of banking services. You can even top up your credit on your mobile phone using an ATM.

Debit Cards

Debit cards are payment cards that allow the user to pay for goods and services electronically instead of using cash, cheques or a credit card. Each card contains a personalised chip and the holder of the card must enter a personalised identification number (PIN) into the retailer's machine. The buyer's current account is electronically debited by the amount of the purchase, while the retailer's account is credited. It is a safe, fast and convenient form of purchasing without incurring credit from the financial institution.

Credit Cards

Credit cards, e.g. Visa, MasterCard, are mainly issued through banks to current account holders. Credit cards also facilitate cash withdrawals. Essentially, the credit card holder is taking out a (short-term) loan of money from the bank, which must be paid back with interest. It is important to note that credit cards are *not* money.

We have had paper currency for only about 150 years and ATMs for only 35 years, so it is hard to forecast how money will evolve. Clearly there is a huge movement towards electronic payments. Telephone banking is now well established and internet banking has grown at an unprecedented rate over the last number of years. Technology is now available to use your mobile phone as your credit card. In the future, perhaps cash will be phased out!

Evolution of Payments System

Barter
↓
Precious metals, i.e. gold and silver (commodity money)
↓
Paper currency (fiat money)
↓
Cheques
↓
Electronic means of payment
↓
Electronic money, i.e. debit cards and credit cards
↓
Internet banking, e.g. PayPal

The European Central Bank (ECB)

The European Central Bank is responsible for conducting monetary policy in the eurozone. The bank was formed in Frankfurt, Germany in June 1998 and works with the central national banks of each of the EU member states to formulate the European System of Central Banks (ESCB).

18: Money and Banking

A point to ponder

What if we didn't use money to buy things?

Let's pretend we use lollipops instead! If you took 100 lollipops to Spain and tried to buy your dinner with them, you couldn't because the owner of the restaurant couldn't use them to pay its staff, suppliers, etc. Similarly, imagine carrying all of your spending money in the form of lollipops. You would have to bring a suitcase with you to go food shopping! Further still, could you envisage how a lollipop ATM would work? Also, you couldn't offer half a lollipop – all you could do is offer multiple lollipops for goods. How could you carry enough lollipops with you to buy a car or an expensive dress? What's more if you ate 10 lollipops today, you would probably be sick of them and not want any more tomorrow. You could offer millions of lollipops to somebody in exchange for a house, but there is no way they would accept them, as no amount of lollipops could come near the value of a home. Lollipops are in negligible demand relative to money. Finally, imagine trying to price things. An ice cream costs four lollipops. A sandwich costs three ice creams. A drink costs one sandwich and one ice cream. How much is all that in lollipops? It is so much simpler to use a commodity generally accepted all over the world that is light to carry, divisible to 1c and is in demand by everybody.

The key functions of the ECB are as follows.

- **Maintain price stability:** The key aim of the ECB is to maintain price stability within the eurozone. This is done by closely monitoring inflation in member countries and assessing the risk it poses to price stability. The base ECB interest rate is adjusted so as to influence consumer spending and investment. Interest rate changes are used to keep inflation under control.

- **Formulates and implements EU monetary policy:** The ECB monitors and influences rates of interest, money supply, credit availability and the protection of the value of the euro. The ECB also ensures that the financial markets and institutions are adequately supervised and that the payment systems function smoothly.

> **MONETARY POLICY:** Those actions by the ECB that influence money supply, interest rates and the availability of credit.

- **Holds and manages the official reserve of the euro area countries:** The EU holds gold, foreign currencies and other reserves as security against the issue of the euro. The ECB manages these reserves on behalf of the countries and buys or sells currencies when necessary to influence exchange rates in balance.

- **Financial stability and supervision:** The member authorities must provide meticulous supervision of credit institutions and ensure stability in the financial system.
- **Sole right to issue euro currency:** The ECB has the exclusive right to authorise the issuance of banknotes and coins by central banks within the euro area.

How the ECB Implements Monetary Policy within the Eurozone Countries

Monitoring the Growth of the Money Supply (Relative to Its Value)
The ECB monitors the growth of the money supply to ensure the euro holds its value.

Engaging in Open Market Operations
The ECB has the power to shrink the amount of money available by open market operations, i.e. sucking up excess liquidity in the system by borrowing money from banks and governments (selling bonds).

Interest Rates
If the cost of money increases, people will borrow less to consume and use for investment and vice versa. As a result, interest rates are a potent tool for influencing inflation. The ECB has the power to increase or decrease interest rates across the eurozone (all the countries in the EU that use the euro).

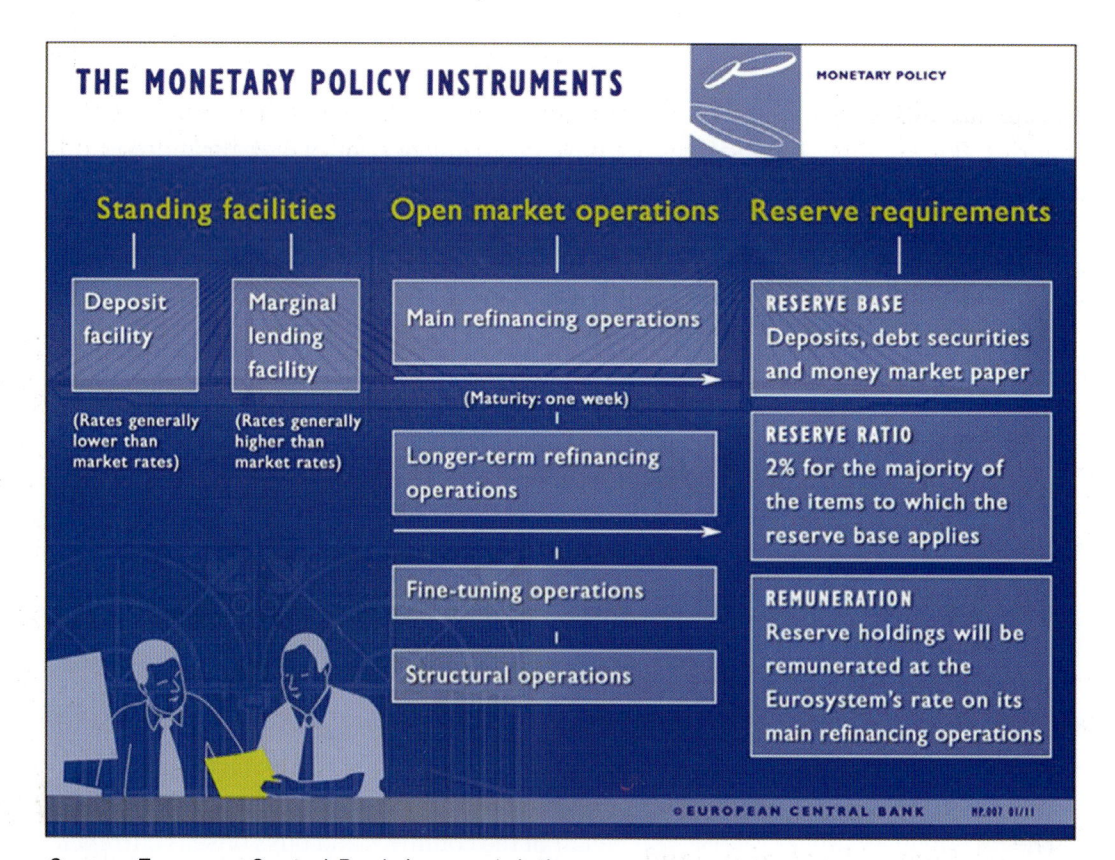

THE MONETARY POLICY INSTRUMENTS

MONETARY POLICY

Standing facilities		Open market operations	Reserve requirements
Deposit facility	Marginal lending facility	Main refinancing operations (Maturity: one week)	**RESERVE BASE** Deposits, debt securities and money market paper
(Rates generally lower than market rates)	(Rates generally higher than market rates)	Longer-term refinancing operations	**RESERVE RATIO** 2% for the majority of the items to which the reserve base applies
		Fine-tuning operations	**REMUNERATION** Reserve holdings will be remunerated at the Eurosystem's rate on its main refinancing operations
		Structural operations	

© EUROPEAN CENTRAL BANK

Source: European Central Bank (www.ecb.int).

THE USE OF STANDING FACILITIES

- **Marginal lending facility:** The facility to borrow money from the ECB against appropriate collateral affects the rate of interest charged by banks to customers.
- **Deposit facility:** The facility to make overnight deposits with the ECB affects the rate of interest paid to depositors.

MINIMUM RESERVE REQUIREMENTS

The ECB requires credit institutions established in the euro area to hold deposits on accounts with their national central bank. These are called minimum or required reserves.

The ECB has one primary objective: to maintain price stability. Specifically, it aims to keep inflation rates below 2% over the medium term.

The ECB and Ireland

The ECB has an immense impact on the Irish economy and specifically the banking sector, particularly through the following ways.

MONETARY POLICY

The ECB has full control over Ireland's monetary policy, as Ireland is one of the eurozone countries. For example, Ireland does not have independent control over its interest rates – these are set for the eurozone as a whole. As a result, if Irish inflation is low, interest rates could still rise. In addition, the ECB has the power to affect the euro exchange rate, which would affect our balance of trade and balance of payments. Finally, the ECB can influence the money supply and our banks' minimum reserve requirements, which directly impacts the amount of money in circulation as well as our banks' ability to create credit.

EMERGENCY LIQUIDITY ASSISTANCE (ELA)

In terms of banking crises, the ECB can provide emergency liquidity assistance, i.e. cheap emergency loans to banks that are running out of funds.

The Central Bank of Ireland

The Central Bank Reform Act 2010 created a new single unitary body, the Central Bank of Ireland, responsible for both central banking and financial regulation.

Banc Ceannais na hÉireann
Central Bank of Ireland

Eurosystem

©The Central Bank of Ireland

The Role of the Central Bank of Ireland

PRINTS/ISSUES LEGAL TENDER
- The Central Bank has the sole authority to print and mint euro currency in Ireland and is based in Sandyford, Dublin.
- It distributes the euro through the financial institutions within Ireland.

GOVERNMENT BANK
All monies received by the government and paid out go through its account with the Central Bank.

REGULATOR OF FINANCIAL SECTOR AND ISSUES LICENCES TO FINANCIAL INSTITUTIONS
The Central Bank issues licenses and regulates the financial sector in Ireland, including credit unions, building societies, banks, etc.

OFFICIAL EXTERNAL RESERVES
The Central Bank manages the country's official holdings of gold, foreign currencies and other reserves held as security against the issue of the euro. It manages these reserves on behalf of the country.

MAINTAINS PRICE STABILITY
The Central Bank is responsible for maintaining price stability in Ireland through the implementation of ECB decisions on monetary policy via open market operations.

FINANCIAL STABILITY
- The key role the Central Bank plays is to ensure the stability of the overall financial system.
- Financial stability analysis involves researching the stability of the financial system overall as well as its relationship with the real economy.

PROVIDES CONSUMER INFORMATION/ECONOMIC RESEARCH – CENTRAL BANK REPORTS
The Central Bank regularly provides information on many aspects of the economy.

CONSUMER PROTECTION
- The Central Bank is responsible for ensuring that the best interests of consumers of financial services are protected.
- The Central Bank introduces and monitors compliance with statutory codes of conduct and sets minimum competency standards for firms.

THE BANKERS' BANK
The Central Bank also acts as the bankers' bank in two ways:
- **Clearinghouse department:** All commercial banks maintain clearing accounts with the Central Bank to settle debts that may arise between themselves due to the cheque system.

- **Lender of last resort:** Offers credit to financial institutions that are experiencing financial difficulties/problems and are unable to obtain the necessary funds elsewhere, e.g. on the interbank money market.

Commercial (Retail) Banks

Commercial banks handle banking needs for large and small businesses and individuals, including:

- Current and savings accounts.
- Personal and business deposits.
- Credit cards, mortgages and personal loans.
- Advice to businesses.
- Processing payments and transactions.
- Night safe facilities.
- Foreign exchange.
- Act as trustees and executors of wills.

COMMERCIAL BANKS are institutions that provide deposit and lending services to personal consumers and businesses.

Examples of commercial (retail) banks in Ireland include AIB (Allied Irish Bank), Bank of Ireland and Ulster Bank.

Other Types of Banks

Merchant (Wholesale) Banks

A merchant bank deals with the commercial banking needs of international finance, long-term company loans and stock underwriting.

Industrial Banks

Industrial banks specialise in providing instalment credit to personal borrowers and companies in the form of fixed-term loans and hire purchase facilities.

Credit Unions

A credit union is a group of people who save together and lend to each other. Every credit union is owned by the members, i.e. the people who save and borrow with it. A member places their deposits with the credit union and these savings contribute to the loan fund and so enable other members to borrow.

A credit union exists only to serve its members and not to profit from their needs. Surplus income generated is returned to the members by way of a dividend and/or is directed to improved or additional services required by members.

Positive Economics

Post Office

An Post is a national organisation that provides a wide range of services which encompass postal, communication, retail and financial services. People can buy savings products offered by An Post, as it acts as an agent of the National Treasury Management Agency (NTMA).

Measuring the Supply of Money

Money Supply

Currency in circulation ⎫
Current account balances ⎬ M1 ⎫
Deposit account balances ⎭ ⎬ M2 ⎫
All other loan instruments up to two years ⎭ ⎬ M3

For example:

- Repo agreements is the sale and repurchase of securities in exchange for a fixed amount of cash. For example, if Bank A needed to borrow money, it could do so by providing some collateral to another party, i.e. a repo provider. However, the defining characteristic of a repurchase is that as soon as the transaction takes place, they make an instant agreement on when the money and collateral are to be returned to each other.
- Money market securities are highly liquid, short-term loans.
- Debt securities are loans that can be bought or sold on a stock exchange. For example, if a government issues a two-year note, it borrows from individual people and promises to pay them back in 10 years with interest.

Banking Ratios

The Primary Liquidity Ratio/Liquidity Coverage Ratio

The **PRIMARY LIQUIDITY RATIO/LIQUIDITY COVERAGE RATIO** is the amount of money with respect to short-term deposits that the Central Bank requires commercial banks to keep in cash form.

Example Consider that the liquidity coverage ratio is 10.5%. For every €100 deposited, the bank will need to hold on to (and not lend out) €10.50 in cash.

- The net stable funding ratio ensures that long-term assets are to be funded with long-term liabilities.

18: Money and Banking

> The **CAPITAL ADEQUACY RATIO** is the percentage of a bank's capital to its risk-weighted assets. Tier 1 capital is comprised of profits (i.e. retained earnings) and certain types of shares. Effectively, this is the amount of back-up a bank has apart from cash as security, e.g. common shares.

Note:
The secondary liquidity ratio has been terminated in accordance with Article 104 of the Maastricht Treaty.

Class Task
Research Article 104 of the Maastricht Treaty 1992 and how it has affected the Ireland of today.

How Do Banks Create Credit?

Commercial banks have the ability to create credit. They can do this as follows.

Example

2002			
Assets	**€**	**Liabilities**	**€**
Cash lodged	100	Deposits	100
Loan	900	New deposits	900
Total assets	**1,000**	**Total liabilities**	**1,000**

- Customer X lodges €100 into the bank.
- In general, the bank knows that only 10% of total deposits are demanded in cash by customers.
- With this €100, the bank has enough cash to support deposits of €1,000. The bank can create another €900 in deposits; it does this by giving out loans of €900.
- For example, the Central Bank could specify that only 10% of its total deposits will be demanded in cash, so €100 cash is sufficient for this purpose (€1,000 x 10% = €100). This is shown in the new balance sheet.

Positive Economics

Balance sheet of a bank

Assets		Liabilities	
Cash lodged by X	€100	X's deposit	€100
Total assets	€100	Total liabilities	€100

Balance sheet of a bank

Assets		Liabilities	
Cash lodged by X	€100	Deposits	€100
Loan	€900	New deposits	€900
Total assets	€1,000	Total liabilities	€1,000

As you can see in the above example, the more people that borrow from the bank, the more credit it creates.

But that's not all! If the bank only needed to hold 5% of deposits, it could create even more credit. On the other hand, if the bank was required to retain 15% of all deposits, its ability to create credit would be constrained. The Central Bank could specify that this primary liquidity ratio is 5%, 10%, 15%, etc.

We can summarise this in the formula below:

$$\text{Increase in credit} = \text{Increase in cash deposits} \times \frac{1}{\text{Bank reserve ratio}}$$

A Bank's Twin Objectives – Profitability and Liquidity

- **Profitability:** Refers to the need for a bank to make as much profit as possible from its assets to satisfy its shareholders. The more profitable the asset is, the less liquid it is.

- **Liquidity:** Refers to a bank's need to have liquid assets in order to meet the demand for cash by its customers. The more liquid the asset is, the less profitable it is.

How does the bank reconcile these twin objectives?

- Banks must satisfy their customers' need for cash, i.e. they must have enough liquidity. They could do this by holding all their assets in cash.
- However, cash doesn't earn interest and banks also wish to be profitable.
- Banks tend to compromise in having sufficient liquidity and yet earning profits by implementing the following portfolio:

- It will keep the majority of its assets in the form of loans and overdrafts. These assets earn profits but are not very liquid.
- It will require sufficient assets in cash and liquid form to meet the cash requirements of their customers. These assets are liquid but earn little profit.

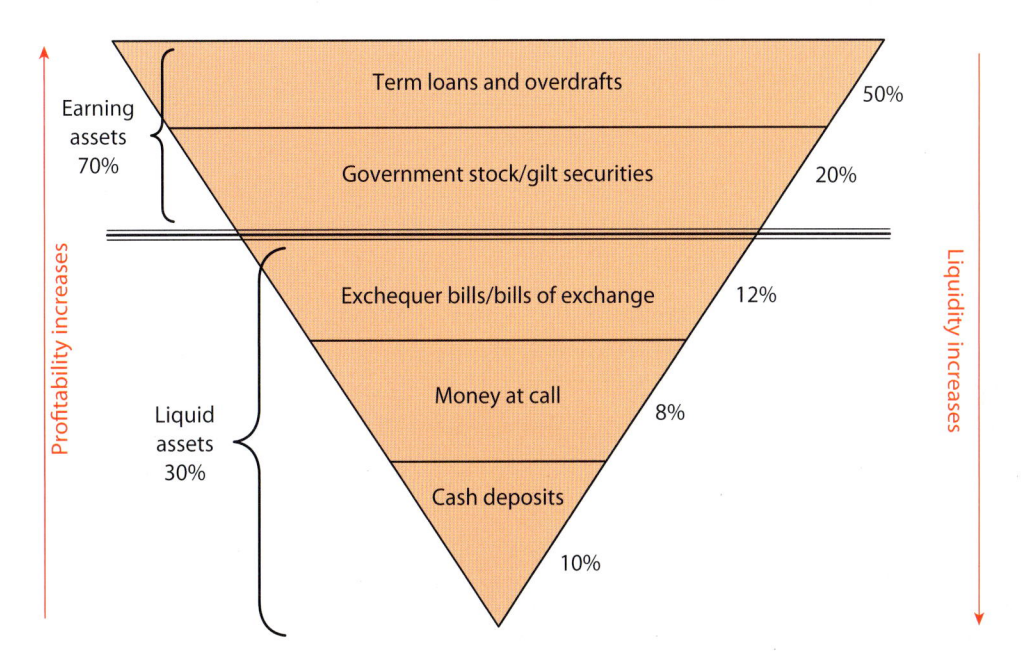

Profitability increases ↑

Earning assets 70%
- Term loans and overdrafts — 50%
- Government stock/gilt securities — 20%

Liquid assets 30%
- Exchequer bills/bills of exchange — 12%
- Money at call — 8%
- Cash deposits — 10%

Liquidity increases ↓

Note:

- By focusing on profitability (extending credit) at the expense of liquidity, a bank may give loans to high-risk ventures, e.g. commercial property development loans. Property loans are highly illiquid but can be very profitable. A bank may run the risk of increasing bad debts, falling share prices, a lack of capital and, at extremes, possible bank failure.
- By ignoring liquidity requirements, banks may not have enough cash to meet the demands of their depositors, which could result in a collapse of confidence and a run on the bank and thus bank failure.

Influential Factors on Credit Creation/Reasons Why Infinite Credit Can't Be Created

Restrictions That Limit the Power of Commercial Banks to Create Infinite Credit

- Banking ratios (primary liquidity ratio and capital adequacy ratio).
- European Central Bank guidelines.

- Limited opportunities for credit extension via a limited supply of creditworthy customers.
- An economic recession would lower confidence, employment and the number of successful businesses. As a result, loans may not be demanded in a recessionary period to the same extent as in a period of growth.

Impact of the Explosion of 'Plastic Money'

An increase in the use of plastic money (credit cards, etc.) by customers affects the ability of commercial banks to create credit as follows.

- Credit is easier to use when you don't have to apply for a loan month-on-month, but instead just hand over a card and tap in a PIN. As a result, plastic card use enables banks to create more credit.
- Since credit cards are so popular today, banks need to take into account the lending provided by these plastic cards when calculating their bank rates.

The Tightening (Reduction) in the Availability of Credit May Affect the Following:

The Motor Industry

- **Decreased demand for cars:** It is more difficult for customers to avail of credit in order to purchase cars. This would lead to a fall in the demand for both new and second-hand cars.
- **Increased redundancies:** With less demand for cars, the number of people employed in the motor industry and the sale of cars could decline.
- **Business closures/consolidations:** Many small independent car dealerships may not survive and would be forced to close. Inability to get credit results in cash flow problems, inability to pay suppliers and possible closure of the firms.

> **Note:** The above can be said for all industries operating in an environment of credit contraction.

Inflation

- **Inflation would decrease:** The supply of money/credit will fall, causing a decrease in the amount that individuals have to spend. This fall would lead to a reduction in demand-pull inflation (this will be discussed in Chapter 21).
- **Deflation:** The price of goods and services may fall due to falling demand and costs of production.

Ireland's Balance of Payments

- **Imports decrease:** If there was a reduction in the demand for goods and services, then we can assume that there would be an automatic fall in the demand for imports.
- **Exports decrease:** Business would not be able to avail of credit in order to expand their business. This fall in investment may lead to a decrease in exports.

Interest Rates

> **NOMINAL INTEREST RATE** is the interest rate unadjusted for inflation.

Nominal Interest Rate
For example, consider that a bank is offering 3% interest on a current account. If you deposit €100 on 1 January, you will have €103 on 1 January the year afterwards, assuming you don't have any withdrawals.

> The **REAL RATE OF INTEREST** is the nominal rate of interest minus the rate of inflation.

Real Interest Rate
For example:

- Consider that a bank is offering 3% interest on a current account. If you deposit €100 on 1 January (year 1), you will have €103 on 1 January (year 2), assuming you don't have any withdrawals.

- Consider that it costs you €100 to buy a mobile phone on 1 January (year 1). If inflation is 2%, the same phone would cost €102 on 1 January in year 2.

- Now, how much better off are you in year 2? You have €103 in the bank, but it now costs €102 to buy the same basket of goods as last year. As a result, your real return (i.e. return adjusted for inflation) is 1%.

Effects of an Increase on Interest Rates on the Irish Economy

- **Borrowing discouraged:** Borrowing is now more expensive, resulting in higher loan repayments. This decreases spending power, demand for imports and the standard of living. As a result, inflation is caused.

- **Savings encouraged:** With higher rates of return, people may find it more attractive to save more and spend less.

- **Cost of servicing the national debt:** With higher interest rates, the cost of repaying the national debt rises.

- **Costs of production/improved competitiveness:** The cost of capital rises, which is a considerable input into many businesses. This increase in cost may need to be passed on, resulting in higher prices (inflation), lower employment and/or reduced margins.

- **Incentive to invest:** Given that the cost of borrowing is now higher, fewer companies will want to invest.

- **Economic growth is dampened:** With possibly lower investment and less disposable income in the pockets of mortgagees, economic growth is hampered.

- **Revenue received from DIRT:** With greater savings, the government may receive more revenue through DIRT.

Effects of a Reduction on Interest Rates on the Irish Economy

- **Borrowing encouraged:** Borrowing is now cheaper, resulting in lower loan repayments. This has the effect of increasing spending power, demand for imports and standard of living. As a result, inflation ~~falls~~ rises.

- **Savings discouraged:** With lower rates of returns, people may find it less attractive to save and hence spend more.

- **Increased demand for houses:** Given that the cost of borrowing has fallen due to lower interest, there may be an increased demand for properties.

- **Cost of servicing the national debt:** With lower interest rates, the cost of repaying the national debt falls.

- **Costs of production/improved competitiveness:** Capital is a considerable input in many businesses. As a result, if the cost of capital falls, this increases the margin of the business or the reduction in cost can be passed on. In both cases, employment may be increased.

- **Incentive to invest:** The marginal efficiency of capital (discussed in Chapter 15) will rise, resulting in higher profits. Investment is encouraged, as it becomes cheaper for businesses to borrow and so businesses may invest.

- **Economic growth is encouraged:** With possibly higher investment, future economic growth in Ireland may be increased.

- **Revenue received from DIRT:** With less savings, the government may receive less revenue through DIRT (but greater capital gains tax on investment profits).

NAMA

The concept behind the National Asset Management Agency (NAMA) was to set up an agency whereby the loans of Allied Irish Bank, Bank of Ireland, Anglo Irish Bank, EBS and Irish Nationwide would be reviewed. NAMA would buy these loans from the banks at a discount in line with their long-term economic value (i.e. the price the properties might be in 10 years) and pay them with **NAMA bonds** (i.e. collateral that could be cashed in at the ECB). The banks would then have cleaner balance sheets and be better capitalised. As a result, they could lend money out to businesses and individuals to get the economy growing.

Consequences of NAMA

- Banks were prevented from insolvency or very serious problems as NAMA paid them for large commercial property loans.

- An artificial floor was put under the falling property market. If commercial property owners had to sell their assets in a 'fire sale', the price of the properties could have plummeted, bringing all real estate prices down.

- The banks received fresh capital so that they could lend to businesses. This allowed many businesses to stay open and generated profit for the banks, increasing the borrower's sustainability as well as their own profitability. If banks are not issuing loans, this means less credit is being created.

- If NAMA makes a loss in the medium term, the government will be asked to put more money into the agency. This would take resources away from the exchequer to spend on public services.

Ireland's Banking Collapse

The Interbank Market

The interbank market refers to short-term money or foreign exchange markets that are only accessible to banks or financial institutions. If banks don't have enough deposits to fund loans or loan repayments to make good on deposits, the institution can tap into the interbank market for short-term funds.

The Euro Interbank Offered Rate (Euribor) is the interest rate at which banks offer to lend funds to other banks in the euro wholesale money market or interbank market. For example, if one Irish bank needs short-term funds, it could borrow from another Irish bank or a foreign bank.

The Credit Crunch

During 2008, the world suffered a credit crunch. This referred to a situation whereby banks would not lend to each other on the interbank market. This began because banks started making riskier and riskier loans, called subprime lending. Banks started worrying that these loans might be defaulted on and hence stopped lending to other banks on the interbank market. Since the supply of money fell, the price (i.e. the interest rate) of that money rose. The graph below shows that the interest rate that banks were demanding on the interbank market shot up in 2008. This was a crucial factor that led to the Irish bank guarantee in 2008 and subsequent capitalisations of the banks.

Interbank Interest Rate Adjusted for Inflation, 1980–2008

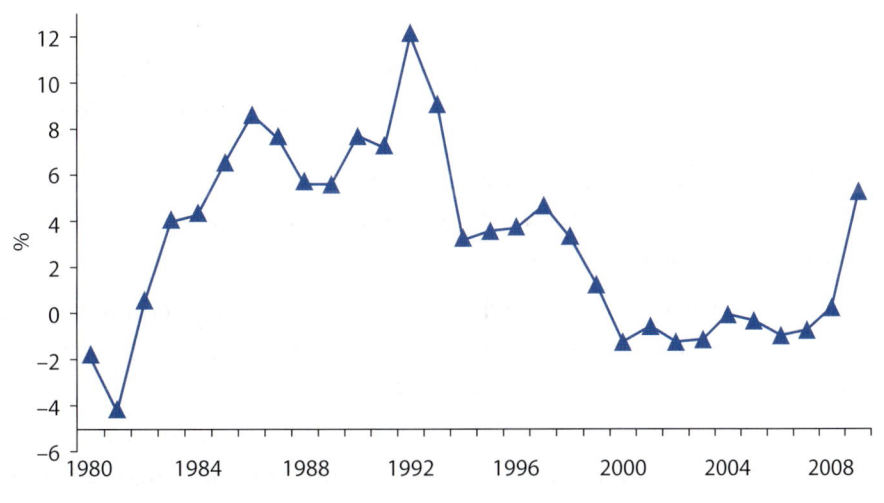

Source: Central Bank of Ireland

Positive Economics

A Snapshot in Time

Ireland's primary banks found themselves in a precarious position in 2008 for many reasons. Firstly, they were highly exposed on the interbank market, as the amount of short-term money they had borrowed mushroomed from €120 billion in 2000 to just under €400 billion in 2007. Following the collapse of Lehman Brothers and the credit crunch of 2008, interest costs increased rapidly and the availability of credit dried up. In addition, many of the banks lent on the back of a property boom and the conditions for obtaining credit had relaxed beyond prudence. Finally, Ireland's Celtic Tiger economy came to an abrupt end and was just about to begin a deep depression.

Regulation of the Banking Sector

Given that Ireland was plagued with such problems in the banking sector in 2008 and the consequences of its recapitalisation will be felt for years and years to come, regulation is absolutely needed to ensure this does not happen again in the future.

> **Class Task**
> What is the interbank interest rate today and how does it compare to 2008?

> **Class Task**
> View the documentary *Freefall* to follow the story of the Irish banking collapse. Following the establishment of NAMA, the Irish banks required five capitalisations – the largest following the very severe stress tests carried out in April 2011.

Why Is There a Need for Regulation in This Country?

- **Protect consumers:** Regulation puts procedures in place to ensure that the interests of the banks' consumers are protected and that savers' deposits are secure.

- **Proper lending policies:** Regulation puts practices in place to ensure that the banks follow correct lending procedures and that excessive/reckless lending is avoided.

- **Banking system stability:** Regulation strengthens the stability of the banking system.

- **Economic stability/confidence:** Proper regulation may ensure that the banks operate efficiently, resulting in public confidence in the banking system and allowing economic growth to strengthen.

- **Less need for government intervention:** If the banks are properly regulated then there will be less need for the government to become involved as previously with extreme measures including the guarantees for savers' deposits; the nationalisation of Anglo Irish Bank; and the setting up of NAMA.

- **Less need for emergency funds:** If banks are properly regulated, any issues arising should be prevented or at least dealt with internally in the banks. This would prevent the need for the government having to resort to finding emergency finance.

PROFILE: Milton Friedman (1912–2006)

The economist Milton Friedman was the 20th century's most prominent advocate of free markets and recipient of the 1976 Nobel Memorial Prize for Economic Science. He was regarded as one of the major thinkers of the monetarist school of economic thought. Friedman presented evidence to resurrect the quantity theory of money – the idea that the price level depends on the money supply. In *Studies in the Quantity Theory of Money*, published in 1956, Friedman stated that in the long run, increased monetary growth increases prices but has little or no effect on output. In the short run, he argued, increases in money supply growth cause employment and output to increase, while decreases in money supply growth have the opposite effect.

His ideas include the following:

- **Monetary policy:** This should be the main instrument used by the government to manage the economy and not fiscal policy. Increased government expenditure would only lead to higher prices and not increased output and employment, as advocated by Keynes.
- **Control of money supply:** Monetarists such as Friedman suggest strict control of the money supply so as to control inflation. Limiting credit availability and keeping interest rates high would control consumer borrowing.
- **Reduction in inflation:** A reduction in inflation increases competitiveness, which may lead to relatively cheaper exports, increased exports and job creation in the long run. Companies should keep wage increases to a minimum in order to avoid cost-push inflation.
- **Laissez-faire principles:** Friedman was in favour of a return to laissez-faire principles, minimum state intervention, deregulation of markets and privatisation of state bodies.
- **Supply side policies:** Friedman favoured any policies that improved market efficiency, boosted supply and reduced the ability of trade unions to interfere with the labour market.

EXAM ✓ Question 6(a), 2011 (35 marks)

(a) Money is usually defined by reference to the functions it performs.
  (i) Outline **four** functions of money.
  (ii) Explain the term 'monetary policy'.
  (iii) Explain a central bank's function as 'lender of last resort'.

(b) Many believe that a lack of supervision ('light touch regulation') of financial institutions in Ireland contributed significantly to the banking crisis. Discuss the economic reasons why commercial banks in Ireland should be regulated.

(c) It is being suggested that the ECB will increase interest rates in the 2011/2012 period. Explain the economic effects of rising interest rates on the Irish economy.

Solution

(a) (i) The four functions of money are:
1. Medium of exchange.
2. A measure of value.
3. A standard for deferred payment.
4. A store of wealth.

(ii) Monetary policy is those actions taken by the ECB that influence the money supply, interest rates and the availability of credit.

(iii) As a lender of last resort, the Central Bank offers credit to financial institutions experiencing financial difficulties and are unable to obtain the necessary funds elsewhere.

(b) The following are economic reasons why commercial banks in Ireland should be regulated:

- **Protect consumers:** Regulation puts procedures in place to ensure that the interests of the banks' consumers are protected and that savers' deposits are secure.

- **Proper lending policies:** Regulation puts practices in place to ensure that the banks follow correct lending procedures and that excessive/reckless lending is avoided.

- **Banking system stability:** Regulation strengthens the stability of the banking system.

- **Economic stability/confidence:** Proper regulation may ensure that the banks operate efficiently, resulting in public confidence in the banking system and allowing economic growth to strengthen.

- **Less need for government intervention:** If the banks are properly regulated, then there will be less need for the government to become involved as previously with extreme measures including the guarantees for savers' deposits, the nationalisation of Anglo Irish Bank and the establishment of NAMA.

- **Less need for emergency funds:** If banks are properly regulated, any issues that could arise should be prevented or at least dealt with internally in the banks. This would prevent the need for the government having to resort to finding emergency finance.

(c) The economic effects of rising interest rates on the Irish economy are as follows:

- **Borrowing is discouraged:** Borrowing is now more expensive, resulting in higher loan repayments. This decreases spending power, demand for imports and the standard of living.

- **Saving is encouraged:** With higher rates of return, people may find it more attractive to save more and spend less.

- **Cost of servicing national debt:** With higher interest rates, the cost of repaying the national debt rises.
- **Costs of production:** The cost of capital rises, which is a considerable input into many businesses. This increase in cost may need to be passed on, resulting in higher prices (inflation), lower employment and/or reduced margins.
- **Incentive to invest:** Given that the cost of borrowing is now higher, fewer companies will want to invest.
- **Economic growth is now dampened:** With possibly lower investment and less disposable income in the pockets of mortgagees, economic growth is hampered.
- **Revenue received from DIRT (Deposit Interest Retention Tax):** With greater savings, the government may receive more revenue through DIRT.

Questions

Short Questions

1. Define the terms 'money' and 'legal tender'.
2. Give examples of cashless transactions.
3. Define monetary policy.
4. Differentiate between the nominal interest rate and the real interest rate.
5. List the characteristics of money.

Long Questions

1. Analyse the functions that money performs and the properties required to fulfil this role successfully.
2. Outline the current role and functions of the Central Bank.
3. Outline the current role and functions of the ECB.
4. Outline the factors that influence the rate of interest and their economic effects.
5. Demonstrate how financial institutions can create credit.
6. Discuss the limitations on an institution's ability to create credit.
7. Analyse the changes in the demand and supply of money.
8. Critically analyse the implications of an excess supply of credit on the economy.
9. Examine how a financial institution reconciles liquidity with profitability.
10. Analyse the need for regulation of the financial sector.

Chapter 19 | Measuring National Income

Specific Learning Outcomes

At the end of this chapter, students should be able to:

- [ ] Explain national income.

- [ ] Define gross domestic product, gross national product and net national product.

- [ ] Describe the relationship between gross domestic product and gross national product.

- [ ] Explain net factor income and identify its main constituents in the case of the Irish economy.

- [ ] Understand the usefulness and limitations of national income statistics.

19: Measuring National Income

Introduction

At the beginning of this book, we looked at the concept of wealth and concluded that **wealth is the total value of all assets owned by an individual.** However, many macroeconomists spend their time thinking about the wealth of a country. We refer to this as national income.

> **NATIONAL INCOME** is the income accruing to the permanent residents of a country from current economic activity from supplying the factors in production during a specific period, which is usually one year.

Measuring National Income

Let's take the very simple example of where national income consists of knitting just one Aran sweater.

- Mary knits and sells the sweater for €100.
- The income received by Mary, who knitted the sweater, is €100 (income method).
- The value of the output (the sweater) is €100 (output method).
- The spending by the consumer who bought the sweater is €100 (expenditure method).

In this example, the income derived, the output generated and the expenditure on the sweater are all valued at €100, i.e. the three methods of calculating national income give us the same answer. In Ireland, the Central Statistics Office calculates our national income accounts.

An Phríomh-Oifig Staidrimh
Central Statistics Office

The Methods of Calculating National Income

These methods are a cross-check on each other and contain useful economic data to macroeconomists when planning and carrying out research. Before we examine these three approaches, we first need to consider other key concepts.

- **Gross** = before deduction
- **Domestic** = home produced

255

Positive Economics

- **Product** = the amount produced
- **National** = what Irish nationals produce
- **Market prices** = the prices consumers pay for goods and services
- **Factor costs** = the cost of the four factors of production (land, labour, capital and enterprise), i.e. the wage paid to the worker, the rent to the landlord, the remaining income to the entrepreneur and the interest payment to the lender. Each of these components is required to create the good or service.
- **Net factor income from the rest of the world** = (income earned by Irish factors of production abroad and sent home (repatriated)) minus (income earned by foreign factors of production in Ireland and sent back (repatriated) to their own country)

Examples

- The Kerry Group makes profits in the US and sends them back to Ireland = incomes earned by Irish factors and returned home (€100 million).
- Apple making a profit and sending it back (repatriated) to the US = incomes earned by foreign factors of production, sent back abroad (€250 million).

$$\text{Net factor income} = €100 \text{ million} - €250 \text{ million}$$
$$= -€150 \text{ million}$$

The Income Method

The **INCOME METHOD** refers to the sum of income earned by the four factors of production: land, labour, capital and enterprise.

Task

Look up www.cso.ie/statistics/nationalacc.htm to find all the national income statistics.

19: Measuring National Income

Calculation of National Income (Income Method)

Step 1:

- Calculate the total value of all incomes earned in the country. This includes benefit-in-kind (benefit-in-kind are benefits that an employee receives that cannot be converted into cash but have a monetary value, e.g. provision of a company car, loans given at a special rate) and profits earned in the various sectors (agriculture, industry and services) throughout the country.
- Transfer payments (e.g. Child Benefit) are excluded.
- Stock appreciation (the value of stock increases due to a rise in price) is subtracted. In this case, no factor of production was supplied.
- Take account of statistical discrepancy (see the note on p. 260).
- All of these elements combine to give net value added at factor cost.

Step 2:

- Depreciation is added to net value added at factor cost to give gross value added (GVA) at factor cost.

Step 3:

- From gross value added (GVA) at factor cost, subtract non-product subsidies (e.g. subsidies to reduce pollution) and add non-product taxes (taxes on pollution resulting from production activities) to give gross value added (GVA) at basic prices.

Step 4:

- From gross value added (GVA) at basic prices, add product taxes (e.g. VAT) and subtract product subsidies (e.g. the subsidy on prescribed medicine) to give gross domestic product at current market prices.

Step 5:

- From gross domestic product (GDP) at current market prices, subtract net factor income from the rest of the world to give gross national product (GNP) at current market prices.

Step 6:

- To gross national product (GNP) at current market prices add **EU** subsidies (e.g. subsidies to farmers under CAP) and subtract **EU** taxes (e.g. a small percentage of VAT receipts to the EU) to give gross national income.

Step 7:

- From gross national income at current market prices, subtract provision for depreciation to give net national income (NNI) at current market prices.

Positive Economics

Step 8:

- From net national income (NNI) at current market prices, subtract **non-EU** taxes (i.e. taxes on production and imports, such as customs on clothing that is imported from non-EU countries) and add **non-EU** subsidies (e.g. subsidies on production and imports) to give net national product (NNP) at factor cost.

Summary of the Income Method

	Title of entry	Value (€, million)
	Calculate total value of all incomes (including benefit-in-kind and profits of companies)	9,134,711
	Exclude transfer payments (employers' contribution to social insurance)	(52) + (5,295)
−	Stock appreciation	1,032
−	Statistical discrepancy	1,015
=	Net value added at factor cost	**127,317**
+	Depreciation	**17,287**
=	Gross value added (GVA) at factor cost	**144,605 (rounded)**
−	Non-product subsidies	2,185
+	Non-product taxes	−1,805
=	Gross value added (GVA) at basic prices	144,986
+	Product taxes	16,417
−	Product subsidies	−807
=	Gross domestic product (GDP) at current prices	**160,596**
−	Net factor income from the rest of the world	−28,363
=	Gross national product (GNP) at current market prices	**132,233**
−	EU taxes	−359
+	EU subsidies	1,719
=	Gross national income at current market prices	**133,592**
−	Provision for depreciation	17287
=	Net national income (NNI) at current market prices	**116,305**
−	Non-EU taxes	−18,243
+	Non-EU subsidies	+893
=	Net national product (NNP) at factor cost	**98,954**

Source: Central Statistics Office.

Precautions When Calculating the Income Method:

- **Transfer payments:** These are excluded as no factor of production has been supplied, e.g. Jobseekers Benefit.
- **Benefit-in-kind:** These should be included as they are payment for providing a factor of production, e.g. labour. An example of a benefit-in-kind is a company car.
- **Contributory workers' pensions:** These are included as they are payment for work done in the past.

The Expenditure Method

The **EXPENDITURE METHOD** is the sum of all expenditure made by citizens.

Step 1:

- Calculate the total expenditure made through consumption, investment and government spending.
- Add the value of exports and subtract the value of imports.
- Take account of statistical discrepancy (see the note on p. 254).
- All of these elements combine to give gross domestic product at current market prices.

Step 2:

- To gross domestic product at current market prices, we add/subtract net factor income from the rest of the world to give gross national product at current market prices.

Step 3:

- To gross national product at current market prices, we add EU subsidies and subtract EU taxes to give gross national income (GNI) at current market prices.

Step 4:

- From gross national income (GNI) at current market prices, we subtract provision for depreciation to get net national income at current market prices.

Step 5:

- From net national income at current market prices, subtract non-EU taxes and add non-EU subsidies to get net national product at factor cost.

Positive Economics

Summary of the Expenditure Method

	Title of entry	Value (€, million)
	Calculate total expenditure	136,746
+	Statistical discrepancy	−1,015
+	Exports	145,902
−	Imports	−121,037
=	Gross domestic product (GDP) at current market prices	160,596
+/−	Net factor income from the rest of the world	−28,363
=	Gross national product (GNP) at current market prices	132,233
+	EU subsidies	1,719
−	EU taxes	−359
=	Gross national income (GNI) at current market prices	133,592
−	Provision for depreciation	17,287
=	Net national income (NNI) at current market prices	116,305
−	Non-EU taxes	−18,243
+	Non-EU subsidies	+893
=	Net national product (NNP) at factor cost	98,954
	Gross national disposable income (GNDI) at current market prices	131,026

Source: Central Statistics Office.

Precautions When Calculating the Expenditure Method

- **Second-hand goods:** Purchase of second-hand goods if included in GNP when new is now not included.

The Production/Output Method

This method is commonly used for calculating national income across Europe.

Method:

1. Calculate the value of all production in the country.
2. Adjust for interest earned and paid by the financial institutions.

> The PRODUCTION/OUTPUT method values the output produced in the agricultural, industrial and services sectors.

> **Note:**
> The statistical discrepancy entry is an adjustment required because the two methods (income and expenditure) don't always give the same answer. The GDP figure that is used by the CSO is an average of these two methods of calculation, derived from halving the difference between the two estimates. (If the income estimate is higher than the expenditure estimate, the difference will have a negative sign in the income tables and a positive sign in the expenditure tables and vice versa.)

3. Add on the expense of depreciation of stock, but subtract any appreciation (as there wasn't any factor of production supplied) to arrive at net domestic product at factor cost.

4. Add/subtract net factor income from the rest of the world to arrive at net national product at factor cost.

Precaution/Difficulties When Calculating the Production/Output Method

DOUBLE COUNTING

An economist must only calculate the value added by each firm and not the total output to prevent double counting. For example, a sawmill sells wood for €100 to a furniture manufacturer. The manufacturer uses this wood to make a table, which they sell for €150. When calculating national output using this method:

- Value the wood produced at: €100
- Value the table manufactured at: €50
- Total value =   €150
- It would be incorrect to value the piece of furniture at €250 (€100 + €150) as this would be double counting.

ONLY GOODS/SERVICES SOLD IN THE MARKETPLACE ARE INCLUDED

In the output method of calculation, only goods and services that are sold in the market are included. Therefore, the value of voluntary work and housework is **not** included as there isn't any payment made.

Explanation of Key Terms in the National Statistics

Task

Look at the CSO website (www.cso.ie) to identify how the country's current national income stands compared to previous years.

GROSS DOMESTIC PRODUCT AT FACTOR COST is the total value of input or expenditure within the country as a result of engaging in current economic activity in one year, valued at payments to factors of production.

OR

GROSS DOMESTIC PRODUCT AT FACTOR COST is the output produced by the factors of production in the domestic economy irrespective of whether the factors are owned by Irish nationals or non-nationals, valued at payments to factors of production.

GROSS DOMESTIC PRODUCT AT MARKET PRICES is the total value of input or expenditure within the country as a result of engaging in current economic activity in one year, valued at current market prices.

OR

GROSS DOMESTIC PRODUCT AT MARKET PRICES is the output produced by the factors of production in the domestic economy irrespective of whether the factors are owned by Irish nationals or non-nationals, valued at current market prices.

Positive Economics

GROSS NATIONAL PRODUCT AT FACTOR COST is the total value of output or expenditure valued at payments to factors of production, produced by Irish-owned factors of production.

OR

GROSS NATIONAL PRODUCT AT FACTOR COST is the value of the total goods and services produced in an economy over a specified period of time (e.g. a year), valued at payments to factors of production, produced by Irish-owned factors of production.

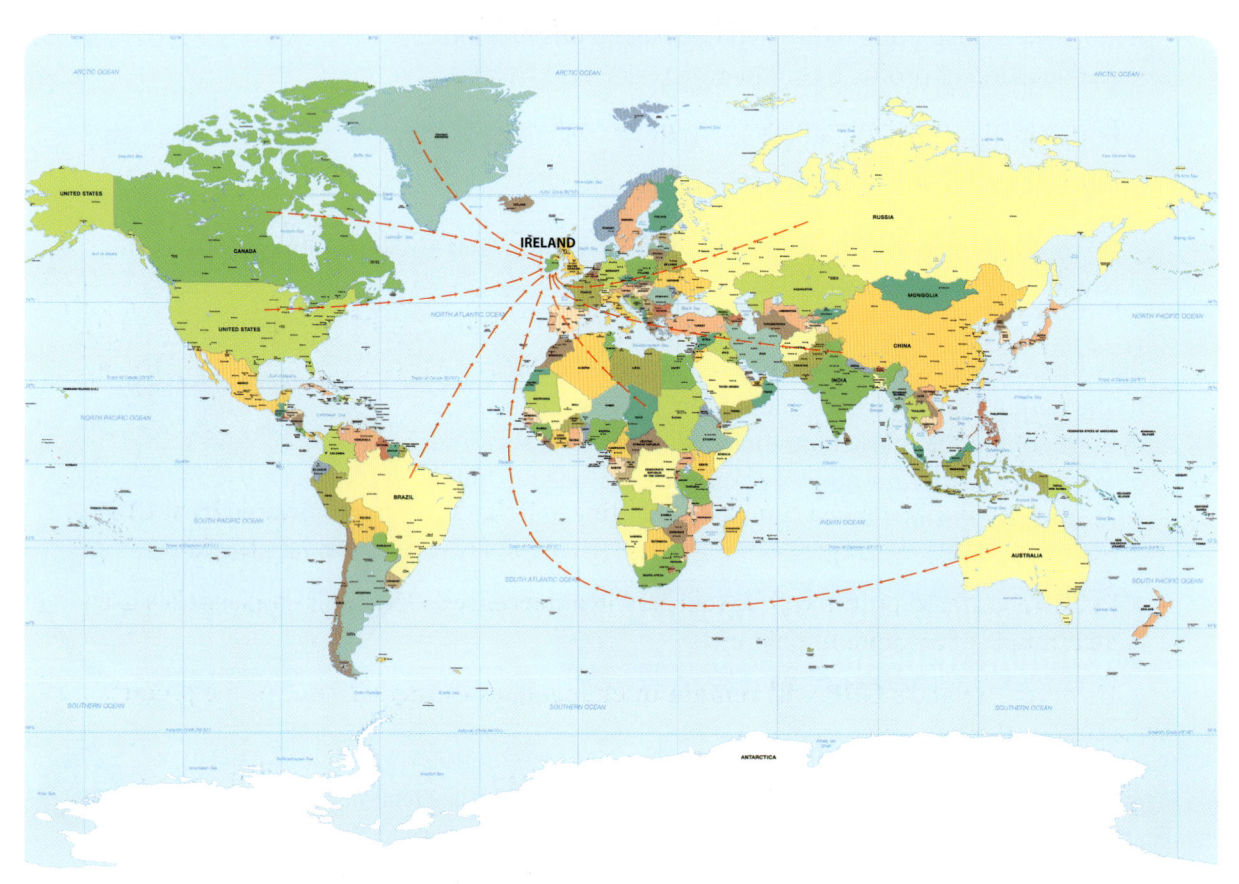

GROSS NATIONAL PRODUCT AT MARKET PRICES is the total value of output or expenditure valued at today's market prices, produced by Irish-owned factors of production, before any adjustments are made for taxation, subsidies or depreciation.

OR

GROSS NATIONAL PRODUCT AT MARKET PRICES is the value of the total goods and services produced in an economy over a specified period of time (e.g. a year), valued at current/today's market prices, produced by Irish-owned factors of production.

19: Measuring National Income

> Gross **national** product at factor cost (GNP)
> Gross **domestic** product at factor cost (GDP)
>
> **The difference between GNP and GDP is net factor income from abroad.**

Would You Expect GDP to Be Higher than GNP?

In Ireland's case, GDP is actually larger than GNP. This is because the net factor income from abroad is usually negative due to the following reasons:

- Repatriation of profits by companies resident in Ireland.
- Repayments on the foreign elements of our national debt.
- The remittances (money) of immigrants in Ireland sent abroad.

Therefore, GDP is a better indicator of the level of economic activity in the country, while GNP is a better indicator of the standard of living in the country.

> **GROSS NATIONAL INCOME is comprised of domestic and foreign income earned by the resident population of a country.**

GNI vs. GDP

- The profits of a US-owned company operating in Ireland will count towards **Irish GDP** but because they are repatriated to the US, they will also count towards **US GNI**.
- These repatriated profits will be reflected in a **decreased GNI** for Ireland, as they are an example of an amount paid **out**.
- However, Ireland's **GDP will remain unchanged**, as the actual value of the produce remains the same.

GNI vs. GNP

Example

An Irish woman, Mary, owns shares in Vodafone, a company listed in the UK, and receives a dividend annually. Does this contribute towards Irish GNP or Irish GNI? The answer depends on where Mary **lives**.

- If Mary lives in the UK and lodges her dividend into her Irish bank account, this counts towards Irish GNP, as GNP refers to remittances received from **Irish nationals abroad**.
- If Mary lives in Ireland and lodges her dividend into her Irish bank account, this counts towards Irish GNI, as GNI refers to **foreign income received by Irish residents**.

Positive Economics

> Gross national **product** at factor cost (GNP)
> Gross national **income** at factor cost (GNI)
>
> **The difference between GNP and GNI is interest and dividends.**

NET NATIONAL PRODUCT is the total joint product of the resources of land, labour, capital and enterprise for a period of time, usually one year. It is the same as national income.

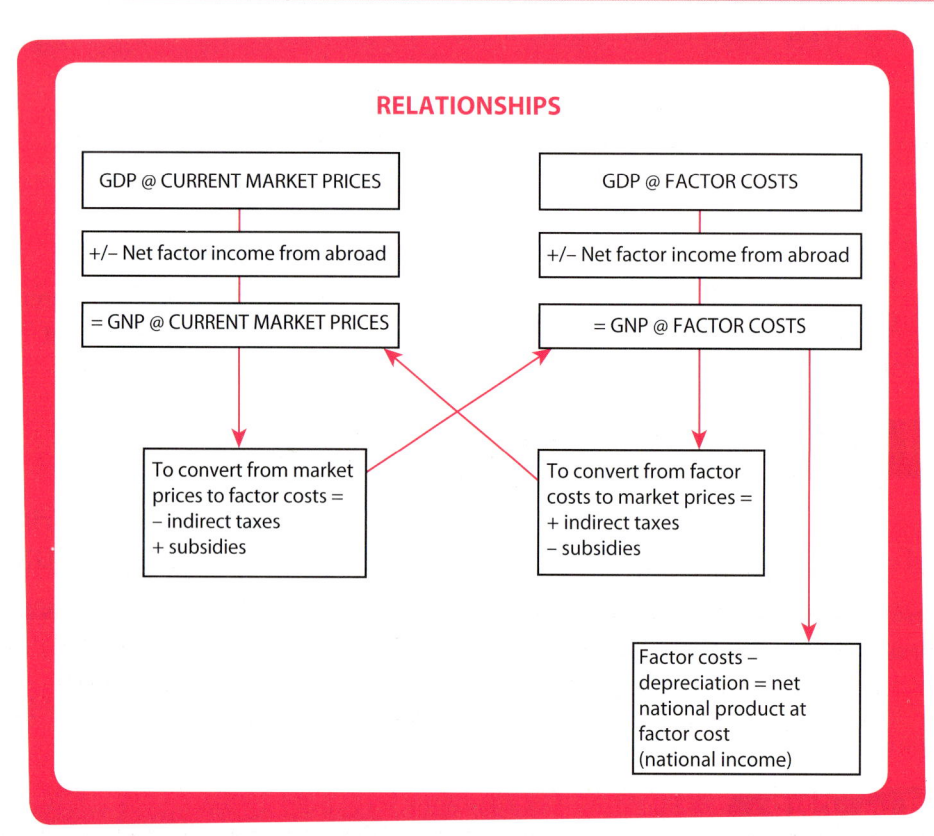

RELATIONSHIPS

GDP @ CURRENT MARKET PRICES	GDP @ FACTOR COSTS
+/– Net factor income from abroad	+/– Net factor income from abroad
= GNP @ CURRENT MARKET PRICES	= GNP @ FACTOR COSTS
To convert from market prices to factor costs = – indirect taxes + subsidies	To convert from factor costs to market prices = + indirect taxes – subsidies
	Factor costs – depreciation = net national product at factor cost (national income)

Uses of National Income Statistics

Indication of Alterations to Our Standard of Living

Any change in our national income figures will indicate the level of economic growth, or otherwise, within the country from one year to the next and give a general indication of changes to the standard of living, if any. It may be used by trade unions to justify wage agreements.

Comparison Mechanism

We can use the national income statistics to compare the standard of living in our country with that of other countries (i.e. GNP per capita (GNP per person)). These definitions are accepted all over the world and measurement is undertaken across the globe uniformly.

Formulating Economic Policy

Governments have a greater influence on the development and growth of the economy. To effectively plan for this, governments need information about our economy, such as that provided by the national income statistics. For example, national income statistics could inform the government that farm incomes have fallen and the government could formulate a policy to deal with this issue.

Effective Research

Economists can analyse and research the economy much more effectively if they have the right data available to them. As a result, they can help the government in making economic policy.

Evaluating Economic Policy

It is useful to have national income statistics to assess changes to the economy and in its various sectors and to provide a benchmark against which progress can be monitored.

EU Budget Contributions/Benefits

The wealth shown in our national income statistics will determine the contribution, if any, that Ireland must make to the EU budget. The figure will also be used in the EU to determine those countries that require financial aid from the EU and the amount of that aid.

Limitations of National Income Statistics

Population Distortions

If there are more people in the country and the economy doesn't change dramatically, per capita measures will fall. For example, if our GNP is €150 billion and there are 5 million people living in Ireland, then our GDP per capita would be €30,000. If our GNP remains the same but the population grows to 6 million people, our GNP per capita would fall to €25,000, even though there wouldn't have been any fall in economic activity.

Inflation/Deflation Is Not Taken into Account

An increase in prices will automatically increase GNP at current market prices, which paints an artificial picture of economic activity.

> **Example**
> - If 100 goods are produced by a nation at €1 each in Year 1, then GNP is €100.
> - Let's suppose in Year 2 that prices increase to €2 and 100 goods are still produced. GNP in Year 2 is now €200.
> - GNP has increased by €100 although the amount of goods produced has stayed the same.

To make valid comparisons with GNP of previous years, it is necessary to use GNP at constant prices to show if there is real growth in national income. If we value production of Year 2 at 100 items at Year 1 prices (€1), we see that there hasn't been any increase in real GNP.

Welfare Is Not Taken into Account
The methods of measurement discussed above provide much insight into the growth of our economy but do not give us any indication as to the working conditions or quality of life of the population.

Employment/Unemployment
If a person is unemployed, increasing GNP per capita will not necessarily have any positive impact on this person's average standard of living, as their income (e.g. social welfare payments) may not necessarily improve.

Levels of Taxation
One should consider levels of direct taxation (tax on income, e.g. PAYE) and indirect taxation (tax on spending, e.g. VAT) when considering the standard of living within a country. An increase in either or both would result in a lower standard of living for an individual. The introduction of the Universal Social Charge (USC) in the tax year 2011 brought about a lower standard of living for the Irish population.

Exclusion of Various Activities
If something is done for free or bartered, even though it is produced, it is not included in national income statistics. For example, voluntary activities and housework are excluded from national income. In addition, since the activities of the black/shadow economy are not registered by the government, the income generated in this market is not included.

Hidden Social Costs
For example, GNP increases if a firm increases output, but this may come with the social cost of pollution.

Distribution of GNP
In general, living standards depend on the distribution of GNP. If only a small minority of people benefit from a rise in GNP, there may not be any evidence of a general increase in the living standards of a nation.

Government Services at Cost Price
Government services are included at cost, while private services are provided at the market price. A country where the government provides many services will record a lower GNP.

19: Measuring National Income

International Comparison

Caution must be exercised when comparing national income analysis between countries due to the following.

Foreign Exchange Translations

Due to the changes in the exchange rates between currencies, it is difficult to compare like with like. For example, let's say our GNP is €150 billion and a US economist is studying the Irish economy.

On 31/12/2010 they would have calculated the dollar equivalent at €150 billion × ($1.29/€1) = $193.5 billion.

Compare this against their colleague, who was asked to do the same thing on 31/05/2011. They would have come up with the following: €150 billion × ($1.4812/€1) = $222.18 billion. A big difference!

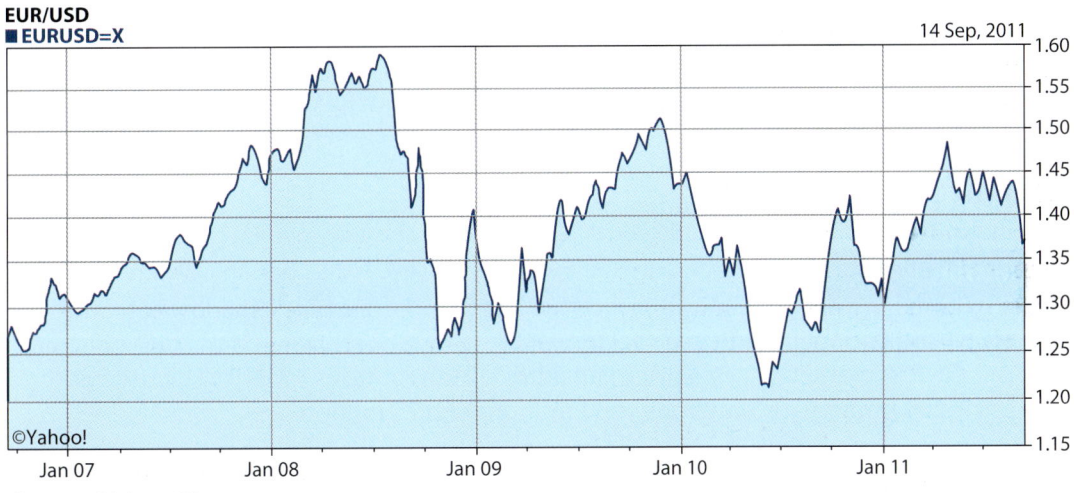

Source: Yahoo Finance.

Market-oriented Economies

It is very important to consider the difference between less-developed countries (where market systems may not be highly developed) with the national income of First World countries. For example, in Kenya there is a high degree of subsistence farming, hence their output would be consumed by the producers without going through the market system. Contrast this with a country like Ireland where market systems are highly developed and most people buy their food requirements.

Length of the Working Week

A country with a longer working week, e.g. 45 hours, may consequently have a higher GDP than a country with a working week of 39 hours.

Positive Economics

The Nature of Government Spending

The governments in two countries, X and Y, may spend the same amount of money. In Country X it is spent on libraries, football pitches, public swimming pools and other social amenities. In Country Y it is spent totally on military defence. The standard of living is being significantly improved for the inhabitants of Country X but not in Country Y.

Different Countries Have Different Needs

For example, an Irish household will have to spend more on heating then a Spanish household due to climate differences. Consequently, the Irish household economy has less money to spend on non-essential goods and services, thus affecting their standard of living.

EXAM ✓ Question 5(a) & (b), 2010   (40 marks)

(a) Given that gross national product at current market prices is €200m, price subsidies €5m, depreciation €12m and indirect taxes €30m, calculate the value of **each** of the following. **Show all your workings.**
  (i) Gross national product at factor cost.
  (ii) Net national product at factor cost/national income.

(b) Explain the economic effect which **each** of the following could have on the level of GNP at market prices.
  (i) A **reduction** in the general level of VAT.
  (ii) A **reduction** in the subsidies paid to farmers.

Solution

(a) (i) Gross national product at factor cost
    GNP @ market prices + price subsidies – indirect taxes = GNP @ factor cost
    €200 million + €5 million – €30 million = €175 million

(ii) Net national product at factor cost/national income
    GNP @ factor cost – depreciation = NNP @ FC
    €175 million – €12 million = €163 million

REMEMBER! Revise the relationship chart on p. 264.

(b)

	(i) Reduction in general level of VAT	(ii) Reduction in subsidies paid to farmers
Effect on GNP at market prices	Will decrease	Will increase
Explanation	The reduction in VAT will decrease the prices for goods and services that consumers must pay in the marketplace	The reduction in subsidies paid to farmers will increase GNP at market prices, as prices for agricultural products will rise in the marketplace

or
The Long Run

	Reduction in general level of VAT	Reduction in subsidies paid to farmers
Effect on GNP at market prices	Will increase	Will decrease
Explanation	With lower prices, consumers may buy more goods and services, aggregate demand increases and so GNP increases	Prices will rise and so demand for their commodities will decrease, resulting in a reduction in consumption and so GNP will decrease

Questions

Short Questions

1. Define national income.
2. What is a transfer payment? Give two examples.
3. Define GDP.
4. Define GNP.
5. Define GNI.
6. Define NNP.
7. What is the difference between GDP and GNP?
8. What is the difference between GNP and GNI?
9. Explain how the following are calculated.
   (a) The income method of national income
   (b) The expenditure method of national income

Long Questions

1. Clearly distinguish between GDP at factor cost and GDP at market prices.
2. Clearly distinguish between GNP at factor cost and GNP at market prices.
3. Would you expect GDP to be higher than GNP? Explain your answer.
4. What factors affect our level of GNP?
5. What precautions would need to be taken when comparing GNP in different years?
6. Would you consider changes to GNP or GDP to be the better basis for assessing changes in the standard of living in Ireland? Explain your answer.
7. In respect of each of the following, state whether the development would affect our GNP or the standard of living in Ireland.
   (a) Growth of the black/shadow economy, i.e. people working and not declaring their income for tax purposes.
   (b) Foreign firms repatriating their profits
8. State and explain four uses of national income statistics.
9. State and explain four limitations of national income statistics.
10. State and explain two difficulties in international comparisons of national income.

Chapter 20: The Determination of National Income

Specific Learning Outcomes

At the end of this chapter, students should be able to:

- [ ] Identify and explain the main determinants of aggregate demand.
- [ ] Describe the main factors influencing each of these determinants.
- [ ] Examine the difficulties of raising aggregate demand in a small open economy.
- [ ] Define, calculate and interpret MPC, MPT, MPS and MPM.
- [ ] Define the multiplier and explain the factors that influence it.
- [ ] Apply the multiplier formulae in an open and closed economy.
- [ ] Describe and illustrate the circular flow of income.
- [ ] Describe, with examples, injections and leakages to and from the circular flow of income.
- [ ] Evaluate changes in injections and leakages on the economy.
- [ ] Assess the impact of transfer payments on the circular flow of income.
- [ ] Critically analyse the impact of shocks to the circular flow of income.
- [ ] Calculate the change in national income given any injection and interpret the effects of such on the economy.
- [ ] Understand the impact of changes in injections/leakages on the multiplier and on the economy.

Positive Economics

Introduction

In this chapter we will examine what actually creates national income and what drives its growth. An understanding of this concept will help us in analysing how a modern economy operates and can explain why there are recessions and booms (trade cycles).

John Maynard Keynes thought that an economy could be in equilibrium (a position from which there is no tendency to change, i.e. total demand = total output) below the full level of employment. In the 1930s, this new theory led governments to focus attention for the first time on employment-creating strategies when drafting national budgets. Keynes felt that governments should increase spending in order to create jobs, consequently increasing the level of national income.

So what factors create national income?

EXPENDITURE CREATES INCOME.

> **Example**
>
> If you buy a cup of coffee for €2, then this €2 is divided between the four factors of production.

Circular Flow of Income

To fully understand how an economic system operates, it is necessary to look at the circular flow of income.

> The **CIRCULAR FLOW OF INCOME** is the flow of receipts and expenditure between companies and households.

Step 1:

- Households receive payments because they supply the factors of production to the firm (labour).
- The income they receive is used to buy the output of firms.

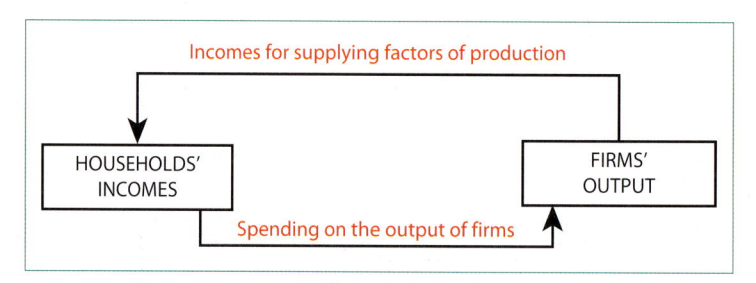

```
              Incomes for supplying factors of production
         ┌─────────────────────────────────────────────┐
         ▼                                             │
   ┌───────────────┐                           ┌───────────────┐
   │  HOUSEHOLDS'  │                           │     FIRMS'    │
   │    INCOMES    │                           │    OUTPUT     │
   └───────────────┘                           └───────────────┘
         │          Spending on the output of firms      ▲
         └─────────────────────────────────────────────┘
```

> **Example**
>
> - A firm produces €5,000 of goods.
>   - They pay workers €3,000 (labour).
>   - They pay owners of the land €1,000 (land).

20: The Determination of National Income

> - They pay lenders of the capital €700 (capital).
> - The remainder is profit €300 (enterprise).
> - The four factors of production above receive a return. If each of these recipients spends all of their income, they are buying €5,000 worth of goods from the firm and hence the cycle repeats itself.

Step 2:

- In step 1, all of the income was spent, i.e. Y = C (income = consumption). However, we know that people **save** some of their income. This is called a **leakage** from the circular flow of income.

> savings = leakage

- The effect of this leakage means that not all goods produced will be bought, hence the company will produce less.

> investment = injection

- However, when people save (deposit in a financial institution), these funds become available for others to borrow.

- When people borrow money, e.g. to extend a factory, this is known as **investment.** This investment is known as an **injection** into the circular flow of income.

- It is possible that investment is less than savings, as businesspeople may not have confidence in the future economic climate and don't invest and banks have to maintain a certain supply of money (minimum reserve ratio) so that they can give people back their deposits when they demand them.

- It is also possible that investment may be greater than savings as banks lend out a multiple of the cash deposited with them (see Credit Creation in Chapter 18).

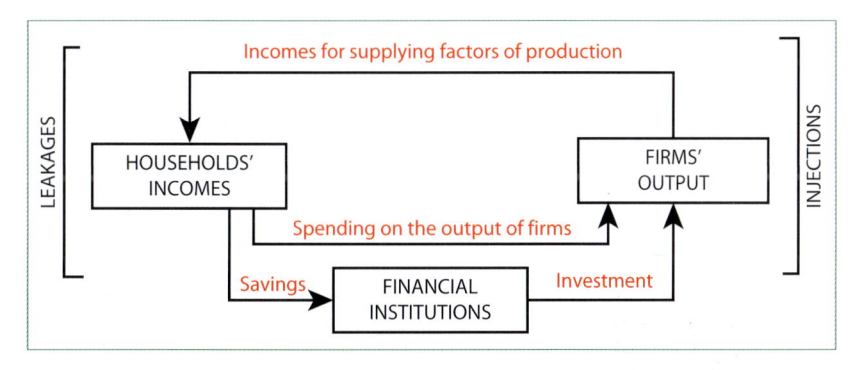

```
                Incomes for supplying factors of production
        ┌──────────────────────────────────────────────┐
LEAKAGES│   ┌──────────────┐              ┌──────────┐ │INJECTIONS
        │   │ HOUSEHOLDS'  │              │  FIRMS'  │ │
        │   │   INCOMES    │              │  OUTPUT  │ │
        │   └──────────────┘              └──────────┘ │
        │           Spending on the output of firms    │
        │      Savings    ┌───────────┐   Investment   │
        │             ────│ FINANCIAL │────            │
        │                 │INSTITUTIONS│               │
        │                 └───────────┘                │
```

Step 3:

We will now look at the effect of the government on the circular flow of income.

- In the annual budget, the government taxes and spends.

Positive Economics

- Taxation reduces the income of households and thus is a leakage from the circular flow of income (e.g. Universal Social Charge and PAYE).

- However, the government spends money (e.g. teachers' salaries) and this constitutes an injection into the circular flow of income.

- If there is a budget deficit (government current spending is greater than government current revenue), then the circular flow of income increases.

- However, the government can increase spending (G) at will, assuming it has the funds in the exchequer or can borrow at a reasonable rate on the financial markets. (Note: Our ability to borrow on the international markets was curtailed in November 2010, when Ireland made an application for external finance from the IMF, EU, ECB, UK, Sweden and Denmark.)

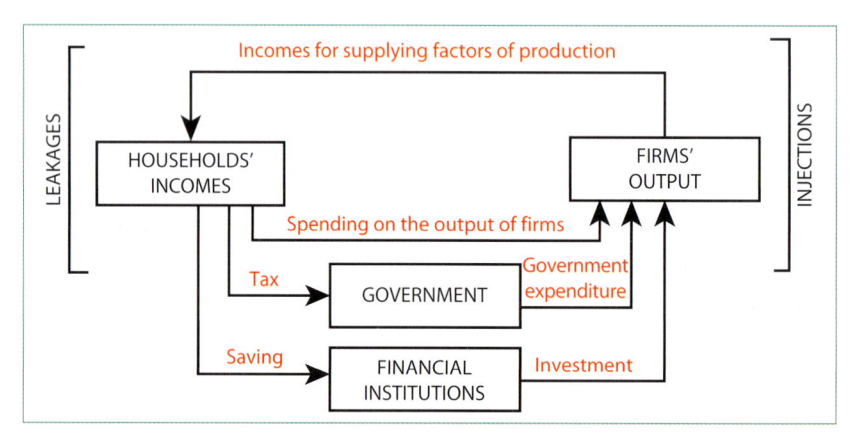

Step 4:

In the above steps we examined the flow of income in a closed economy. We will now expand our analysis to include imports and exports, i.e. an open economy.

> **REMEMBER!**
> - **Closed economy:** An economy that does not engage in any international trade.
> - **Open economy:** An economy that does engage in any international trade.

- When income is spent on imports, money leaves the economy and hence domestic firms may suffer a fall in demand for their substitute good. (This is why the government regularly runs 'Buy Irish' campaigns to boost consumption of Irish produce and hence protect and create jobs in Ireland.)

- Conversely, exports have the effect of increasing demand for Irish goods. (Enterprise Ireland and the Irish Exporters Association try to boost the sale of Irish goods abroad, which increases the circular flow of income in Ireland and stimulates the domestic economy.)

20: The Determination of National Income

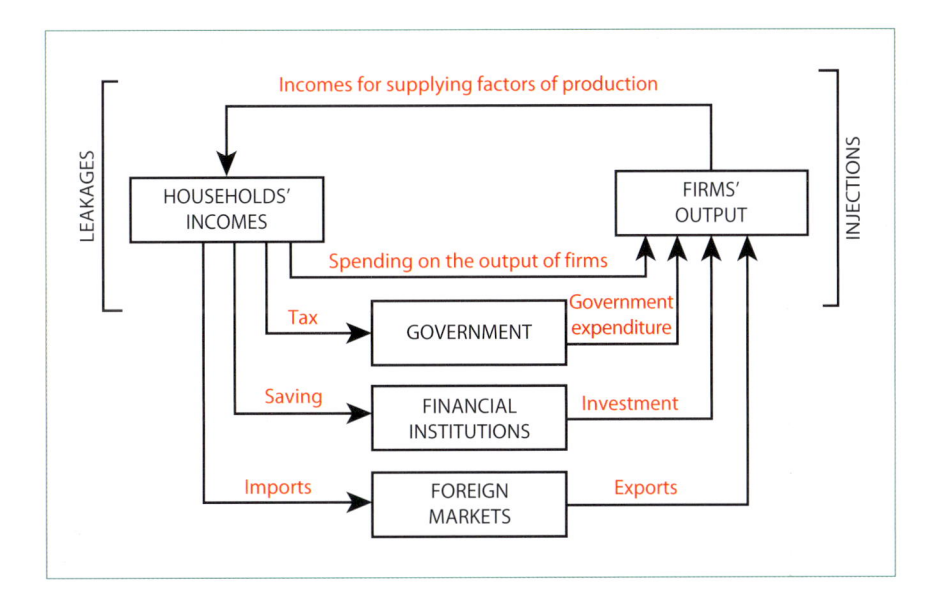

We classify expenditure under the following headings:

> **Income (Y) = consumption (C) + investment (I) + government current expenditure (G) + exports (X) – imports (M)**
>
> $Y = C + I + G + X - M$

If you get pocket money or earn money from a part-time job, what do you do with it? Do you save or spend? The percentage that you spend on consumption directly is your average propensity to consume.

> **AVERAGE PROPENSITY TO CONSUME** is the proportion of total income spent.

$$APC = \frac{\text{Total consumption}}{\text{Total income}}$$

Marginal Prosperity to Consume

Example

A student working a half-day in a café on a Saturday afternoon earns €50.
    Earns €50   Spends €40   Saves €10

The same student works a full day on Saturday and earns €100.
    Earns €100   Spends €80   Saves €20

Clearly, as income goes up, so does spending.

275

Positive Economics

MARGINAL PROPENSITY TO CONSUME is the proportion of each additional unit of income that is spent.

$$MPC = \frac{\text{Change in consumption}}{\text{Change in income}}$$

Following the example above, if the student receives a raise and earns €110:

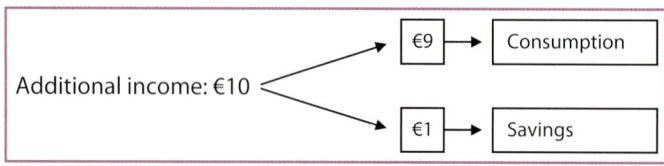

Additional income: €10 → €9 → Consumption
Additional income: €10 → €1 → Savings

The higher the MPC, the higher the level of spending.

In the above example, the marginal (extra) income = €10. Consumption = €9 and savings = €1.

Here, the MPC is 90%.

What Does Consumption Depend On?

Level of Income, Irrespective of Source (Interest from Savings, Royalties from a Book, Wages, Annual Dividends)

The more money you have, the more money you can afford to spend. This is evidenced by the fact that people spend more when they receive a pay rise.

Availability of Credit

If banks are willing to offer higher loans for businesses to expand and households to buy cars, etc., then the level of spending will increase. If banks become more stringent in granting credit, then consumption in the economy will fall.

Rate of Interest (Opportunity Cost of Spending)

If rates of interest are low, consumers will borrow and hence spend. If rates of interest are high, the cost of money is high, therefore consumers will borrow less as it is more attractive to save.

Rate of Income Taxation

If income tax (PAYE) increases, the amount of disposable income that people have will fall and consequently consumers will have less to spend on goods, e.g. the introduction of the Universal Social Charge (USC) in 2011 reduced consumers' disposable incomes and hence spending.

What Does Investment Depend On?

Cost of Capital Goods
As interest rates rise, borrowing becomes more expensive and investment tends to fall. For example, consider a hotel looking to borrow €1 million to build a leisure centre when interest rates are 2%. It is less likely to invest in this expansion project if interest rates were to rise to 8%, because now the cost of the capital would be much higher.

Businesspeople's Expectations
If businesspeople are optimistic about the future, investment may increase. For example, if the economy is improving, it will lead to increased employment and increased demand for goods and services, which will translate into increased spending. Government policy may be business friendly, e.g. low corporation tax which encourages investment and enterprise.

Government Expenditure
Investment is much more attractive if government support is forthcoming. Government expenditure primarily depends on the political decisions of the government and the possibility of borrowing money on financial markets as well as the type of fiscal policy being pursued by the state. (This topic is dealt with in detail in Chapter 23.)

Productive Capacity of the Economy
A country that has vast amounts of scarce resources, e.g. oil, will have a higher GDP than countries that need to import this essential good because they can sell a highly priced export. Likewise, a highly educated and motivated workforce will have a greater productive capacity and therefore a higher GDP than a country with an unskilled labour force.

State of Technology
For example, Ireland promotes research, development and innovation by offering tax credits to companies that spend money in this area. The government initiated this policy so that the country will potentially have a higher national income than a country that devotes little resources to R&D.

What Do Exports Depend On?

Level of Incomes Abroad
The higher the level of incomes abroad, the greater our exports will be.

Positive Economics

Competitiveness
If Irish products are cheaper than foreign alternatives, demand for Irish exports will rise.

Value of the Euro
If the euro is weak relative to other currencies, Irish exports will be cheaper and demand may increase.

What Do Imports Depend On?

Availability of Goods
If essential goods are not available in Ireland, e.g. oil, they would have to be imported.

Foreign Prices vs. Domestic Prices
Consumers may buy cheaper imported goods rather than more expensive domestically produced goods.

Levels of Incomes (Irrespective of Source)
As income increases, the level of spending on all goods, including imports, tends to rise.

Value of the Euro
If the euro is weak relative to other currencies, e.g. pound sterling and US dollar, imports from these countries are more expensive to buy in comparison to Irish-produced goods and hence imports would fall.

Marginal Propensity to Import (MPM)
The higher the MPM, the higher the demand for imports will be.

$$\text{MPM} = \frac{\text{Change in imports}}{\text{Change in income}}$$

> **MARGINAL PROPENSITY TO IMPORT (MPM)** is the proportion of each additional unit of income that is spent on imports.

The Multiplier

A change in spending will cause a change in national income, but the change in income is likely to be much greater than the initial expenditure, i.e. it is said to have a multiplying effect.

> The **MULTIPLIER** shows the precise relationship between an initial injection into the circular flow of income and the eventual increase in national income resulting from the injection.

20: The Determination of National Income

> **Example**   Let's follow the money!

Steps	Income	Savings
John receives an increase of €100 per week.	John spends 80% of this €100 (€80) going to the dentist. MPC = 0.8 = €80 spent	MPS = 0.2 = €20 saved
The dentist receives €80.	The dentist spends 80% of this €80 on hiring a painter to paint the surgery. MPC = 0.8 = €64 spent	MPS = 0.2 = €16 saved
The painter receives €64.	The painter spends 80% of this €64 on buying a new pair of glasses. MPC = 0.8 = €51.20 spent	MPS = 0.2 = €12.80 saved
The optician receives €51.20.	The optician spends 80% of this €51.20 on hiring an electrician. MPC = 0.8 = €40.96 spent	MPS = 0.2 = €10.24 saved
The electrician receives €40.96.	The electrician spends 80% of this €40.96 on buying books. MPC = 0.8 = €32.77 spent	MPS = 0.2 = €8.19 saved
The bookshop owner receives €32.77.		And the process continues…
Total	€500	€100

The above process keeps going until the €100 is all saved.

Clearly, the initial income created a lot more than the original €100 income itself. In fact, if the above process continued, you would find income of €500 was created. The multiplier formula can be used to calculate the total income created.

Positive Economics

$$\frac{1}{1 - MPC}$$
$= 1/1 - 0.8$
$= 1/0.2$
$= 5 =$ the multiplier

The multiplier effect is €500 (5 x €100). The figure 5 means that for any given injection into the economy, national income will increase by five times the original injection.

> **Note:**
> The multiplier formula is used for a closed economy (no imports or exports) and can be rewritten as multiplier = 1/MPS (MPS = 1 – MPC). Due to the fact that what is not consumed is saved, (MPS = 1 – MPC).

Marginal Propensity to Tax (MPT)

You don't choose what you spend on tax, as this percentage is decided by the Department of Finance and announced each year on Budget Day.

Taxes have a numbing impact on the multiplier, i.e. the higher the tax band, the less money that goes to the business or borrower, the less money that can be used to spend, save and pay tax again.

> **MARGINAL PROPENSITY TO TAX** is the percentage of tax paid out of the last increase in income.

$$\text{Multiplier effect of taxation} = \frac{1}{1 + MPT}$$

For example, if 20% of people's salaries are paid to the government on tax, it has the following impact:

Multiplier effect of taxation = 1/(1 + MPT)
$= 1/(1 + 0.2)$
$= 1/(1.2)$
$= 0.83$

This means that only €83 out of every €100 earned can be spent in the economy. (It is important to note that taxes find their way back into the circular flow of income via government spending.)

Marginal Propensity to Save (MPS)

If you don't spend money (or pay tax), you must save it.

$$MPS = 1 - MPC$$

> **MARGINAL PROPENSITY TO SAVE (MPS)** is the percentage of savings held out of the last increase in income.

20: The Determination of National Income

Factors That Affect the Savings Rate in the Irish Economy

Future Expectations for the Economy
If people are concerned about the future of the economy, it will affect consumer confidence. As a result, people tend to postpone purchasing and save instead. On the other hand, if consumers have confidence about the future, they won't hoard cash, but instead spend based on their belief that they will have plenty tomorrow.

Security of Savings
If people don't have confidence in the banking system, they will withdraw their deposits and move them outside of the country or to government-backed savings schemes.

Price Levels / Real Rate of Interest
If deflation is present in an economy, people can spend less to buy the same goods and services as last year, so their ability to save is increased. Hence, in a period of falling prices, consumers may hold back from spending, expecting the price to fall even further and thereby save instead. Deflation increases the real rate of return on savings, as the value of inflation is negative.

> **REMEMBER!**
> Real rate of return = nominal rate of return – inflation

Quality of Financial Products
If the return on offer from financial products (e.g. savings bonds) is satisfactory, people are inclined to avail of them and thus increase their level of savings.

Deferred Spending
If unemployment is rising or people in general are worried about the prospect of losing their jobs, they are likely to reduce spending and increase savings to prepare for the possibility.

Future Levels of State Benefits
If people are fearful for their future pensions, they need to increase savings or pension contributions so that they can afford a comfortable senior life. This activity increases the savings rate in the country.

Economic Effects That an Increase in the Rate of Savings May Have on the Irish Economy

Reduced Spending
People who save more spend less, hence the demand for goods and services falls. Reduced spending within the economy implies a leakage from the circular flow of income.

Positive Economics

Increased Level of Funds Available for Investment
Higher savings implies more funds are available in financial institutions for borrowing by individuals and firms. This stimulates economic growth.

Reduced Inflation
With lower spending and falling demand, there will be downward pressure, or at least less upward pressure, on prices, resulting in lower inflation and increased international competitiveness.

Reduced Demand for Imports
Less spending and greater savings may result in reduced demand for imports, thereby improving our balance of trade and balance of payments.

More Capitalised Banks
Increased savings result in increased funds available to banks. This further capitalises the banks' balance sheets, thereby increasing stability and confidence in the banking sector.

Increased Revenue for Government
More savings means increased revenue from DIRT to the government.

Marginal Propensity to Import (MPM)

In the previous example, we made an assumption that money didn't leave the economy. In other words, we assumed a closed economy, i.e. one that did not engage in international trade. Let's relax that assumption now and review our case study using an economy that imports (open economy). Consider the example that you might buy three books in the next couple of months. Within your purchase in the bookshop, 30% of the amount you spent goes on imported books. If, in general, you spend 30% of your consumption on imported goods, it could be said that your MPM is 30%. This would have the effect of money leaking out of the economy and decreasing the multiplying effect.

Now let's review the impact of this on the Irish economy.

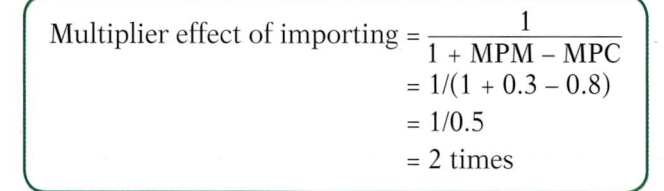

Task

Find out the amount received by the government in DIRT last year and compare it to previous years.

MARGINAL PROPENSITY TO IMPORT (MPM) is the percentage of money spent on imported goods out of the last increase in income.

$$\text{Multiplier effect of importing} = \frac{1}{1 + \text{MPM} - \text{MPC}}$$
$$= 1/(1 + 0.3 - 0.8)$$
$$= 1/0.5$$
$$= 2 \text{ times}$$

20: The Determination of National Income

This means that for any given injection into the economy, national income will rise by twice the original injection. This is a marked difference to earlier, when the multiplier effect was five times in a closed economy.

The above formula can also be written as:

1/(MPS + MPM) = 1/(0.2 + 0.3) = 1/0.5 = 2 times

1/(1 – MPC) + MPM + MPT, where:

MPC* = marginal propensity to consume
MPM = marginal propensity to import
MPT = marginal propensity to tax

> The **MULTIPLIER FORMULA** developed by John Maynard Keynes shows the precise relationship between an initial injection into the circular flow of income and the eventual total increase in national income resulting from the injection.

REMEMBER!
MPS = marginal propensity to save = (1 – MPC)

Example: Calculate the multiplier in a closed economy where the MPC = 65% and MPT = 15%.

Solution:
Step 1: In a closed economy, there isn't any international trade, so MPM = 0
Step 2: MPC = 0.65
Step 3: MPT = 0.15
Step 4: Multiplier formula = 1/(1 – MPC + MPM + MPT)
= 1/(1 – 0.65 + 0 + 0.15)
= 1/0.5
= 2 times

This means that for any given injection into the economy, national income will rise by twice the original injection.

Example: Calculate the multiplier effect in an economy where MPC = 65%, MPM = import 25% and MPT = 15%.

Solution:
Step 1: MPC = 0.65
Step 2: MPM = 0.25
Step 3: MPT = 0.15

Positive Economics

> Step 4: Multiplier formula = 1/1 − MPC + MPM + MPT
> = 1/(1 − 0.65 + 0.25 + 0.15)
> = 1/0.75
> = 1.33
>
> This means that for any given injection into the economy, national income will rise by 1.33 times the original injection.
>
> Another way of writing this formula is 1/(MPS + MPM + MPT).

Where Does the Money Come From to Fund Transfer Payments?

REMEMBER!

Transfer payments:
- Payments received for which no factor of production has been supplied or offered.
- Income people received for which they did not supply goods or services.

Example

- People pay income tax (leakage) so that the government can pay social welfare to the unemployed (injection).
- People pay Deposit Interest Retention Tax (DIRT) on the interest they receive from savings (leakage) so that the government can give businesses money to invest in the form of grants (injection).
- People pay Pay Related Social Insurance (PRSI) (leakage) so that the government can pay for the pensions of people who are retired (injection).

Impact of Transfer Payments on the Multiplier

Generally, the person in receipt of a transfer payment has a high MPC and as a result this person is likely to spend all the money that they receive each week. Consequently, the use of transfer payments actually speeds up the pace at which money moves in the economy and this has a positive impact, as can be seen by the multiplier effect.

20: The Determination of National Income

Impact of Shocks on the Economy or Circular Flow of Income

Case Study 1: A Sudden Rise in the Price of Oil
Firstly, since Ireland doesn't produce any oil and there is little choice of a substitute, companies using it would simply have to pay more for this import. This would represent a large leakage from the Irish economy. Secondly, as the cost of production has risen, the company may have to increase the price of the final product and may export less. This affects the circular flow of income, as economic activity is lower.

Case Study 2: A Factory Closure
If a factory closes down, the staff lose their jobs and hence their incomes fall. They need to find a new job or request social welfare from the state. The factory's suppliers have one less customer, which hurts their own sales and profits. The government receives less tax because the factory won't be making any more profits and paying the workers. If the factory was exporting its output, the country loses out on the additional injection received from abroad.

The Keynesian Presentation of National Income

Keynes drew what is called his 45° diagram to illustrate consumption at different levels of income. All points on the 45° line show where consumption = income.

1. When we add consumption at different income levels to the 45° diagram, we get a consumption function.

2. When the consumption function crosses the 45° line, we get equilibrium income because at that point, expenditure = income (Figure 1).

3. If investment is greater than savings, national income will rise (Figure 2).

4. Likewise, if government spending (injection) is greater than taxation (leakage), national income will rise.

5. Similarly, if exports are greater than imports, national income will increase.

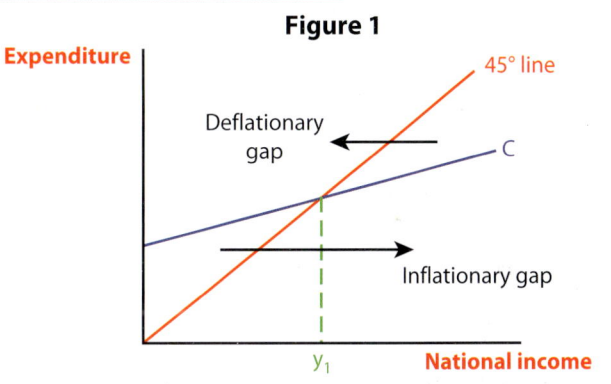

Figure 1

y_1 represents an equilibrium level of national income => all production is being consumed

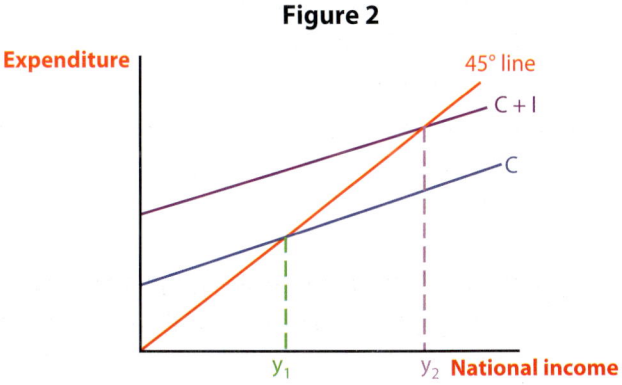

Figure 2

y_2 represents an equilibrium level of national income with investment included
Investment is an injection into the circular flow of income, which raises national income

Positive Economics

6. On the Keynesian 45° line, equilibrium occurs where the level of expenditure (C + I + G + X – M) crosses the 45° line.

7. At y_4 (Figure 3), there is equilibrium of national income. However, this may not be the level required for full employment. This could be beyond y_4 (e.g. y_F).

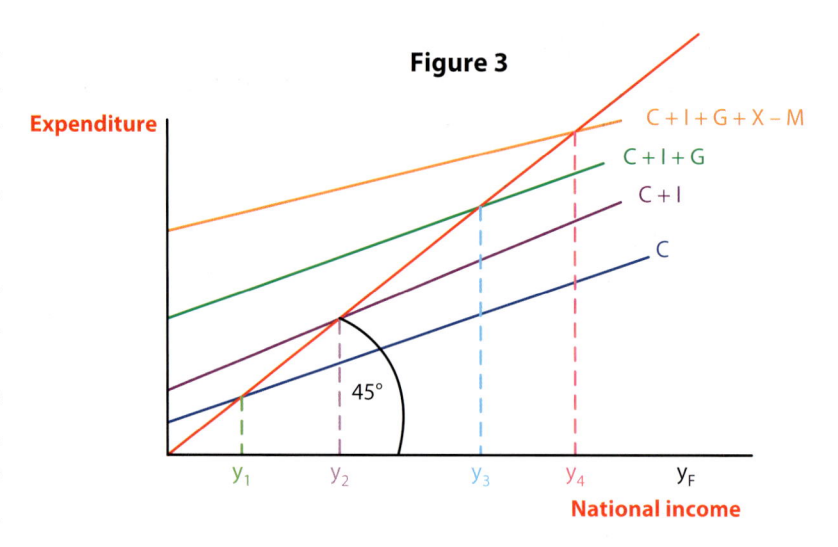

Figure 3

8. If the equilibrium level of national income happens to be greater than the level that would give full employment (too much money chasing too few goods) this would lead to an inflationary gap. In Keynesian analysis, this exists where aggregate demand at full employment national income is above the 45 line.

9. Likewise aggregate demand may be too small to give full employment – thus a deflationary gap exists. In the Keynesian graph, this occurs where aggregate demand at full employment national income is below the 45 line.

10. Refer back to Figure 1. Let's assume that $y_1 = y_F$ (full employment national income). To the left, you have an inflationary gap and to the right you have a deflationary gap.

Trade Cycles

The trade cycle refers to recurring patterns of expansion and contraction in the economy. Almost all the major industrialised economies of the world have experienced a continuous succession of booms and slumps. This cycle became known as the trade cycle and it provides information on the relationship between prices, employment and investment.

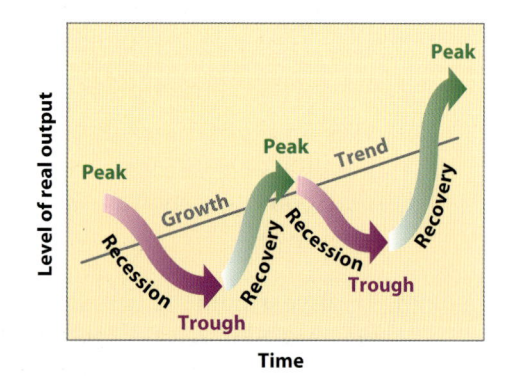

Source: www.allbusiness.com

Phase 1: Recovery

The economy starts from a depressed state of high unemployment with low prices and output. An increase in investment with the multiplier effect leads to increased incomes and demand. This increased level of demand leads to a further increase in investment capital, anticipating future profits. This leads to increased economic activity and recovery.

Phase 2: Boom
As demand increases, the level of employment increases and any further increases in demand cannot be satisfied by increases in production. This leads to price increases via inflation.

Phase 3: Recession
The boom comes to an end when output is at full capacity and investment begins to decrease. A decline in investment leads to a fall in consumption. As profits and prices fall, a wave of pessimism is experienced and the demand for new capital equipment falls significantly.

Phase 4: Depression
In many trade cycles, the recovery phase happens after a period of recession, but in extreme circumstances (that occur less often), there can be a deeper fall-off of economic activity, namely a depression. This depression can happen when there has been a recession that has persisted for an extended period of time and the economy has seen a real decline of GDP by more than 10%.

Back to the Beginning of the Trade Cycle Again…
At some point, incomes, profits and demand will stop falling. There will be high unemployment and little investment. Due to the fact that some capital goods have now become obsolete, entrepreneurs are forced to invest in new equipment, which will lead to the recovery phase and the cycle starts again.

Positive Consequences of Economic Growth

- **Increased employment:** A rise in GNP will lead to increased demand for goods and services with more labour being demanded to be able to meet this demand.

- **Improved government finances:** More people employed will result in an increase in incomes. Increases in income will in turn mean an increase in spending, which will result in an increase in indirect tax revenue (VAT) for the government. The government will see a decrease in expenditure on social welfare benefits. In addition, more and improved government services will be available.

- **Effect on balance of payments:** If extra GNP results from increased output and if some of this output is exported, then our balance of payments position will improve.

- **Improved standard of living:** Higher GNP will result in increased wealth in the economy, allowing customers to purchase more goods and services, leading to an improved standard of living. Following from this, the economy will see a reduction in poverty.

Positive Economics

- **Effects on migration:** If job opportunities exist, then people who had planned to emigrate may remain in Ireland and more immigrants may be attracted into the economy.
- **Investment opportunities:** Rising GNP indicates a growing economy and this may attract further investment into the economy.

Negative Consequences of Economic Growth

- **Inflationary pressures:** The rise in the level of economic activity brings about an increase in the level of demand for goods and services. This causes an increase in inflation.
- **Labour shortages:** The increased demand for goods and services will increase the demand for labour in certain sectors, which may result in labour shortages.
- **Demand for wage increases:** Expectations by workers may increase with respect to pay increases (due to both points above).
- **Increased demand for imports:** A rise in GNP increases income and spending power. Hence, demand for imports may rise, worsening the balance of payments position.
- **Pressure in the housing market:** The rise in GNP increases spending power, thus stimulating demand for houses and resulting in housing shortages and increasing prices.
- **Pressure on state infrastructure:** Higher GNP results in a greater demand for scarce resources. Higher incomes will increase demand for commodities, e.g. cars. The extra pollution would result in more damage to the environment.
- **Increased immigration/displacement of population:** Rising GNP increases demand and provides more opportunities for employment, leading to a possible rise in immigration and the displacement of population (movement to urban centres), which further adds to the pressures mentioned in the above two points.

The Accelerator Principle

Remember Pat's Deli? He has an annual increase in sales of 3%. However, in year 5 he needs to replace the coffee machine, which is a 100% increase in capital goods. This is an example of how an increase in demand (3%) for final goods leads to a much greater demand (100%) for capital goods due to wear and tear (i.e. depreciation).

> The **ACCELERATOR PRINCIPLE** states that an increase in demand for final goods results in a more than proportional increase in demand for capital goods.

PROFILE: John Bates Clark (1847–1938)

Clark was Professor of Economics at Colombia University in the US. He said that the price of labour is determined by its marginal utility to the employer. Due to diminishing returns, each worker adds less output than the previous worker and each worker must be paid the same rate. Therefore, the employer will stop hiring units of labour when the contribution of the last worker hired exactly equals the wages they are paid.

Clark also developed the accelerator principle, which states that a small increase in demand for final goods can lead to a proportionately greater increase in demand for capital goods.

PROFILE: John Maynard Keynes (1883–1946)

His major work, *The General Theory of Employment, Interest and Money*, was published in 1936. The main goal of this text was the determination of national income and employment.

Output Is Demand Determined
Keynes took the view that the size of national income depended on expenditure, i.e. consumer spending, investment, government spending and exports less imports. Unemployment was caused by people not spending enough money. He was not in favour of wage cuts as he felt that they had harmful effects on consumption, income and total demand. He thought wage cuts increased unemployment rather than reducing it.

The Multiplier
In recessions, the aggregate demand of economies falls, i.e. businesses and individuals spend less. Lower spending causes a fall in demand and further falls in spending. Keynes thought that governments should borrow and push money into the economy. Once the economy recovered and was expanding again, governments should pay back the loans. This theory formed the basis for the Keynesian multiplier (any increase in spending will cause a much greater increase in GNP due to the fact that one person's expenditure is another person's income).

Government Intervention
Keynes strongly attacked the laissez-faire thinking of previous economists who felt that economies worked best when markets are free of state intervention. Keynes thought that governments should intervene in the economy by means of fiscal policy. He wrote that governments should borrow and engage in budget deficits, e.g. public works programmes, to stimulate economic activity in recessionary times. This was in complete contrast to the prevailing view that governments should pursue balanced budgets.

Positive Economics

Liquidity Preference Theory
Previous writers thought that the public saved money when offered a high rate of interest; money was considered a medium of exchange. Keynes adopted a new approach by studying the holding rather than the spending of money. He saw three motives that the public had for holding money: transactionary, precautionary and speculative motives.

National Income Could Be in Equilibrium at Less Than Full Employment
Keynes thought that national income could reach equilibrium without reaching full employment and thus suggested government intervention to help create jobs.

Investment Decisions by Entrepreneurs
The classical school thought that the rate of interest ensured that all savings were invested. Keynes did not agree. He stated that investment by entrepreneurs was more dependent on businesspeople's expectations rather than the rate of interest. Hence, investment could be less than savings, resulting in a leakage from the circular flow of income and leading to a fall in demand and more unemployment.

EXAM ✓ Sample Question (20 marks)

The table below shows the level of national income, consumption, investment, exports and imports at the end of year 1 and year 2 (for the purpose of this question, you may ignore the government sector).

Year	National income	Consumption	Investment	Exports	Imports
1	€5,800	€4,800	€1,200	€1,000	€1,200
2		€5,250	€1,300	€1,200	€1,350

Calculate the following, showing all your workings.

1. The level of national income in year 2
2. The marginal propensity to save
3. The marginal propensity to import
4. The size of the multiplier. Explain the economic meaning of this multiplier figure.

Solution
1. $Y = C + I + X - M$
   $Y = 5{,}250 + 1{,}300 + 1{,}200 - 1{,}350$
   $Y = 6{,}400$

2. MPC + MPS = 1
   MPC = ΔC/ΔY = 450/600 = 0.75
   1 − 0.75 = 0.25 = MPS

   OR

   ΔS/ΔY = 150/600 = 0.25
   Y − C = S
   Period 1: Y − C = 5,800 − 4,800 = 1,000
   Period 2: Y − C = 6,400 − 5,250 = 1,150

3. MPM
   ΔM/ΔY
   ΔM = 1,350 − 1,200 = 150
   150/600 = 0.25

4. Multiplier
   1/(MPS + MPM) = 1/(0.25 + 0.25) = 1/0.5 = 2

   OR

   1/(1 − (MPC − MPM)) = 1/1 − (0.75 − 0.25) = 2

   This means that for any given injection into the economy, national income will rise by twice the original injection.

Questions

Short Questions

1. What is the circular flow of income?
2. Outline three examples of leakages.
3. Outline three examples of injections.
4. What are the constituents of aggregate demand?
5. What influences consumption?
6. What influences investment?
7. How would you describe an economy with MPM = 0?

Positive Economics

Long Questions

1. Draw the circular flow of income, explaining its injections and leakages.
2. What is the multiplier? Explain the variables that make up its formula.
3. Critically analyse the impact on the multiplier and the economy of:
    (a) A decrease in income tax
    (b) A decrease in the cost of money
    (c) A decrease in exports
    (d) A decrease in imports
    (e) An increase in government spending
    (f) An increase in VAT
4. Calculate the multiplier in each of the following cases.
    (a) MPM = 0, MPT = 0.05, MPC = 0.65
    (b) MPM = 0, MPT = 0.05, MPS = 0.65
    (c) MPM = 0.3, MPT = 0.05, MPC = 0.65
    (d) MPM = 0.5, MPT = 0.05, MPC = 0.65
    (e) MPM = 0.5, MPT = 0.1, MPS = 0.65
    (f) MPM = 0.3, MPT = 0.2, MPS = 0.65
    (g) MPM = 0.1, MPT = 0.03, MPS = 0.65
    (h) MPM = 0.3, MPT = 0.3, MPC = 0.65
    (i) MPM = 0.5, MPT = 0.6, MPC = 0.65
    (j) MPM = 0.01, MPT = 0.01, MPC = 0.65
5. Explain the phases of the trade cycle.
6. Critically analyse the positive and negative consequences of economic growth.
7. Define the accelerator principle.
8. Write a brief note on the contribution of John Maynard Keynes.
9. Calculate the following, showing all your workings.

Year	National income	Consumption	Investment	Exports	Imports
1	€10,000	€8,600	€1,000	€1,200	€800
2	€11,200	€9,500	€1,300		€1,100

    (a) The level of exports in year 2
    (b) The marginal propensity to import
    (c) The marginal propensity to save
    (d) The size of the multiplier. Explain the economic meaning of this multiplier figure.
10. Calculate the following, showing all your workings.

Year	National income	Consumption	Investment	Exports	Imports
1	€5,000	€4,300	€500	€600	€400
2	€5,600	€4,750	€650	€750	

    (a) The level of imports in year 2
    (b) The marginal propensity to import
    (c) The marginal propensity to save
    (d) The size of the multiplier. Explain the economic meaning of this multiplier figure.

Chapter 21 | Inflation

Specific Learning Outcomes

At the end of this chapter, students should be able to:

- ☐ Define price inflation.
- ☐ Calculate, from a given date, a weighted price index.
- ☐ Describe the construction of the consumer price index.
- ☐ Interpret and critically analyse changes in the consumer price index.
- ☐ Evaluate the usefulness and limitations of the consumer price index.
- ☐ Identify and explain the principal causes of inflation in the Irish economy.
- ☐ Critically analyse the effects of inflation on the Irish economy.
- ☐ Describe the main policies available to control inflation.
- ☐ Describe the benefits of stable prices.
- ☐ Describe what the HICP is and understand the difference between it and the CPI.
- ☐ Define deflation.
- ☐ Explain the Constant Tax Price Index.

Positive Economics

Introduction

Inflation has been a marked characteristic of most economies since World War II and is one of the most talked about economic concepts. It is also a goal of many governments to achieve price stability. It affects consumers, businesses and governments. So what is it?

> **INFLATION** is defined as a steady and persistent increase in the general level of prices. It's the rate at which your money loses its ability to buy things.

In Germany in 1923, the wildest inflation in history was raging. Prices of goods often doubled in a few hours! A frenzied stampede developed to buy goods and get rid of money. By late 1923 it took 200 billion Deutschmarks (old German currency) to buy a loaf of bread!

More recently, the inflationary experiences in Zimbabwe are just as alarming when we look at the following inflation rates.

Year	Rate
1980	7%
1990	17%
2000	55.22%
2008	231,150,888.87% (July)

Source: Wikipedia.

Who Calculates Inflation in Ireland?

The Central Statistics Office (CSO) employs 94 part-time price collectors who collect about 53,000 prices in 84 locations throughout the country on the second Tuesday of every month. A further 3,000 are collected from postal, email and telephone inquiries along with internet price collection. These prices are used to calculate price inflation.

Measuring Inflation

If we want to measure the change in price of one good over time, we simply look at the two prices and compare them.

Year	1	2	3	4
Price per bag of sugar	90c	92c	93c	99c

21: Inflation

From the above table we can see that a bag of sugar rose in price by 9c between year 1 and year 4. When we compare prices in this way it is important that we have a starting point so that all prices can be compared to this reference point. Our base year (starting point) will be year 1, i.e. prices equal 100, which allows us to find the price changes in percentage terms.

$$\frac{\text{Price in any year}}{\text{Price in base year}} \times 100$$

Year 1	Year 2	Year 3	Year 4
$\frac{90}{90} \times 100$	$\frac{92}{90} \times 100$	$\frac{93}{90} \times 100$	$\frac{99}{90} \times 100$
100	102.22	103.33	110

We have now calculated a simple price index, i.e. the price changes for a **single good**, and it allows us to say that a bag of sugar rose by 10% between year 1 and year 4. However, we need to examine changes in the general price level, i.e. in many goods. We use a composite price index for this, which takes into consideration the importance of the amount of money spent on each good (weights). Steps involved in constructing a composite index are as follows:

1. Choose a base year and let all the prices equal 100.
2. Select the goods and find the prices for all goods in all years.
3. Construct a simple price index for each good (as above).
4. Multiply the simple price index by the weight (proportion of income spent on the good).
5. Add to get the composite price index for the current year.

For example:

Category	Price of item in base year 1	Price of item in year 2	Price of item in year 3	Price of item in year 4	% of income spent on item (weight)
Food	19	21	23	24	40%
Transport	45	44	42	41	25%
Health	28	30	31	33	35%

Year 1 base year	Calculation of simple price index × weight	Weighted index
Food	$\frac{19}{19} \times 100 = 100 \times 40\% =$	40
Transport	$\frac{45}{45} \times 100 = 100 \times 25\% =$	25
Health	$\frac{28}{28} \times 100 = 100 \times 35\% =$	35
	Price index for the current year	**100**

Year 2	Calculation of simple price index × weight	Weighted index
Food	$\frac{21}{19} \times 100 = 110.52 \times 40\% =$	44.21
Transport	$\frac{44}{45} \times 100 = 97.78 \times 25\% =$	24.44
Health	$\frac{30}{28} \times 100 = 107.14 \times 35\% =$	37.50
	Price index for the current year	**106.15**

Year 3	Calculation of simple price index × weight	Weighted index
Food	$\frac{23}{19} \times 100 = 121.05 \times 40\% =$	48.42
Transport	$\frac{42}{45} \times 100 = 93.33 \times 25\% =$	23.33
Health	$\frac{31}{28} \times 100 = 110.71 \times 35\% =$	38.75
	Price index for the current year	**110.50**

Year 4	Calculation of simple price index × weight	Weighted index
Food	$\frac{24}{19} \times 100 = 126.32 \times 40\% =$	50.53
Transport	$\frac{41}{45} \times 100 = 91.11 \times 25\% =$	22.78
Health	$\frac{33}{28} \times 100 = 117.86 \times 35\% =$	41.25
	Price index for the current year	**114.56**

We can now say that the average price level rose by 14.56% between the base year (year 1) and year 4. Prices increased by 4.1% between year 2 and year 3 (110.50 – 106.15 = $\frac{4.35}{106.15} \times 100 = 4.1\%$).

The Consumer Price Index

The consumer price index (CPI) is the official measure of inflation in Ireland. It measures the price changes of goods and services typically consumed by all consumers living in rural/urban areas, high-/low-income earners and from all age groups. It is a price index that shows the current cost of purchasing the same identical basket of goods with the base year (starting point).

How Is the CPI Constructed?

NATIONAL AVERAGE SHOPPING BASKET
This is based on a selection of the most frequently purchased goods and services, i.e. the National Average Family Shopping Basket. Presently, over a thousand items are included, ranging from day-to-day items like food, clothing, footwear and petrol, but also items like mobile phones, bank charges, childminding fees, etc.

EXPENDITURE CATEGORIES
This 'shopping basket' is divided into 12 main groups, which allows for a more detailed analysis of the contribution each makes to the overall change in prices in the month and year. The 12 categories are:

1. Food and non-alcoholic beverages
2. Alcoholic beverages and tobacco
3. Clothing and footwear
4. Housing, water, electricity, gas and other fuels
5. Furnishings, household equipment
6. Health
7. Transport
8. Communications
9. Recreation and culture
10. Education
11. Restaurants and hotels
12. Miscellaneous

HOUSEHOLD BUDGET INQUIRY
Household Budget Inquiries are carried out every five years to ensure the index accurately reflects the up-to-date purchasing patterns of the public since tastes change, items go out of fashion and new products become available. These surveys also tell us the fraction of income that is spent on each category. These are called weights.

DECIDE ON A BASE YEAR AND FIND THE PRICES
The prices of the goods to be included in the calculation are made equal to 100.

PRICES IN THE CURRENT YEAR ARE COLLECTED
To ensure that the fixed basket stays the same, accurate checking of prices has to be done every month. For an item to be comparable, the brand, model, size, etc. must not change from one month to the next. These prices are then compared to the base period.

Positive Economics

What Are the Economic Uses of the Consumer Price Index?

MEASURES THE RATE OF INFLATION
Monthly changes in the CPI give us the change in the average level of prices (inclusive of indirect taxes) paid for consumer goods and services.

INTERNATIONAL COMPARISONS
By comparing our rate of inflation with that of other countries, we can see quite easily if we are maintaining our international competitiveness. If our inflation rate is 3% and that of our trading partners is 2%, then it is possible for our goods to be priced out of international markets.

INDICATOR OF THE COUNTRY'S/GOVERNMENT'S PERFORMANCE
The CPI, along with other statistics such as economic growth, rate of unemployment, government finances, etc., gives us essential information on how the economy is performing. It is also an indicator of how well a government is performing: is it achieving one of its economic goals (price stability – inflation less than 2%)?

INDEXATION OF SAVINGS AND INVESTMENTS
Some saving schemes are indexed linked. What this means is that the rate of interest rises in keeping with rises in the CPI. Also, individuals with pension policies may decide to increase their contributions to maintain the real value of their policies.

USED IN WAGE NEGOTIATIONS
Employee representatives will often use increases in the CPI in order to bargain for higher wages. Their argument is usually based on the fact that prices have risen, thereby reducing the real value of their members' wages.

USED BY GOVERNMENT TO INDEX TAX BANDS
The government may use increases in the CPI to index tax bands so that taxpayers are not paying more tax. Likewise, the government may justify increases in social welfare payments to maintain the standard of living of recipients.

What Precautions Should Be Taken When Using the CPI?
While the CPI is very useful, as outlined above, care should be taken when interpreting the data for the following reasons.

AN INDEX OF THE AVERAGE CONSUMER
As the index covers the buying habits of the average consumer, it cannot then cover the spending profile of any one individual or household, e.g. non-smokers/non-drinkers.

NOT A COST OF LIVING INDEX
The CPI is a price index and thereby measures the change in the level of prices of consumer goods and services. A cost of living index includes such items as income levels, taxation, social welfare payments and substitution between cheaper and dearer goods. While the change in the level of prices is an important determinant in the change in the cost of living, the CPI only covers this element.

LAGS BEHIND CONSUMER TRENDS AND FASHIONS
While the basket of goods (616 items) is reviewed every five years, new and popular products in the intervening years are not included. Similarly, goods and services consumed in Celtic Tiger times which are included, e.g. a single CD, may not now be consumed, making the index outdated.

STATIC WEIGHTS
The weight is the proportion of total expenditure spent on a certain item or category in the basket of goods and services. The importance of some items in the base year could change over time due to changes in prices, tastes and income, thus making the weights outdated. The further we move from the base year, the less it's going to fully reflect consumer spending.

QUALITY CHANGES IN PRODUCTS
While the index shows increases in prices, it does not indicate whether there have been improvements in the quality of the products to justify the price increases.

SUBSTITUTION OF PRODUCTS
The CPI compares the current price of a fixed quantity of goods and services with the price of the same fixed quantity in the base period. When goods increase in price, consumers may switch to cheaper substitute goods/brands and the CPI does not account for this.

> 'The ECB's main task is to maintain the euro's purchasing power and thus price stability in the euro area.'
>
> *Source*: www.ecb.int.

What Factors Cause Inflation?

Consumers don't like to see the purchasing power of their euro falling, as fewer goods and services can be purchased. Manufacturers don't like to see the price of raw materials increasing. So what causes prices to increase?

Demand Pull Factors

If aggregate demand is greater than aggregate supply, prices will be forced upwards. This can happen where there is relatively easy access to bank credit and where government increases expenditure. Basically, too much money chasing too few goods and excess demand 'pulls' up prices. This tends to happen when the purchasing power of consumers increases at a faster rate than the production of goods and services.

Cost Push Factors

If a company experiences an increase in its cost of production, it will probably pass on this increase by raising the selling price of the final good sold to the consumer. Increases in wages, raw materials, PRSI rates, commercial rates, electricity costs, etc. will all have the effect of pushing up the cost of production and hence the retail price.

Imported Inflation

Many raw materials used in the production process are imported. When these prices increase, so does the cost of production and manufacturers have no option but to increase the selling price of their finished goods.

Similarly, if the value of the euro falls relative to sterling (or any other non-eurozone currency), then it costs us more to purchase the same quantity of goods than it did before the devaluation. This too can lead to price increases to compensate for the increased cost of the raw materials.

Government-induced Inflation

This can occur when the government, through its budgetary policy, decides to increase VAT rates (indirect taxes), thus raising prices. On the other hand, lowering income tax rates (direct taxes, e.g. PAYE) gives greater spending power to consumers, potentially causing price inflation.

What Remedies Are Available?

In a small open economy like Ireland, our inflation rate can be affected by external factors beyond our control, e.g. price increases in oil. However, we can take steps to tackle price inflation that is caused by domestic influences.

Fiscal Policy

Increasing direct taxation would have the effect of reducing demand, as consumers would have less disposable income. However, governments tend not to favour this option as it stifles economic growth and is politically imprudent. On the other hand, increasing tax credits may reduce the demand for wage increases, thereby curbing cost-led inflation. Indirect taxation increases (e.g. VAT) may also reduce consumer expenditure, but has the effect of increasing retail prices.

The government could introduce cutbacks, balance its budget (by reducing the number/wages of public sector employees and the amount of services available and decreasing infrastructural/social welfare spending), each of which would have the effect of decreasing demand in the economy. Almost all these measures would be strongly resisted by unions and various interest groups, making these cost-cutting measures very difficult to implement, as they could lead to unemployment, a fall in welfare and a decline in the future wealth-creating capacity of the economy.

Monetary Policy

Reducing the amount of credit made available by the banking sector would certainly reduce demand but has the effect of curtailing future wealth creation and employment. Increasing the rate of interest (price of money) reduces the demand for loans and hence discourages investment and consequently leads to unemployment. However, this option is not within the remit of the Irish government, as interest rate increases/decreases are determined by the ECB.

Partnership Agreements

Any arrangements that attempt to limit wage increases will help dampen cost push inflation. Productivity agreements (e.g. an increase in the wage rate of 2% accompanied by an increase in output of 2%) and Social Partnership Agreements (e.g. ICTU/IBEC/IFA/government, etc. agreeing to limit pay increases) both have the effect of curtailing cost push inflation. Likewise, any government that reduces the minimum wage rate (the rate at which all other wages are pegged) could reduce business costs and consequently inflation. Any reduction in energy costs, i.e. the price of oil or electricity, will certainly assist in keeping costs low and consequently prices stable.

What Problems Are Caused by High Inflation?

Lower Standard of Living
Due to higher costs of living, people have reduced spending power (unable to purchase the same amount of goods and services) and can thus experience a fall in their standard of living.

Fixed Income Holders
People with fixed incomes lose out in inflationary times since their fixed incomes may not keep pace with price increases. For example, old age pensioners may have to wait for the government to decide to adjust their payments.

Speculation Encouraged
During inflationary times, the value of assets, e.g. houses/land, tends to rise, thus attracting investment in these assets. Money tends to be invested in these speculative projects and not in manufacturing ventures.

Borrowing Encouraged
Let's say a customer takes out a mortgage of €100,000 and agrees to repay €600 per month earning a net monthly wage of €2,000. If during the period of repayment prices and hence wages increase (in our example to €2,200), then repayment commitments on the loan fall in relative terms.

Wage Demands
Workers and their representatives will try to negotiate increased wages during inflationary times to compensate for a loss in their existing purchasing power.

Loss of International Competitiveness
If our inflation rate is higher than that of our trading partners, then our exports may fall, as we are less competitive on foreign markets.

Savings Discouraged
During inflationary periods, people may not be inclined to save if the rate of interest (e.g. 3%) is lower than the rate of inflation (e.g. 5%). The real return is negative, acting as a disincentive to save.

Difficulty Attracting Foreign Direct Investment (FDI)
A country with prolonged high inflation may find it difficult to attract new foreign multinationals and existing investors in the country may decide to locate to cheaper wage inflation countries.

Increase in Unemployment
Employers faced with increased wage demands and a possible loss of exports due to our rate of inflation being higher than our trading partners may decide to reduce costs by making staff redundant.

What Is Deflation?

Deflation happens when there is a general decrease in the average level of prices. This sounds great, but it can damage an economy. If all prices are steadily declining, then consumers may postpone buying goods and services, expecting it to cost less a week later and less again a month later, causing consumer demand to fall and thus affecting employment and growth. Likewise, a company might postpone investing and the economy would suffer.

> If all prices are steadily declining, then consumers may postpone buying goods and services
>
> ↓
>
> Expecting it to cost less a week later and less again a month later
>
> ↓
>
> Causing consumer demand to fall
>
> ↓
>
> Affecting employment and growth

Benefits of Price Stability

The benefits of inflation being below 2% (goal of the ECB) include:

- Consumers will tend to spend, generating demand for goods and services and hence employment, contributing to economic growth.

- Government revenues could increase with more indirect and direct taxes being collected due to increased numbers working and spending.

- The demand for wage increases wouldn't be as urgent given that workers' purchasing power wouldn't be falling. This in turn keeps costs stable and companies may decide to increase investment given that they are able to plan more effectively.

- Old age pensioners and those on fixed pensions will see their purchasing power being maintained and will be able to manage better.

- Savings in the economy may increase, leading to investment (if the rate of inflation is less than the rate of interest).

Constant Tax Price Index

This is a price index that keeps the indirect tax part of a price increase constant. For example:

- Price of mobile phone in year 1: €105 (€100 plus €5 VAT)

- Price of same mobile phone in year 2: €125 (€110 plus €15 VAT)

When calculating the Constant Tax Price Index, the year 2 price would be taken as €115, i.e. the increase in indirect tax of €10 would be subtracted from the price. The main use of this index is in wage negotiations. It will reduce the possibility of employees getting wage increases to compensate for increases in taxation.

Inflation in Europe

Harmonised Index of Consumer Prices

Almost all nations calculate a CPI to measure inflation in their respective economies. The weights and the items included in the basket of goods and services indicate the prevailing consumer patterns of each individual country. Eurostat, along with member states, produces a Harmonised Index of Consumer Prices (HICP). Presently, just under 90% of the total CPI basket is included in the HICP. The HICP excludes mortgage interest, building materials, concrete blocks, union subscriptions, motor taxation and the non-service elements of motor and house insurance. So which is the better indicator of inflation? The CPI, with greater coverage, is a better measure for national purposes. For EU comparisons, the HICP is the correct measure.

Changes in Demand and Supply of Money

The following are the economic effects if the supply of money grows at a faster rate than a country's production of goods and services (quantitative easing).

- **Inflation:** Prices of goods and services may rise, given that there is more money available in the system to purchase them, thus fuelling demand for consumption. Coupling this with an insufficient supply of goods and services pushes the price up further.

- **Imports:** Since there is more money in the system and growth is above that of the economy, consumers have more disposable income to spend on imports. Coupled with an insufficient supply of goods and services, demand must be met by greater imports.

- **Fall in exchange rate:** Due to the increase in the supply of money and possible increase in demand for imports, this could lead to a fall in the value of the euro.

- **Interest:** Under Keynes's liquidity preference theory, if the supply of money grows, then interest rates will fall. This occurs via simple demand and supply economics. If there is more of a commodity available (i.e. excess supply), the price (interest rate) has to fall.

The following are the economic effects if the supply of money grows at a slower rate than a country's production of goods and services.

- **Deflation/moderation in price levels:** Prices of goods and services may stop rising or even fall, given that there is less money available in the system to purchase them, thus fuelling demand for consumption. Coupled with the excess supply of goods and services, the price is pushed down even further.

- **Unemployment and falling demand:** Given that there is declining economic growth, producers may rationalise, leading to rising unemployment. As a result, aggregate demand falls due to lower disposable income and this hampers confidence in the economy.

- **Imports:** Since there is less money in the system, consumers have less disposable income to spend on imports. Coupled with the excess supply of goods and services, the demand for imports is further dampened.

- **Fall in exchange rate:** Because of insufficient supply, there are fewer people who have the currency than actually demand it. As a result, the value of currency in a non-eurozone country may strengthen.

- **Interest:** Under Keynes's liquidity preference theory, if the supply of money contracts, then interest rates will increase. This occurs via simple demand and supply economics. If there is less of a commodity available (i.e. insufficient supply), the price has to increase (interest rate).

EXAM Question 7(a)(ii), 2006 (12 marks)

Explain how a consumer price index is constructed.

Solution

- **Based on the National Average Family Shopping Basket:** Those items that the average Irish family buys frequently and in large quantities are included.

- **Expenditure patterns divided into various categories:** The CPI contains various categories of expenditure, e.g. food, alcohol, tobacco, clothing and footwear, fuel and light.

- **Calculation of 'weight' (Household Budget Inquiry):** The weight is the fraction of income that is spent on each category of expenditure. This information is obtained through the Household Budget Inquiry (a random sample of all private households in the state).

- **Prices in the base year determined:** The average cost of the above items is taken to equal 100.

- **Prices in the current year determined:** The current prices of each item are collected from a fixed panel of retail and service outlets in various locations throughout the country.

Positive Economics

Question 6, Section A, 2005 (17 marks)

For a composite (weighted) price index covering the three types of expenditure given in the following table, calculate the price index for the current year. The base value is 100. Show your workings.

Category	% income spent on item(s)	Prices of item(s) base year €	Prices of item(s) current year €	Calculation of simple price index	Weight	Result
Food	30%	10.00	11.50			
Clothing and footwear	20%	40.00	36.00			
Other items	50%	20.00	22.00			
	100%			Price index for the current year →		

Solution

Category	% income spent on item(s)	Prices of item(s) base year €	Prices of item(s) current year €	Calculation of simple price index	Weight	Result
Food	30%	10.00	11.50	$11.50 \times \frac{100}{10} = 115$	× 30%	34.50
Clothing and footwear	20%	40.00	36.00	$36.00 \times \frac{100}{40.00} = 90.00$	× 20%	18.00
Other items	50%	20.00	22.00	$22.00 \times \frac{100}{20.00} = 110$	× 50%	55.00
	100%			Price index for the current year →		107.5

Questions

Short Questions

1. Define price inflation.
2. Who calculates the rate of inflation in Ireland?
3. Name the main index used to measure price inflation in the Irish economy.
4. Explain the differences between a simple and a composite price index.
5. Outline the steps in constructing a composite price index.

Long Questions

1. Why are weights important in constructing a composite index?
2. Outline the steps in constructing the CPI.
3. Outline the economic consequences of a rise in the rate of price inflation in Ireland.
4. Explain the uses of the CPI.
5. Are changes in the CPI an accurate measure of changes in the cost of living? Discuss.
6. State and explain how the CPI would be used by consumers, the government and workers.
7. Explain demand pull inflation and cost push inflation. How can each be prevented?
8. Why is it important to have price stability?
9. Calculate the composite price index from the following.

Category	Weight	Price in base year	Price in current year
Education	25%	9	14
Health	40%	27	28
Communication	35%	15	16

10. Explain the likely economic effects in an open and in a closed economy if:
    (a) The supply of money grows at a faster rate than a country's production of goods and services.
    (b) The supply of money grows at a slower rate than a country's production of goods and services.

Chapter 22 | Employment

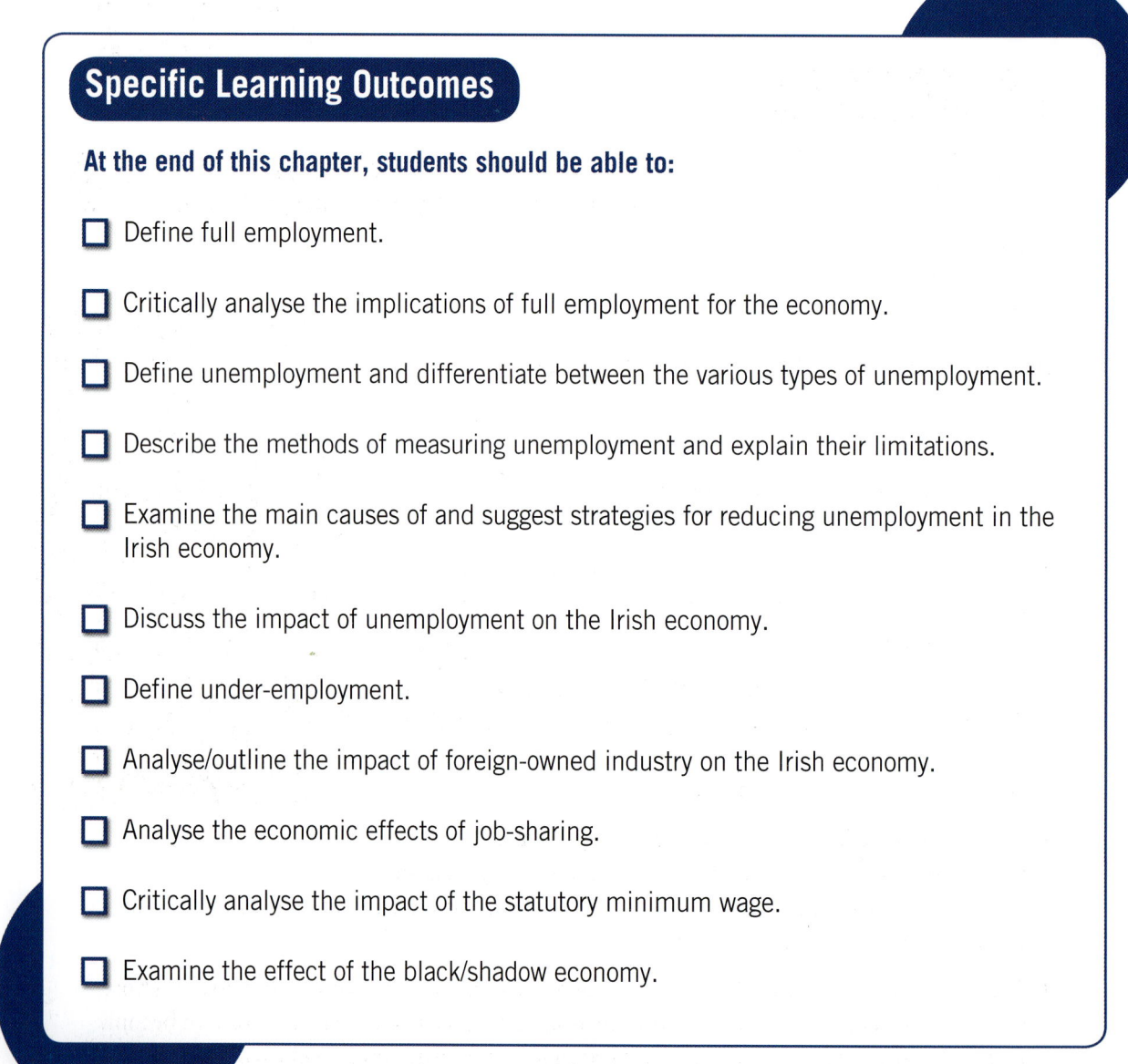

Specific Learning Outcomes

At the end of this chapter, students should be able to:

- [ ] Define full employment.

- [ ] Critically analyse the implications of full employment for the economy.

- [ ] Define unemployment and differentiate between the various types of unemployment.

- [ ] Describe the methods of measuring unemployment and explain their limitations.

- [ ] Examine the main causes of and suggest strategies for reducing unemployment in the Irish economy.

- [ ] Discuss the impact of unemployment on the Irish economy.

- [ ] Define under-employment.

- [ ] Analyse/outline the impact of foreign-owned industry on the Irish economy.

- [ ] Analyse the economic effects of job-sharing.

- [ ] Critically analyse the impact of the statutory minimum wage.

- [ ] Examine the effect of the black/shadow economy.

22: Employment

Introduction

> 'Far and away the best prize that life has to offer is the chance to work hard at work worth doing.' – Theodore Roosevelt (1858–1919), 26th president of the US

It is the goal of every government of a modern economy to achieve a high level of employment for the following reasons:

- Higher tax take in the form of income taxes.
- Less government expenditure on social welfare payments.

© Liam Sweeney

Full Employment

Full employment happens when a sustained period of economic growth occurs. As the economy grows, people earn more and they spend more on goods and services.

FULL EMPLOYMENT exists when everybody seeking work is employed at existing wage rates.

Consequences of Full Employment in Ireland

POSITIVES

- **Increased standard of living:** If people are gainfully employed they have a disposable income to spend on goods and services.

- **Increased government tax revenues:** People pay income tax on what they earn and VAT on what they spend. If there is full employment, the tax take would be very high.

- **Reduced social welfare bill:** If the unemployment rate is low, this leads to lower government spending, e.g. Jobseekers Benefit and Allowance. This decreases government current expenditure.

- **Increased aggregate demand:** Full employment would result in an increase in all constituents of aggregate demand, including consumption, investment, government expenditure and net exports, thereby fuelling further economic growth.

- **Increased investment:** In an environment of full employment, economic growth is strong and businesspeople's expectations for the future are good. Companies will want to become more efficient in order to produce and sell more. As a result, investment will increase.

NEGATIVES

- **Possible labour shortages:** If a company wants to take on more staff and there isn't any available, it will stunt the growth of the firm. Alternatively, the company will move abroad, recruit people to move to Ireland or increase the wages it offers.

- **Inflationary pressures:** If people are spending more and there is the same number of goods in the country, it will lead to a situation where demand exceeds supply and there will be demand pull inflation.

- **Pressure on the state's infrastructure:** If everybody is employed and the vast majority of people work outside of their home, traffic on the roads will be extremely heavy. The transportation networks may not be capable of handling this volume. Similarly, if more and more parents want to and can find employment, there will be a proportionate need for childminding services. Full employment has a ripple effect across all public services.

- **Deterioration/loss of services:** In full employment, people would not be attracted to low-paid jobs, even though they are crucial to the smooth running of society and the economy. If employers don't have enough personnel to do these jobs or have to pay exorbitant wages for low-quality work, there may be a deterioration or complete loss of services.

> **REMEMBER!**
>
> **Demand pull factors:** If aggregate demand is greater than aggregate supply, prices will be forced upwards.

> **Task**
>
> What career paths have the Irish population chosen? What is employment in Ireland comprised of? Find the latest economic labour statistics at www.cso.ie/.

Unemployment

The following are the different types of unemployment.

Frictional Unemployment

Frictional unemployment is a situation whereby there is a reduction in the demand for labour in a particular occupation though jobs are available in other occupations and/or firms. This could be due to lack of knowledge of vacancies or unwillingness to move to another area where there are jobs.

> **UNEMPLOYMENT** is all those seeking work at existing wage rates but unable to find work.

Seasonal Unemployment

Seasonal unemployment occurs when some members of the workforce are only in employment for a certain part of the year. This occurs as the demand for some labour moves in line with the seasonality of the work. For example:

- A student picking strawberries during the summer.
- Hotels reducing the numbers employed at the end of the summer season.

Cyclical Unemployment

Cyclical unemployment results from reduced demand for goods and services during an economic recession, e.g. the decline in employment in Ireland from 2 million people in 2006 to 1.85 million in 2010 due to economic recession.

Structural Unemployment

Structural unemployment refers to those who become unemployed because their skills are no longer in demand due to technical progress/competition, e.g. online check-in machines at airports have reduced the amount of ground staff required.

Institutional Unemployment

Institutional unemployment arises because there are obstacles preventing the mobility of labour, i.e. lack of housing in another region or the refusal of foreign governments to grant work permits.

Methods of Measuring Unemployment

Live Register

The Live Register is a publication containing a count of all those under 65 years old who are in receipt of Jobseekers Benefit and Jobseekers Allowance. The Department of Social and Family Affairs accumulates monthly returns from each social welfare office, which is then passed on to the Central Statistics Office.

LIMITATIONS

The Live Register is not an accurate measure of unemployment because it includes people who are:

- Legally working part time and signing on part time. For example:
  - Those in receipt of Jobseekers Benefit/Allowance.
  - Those who work in seasonal industries, up to three days per week and in casual employment.

- Engaged in the black/shadow economy.
- Not seeking employment.

Quarterly National Household Survey

The Quarterly National Household Survey (QNHS) is a countrywide survey of 39,000 different households in Ireland, conducted every quarter. Its purpose is to generate labour force estimates, including the official measure of employment and unemployment in the country.

> **Task**
> Review the latest unemployment statistics available and examine the trends that are emerging over the last one, three, five and 10 years.

USEFULNESS AS AN ACCURATE MEASURE OF UNEMPLOYMENT

The QNHS is a better measure of unemployment in Ireland because it excludes the people who:

- Legally sign on and work simultaneously.
- Legally draw Unemployment Benefit/Unemployment Assistance because they work three days per week or are in seasonal or casual labour.
- Sign on, but are not seeking employment or are not available for work.

The QNHS also includes those who are unemployed but are not in receipt of social welfare for other reasons.

Causes of Unemployment

There are many reasons why unemployment might occur, including the following.

Economic Recession/Cyclical Unemployment

A worldwide/nationwide recession results in a reduction in aggregate demand, which in turn results in the closure of businesses and hence the lay-off of workers.

Relocation of Industry

Businesses that need to reduce their costs and wish to survive have moved to lower-cost locations, e.g. Dell manufacturing moved to Poland, resulting in job losses in Limerick. The loss of income results in further job losses in firms that supply these industries.

Irish Companies Exporting to the US and UK

A rise in the value of the euro against the UK pound sterling and US dollar could result in a reduction in demand for the output of Irish companies, leading to job losses in export-oriented industries, e.g. in the hotel and catering industry.

Banking Crisis

A crisis in the banking sector would result in a major reduction in the availability of credit for businesses. This would mean that businesses would be forced to close, with resulting job losses.

Uncertainty About the Future

With a downturn in economic activity and resulting recession, people may be fearful for the future. People may reduce or defer their spending. This reduced demand would result in job losses, e.g. the closure of firms in the retail sector.

Reliance on Construction Sector/Structural Unemployment

During Ireland's Celtic Tiger, much of Ireland's economic growth and employment relied on the construction sector. With the downturn that followed, the immediate effect was the major loss of jobs in this sector with the accompanying loss of jobs in all allied trades/industries.

What Is the Impact of Unemployment on the Economy?

Decrease in Consumer Demand

Unemployment results in a fall in income. Consequently, people have less money to spend on goods and services.

Falling Inflation or Deflation

As a result of unemployment there will be a downward pressure on demand pull inflation, as there has been a dampening effect on consumer demand due to smaller disposable incomes.

Entrepreneurs Hesitant to Invest

Entrepreneurs will only set up a business if they feel there is a market for their product. If there is increasing unemployment and hence weakening consumer demand, they are unlikely to put capital into their idea and create jobs as businesspeople's expectations are poor.

More Government Expenditure on Social Welfare

As people become unemployed, they require social welfare from the state to provide for their needs until they find their next job. This increases government current expenditure.

Lower Tax Receipts

As unemployment increases, income tax revenue received by the government falls. There may also be a reduced intake in indirect taxes (e.g. VAT), as people will be spending less on consumer goods and services due to the fact that people are earning less.

Greater Taxation Burden on the Employed/Reducing the Incentive to Work

In order to find the money to fund the growing social welfare bill, the government must cut expenditure from other parts of its budget as well as taxing people more, i.e. they may have to raise the marginal rate of tax or reduce tax credits. Any increases in income taxes may encourage the black/shadow economy.

Increased Social Problems

As unemployment increases, crime levels may also increase. This may result in increased government current expenditure on security.

Wage Increases Not Sought

In recessionary times, demand for wage increases tends to fall as the threat of unemployment becomes a serious concern. This may mean that cost increases (wages) will not be as high, which brings down the cost base of a product, which may in turn lead to increased sales and exports.

Reduced Demand for Imports

As the number of unemployed increases, the demand for imported goods and services may decrease, e.g. fewer Irish people taking holidays in Spain (invisible import).

A Rise in the Level of Unemployment

A rise in the level of unemployment has an effect on the following.

The government current finances:

- Reduction in taxation revenues.
- Increase in social welfare payments.

The balance of payments current account:

- Lower incomes leading to a reduction in imports.
- Rising unemployment may mean closures of business – some of which may be export oriented, hence lower exports.

Price inflation:

- Moderation in the rate of price inflation due to the reduction in spending power and a fall in demand pull inflation.
- In the long term, the increase in unemployment may lead to the need to increase taxation or increase charges for certain services, resulting in a rise in the consumer price index (CPI).

Strategies for Reducing Unemployment in Ireland

Decrease Taxation
If the government could afford to reduce VAT (indirect tax) and income tax rates (direct tax), people would have more money to spend on goods and services in the economy. In addition, a move like this would instil a degree of confidence in the consuming public, which would further bolster private expenditure. If companies witness greater demand, they will need to employ more people to meet that positive change.

Sustain a Low Rate of Corporation Tax
Currently, our corporation tax stands at a rate of 12.5%, one of the lowest in the EU. This is attractive to foreign direct investors.

Subsidise Additional Labour
Many businesses would love to have additional help in their companies in the form of labour but can't afford the market clearing wage rate. If the government provided more employment grants or introduced tax breaks for additional employees, entrepreneurs and managers would find it easier to employ more people. In addition, if there was a decrease in employer's PRSI, this would further reduce the cost of employing additional labour and may encourage the hiring of additional staff.

Reduce Costs for Business
Since the state owns most of the utility companies in Ireland, through legislation and regulation, the government could force those supplying businesses to reduce their prices as well as oversee a fall in commercial rates and utility prices (e.g. refuse charges). The result would be that a company's cost base would be reduced, enabling a lower cost of production.

In addition, lowering the minimum wage, against which all other wages are pegged, would reduce companies' costs. As a result, companies could offer a lower selling price in the market, which would lead to increased sales and hence employment.

Capital Investment by Government
By investing in projects that improve our infrastructure, e.g. new motorways, Dublin Port Tunnel, etc., the government automatically creates jobs. This government injection has a multiplier effect (see Chapter 20).

Encouraging New Investment Opportunities
Creating an environment where grants are given for investing in projects (e.g. renewable energy initiatives) means Irish companies could lead the way in research and development.

Investment in Education and Training

As people become more educated and specialised, they can make and sell more innovative products as well as offer better results to potential employers. Consequently, if the government invests in these areas, including drawing down EU funding for such projects, employment should rise.

Consumption of Irish Goods

Any campaign that encourages import substitution, i.e. buying Irish, will maintain existing jobs and hopefully create new and additional employment.

Encourage Entrepreneurship

Continued assistance and grants by County Enterprise Boards and Enterprise Ireland in new business start-ups encourages potential entrepreneurs to use their initiative to build new enterprises and hence create employment.

Encourage Labour-intensive Industries

Examples:

- By abolishing the travel tax, the government creates a more tourism-friendly environment to international visitors.

- Lowering the VAT rate in other labour-intensive sectors, e.g. meals in restaurants, will create greater customer demand and hence will hopefully lead to an increase in employment levels in restaurants and hotels.

What Are the Effects of Job-sharing?

- **Fewer people on social welfare:** Opportunities for people to job-share will result in a decrease in people claiming social welfare.

- **Less absenteeism:** With reduced working days, employees are less likely to be absent from work, as recuperation from illness can occur on days off.

- **Lower tax revenue intake due to lower marginal tax rates:** Two staff working may pay the standard rate of tax as opposed to a sole employee who may pay the higher rate (marginal rate of tax).

- **Fewer imports as a result of reduced incomes:** As an individual has less income than if they were engaged in full-time employment, there would also be less demand for imports.

- **Increased administration/training costs:** The administrative and training costs involved in employing two staff members for one job would be higher than for one person, e.g. two job-sharing staff members having to complete a manual handling course as opposed to one full-time staff member.

- **Social problems decrease:** As a result of job-sharing opportunities, more people are gainfully employed and this has traditionally led to fewer social problems.

Underemployment

> **UNDEREMPLOYMENT** is a situation whereby a factor of production (e.g. labour), though not actually unemployed, is working below capacity.

Examples

- A PhD graduate in Analytical Chemistry who is unable to find work and instead is working as a waiter. Their training, skills and qualifications are not being utilised to the maximum.

- A son or daughter employed in their family's business while they are waiting for a job elsewhere may be underemployed, i.e. the sales of the business do not increase as a result of their employment.

- Labour hoarding is another example of underemployment. This occurs where an employer keeps workers during a downturn in economic activity to save on hiring and retraining costs.

Foreign Direct Investment (FDI) in Ireland

Ireland has attracted many **multinational** companies to establish operations in recent years for many reasons, including the following.

- **Availability of a skilled, English-speaking workforce:** Firms have a large, highly educated and multi-skilled workforce available to them. This helps reduce the training costs for these firms. An English-speaking workforce is a major attraction for foreign firms.

- **Low rates of taxation:** The rate of corporation profits tax in Ireland is one of the lowest in the EU at 12.5%.

- **Access to EU market/member of the euro currency:** Firms that locate in Ireland have access to free movement of their goods within the EU. Ireland is a member of the euro, which makes payment for international transactions within the eurozone much easier and hence more attractive.

Positive Economics

- **Availability of state incentives:** Firms can avail of attractive grants and other incentives provided by the state through the Industrial Development Authority (IDA), the state agency responsible for attracting FDI into Ireland. Examples include advance factories, serviced industrial estates, contribution towards training costs and grants towards research and development.

> **Class Discussion**
>
> If you were the decision-maker in a large multinational, would you decide to locate in Ireland? Consider economic growth, inflation, availability of staff, the euro, industrial relations, grants that you could get, etc.

- **Good industrial relations:** Social partnerships have resulted in relative industrial peace, offering firms uninterrupted production.

Ireland has seen the exit of multinationals over the past number of decades. Why would a multinational choose to locate to lower-cost bases?

- **Lower wage costs outside Ireland:** Businesses have stated that labour costs in Ireland are prohibitive and cite the introduction of the minimum wage and the existence of social partnerships as factors that have led to these higher wage costs. Labour costs in Eastern Europe and Asia are much more competitive.

- **Skills mismatch:** If a country does not have a labour force equipped with the specific skills and experience that they require, these large companies move to a location where the local population can offer them the labour they need.

- **Rising costs of production:** Many firms have voiced concerns about increasing costs such as insurance, refuse charges, energy costs and the high costs of available land for expansion and development. These increases drive up the cost of doing business and make our exports less competitive.

- **Accession of new EU member states:** Since May 2004, many new countries have joined the EU and these countries offer companies access to the EU market as well as cheap labour and room to expand. Hence, they have become an attractive location for mobile industry.

- **Regulatory framework:** Actions by the central government, local government or the EU have placed further requirements on industry. These actions impose a stricter regulatory framework for firms to operate in. By moving to Eastern Europe or Asia, regulations may be less strict, making it easier to operate, e.g. there may be fewer regulations on safeguarding the environment.

- **Advances in international communications:** Advancements in global communications have made it possible for service firms to locate in places that were not options in the past and still carry out their business. They can now do so at lower unit costs and thereby increase their profits. For example, some credit card companies have relocated their international call centres to Asia.

22: Employment

The Statutory Minimum Wage

The statutory minimum wage is the lowest wage that an employer must pay a member of staff. There are some exceptions to the payment of the statutory minimum wage:

- Employees under the age of 18.
- Family members employed in a business.

Advantages and Disadvantages of Lowering the Minimum Wage in Ireland

Advantages

- **Lower labour costs:** These result in continued production and reduced risk of business closure.
- **Lower selling prices:** With production costs falling, this may lead to lower consumer prices and increased competition.
- **Increased demand/protection of jobs:** The lower wage rate leading to lower prices may lead to increased demand and hence greater demand for workers. Indigenous jobs are protected, e.g. jobs in the tourism sector.
- **Investment stimulus:** Reduced costs may lead to increased investment by entrepreneurs/increased foreign direct investment.
- **Reduced risk of relocation:** Irish wage levels may fall more into line with other countries and this may result in fewer firms relocating to countries outside Ireland.

Disadvantages

- **Reduced standard of living:** Workers will now receive a lower income, so their standard of living will fall.
- **Reduced aggregate demand/spending:** Lower incomes will reduce spending, so the demand for goods and services may fall, resulting in unemployment/less VAT receipts.
- **Impact on general wage levels:** This reduction may indicate to employers that all wage levels should fall and this may result in a possible reduction in the standard of living amongst the entire workforce.
- **Workers on lower incomes suffer most:** If the reduction is confined to those on the minimum wage rate, then the burden is not being shared equally within the workforce, which is not equitable.
- **Discourage employment:** The reduction may not encourage people to join the workforce or it may lead to greater participation in the black/shadow economy.

The Black/Shadow Economy

Economic effects of the black/shadow economy in Ireland include the following.

> The **BLACK/SHADOW ECONOMY** describes all economic activity that goes unrecorded in the national income accounts.

- **Loss of tax revenue to the government:** Tax revenue essential to the provision of state services is lost to the exchequer. These could have been used by the government for various services.

- **Decline in legitimate business activity/threat to jobs:** Legitimate businesses will suffer a decline in sales, leading to possible job losses and a decline in economic activity.

- **Increased government expenditure on enforcement:** To curb black/shadow economic activity, the government may have to increase spending on enforcement, which will lead to further pressure on the state's finances/necessity to raise taxes.

- **Pressure on government services/finances:** With the loss of revenue to the state, the government may have to cut spending, find additional sources of tax revenue and/or reduce the volume of services it provides and/or increase borrowing.

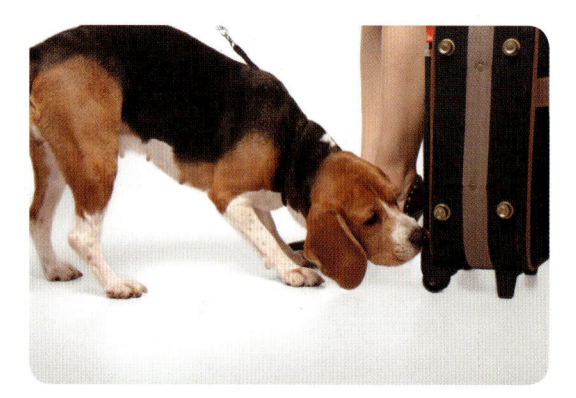

- **Standards of products/services:** Because of a lack of regulation, products may be unsafe/harmful to consumers.

What strategies could the government undertake to discourage black/shadow market activity?

- **Reduce direct taxation rates:** By doing this, citizens may be more inclined to pay their full tax/be tax compliant, as less of their income is being deducted in taxation.

- **Reduce indirect taxation:** By reducing VAT rates and excise duties on goods and services, prices should fall, which may encourage less activity in the black/shadow economy, e.g. smuggling cigarettes.

- **Better enforcement by Revenue Commissioners:** Continued enforcement by the Revenue Commissioners may deter people from engaging in the black/shadow economy. More deterrents, heavier fines and longer sentences by the courts may also help.

- **Educate the public about the importance of tax revenue to the state:** If the government was successful in educating the public about the important uses to which tax revenue is put and linked revenue with the provision of state services, it may convince citizens to avoid unrecorded economic activities.

- **Simplification of the tax system/close all tax loopholes:** A tax system that is easy to follow and understand may reduce tax evasion.

PROFILE: Karl Marx (1818–83)

The philosopher, social scientist, historian and revolutionary Karl Marx is without doubt the most influential socialist thinker to emerge in the 19th century and communism's most zealous intellectual advocate.

Main Ideas

- **Theory of surplus value:** Marx maintained that employers paid subsistence wages to employees, as the wages paid to workers were far lower than the value of goods produced. This difference would result in a surplus to the employer. He believed that capitalists therefore exploited workers, as labour is the only factor of production capable of creating wealth.

- **Unemployment:** As capitalists want to make more profit, labour will eventually be replaced, resulting in unemployment. However, this is at odds with the fact that only labour can generate profit.

- **Reduced demand:** There will be a reduction in the demand for goods and services produced by capitalists as a result of unemployment.

- **Two-tiered society:** Marx believed that history was a series of class struggles between owners of capital (capitalists) and workers (the proletariat). As wealth became more concentrated in the hands of a few capitalists, he believed the ranks of an increasingly dissatisfied proletariat would swell, leading to bloody revolution and eventually a classless society.

- **Labour theory of value:** Marx's labour theory of value examined the capitalist process of production. He believed that the concept of surplus value and exploitation would lead to decreasing rates of profit, an increasing concentration of wealth and the collapse of industrial capitalism.

EXAM ✓ Question 8, 2009 (75 marks)

(a) Discuss the factors that influence the size of the Irish labour force. *(20 marks)*

(b) 'According to the Quarterly National Household Survey (QNHS), the rate of unemployment was 7.7% in December 2008.'
  (i) Name one source, other than the QNHS, for unemployment statistics in Ireland.
  (ii) State, with reasons, which of the measurements of unemployment used by each of these sources gives the most accurate estimate of Irish unemployment.
  (15 marks)

(c) (i) Outline the main causes of the recent increases in unemployment in the Irish economy.
  (ii) Discuss economic policies which the Irish government might pursue in order to reduce the level of unemployment. *(40 marks)*

Solution

(a)
- **Wage levels within the economy:** Higher wage levels in recent years act as an incentive for more people to supply labour. However, wage restraint may see a fall in this figure.

- **Structure of population/size:** Ireland's population has increased, with more citizens within the working-age bracket. The size of the labour force increases, e.g. Ireland has a smaller population than France, resulting in a smaller labour force.

- **Participation rate:** The number of people willing to work within the 16–65 age group has increased. More women working or people who were once retired are willing to take up part-time employment.

- **Rates of income tax within the economy:** In the past a reduction in income tax rates acted as an incentive for people to join the workforce. In the 2009 Budget, the new Income Levy could now act as a disincentive to work and negatively affect the size of the labour force.

- **Labour mobility:** The workforce in Ireland has become more occupationally mobile: there are fewer barriers in place preventing the movement of workers. With EU enlargement, the free movement of labour is increasing. The recent downturn in the Irish economy may see many immigrants moving home and an increase in the emigration of Irish citizens.

- **Government policies:** The government has moved to ease restrictions on the entry of immigrants to Ireland, aiming to liberalise entry requirements into certain occupations, e.g. pharmacies, hospital consultants.

(b) (i) The Live Register or census (of population) are also sources of unemployment statistics. *(Either one of these would be an acceptable answer.)*

(ii) Refer to pp. 311–12 for the answer.

(c) (i) Refer to pp. 312–13 for the answer.

(ii) Refer to pp. 315–16 for the answer.

22: Employment

Questions

Short Questions

1. Define full employment and underemployment.
2. Define unemployment.
3. Define frictional, cyclical, seasonal and institutional unemployment.
4. List four causes of unemployment.
5. Define the black/shadow economy.
6. Name the agency responsible for attracting foreign direct investment into Ireland.

Long Questions

1. State and explain five consequences of full employment in Ireland.
2. State and explain four different types of unemployment.
3. Why is the QNHS a better measure of unemployment than the Live Register?
4. State and explain four consequences of unemployment.
5. Discuss the impact of unemployment on the Irish economy.
6. Outline three different strategies the government could implement to reduce unemployment.
7. Critically analyse the impact of FDI on Ireland's balance of payments.
8. Account for the recent inflows of FDI into Ireland.
9. Critically analyse the impact of the minimum wage.
10. State and explain four consequences of the black/shadow economy in Ireland.
11. State and explain five reasons why FDI may consider relocating away from Ireland.

Chapter 23 | Government Budget and Finances

Specific Learning Outcomes

At the end of this chapter, students should be able to:

SECTION A: REVENUE, EXPENDITURE AND THE BUDGET

- ☐ Define fiscal policy, current budget, current expenditure, revenue buoyancy and capital budget.
- ☐ Define and interpret deficit, surplus and balanced current budget.
- ☐ Identify the main sources of government current revenue/expenditure.
- ☐ Identify the size of government current spending/revenue.
- ☐ Describe and assess trends in and uses of government spending.
- ☐ Critically analyse how government spending influences our daily lives.
- ☐ Identify current government fiscal policy as announced in the most recent budget.
- ☐ Examine and evaluate current government fiscal policy (on the economy).

SECTION B: IDENTIFY AND DEFINE NATIONAL DEBT

- ☐ Identify and define exchequer borrowing requirement, public sector borrowing requirement, general government deficit and national debt.
- ☐ Examine and evaluate the reasons for state borrowing.
- ☐ Differentiate between external and internal national debt.
- ☐ List the functions of the NTMA.
- ☐ Identify, interpret and assess the changing debt/GDP ratio.
- ☐ Understand and critically analyse the impact of default.

22: Employment

Questions

Short Questions

1. Define full employment and underemployment.
2. Define unemployment.
3. Define frictional, cyclical, seasonal and institutional unemployment.
4. List four causes of unemployment.
5. Define the black/shadow economy.
6. Name the agency responsible for attracting foreign direct investment into Ireland.

Long Questions

1. State and explain five consequences of full employment in Ireland.
2. State and explain four different types of unemployment.
3. Why is the QNHS a better measure of unemployment than the Live Register?
4. State and explain four consequences of unemployment.
5. Discuss the impact of unemployment on the Irish economy.
6. Outline three different strategies the government could implement to reduce unemployment.
7. Critically analyse the impact of FDI on Ireland's balance of payments.
8. Account for the recent inflows of FDI into Ireland.
9. Critically analyse the impact of the minimum wage.
10. State and explain four consequences of the black/shadow economy in Ireland.
11. State and explain five reasons why FDI may consider relocating away from Ireland.

Chapter 23 | Government Budget and Finances

Specific Learning Outcomes

At the end of this chapter, students should be able to:

SECTION A: REVENUE, EXPENDITURE AND THE BUDGET

- ☐ Define fiscal policy, current budget, current expenditure, revenue buoyancy and capital budget.
- ☐ Define and interpret deficit, surplus and balanced current budget.
- ☐ Identify the main sources of government current revenue/expenditure.
- ☐ Identify the size of government current spending/revenue.
- ☐ Describe and assess trends in and uses of government spending.
- ☐ Critically analyse how government spending influences our daily lives.
- ☐ Identify current government fiscal policy as announced in the most recent budget.
- ☐ Examine and evaluate current government fiscal policy (on the economy).

SECTION B: IDENTIFY AND DEFINE NATIONAL DEBT

- ☐ Identify and define exchequer borrowing requirement, public sector borrowing requirement, general government deficit and national debt.
- ☐ Examine and evaluate the reasons for state borrowing.
- ☐ Differentiate between external and internal national debt.
- ☐ List the functions of the NTMA.
- ☐ Identify, interpret and assess the changing debt/GDP ratio.
- ☐ Understand and critically analyse the impact of default.

23: Government Budget and Finances

SECTION C: TAXATION

- ☐ Illustrate and define direct, indirect, progressive and regressive taxes.
- ☐ Discuss the characteristics of a good tax system.
- ☐ Evaluate/outline the reasons for taxation.
- ☐ Evaluate/discuss how taxation may help the government achieve its economic and social aims.
- ☐ Critically analyse how taxation can impact on economic sustainability.
- ☐ Explain how changes in rates/types of taxes can impact on different sectors of the economy.

SECTION A: REVENUE, EXPENDITURE AND THE BUDGET

Government Intervention

Could you imagine what life in Ireland would be like if every single unemployed person didn't get benefits or some assistance to manage their day-to-day lives while looking for work? How would the disabled or the visually impaired live? On the other hand, look at how much better off Irish society is because of foreign multinational companies employing thousands of people. Look at all the indigenous Irish companies that export and use the services of state agencies and grants. Some industries are unprofitable (e.g. bus service to remote parts of the country) or very expensive to start (e.g. train service), yet these facilities are important for citizens and companies.

As a result of all of the above, the government intervenes in the economy. The Department of Finance arranges to spend money on various projects that businesses wouldn't. However, it get its funding from the taxpaying public.

Éamon de Valera, Charles Haughey, Bertie Ahern and Brian Cowen were all Ministers for Finance of previous Irish governments

(Images Courtesy of Fianna Fáil)

Positive Economics

In Chapter 18, you learned about the tool used by the European Central Bank (ECB), that can influence the economy. There is a whole other set of techniques that come under the banner of fiscal policy. The following table illustrates the difference between the two.

Monetary policy	Fiscal policy
Actions by the ECB that influence the money supply, interest rates and the availability of credit.	Actions taken by the government that influence the timing, magnitude and structure of current revenue (money in) and expenditure (money out).

How Does the Government Intervene in the Economy?

- **Collect taxes:** The government imposes various different taxes on income, payments, goods, services, savings, investments, profits, etc.

- **Pay social welfare:** People who have lost their jobs, have young children, are retired, etc. all receive transfer payments from the state.

- **Semi-state companies:** In some cases, it would not be profitable for a private company to run a certain business. For example, Bus Éireann runs bus services to remote parts of the country at a loss so that more citizens of the country are served, rather than just those in populated urban areas.

> **REMEMBER!**
>
> **Transfer payments:**
> - Payments received for which no factor of production has been supplied or offered.
> - Income people received for which they did not supply goods or services.

- **Impose laws and provide consumer protection:** Without any governmental authority, there wouldn't be any judicial law. Through various pieces of legislation, consumers, employees, employers and other legal entities all have rights and responsibilities, e.g. the Sale of Goods and Supply of Services Act 1980 gives consumers the right to return a product if it was broken when they brought it home.

- **Represent the Irish people at EU level:** The Irish economy has benefited significantly from membership of the European Union via more trade opportunities and our attractiveness as a location for foreign direct investment as well as direct grants, e.g. Common Agricultural Policy.

- **Take action during national emergencies:** During natural disasters, governments can gather and disburse emergency supplies on a national level. In the case of an economic crisis, elected officials can call in emergency lending, e.g. in November 2010, Ireland needed loans from the IMF, EU, ECB, Denmark, Sweden and the UK.

Advantages and Disadvantages of Governmental Intervention

ADVANTAGES

- **Foreign direct investment:** The government has the ability to meet with the senior management of large multinationals and offer them tax incentives and grants so that they will set up and create employment in a country, e.g. Twitter, Facebook, Google.

- **Regulates the development of monopolies:** The government has the ability to pass regulation to avoid monopolies in industry and protect consumers from high prices, allowing healthy competition.

- **Provides employment:** The government needs a lot of people to organise, manage, implement and review all of its activities and hence it employs a significant number of people.

- **Non-profit companies:** Given that governmental organisations can sustain loss-making businesses, state-owned agencies can focus on delivering services for customers who need them, e.g. Bus Éireann can run buses on unprofitable routes.

- **Social welfare:** People who are unemployed or who can't work to sustain their own well-being can receive state aid for their basic needs.

- **Education:** In order to create a vibrant, skilled labour force, the government needs to fund a relevant, up-to-date and comprehensive education system. Businesses would not have the interest nor the money to fund the eduation of its employees from playschool!

- **Public goods:** Governments spend vast amounts of money on goods that a private company could not charge for, e.g. traffic lights, national security, non-tolled roads.

DISADVANTAGES

- **Reduces entrepreneurship and initiative:** If a government provides loss-making services, it reduces the need for a private company to come up with an innovative solution to that problem.

- **Government bureaucracy:** Dealing with governmental agencies can prove to be frustratingly slow, given the high volume of paperwork needed to get things done.

- **Government inefficiency:** Since the state does not have the same priorities as an entrepreneur or businessperson, it often does not explicitly seek out the best value for money, leading to inefficiency.

- **State employees are not incentivised:** State employees are not incentivised to work harder, as their pay is fixed irrespective of the amount of work they do. Hence, there is the possibility of lower work productivity.

- **Public sector workers are protected:** There are a number of powerful trade union groups that can grind the country to a halt via strikes if the government does not accede to their demands.

Positive Economics

The Budgetary Process

1. Each government department will prepare estimates of their expenditure. This is discussed and reviewed at cabinet level.
2. The Book of Estimates is drawn up and contains planned expenditure for the year and into the future.
3. The Budget is presented to the Dáil in early December.
4. Later, both the Finance Act and Appropriation Act are voted on, allowing the government to tax and spend.

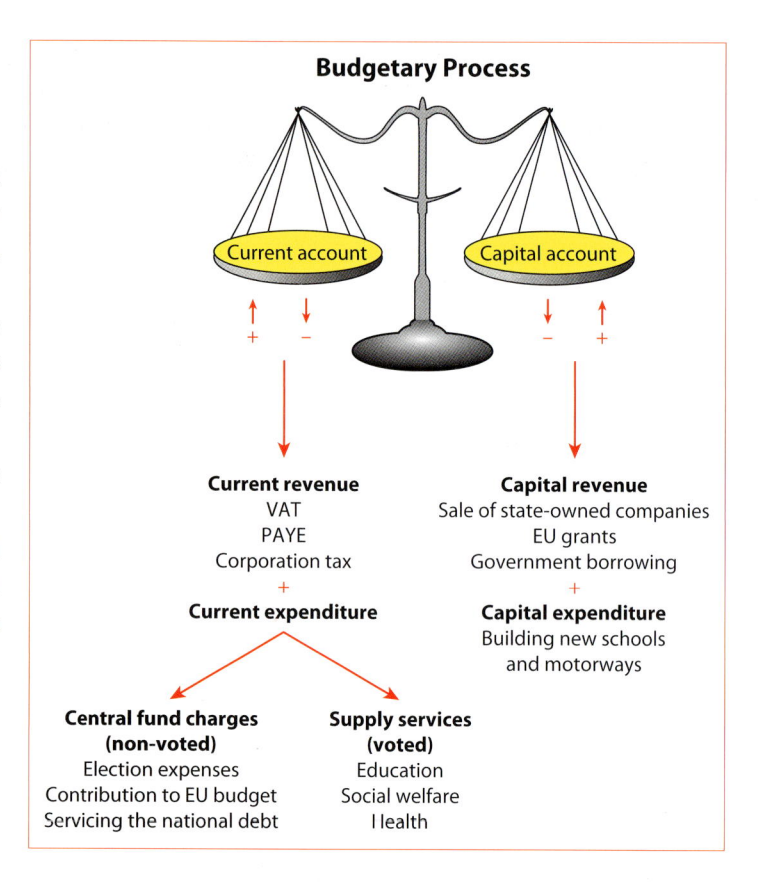

Budgetary Process

Current account / Capital account

Current revenue
VAT
PAYE
Corporation tax
+
Current expenditure

Capital revenue
Sale of state-owned companies
EU grants
Government borrowing
+
Capital expenditure
Building new schools and motorways

Central fund charges (non-voted)
Election expenses
Contribution to EU budget
Servicing the national debt

Supply services (voted)
Education
Social welfare
Health

Where Does the Government Get Its Money and How Does It Spend It?

In order for the government to intervene, it must have money. As a result, it taxes people and businesses on their income, savings, the goods they buy and the transactions they make. With that money, the state pays for public sector wages, social welfare, capital projects (i.e. roads, buildings), etc.

> **CURRENT REVENUE** is divided into taxation revenue (e.g. VAT) and non-taxation revenue (e.g. fees charged for services).

Revenue

CURRENT REVENUE

- Direct tax revenue.
- Indirect tax revenue.
- Profits of state companies.
- Interest on loans to semi-state companies and local authorities.
- Fees charged for services, e.g. obtaining your passport.
- State savings schemes, e.g. An Post, Prize Bonds, National Solidarity Bond.
- Central Bank surplus income.

Tax revenue	Non-tax revenue
Customs	Central Bank surplus income
Excise	National Lottery surplus
Capital gains tax	Dividends of state-owned enterprises, e.g. Bord Gáis
Capital acquisitions tax	Guarantee schemes (CIFS and ELG)
Stamp duties	Winding up of Ulysses securitisation
Income tax	Interest payments euro area loan facility to Greece
Corporation tax	Other receipts
Value Added Tax	

CAPITAL REVENUE

Capital revenue is comprised of the following.

- **Surplus from the current budget:** If the government has taken in more revenue than it has spent on a day-to-day basis, i.e. it has a surplus from the current budget, the balance goes towards capital revenue.

- **Loan repayments from local authorities and semi-states:** The government issues loans to local authorities (e.g. Cork City Council, Clonmel Borough Council) and the semi-state companies (e.g. CIÉ, TG4). On repayment of those loans, the money goes towards capital revenue.

- **Borrowing through national loans, i.e. the bond market:** The government borrows money from the financial markets by issuing bonds (loans that trade on the stock market that the government promises to repay in the future). This is dealt with in more detail under 'Irish National Debt' on pp. 335–336.

- **Grants and loans from foreign international institutions and the EU:** The government receives monies from the EU for the development of society, e.g. the EU Cohesion Fund.

- **Sale of state property:** If the state sells off land/buildings that it owns, it is recorded as capital receipts. For example, the Irish government sold €10 billion worth of state property in 2010.

Spending/Expenditure

After the government collects the taxation revenue, it spends money on the betterment of society, e.g. paying public sector wages and social welfare as well as building capital projects.

Positive Economics

> **CURRENT EXPENDITURE** is money spent on items used up during the year on day-to-day items, i.e. teachers' salaries and social welfare payments.

> **Task**
> In order to examine exactly what the government spends its money on, visit www.budget.gov.ie/budgets, where you can see each line of expenditure in the Estimates of Receipts and Expenditure for the Year.

Let's see exactly what the government spends its money on below.

CURRENT EXPENDITURE

In advance of Budget Day, the Minister for Finance talks to each government department. Together, they decide on the amount of money that is available for each of the current activities that the government decides on, e.g. wages of public and civil servants, social welfare payments, upkeep of state property, etc. All this spending comes under the umbrella of voted expenditures.

However, there is also other money, i.e. non-voted expenditures, that comes directly from a Central Fund. This is for payments outside of the government's current influence, i.e. interest payments on the national debt and EU fund contributions.

> The **GOVERNMENT'S CAPITAL BUDGET** outlines the government's planned expenditure on items not used up during the year, but which increase the productive capacity of the country. The money to pay for capital expenditure is usually funded through borrowings on the part of the government, e.g. building a new road system.

CAPITAL EXPENDITURE

If a government borrows for capital spending but can envisage a long-term return, there can be sincere justification to borrow for such a purpose. However, it is even better when the state can afford these projects from taxation revenue, as it saves the opportunity cost of external financing (i.e. the interest on the loans it doesn't have to borrow).

Government Finances Examined

The difference between the amount that a government takes in via tax and what it spends is the balance. There are a number of ways in which we balance these two numbers:

- **Government current expenditure/revenue:** The current account is made up of the day-to-day activities of the government, i.e. current revenue (money in) minus current expenditure (money out).

> **Note:**
> The exchequer is another name for the Department of Finance.

- **Exchequer balance:** The exchequer balance is the difference between the total receipts in the exchequer minus the total expenditure.

> **Task**
>
> Go to www.budget.gov.ie/budgets and click on the latest Estimates of Receipts and Expenditure for the year ending 31 December. Examine the ways in which the government takes in (revenue) and spends (expenditure) money.

General Government Balance

The general government balance refers to the net borrowing (surplus) of central and local government plus the net surplus of the Social Insurance Fund.

Current Budget Interpretation

- A **current budget deficit** is one in which current government expenditure exceeds current government revenue.

- A **current budget surplus** is one in which current government revenue exceeds current government expenditure.

> The **GOVERNMENT'S CURRENT BUDGET** outlines the government's expected (planned) revenue and expenditures for day-to-day purposes for the forthcoming year.

- A **balanced current budget** is one in which current government revenue equals current government expenditure.

- An **inflationary budget** is one where revenue expenditure is increasing or taxation is decreasing.

- A **deflationary budget** is one where revenue expenditure is decreasing or taxation is increasing.

> **REVENUE BUOYANCY** is the actual taxation revenue collected during the year that is greater than what had been planned for.

- A **neutral budget** is neither inflationary nor deflationary.

Fiscal Drag

In a period of revenue buoyancy, when revenue is greater than expected, government expenditure may remain at the same level. Therefore, revenue is greater than expenditure and has a deflationary effect on the economy.

Impact of Government Current Budget Surplus

POSITIVE

- **Reduced inflationary pressures:** The government is withdrawing more money from the economy than it is putting in. This tends to have a deflationary effect in the economy.

- **Managing our finances:** The existence of a budget surplus means that the government does not have difficulty in controlling its finances. This can lead to confidence in the economy and attract investment.

- **Adhering to EU guidelines:** The fact that a budget surplus exists indicates that the country is meeting the EU agreed guidelines without any difficulty.

- **Scope for taxation:** The fact that a surplus exists indicates that scope exists for reform in the taxation system in the country. This should allow for improvements in the tax system that allow people to retain more of their income, e.g. widened tax bands.

- **Uses of this increased government revenue:** With increased revenue flowing into the government, they now have the ability to make use of this additional revenue. They may use it for current projects (e.g. services) or capital projects (e.g. infrastructure).

NEGATIVE

- **Rise in conflicting expectations:** When citizens observe a budget surplus, they may demand improvements in state services, e.g. health services, education provision. However, the demands/expectations made on the government may conflict.

- **Public sector workers:** When public sector workers see this budget surplus, they may see it as an opportunity for wage negotiations. Workers may thus demand pay increases and/or an increase in the level of the workforce.

- **Tax reductions:** Taxpayers who feel that they are paying too much tax may feel aggrieved. They may demand reductions in their tax or improved equity in the tax system.

- **Discontinuity in social partnership:** The existence of the budget surplus may cause discontent within society. Citizens may feel that certain sectors benefit more

> **Task**
> Check out what the newspapers are saying about the current exchequer figures. A current knowledge of this economic data is crucial for the exam.

from government policies. As a result, it may prove difficult in approving national agreements.

- **Opportunity cost of a surplus:** The budget surplus may have been achieved by the reduction of expenditure on services within the country. Thus, spending on essential services such as health and education may have been compromised.

Impact of Government Current Budget Deficit

POSITIVE

- **Fall in conflicting expectations:** When citizens observe a budget deficit, they reduce their expectations of the government's ability to grant increases in benefits and decreases in taxes. This enables people to plan their expenditures realistically.

- **Public sector workers:** When public sector workers see this budget deficit, they see that there isn't a basis for wage agreements and hence do not have an argument for higher wages.

- **Unpopular economic decisions:** Taxpayers who would have felt aggrieved in the past now understand that a budget deficit is a disadvantageous position for the government to be in. As a result, it is easier for the government to make unpopular political decisions.

- **Prevents overconfidence:** If an economy is spending too much and is in danger of over-indebtedness or a fall-off in prudent spending behaviour, a budget deficit and the subsequent measures shock people into managing their finances better.

NEGATIVE

- **Inflationary pressures:** The government is spending more money from the economy than it is withdrawing through taxation. This tends to have an inflationary effect in the economy.

- **Managing our finances:** The existence of a budget deficit means that government has difficulty controlling its finances. This can lead to a fall in confidence in the economy, both in terms of consumption and investment.

- **Adhering to EU guidelines:** The fact that a budget deficit exists indicates that the country is meeting the EU agreed guidelines with difficulty or maybe not at all.

- **Scope for taxation:** The fact that a deficit exists indicates that the government needs to increase taxation in order to achieve a balanced budget. This means the tax system will change and people will retain less of their income, e.g. narrower tax bands, increased rates of taxation.

- **Cost savings required to achieve a balance:** In the case of a deficit budget, a balance needs to be achieved via the reduction of expenditure on services within the country. Thus, spending on essential services such as health and education may be compromised.

Government Spending Can Affect Our Daily Lives in Many Ways

- Social welfare payments give unemployed people a certain amount of income and benefits so that they can feed, clothe and house themselves until they find employment.

- Schools, universities and educational centres provide the teaching profession with a place, facilities and materials to educate the nation.

- Roads, railway lines, airports and ship ports enable people to travel to destinations all over the country and the world. This facilitates the tourism industry, international trade and imports of essential goods.

- Government grants and initiatives encourage and nurture enterprise, thus increasing employment opportunities and prosperity, boosting the tax take and generating the funding to begin the cycle again.

SECTION B: GOVERNMENT DEBT

State Borrowings

The government might need to borrow from the financial markets because it does not have enough money to pay for all of the expenditure that it has committed to make versus the amount of income that it expects to receive. This is called a deficit. As a result, it needs to borrow and this causes a debt to be raised on the state's balance sheet.

CASE STUDY: Debt Situation in Ireland

Ireland experienced a significant growth in its economy from the early 1990s, but it grew even faster by the start of the 2000s. This era was called the Celtic Tiger. However, from 2007, the Irish economy has suffered a severe decline, as evidenced by a fall of GDP from €189 billion in 2007 right down to €153 billion in 2010. The government faced a massive deficit of €49 billion in 2010, which represented 32% of GDP, the highest by far in the EU.

GENERAL GOVERNMENT DEFICIT: Combined deficit (or surplus) of central and local government.

GENERAL GOVERNMENT DEFICIT AS A PROPORTION OF GDP: Combined deficit (or surplus) of central and local government as a proportion of GDP.

- **Exchequer borrowing requirement:** Borrowing by the state to finance a current budget deficit and borrowing for capital purposes.

- **Public sector borrowing requirement:** The exchequer borrowing requirement plus borrowing for semi-state/state-sponsored bodies and local authorities.

- **National debt:** This is the total amount/accumulated total of outstanding borrowing by the government.

- **National debt/GDP:** This is the total amount/accumulated total of outstanding borrowing by the government as a proportion of GDP.

- **General government debt:** The general government debt consists of the national debt as well as promissory notes and central and local government debt. It is important to note that the GGD is a gross measure of debt (i.e. it is not net of the government's cash balances).

- **General government debt/GDP:** The general government debt consists of the national debt as well as promissory notes and central and local government debt as a proportion of GDP.

Reasons for State Borrowing

Productive Investment
Productive investment is expenditure on projects that ultimately become self-financing. These capital projects create revenue streams that can be taxed. As a result, the government sees a better end result financially in the long term.

Social Investment
Social investment is expenditure on projects that are not and will never be self-financing. However, they are desired and, in many cases, required by society, e.g. medical centres, schools and universities. While there is not a direct return on investment, society benefits in other ways.

Current Budget Deficit
Funding the current budget deficit means obtaining external finance to pay the day-to-day running expenses of the country, i.e. public servants' salaries and social welfare payments. Borrowing this money today means larger taxes in the future to pay back the amount borrowed plus the interest. It is not the best use of the money borrowed and is a sign that the government is not managing its finances effectively.

Irish National Debt – Advantages

- **Maintained or better public services:** If the increase in debt is spent on current expenditure, the government may continue to spend on public services, resulting in a continuation or betterment of these services.

- **More spending on infrastructure:** If the increase in debt is simply as a result of an increase in capital borrowing, then there may be greater spending on the state's infrastructure, which may assist the future growth of the economy.

- **Future economic growth:** Increased national debt brings more money into the country, fuelling government spending, which may boost aggregate demand and provide opportunities for further economic growth.

- **Employment:** A continuation of or rising aggregate demand should lead to increased demand for labour, resulting in higher employment.

- **Self-liquidating debt:** If the return on investment generated via the borrowings is able to meet the cost of repayments, then the borrowing has been self-liquidating.

Irish National Debt – Disadvantages

- **Opportunity costs:** Given that more funds are being used to meet annual interest repayments, the government has less money available for other worthwhile purposes.

- **An increased burden on taxpayers:** A greater amount of debt means the government will have to fund the interest payments by increasing taxation or cutting expenditure on public services.

- **An increase in annual interest repayments:** A greater amount of debt means the state has incurred more annual servicing of debt costs.

- **Lower international credit rating:** Ireland has seen its credit rating fall, as agencies viewed Ireland's repayment capacity as diluted.

- **Stability and Growth Pact requirements:** Ireland has had difficulty meeting the conditions of the Stability and Growth Pact and hence corrective action must be taken in economic policy matters and agreed by the EU.

- **Possible deterioration of public services:** An increase in the national debt and hence the annual servicing costs will see the government cut back spending on certain public services, thereby affecting the provision of some services, e.g. the health service, special needs funding.

- **Uncertainty in servicing the external portion of the national debt:** If a portion of national debt is borrowed outside of the euro currency, it is subject to exchange rate movements. In addition, the Irish government doesn't earn tax revenue on the repayment of external lenders, unlike on the repayment of internal sources.

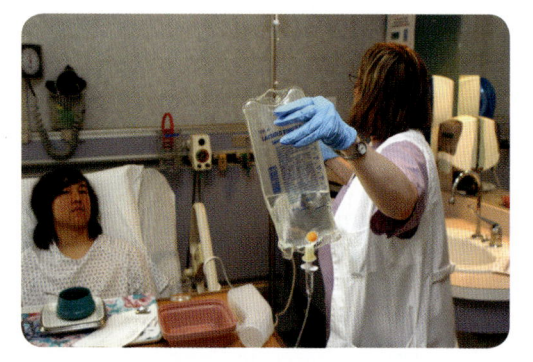

National Treasury Management Agency (NTMA)

The National Treasury Management Agency (NTMA) is the treasury of the government. It manages the assets and liabilities on behalf of the Irish government as well as the

National Pension Reserve Fund, NAMA and the State Claims Agency. It also serves many other functions:

- Borrows money for the exchequer.
- Manages the national debt on behalf of and subject to the control and general superintendence of the Minister for Finance.
- Establishment of a State Pensions Reserve Fund.
- Manages certain claims against the state covering personal injury and property damage.
- Manages the Central Treasury Service.
- Provides fund investment, advisory and consultancy services.
- Establishment of the National Development Finance Agency.

Domestic Debt and External Debt

The national debt is comprised of:

- Domestic debt, which is money borrowed from individuals and financial institutions within the geographic borders of Ireland, i.e. post office savings.
- External debt, which is money borrowed from individuals and institutions outside of Ireland, e.g. foreign bondholders.

Debt/GDP Ratio

The debt/GDP ratio is calculated by dividing a debt measure (i.e. general government debt) by GDP.

In 2010, Ireland signed up to a package of measures with the IMF, European Commission and European Central Bank as well as the governments in Sweden, Denmark and the United Kingdom in order to claw its deficit back to 2.8%. Ireland broke the 60% debt/GDP ratio ceiling imposed by the EMU and was in a serious position whereby its debt/GDP ratio was in excess of 100%. Ireland set about decreasing this figure by repaying its debt, curbing its deficit and striving to grow its GDP simultaneously.

Default

Default refers to not making good on a financial agreement. There are a number of ways in which the government could default on its national debt, including:

- Paying back none of or less than the full amount of the loans borrowed from lenders.
- Extending the maturity of the loan past the time it originally agreed to repay.
- Deciding not to pay the annual interest (coupons).

If Ireland does default, it would make the markets very worried about lending to us again and hence our borrowing costs would rise extraordinarily. As a result, we would have three options:

- Cut our deficit so that the current budget balances.
- Obtain more external financing from the EU and the IMF.
- Leave the euro so that our competitiveness is restored, but our credibility would not be.
- Borrow at interest rates that would be unsustainably high.

If Ireland does not default, the taxpayer will have to continually fund the interest costs of the debt as well as the repayment of the money in full.

SECTION C: TAXATION

Taxation

Before we delve into the various different types of tax that governments impose, we need to consider what our tax system needs to be based on and then what goals we want to achieve from taxation measures. Let's look to Adam Smith's canons of taxation to start with.

Canon	Explanation
Equity	The system of taxation should take a higher proportion of income in tax as income rises or the ability of each person to pay must be taken into account.
Economy	The amount of revenue collected should exceed the costs of collection.
Certainty	The amount paid should be unambiguous, certain and clear.
Convenience	Tax should be levied at a convenient time and manner for the contributor.

Are these canons useful for analysing the taxation system in Ireland? Yes:

> **Memory Hook:**
> There are two canons beginning with 'c' and two others with 'e'.

Canon	Direct taxation	Indirect taxation
Equity	With PAYE, people on greater incomes pay a greater proportion in tax. One of the accepted functions of taxation is the redistribution of national wealth, which conforms to the argument for equity.	Indirect taxes are regressive, as a taxpayer's ability to pay is not taken into account.

Canon	Direct taxation	Indirect taxation
Economy	If a tax yield does not collect more than the cost of administration, the tax should not be introduced. This is one of the advantages of direct taxes.	The complexity of the collection systems is one of the arguments against indirect taxation.
Certainty	Financial planning is aided by the fact that the amount to be collected is clear to the state. This is one of the main advantages of direct taxes.	The amount of indirect tax revenues to be collected is unclear and hence hinders effective financial planning.
Convenience	PAYE tax is deducted at source from incomes, thereby removing the burden of reporting from the taxpayer and allowing the payment to be made regularly.	If the method and timing of payment are not convenient for the taxpayer, it can lead to evasion.

No:

Besides these canons, there are other key principles that could be considered for analysing the taxation system.

- Is tax evasion possible? None of the canons help us measure the level of tax evasion, which has proved problematic in Ireland.

- Does the tax cause a disincentive to work, save or invest?

    o If a tax acts as a disincentive to work, this has a negative impact on the labour supply.

    o If a tax acts as a disincentive to save, it may result in people consuming more today and hence not providing for financially burdensome circumstances in the future.

    o If a tax acts as a disincentive to invest, entrepreneurs may either choose not to invest and create economic growth or else use their money to create return on investment in another country.

From the above, we can derive the principles of a fair tax system.

Principles of a Fair Tax System

- **Taxes should be equitable:** The tax levied should be proportionate to the person's ability to pay.

- **Taxes should be certain:** The amount of tax a person must pay (the state collects) should be clear.

- **Taxes should be convenient:** The manner and timing of payment of the taxes should be convenient to pay on the part of the taxpayer. For example, the PAYE system of tax is convenient because it is deducted regularly rather than one lump sum.

- **Taxes should be economical:** The costs of collection should be small relative to the amount of revenue to be collected.

- **Taxes should not be perceived, nor act, as a disincentive.**
    - The marginal rates of tax should not discourage workers from working or working overtime.
    - Rates of tax on profits should not discourage entrepreneurial investment.
    - Savings should not be discouraged by the presence of interest tax (DIRT).

- **Taxes should assist the redistribution of income:** A good tax system should help the government redistribute income progressively from the rich to the poor.

- **Tax rates should be consistent with, and aid in the achievement of, national economic objectives:** The taxes levied should enable the government to achieve other economic/social objectives, e.g. raising excise rates on cigarettes will discourage smoking.

- **Taxes should have a stabilising influence on the economy (automatic stabilisers):** An effective system of taxation can prevent the level of economic activity rising as fast as it would otherwise in economic growth. Similarly, the system should shield the level of economic activity from falling as fast as it otherwise would in a recession.

- **Evasion should not be possible:** Effective taxes should be impossible to evade, otherwise the tax is not fair.

Functions of Taxation

- **To finance government activities**, e.g. operate civil services, pay the wages of public sector workers.

- **To achieve economic objectives**, e.g. reduce inflation, favourable balance of payments.

- **Redistribution of national wealth**, e.g. transfer payments to the poor from the tax take of the rich.

- **Automatic stabiliser**, e.g. taxes help to avoid wide fluctuations in the economic cycle by automatically taking more tax when the economy is doing well and taking less when the economy is performing poorly.

- **Social objectives**, e.g. discourage smoking and drinking, pollution and damage to the environment.

- **Promote enterprise**, e.g. provide subsidies, grants, mentoring and other services to industry and encourage enterprise, e.g. County Enterprise Boards, Enterprise Ireland.

23: Government Budget and Finances

Types of Tax

At a basic level, there are two forms of tax: progressive and regressive.

Progressive taxation	Regressive taxation
A taxation measure that takes proportionately more in tax as a person's income increases.	A taxation measure that takes proportionately less in tax as a person's income increases.
Example: Income tax and Universal Social Charge.	Example: The carbon tax and household charges are regressive taxes because they do not take into account one's ability to pay the tax. In addition, people on lower incomes would pay a greater proportion of their income in tax.

Note:
VAT, custom duties and stamp duties are all examples of an **ad valorem tax**, i.e. a tax that increases with the value of the goods.

DIRECT TAXES are taxes on income and wealth, e.g. PAYE (income tax), capital gains tax (tax on investments), capital acquisition tax (tax on inheritance) and DIRT (tax on savings).

INDIRECT TAXES are taxes on transactions/spending, e.g. VAT (tax on purchases of goods and services), custom duties (tax on goods entering the country) and stamp duties (tax on making an investment, i.e. stocks and property).

Advantages and Disadvantages of Indirect Taxation

ADVANTAGES

- **Evasion is more difficult:** As the indirect tax is included in the selling price of the good or services, it is impossible to evade.

- **No disincentive to work:** A taxpayer can adjust their expenditure patterns to reduce their tax liability. Thus, this does not act as a disincentive to work, unlike direct taxes.

- **Convenient for the taxpayer:** They are included in the selling price and paid when the good or service is bought.

- **Used by the government to change consumption patterns:** The government could increase the tax on those commodities which it deems harmful to the public, e.g. cigarettes and alcohol. The introduction of the plastic bag tax has reduced demand.

- **Economical:** The cost of collection is borne by the retailers and producers and not by the state.

- **Acts as a built-in stabiliser:** As the economy expands, spending rises and so too will the revenue collected from taxation.

Disadvantages
- **Will increase inflation:** Indirect taxes raise the prices of goods and services and hence the cost of living. As a result, this forms the basis for demands for wage increases.
- **Regressive:** Lower-income groups may end up paying a greater proportion of their income in this form of tax because they spend a greater proportion of their income on goods and services.
- **Revenue collected is not as certain:** The revenue to be collected is not as predictable as that from direct taxation. This may hinder the government's financial planning.
- **Burden of collection passed to retailers/traders:** These now act as revenue collectors and procedures must be put into practice to collect, record and remit the revenue. This increases costs for the firms.
- **Inequitable:** Indirect taxes ignore ability to pay. A person who earns a high income but doesn't drink, smoke or drive a car will pay a lower proportion of their income in tax than a person on the same income who does consume these commodities.

Advantages and Disadvantages of Direct Taxation

Advantages
- **Equitable:** Direct taxes are equitable, as those most in a position to pay are asked to contribute most due to progressive taxation.
- **Convenient for the taxpayer:** For PAYE workers, they are included and paid weekly by their employers on their behalf.
- **Revenue collected is certain:** Tax bands and tax rates are announced on Budget Day and in advance of the start of the tax year. The revenue to be collected is relatively predictable and this aids the government's financial planning.
- **Acts as a built-in stabiliser:** As the economy expands, incomes rise and so too will the revenue collected from taxation.
- **Economical:** The cost of collection is borne by employers and investors and not by the state.

Disadvantages
- **Disincentive to work:** If the rate of tax is too high and there is not enough of a gap between income received from a wage and social welfare, it may act as a disincentive to work.
- **Small amount of people paying lots of tax:** If there is a percentage of people paying the bulk of income tax, the burden falls heavily on those high earners.

- **Black/shadow economy:** Those engaging in the black/shadow economy avoid paying tax completely.
- **Burden of collection is passed to employers and investors:** These now act as revenue collectors and procedures must be put into practice to collect, record and remit the revenue. This increases costs for the firms or reduces the return for investors.

There are other subsets of taxation, including the following.

Specific Tax
A specific tax is applied at a fixed rate per physical unit of the good taxed, regardless of its price. For example, car tax is levied on the size of the engine irrespective of whether the car is new or 20 years old.

Stealth Tax
A stealth tax is applied so that it is largely unnoticed or not recognised as a tax, e.g. water charges.

> **TAX HARMONISATION** refers to the aim of members of the EU and other trading blocs to move all tax rates to the same rates, i.e. align with each member state/country.

Tax Evasion and Tax Avoidance

> **TAX AVOIDANCE** is arranging one's affairs within the law so as to minimise tax liabilities.
>
> **TAX EVASION** is reducing tax liabilities by making false returns or not making any returns at all.
>
> **BROADEN THE TAX BASE:** Increase the number of people/areas on which the tax is levied/in the tax net.
>
> **IMPOSITION OF TAX:** The imposition or impact of taxation refers to the people or companies on whom the tax is actually levied or placed, i.e. imposed.
>
> **INCIDENCE OF TAX:** Refers to the individual who actually pays the tax. Whether the imposition or incidence of tax are the same depends on the relative price elasticity of demand.

How Can Taxation Help the Government Achieve Its Economic and Social Aims?

The government can use a strategy and combination of the following.
- Increase taxes to decrease consumption, e.g. smoking and drinking.
- Impose a levy to discourage waste, e.g. plastic bag levy.

- Impose fines on anti-social behaviour, e.g. litter fines.
- Grant tax breaks to encourage activities, e.g. research and development tax credits.
- Give financial aid to boost enterprise, e.g. County Enterprise Board grants.
- Create the infrastructure to enable people and companies to cohesively achieve national aims, e.g. build better roads to enable companies to deliver a faster, better service.

Taxation and Economic Sustainability

Economic sustainability refers to putting resources to the best possible use to enable the country to move to long-term prosperity. This can be done in a variety of ways.

In times of economic boom, in order to prevent overconfidence and people overburdening themselves with debt to invest, the government could take the following actions:

- Increase tax on consumption.
- Increase tax on investments to deter people from taking too much risk in order to invest, i.e. capital gains tax.
- Reduce or pay off the national debt in order to free up our capacity to borrow to deal with harder times.
- Increase the cash balances of the NTMA so that money could be used for capital projects and fiscal stimuli in recessionary periods.
- Closer monitoring of credit availability from banks.

In times of economic recession, in order to rejuvenate the economy and build confidence on the part of consumers and investors, the government could take the following actions:

- Lower tax rates and widen tax bands so that people keep greater amounts of income, which can be used to spend in the economy.
- Use state funds received via taxation to initiate capital projects that would aid employment and boost economic activity as well as contribute towards the long-term betterment of society.
- Design an attractive taxation system for multinationals to bring foreign direct investment into the country, i.e. low corporation tax rate and research and development tax credits.
- Design and offer tax breaks as well as use taxation revenue for grants to encourage indigenous Irish companies to start up, export and flourish.

23: Government Budget and Finances

Impact of Changes in Revenue and Expenditure on an Economy

On any given Budget Day, the government needs to take into account the consequences of their actions. They need to consider the impact their policies will have on the following:

- Inflation and competitiveness.
- Standard of living.
- People on low incomes.
- Incentive to work.
- Incentive to save.
- Incentive to invest.
- Ability to attract foreign direct investment.
- Deficit/surplus.
- Efficiency of resources and services.
- Equity.
- Social partnership and trade unions.
- Black/shadow economy.

> **Task**
>
> In order to find the economic variables that the Department of Finance bases its budget and projections on, visit www.finance.gov.ie. Download the 'Monthly Economic Bulletin' in order to get the latest data on:
>
> - Employment
> - Price inflation
> - Imports
> - Exports
> - Economic growth
> - Government spending
> - Consumption spending

Many economists work in the area of policy, i.e. what measures a government should implement in the future to deal with the problems of today. The Department of Finance may be facing a situation whereby it is spending more than it is taking in (deficit), a massive debt/GDP ratio, unemployment or, on the other hand, an overheating economy. How would you deal with any of the above problems?

Economic Consequences of Increasing Public Service Charges

Positive

- **Less pressure to increase taxes/borrowing:** Increasing public charges removes pressure from the government to raise additional revenue by increasing taxation.
- **More efficient use of services:** If people pay for services, efficiency on their part is encouraged, e.g. people are incentivised to recycle or use public transport.

- **Saving scarce resources:** People who can afford to use these services are now those who avail of them. Hence, the resources that were being used to finance these services would no longer be necessary.
- **Targeting use of resources economically:** By asking those who can afford to pay, the government can provide direct payments to help those who cannot, thereby targeting the use of our resources more economically.
- **Pressure to improve quality of service:** Providers may be forced to improve the quality of service provided, as people now pay. For example:
  - Increased frequency of service
  - Greater number of recycling centres
  - Pay-per-weight for refuse collection
- **Lower tax base:** Ireland can maintain an attractive tax regime and hence encourage continued investment into the economy.
- **Use of revenue collected:** The collected revenue can be targeted for best use and to help achieve aims, e.g. the plastic bag tax.

Negative
- **Increased cost of living:** The prices of services for which charges are being imposed will increase, thereby increasing the cost of living.
- **Increased inflation:** Inflation will rise due to increased charges. This affects the economy negatively via reduced competitiveness and demand for compensatory wage increases, etc.
- **Affects lower-income groups most:** The additional charges have the greatest impact on lower-income groups, i.e. those with the least ability to cope with higher prices, and this negatively impacts their standard of living.
- **Viability of partnership agreements:** Trade unions may consider that the increases in these charges are stealth taxes and this may form the basis of an argument to seek higher wage increases.
- **Inequity/fairness:** The disparity in charges, in the quality of service or the introduction of charges:
  - May cause dissatisfaction in citizens
  - Cause people to dump their rubbish illegally
  - Divert from toll roads and disrupt local communities
- **Higher costs for business:** Firms must now pay higher toll charges, refuse charges and water charges – increasing costs that may require higher prices or a reduction in jobs.

PROFILE: Adam Smith (1723–90)

Adam Smith was born in Scotland and is often credited as being the founder of modern economic science. He wrote *An Inquiry into the Nature and Causes of the Wealth of Nations* in 1776. His main ideas were as follows.

Individual Self-interest
According to Smith, individuals are motivated by pursuing their own self-interest and, in so doing, unintentionally promote the public interest. He thought that individuals working without government interference were guided by an 'invisible hand' for their own and the common good. This supported Smith's belief in free enterprise as the best form of economic systems, i.e. minimal government interference – a laissez-faire system.

Labour Theory of Value
Smith believed that labour was the main source of wealth, i.e. the value of an object is equal to the amount of labour it can demand in exchange for itself. He illustrated this concept by means of a sketch of a primitive society of hunters. If it cost twice the labour to kill a beaver as it did a deer, then one beaver would exchange for two deer, i.e. labour was the fundamental measure of value.

Division and Specialisation of Labour
One of the keys to increasing wealth was through the specialisation of labour. Smith quoted the example of the manufacture of pins. If one person was set the task of carrying out all the operations of making pins, his output would be minimal. If, however, each person specialised on a single operation only, output would be increased a hundredfold.

Canons of Taxation
In his discussion on public finances, Smith laid down four principles of taxation:

- Economy: The cost of assessing and collecting a tax should be as low as possible.
- Equity: A system of taxation should consider a person's ability to pay.
- Certainty: The amount of tax payable by each taxpayer should be certain and not arbitrary.
- Convenience: Tax should be levied at a convenient time and manner for the contributor.

Perfect Competition
The market price of a good, according to Smith, was determined by demand and supply, but each good had a natural price, which was its real value. This natural price was made up of the prices of the four factors of production: wages to be paid to workers, rent paid to the landowner, money spent on machinery and profit and the return to the entrepreneur. These two prices (market and natural price) could differ from time to time, but competition ensured that they were usually equal. His analysis was based on what we study and know as perfect competition. Smith thought that this was the ideal market.

Free Trade
Smith advocated international free trade unhindered by the imposition of tariffs so that markets could operate efficiently and allow the gains from free trade to spread between nations.

Positive Economics

Sample Exam Question (30 marks)

You have been employed as an economic advisor to the Minister for Finance.

(a) State and explain **two** specific courses of action (one on the revenue side and one on the expenditure side) you would advise the minister to take in order to significantly reduce the current budget deficit. *(10)*

(b) Outline the possible economic effect(s) of **each** course of action you have chosen. *(20)*

Solution

Revenue:

1. **Increase indirect tax(es):** If the government was to increase consumption taxes such as VAT and excise duties, the tax yield would rise.

   Effect:
   - A rise in smuggling in order to evade tax.
   - Increased inflation, as the good automatically sees an increase in price.
   - A fall in aggregate demand, as prices have increased.

2. **Increase direct tax(es)/pension levy:** If the government was to increase taxes such as PAYE or the pension levy, it would increase their tax revenue.

   Effect:
   - A greater number of people engaging in the black/shadow economy in order to evade tax.
   - A fall in employment, as there is a decreased incentive to work.
   - A surge in wage demands, which may lead to industrial disputes.
   - A fall in aggregate demand, as real incomes and spending power fall.

Expenditure:

1. **Cut the numbers employed in the public sector:** Make an offer of redundancy packages to those working in the public sector.

   Effect:
   - A short-term shock in the costs of meeting redundancy payments.
   - A possibility of increasing long-term unemployment if there is no work available in the private sector.

- A fall in aggregate demand, as real incomes and spending power have decreased.

- A deterioration in the various public services.

2. **Stabilise or cut wages in the public sector:** Introduce a pay freeze where workers' wages will not increase over a period of time.

   Effect:

   - A possibility of industrial disputes.

   - A possibility that skilled workers may leave for the private sector or emigrate.

   - Discourage effort and motivation in the sector, leading to a fall in efficiency in the long term.

3. **Scale back on state services:** Reduce services such as medical cards, the cervical cancer vaccine, book grants, etc. in each government department.

   Effect:

   - A possibility that those on lower incomes may suffer a dramatic fall in their standard of living.

   - A possibility that costs are increased in the long run in order to reintroduce services.

   - A possibility of industrial disputes and public protests by affected citizens.

4. **Reduce social welfare:** This will result in reduced current expenditure and a reduction in the budget deficit.

   Effect:

   - People on lower incomes may suffer a dramatic fall in their standard of living.

   - The incentive to find work would be further increased.

Positive Economics

EXAM Question 5(b), 2007 (30 marks)

State and explain how **a government budget** could be affected by each of the following developments.

- A rise in interest rates in the economy
- A fall in the rate of stamp duty on property purchased
- Introduction of subsidised child care for all families within the state

Solution

Factor	Effect	Explanation
A rise in interest rates	Current government expenditure increases	The government needs to increase expenditure to meet interest rate payments on national debt.
	Current government revenue decreases	A higher 'cost of money' acts as a deterrent to borrowing. As a result, the government will see a fall in consumer spending and falling tax revenues.
	Current government revenue decreases or current expenditure increases	If investment falls, job losses may result. This has the impact of decreasing the direct tax revenue collected and increasing the social welfare expenditure.
A fall in the rate of stamp duty on property	Current government revenue increases	This action may result in additional property sales, increasing the amount of revenues generated. In essence, the final effect depends on the price elasticity of demand for houses.
Introduction of subsidised child care for all families	Current government expenditure increases	There would be increased expenditure on the part of the state in maintaining crèches, paying staff salaries, etc.
	Current government revenue increases	This policy might encourage more people to return to work, thereby increasing the tax revenue collected.

23: Government Budget and Finances

EXAM ✓ Question 5, 2011 (75 marks)

(a) The Budget is a statement of the government's <u>fiscal policy</u>. The Irish government, in its National Recovery Plan 2011–2014, committed to reducing the general government deficit to under 3% of GDP by 2014.
  (i) Explain the underlined term.
  (ii) State and explain **four** possible economic effects on the Irish economy of the government's plan to significantly reduce the deficit over the next four years. *(30)*

(b) It has been suggested that in order to reduce the national debt, the government should privatise state-owned companies in the coming years.
  (i) Explain the term 'privatisation'.
  (ii) Outline **four** economic arguments in favour of privatisation OR outline **four** economic arguments against privatisation. *(25)*

(c) 'The number of staff in the Irish public sector grew by 15.5% from 2001 to 2008, according to OECD statistics.' (*Report on the Sources of Ireland's Banking Crisis, 2010*)

Discuss **four** measures the Minister for Finance could take to reduce the public sector wage bill. *(20)*

Solution

(a) (i) Fiscal policy refers to any action taken by the government that influences the timing, magnitude and structure of current revenue and expenditure.

(ii) *Any four of the following would be acceptable.*
- **Reduced standard of living:** Taxpayers will have lower disposable incomes due to higher taxes and their standard of living will fall.
- **Public services: loss/deterioration/introduction of charges:** Some public services may be discontinued (e.g. bus transport routes, fewer special needs assistants), others may fall in standard (e.g. health services), while more may have to be paid for (e.g. household charges).
- **Changed ownership of strategic state assets:** Some state bodies may be privatised, affecting consumers (prices), employees (non-employment) and the government (revenue).
- **Public sector effects:** The numbers employed in the public sector will fall or wages may be reduced, which may further add to the numbers unemployed.
- **Level of economic activity/demand fall:** Lower disposable incomes means reduced domestic demand, which may result in an increase in the numbers unemployed.
- **Growth in the black/shadow economy:** More people may be willing to participate in the black/shadow economy due to reduced incomes and the possibility of lower prices being charged in the black/shadow market.

Positive Economics

- **Widening gap between rich and poor:** Cutbacks in the rate of social welfare payments coupled with stricter eligibility requirements may mean that social welfare recipients suffer. Changes in taxation and expenditure cuts may have a greater effect on lower-income groups.
- **Public unrest:** People may become involved in protests/strikes that may disrupt economic activity. Some citizens may decide to emigrate to seek a better future.

(b) (i) Privatisation refers to the sale of a state-owned company to private owners.

(ii) *Any four of the following would be acceptable.*

Arguments in favour	Arguments against
1. **Improved quality/choice of services:** Privatised firms may improve the quality/efficiency/choice of the service provided.	1. **Loss of non-profit-making service:** Non-profit-making services may be discontinued in an effort to reduce costs.
2. **More competitive prices:** Consumers may be offered more competitive prices on goods/services.	2. **Standards of service/increased prices:** The quality of services provided by the new company may deteriorate in an effort to save costs. Prices may be increased to increase revenue. Charges for services that were considered free may be introduced.
3. **Continuity of supply:** The newly privatised companies may have access to new sources of funds and as they are not subject to government interference, their long-term prospects for survival may improve, ensuring continuity of supply for consumers.	3. **Curtailment in pay/pension increases/ changes to working conditions:** The new owners may limit the pay/pension increases due to its employees or change its employees' conditions of employment, resulting in a worsening of these.
4. **Employment opportunities:** If the new firm increases its market share, this may result in a growth in employment within the industry/additional job security for existing employees.	4. **Loss of jobs/reduced job security/ increased social welfare bill:** Jobs may be lost through rationalisation of services, meaning higher social welfare costs.

Arguments in favour	Arguments against
5. **More rewards/incentives for innovation:** Employees may reap more rewards for their innovations within the privatised industry, e.g. higher bonuses.	5. **Loss of a state resource/critical infrastructure:** This company has been financed by taxpayers in the past. With its sale, taxpayers now lose critical infrastructure that they once owned.
6. **Revenue from sale/reduce borrowing:** The government could use the revenue from the sale of the firm to help reduce its level of borrowings.	6. **Costs of the sale:** All costs in preparation for the sale, such as legal work, must be paid for by the taxpayer.
7. **Shedding loss-making companies:** By selling loss-making companies, the financial burden on the state/taxpayers is removed.	7. **Foreign ownership:** Overseas buyers can become owners of a previously Irish company, so control of the asset can go outside the state.

(c) *Any four of the following would be acceptable.*

1. **Reduce the numbers employed in the sector:** Do not fill vacancies when they occur/natural wastage. Introduce a voluntary redundancy package, e.g. as in the HSE.

2. **Reduce rates of pay per employee:** Pay new entrants into the sector lower rates than existing employees. Adjust pension entitlements to reduce the cost of future pensions.

3. **Change terms of employment:** Defer incremental pay increases, negotiate pay reductions for state employees/wage freeze, cap the pay of higher-paid civil servants and ban overtime for state employees/offer career breaks.

4. **Change pension entitlements:** Reduce the pensions given to current pension holders.

5. **Outsource services, e.g. IT, payroll:** This will mean that less staff are required in the public sector to provide these services.

Questions

Short Questions

1. Define fiscal policy, current budget, current expenditure, revenue buoyancy and capital budget.
2. Define and interpret deficit, surplus and balanced current budget.
3. Identify the size of government current spending/revenue.
4. Illustrate and define direct, indirect, progressive and regressive taxes.
5. Identify and define exchequer borrowing requirement, public sector borrowing requirement, general government deficit and national debt.
6. List the functions of the NTMA.

Long Questions

1. Discuss the characteristics of a good tax system.
2. Evaluate how taxation may help the government lower our carbon footprint.
3. Evaluate how taxation may help the government decrease cigarette consumption.
4. Evaluate how taxation may help the government increase green energy awareness.
5. State and explain why Smith's canons of taxation are useful for analysing the taxation system.
6. Discuss the advantages and disadvantages of a progressive tax.
7. Discuss the advantages and disadvantages of a regressive tax.
8. Outline the positive and negative implications of a budget deficit.
9. You are the economic advisor to the Minister for Finance. Discuss the economic advantages and disadvantages of the following policies:
   (a) Lowering income tax
   (b) Widening tax bands
   (c) Increasing the Universal Social Charge
   (d) Reducing public sector numbers
10. Discuss the advantages and disadvantages of indirect taxation.
11. Discuss the advantages and disadvantages of direct taxation.
12. Identify the size of the national debt. Outline the benefits and drawbacks of the national debt.
13. State and explain how a government budget could be affected by each of the following developments:
    (a) A fall in interest rates
    (b) A replacement of stamp duty by a flat property charge
    (c) An introduction of water charges
14. Differentiate between external and internal debt.
15. Critically analyse the impact of default on the Irish economy.

Chapter 24: The Role of Government: Economic Aims and Policies

Specific Learning Outcomes

At the end of this chapter, students should be able to:

- [ ] Evaluate the government's economic aims and objectives.

- [ ] Comment on the significance of those aims and objectives.

- [ ] Discuss the methods/instruments used in achieving these aims and objectives.

- [ ] Evaluate the possible conflict in achieving them simultaneously in a national and international context.

- [ ] Discuss the economic benefits and consequences of nationalisation and privatisation.

Positive Economics

Introduction

A government attempts to increase the economic welfare/benefit of its citizens by implementing economic policy. Since the late 1920s, when many advanced economies were on the brink of complete collapse, economists have recognised that government has a role in steering a macroeconomy towards increased economic welfare. This idea was first introduced during the late 1930s and early 1940s when Keynes outlined most of the ground rules for designing his own policies, which paved the way for later generations of policymakers. Keynes was able to demonstrate that a market economy could become trapped in a downward spiral of falling economic activity and diminishing economic welfare.

For Keynes, the key questions were:

- What could trigger a fall in aggregate demand?
- What processes would prevent aggregate demand from increasing?
- How could governments generate a rise in aggregate demand?

We will discuss the major objectives of government as well as the way in which these objectives are measured and their relative importance. We will also look at the difficulties governments experience trying to achieve all these aims at once.

Economic Objectives/Aims of the Government

The government's economic objectives are as follows:

1. Achieve full employment.
2. Achieve sustainable economic growth.
3. Control of government finances.
4. Promote balanced regional development.
5. Improve infrastructure.
6. Create a just social environment/ensure equal distribution of wealth.
7. Control price inflation/price stability.
8. Maintain state services.

9. Broaden the tax base.
10. Care for the environment.

11. Achieve equilibrium of the balance of payments.

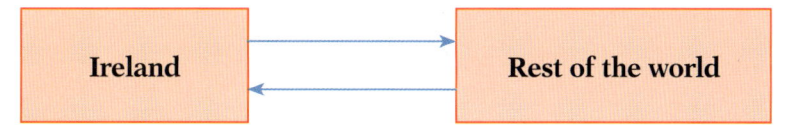

| Ireland | ⇄ | Rest of the world |

12. Stabilise the banking sector.

1. Achieve Full Employment

By implementing policies aimed at achieving an increase in employment or full employment, the government significantly decreases the amount of current expenditure on social welfare, such as unemployment benefit. Consequently, full employment sees the government's current revenue increase due to PAYE taxes on wages of the newly employed people and VAT from the increase in spending on goods and services.

Note: In 2010/2011, stabilising the banking sector was an economic aim of the Irish government. Other objectives may arise as a priority from time to time, given prevailing economic circumstances.

FULL EMPLOYMENT is a situation in which employment is available for all those prepared to work at existing wage levels. It occurs when the labour force is fully employed in productive work.

Task

What does full employment look like? Consult www.ncirl.ie and compare employment figures for the past 10 years.

Economic Benefits of a Full Employment Economy in Ireland

- **Reduced social welfare bill:** An increase in employment will see a reduction in unemployment. With more people working, there would also be a significant decrease in government current expenditure on social welfare benefits.

- **Increased aggregate demand within the economy/economic growth:** High employment will increase aggregate demand for goods and services within the economy.

- **Increased standard of living:** Higher incomes facilitate the purchase of a greater quantity of goods and services, thereby improving the standard of living.

- **Increased government tax revenues:** High employment facilitates an increase in government current revenue from direct tax, e.g. PAYE, and indirect tax, e.g. VAT.

- **Increased investment:** A buoyant and growing economy encourages further investment rather than a stagnant or declining business environment, as demand for goods and services is rising and expectations about the future are positive.

Economic Difficulties of a Full Employment Economy in Ireland

- **Possible labour shortages:** As an economy reaches full employment, the result may see a shortage of labour for employers trying to meet production targets. As a result, this might invoke an increase in the need for overseas recruitment and pressure to relax immigration regulations.

- **Wage demands:** Employers may be forced to increase wage rates in order to retain their workforce where labour shortages are occurring.

- **Inflationary pressures:** A rise in income results in an increase in the purchasing of goods and services. This increase in spending tends to fuel inflation within the economy.

- **Pressure on the state's infrastructure:** There will be increased pressure on the government to improve and provide necessary infrastructure, such as housing, better roads, crèche facilities, improved public services and public transport and better telecommunications.

- **Deterioration/loss of services:** In sectors with low wage rates, it may be difficult to attract workers and the quality of service may deteriorate or the service may even discontinue.

2. Achieve Sustainable Economic Growth

What does sustainable economic growth look like?

Economic growth is when the average income per head of population increases without any fundamental change in the structure of society. This growth will result in an increase in the standard of living for a country's citizens.

If there is a downturn in economic activity, the government aims to return the country to a position of economic growth.

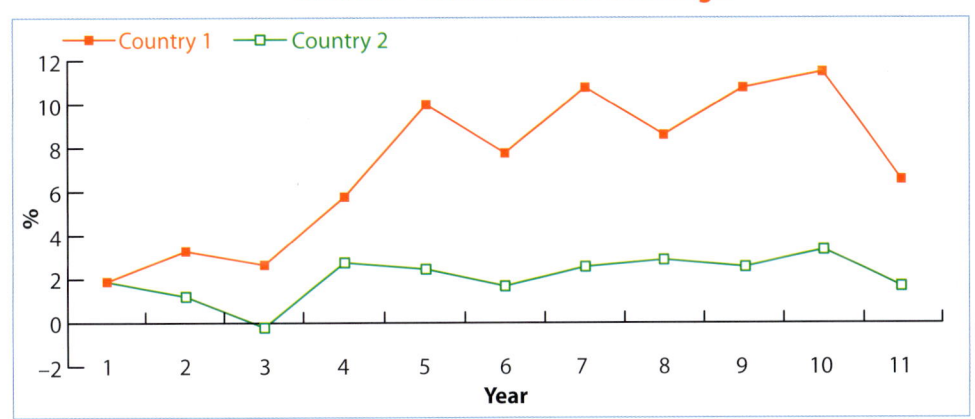

24: The Role of Government: Economic Aims and Policies

Real GDP Growth Annual % Change

Note: The graph shows that Country 1's economy, as measured by real GDP, grew at an annual average rate of 9.9% in the five years from year 1 to year 11 compared to Country 2's average of 2.5%. *Based an OECD source.*

However, economic growth has costs in addition to benefits, though it is important to note that the benefits significantly outweigh any costs. For example, growth in the economy may see an increase in the destruction of the environment, pollution and traffic congestion.

Governments can achieve economic growth by implementing the following strategies:

- Providing an economic infrastructure in which private industry can survive and flourish, e.g. reducing VAT for the service industry.
- Adopting fiscal and monetary policies that stimulate private industry, e.g. low rates of corporation tax and low interest rates for start-up companies.
- Promoting government policies designed to encourage the private sector, e.g. grants and training schemes.
- Lowering the minimum wage rate.
- Sponsoring state trading corporations.
- Reducing bureaucracy (state regulations) for companies.

Positive Economic Consequences of Economic Growth

- **Increased employment:** A rise in GNP will lead to increased demand for goods and services, with a consequent increase in the demand for labour.
- **Improved government finances:** More people employed will result in increased incomes. These in turn will mean increased spending, which will result in an increase in indirect tax revenue (VAT) for the government. The government will see a decrease in expenditure on social welfare benefits.

- **Effect on balance of payments:** If extra GNP results from increased output and if some of this output is exported, then our balance of payments position will improve (all money into a country less all money out of a country).

- **Improved standard of living:** Higher GNP will result in increased wealth in the economy, allowing customers to purchase more goods and services, leading to an improved standard of living. Following on from this, the economy will see a reduction in poverty.

- **Effects on migration:** If job opportunities exist, then people who had planned to emigrate may remain in Ireland and more immigrants may be attracted into the economy.

- **Investment opportunities:** Rising GNP indicates a growing economy, which may attract further investment into the economy.

Negative Economic Consequences of Economic Growth

- **Inflationary pressures:** The rise in the level of economic activity brings about an increase in the level of demand for goods and services. This causes an increase in inflation.

- **Labour shortages:** The increased demand for goods and services will increase the demand for labour in certain sectors, resulting in labour shortages.

- **Demand for wage increases:** Workers' expectations may increase with respect to pay increases (due to both points above).

- **Increased demand for imports:** A rise in GNP increases income and spending power. Hence, demand for imports may rise, worsening the balance of payments position.

- **Pressure in the housing market:** The rise in GNP increases spending power, thus stimulating demand for houses and resulting in possible housing shortages and increasing prices.

- **Pressure on state infrastructure:** Higher GNP results in a greater demand for scarce resources. Higher incomes will increase demand for commodities, e.g. cars. The extra pollution would result in more damage to the environment.

- **Increased immigration/displacement of population:** Rising GNP increases demand and provides more opportunities for employment, leading to a possible rise in immigration and the displacement of population (movement to urban centres), which further adds to the pressures mentioned in the above two points.

Positive Economic Consequences of an Economy in Decline

- **Lower inflation:** A slower increase in GNP should reduce demand inflation, as demand for goods and services declines.

- **Labour shortages:** The fall in demand for goods and services will decrease the demand for labour in certain sectors, thus easing labour shortages.

- **Falling demand for wage increases:** Workers' expectations for pay increases will decrease.

- **Reduced demand for imports:** A reduction in GNP lowers income and spending power and demand for imports will fall, leading to an improved balance of payments position.

24: The Role of Government: Economic Aims and Policies

- **Less pressure in the housing market:** The slower growth in GNP will decrease spending power. Demand for housing may then begin to fall, resulting in surplus housing stock and decreasing prices.
- **Expectations of citizens:** During an economic downturn, citizens may revise their expectations downwards.

Negative Economic Consequences of an Economy in Decline

- **Increased unemployment:** A slower increase in GNP will lead to reduced demand for goods/services and fewer workers will be required, increasing the level of unemployment.
- **Falling government finances:** A fall in spending causes a decrease in indirect tax revenue. Fewer people working results in less direct tax and an increase in social welfare payments.
- **Lower standard of living:** Slower growth in GNP will result in reduced wealth in the economy, which means fewer goods and services will be bought. There may be an increase in poverty and a deterioration in state services.
- **Effects on migration:** If job opportunities no longer exist, then more people will be forced to emigrate and fewer immigrants will be attracted to the economy.
- **Investment opportunities:** A slower growth in GNP may indicate the economy is heading into recession and potential investors will be deterred from investing in Ireland.
- **Less funds for infrastructure:** The fall in state finances due to the decreased receipts and higher social welfare costs will make it more difficult to fund major infrastructural developments, e.g. road infrastructure.

3. Control of Government Finances

Government spending can influence economic activity. In recessionary times, a government may decide to incur a budget deficit, i.e. government current spending is

Task

Check out this website and watch our debt increase by the second: www.financedublin.com/debtclock.php.

Current Government Expenditure and Revenue, 1960–2010

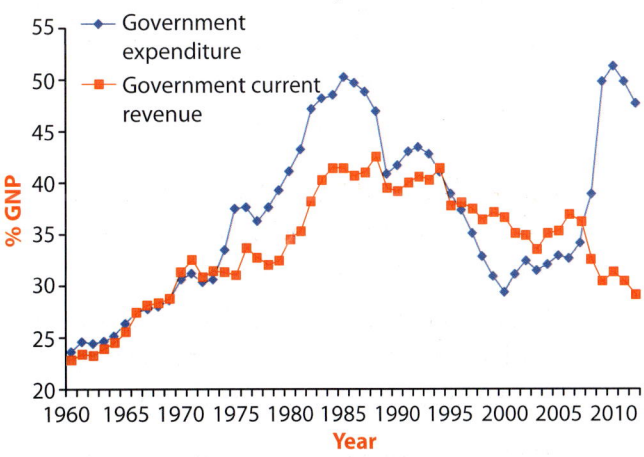

Source: Department of Finance, CBFSAI calculations.

greater than government current revenue. However, it should be careful not to increase its borrowings (the national debt) and the consequent servicing of this debt (interest on the national debt). For example, in 2010, €3 billion was used to service the national debt, or 10% of all receipts (NTMA). There is a need to prioritise policies that can help control problems and stimulate economic activity. This would allow the government to make much better use of scarce resources.

4. Promote Balanced Regional Development

Regional development is aimed at ensuring that all regions share in the economic growth of the country. Some areas of the country may lag behind the rest in terms of economic development. Consequently, they may not be afforded the same investment opportunities due to location, poor infrastructure, unskilled workforce, lack of telecommunications or shortage of natural resources. The government identifies and targets regions that are disadvantaged or economically depressed and then implements policies that positively discriminate in favour of these regions. The National Development Plan aims to implement these policies and spread the benefits of growth across the country.

Policies to Achieve Balanced Regional Development

- **Decentralise the public service:** The process of relocating government departments to local regions brings additional income to those areas via the multiplier effect, thus aiding economic development.

- **Tax and other incentives to attract industry:** If incentives are provided to industries in specific target areas, more firms will locate there, thus promoting economic development.

- **Investment in the infrastructure:** If investment in social infrastructure takes place, then this improvement will make these regions more attractive to live in. This has the effect of making such communities more attractive places to live, work and invest in, e.g. the Ballymun Regeneration Project.

- **Investment in communications:** The lack of adequate telecommunications is a deterrent to investment in some regions. Mobile phone coverage, broadband facilities, etc. are all integral elements of a business's communications system. If these facilities were improved, these areas would be a much more attractive investment location.

- **Develop/promote educational opportunities in the regions:** The provision of adequate third-level educational facilities and training networks are a prerequisite for attracting high-value-added businesses to the regions. The availability of courses in Institutes of Technology and other colleges in regional areas encourages enterprise in these same areas, facilitates economic development and stimulates economic activity and growth.

- **Improved access to and from other regions:** Tourist organisations in these regions state the lack of direct international flights is a major deterrent to attracting tourists/businesses. Investment in the road and rail networks would also improve access.

- **Easing planning restrictions in building residential property:** Easing planning restrictions on the building of residential property would encourage more people to live and work in these areas, boosting economic development.

- **Providing leadership programmes:** By identifying opportunities and aiding in research, training and promotion, these leadership programmes would encourage initiative and should aid regional development.

- **Government spatial strategy:** The aim of creating hubs and gateways within the regions in Ireland is to promote the urban areas in these regions as centres for development, which should have a ripple effect on the surrounding communities.

Can the government experience conflicts when trying to implement a balanced regional development policy?

- By encouraging more people to work and live in these areas, property prices can increase. This is contrary to the stated policy of creating affordable housing for those who relocate to these areas.

- Improving infrastructure in these regions requires increased expenditure. By increasing spending on infrastructure, there is a reduction in expenditure required to improve state services nationally, e.g. the health service.

- Policies to achieve industrial development in these regions may conflict with other policies to promote tourism in regional locations.

- Increased regional industrialisation may be at the expense of increased social costs such as pollution, congestion and increased local government charges.

5. Improve Infrastructure

To ensure a high standard of living, generate economic growth and attract foreign direct investors, it is imperative that there is continued development in infrastructure in the country, such as:

- The development of road infrastructure.
- The provision of public transport.
- The development of airports and seaports.
- A significant increase in the quality of telecommunications infrastructure.

6. Create a Just Social Policy/Ensure Equal Distribution of Wealth

Social policy refers to the provision of income and/or services for those who, for one reason or another, would find it difficult to provide for themselves if exposed to the full rigours of the market economy. An equitable distribution of income means that the gap between rich and poor is not excessive, but still enough to create incentives to work. The government is responsible for providing all citizens with those goods and services that allow them to enjoy a full life, e.g. the provision of education, health facilities and housing (merit wants). These policies are often pursued by governments on humanitarian, rather than economic, grounds.

The government must continue to ensure that social welfare recipients' standard of living is maintained, that it provides adequately for future pensions and helps to redistribute income within the state, subject to the current constraints on government current spending.

7. Control Price Inflation/Price Stability

The control of inflation:

- Stabilises the cost of living.
- Prevents demand for wage increases.
- Keeps Irish industry internationally competitive.

LOSS OF COMPETITIVENESS: A situation where our goods abroad are less attractive to foreign buyers.

Task

Compare the level of inflation over the past five years on www.tradingeconomics.com.

Ireland relies heavily on exports and any rise in Irish prices may lead to a decrease in our exports. Consequently, inflation has the effect of decreasing competitiveness.

Why does the government seek to control inflation?

- If our inflation rate is higher than our competitors', we would see a loss of competitiveness in international trade. As a result, it would be more difficult to sell our exports while at the same time imports would outsell domestic products on the home market.
- We would experience difficulty in encouraging foreign industrialists to invest in Ireland if our costs of production are high, e.g. higher wages.
- Workers and their representatives will try to negotiate increased wages during inflationary times to compensate for a loss in their existing purchasing power.
- Inflation results in the suffering of the economically weaker section of the community, e.g. pensioners, recipients of social welfare benefits or anyone on a fixed income. (Refer to Chapter 21.)

8. Maintain State Services

In recessionary times, if taxation revenues are declining, the government must ensure that essential services continue to be provided to its citizens, such as:

- Our health services are maintained and made more efficient.
- Schools are built and staffed to ensure a high level of education.

24: The Role of Government: Economic Aims and Policies

- Adequate housing and care of the vulnerable members of society are maintained.
- The government must provide adequately for future pensions and help redistribute income within the state.
- Practices are developed to ensure the long-term viability of essential services, i.e. possible charges or changed entry requirements for the provision of 'free' services.

Positive Consequences of a Government Policy to Increase Public Service Charges

- **Less pressure to increase taxes or borrowing:** Raising public charges will remove pressure on the government to raise additional revenue by increasing taxation.
- **More efficient use of services:** If people pay for services, it will encourage greater efficiency in their use, e.g. encourage people to recycle or use public transport.
- **Target the use of resources more economically:** By charging those who can afford to pay, the government can provide direct payments to those who cannot, thereby targeting the use of our resources more economically.
- **Pressure to improve quality of service:** Agencies will be forced to improve the quality of service provided, as people now pay, e.g. better frequency of service, more recycling centres and pay-per-weight for refuse.
- **Lower tax base:** Ireland can maintain a low tax base and hence encourage continued investment into the economy.
- **Uses of revenue collected:** Revenue collected can be targeted for best use to help achieve further aims, e.g. the plastic bag levy achieved the objective of reducing the wasteful use of plastic bags in Ireland.

Negative Consequences of a Government Policy to Increase Public Service Charges

- **Increased cost of living:** The prices of those services for which charges are being imposed will increase the cost of living, e.g. water charges and first-time buyer's property tax.
- **Increased inflation:** Inflation will rise, which will affect the economy negatively via reduced competitiveness, demand for compensatory wage increases, etc.
- **Affects lower-income groups most:** The increased charges will have the greatest impact on lower-income groups, i.e. those with the least ability to cope with higher prices. Their standard of living will deteriorate.
- **Viability of partnership agreements:** Trade unions may agree that the increase in these charges are stealth taxes, which may affect their decision to enter into future agreements/seek higher wages.

Positive Economics

- **Inequity/fairness:** The disparity in charges, an unacceptable level in the quality of service and the very introduction of charges may cause disquiet in citizens. In addition, people who won't pay for services may cause people to create other social problems, e.g. dump rubbish illegally, avoid toll roads and disrupt local communities.

- **Higher costs for business:** Firms must now pay higher toll charges, refuse charges, water charges, etc. – increasing costs which require higher prices passed on to consumers or a reduction in jobs.

9. Broaden the Tax Base

Many people believe in the past we relied too much on the property boom for taxation revenue. With the property boom at an end and hence the drastic reduction in stamp duty receipts, the government must now find new ways to generate taxation revenue, i.e. via the introduction of new taxes, widening the tax base, eliminating tax evasion and bringing workers into the income tax net and thus generating a greater flow of and increase in tax revenues. This money is vital for running the country, particularly if an economy is pulling itself out of a recession.

> **Task**
>
> Check out www.finance.gov.ie to compare tax revenue for the last five years.

10. Care for the Environment

Care for the environment means protecting the environment from misuse and overuse. The environment is an important asset that needs to be protected, so the government aims to implement policies to meet this need as well as educate citizens on what they can do to help protect their surroundings, e.g. recycling, plastic bag charges.

11. Achieve Equilibrium of the Balance of Payments

This is an issue for countries with an independent currency, e.g. the US. An equilibrium in the Balance of Payments implies that exports and imports are roughly equal. If exports are greater than imports, the demand for a country's currency will exceed supply, putting upward pressure on that currency. If imports are greater than exports, the opposite will occur.

12. Stabilise the Banking Sector

The instability of the banking sector in recent years rocked the nation and instilled fear and uncertainty in both the government

> It is important to note that not all of the above objectives discussed may be relevant to the government at all stages in our economic history. It will depend on the state of the economy and what is most relevant to our current government and current economic situation at the time of your study.

24: The Role of Government: Economic Aims and Policies

and economy. The state guarantee on depositors' savings, the nationalisation of Anglo Irish Bank and the establishment of NAMA were all aimed at restoring confidence in the banking sector. The government tried to revitalise credit availability and confidence among domestic and international investors.

Instruments in Achieving Economic Aims and Objectives

> **Task**
>
> Check out the ECB's current policies at www.ecb.int/home/html/index.en.html.

The following are instruments used in achieving government objectives.

Monetary Policy

Monetary policy is actions by the European Central Bank that influence:

- Money supply via changing the amount of money in circulation.
- Interest rates via changing the ECB base rate on which all variable rates depend.
- The availability of credit via changing the rules on issuing loans.

Fiscal Policy

This is any action taken by the government that influences the timing, magnitude and structure of government current revenue and expenditure. It is carried out by increasing or decreasing tax and increasing or decreasing government spending, e.g. increasing PAYE.

Exchange Rate Policy

This policy is directly controlled by the ECB and refers to the devaluation (making the currency worth less) and revaluation (making the currency worth more) of the euro in terms of other currencies.

Direct Intervention

This refers to the government's ability to directly intervene in the economy in order to achieve its aims and objectives. This is achieved by passing legislation, e.g. minimum wage, and setting up semi-state bodies, e.g. An Post and the Department of Health.

Deregulation
This is also regarded as a form of direct intervention and involves the government changing laws and practices that it deems detrimental to competition, e.g. the taxi industry.

Prices and Incomes Policy
This is a method used by the government to control inflation by restraining prices and incomes. It is implemented by imposing wage freezes or strict limits on wage increases, setting maximum prices for certain essential items and government approval on price increases for companies. It is important to note that this instrument may not be relevant to the Irish situation, but is an instrument that can be used by other governments.

Economic Planning
This involves consultation with the social partners, i.e. employers' representatives (IBEC), trade union representatives (ICTU), farmers' representatives (IFA) and community and voluntary organisations. The aim is to discuss and agree on a wide range of economic policies with a view to improving the standard of living for all citizens, e.g. the National Development Plan and Towards 2016.

Linking Government Aims and Objectives with Instruments

Aim: Full Employment
- **Fiscal policy:** Reducing taxation will result in an increase in demand for goods and services, leading to an increase in production and thus employment. By reducing both direct and indirect taxes, consumers have more disposable income and will increase their consumption.

- **Monetary policy:** Reducing interest rates has the effect of making the economy more attractive from an investment perspective. An increase in investment will lead to an increase in demand for labour.

- **Exchange rate policy:** Devaluing the currency makes exports cheaper, so there is an increase in demand for domestic products on foreign markets. An increase in the level of exports results in an increase in the demand for labour and thus an increase in employment.

24: The Role of Government: Economic Aims and Policies

- **Direct intervention:** Increased employment in the public sector and the provision of retraining and resettlement allowances encourages mobility of labour, i.e. giving more resources to the IDA or introducing wage subsidies to companies to encourage them to recruit more workers.
- **Prices and incomes policy:** Encouraging low wage inflation enables employers to employ more people.
- **Economic planning:** Holding discussions with the various social partners allows for the proper identification of labour requirements for the different sectors of the economy.

Aim: The Achievement of Economic Growth

- **Fiscal policy:** Reducing taxation on company profits (e.g. corporation tax) and labour (e.g. income taxes) will result in a more attractive investment environment.
- **Monetary policy:** Reducing interest rates leads to an increase in the production of goods and services. This creates an increase in employment and hence greater disposable incomes. The cycle begins again at consumption and so on. This is economic growth.
- **Direct intervention:** The government can establish semi-state companies to produce the goods and services that the private sector is unwilling to provide. These organisations, which contribute to economic growth, provide employment.
- **Economic planning:** Engaging in discussions with the social partners allows for realistic economic targets to be set for the various sectors of the economy, e.g. the National Development Plan.

Aim: Control of Government Finances

- **Fiscal policy:** Reducing government expenditure and lowering current borrowings enables the government to better control the national debt. The National Treasury Management Agency (NTMA) is currently managing this objective.

Aim: Achieve Balanced Regional Development

- **Fiscal policy:** The government could increase the provision of grants and subsidies to companies that are willing to locate and operate their business from less developed areas of the country.

Positive Economics

- **Economic planning:** Balanced regional development can be achieved through working closely with the social partners and implementing the National Spatial Strategy for Ireland 2002–2020.

Aim: The Provision of Adequate Infrastructure

- **Fiscal policy:** Increasing government expenditure on the improvement of infrastructural goods and services required by the citizens of the country and potential investors, e.g. toll roads, airports, schools, hospitals and telecommunications.

- **Direct intervention:** The government can establish Public Private Partnerships (PPP), i.e. the government combines forces with private enterprise to provide goods and services such as toll roads and waste disposal services.

- **Economic planning:** By promoting PPPs, it enables these companies to avail of greater resources needed in the provision of infrastructure. The National Development Plan defines PPPs as partnerships between public sector organisations and private sector investors and businesses for the purposes of designing, planning, financing, constructing and operating infrastructure projects.

Aim: Achievement of a Just Social Policy/Distribution of Wealth

- **Fiscal policy:** An increase in tax for higher-income earners will achieve a more equal distribution of wealth. A reduction in indirect tax on necessities and an increase in spending on social welfare benefits will also help achieve a more just social policy.

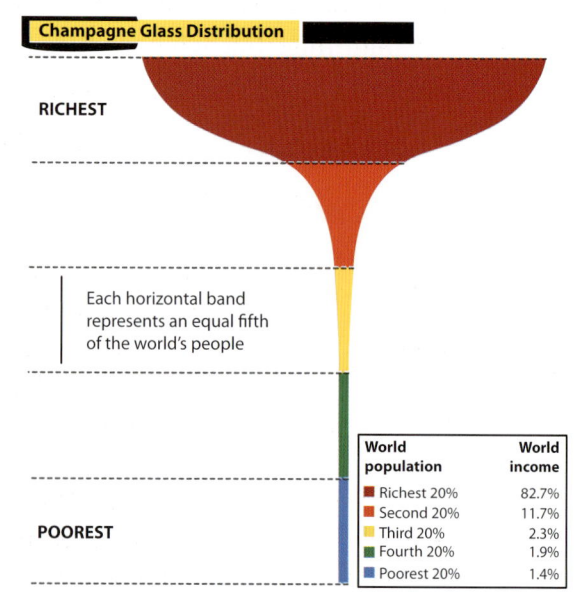

Champagne Glass Distribution

RICHEST

Each horizontal band represents an equal fifth of the world's people

POOREST

	World population	World income
Richest 20%		82.7%
Second 20%		11.7%
Third 20%		2.3%
Fourth 20%		1.9%
Poorest 20%		1.4%

Source: http://thesocietypages.org

Aim: The Control of Inflation

- **Fiscal policy:** Lowering indirect tax allows prices for goods and services to decrease, thus aiding the control of inflation. In addition, an increase in direct taxation will result in a reduction in consumption, again helping to control high inflation.

- **Monetary policy:** Increasing interest rates will see a decrease in the demand for loans by consumers and hence less money available for consumption in the economy.

- **Prices and incomes policy:** Imposing strict price controls and wage freezes ensures that inflation will be better controlled.

- **Economic planning:** Negotiating national wage agreements can control increased demands for wages and escalating prices, e.g. Towards 2016, and inflation can be better controlled.

Aim: Maintain State Services

- **Fiscal policy:** An increase in government expenditure will ensure that state services such as schools and hospitals are available to meet the demands of citizens. An increase in both direct and indirect taxation would increase the amount in the exchequer to be spent on funding state services.

Aim: Broaden the Tax Base

- **Fiscal policy:** The government could increase the numbers of people paying tax in Ireland. For example, they could:
    - Lower the thresholds so that lower-income earners start paying tax.
    - Lower the tax bands so that more people pay the higher rate of tax.
    - Introduce the property tax.

Aim: Care for the Environment

- **Fiscal policy:** By increasing indirect taxes, the extra revenue can be used to pay for the costs of repairing a damaged environment, e.g. carbon tax and plastic bag levy.

Aim: Achieve Equilibrium of the Balance of Payments

- **Fiscal policy:** By increasing direct taxes, there will a reduction in disposable income and therefore a reduction in the ability to purchase imports. By decreasing taxes on profits made from exports, the government will encourage more firms to engage in exporting, thus increasing the level of exports and achieving a more balanced equilibrium of payments.

- **Monetary policy:** By increasing interest rates, there is a reduction in the amount of loans demanded and therefore a reduction on imports such as foreign holidays.
- **Exchange rate policy:** By devaluing the currency, exports become much cheaper and imports become more expensive.

Aim: Stability in the Banking Sector
- **Fiscal policy:** If a government uses expenditure to recapitalise Irish banks, it strives to instil greater confidence in consumers.
- **Monetary policy:** If the ECB decreases interest rates, the cost of credit falls, enabling people to borrow more, which creates investment and consumption. If the ECB or Irish Central Bank increases the primary liquidity ratio, the banks must then increase their capital, thus making them stronger.
- **Direct intervention:** The government can pass laws that will protect consumers in the wake of a banking crisis, e.g. state guarantee on depositors' savings.

Task

Check out the current levels of income tax as well as tax bands on www.citizensinformation.ie.

Possible Conflicts between Economics Aims and Objectives

The opportunity cost of achieving any government objective is that the expenditure assigned for this project takes the funding away from working towards another aim. If the government targets certain areas for spending and development, other parts of the country and economy may lose out. The possible conflicts between government aims are as follows.

- Control of government finances vs. full employment
- Control of government finances vs. provision of infrastructure
- Control of government finances vs. economic growth
- Full employment vs. control of inflation
- Full employment vs. balance of payments equilibrium
- Balanced regional development vs. maintaining state services
- Economic growth vs. just social policy

Control of Government Finances vs. Full Employment
Policies that are designed to increase the level of employment in the country increase government expenditure. For example, in order to fund the Jobs Initiative during 2011, the government

24: The Role of Government: Economic Aims and Policies

imposed a levy on pensions as opposed to using existing monies in the exchequer to finance direct employment stimuli.

Control of Government Finances vs. Provision of Infrastructure
Infrastructure in Ireland has often been financed by government borrowings. If the government invests in capital projects, it increases government spending. This expenditure does not necessarily bring about a direct or immediate return on investment to the government.

Control of Government Finances vs. Economic Growth
In order for the government to address a significant budget deficit and meet its debt obligations, it needs to keep expenditure as low as possible while increasing revenue. Increasing revenue means higher taxes. These policies may have a deflationary effect on the Irish economy, which will stunt economic growth and prosperity.

Full Employment vs. Control of Inflation
Increasing employment requires the government to increase its public spending, decrease taxes and/or reduce interest rates (if it had the ability to). The result will be an increase in employment, which in turn will lead to higher wages, more disposable income, a greater demand for goods and services and therefore increased prices and high inflation. However, these actions can be counterproductive – if the government tries to control inflation by increasing interest rates, this will reduce consumer spending and will detract investment away from the country and will therefore result in job losses and increasing unemployment. Norman Lamont, Conservative Chancellor of the early 1990s, famously said, 'Unemployment is the price worth paying for lower inflation.'

Full Employment vs. Balance of Payments Equilibrium
The creation of employment leads to consumers having more disposable income and therefore demanding greater choice of goods and services. Some of this increased spending will be on imports, resulting in an outflow (leakage) of wealth from the economy. In addition to this, an increase in industrial activity means an increase in production and the demand for raw materials and machinery.

Balanced Regional Development vs. Maintaining State Services
If the government provides grants or tax incentives to firms to locate in underdeveloped areas of Ireland, e.g. the north-west, the government's current expenditure will increase. As the government has to tightly control its finances and all spending, high expenditure on creating balanced regional development would mean that less money is spent on state services such as health and education, which are necessary services for the citizens of the country nationwide.

Economic Growth vs. Just Social Policy

In order to achieve a just social policy and to create a more equal distribution of wealth, the government must increase the taxes on high-income earners and use the revenue received from these taxes to increase social welfare benefits. However, these high-income earners are generally the wealth creators of the country and may choose to leave our economy for a country with a more favourable tax system. This absence of investment could seriously impede our economic growth. In addition, there is an argument against an 'over-generous' social welfare system, which perhaps discourages people to get back into the workforce.

Nationalisation

Nationalisation happens when a government acquires ownership of privately owned businesses. This may be done to ensure the continuity of supply of an essential product or service, e.g. water, to all citizens at a reasonable price.

NATIONALISATION means taking a company or assets in the private sector into public ownership by a government.

Privatisation

PRIVATISATION is used to describe the sale or transfer of public sector assets to the private sector. Examples include Eircom and Greencore.

Economic Arguments in Favour of Privatisation

- **Improved quality/choice of services:** Privatised firms may improve the quality/efficiency/choice of the service provided.
- **More competitive prices:** Consumers may be offered more competitive prices on goods and services.
- **Continuity of supply:** The newly privatised companies will have access to new sources of funds, and as they are not subject to government interference, their long-term prospects for survival may improve, ensuring continuity of supply for consumers.
- **Employment opportunities:** If the new firm makes a commercial decision and increases its market share, then this may result in a growth in employment within the industry or additional job security.
- **More rewards/incentives for innovation:** Employees may reap more rewards for their innovations within the privatised industry, e.g. higher bonuses.
- **Revenue from sale may help reduce current/future taxes/opportunity cost:** The government could use the revenue from the sale of the firm to help reduce tax rates in Ireland, either direct or indirect.

24: The Role of Government: Economic Aims and Policies

Economic Arguments Against Privatisation

- **Loss of non-profit-making services:** Non-profit-making services may be discontinued by the company in an effort to reduce costs.

- **Standards of service:** A privatised company may need to make savings in ways that a state-owned company would not. As a result, the non-core services provided by the private company may deteriorate in an effort to save costs.

- **Preference to meet shareholders' demands:** Greater emphasis might be placed on meeting the expectations of shareholders rather than improving the quality of the service for consumers. A firm may charge for services that were considered free.

- **Loss of jobs/reduced job security/increased social welfare bill:** There may be a loss of jobs through rationalisation of services, leading to higher social welfare spending.

- **Curtailment in pay/pensions increases/working conditions:** The new owners may:
  - Limit the pay/pension increases due to its employees.
  - Change its employees' conditions of employment in a negative way.

- **Loss of a valuable state resource:** A company that had been financed by taxpayers in the past. With its sale, taxpayers now lose a valuable asset that they once owned.

- **Costs of sale:** All costs in preparation for the sale, such as legal work, must be paid for by the taxpayer, e.g. Aer Lingus.

- **Foreign ownership of Irish companies:** Overseas buyers can become owners of a previously owned Irish company and hence control of the asset can go outside the state.

Government Strategies

Task

Research the current government strategies that set out to achieve a better quality of life for the country's citizens.

Positive Economics

Task

The government has €35 billion set aside to devote to spending on different policy aims and objectives. It is seeking advice on how to allocate these resources between different uses and is looking for evidence for how these resources will represent value for money, measured in this case by giving the greatest benefit to the most people in society.

You will work in two sections.
- Section 1 will consist of three groups, each working on a different policy objective.
- Section 2 will represent a panel of ministers who will be charged with making the final decision on the apportionment of the funds.

Task

You have been asked to present a short speech to a panel of ministers promoting the case for a particular spending plan and objective. Your speech should cover the following areas, but you can consider other aspects that you think are important:

1. The objective of the plan.
2. What behaviour/infrastructure/resources will be needed to achieve the objective.
3. What external effects this is likely to have on other areas of economic and non-economic policy objectives.
4. Why this plan should be a priority for the government.

The three spending plans relate to:
- Health
- Education
- Pensioners

24: The Role of Government: Economic Aims and Policies

PROFILE: Physiocrats (1750–1800)

These were a group of 18th-century, mainly French economists whose ideas were in direct contrast to the Mercantilists. Two of the leading proponents from this school of thought were François Quesnay and Jacques Turgot. Their main ideas were:

- Agriculture was the only productive sector of the economy – the trade and industry sectors were sterile.
- Free trade was favoured.
- State intervention should be kept to a minimum.
- Advocated a self-interest approach (laissez-faire economic system).

PROFILE: François Quesnay (1694–1774)

Quesnay produced the famous Tableau Économique in 1785 (Economic Table). This was similar to what we now refer to as the circular flow of income and was modelled on the circulation of blood in the human body. His analysis showed that agriculture was the only sector of society producing a surplus and the other sectors consumed what it produced.

PROFILE: Jacques Turgot (1727–81)

Best known for his analysis of the law of diminishing returns in agriculture and an advocate of non-governmental intervention in economic affairs, Turgot suggested that the value of an item depends on its utility to the buyer.

EXAM ✓ Question 6(a)(ii), 2010 (15 marks)

It has been suggested that the main *commercial (retail) banks* in Ireland should be *nationalised*.

Outline **two** possible arguments for and **two** possible arguments against the nationalisation of banks.

Positive Economics

> **Solution**

Economic arguments in favour of the nationalisation of banks

- **Stability to the economy/investor confidence:** It was designed to signal to domestic and international investors that the state seeks to protect an important resource and thus attract investment.
- **Availability of credit:** Ideally, if the government backstopped the banking system, people would have confidence and leave their deposits in the banks. As a result, the banks could plan forward with accuracy and allow the flow of credit to resume. (Due to the worsening conditions on the financial markets, this proved more difficult than the ideal scenario.)
- **Rationalisation of banking services:** It may lead to a rationalisation of banking services within the state, the elimination of wasteful practices and cost efficiencies.
- **Employment/consumer protection:** Jobs currently threatened may be protected by state intervention. Consumers may also be offered better protection by state banks.
- **Development of ethical banking practices:** With nationalisation, banking practices may be less motivated by the generation of profit and more towards the provision of the services required by consumers.
- **Continued provision of banking services to the community/prevent foreign ownership:** A nationalised bank may continue to provide retail services to communities that were previously only provided if the branch was profitable.

Economic arguments against the nationalisation of banks

- **Unnecessary state interference:** Too much state involvement in commercial businesses may discourage domestic/international investors.
- **Shareholders penalised:** They may be forced to sell their shares at a price deemed to be unfair. Shareholders lose part or all of their investment, which has a detrimental effect on them and has a contagious effect on the financial markets.
- **Increased taxation:** Taxes have to be increased to fund the purchase and running of the nationalised banks.
- **Opportunity costs:** The money used for nationalisation could have been put to alternative uses by the state, e.g. the provision of improved health services.
- **Profit motive diminished:** Nationalisation reduces the pressure to improve services, achieve efficiencies and maximise profits.
- **Financial cost:** Large amounts of funds are needed to ensure the banks continue to survive and they could continue to be loss-making into the foreseeable future.

Questions

Short Questions

1. Distinguish between fiscal policy and monetary policy.
2. What are Public Private Partnerships?
3. Define loss of competitiveness.
4. Define deregulation.
5. Define nationalisation.
6. Define privatisation.
7. Explain the use of direct intervention.
8. What is meant by social policy?

Long Questions

1. Discuss the economic objectives of the government.
2. State the means available to the government in its efforts to achieve these objectives.
3. Discuss the instruments used to achieve full employment.
4. Examine the instruments used to achieve economic growth.
5. Explain why economic planning is an important instrument for implementing economic aims and objectives.
6. Evaluate the economic benefits and consequences of full employment in Ireland.
7. Discuss the economic benefits and consequences of economic growth in Ireland.
8. Comment on the economic benefits and consequences of a slower rate of economic growth in Ireland.
9. Discuss the reasons why governments seek to control inflation.
10. Discuss the effects that an increase in expenditure on social welfare schemes might have on other objectives of national economic policy.
11. Examine the consequences of the government increasing public service charges.
12. Discuss the policies that can be implemented in order to achieve balanced regional development.
13. Examine, in detail, the possible conflicts that can arise between economic aims and objectives.
14. Which objective of national economic policy would you prioritise at present? How would you attempt to achieve this objective?
15. Evaluate the economic arguments of privatisation.

Chapter 25: Economic Development and Growth

Specific Learning Outcomes

At the end of this chapter, students should be able to:

- [ ] Describe the characteristics of least developed countries (LDCs).

- [ ] Examine the costs and benefits of economic development.

- [ ] Identify and evaluate current policies available for aiding development in developing countries.

- [ ] Define economic growth and economic development.

- [ ] Explain the meaning and significance of economic growth and economic development.

- [ ] Discuss the role of the UN Human Development Index (HDI).

25: Economic Development and Growth

Least Developed Countries (LDCs)

Least developed countries (LDCs) represent the poorest and weakest segment of the international community.

What hampers LDCs' development?

- Extreme poverty.
- Structural weaknesses of their economies.
- Lack of capacities related to growth.
- Lack of infrastructure.
- Lack of industrial base.

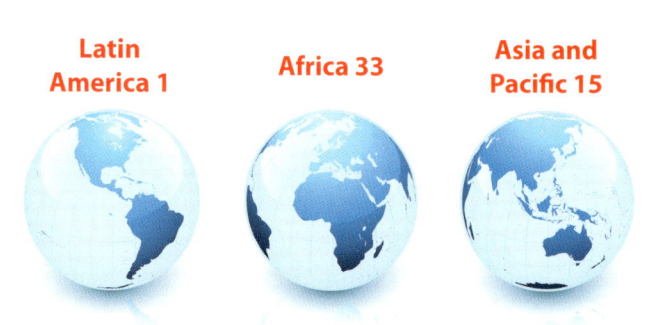

Latin America 1　　**Africa 33**　　**Asia and Pacific 15**

Number of LDCs in Latin America, Africa and Asia and Pacific

These countries are also characterised by their acute susceptibility to external economic shocks, natural and man-made disasters and communicable diseases. There are 49 countries classified as LDCs, with population expected to reach 965.2 million by 2015.

The UN Committee for Development Policy outlines the following criteria for identifying LDCs:

- **A low income per capita**, based on a three-year average estimate of the gross national income (GNI) per capita (under $905 for inclusion, above $1,086 for graduation).

- **Human vulnerability**, based on the following indicators:
    - Nutrition – percentage of population that is undernourished.
    - Health – mortality rate for children aged five years or under.
    - Education – the gross secondary school enrolment ratio.
    - Adult literacy rate.

- **Economic vulnerability**, based on indicators of:
    - Population size.
    - Remoteness.
    - Merchandise export concentration.
    - Share of agriculture, forestry and fisheries in gross domestic product.
    - Homelessness owing to natural disasters.
    - Instability of agricultural production.
    - Instability of exports of goods and services.

Positive Economics

Stages of Economic Growth

American Economist Walt Rostow examined the stages of economic growth, which were first published in 1960 in his famous work, *The Stages of Economic Growth: A Non-Communist Manifesto*.

Stage 1: Traditional Society

The economy is dominated by subsistence activity where output is consumed by producers rather than traded. Agriculture is the most important industry and production is labour intensive with limited possibilities. (Can you imagine trying to plant orange trees in the same field where coffee beans are growing?) The opportunities to increase output are limited, e.g. introduction of new crops, and irrigation is not always possible. Resource allocation is largely determined by traditional methods of production where clans and families tend to control the environment.

Stage 2: Transitional Stage (The Preconditions for Take-off)

At this stage, a country needs to be open to using modern ideas and aiming to break away from the poverty cycle. Through investment by developed countries into LDCs, a social climate emerges that encourages the pursuit of economic objectives. Banking and manufacturing begin at this point in addition to the emergence of a transport and communications infrastructure to support trade. As incomes, savings and investment grow, entrepreneurs emerge.

Stage 3: Take-off

This is the most critical stage. Industrialisation increases, with workers switching from the agricultural sector to the manufacturing sector. New industries emerge and the geography of the population changes as there is a move from rural to urban areas. Agricultural production increases to feed those now not working in the farming industry. The level of investment increases and reaches over 10% of GNP. The economic transitions are accompanied by the

> **Task**
>
> Talk to your parent(s) and grandparents about the life they lived in Ireland when they were young. They will be able to give you an insight into this very transition in our own economic history.

25: Economic Development and Growth

> Take a look at the show *Reeling in the Years* through the 1990s to see this change in Ireland's society and economics.

evolution of new political and social institutions that support the industrialisation. The growth is self-sustaining as investment leads to increasing incomes, which in turn generates more savings to finance further investment.

Stage 4: Drive to Maturity

There is a long period of sustained economic progress and GNP continues to increase. The economy is diversifying into new areas. Technological innovation is providing a diverse range of investment opportunities and older industries diminish in relative importance. The economy is producing a wide range of goods and services and there is less reliance on imports.

Task

Visit www.cso.ie to see how our exports ballooned throughout the Celtic Tiger and our imports grew in far less proportion.

Stage 5: High Mass Consumption

The economy is geared towards mass consumption. There is an increase in real income and the population enjoys an increased standard of living. The consumer durable industries flourish as the services sector becomes increasingly dominant. Increased resources are devoted to social welfare and security.

Task

For a humorous look at Irish society throughout the high mass consumption era, take a look at the book *Ross O'Carroll-Kelly's Guide to (South) Dublin: How to Get By on, Like, €10,000 a Day*.

Limitations of Rostow's Theory

Many economists argue that Rostow's model was developed with Western cultures in mind and that it is not applicable to LDCs for the following reasons:

- The development programmes should be more person-centred. The approach should look towards improving the life of individuals in their existing environment rather than the adoption of development programmes, as this stimulates mass movements of population into urban areas, potentially leading to industrial slums.

- The benefits that accrue from rapid urbanisation and industrialisation may take a long time to trickle down to the average worker.

- Its generalised nature makes it somewhat limited. It does not set down the detailed nature of the preconditions for growth.

- In reality, policymakers are unable to clearly identify the respective stages as they merge together.

As a result of all of the above, it is not very helpful as a predictive model, but perhaps its main use is to highlight the need for investment. It is essentially a growth model and does not address the real issues of development.

> **ECONOMIC DEVELOPMENT** is an increase in GNP per head of population, which is accompanied by a fundamental change in the structure of society.

What Constitutes a 'Fundamental Change' in the Structure of Society?

- **Urbanisation:** The move from rural areas of the country to more urban districts.
- **Education:** The provision of mandatory primary education for all citizens. 
- **Political stability:** A move from an unstable and corrupt political structure to a democratic constitution.
- **Move away from subsistence industry:** Less dependence on agriculture and a move into the manufacturing sector.

> **ECONOMIC GROWTH** is an increase in GNP per head of population, without any changes to the structure of society.

25: Economic Development and Growth

The Human Development Index (HDI)

The **HUMAN DEVELOPMENT INDEX (HDI)** is a summary composite index that measures a country's average achievements in three basic aspects of human development: health, knowledge and income.

The HDI was introduced as an alternative to conventional measures of national development, such as level of income and the rate of economic growth. It was created to emphasise that people and their capabilities should be the ultimate criteria for assessing the development of a country, not economic growth alone.

		Developed countries					
HDI rank	Country	Human Development Index (HDI) value	Life expectancy at birth (years)	Mean years of schooling (years)	Expected years of schooling	GNI per capita	GNI per capita rank minus HDI rank
1	Norway	0.938	81.0	12.6	17.3	58,800	2
2	Australia	0.937	81.9	12.0	20.5	38,692	11
3	New Zealand	0.907	80.6	12.5	19.7	25,438	30
4	United States	0.902	79.6	12.4	15.7	47,094	5
5	Ireland	0.895	80.3	11.6	17.9	33,078	20
6	Liechtenstein	0.891	79.6	10.3	14.8	81,011	−5
7	Netherlands	0.890	80.3	11.2	16.7	40,658	4
8	Canada	0.888	81.0	11.5	16.0	38,668	6
9	Sweden	0.885	81.3	11.6	15.6	36,936	8
10	Germany	0.885	80.2	12.2	15.6	35,308	9

Source: United Nations, June 2011.

Positive Economics

HDI rank	Country	Human Development Index (HDI) value	Life expectancy at birth (years)	Mean years of schooling (years)	Expected years of schooling	GNI per capita	GNI per capita rank minus HDI rank
			Least developed countries				
160	Mali	0.309	49.2	1.4	8.0	1,171	–7
161	Burkina Faso	0.305	53.7	1.3	5.8	1,215	–12
162	Liberia	0.300	59.1	3.9	11.0	320	5
163	Chad	0.295	49.2	1.5	6.0	1,067	–9
164	Guinea-Bissau	0.289	48.6	2.3	9.1	538	1
165	Mozambique	0.284	48.4	1.2	8.2	854	–5
166	Burundi	0.282	51.4	2.7	9.6	402	0
167	Niger	0.261	52.5	1.4	4.3	675	–3
168	Congo	0.239	48.0	3.8	7.8	291	0
169	Zimbabwe	0.140	47.0	7.2	9.2	176	0

Source: United Nations, June 2011.

Characteristics of LDCs

- **High rate of population growth:** Rates are very high, resulting in economic problems that the government finds hard to resolve.
- **Famine:** Too frequently, famine occurs in LDCs, resulting in disease, deaths at an early age and high medical costs.
- **Foreign debts:** Foreign debts tend to be very high in LDCs. The capital and interest repayments use up significant government revenue and often cripple the economy.
- **Uneven distribution of wealth:** In some LDCs, a minority control a large part of the country's wealth, resulting in widespread poverty.
- **Overdependence on one crop:** Some LDCs are overdependent on one crop. The country may be subject to crop failure and/or a wide variation in export prices.
- **Small home market:** A limited domestic customer base lessens the ability of firms in LDCs to achieve economies of scale. They therefore remain uncompetitive against competition from developed countries.
- **High percentage of the population engaged in the extractive/primary industries in LDCs:** An overall low standard of living results from an insufficient number of workers employed in secondary and tertiary sectors. There is an underdeveloped industrial base.
- **Unfavourable terms of trade for LDCs:** LDCs may suffer from low export prices and high import prices and hence the gains from trade are reduced for these countries.

25: Economic Development and Growth

- **Poor living conditions/inadequate infrastructure in LDCs:** A large proportion of the population may live in shantytowns in poor conditions with dirty, if any, water and poor sanitation. Lack of paved roads and railways, inadequate power and water supplies as well as a lack of airports, telephones and other telecommunications equipment may hinder the development of business.

- **Lack of capital/low levels of investment in LDCs:** LDCs lack the capital essential for economic development and employment generation. They also have limited access to technological advances. Infrastructure, factories, schools, etc. are all inadequate in LDCs.

- **Low per capita incomes in LDCs:** If people have very little income, they have a low demand for goods and services and a poor standard of living.

- **Poor levels of education/literacy in LDCs:** Educational opportunities are very limited in LDCs. This acts as an impediment to economic development and contributes to continuing unemployment.

- **Political corruption/less stable political institutions:** Some LDCs spend a lot on bureaucratic administration/military spending, which may result in civil unrest. In some cases, the political institutions are unstable and this hinders investment.

- **Multinationals' exploitation of LDCs/economic dualism:** Exploitation may take the form of low wages, lack of care for the environment and control over key exports.

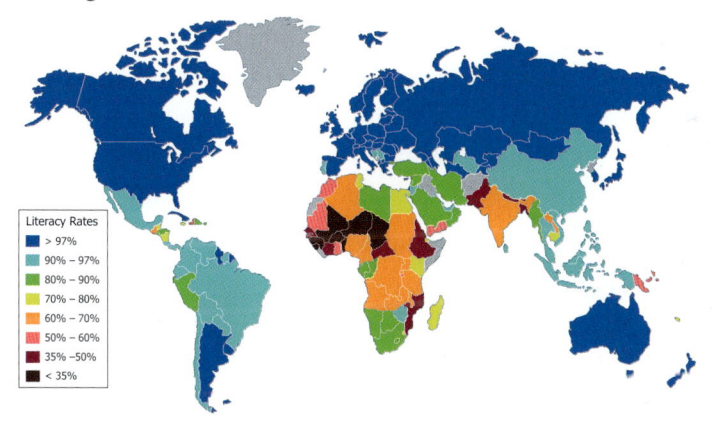

Source: UN Development Report 2007/2008.

Country	Adult literacy rate	Youth literacy rate
China	91.0%	98.9%
India	66.0%	82.0%
Nepal	44.0%	62.7%
Pakistan	41.5%	53.9%
Sri Lanka	92.0%	98.0%

According to UNESCO, there are about 1 billion non-literate adults in the world today.

- This 1 billion is approximately 26% of the world's adult population.
- Women make up two-thirds of all non-literates.
- 98% of all non-literates live in developing countries.

Positive Economics

How Governments in LDCs Might Promote Economic Development

- **Promote population control:** Governments could encourage a reduction in population by such measures as educating the population in family planning methods, improving the welfare of its citizens and providing better social services for its citizens.

- **Improve infrastructure:** Capital projects could be embarked on to improve the societies of LDCs, including the provision of clean water and proper sanitation as well as the development of public housing, roads and power supplies, etc.

- **Promote land/agricultural reform:** Governments could decrease the emphasis on one crop/diversify production. They could try to spread ownership of land, improve production methods and modernise the agricultural industry.

- **Improve education/literacy skills**: There are various programmes that would augment the future possibilities of LDC citizens. For example:
    - Start with a basic literacy programme to improve literacy skills.
    - Provide technical skills to the population.
    - Provide primary education.
    - Develop the secondary sector and initiate further education programmes.

- **Incentives for the development of enterprise:** The government could try to foster a movement away from a dependency culture and encourage enterprise. Borrowings could be used to encourage enterprise so as to create sustainable employment.

- **State bureaucracy/corruption/spending on arms:** There are some very effective initiatives that could help all citizens, including:
    - Reducing bureaucracy within state institutions.
    - Eliminating corruption so that aid flows to those it was intended for.
    - Diverting funds from arms spending to more urgent current requirements.

What Can LDCs Do to Improve Output?

Primary Sector
This refers to the extraction of wealth from nature – farming, mining, forestry and fishing.

- Need for basic education to raise output in agriculture.
- Use of fertilizers.
- Investment in irrigation schemes.

Secondary Sector
This refers to manufacturing industries.
- Investment in education.
- Investment in infrastructure.
- Investment in small home industries.

Tertiary Sector
This refers to the supply of services.
- Eco-tourism should be encouraged.
- Promote activity holidays.
- Need to upgrade airports, hotels, etc.
- Very difficult at present for LDCs to advance in other tertiary sectors until education levels improve (and if education were to significantly improve, they would no longer necessarily be classified as an LDC!).

How Governments of Developed Countries Can Promote Economic Development in LDCs

- **Assist foreign aid programmes/capital provision:** Governments can continue with aid to help in emergency situations. They can also provide more long-term aid to help with the development of infrastructure and the provision of education, health programmes, etc.

- **Restructure their national debts:** If the national debts were cancelled, these funds would become available for the country to use for economic development.

- **Improve trading opportunities:** If LDCs improved access to markets in the developed world as an outlet for their exports, they would improve the terms of trade available and negotiate higher prices for exports.

Least Developed Countries Market Share of EU Imports 2010

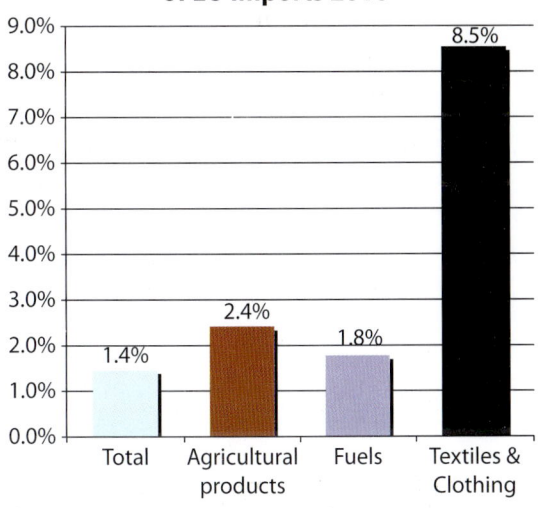

Total	1.4%
Agricultural products	2.4%
Fuels	1.8%
Textiles & Clothing	8.5%

Source: Eurostat.

- **Encourage multinationals to set up firms in LDCs:** Multinationals could provide workers with skills. The fair wages received could help boost domestic demand and provide tax revenue for the state.

- **Assist LDCs with skills and technologies:** The provision of skills and technologies to the LDCs would help with improving standards of living and increasing productive capacity.

Positive Economics

- **Assist with peace measures and promote political stability:** Economic development requires a peaceful environment. Foreign countries could provide peacekeeping troops and encourage the movement towards political stability.

Benefits of Economic Development to LDCs

- **Increased standard of living:** Life would improve for LDC citizens via better education, improved health services, increased life expectancy, better housing and potentially higher incomes.
- **Increased employment:** Increased opportunities for employment through increased demand would improve LDCs in many ways.
- **Increased resources available to the governments:** Tax revenue would allow the government scope for initial and further investment.
- **Alleviation of poverty:** More schools, houses and other essential services to promote self-sufficiency would help reduce poverty.
- **Investment in research and development:** As money starts to become available for investment, economic growth would strengthen.

REMEMBER!
Aggregate demand:
$C + I + G + NX$

Costs of Economic Development to LDCs

- **Unfair distribution of benefits/widening of poverty gap:** The increased wealth may not trickle down to the people who need it most.
- **Costs to environment:** Increased pollution, disfigurement of the landscape and large-scale urban sprawl would detract from the quality of life in LDCs.
- **Traditional values:** Large-scale movement from rural to urban areas may result in the loss of traditions, culture and a way of life.
- **Welfare may not improve:** The increase in wealth may be brought about through changed working practices, movement of the population and crime in areas, etc.
- **Scarcer resources:** By achieving economic development, these countries will contribute to using up the world's scarce resources.

RESOLVING THE CRISIS

25: Economic Development and Growth

Steps towards Resolving Debt Crisis

- **Drop the debt:** The quickest and simplest way to solve the debt crisis is to write off the existing debts of these countries and start afresh.

- **Reschedule the capital repayments:** By allowing these countries to extend the length of the repayment period, they could present payment at a more suitable time. As a result, they would also be reducing the annual repayments charges and funding urgently required needs.

- **Lower the annual interest repayments:** Negotiate a reduction in the interest repayments on the existing debt to facilitate domestic needs.

- **Replace the existing 'expensive' debt:** By replacing existing debts with new loans carrying lower rates of interest, the annual interest charges and capital repayments would fall.

- **Place a limit on interest repayments:** The amount of interest to be paid could be limited to a percentage of that country's exports.

- **Barriers to prevent the flight of capital:** Governments in LDCs could erect barriers to prevent those wealthy enough from taking their money out of the country, i.e. from moving their wealth to bank accounts in other countries.

- **Debt swaps:** Governments could arrange to swap debt for investment in firms in debtor countries or for the right to conserve large areas of habitat in danger, i.e. tropical forests.

- **Debt buybacks:** LDCs could engage in negotiation to buy back debt from the debtor country at a discount.

- **Reform of IMF/World Bank:** Critics of IMF/World Bank policies say that their decisions are too influenced by US policy. If these institutions were reformed and their lending policies adjusted, the debt problems of LDCs could be alleviated far more effectively.

Opportunities and Challenges that the Expansion of the EU Presents to LDCs

Opportunities

- Any trade agreements with the EU open up much bigger markets, as barriers to entry to previous Eastern bloc countries are eased.

- Easier to find markets in Europe as negotiating barriers are removed.

- New sources for tourists for LDCs to target.
- New sources for investment in LDCs will arise as new EU states raise their own standards of living.

Challenges

- EU agricultural subsidies now directed to several new EU states will make it harder for LDCs to sell their produce in Europe.
- LDCs may face stronger opposition for manufactured goods as the new EU countries benefit from investment by their EU neighbours.
- EU expansion allows freer movement of labour within most EU countries – this in turn will keep labour costs down in the EU, making it harder for LDCs to gain a market foothold for their goods in the EU.
- New EU states may obtain loans from their EU neighbours, thus limiting funds available to LDCs.

Task

Go to the United Nations website (www.un.org) and pick any country characterised as an LDC. Prepare a profile on the country. Identify the main problems within the economy of your chosen LDC. In your report, suggest strategies for helping to reduce poverty and boost economic development.

EXAM Question 7(b), 2010 (30 marks)

(b) (i) Describe the main differences between a developed country and a developing country (LDC).

(ii) Discuss **three** measures which the governments of developed countries could take to promote economic development in developing countries (LDCs).

Solution

(b) (i)

- **High rate of population growth:** Rates are very high, resulting in economic problems that the government finds hard to resolve.

- **Famine:** Famine frequently occurs in LDCs, resulting in disease, deaths at an early age and high medical costs.

- **Foreign debts:** Foreign debts tend to be very high in LDCs. The capital and interest repayments use up significant government revenue and often cripple the economy.

- **Uneven distribution of wealth:** In some LDCs, a minority control a large part of the country's wealth, resulting in widespread poverty.

- **Overdependence on one crop:** Some LDCs are overdependent on one crop. The country may be subject to crop failure and/or a wide variation in export prices.

Refer to pp. 386–87 for further points that would be acceptable answers.

(b) (ii) *Any three of the following points would be acceptable answers.*

- **Assist foreign aid programmes/capital provision:** Governments can continue with aid to help in emergency situations. They can also provide more long-term aid to help with the development of infrastructure and the provision of education, health programmes, etc.

- **Restructure their national debts:** If the national debts were cancelled, these funds would become available for the country to use for economic development.

- **Improve trading opportunities:** If LDCs improved access to markets in the developed world as an outlet for their exports, they would improve the terms of trade available and negotiate higher prices for exports.

- **Encourage multinationals to set up firms in LDCs:** Multinationals could provide workers with skills. The fair wages received could help boost domestic demand and provide tax revenue for the state.

- **Assist LDCs with skills and technologies:** The provision of skills and technologies to the LDCs would help with improving standards of living and increasing productive capacity.

- **Assist with peace measures and promote political stability:** Economic development requires a peaceful environment. Foreign countries could provide peacekeeping troops and encourage the movement towards political stability.

Questions

Short Questions

1. Define economic development.
2. Explain three costs of economic development.
3. State two ways governments in LDCs might promote economic development.
4. Explain the elements that constitute a 'fundamental change' in the structure of society.

Positive Economics

Long Questions

1. Outline the main characteristics that would indicate that a country is an LDC.
2. Describe the main differences between a developed country and a developing country.
3. Discuss the measures that the governments of developed countries could take to promote economic development in developing countries.
4. Evaluate the policies employed by LDCs in the promotion of economic development.
5. Discuss how economic development in LDCs might be promoted:
    (a) By their own government
    (b) By foreign governments/agencies
6. Discuss the benefits of economic development to LDCs.
7. Discuss the costs of economic development to LDCs.
8. Discuss the steps that could be taken to solve the debt crisis that LDCs are experiencing.
9. Explain how economic problems in many LDCs restrict economic development.
10. Describe how economic output in LDCs can be promoted by their own government in the primary, secondary and tertiary sectors of their economies.
11. Explain how the expansion of the European Union provides opportunities and difficulties for LDCs.

Chapter 26 | Economics of Population

Specific Learning Outcomes

At the end of this chapter, students should be able to:

- [ ] Illustrate the size, composition and trends of national population.

- [ ] Illustrate the size, composition and trends of global population.

- [ ] Define demography, overpopulation, underpopulation and optimum population.

- [ ] Define birth rate, fertility rate, death rate, infant mortality rate and life expectancy rate.

- [ ] Define density of population.

- [ ] Evaluate the economic effects of an ageing population on the Irish economy.

- [ ] Illustrate the push and pull forces of migration.

- [ ] Analyse the consequences of an increase in emigration.

- [ ] Consider the implications of the changing structure and size of the Irish population.

- [ ] Outline the economic uses of a census of population in Ireland.

- [ ] Evaluate the importance of a census of population.

- [ ] Critically examine the influence of population on economic development and growth, both nationally and globally.

Positive Economics

Introduction

The economic aspects of population are an important element of our analysis when studying economics. We discover and consider the important and ever-changing relationship between population trends, economic development and growth. We are living in a world of unprecedented demographic change. Having grown very slowly for most of human history, the world's population more than doubled in the last half century to reach 6 billion in late 1999 and by late 2011 it had reached 7 billion. Lower mortality, longer life expectancy and a youthful population in countries where fertility remains high have all contributed to the rapid population growth of recent decades.

According to the UN, world population is expected to exceed 10 billion by 2100.

Population

We gather demographic information from the registration of births and deaths and also from

> **DEMOGRAPHY is the statistical study of human population.**

a census of population. These statistics are invaluable, as they provide us with information needed and used by the government in economic planning. We will now examine the various important elements of population and its relationship to economics.

Source: United Nations Population Division.

Underpopulation

Some countries, e.g. Canada and Australia, encourage people to immigrate to their countries in order to satisfy labour shortages. Increased labour means increased production and better utilisation of previously underutilised resources. These countries benefit from a high standard of living and can be characterised by their high GDP per capita.

> **A country is UNDERPOPULATED when an increase in the population causes an increase in the average income per head under given economic resources.**

Overpopulation

Countries that are overpopulated find it almost impossible to produce enough to support themselves and the hope of having a surplus to sell is virtually non-existent. This can contribute

> **A country is OVERPOPULATED when an increase in population causes a decrease in the average income per head under given economic resources.**

26: Economics of Population

to a low GDP per capita, which is a typical characteristic of an overpopulated country. As a result, in order to support themselves, some of these countries rely heavily on foreign debt and citizens are severely hindered by the poverty trap. They suffer from very high levels of unemployment, as there simply are not enough jobs. Consequently, these countries have very high crime rates as people resort to extreme measures in order to survive.

Optimum Population

> **OPTIMUM POPULATION** is when the average income per head is at its highest possible level under given economic resources.

Trends in Births and Deaths

In order to appreciate the changes that have taken place in population, both globally and nationally, we must examine trends in births and deaths for the past number of years.

Birth Rate

From a global perspective, the birth rate will vary between developed and less developed countries. The birth rate is dependent on a number of features, including the age structure of the population, level of GNP per capita, religion, culture and education. Globally, Ireland has an average of 16.1 births per 1,000 population.

> **BIRTH RATE** is the average number of live births per 1,000 people per year.

Highest birth rates	Country	Births per 1,000 population
1	Niger	50.54
2	Uganda	47.49
3	Mali	45.62
4	Zambia	44.08
5	Burkina Faso	43.59
6	Ethiopia	42.99
7	Angola	42.91
8	Somalia	42.71
9	Burundi	41.01
10	Malawi	40.85

Source: nationmaster.com (2011).

Positive Economics

Lowest birth rates	Country	Births per 1,000 population
1	Monaco	6.94
2	Japan	7.31
3	Hong Kong	7.49
4	Germany	8.30
5	Saint Pierre and Miquelon	8.32
6	Singapore	8.50
7	South Korea	8.55
8	Austria	8.67
9	Czech Republic	8.70
10	Slovenia	8.85

Source: nationmaster.com (2011).

Fertility Rate

Fertility rate is one of the most important factors in determining future population growth rates. As with birth rate, the fertility rate varies between developed and developing countries. For example, in developed countries:

> **FERTILITY RATE** is the number of live births in a geographic area in a year per 1,000 women of childbearing age.
>
> **TOTAL FERTILITY RATE** is the average number of babies born to women during their reproductive years.

- Many women opt to concentrate on their careers rather than have children.

- Increasing sexual equality means that women have more control over their own fertility.

- It is often viewed that children are very expensive to rear and educate.

- A vital factor is that there is a ready availability of contraception and family planning advice.

On the other hand, in less developed countries:

- Many parents have a lot of children in the expectation that some will die because of a high infant mortality rate in their region.

- Children are viewed as essential in families because they contribute to household income, either by way of government support or employment, e.g. working on the farm. They are also viewed as essential contributors in supporting the elderly or sick, as there may not be an old age pension scheme.

- There may be an immense shortage of family planning facilities and advice.

From a global perspective, Ireland has an average of 2.2 children born per woman over the course of her lifetime. However, it is projected that the total fertility rate will decline to 1.65 by 2016, remaining constant thereafter. It is noteworthy that the countries with the highest fertility rate are the least developed countries (LDCs).

Task

Research the countries that are the most overpopulated and underpopulated in the world. What are the economic consequences of high/low fertility rates for these countries? Present your findings to the class.

Class Discussion

- What effect does a high fertility rate have on a country that is characterised as less developed?

- Ireland's figure is average for a developed country. However, it is interesting to note that it is higher than other developed countries such as Japan. Why is this? (Recall what you have learned on overpopulation.)

Highest fertility rates	Country	Average number of children born per woman
1	Niger	7.60
2	Uganda	6.69
3	Mali	6.44
4	Somalia	6.35
5	Burundi	6.16
6	Burkina Faso	6.14
7	Ethiopia	6.02
8	Zambia	5.98
9	Angola	5.97
10	Republic of Congo	5.68

Source: nationmaster.com (2011).

Positive Economics

Lowest fertility rates	Country	Average number of children born per woman
1	Macau	0.92
2	Hong Kong	1.07
3	Singapore	1.11
4	Taiwan	1.15
5	Japan	1.21
6	South Korea	1.23
7	Lithuania	1.25
8	Montserrat	1.26
9	Belarus	1.26
10	Czech Republic	1.26

Source: nationmaster.com (2011).

Death Rate

It is not only the rate of births that affects population, but also the rate of deaths in a country.

DEATH RATE is the average number of deaths per 1,000 people per year.

Developing countries tend to have very high death rates. There are a number of factors that contribute to this, including:

- Dirty and unreliable water supplies.
- Poor housing conditions.
- Poor access to medical services.
- Endemic disease in some countries.
- Diets that are low in calories and/or protein.

Developed countries tend to have much lower death rates. The factors that contribute to this include:

- Good housing conditions.
- Safe water supplies.
- More than enough food to eat.
- Advanced medical services that are easy to access.

From a global perspective, Ireland has a figure of 6.34 deaths per 1,000 population. This is very low if compared to Angola and Nigeria. However, it does not fall within the top 10 lowest death rates, such as the United Arab Emirates and Kuwait. Why do you think this is?

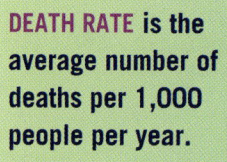

Highest death rates	Country	Deaths per 1,000 population
1	Angola	23.40
2	Afghanistan	17.39
3	South Africa	17.09
4	Nigeria	16.06
5	Russia	16.04
6	Ukraine	15.74
7	Chad	15.47
8	Guinea-Bissau	15.27
9	Lesotho	15.19
10	Central African Republic	15.01

Source: nationmaster.com (2011).

Lowest death rates	Country	Deaths per 1,000 population
1	United Arab Emirate	2.06
2	Kuwait	2.11
3	Qatar	2.43
4	Mayotte	2.60
5	Bahrain	2.61
6	Jordan	2.69
7	Turks and Caicos Islands	2.99
8	Northern Mariana Islands	3.28
9	Saudi Arabia	3.33
10	Brunei	3.35

Source: nationmaster.com (2011).

Infant Mortality

According to UNICEF and the International Rescue Committee, infant mortality is the result of the following factors:

- Lack of nutrition.
- No availability of safe, clean water.
- Lack of child and maternal services.
- Lack of medication and immunisation.
- Infectious diseases and pregnancy-related conditions.
- Disruption of health services, deterioration of infrastructure and population displacement due to conflict.

INFANT MORTALITY refers to the number of children out of every 1,000 born alive who die on or before their first birthday.

Positive Economics

Children are particularly susceptible to these easily preventable and treatable conditions.

Ireland ranks 156th out of 179 countries in infant mortality rate. An average of 5.5 infants per thousand die each year, which is incredibly low if compared to countries such as Angola, Mozambique and Malawi.

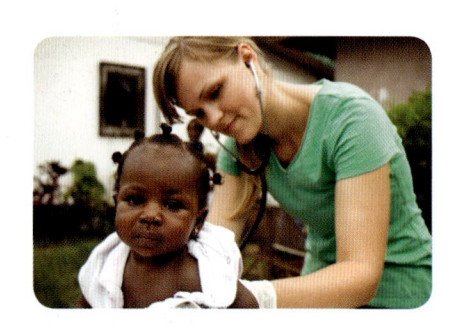

Highest infant mortality rate	Country	Average infant mortality rate
1	Angola	192.50
2	Afghanistan	165.96
3	Mozambique	137.08
4	Liberia	130.51
5	Niger	122.66
6	Mali	117.99
7	Guinea-Bissau	108.72
8	Djibouti	105.54
9	Malawi	104.23
10	Bhutan	102.56

Source: nationmaster.com (2011).

Lowest infant mortality rate	Country	Average infant mortality rate
1	Hong Kong	2.97
2	Japan	3.28
3	Iceland	3.31
4	Finland	3.59
5	Norway	3.73
6	Malta	3.94
7	Czech Republic	3.97
8	Andorra	4.05
9	Germany	4.20
10	France	4.31

Source: nationmaster.com (2011).

26: Economics of Population

Life Expectancy

Life expectancy rose rapidly in the 20th century due to improvements in public health, nutrition, access to safe drinking water, sanitation, adult literacy and medicine. It's likely that life expectancy of the most developed countries will slowly advance and then reach a peak in the mid-80s in age.

LIFE EXPECTANCY is the number of years, based on statistical averages, that a given person of a specific age, class or other demographic variable may be expected to continue living.

The following factors are significant in determining one's life expectancy:

- Income
- Education
- Urbanisation
- Geographical location of a country

However, in many of the countries in the developing world, particularly Sub-Saharan Africa, life expectancy has been decreasing. Life expectancy can fall due to problems like famine, war, disease and poor health. Unfortunately, AIDS has taken its toll in Africa, Asia and even Latin America, by reducing life expectancy in many emerging countries.

Life expectancy	Country	Average life expectancy
1	Japan	73.6 years
2	Switzerland	72.8 years
3	Sweden	71.8 years
4	Australia	71.6 years
5	France	71.3 years
6	Iceland	71.1 years
7	Austria	71 years
8	Italy	71 years
9	Spain	70.9 years
10	Norway	70.8 years

Source: nationmaster.com (2011).

Density of Population

Formula

$$\frac{\text{Total population of a country}}{\text{Total land area of a country}}$$

DENSITY OF POPULATION is the average number of people per square kilometre.

Positive Economics

From a global perspective, Ireland has an average of 52.74 people per square kilometre.

Highest density of population	Country	Average number of people per square km
1	Macau	20,824.40
2	Monaco	16,486.70
3	Hong Kong	6,571.14
4	Singapore	5,539.77
5	Gibraltar	4,486.92
6	Gaza Strip	3,090.71
7	Bermuda	1,249.44
8	Malta	1,192.51
9	Bahrain	1,014.66
10	Maldives	1,000.73

Source: nationmaster.com (2011).

Monte Carlo, Monaco

Lowest density of population	Country	Average number of people per square km
1	French Guiana	1.88
2	Namibia	2.00
3	Australia	2.47
4	Botswana	2.50
5	Mauritania	2.51
6	Suriname	2.67
7	Iceland	2.72
8	Libya	2.84
9	Canada	3.36
10	Guyana	3.58

Source: nationmaster.com (2011).

Migration

> **NET MIGRATION** is the difference between outward migration (emigration) and inward migration (immigration) during a period of time.

- **Emigration:** Irish citizens leaving Ireland and moving to live abroad.
- **Immigration:** Citizens of other countries entering Ireland to live.

There are many factors that contribute to migration, which is a major determinant of population size and composition. These are classed as **push forces** and **pull forces**.

Push Forces

Factors that compel people to leave their own country (emigration) include:

- High levels of unemployment
- Low wage rates
- Lack of promotion opportunities
- Poor social infrastructure
- Political instability
- Religious persecution
- Desire to seek new experiences and employment outside of one's native homeland

Pull Forces

These are the factors that draw a person to another country (immigration) and include:

- Employment opportunities
- Higher wages
- Better standard of living
- Job experience
- Greater political stability abroad
- A more attractive climate
- The desire to broaden one's outlook on the world

Positive Economics

The table below illustrates our knowledge of birth, death and migration rates from the Irish perspective.

Average annual births, deaths, natural increase and estimated net migration for each inter-censal period, 1926–2011			
Period	Total births (thousands)	Total deaths (thousands)	Natural increase (thousands)
1926–36	58	42	16
1936–46	60	43	17
1946–51	66	40	26
1951–56	63	36	27
1956–61	61	34	26
1961–66	63	33	29
1966–71	63	33	30
1971–79	69	33	35
1979–81	73	33	40
1981–86	67	33	34
1986–91	56	32	24
1991–96	50	31	18
1996–02	54	31	23
2002–06	61	28	33
2006–11	73	28	45

Source: Central Statistics Office.

Task

In groups of three, compare Ireland's birth, death and migration rates in 1951 and 2011. What changes do you notice? What are the economic factors that have contributed to these changes? Present your findings to the other groups.

$$\text{Dependency ratio:} \quad \frac{\text{Number of people aged under 15 and over 65}}{\text{Number of people aged between 15 and 65}}$$

As you can see from the above table, Ireland's population has been rising since 1991.

If the increase in population is due to immigration, then the numbers joining the labour market may increase. It is therefore important for the government to prioritise the creation of employment. Increased numbers in the labour force will lower the dependency ratio and lead to increased tax revenue for the state.

On the other hand, if the increase in population is due to the increased birth rate, then there will be a higher dependency ratio, i.e. an increase in the percentage of the population that is economically inactive, which will place greater demands on government funds.

Economic Consequences of an Increase in Emigration

- **Higher dependency ratio:** As 18- to 35-year-olds are the most likely age group to emigrate, the country will have an increased dependent population of young children and elderly people. They have a higher dependency on the government's funds in terms of pensions, Child Benefit, health care, etc.

- **Opportunity costs:** The Irish government prides itself on a first-rate education system that is free to its citizens. Education is an immense financial investment and the state may lose out substantially on this investment if our citizens take their skills and work in foreign countries.

- **'Brain drain':** Graduates who have acquired skills needed to help us move towards economic growth may emigrate in search of employment or better job opportunities. The 'brain drain' robs the economy of the skills and qualifications invested in them, which are an important aspect of economic recovery and strength.

- **Smaller domestic market:** As the domestic market contracts, there may be reduced opportunities for investment by businesses, entrepreneurs and foreign direct investment (FDI). This leads to increased unemployment.

- **Upward pressure on Irish wage levels:** The most skilled and best-trained workers are those who are the most mobile and so will choose to leave in search of better employment opportunities. In order to try to retain these employees, employers may be forced to increase wage levels as an incentive to stay.

- **Demand for state services:** As the population declines, the demand for state services such as schools, transport and health care may decrease.

- **Unemployment reduced:** Emigration reduces the financial strain on the government's finances as social welfare payments no longer need to be paid to unemployed people who have emigrated.

- **International connections:** Irish employees who have emigrated may be able to form international connections between Irish exporters and their chosen country. This would be an opportunity for Irish businesses to expand and increase revenue.

- **A reduction in social costs:** A major contributor to emigration is unemployment. As emigration increases, unemployment decreases as well as the social costs associated with unemployment, such as crime.

- **Loss of potential investment:** A lack of skilled labour detracts multinationals from setting up in Ireland. These firms are a much-needed element of economic growth.

Economic Consequences for a Country Experiencing Increased Immigration

POSITIVE

- **Increased demand for goods and services:** The level of demand for goods and services will increase, leading to greater opportunities for businesses in terms of investment and increasing production and economies of scale.

- **Improved dependency ratio:** If immigrants are mainly in the working age group and employed, then the dependency ratio decreases, which leads to increased tax revenue for the government.

- **Government revenue increases:** If the increase in population is due to immigration, then numbers joining the labour market may increase and lead to greater income tax revenue.

- **Reduction in labour shortages:** Immigrants may fill vacancies that exist in the labour market and help ease the pressure on wage rates.

- **Greater utilisation of services:** If immigrants locate in low-density populated areas, then services will be more fully utilised, i.e. transport services, schools.

- **New skills/traditions within society:** The economy may benefit from new skills/traditions, helping society to become more tolerant, efficient and competitive.

NEGATIVE

- **Pressure on provision of state services:** With an increasing number of immigrants, there will be increased pressure on the government to provide and improve services available to people. If the increase has not been planned for by the government, shortages may develop in certain sectors, i.e. housing, education, social services. This also puts a financial strain on government expenditure.

- **Increased pressure on infrastructure:** The government has to plan for additional and improved infrastructure, such as more schools and facilities for a younger population and more health facilities for the older population.

- **Drain on state finances:** The need to provide immigrants with benefits such as unemployment benefit, children's allowance, etc. will put pressure on government finances. There will also be a need for future pensions and health care planning for long-term immigrants.

- **Exploitation of immigrants:** If immigrants are not adequately protected by Irish laws, they may be forced to work and live in poor conditions and accept low levels of pay.

- **Increased dependency ratio:** If immigrants are mainly in a non-working age group, the dependency ratio increases and this puts financial pressure on the government.

- **Resentment/racism:** An increase in immigration may lead to resentment or racism within a country. This can result in an increase in crime and a requirement for greater policing and legislation.

- **Land and property values increase:** As population density increases, available land and property become scarce. The increase in demand and the restricted supply lead to increased prices for land and property.

The Greying Population

An **AGEING POPULATION** is defined by a population who:
- Is living longer.
- Has an average lifespan that is increasing.
- Has a growing percentage of the population who are in an older age bracket.

The Central Statistics Office (CSO) reveals that irrespective of the combination of assumptions used, there will be between 1.3 and 1.4 million older persons (those aged 65 years and over) in 2041, compared with 460,000 in 2006. This implies that 20% to 25% of the population will be aged 65 years and over in 2041 compared with 11% in 2006. The number of 'oldest old' persons (those aged 80 years and over) is projected to quadruple from 110,000 in 2006 to about 440,000 in 2041.

Possible Economic Effects of an Ageing Population on the Irish Economy

- **Pressure on the provision of state pensions:** The government must encourage individuals through tax incentives to avail of private pensions in order to reduce the pressure on the government to provide state pensions.

- **Increased tax burden:** With larger numbers of people aged over 65, the dependency ratio may increase, resulting in the need for higher taxes on the workforce to fund services for older people.

- **Increased government expenditure:** The government may spend a greater proportion of its revenue on the provision of services for the elderly, such as social welfare payments, medical care, free transport, fuel allowances and nursing homes.

- **Changing pattern of demand:** Demand for those goods and services required by older people will increase, e.g. nursing homes, medication, free travel. There may also be an increased demand for price concessions in various services.

- **The participation rate falls:** As more people reach retirement age, the supply of labour may be affected. Some may wish to work part time and some may retire.

- **Reduced mobility of labour:** As people get older, they are less likely to move to a different location in search of work.

> **Note:**
>
> In 2011, the government was forced to revise the retirement age in employment contracts as evidence of underused skills became apparent. Under the new National Pensions Framework, the age at which people qualify for the state pension will increase over time to 66 years of age in 2014, 67 in 2021 and 68 in 2028. This means that the government is concerned about the economic effects of an ageing population. By increasing the retirement age, the tax burden is decreased, as workers are contributing to the income of the government for longer. In addition, the participation rate increases as people are now working longer with the extension of the retirement age.

The Census

> The **CENSUS** is the official count of the nation's people and a compilation of economic, social and other data. It is used by the government in formulating development policies and plans. It usually occurs every five years.

An Phríomh-Oifig Staidrimh
Central Statistics Office

Economic Uses of a Census of Population in Ireland

- **Demographic changes:** It provides information on demographic changes, both nationally and on a regional basis.

- **Infrastructural requirements:** It helps the government to plan for future infrastructural requirements, e.g. roads, new schools, health care facilities.

- **Planning and the provision of essential services:** It indicates if additional investment in services is required, i.e. health, education.

- **Regional policy:** The government may be prompted to change or develop regional policy if some counties experience depopulation.

- **Pension planning:** It can influence the provision of pension funds and how the government plans its state pensions.

- **Future levels of consumer demand:** Producers can more accurately predict future demand for goods and services.

- **Labour market:** The data can be used to predict and make provisions for future labour requirements.
- **Profiling of the population:** The population can be profiled by age, gender, nationality, place of residence, marital status, number of children, religion, ethnic background, etc.

Importance of a Census of Population

- The census gives an overall picture of the social and living conditions of our people. The government uses the result for effective planning, decision-making and policy purposes.
- The state has been collecting information on our population since 1841. This has allowed us to track population changes over a long period of time.
- The government uses population statistics to plan for essential services such as infrastructure, education and health care. In turn, these figures are used at local level to identify new schools and new shopping centres that could be built and areas of high unemployment.
- Membership of Dáil Éireann depends on the population as measured by the census.
- When the results of successive censuses are compared, we get an accurate indication of net migration, i.e. the difference between inward and outward migration in the country.

> **Task**
>
> Compare the levels of non-Irish residents in 2002 and in 2011. What do you notice? What are the economic effects of migration based on your analysis? Discuss with your class.

The Irish Situation

The table below illustrates the changes in population from 1871 to our most recent census in 2011.

Population classified by sex at various censuses			
Census year	Persons (thousands)	Males (thousands)	Females (thousands)
1871	4,053	1,992	2,061
1926	2,972	1,507	1,465
1956	2,898	1,463	1,435
1981	3,443	1,729	1,714
2011	4,485	2,222	2,263

Source: Central Statistics Office.

Positive Economics

The Global Perspective: A Rising Population

World Famine
Ninety-five per cent of human population growth is occurring in countries already struggling with poverty, illiteracy and civil unrest. In countries with rapid population growth, a high percentage of income is spent on basic needs such as food, housing and clothing. Little finance is left over for investment in the economy. This perpetuates the poverty cycle and frustrates many developing countries that are trying to expand their economies. To meet the infrastructural needs of these developing countries, approximately $1 trillion per year needs to be spent. It is likely that this goal won't be met, so the prospect of an increase in world poverty and inadequate health care is a real possibility.

Deforestation in the Amazon

Fall in Population in Developed Countries
The population in developed countries is unlikely to change over the next 40 years and should remain at around 1.2 billion. Fertility is below the replacement level in many developed countries. Indeed, the population of developed countries such as Germany, Italy and Japan is ageing (greying population) and without inward migration could decline further in the future.

Population and the Environment
Overpopulation has a significant effect on our world:

- There could be less land available for agriculture; therefore, there could be increased demand for chemical agriculture and genetically modified crops. This could lead to an increase in food production to satisfy bigger populations.

- Fresh water supplies are decreasing. In fact, the amount of water available per person will drop by 74% between 1950 and 2050. Water scarcity could have the same effects as the droughts we regularly see in many parts of the world.

26: Economics of Population

Adnan Nevic was born in Sarajevo, the capital of Bosnia Herzegovina, on 12 October 1999. He was chosen by the United Nations to symbolise the 6 billionth living person.

On 31 October 2011, Danica May Camacho, born in Manila, the Philippines, was chosen to symbolise the 7 billionth living person.

Task

Research and prepare a report on Adnan Nevic, the 6 billionth living person, and Danica May Camacho, the 7 billionth living person. Examine the population of their countries, looking at the birth rate, death rate, etc. Check out www.nationmaster.com.

PROFILE: Thomas Malthus (1766–1834)

Malthus is most remembered for his book *An Essay on the Principle of Population*, which states that population will increase in a geometric progression (1, 2, 4, 8, 16 …) while the resources necessary to feed the population will grow by arithmetic progression (1, 2, 3, 4 …), which ultimately would lead to food shortages.

He thought that this population growth could be halted by war, disease and famine, which he termed the positive checks on population. He wrote that the preventative checks, i.e. those lowering the birth rate (restraining population growth), could be brought about by 'moral restraint' on the size of families.

His predictions on population growth did not materialise due to improvements in agricultural technology, which made land more productive, and the slowdown in the rate of population growth in developed countries.

However, his predictions on population growth and consequent problems may well be seen in many less developed countries today.

His **iron law of wages/subsistence wages** theory stated that any wages paid to workers in excess of the subsistence level would cause an increase in population. This would in turn lead to a growth in the supply of labour, which would lead to a fall in the wage rate. This fall in the wage rate would lead to a decrease in population and move wages up to subsistence level.

Positive Economics

EXAM ✓ Question 7(c), 2008 (20 marks)

The <u>birth rate</u> in Ireland shows an increase over previous years (CSO Census 2006).

(i) Explain the meaning of the underlined term.
(ii) Outline **three** economic implications of the changing structure and size of the Irish population.

Solution

(i) The birth rate is the average number of live births per 1,000 people per year.

(ii) *Any three of the following points would be an acceptable answer.*

- **Increased demand for goods and services:** The level of demand for goods and services will increase, leading to greater opportunities for businesses in terms of investment and increasing production and economies of scale.

- **Improved dependency ratio:** If immigrants are mainly in the working age group and employed, then the dependency ratio decreases, which leads to increased tax revenue for the government.

- **Greater utilisation of services:** If immigrants locate in low-density populated areas, then services will be more fully utilised, i.e. transport services, schools.

- **Pressure on provision of state services:** With an increasing number of immigrants, there will be increased pressure on the government to provide and improve services available to people. If the increase has not been planned for by the government, shortages may develop in certain sectors, i.e. housing, education, social services. This also puts a financial strain on government expenditure.

- **Increased pressure on infrastructure:** The government has to plan for additional and improved infrastructure, such as more schools and facilities for a younger population and more health facilities for the older population.

- **Land and property values increase:** As population density increases, available land and property become scarce. The increase in demand and the restricted supply lead to increased prices for land and property.

26: Economics of Population

Question 7(c), 2003 — EXAM (30 marks)

Immigration replaced high levels of emigration during the Celtic Tiger period.

(i) Outline **three** reasons why the trend has changed from emigration to immigration in Ireland.

(ii) Discuss the economic consequences (positive **and** negative) for a country experiencing increased immigration.

Solution

(i) *Any three of the following points would be acceptable.*

1. **Emergence of the Celtic Tiger/increased awareness of opportunities:**

   - The boom in the Irish economy with employment opportunities attracted immigrant workers.
   - Global communications have made people aware of the employment opportunities available in Ireland.
   - Multinational corporations may bring their own personnel to do specific work.

2. **Member of EU and ease of access:** With the relative prosperity of citizens in the EU, many non-EU nationals seek an improvement in their living standards, and as Ireland is a member of the EU, it has become an attractive destination for those immigrants.

3. **Ireland's social welfare system:** Ireland offers a 'caring' welfare system in comparison to some countries and this eases the difficulties of relocating to Ireland, making it an attractive destination.

4. **Stricter immigration controls in other countries:** The economic downturn in some countries such as Germany coupled with tighter immigration controls in certain countries such as Australia and the US have led to Ireland attracting more immigrants.

5. **Recruitment in the past by FÁS to fill labour shortages:** During the boom, Ireland experienced significant labour shortages in certain sectors and state/private agencies sought immigrants to fill these vacancies.

6. **Lower tax rates:** In recent years, personal taxation levels have fallen, attracting people back home who emigrated in the past due to high taxes.

7. **Better quality of life:** Ireland offers its citizens a better quality of life and people who have emigrated have returned home to raise their children in what is considered a safe environment.

8. **Humanitarian factors:** People forced out of their own countries due to conflicts have been welcomed in the past by the Irish state, i.e. those displaced in the Kosovo conflict.

(ii)

Positive consequences	Negative consequences
• **Increased demand for goods and services:** The level of demand for goods and services will increase, leading to greater opportunities for businesses. • **Improved dependency ratio:** If immigrants are mainly in the working age group, then the dependency ratio decreases. • **Reduction in labour shortages:** Immigrants may fill vacancies that exist in the labour market and help ease the pressure on wage rates. • **Greater utilisation of services:** If immigrants locate in low-density populated areas, then services will be more fully utilised. • **New skills/traditions within society:** The economy may benefit from new skills/traditions, helping society become more tolerant, efficient and competitive.	• **Pressure on provision of state services:** With an increasing number of immigrants, there will be pressure on the government to provide/improve services available to immigrants. • **Drain on state finances:** The need to provide immigrants with benefits will put further pressure on government finances. • **Exploitation of immigrants:** If immigrants are not adequately protected, then they may be forced to work/live in poor conditions and accept low levels of pay. • **Increased dependency ratio:** If immigrants are mainly in the non-working age group, then the dependency ratio increases. • **Resentment/racism:** An increase in immigration may lead to resentment/racism within a country requiring greater policing/legislation.

Questions

Short Questions

1. Define demography.
2. Explain what is meant by optimum population.
3. Define life expectancy rate.
4. Distinguish between birth rate and fertility rate.
5. Distinguish between the death rate and infant mortality rate.
6. Define net migration.
7. Explain the term 'greying population'.
8. Illustrate the difference between immigration and emigration.

Long Questions

1. Distinguish between overpopulation and underpopulation.
2. Set out the push and pull factors that lead to emigration.
3. Comment on the economic implications of Ireland's demographic pattern.
4. Analyse the economic effects of emigration.
5. Discuss the impact of a rise in the dependency ratio.
6. Evaluate the economic effects of an ageing population on the Irish economy.
7. Consider the implications of the changing structure and size of the Irish population.
8. Evaluate the consequences of an increase in immigration.
9. Discuss the economic uses of the 2011 census of population data for government and business.
10. 'Ireland is experiencing the highest level of net outward migration since 1989' (CSO, 2010). Discuss the reasons why Ireland is now experiencing a high level of net outward migration.
11. Evaluate the importance of a census of population.

Chapter 27 | International Trade

Specific Learning Outcomes

At the end of this chapter, students should be able to:

- ☐ Understand imports, exports, invisible and visible exports and imports.
- ☐ Explain the balance of trade.
- ☐ Identify Ireland's main exports, imports and main trading partners.
- ☐ Understand the importance of trade to the Irish economy.
- ☐ Examine the implications of Ireland being a small open economy.
- ☐ Analyse the effect of multinational corporations on Ireland's trade.
- ☐ Understand and explain the advantages of specialisation and international trade.
- ☐ Examine the ways in which a country can enhance its competitiveness.
- ☐ Explain and illustrate the law of comparative advantage.
- ☐ Describe the sources of comparative advantage for Ireland.
- ☐ Critically analyse the limitations of the law of comparative advantage.
- ☐ Explain the terms of trade.
- ☐ Calculate the terms of trade and examine the benefits resulting from specialisation.
- ☐ Examine the impact on a country of changes in that country's terms of trade.
- ☐ Describe the main barriers to trade.
- ☐ Understand the role of trading blocs in international trade.

27: International Trade

What Is International Trade?

International trade is the exchange (buying and selling or importing and exporting) of goods and services across international territories.

When we purchase foreign goods and services, we are said to be importing. We export when we sell our goods and services to foreigners.

There are physical/visible exports and imports and non-physical/invisible exports and imports. For example, when Italian students come to Ireland in the summer, they bring euro with them, which enables them to purchase Irish goods. This is an example of invisible exports. This has the same effect as if we had sold the goods to Italy – a visible export.

International trade has been significant to economies throughout history. Some of the earliest examples of international trade can be traced back to the Amber and Silk Roads. The Amber Road was an ancient trade route for the transfer of the valuable commodity amber from Europe to Asia, Northern Africa to the Baltic Sea and back again. The Silk Road was a complex network of trade routes across the Asian continent that connected Asia with Africa and Europe. The economic, political and social importance of international trade has risen continuously over the centuries and it now represents a significant share of gross domestic product (GDP) for many economies.

Over the past 100 years, Ireland has gone from being a country with very little involvement in foreign trade to being an economy that is extremely open. Ireland's open economy means a significant proportion of our goods and services are traded internationally.

An **OPEN ECONOMY** exists where international trade takes place (i.e. exports and imports).

Why Do Countries Trade?

Countries engage in trade for the following reasons:

- To obtain essential raw materials, e.g. oil.
- Our domestic population is relatively small, so to allow our industries to expand and hence achieve economies of scale, companies engage in international trade to increase their sales.
- Our climate and soil type are unsuitable for producing certain goods, e.g. citrus fruits, so we import them for consumption.

Positive Economics

- To obtain a variety of goods and allow for consumer choice.
- To benefit from the skills/traditions of another workforce in areas that our domestic workforce isn't as efficient in, e.g. watch-making in Switzerland.
- To create more employment, e.g. Enterprise Ireland promotes Irish products and services abroad, which in turn creates employment in Ireland.
- To pursue export-led growth, which will consequently increase the standard of living in our country.
- To benefit from the specialisation of labour (as can be seen from the law of absolute advantage).

The Laws of International Trade

The Law of Absolute Advantage

ASSUMPTIONS OF THE LAW OF ABSOLUTE ADVANTAGE

- There are two countries.
- Two products are produced.
- No transport costs exist.
- There is one factor of production, e.g. labour.
- There is free mobility of factors within both countries.

> The **LAW OF ABSOLUTE ADVANTAGE** states that each country should specialise in the production of that good in which it has an absolute advantage, i.e. if it can produce the good more efficiently/cheaply (at a lower cost) than other countries.

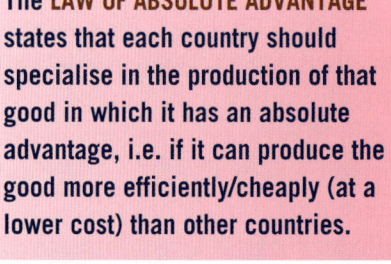

Country	Lemons (kg per week per worker)	Olives (kg per week per worker)
Brazil	1,200	600
France	600	2,400
World production	**1,800**	**3,000**

CALCULATE ABSOLUTE ADVANTAGE

- Brazil has absolute advantage in the production of lemons. Lemons: $\frac{1,200}{600}$ is 2 : 1, i.e. one worker in Brazil is twice as productive as a worker in France.

- France has absolute advantage in the production of olives. Olives: $\frac{2{,}400}{600}$ is 4 : 1, i.e. one worker in France is four times more productive than a worker in Brazil.

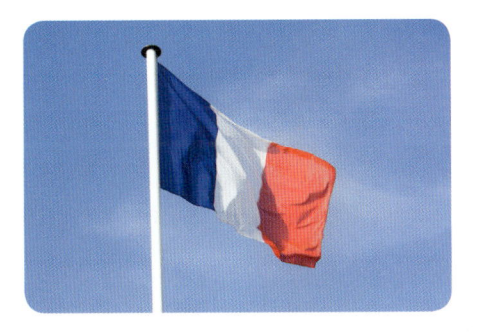

- Therefore, Brazil should specialise in the production of lemons and France should specialise in the production of olives.

- Both countries should specialise in the production of goods that it can produce most cheaply and trade for its other requirements.

Country	After specialisation	
	Lemons (kg per week per worker)	Olives (kg per week per worker)
Brazil	2,400	–
France	–	4,800
World production	**2,400**	**4,800**

The above table shows the output for two workers specialising in each country. World output of both lemons and olives has increased, from 1,200 kg to 2,400 kg in lemons and 2,400 kg to 4,800 kg in olives.

The Law of Comparative Advantage

We will now study David Ricardo's (classical economist) contribution to international trade and illustrate the benefits of trading. We will state the assumptions on which the law is based and again take only two commodities and two countries.

> The **LAW OF COMPARATIVE ADVANTAGE** states that a country should specialise in the production of those goods and services in which it is relatively most efficient and trade for the remainder of its requirements.

Positive Economics

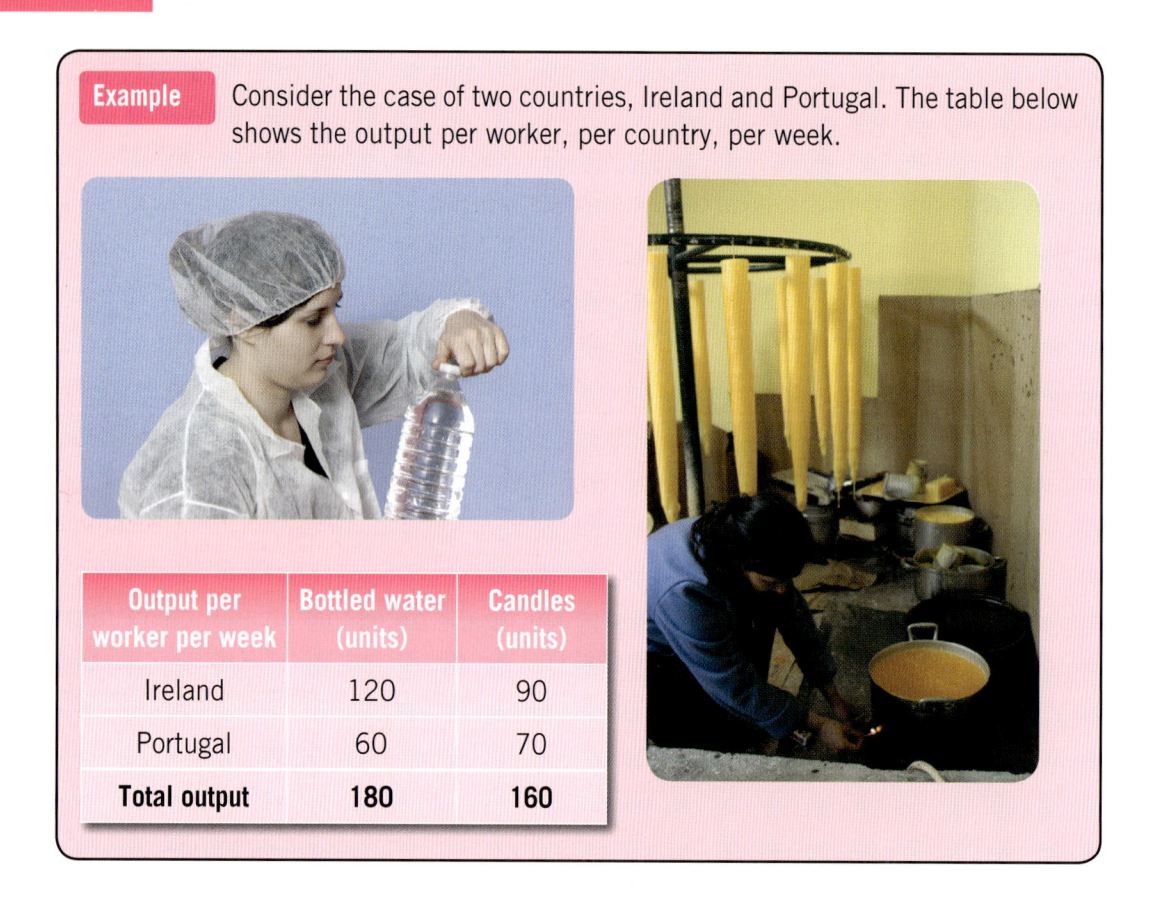

Example — Consider the case of two countries, Ireland and Portugal. The table below shows the output per worker, per country, per week.

Output per worker per week	Bottled water (units)	Candles (units)
Ireland	120	90
Portugal	60	70
Total output	**180**	**160**

WHAT HAPPENS IF BOTH COUNTRIES DO NOT ENGAGE IN INTERNATIONAL TRADE?

- If the two countries supply their own needs and do not engage in trade, each country will have one worker engaging in the production of bottled water and one worker engaging in the production of candles.
- One worker in Ireland can produce 120 bottles of water per week and the second worker can produce 90 candles per week.
- One worker in Portugal can produce 60 bottles of water per week and the second worker can produce 70 candles per week.

WHAT HAPPENS IF BOTH COUNTRIES DO ENGAGE IN INTERNATIONAL TRADE?

Output per worker per week	Bottled water (units per worker per week)	Candles (units per worker per week)
Ireland	120	90
Portugal	60	70
Total output	**180**	**160**

- Examining the above information, it is clear that Ireland has absolute advantage in the production of both water and candles.
- In Ireland, workers can produce 120 bottles of water and 90 candles per week.
- In Portugal, workers can produce 60 bottles of water and 70 candles per week.
- This does not mean that Ireland should produce both goods. They will specialise in the production of the product at which they are most efficient, i.e. in which they have comparative advantage, and trade for all other requirements.

SHOULD IRELAND SPECIALISE IN BOTTLED WATER OR CANDLES?

- From the ratios, we can see that Ireland would be better off specialising in the production of bottled water, as an Irish worker is twice as efficient as a Portuguese worker at producing water (120 : 60 = 2 : 1).
- An Irish worker is only 1.3 times as efficient as a Portuguese worker in the production of candles (90 : 70 = 1.3 : 1).

Production of bottled water	Production of candles
Ireland : Portugal	Ireland : Portugal
120 : 60	90 : 70
2 : 1	1.3 : 1

Country	Bottled water	Candles
Ireland	240 units	0 units
Portugal	0 units	140 units
Total output	**240 units**	**140 units**

TOTAL OUTPUT AFTER SPECIALISATION

- Ireland has comparative advantage in the production of bottled water, so it will cease the production of candles. Hence, both workers will now produce bottled water in Ireland and output will be doubled.
- Both workers in Portugal will now concentrate on candle production, doubling its output.
- With specialisation, the total output of bottled water has increased by 60 units (180 units increased to 240 units), or 33.33% ($\frac{60}{180} \times 100 = 33.33\%$) ($\frac{\text{difference}}{\text{original}} \times 100$).
- With specialisation, the total output of candles decreased by 20 units (160 units decreased to 140 units), or 12.5% ($\frac{20}{160} \times 100 = 12.5\%$).
- Therefore, since the increase of 33.33% is greater than the fall of 12.5%, the world is better off.

Positive Economics

HOW DO WE PROVE THIS CASE?
Is the fall in output of candles of 20 units offset by the increase of 60 units in bottled water, i.e. is the world better off after specialisation?

To understand, we need to calculate the value of bottled water : candles in world terms.

In world terms:

Total output bottled water/ Total output candles	$\frac{180}{160}$	1 candle = 1.125 bottles of water
Total output candles/ Total output bottled water	$\frac{160}{180}$	1 bottle of water = 0.89 of a candle

- In world terms, 1 candle = 1.125 bottles of water, so a decrease of 20 candles is worth 22.5 bottles of water (20 × 1.125 = 22.5).
- The production of water has increased by 60 bottles, which is greater than 22.5.
- As the increase of 60 (33.33%) bottles of water is greater than the decrease of 20 (12.5%) candles, the world is better off.

We will now calculate the terms of trade (e.g. value of a candle in terms of a bottle of water).

Terms of trade		
IRELAND		
1 candle	is the equivalent of/equals	1.33 bottles of water $\left(\frac{120}{90} = 1.33\right)$
1 bottle of water	is the equivalent of/equals	0.75 of a candle $\left(\frac{90}{120} = 0.75\right)$
PORTUGAL		
1 candle	is the equivalent of/equals	0.86 of a bottle of water $\left(\frac{60}{70} = 0.86\right)$
1 bottle of water	is the equivalent of/equals	1.2 of a candle $\left(\frac{70}{60} = 1.2\right)$

Will countries specialise and then trade?

- If Ireland produces candles, it will want 1.33 bottles of water for 1 candle.
- If Portugal produces candles, it will want 0.86 of a bottle of water for 1 candle.
- **Therefore, the terms of trade for candles lies between 0.86 of a bottle of water and 1.33 bottles of water.**
- If Ireland produces bottles of water, it will want 0.75 of a candle for 1 bottle of water.
- If Portugal produces bottles of water, it will want 1.2 candles for 1 bottle of water.

- Therefore, the terms of trade for bottled water lies between 0.75 of a candle and 1.2 candles.

Terms of Trade

- **Formula:** $\left(\dfrac{\text{Index of export prices}}{\text{Index of import prices}}\right) \times 100$

- **Or:** What a given volume of exports will buy of imports

- **Or:** The amount of imports that can be bought per unit of exports

> The **TERMS OF TRADE** refer to the ratio between the average price of exports and the average price of imports.

> **Note:**
> Where the terms of trade eventually lie will depend on the bargaining strengths of both countries.

> **Example** — Example of improved terms of trade
> Year 1: 1 computer = 2 barrels of oil
> Year 2: 1 computer = 10 barrels of oil

The terms of trade have improved. How can this happen?

- If export prices are rising faster while import prices remain the same.
- If export prices are rising faster than import prices.
- If import prices fall while export prices stay the same.

> **Note:** The opposite would cause the terms of trade to disimprove.

Assumptions/Limitations of the Law of Comparative Advantage

The law of comparative advantage (LOCA) illustrates how mutually beneficial international trade can be to both countries. However, there are a number of limitations that one must consider.

- **Strategic reasons in favour of self-sufficiency are ignored:** Some countries may not want to specialise but prefer to be as self-sufficient as possible. A country may possess very limited resources, thus curtailing its ability to specialise. Alternatively, a country may possess innate talents that gives it advantages in the production of certain goods.

- **Transport costs are ignored:** The LOCA assumes that transport costs do not exist. However, for an island nation like Ireland, transport costs can be a major cost factor and can act as a barrier to trade. A firm's cost efficiencies may be eliminated by the transport costs involved.

- **Perfect mobility of the factors of production is assumed:** We have assumed that the person who becomes unemployed in each country as a result of specialisation occurring can switch to an alternative job and that there are no barriers to mobility. This is not always the case, as there are barriers to the complete mobility of labour.

- **The law of diminishing marginal returns (LDMR) is ignored:** The LOCA assumes that the LDMR does not apply or assumes constant returns to scale. But this law does apply. Each extra person employed will not continue to produce the same amount as the original person. A point will eventually be reached when an extra person employed will produce less additional output.

- **Free trade is assumed to exist:** The LOCA assumes that free trade takes place. While this may be true within the EU or NAFTA blocs, free trade is often limited where countries impose barriers to trade for economic, social, cultural and moral reasons.

- **Alternative employment is available:** It is assumed that people who become unemployed in one sector arising from specialisation can find alternative employment. This may not be the case. Consider countries during a recession, when the availability of employment is very low and there are huge adjustment costs in the transition.

- **An equal distribution of benefits occurs:** When we calculate the terms of trade, we assume that both countries benefit from trade. Consider a developing country – sometimes the terms of trade may not be to its advantage, e.g. it may receive very low export prices and have to pay high import prices. Hence, their bargaining position is weak and they may not benefit from trade to the extent that developed, more powerful countries do.

Sources of Comparative Advantage for the Irish Economy

It is important that Ireland capitalises on its own sources of comparative advantage to avail of the benefits of trade. Our domestic sources are as follows.

- **Climate:** Our climate is suitable for the production of crops like potatoes and grazing for livestock (beef). Our agriculture industry is vital to our economy.

- **Raw materials:** Raw materials that are scarce in other countries are available in Ireland, e.g. moss peat, blanket bogs.

- **Educated and skilled workforce:** Companies locate here without incurring exorbitant training costs. The workforce has developed specific skills in production/services over a period of time, e.g. ICT, food production, pharmaceutical companies.

- **Low rate of corporation tax:** This means that the costs of operation may be more competitive in Ireland than in other countries. The 12.5% rate makes Ireland attractive to multinationals looking to cut costs.

How Does Specialisation Encourage International Trade?

- **Greater efficiency in the allocation of scarce resources:** When countries specialise in producing goods in which they have a comparative advantage, they maximise their combined output and allocate their resources more efficiently, thus reducing wastage.
- **Greater interdependence:** A country that specialises is no longer self-sufficient and hence must trade for the remainder of its requirements. It therefore depends on building good trade relationships with other nations.
- **Increased wealth and rising aggregate demand:** Specialisation causes individual countries to gain, thus increasing wealth and allowing greater opportunities for engaging in trade. In turn, consumers will have increased purchasing power and will demand increased choice and variety of commodities.
- **Lower costs and prices:** Specialisation improves efficiency, resulting in lower costs and prices. With lower prices for commodities, consumers will increase their demand, which leads to increased trade, sales and thus profits.
- **Division of labour:** When labour specialises, skills may improve. Labour therefore becomes more mobile, allowing for greater trade in the labour market.
- **Economies of scale:** Greater economies of scale may be available when producing a product for a world market that would not be available when producing for a more limited domestic market, e.g. motor vehicle industry.

Factors That Affect the Competitiveness of Irish-based Firms Involved in International Trade

- **Rate of inflation in Ireland vs. rate of inflation in competitor countries:** If the level of inflation is lower in Ireland than in the firm's export markets, then the firm's goods are at a price advantage. On the other hand, if the level of inflation is higher in Ireland than in these export markets, then the firm's goods may be much more expensive than the foreign markets' domestic good, resulting in fewer sales.
- **Exchange rate of the euro against other currencies:** If the value of the euro rises against other currencies, then the price of that firm's exports will rise. On the other

hand, if the value of the euro decreases against other currencies, e.g. the dollar, then the price of that firm's exports may drop significantly.

- **Transport costs:** As Ireland is an island nation, transportation costs can be high. An increase in these costs needs to be passed on to the end customer, resulting in an increase in the price of the goods sold. This affects the level of sales and turnover on the part of the exporting country.

> **Class Discussion**
> How has the euro moved recently against our main trading partners' currencies and how will this affect exporting businesses' sales?

- **Infrastructure costs:** If rents or building costs are high, this must be incorporated into the final selling price of the good. In addition, if the process of bringing the goods to the end customer takes a long time due to a lack of high-quality infrastructure, this also invokes additional costs. These issues put pressure on prices within the country and damage the competitiveness of the exporter.

- **Production costs:** Many firms have voiced concerns about the cost of their insurance premiums. Lack of competition in this area coupled with the costs of meeting compensation claims may result in cost increases. In addition, if oil and energy prices continue to rise, these cost increases would make exports less competitive.

- **Labour costs:** If labour costs (e.g. the introduction of the minimum wage) in Ireland rise above those in export markets, then these additional costs must be borne by the final consumer and this would increase the price of the exports, resulting in falling demand. IBEC has stated that Ireland must limit wage increases in order to maintain our international competitiveness.

- **Government policies:** Any actions by the government or EU that impose further requirements on industry which have cost implications for firms have the effect of making exports less competitive. However, many actions can be taken to influence the competitiveness of Irish-based firms, e.g. change the level of consumption and excise taxes, offer tax breaks to exporting countries and impose tariffs on raw material imports.

- **Social partnership agreements and national wage agreements:** Industrial conflict, strikes and resolutions take time, cost money and damage relationships and confidence. Social partnership can help stabilise price increases in the economy. In an absence of industrial peace, companies exert much time and resources dealing with internal issues that eventually have to be paid for, and if the end customer pays a higher price for the goods, this hinders competitiveness.

Importance of International Trade to the Irish Economy

Ireland has a very small domestic market. Without the opportunity to sell on foreign markets, many of our businesses may not be able to make profitable incomes, offer employment and increase the wealth of our country. As consumers, we also demand a large variety of goods and services that are not necessarily available in Ireland. As a result, international trade is extremely valuable to the Irish economy for the following reasons.

- **Economic growth:** International trade allows small countries like Ireland with small home markets to export, enabling growth in the economy to take place. It provides foreign markets with produce that cannot be sold at home. By selling abroad, foreign currency is earned, which in turn is used to finance further trade.

- **Increased standard of living:** Trade increases the wealth/GNP of an economy, which means consumers are able to buy more goods and services. An increase in the demand for goods and services creates a richer economy.

- **Greater choice of goods and services:** International trade allows us to benefit from the choice of a greater variety of goods and services and the ability to purchase goods not available here in Ireland, e.g. citrus fruits, tea, coffee, rice, cars. We also lack some essential raw materials for production, e.g. oil and petroleum, so we must import these from other countries.

- **More competitive prices:** Trade results in greater competition on the market, which should lead to more competitive prices for consumers. Without free trade in a particular commodity, the opportunity for a dominant business to control and exploit the domestic market would significantly increase. Irish businesses face a lot of competition from foreign firms. This forces them to keep their costs low so that they can compete. Production becomes more efficient, resulting in lower prices being passed on to consumers. For example, Dunnes Stores keeps its prices low to compete with Lidl and Aldi.

- **Employment/investment opportunities:** Many jobs in Ireland are dependent on exports. A growth in exports simply leads to more job creation, as there are more people required to produce the goods and services to sell abroad. A decrease in unemployment would allow the government to invest money in infrastructure, increase grants and lower taxes. A resulting increase in employment would generate revenue for the government in the form of taxes, e.g. PAYE, Universal Social Charge and PRSI.

- **Companies benefit from economies of large-scale production:** When a country engages in international trade, specialisation takes place. There will be a resulting increase in production of the goods in which a country specialises. Consequently, a company may benefit from economies of scale (lower costs for large-scale production), which may then be passed on to the consumer in the form of lower prices. In addition, commodities such as motor vehicles and aircraft might simply be too expensive to produce if a company is restricted to small domestic markets. Industries can avail of economies of large-scale production as they are producing for world markets and not just the domestic one. Irish firms could not avail of economies of scale without getting involved in international trade, as the Irish market is too small to achieve savings in production costs without selling in international markets.

- **Allows for the sale of surplus/excess domestic output:** International trade provides the opportunity to sell surplus domestic output on the international market and trade for commodities that we cannot produce ourselves. For example, Ireland is highly regarded for its high-quality food production. We produce too much for domestic consumption, so the excess is exported to meet demand on international markets and avoid superfluity in the home market.

- **More efficient use of scarce resources:** By specialising in production, countries maximise their combined outputs. As a result, raw materials and resources are efficiently allocated and wastage of scarce resources is significantly reduced.

- **International co-operation:** On a political level, it is important that countries develop and maintain close trading links with each other. These connections often develop cultural and friendship bonds that facilitate international co-operation and diminish the possibility of political and military conflicts. Queen Elizabeth II's and Barack Obama's visits to Ireland in May 2011 were prime examples of the continued development and support of international co-operation for our countries' mutual trading benefits.

As we have already mentioned, international trade involves importing and exporting goods and services.

- **EXPORTING** refers to the production and sale of Irish goods and services to other countries.
- **VISIBLE EXPORTS** are goods sold to other countries, e.g. beef, pharmaceuticals, butter.
- **IMPORTING** refers to buying foreign-produced goods and services.
- **VISIBLE IMPORTS** are goods that are bought from foreign countries, e.g. wine, cars, tea, coffee, citrus fruits.

Balance of Trade

The **BALANCE OF TRADE** is the difference between the value of visible exports and visible imports (goods).

Balance of trade = (exports of goods, e.g. dairy products) – (imports of goods, e.g. oil)

Balance of Invisible Trade

- **Invisible exports** are services sold to other countries, such as:
  - An Irish band playing a concert in London.
  - Spanish students coming to study in Ireland during the summer.
  - A French family holidaying in Kerry.
- **Invisible imports** are services that are bought from foreign countries, such as:
  - Michael Bublé playing in the O_2 Arena in Dublin.
  - An Irish family holidaying in the Algarve.

Benefits of Imports to the Economy

- **Increased choice of goods and services:** Consumers have an increased choice of goods and services, which benefits consumers, resulting in a greater standard of living. Consumers can purchase goods that cannot be produced in the domestic market, e.g. citrus fruits, tea, coffee and cars.
- **Lower prices for consumers:** Importing creates competition. Competition encourages businesses to increase their efficiency in order to keep costs low and in turn the consumer benefits from lower prices.
- **Access to raw materials:** Businesses have access to essential raw materials that are not available on the domestic market, e.g. oil, coal, petroleum. Without these essential raw materials, many firms could not produce and manufacture goods.
- **Domestic production would be too expensive:** Ireland is a small economy and some goods are simply too expensive to produce ourselves, so we import them, e.g. aircraft and cars.

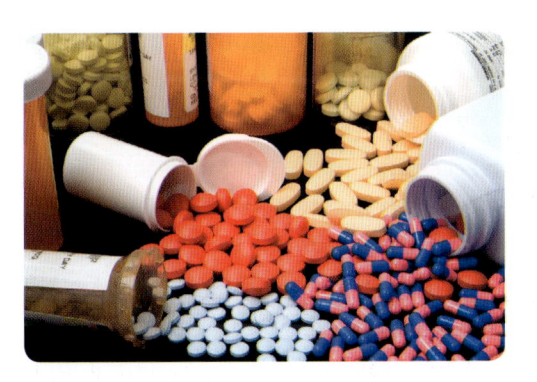

Benefits of Exports to the Economy

- **Exporting creates employment:** If an indigenous company starts to sell its products/services abroad, it will have to increase production, which will require labour. Exporting is therefore a vital creator of employment.

Positive Economics

- **Money flows into (money is injected) the Irish economy:** As Irish goods/services are bought, profits are repatriated back into the Irish economy. In addition, government revenue is increased in the form of corporation tax and PAYE (due to increased employment). Consumers will also have increased purchasing power, resulting in increased levels collected in VAT. Consequently, Irish wealth increases and can therefore boost economic growth.

- **Exporting gives firms access to larger markets:** More customers means more sales and profits. Firms that export can expand and take advantage of economies of scale. By reducing costs, the consumer may benefit from cheaper prices, encouraging even greater turnover.

> **Task**
>
> With your class, check out www.cso.ie and find the annual external trade figures for the past 10 years. Discuss with your class the value and types of commodities imported and exported. Do you notice a trend in the most recent figures?
> Prepare a report on your assessment and present your finding to the class.

- **Investment increases:** Firms that export may need to expand and build new/larger premises as their business grows. They may also need to invest in more capital and expand their labour force.

Implications for Ireland as a Small Open Economy

- **Inadequate infrastructure:** Ireland's inadequate transport systems and lack of integral development in telecommunications and ICT are a huge deterrent for increased foreign direct investment (FDI) and the growth of our small economy.

- **Skilled labour shortages:** If the economy is in recession, many graduates and skilled workers may emigrate. This can lead to the possibility of a shortage of educated and skilled graduates in the Irish economy, resulting in a potential lack of enterprise and innovation that is critical for the survival and growth of an open economy such as Ireland.

- **Increased costs:** Increased costs in labour, transport, production, property and utilities have seen many multinational corporations relocate to countries where these costs are significantly cheaper. It is difficult for a small economy to maintain its competitiveness with high costs such as these.

- **Ireland's dependence on foreign markets for survival:** If a slowdown in our trading partners' economies occurs, it will greatly affect our ability to survive, as we rely heavily on such large economies to purchase our exports.

27: International Trade

Free Trade and Government Intervention

We've already examined the importance of international trade to the Irish economy. In certain circumstances, the government has to intervene and restrict the level of international trade. The following are the economic justifications for a government intervening and restricting international trade.

Free Trade

ECONOMIC JUSTIFICATIONS OF RESTRICTING FREE TRADE

- **To create/protect domestic employment:** By discouraging and limiting competitive imports, the government can help stimulate the domestic economy, encourage employment and protect existing jobs.

> **FREE TRADE** states that there are no barriers to the movement of goods and services between countries.

- **Protect indigenous firms/infant industry:** When new enterprises emerge, they may initially face challenges in competing against foreign competition. These industries can be protected by the government until they are confident and capable of competing with foreign firms.

- **Protect against low-wage competition:** The government may feel it is necessary to establish protective measures in order to protect domestic producers from what are considered unfair, low-wage or 'cheap labour' economies, e.g. India and South American countries.

- **To increase government revenue:** Increased revenue may be raised from tariffs placed on imports. These taxes are a major contributor in funding state services.

- **Retain wealth within the country/protect the balance of payments:** By reducing the amount of money spent on foreign imports, the government could reduce the level of wealth leaving the country. This would improve our balance of payments position.

> **DUMPING** occurs when goods from a country are sold abroad at a lower price than the price charged for them at home.

- **Prevent 'dumping':** Government barriers will stop foreign firms from 'dumping' surplus production and hence significantly prohibit their ability to undermine domestic firms, which may have otherwise resulted in their closure.

- **Protect the nation:** It is important that countries protect their industries. At times, it is necessary to impose strict regulations in order to ensure that protection. For example, Ireland has previously imposed strict regulations governing the importation of agricultural commodities in order to protect the country from foot and mouth disease.

- **Strategic purposes:** A country must examine its most important and productive industries and employ strategies to ensure the protection of these industries against competition from cheaper foreign firms, e.g. the beef production industry. Applying protective measures may also ensure continuity of supply.

- **The senile industry argument:** If industries are declining and inefficient, they may require a lot of investment to make them efficient again. Protection for these industries would act as an incentive for firms to invest in and reinvent themselves. However, it is important that protectionism is not used as an excuse for protecting inefficient firms.

- **Political reasons:** For historical and political reasons of conflict, many countries do not engage in international trade. For example, the US has not engaged in commercial, financial or economic activity with Cuba since the 1960s.

Barriers to Trade (Protectionism)

PROTECTIONISM refers to efforts by a government to restrict free trade, particularly imports.

In order to reduce imports and help promote domestically produced goods, the government may introduce some of the following barriers.

Tariffs

A tariff is a tax on imports. It makes the import more expensive so that consumers are discouraged from buying it and it may make a domestically produced alternative relatively cheaper (import substitution). It is also an important source of government revenue.

Example

If Ireland wants to protect its drinks industry by reducing the amount of American beer sold on the Irish market, the Irish government can place a tariff on every bottle of American beer to discourage buying the imported product and encourage switching to a relatively cheaper domestic alternative.

Quotas

A **quota** is a physical limit placed by a government on the amount of a certain good allowed to enter the country. Quotas don't generate any revenue for the government; their purpose is to ensure that imports are restricted to a specific amount in order to encourage the purchase of domestically produced goods. However, importers may exploit the situation and see it as a profit-making opportunity and increase prices in order to satisfy the increase in demand of a good that is now limited in supply.

> **Example**
>
> The US wants to protect the American car industry from Japanese imports and so places a quota on the number of Japanese cars allowed to be sold in the country. This reduces the possibility of American consumers buying the imported car, as there is limited supply once the quota has been reached. It therefore encourages consumers to purchase American-manufactured vehicles.

ADMINISTRATIVE BARRIERS
These barriers are obstacles including paperwork, bureaucracy and red tape that a government puts in place to create inconvenience for the importer in the hope that they will be discouraged from importing.

TRADE EMBARGO
This is a complete ban on the importing of a particular good or goods from a country or a total ban on all trade to and from a particular country, e.g. there is an embargo on all trade between the US and Cuba.

Trading Blocs and Agreements

A distinctive feature of the world economy in recent years has been the growth of trading blocs, i.e. a group of countries sharing free trade agreements with each other. The European Union is probably the best-known trading bloc. Other trading blocs include the North American Free Trade Agreement (NAFTA) and the Asia Pacific Economic Co-operation (APEC), in which multilateral trade agreements encourage international trade within the bloc.

International Trading Opportunities
- Eastern European and former communist countries are a significant market opportunity, as they have the potential to be a much larger and more profitable market than the EU. There are many opportunities for businesses in the West, particularly as there are major shortages in goods and services such as commercial transport vehicles, communications systems and domestic appliances.

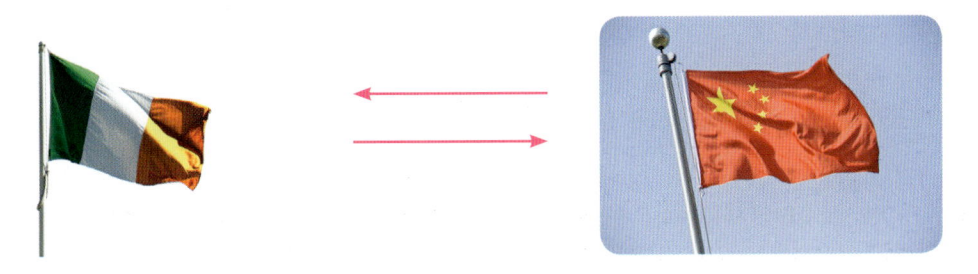

- China has the biggest population of any country on the planet. Until recently, China did not engage in international trade with the rest of the world, but China has recognised that foreign direct investment (FDI) has become an inextricable part of the Chinese economic success story and this is likely to continue. With new agreements in place, the Irish government in particular has spent a great deal of time developing trade relations between the two countries. There are huge opportunities for Irish businesses on the Chinese market. Sources predict that if the current relative growth rate persists, China will be at a rough parity with the US by 2020.

World Trade Organization (WTO)

The World Trade Organization (WTO) came into effect on 1 January 1995 to administer the international trading system. The WTO consists of 153 countries, including Ireland. The main function of the WTO is the promotion of free trade among its members based on the principle of non-discrimination. It holds negotiations between countries and reaches agreements to remove barriers to international trade, providing countries with massive opportunities on foreign markets. The goal is to help producers of goods and services, exporters and importers conduct their business in a fair and mutually profitable manner.

Objectives of the WTO:

- Reduce and eliminate all barriers to world trade, e.g. tariffs, quotas and embargos.
- Remove trade discrimination by promoting fair trade among its members.
- Eventually achieve a global free trade area.
- Negotiate with governments of member states to promote and eventually achieve global free trade.
- Arbitration in international trade disputes between member states.

Benefits of the WTO:

- The system helps promote peace and instil international trade and confidence.
- Disputes are handled constructively and resolved peacefully.
- The WTO cannot claim to make all countries equal, but it does reduce some inequalities, giving smaller countries more of a voice.
- Free trade results in reduced costs of production (because imports used in production are cheaper) and reduced prices of finished goods and services, which ultimately results in a lower cost of living.
- It provides more choice of products and services.

27: International Trade

- Lowering trade barriers allows trade to increase, which adds to both national incomes and personal incomes.

- Trade stimulates economic growth – trade clearly has the potential to create jobs.

- More efficiency for enterprises directly involved in trade and for the producers of goods and services.

- Governments are better able to shield themselves against lobbying from narrow interest groups by focusing on trade-offs that are made in the interests of everyone in the economy.

- The system discourages a range of unwise policies and thus encourages good discipline in governments. This in turn means greater clarity and certainty among businesses.

The WTO is important because of its potential for increasing the amount of trade in the world. An increase in trade can lead to greater prosperity, and an increase in the wealth of many nations has been due to the success of the WTO in lowering trade barriers.

Other examples of trading blocs include the following:

The North American Free Trade Agreement (NAFTA)

This agreement liberalised trade and brought about economic co-operation between the US, Canada and Mexico in 1994. Since then, NAFTA has demonstrated how free trade increases wealth and competitiveness, delivering real benefits to families, farmers, workers, manufacturers and consumers.

NAFTA: America, Mexico and Canada

For example, one of the biggest importers of Guinness is the US market. In order to avoid the costs that would be incurred through tariffs, Guinness set up a manufacturing plant in Canada. They can now export the product freely to the US market thanks to NAFTA.

437

Positive Economics

The Asia Pacific Economic Co-operation (APEC)

APEC Members

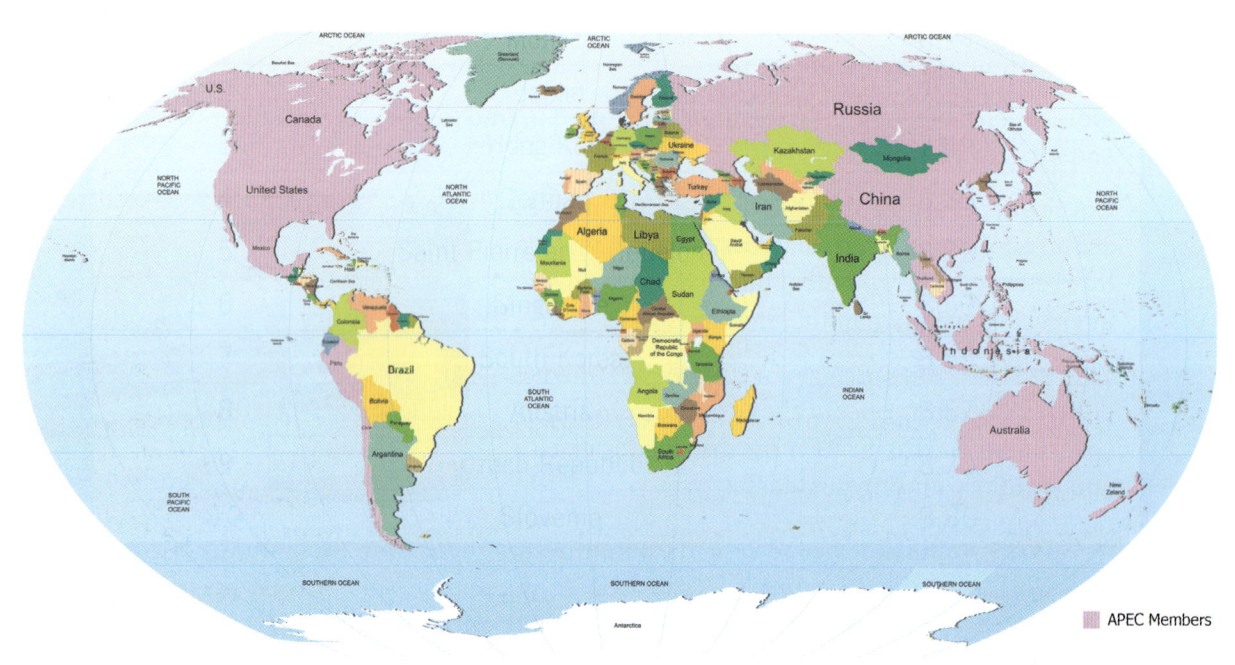

Established in 1989, APEC is a trade agreement similar to NAFTA and the EU, but applying to countries in the Pacific Basin. It is the primary vehicle for promoting open trade and practical economic co-operation between 21 countries in the Pacific Rim. Among the most important countries are Australia, New Zealand and China. Since APEC's inception in 1989, members' total trade has grown by 395%. APEC's work under its three main pillars of activity – trade and investment liberalisation, business facilitation and economic and technical co-operation – has helped drive this economic growth and improve employment opportunities and standards of living for the citizens of the region. Over 30 bilateral free trade agreements (FTAs) have been concluded between APEC member economies.

PROFILE: Mercantilists (1500–1780)

Towards the end of the 16th and 17th centuries (the Middle Ages), a group of writers known as the Mercantilists emerged. This was at a time of colonisation and increased commercial activity, when greater emphasis was put on profit as a motive. The Mercantilists believed that wealth consisted of accumulating gold and silver and that these precious metals could be acquired through trading if the country did not possess them. The main principles of Mercantilism were:

- Precious metals were seen as the way to increase national wealth.
- A country could acquire these precious metals through trade.

- Colonies could be the source of these raw materials and then a market for exports.
- Self-sufficiency was encouraged.
- Trade protection was introduced.
- The main contributors were Thomas Mun and James Stuart.

PROFILE: Thomas Mun (1571–1641)

Mun encouraged a trade surplus as a means to increase wealth (exports exceeding imports). He suggested that domestic companies should be developed to supply local necessities and when exporting should charge low prices on competitive goods and high prices on necessities.

PROFILE: James Stuart (1712–80)

Similar to Mun, Stuart suggested a trade surplus was essential to increase the wealth of a nation. He was an advocate of government intervention to regulate and control economic activity.

Sample Exam Question (20 marks)

The table below illustrates the law of comparative advantage.

Country	Output (kg per worker per week)	
	Pork	Grapes
Italy	1,200	1,800
Austria	2,400	7,200
World output	**3,600**	**9,000**

(i) Explain how **both** countries benefit from international trade in the above example.

(ii) Calculate the **total output** when specialisation takes place (show all your workings).

(iii) Calculate the **terms of trade** for **both** commodities (show all your workings).

Positive Economics

Solution

Country	Pork (kg per worker per week)	Grapes (kg per worker per week)
Italy	1,200	1,800
Austria	2,400	7,200
Total world output	**3,600**	**9,000**

(i) (1) Calculate world terms

1 kg pork is worth $\frac{9,000}{3,600}$ = 2.5 kg grapes

(2) What should both countries specialise in?

Austria has comparative advantage in the production of both goods. It can produce:

Pork: $\frac{2,400}{1,200}$, i.e. 2 : 1

and

Grapes: $\frac{7,200}{1,800}$, i.e. 4 : 1

Therefore, Austria should specialise in the production of grapes, as it has the greatest comparative advantage, and Italy should produce pork.

(ii) (1) What happens to world output when specialisation takes place?

Country	Pork (kg per worker per week)	Grapes (kg per worker per week)
Italy	2,400	–
Austria	–	14,400
Total world output	**2,400**	**14,400**

- The production of pork has fallen by 1,200 kg, i.e. by 33.3% $\left(\frac{1,200}{3,600}\right)$.

- The production of grapes has increased by 5,400 kg, i.e. by 60% $\left(\frac{5,400}{9,000}\right)$.

(2) Is the world better off due to specialisation?

The world is considered to be better off because the increase in grapes of 60% is greater than the fall in pork of 33.3%.

Also, the fall in pork of 1,200 kg is worth 1,200 × 2.5 = 3,000 kg of grapes (as calculated in part (1) above) and the production of grapes has increased by 5,400 kg.

(iii) Where will the terms of trade lie?

Country	Pork (kg per worker per week)	Grapes (kg per worker per week)
Italy	1,200	1,800
Austria	2,400	7,200
Total world output	**3,600**	**9,000**

Italy		
1 kg pork	is the equivalent of	1.5 kg grapes $\left(\frac{1,800}{1,200}\right)$
1 kg grapes	is the equivalent of	$\frac{2}{3}$ kg pork $\left(\frac{1,200}{1,800}\right)$
Austria		
1 kg pork	is the equivalent of	3 kg grapes $\left(\frac{7,200}{2,400}\right)$
1 kg grapes	is the equivalent of	$\frac{1}{3}$ kg pork $\left(\frac{2,400}{7,200}\right)$

- The terms of trade for pork lie between $\frac{2}{3}$ kg and 1.5 kg of grapes.
- The terms of trade for grapes lie between $\frac{2}{3}$ kg and $\frac{1}{3}$ kg of pork.

Questions

Short Questions

1. Explain the term 'open economy'.
2. Explain the term 'dumping'.
3. Explain the term 'protectionism'.
4. Explain the term 'trading bloc', giving examples to illustrate your understanding.
5. Define and explain the terms of trade.

Long Questions

1. Outline the reasons why multinationals locate in Ireland.
2. Explain why international trade is essential for the Irish economy.
3. Outline the benefits of exporting for the Irish economy.
4. Outline the benefits of importing for the Irish economy.
5. Discuss the economic advantages of free trade.
6. Illustrate the economic disadvantages of free trade.
7. Discuss the economic justifications for a government intervening in free trade.
8. Explain the economic reasons why countries may impose barriers to restrict trade.
9. State and explain the methods of restricting free trade.
10. Outline the main objectives of the World Trade Organization.
11. State the law of absolute advantage and explain how a country has absolute advantage in the production of a product.
12. State the law of comparative advantage and describe four assumptions/limitations of the law of comparative advantage.
13. Illustrate the sources of comparative advantage for the Irish economy.
14. Ireland is a small open economy. Explain the factors that affect the competitiveness of Irish-based firms in international trade. Use examples to support your answers.
15. Explain how specialisation and the division of labour promote international trade.

Long Questions – continued

16. The table below illustrates the law of comparative advantage.

Country	Output (production per worker per week)	
	Computers	Beer
Ireland	40 units	10 units
United Kingdom	80 units	30 units
Total output	**120 units**	**40 units**

(a) Explain how both countries benefit from international trade in the above example.
(b) Calculate the total output when specialisation takes place (show all your workings).
(c) Calculate the terms of trade for both commodities (show all your workings).

17. The table below illustrates the law of comparative advantage.

Country	Output (production per worker per week)	
	Machines	Cars
Spain	20 units	5 units
Japan	40 units	15 units
Total output	**60 units**	**20 units**

(a) Explain how both countries benefit from international trade in the above example.
(b) Calculate the total output when specialisation takes place (show all your workings).
(c) Calculate the **terms of trade** for **both** commodities (show all your workings).

Chapter 28: Balance of Payments and Foreign Exchange

Specific Learning Outcomes

At the end of this chapter, students should be able to:

- ☐ Define and identify the size of the balance of payments surplus (deficit).

- ☐ Understand the basic composition of Ireland's balance of payments account, including visible and invisible trade, the current account balance and capital flows.

- ☐ Understand multinationals' impact on the balance of payments account.

- ☐ List and explain strategies that a government could undertake to reduce a balance of payments deficit or build a balance of payments surplus.

- ☐ State and explain the consequences for a balance of payments deficit and surplus.

- ☐ Define exchange rate.

- ☐ Examine the history of exchange rates and the EMU.

- ☐ Understand how exchange rates are determined.

- ☐ Analyse the impact on the economy of changes in the euro exchange rate.

- ☐ Discuss the implications of fixed and variable exchange rates.

28: Balance of Payments and Foreign Exchange

Introduction

The balance of payments deals with all the inflows and outflows of funds to and from other countries. A more accurate name would be the **balance of international payments**. The balance of payments can be a complex set of data and needs much examination.

> The **BALANCE OF PAYMENTS** is a record of a country's monetary transactions with the rest of the world for a period of time (usually one year).

The balance of payments is composed of **three** main sections: **current, capital and financial accounts**. The current account is further divided into two parts: visible trade and invisible trade.

Balance of payments				
Current account		**Capital account**	**Financial account**
Visible trade	**Invisible trade**	Inflows and outflows of a non-recurring nature, e.g. funds received from the Regional Development Fund	Foreign financial transactions and liabilities, e.g. foreign companies investing in Ireland
Beef (export), citrus fruit (import)	*Irish people holidaying in France (invisible import), Spanish students coming to Ireland to study (invisible export)*		

Balance of Payments on Current Account

> The **BALANCE OF PAYMENTS ON CURRENT ACCOUNT** refers to the difference between total exports and total imports:
> (visible + invisible exports) − (visible + invisible imports)

Structure of the Current Account

- **Goods:** Balance of visible trade = (exports of goods) − (imports of goods).
- **Services:** Balance of invisible trade = (exports of services) − (imports of services).
- **Income** is net factor income from abroad, i.e. dividends, interest and repatriation of profits.

The value of net factor income from abroad has been negative for over 20 years. There is a significant number of non-national people and multinational companies in Ireland.

They may bring money from Ireland back to their country of origin, either by spending while they visit home or sending back part of their wages to support their families. In the case of companies, many of them repatriate profits back to their headquarters. As a result, the net factor income from abroad is traditionally negative, decreasing the value of the current account.

> **CURRENT TRANSFERS** are subsidies and monies receivable from and taxes payable to the EU. It also includes aid payments to non-governmental organisations and transfers related to non-life insurance business.

Balance of Payments on Capital Account

The capital account is comprised of the following.

> The **CAPITAL ACCOUNT** is a record of a country's receipts and payments for capital items, i.e. a record of a country's inflow and outflow of capital/items of a non-recurring nature.

- **The amounts received under the EU Regional Development Fund (ERDF):** ERDF money is used to co-finance projects that preserve and create jobs, i.e. infrastructure, local development and small and medium-sized enterprise (SME) initiatives.

- **The amount of acquisitions and disposals of non-produced, non-financial assets, e.g. patents and copyrights:** The value of intangible assets bought and sold in Ireland annually. An intangible asset is an asset that isn't physical, e.g. patents, copyrights and goodwill of state-owned companies.

Balance of Payments on Financial Account

This is done via the following entries.

- **Direct investment:** The net investment in buildings and machinery by foreign companies operating in Ireland, e.g. if Google was to invest €75 million in a new energy-efficient data centre.

> The **FINANCIAL ACCOUNT** deals with transactions in foreign financial assets and liabilities.

- **Portfolio investment – acquisition and disposal of equity and debt securities:** The amounts of money that foreign companies spend or receive when they buy and sell shares and bonds.

- **Other investment – loans, currency, deposits, financial derivatives as well as other debtors and creditors:** The amounts of money that foreign companies put into (deposits) and borrow from (loans) Irish banks, the stock of currencies they hold as well as all other assets and liabilities.

28: Balance of Payments and Foreign Exchange

- **Reserve assets – assets that qualify under the control of the Central Bank of Ireland:** The currency or any other store of value that is primarily used by nations for their foreign reserves.

- **Net errors and omissions:** Economists can't gather 100% accurate information on every single balance that makes up the account, so they need to estimate the figures to a certain degree. This entry allows for the net amount of the discrepancies that arise in calculations.

> **Note:**
> Each of the above would be calculated on a net residual value basis, which is the anticipated proceeds of an asset at the end of its useful life, less any related selling costs.

Sample summary of current and capital account balances (€, mn)			
Balance of visible trade (€, million)			9,224
Invisibles	Services	–800	
	Income	–8,425	
	Current transfers	–487	
Total of invisibles			–9,712
Balance on current account			–488
Balance on capital account			–8
Net current and capital account balance			496

The **BALANCE OF AUTONOMOUS TRANSACTIONS IN THE BALANCE OF PAYMENTS** refers to the balance on the current account plus long-term capital inflows (e.g. funds transferred by a multinational company to its Irish subsidiary).

> **Example**
> Current account: −€750 million
> Capital inflow: +€790 million
> Thus, the balance of autonomous transactions = **+€40 million**.

Sample summary of financial account balances (€, mn)	
Direct investment	5,137
Portfolio investment	22,478
Other investments	−27,899
Reserve assets	9
Balance on financial account	**−275**
Net errors and omissions	771
Net balance on financial account	**496**

Do the Balance of Payments Accounts Balance?

In theory, the balance of payments should balance in an accounting sense, i.e. the sum of the credit entries should equal the sum of the debit entries over all three accounts. In practice, however, because some transactions may not be recorded or because of differences in coverage, valuation and timing of transactions, exact symmetry does not occur and the CSO inserts a balancing item called **net errors and omissions** to balance the overall account.

How Has an Increase in Exports Affected the Irish Economy?

Irish exports have been steadily increasing in recent years. How does this development affect the level of Irish imports and the amount of borrowing by the Irish government?

In the case of the level of Irish imports:

- **Increased demand for consumer goods:** Since the sales of Irish goods leads to an increase in our income, Irish people and firms will spend more. Part of this spending may be on imports.

- **Increased demand for capital goods:** The additional demand will lead to increased domestic production, thus companies may require more capital goods and raw materials, which may be available domestically or need to be imported.

In the case of the amount of borrowing by the Irish government:

- **Increased tax take:** Due to the increased spending within the economy and the potential rise in employment, the government will take in additional direct and indirect tax revenue. In addition, due to greater profits, the government receives more corporation tax. This has the impact of reducing the need for the government to borrow.

- **A fall in government expenditure:** There will be a reduction in the numbers on social welfare due to the increase in employment. As a result, current government expenditure would fall (e.g. social welfare payments) and so would the need for the state to borrow.

Multinationals' Impact on the Balance of Payments on Current Account

- Foreign firms bring staff and expertise from their home country. Consequently, a portion of the salaries earned may be returned home (invisible imports).
- In order to create their output, firms require capital goods and raw materials and some of these may need to be imported (visible imports).
- Many multinational firms export their produce (visible exports).
- Many multinational firms repatriate their profits (invisible import).

Note:
Generally, when we speak of a balance of payments deficit/surplus, we are referring to the balance on the current account.

Multinationals' Impact on the Balance of Payments Capital Account

- When foreign firms first come to Ireland, they bring additional capital investment with them (e.g. machinery). This is a long-term capital inflow into Ireland.

Consequences of balance of payments deficit/surplus	
Deficit	**Surplus**
Leakage of income from the economy Due to the fact that imports are a leakage from the circular flow of income, the multiplier is contracted and hence national income falls as more is spent on imports.	**Injection of income into the economy** Due to the fact that exports are an injection into the circular flow of income, the multiplier is magnified and hence national income increases.
Fall in our external reserves A government needs to fund a deficit and it may choose to draw upon our external reserves. This activity reduces our ability to make international payments.	**Rise in our external reserves** A government can add to our external reserves using a surplus and hence it is easier to make international payments.

Positive Economics

Consequences of balance of payments deficit/surplus	
Deficit	**Surplus**
Loss of jobs If imports are chosen over domestically produced goods due to lower price or greater choice, it may result in the loss of Irish jobs.	**Export-led jobs** Irish exports are foreign countries' imports. If they are chosen over domestically produced goods due to lower price, better quality or greater choice, it will result in an increase in Irish employment.

A Deficit Does Not Cause a Government to Be Concerned or to React When…

- **A number of years of surpluses follow or have preceded the deficit:** In some cases, the government needs to sustain a deficit for a short period of time. For example, the Irish government reported a general government deficit of €50.3 billion in 2010. If the Budget was set to take this huge amount of money out of the economy in one year, it would have had devastating effects on the potential for growth for many years to come as well as imposed massive cuts and tax increases for the population.

- **The deficit on the current account is compensated for by a surplus on the capital account**, e.g. an inflow from EU Cohesion Fund. The shortfall is made up from the EU Regional Development Fund, EU Cohesion Fund or net inflows from migrant transfers or intangible assets. A large portion of the deficit is used to fund the import of capital goods, which will enhance the efficiency of Irish production and increase exports. The government may invest heavily in capital projects that will serve the country well in the future.

- **A large portion of the deficit is to fund the import of raw materials that are necessary for use in the production of goods by Irish manufacturing firms:** Every manufacturing business needs to buy in some stock in order to process it and then sell it on at a profit. On a macro level, if the purchase of raw materials makes up a large part of the deficit, the economy will receive monies in the future from the sale of the finished goods.

- **The deficit occurs because of exceptional, non-recurring items**, e.g. the purchase of new trains by CIÉ (Irish Rail), which are expensive capital goods, which is going to rarely happen.

Strategies for Reducing a Deficit or Building a Surplus

Imports May Be Restricted

The government could implement various measures to diminish imports coming into the country, i.e. quotas, increased administration barriers, increased excise duty, tariffs. These can only be implemented on non-EU countries.

Import Substitution

The government could encourage its citizens to 'buy Irish' irrespective of cost or choice through various initiatives and advertising campaigns so that there would be less demand for foreign goods and more demand for Irish goods.

Encourage and Stimulate Exports

The government could give tax breaks and financial grants to Irish companies that export. They could organise events in Ireland and fund the attendance of trade fairs to promote Irish goods and services abroad. They could increase expenditure on mentoring, training and communications on exporting via the county enterprise boards and Enterprise Ireland.

Introduce Incomes Policy

The government could engage in various measures to keep wage inflation very low, e.g. lowering the minimum wage, as all other rates are pegged from this. This would mean that Ireland would maintain and improve its competitiveness against other countries. This would increase the attractiveness of Irish exports abroad and prevent people from spending too much on imports.

Deflationary Government Policy

The government could increase taxes and decrease government expenditure (e.g. fiscal policy – the Budget) so as to decrease the amount of money circulating in the economy. Consumers will have less to spend and consequently the demand for imports may fall. Negative aspects of this may be an increase in unemployment and reduced consumption of domestic goods.

Exchange Rate

The **EXCHANGE RATE** is the price of one currency in terms of another.

Task

If you would like to see how much the euro is worth today against any other currency, check out the Yahoo Finance Currency Convertor at http://finance.yahoo.com/currency-converter.

The price of any commodity is determined by supply and demand. We will now look at how the euro evolved.

Exchange Rates: A Brief Historical Overview

1820–1914	1936	1944	1970	1980	2001
Gold Standard	Sterling and dollar	IMF: Fixed E/R	Variable: EMS	Variable: EMS	Introduction of euro

Positive Economics

1820–1914

This was the period of the Gold Standard, where international payments were based on a system of currencies being valued in terms of gold. Any participating country had to comply with two basic conditions:

- The currency of a participating country had to be freely convertible into gold at a fixed rate.
- The country had to allow gold to move freely in and out of the state.

During this period, all the major trading countries of the world had their currencies denominated in terms of gold and exchange values between currencies could be calculated. The system worked as follows.

If Ireland imported more from the US than it exported to America, then a trade deficit would emerge, resulting in an excess supply of Irish pounds and a shortage of dollars. However, rather than this excess supply of pounds forcing up the value of the US dollar (demand > supply), Irish importers converted their currency into gold and sent it to the US to pay for the goods.

From this analysis, we can see that countries with a surplus on international trade would receive gold and deficit countries would lose gold. At this time, the quantity of money in circulation was tied to the amount of gold held by the banking authorities in each country. Hence, in our example America would receive gold and its money supply would increase and prices would consequently rise. The opposite would happen in Ireland, as the money supply would contract and prices would fall (deflation). The fall in Irish prices would make Irish exports more competitive in the US and exports would increase. Prices in the US would rise, making their exports to Ireland less competitive. This changing of prices would see the Irish balance of payments beginning to correct itself, i.e. the self-adjusting mechanism of the Gold Standard would eventually lead to an equilibrium position.

The main advantages of the Gold Standard were that:

- International trade was stimulated because of certainty in rates of exchange.
- It provided a mechanism that corrected trade surpluses and deficits within countries.

In **1914** the Gold Standard was abandoned due to the outbreak of World War I.

Between **1916 and 1925**, a period of floating exchange rates existed where currencies were allowed to float to reflect market demand and supply conditions.

The years **1925 to 1931** saw a return to the Gold Standard/gold exchange standard. Under the latter scheme, many countries kept their reserves in the currency of a country, e.g. sterling and dollars, which was convertible into gold.

COLLAPSE OF THE GOLD STANDARD

The workings of the standard required the deficit (gold-losing country) to deflate, while countries with a surplus (gold-receiving country) would inflate. However, countries did not follow these edicts as they proved very unpopular, e.g. trade unions in the deflating country would not agree to wage decreases. In **1931**, Britain finally abandoned the Gold Standard as the Great Depression began to affect the world. They were followed by France, Poland and the Netherlands in **1936**.

In **1944**, the IMF was founded in New Hampshire in the US. Among its objectives were the following.

- To promote international monetary co-operation.
- To facilitate the expansion of the balanced growth of international trade.
- To promote exchange rate stability.
- To provide funds for correcting balance of payments disequilibrium.
- To give loans to member countries.

THE EUROPEAN MONETARY SYSTEM (EMS): 1979–99

- In 1979 the European Economic Community (EEC) introduced the European Monetary System (EMS), whereby member countries maintained parity of their currencies vis-à-vis each other.
- The European Currency Unit (ECU) was established and each currency was given a value against the ECU.
- Participating countries set a value for their currency in terms of each of the other participating currencies and they undertook to maintain exchange rates within a band of 2.25% or 6%.
- Each country's central bank intervened on the foreign exchange markets to maintain their agreed values.
- The EMS restored stability to exchange rates and international trade increased.

Economic and Monetary Union (EMU): 1999

In October 1980, the EU published a report, *One Market, One Money*, about the benefits of an Economic and Monetary Union. It was provided for in the Maastricht Treaty in 1991 and Ireland joined in 1999.

Provisions/Objectives

- **Introduction of a single currency (euro):** Many member states have adopted the euro as their currency, with the abolition of their own state currency. The value of the euro is influenced by the actions of the European Central Bank (ECB). Before being accepted into the eurozone, a country needs to comply with convergence criteria. These are the conditions new member states have to meet related to inflation, interest rates, exchange rate stability, government deficits and national debts in order to join the EMU.

- **Single monetary policy:** The EU created a single monetary policy to be implemented by the ECB. Since then, the main job of the ECB has been to ensure price stability across the eurozone and implement a European monetary policy.

Benefits of EMU for Ireland

- **Saving on currency conversion costs for business:** Eliminating foreign exchange transaction costs for exporters simplifies financial dealings when exporting and significantly reduces business costs.

- **Eliminating exchange rate risks in the eurozone:** The uncertainty associated with exchange rates is removed for all firms exporting and importing within the European states. This allows firms to confidently budget future cash flows with more certainty.

- **Price transparency:** When all goods and services are priced in euro, there is greater price transparency for all EU consumers. Consumers and firms greatly benefit from this information, as they can make definite comparisons and see where the best value is available. As a result, there is increased price competition across EU states and efficient suppliers will drive prices down across the eurozone.

- **Foreign investment:** Ireland has seen increased FDI due to the common currency and the reduction of risk and uncertainty caused by currency fluctuations. Multinationals have easy access to the EU market, where trade is simple and cheaper. This has created, and continues to create, employment and wealth.

- **Increased tourism:** Savings are made by not having to convert currency when travelling within the eurozone. This appeals to many travellers, who are more likely to experience new EU countries, thereby bringing money into those member states.

- **Lower interest rates:** Interest rates are lower and less volatile, stimulating investment and growth. They will be similar in member states, which should lead to stability in the markets, which is good for the European economy.

- **Lower inflation:** Price stability and low inflation are the ECB's primary objectives. Again, inflation rates will be similar in all member states, which should lead to stability of prices and income. Industry should therefore remain competitive and inflation low.

- **Stable currency:** Due to the enormous economic power of the EU, we will have a strong and stable currency. There can be no devaluation of the euro within the EU by a member state.

- **More stable economic environment:** Common currency creates stability in our economic environments as exchange rate costs and risks are removed between member states.

Disadvantages of EMU to Ireland

- **United Kingdom:** A significant amount of Ireland's trade is with the UK, a country that has decided to remain outside the single currency. Thus, Irish businesses still face the costs of changing their money and the risk of fluctuating exchange rates when it comes to buying from and selling to the UK.

- **Interest rates:** Interest rate levels are no longer under the control of the Irish Central Bank. As a result, we can't adjust our monetary policy to aid our own economy when we need to cool it down in times of overheating and stimulate it in times of recession.

- **Outflow of wealth:** Wealth may flow out of Ireland and go to other eurozone countries where better rates are available to investors and savers or when alternative currencies offer better purchasing power.

- **Loss of sovereignty:** Ireland has given control of its monetary policy tools to the EU, which has resulted in the loss of some sovereignty. Ireland has very proud national roots and some people find it difficult to be seen as European rather than Irish.

Factors Affecting the Exchange Rate of a Currency

Foreign Trade

If firms and individuals outside the eurozone want to consume eurozone visible and invisible exports, they need to purchase euro in advance. Similarly, if eurozone citizens want to import goods, they need to sell euro and buy the currency in order to carry out the purchase. As a result, if payments into the eurozone are greater than payments out of the eurozone, there will be more demand for euro and the currency will appreciate and vice versa.

Interest Rates

If a country can offer a high interest rate, money will flow into that country to avail of a high return on investment. However, in order to do so, the individual or firm seeking that return must first buy the country's currency, driving exchange rates higher.

Level of Money Supply
If there is an expansion in the money supply in the eurozone area, this will likely lead to an increase in imports into the eurozone. This will necessitate an increase in demand for foreign currency and a possible fall in the value of the euro (supply exceeds demand = price falls).

Central Bank Intervention
If a country or zone wants to appreciate or deflate its currency, it can do so by flooding the market with supply (i.e. deflate) or use its own foreign reserves to demand and buy the currency. For example, in 2011, the Swiss Central Bank made a decision to peg the euro at €1: CHF 1.20. In order to do so, it bought up significant amounts of euro.

Role of Speculators
There are people who participate in the currency market simply to make a profit on exchange rate movements. If speculators feel that the exchange rate will move in one direction or another, they will buy or sell the currency accordingly. If a significant number of people participate in this activity with a lot of money, they too can influence the exchange rate via demand and supply.

> **Example**
> Let's say the euro/dollar exchange rate is €1 : $1.40 today and in a fortnight's time it will be €1 : $1.35. Consider the money trail of €1,000. Initially, €1,000 is transferred into $1,400 and in two weeks' time it is translated back to euro, i.e. ($1,400/$1.35 = €1,037). The return is 3.7% over two weeks.

Purchasing Power Parity
The purchasing power parity theory was put forward by the Swedish economist Gustav Cassel in 1916. It came to the fore explaining how to determine the appropriate equilibrium exchange rate at which countries should rejoin the Gold Standard after World War I.

> The **PURCHASING POWER PARITY THEORY** states: 'In a free market, the exchange rate between one currency and another currency is in equilibrium when their domestic purchasing powers at that rate of exchange are equivalent.'

In other words, the exchange rate will be determined to be at equilibrium where a given amount of one currency will buy the same quantity of goods whether it is spent on the domestic or international market.

> **Example**
> - A bottle of cola costs €1 in Ireland.
> - Euro/dollar exchange rate is €1 : $1.40.
> - If the bottle of cola holds to the law of purchasing power parity, the price of a bottle of cola in the US should be €1 × $1.40 = $1.40.

Weakness of Purchasing Power Parity

Purchasing power parity is an oversimplified theory due to the following.

- **Exchange rates are determined by a number of factors:** As explained above, speculation, central bank intervention, interest rates, etc. all influence the demand for and supply of a currency and hence its exchange rate, not just the demand for and supply of a currency for goods and services, as suggested by this theory.

- **Transportation costs ignored:** Goods in different countries rarely move inter-price equality due to hindrances such as transport costs, which could significantly increase the price of a good when exported.

- **Many goods are not tradable or transportable:** This is not considered by the purchasing power parity theory, i.e. you cannot export or import going to the doctor or going to the hairdresser.

- **Free trade is not characteristic of all markets:** Many countries impose financial and other types of barriers to imports, e.g. tariffs, subsidies. In 2009, Russia banned all the export of wheat out of the country, as it was experiencing drought and needed the entire crop for its own people.

Impact of a Devaluation

Imports From Non-euro Countries Will Become More Expensive

> **DEVALUATION** is the decrease in the value of one currency relative to that of other currencies.

As the value of the currency has fallen, one needs to spend more of it to get the same amount of imported goods. Hence, the price of imports is higher and the overall bill for imports is higher, putting pressure on businesses that need internationally sourced raw materials and capital goods for their enterprises. In addition, it is now more expensive for Irish tourists to travel abroad and they may instead opt for a 'staycation'.

Exports to Non-EU Countries Will Be Cheaper

The value of the currency has fallen; therefore, international buyers need to spend less of it to get the same amount of Irish goods. The demand for our exports would increase and this would act as an injection to the circular flow of income and our national income. In addition, it is now financially more attractive for foreign tourists to visit Ireland.

Pressures of Inflation on the Irish Economy

Due to the fact that import prices have risen in the Irish economy, goods that use imported raw materials will cost more, contributing to Irish inflation.

Upward Wage Demands

Imported inflation causes the prices of goods and services to rise in Ireland. Trade unions use inflation data as the basis of their argument to negotiate higher wages for their members.

Interest Rate Changes

Since the ECB has an explicit mandate to keep inflation under control, if it sees that prices of goods and services have increased more than 2%, it may increase interest rates to curb that problem.

Boosts to Trade and Employment

Since the price of exports has fallen, there will be more demand for Irish exports, thus increasing demand for raw materials and labour. In addition, confidence and disposable income will increase, driving consumption higher. **A revaluation will have the opposite effect**.

Impact of an Appreciation/Revaluation of a Currency on the Balance of Payments

This is the effect of an increase in the euro against the American dollar, Australian dollar, sterling, etc. (this means that the euro is dearer from an international perspective).

Current account	Capital account
• **Export prices rise (visible/invisible):** The demand for price-sensitive Irish exports will fall. As a result, less foreign revenue via exports will be received into the country.	• **Real value of money invested abroad rises:** As a result, there may be greater capital outflows.

28: Balance of Payments and Foreign Exchange

Current account	Capital account
• **Import prices fall (visible/invisible):** The demand for goods imported into the country may fall, as their prices have fallen. As a result, there would be more money leaking out of Ireland to go to the country of origin. • **Deficit on current account of the balance of payments may increase:** As a consequence of what was said above, the balance of payments current account deficit may increase.	• **Irish borrowing on foreign markets is more financially attractive:** As a result, there may be an increased amount of borrowing on the part of the government. • **Foreign direct investment in Ireland is less attractive:** As a result, there may be a fall in the amount of foreign direct investment in Ireland.

MARSHALL LERNER CONDITION: A devaluation will improve a country's balance of trade if the sum of the elasticities of demand for exports and imports is greater than 1 (in absolute terms).

Example of a Devaluation Including Elasticity of Demand

China records exports and imports as well as price elasticity of demand as follows.

	No. of goods (million)	Price	Price elasticity of demand
Exports	100	€1	–1.1
Imports	200	€1	–1.6

Before Devaluation

The balance of trade deficit = €100 million. The Chinese government decides to devalue the currency by 30%.

Effect of devaluation:
- The price of exports falls by 30% due to the devaluation.
  - Since PED (exports) = –1.1, the quantity demanded increases by 33%.
- The price of imports rises by 30% due to the devaluation.
  - Since PED (imports) = –1.6, the quantity demanded falls by 48%.

After Devaluation

	No. of goods	Price	Total value
Exports	133	€0.70	€93.1 million
Imports	104	€1.30	€135.2 million

Positive Economics

The balance of trade (after devaluation) = €42.1 million. In general, the result of the devaluation was a bettering of China's balance of trade by €57.9 million. The sum of elasticity of demand for exports as well as that of imports is 2.7.

Since 2.7 > 1, the devaluation benefited China, i.e. the more elastic the demand for a country's imports and exports, the greater the impact of an exchange rate movement.

Different Types of Exchange Rates

Fixed Exchange Rate

ADVANTAGES

- The uncertainty is removed from financial planning in relation to buying foreign goods on credit. If a company bought $10,000 worth of goods in the US at an exchange rate of €1 : $1.40, they know that will cost them €7,143. However, if the rate was to fluctuate upwards and the dollar strengthened to €1 : $1.35, this invoice would now increase by (($10,000/1.35) – €7,143)= €264.

> **FIXED EXCHANGE RATE:** The values of currencies are agreed upon and each participating country undertakes to exchange the currency at that value. The government signs up to do whatever is necessary to adhere to this system.

- The uncertainty is removed from financial planning in relation to borrowing on the international market. Consider a company who borrowed and needed to repay $10,000 in interest and principal. At an exchange rate of €1 : $1.40, they know that will cost them €7,143. However, if the rate was to fluctuate upwards and the dollar strengthened to €1 : $1.35, this total due would now increase by (($10,000/1.35) – €7,143)= €264.

- Speculation in the markets is no longer a worthwhile exercise, as there is no exchange rate movement to speculate on.

DISADVANTAGES

- Countries may need to use their external reserves of foreign currency to maintain the fixed rate regime.

- Governmental policy to maintain a fixed interest rate could supersede other prudent policies. For example, in order to decrease the amount of money spent on imports, a government might consider raising interest rates.

Floating Exchange Rate

> **FLOATING EXCHANGE RATE:** Currencies fluctuate in value and the equilibrium rate is decided by the market forces of supply and demand.

28: Balance of Payments and Foreign Exchange

ADVANTAGES

- There isn't any governmental intervention as the currency finds its own equilibrium on the markets, which is underpinned by the forces of supply and demand, reflecting the state of the underlying economy.

- Countries' reserves remain intact and available for other policies.

- The balance of payments on the current account will balance in the long run because if demand for either exports or imports is greater than the other, the exchange rate will find a balance between the two.

DISADVANTAGES

- There is uncertainty in financial planning when firms are trading internationally. If a company bought $10,000 worth of goods in the US at an exchange rate of €1 : $1.40, they know that it will cost them €7,143 if they had paid today. However, if the rate was to fluctuate upwards and the dollar strengthened to €1 : $1.35, this invoice would now increase by (($10,000/1.35) – €7,143) = €264. On the other hand, if the rate was to fluctuate downwards and the dollar was to weaken to €1 : $1.30, the invoice would now decrease by (€7,143 – ($10,000/1.3)) = €549. As a result, fewer firms might engage in this market, lowering international trade.

- There is uncertainty in financial planning in relation to borrowing on the international market. Consider a company that borrowed and needed to repay $10,000 in interest and principal. At an exchange rate of €1 : $1.40, they know that will cost them €7,143. However, if the rate was to fluctuate upwards and the dollar strengthened to €1 : $1.35, this total due would now increase by (($10,000/1.35) – €7,143)= €264. On the other hand, if the rate was to fluctuate downwards and the dollar was to weaken to €1 : $1.30, the repayment amount would now decrease by (€7,143 – ($10,000/1.3)) = €549. As a result, there may be less borrowing on the international markets for capital projects, meaning either taxpayers get less of their wages as their own or the capital projects are not initiated.

- Speculators enter the market in search of short-term return on investment. This distorts the equilibrium exchange rates and hence exporters and importers must deal with the consequences.

EXAM ✓ Question 6, Section A, 2011 (17 marks)

Outline **two** possible economic effects for the Irish economy of the euro (€) falling in value relative to the US dollar ($).

Positive Economics

> **Solution**
>
> *Any two of the following points would be acceptable.*
>
> - **Import prices (from the US) are dearer:** Prices of imports from the US increase. This will result in a higher import bill for Irish producers and a decrease in imports from the US. The cost of Irish people visiting the US is dearer, so fewer Irish people may holiday there.
>
> - **Export prices (to the US) are cheaper:** The price of exports from Ireland to the US decreases and therefore are easier to sell. This may result in increased exports to the US. The cost of Americans visiting Ireland is cheaper, so more Americans may holiday here.
>
> - **Employment opportunities:** With a possible increase in exports, employment in those industries that depend on Irish exports to the US may increase.
>
> - **Economic growth may increase:** With job creation, spending within the economy may rise. Expenditure by the government on social welfare would decrease. Combined, these will impact positively on the rate of economic growth.
>
> - **US investment in Ireland:** It may be less costly for US firms to purchase capital goods/invest in Ireland, so investment may increase.

EXAM ✓ Question 6(b), 2006 (20 marks)

State and explain how **imports** into the eurozone would be affected by each of the following developments:

(i) The US dollar rises in value against the euro.

(ii) Employment within the eurozone increases.

Solution

		Statement	Explanation
(i)	**US dollar rises** in value against the euro	Imports will decrease	Imports from the US are now more expensive, hence imports from the US may fall.
(ii)	**Employment** within the eurozone **increases**	Imports will increase	With higher incomes, eurozone citizens can now afford to buy more goods and services. As employment increases, demand for capital goods and raw materials will increase and this may result in greater imports.

28: Balance of Payments and Foreign Exchange

EXAM ✓ Question 7(b), 2007 (25 marks)

Suppose the euro (€) increases in value relative to the American dollar ($) and sterling (£). Outline the likely effects this increase would have on any **three** components of the balance of payments. At least one component should be from the capital account.

Solution

Effects of increase in value of euro (€) relative to the American dollar ($) and sterling (£)	
Current account	**Capital account**
• **Export prices increase (visible/invisible):** Demand for Irish exports may fall. Less foreign revenue earned from exports to US/UK. • **Import prices decrease (visible/invisible):** Demand for imports from the US and UK may rise. More euro paid out for imports from the US/UK.	• **Real value of money invested abroad is greater:** May result in greater capital outflows. • **Real value of money from abroad invested in Ireland is reduced:** May result in reduced capital inflows. • **Irish borrowing abroad is more attractive:** May result in increased foreign borrowing. • **Foreign investment in Ireland is less attractive:** May result in reduced foreign development in Ireland.

EXAM ✓ Sample Exam Question (10 marks)

(a) You are going to the US on your holidays and you need to buy some dollars. You have €100 saved in your bank account. How many dollars will you get?
(b) You have returned home from a wonderful trip, but you actually only spent half of the money. How much will you get back in euro?

Bank Rates:
We Sell: 1.4219   **We Buy: 1.4398**

Solution

(a) If you are buying dollars, the bank is selling them to you.
    amount × (bank sell rate) = €100 × 1.4219 = $142.19.

(b) If you are getting back euro, the bank is buying dollars from you.
    amount/(bank buy rate) = ($142.19/2) = $71.095/1.4219 = €50.

Questions

Short Questions

1. Define visible imports and visible exports.
2. Define invisible imports and invisible exports.
3. What is a balance of trade surplus (deficit)?
4. What is a balance of payments surplus (deficit)?
5. Define exchange rate.

Long Questions

1. State and explain the elements of the balance of payments account.
2. List and explain strategies that a government could undertake to reduce a balance of payments deficit or build a balance of payments surplus.
3. State and explain the consequences for a balance of payments deficit.
4. State and explain the consequences for a balance of payments surplus.
5. Analyse the impact on the economy of the following:
    (a) A devaluation of the euro against the dollar
    (b) A revaluation of the euro against the dollar
6. Analyse the impact on both the balance of payment current and capital accounts of the following:
    (a) A rise in the euro against the dollar
    (b) A fall in sterling against the euro
7. Discuss the advantages and disadvantages of fixed exchange rates.
8. Discuss the advantages and disadvantages of floating exchange rates.
9. Discuss the impact multinationals have on the balance of payments capital and current accounts.
10. State and explain the factors affecting the exchange rate of a currency.
11. Outline the purchasing power parity theory.

Chapter 29: The Global Economic System

Specific Learning Outcomes

At the end of this chapter, students should be able to:

- [ ] Evaluate the importance of membership for Ireland to the European Union.
- [ ] Discuss the role and function of European institutions.
- [ ] Discuss the policies of the EU that are relevant to Ireland as an EU member state.
- [ ] Outline the role and functions of the World Bank.
- [ ] Outline the role and functions of the International Monetary Fund.

The European Union (EU)

The European Union is an economic and political union that has as its main aim total co-operation among its members on all economic, political and monetary matters. It is a trading bloc of 27 (at the time of writing) countries, called member states. There is free trade among all member states and EU trade is known as the single market.

The 27 member states are:

Austria	Germany	Netherlands
Belgium	Greece	Poland
Bulgaria	Hungary	Portugal
Cyprus	Ireland	Romania
Czech Republic	Italy	Slovakia
Denmark	Latvia	Slovenia
Estonia	Lithuania	Spain
Finland	Luxembourg	Sweden
France	Malta	UK

Applicant countries:
Croatia
Former Yugoslav Republic of Macedonia
Iceland
Turkey

Objectives of the EU

- To facilitate the free movement of goods, services, labour and capital between member states.

- To maintain peace and stability within all of Europe through a common foreign and defence policy.

- To improve the standards of living and quality of life of European citizens.

- To establish common values among citizens, such as democracy, equality and human rights.

- To strengthen, support and enlarge the European Union.

Importance of the EU

PEACE AND STABILITY

The EU has brought peace and stability as well as closer co-operation between member states.

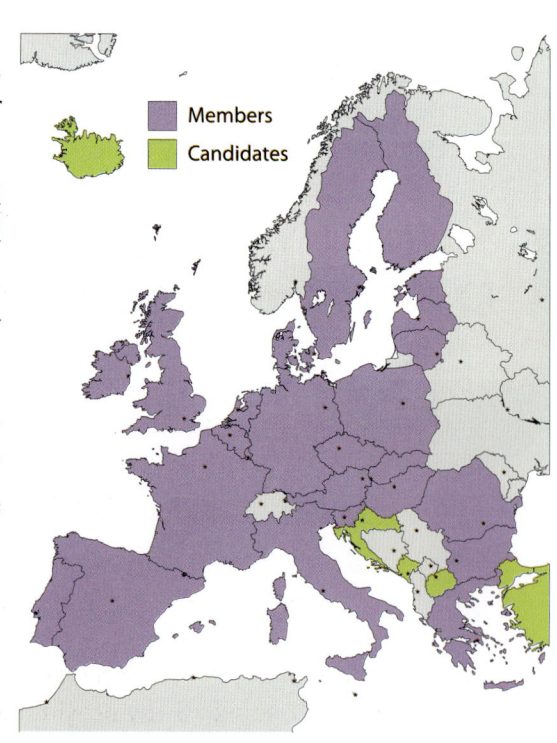

LARGE OPEN MARKET
The EU represents one of the largest markets in the world, with a combined population of over 500 million people, and is responsible for over 25% of world trade. It provides Irish businesses with the opportunity to increase their profits by selling their products and services freely to this market.

Task
How many flags, cities and landmarks can you match in Europe?

FREE TRADE AREA
The EU is a free trade area, where goods, services, labour and capital can move freely in and out of member states without obstruction. This has encouraged Irish firms to enter the export market and has forced them to improve their competitiveness.

HARMONISATION OF LAWS
The EU has succeeded in harmonising many of the laws operating throughout the member states. This has made it easier for Irish firms to do business within the EU.

FUNDING
The EU has made substantial funds available to improve the under-developed regions of the Union. Ireland has benefited greatly from these funds and grants in the past and has used them to improve infrastructure such as motorways, airports and sea ports, thus improving productivity and lowering the cost of transport.

SINGLE CURRENCY
The EU was successful in developing a single currency (the euro), which has been adopted as the currency of 17 member states. This has removed the uncertainty associated with foreign trade, eliminated the cost of converting currencies and made it easier for firms to make purchasing decisions.

PROTECTION
The EU has taken various measures to protect the citizens of member states and to afford them equal rights and conditions, e.g. consumer rights, product safety and worker rights. The Nice Treaty and Lisbon Treaty have further protected these rights.

INWARD INVESTMENT
Membership of the EU has made Ireland an attractive place for foreign firms to locate manufacturing and service bases. This has created valuable employment in Ireland and has had a vital impact on the development of the economy. As well as providing thousands of jobs, raw materials are sourced from Irish suppliers, which in turn increases Irish sales and profits.

EU POLICIES
The introduction of the Common Agricultural Policy and the Fisheries Policy have greatly benefited Ireland's primary industries of agriculture and fisheries. The policies aim to give those operating in these sectors an improved standard of living and help modernise and improve these sectors by providing the industries with grants.

Institutions of the European Union

The European Commission

The functions of the European Commission are to:

- Propose new laws for the European Union member states.
- Enforce all EU laws.
- Draft and manage the EU budget.
- Represent the EU internationally.

The European Commission has the power to do the following:

- Bring individuals and organisations to the EU courts.
- Impose fines on those who don't follow EU regulations.
- Reprimand states that don't fulfil their obligations under EU law.

The European Commission

The European Parliament

The functions of the European Parliament are:

- Legislative, budgetary and executive control.
- Representing the citizens of Europe who have been elected to the parliament to represent their interests in discussions with other EU institutions.
- Vetting and appointing the members of the Commission.
- Protecting the rights of the people of the EU member states.
- Debating issues that are of concern to all member states, e.g. pollution, terrorism, drug trafficking, money laundering, refugees, waste disposal and consumer protection.

The European Parliament

The Council of Ministers

The Council of Ministers is the most powerful institution and is the main decision-making body of the EU. It sets all the key economic and political objectives and decisions of the EU. Its functions include:

- Approving and overseeing legislation.
- Co-ordinating policies.

The European Council of Ministers
© Photographic Service of the Council of the EU

29: The Global Economic System

- Concluding international agreements.
- Approving the EU budget.

The European Court of Justice
The functions of the European Court of Justice include:

- Enforcing laws.
- Enforcing EU policies.
- Passing judgement.
- Taking action where laws and policies are broken/not implemented.
- Interpreting EU law.
- Ensuring the law is observed.
- Adjudicating on disputes.
- Writing laws.

The European Court of Justice
© Court of Justice of the European Union

The European Court of Auditors
The role of the European Court of Auditors includes:

- Implementing the EU budget.
- Spot checks on member states to ensure the budget is used for the purpose intended.
- Preparing an annual budgetary report.

The European Court of Auditors
© European Union

EU Policies

Common Agricultural Policy (CAP)
The CAP is a common development plan for agriculture for all member states and accounts for over 45% of the EU budget. It was introduced to make the EU self-sufficient in food and to improve farm incomes.

Objectives

- Fair and efficient standards of living for the agricultural community.
- A single market where all agricultural produce is allowed to move freely across the EU without any restrictions or barriers.

469

- Products from the EU are to be given preference over imported products.
- Expenses and spending relating to the application of the CAP are borne by the EU budget.
- Stabilise agricultural markets and regulate prices.
- Reasonable prices and quality choice for consumers.
- Grants to ensure quality of produce.
- A single farm payment or single payment scheme (SPS) for EU farmers, independent from production.
- Respect of environmental, food safety, animal and plant health and animal welfare standards.

Common Fisheries Policy (CFP)

The Common Fisheries Policy is a set of common rules that apply to the fishing industry in each EU member state. It was officially introduced in 1973 and updated in 2003.

OBJECTIVES

- Prevent overfishing and preserve and ensure fish stocks into the future.
- The EU decides what quantity (quota) of various types of fish can be caught by each member state in certain waters – the Total Allowable Catch (TAC).
- The CFP placed restrictions or bans on certain types of fishing.
- All fishing boats on EU waters must be licensed to fish.
- Each member state agreed to reserve a 19 km zone around its coast for its own fishing fleet.
- Member states are responsible for monitoring fishing activities and ensuring that all the rules and fisheries policy are applied.
- Aims to safeguard the livelihood of those involved in the fishing industry and ensure the economic viability of the European fleets.
- Aims to protect the marine environment in every manner.
- Provides funding to protect and promote the fishing industry.

Competition Policy

The aim of the Competition Policy is that consumers get a choice of quality goods and services at reasonable prices.

29: The Global Economic System

Objectives

- Fair and free competition between firms in the Single European Market (SEM).
- Healthy competition ensures better service and lower prices for consumers.
- Eradicate cartels, i.e. the arrangement between two or more firms resulting in a restriction of competition, e.g. price fixing.
- Firms that hold a dominant position in a particular industry may not abuse that position in order to raise prices or increase profits.
- All monopolies, whether state-owned or private, must be deregulated to allow new firms into the market.
- Mergers, takeovers and strategic alliances must be approved by the relevant competition authority in each country.
- The Commission closely monitors how much aid member governments make available to state-owned or other businesses.

European Structural Policy
Objectives
- Promoting the development and structural adjustment of regions whose development is lagging behind.
- Conversion of declining industrial regions.
- Combating long-term unemployment.
- Integration of young people into working life.
- Adjustment of production, processing and marketing structures in agriculture and forestry and development in rural areas.

European Structural Funds

The Structural Funds were created to help regions within Europe whose development is lagging behind in order to reduce the differences between regions and create a better economic and social balance within and between member states. The two individual funds are collectively known as the EU Structural Funds and work together to support economic and social development across Europe. These funds are the ESF and ERDF.

European Social Fund (ESF)

The European Social Fund is the EU's financial instrument for investing in people. Its mission is to help prevent and fight unemployment, to equip Europe's workforce to face new challenges and to prevent people from losing touch with the labour market.

European Regional Development Fund (ERDF)

The principal objective of the European Regional Development Fund is the promotion of economic and social cohesion within the EU through the reduction of imbalances between regions or social groups.

> **Task**
>
> Find and summarise the government's latest document that sets out the roadmap to Ireland's future economy and society. As a class, discuss how you think it might impact you, your family, your bank account and prospects for the future.

The World Bank

> The **WORLD BANK** is an international organisation dedicated to providing financing, advice and research to developing nations to aid their economic advancement.

The World Bank Group (WBG) was established in 1944 to rebuild post-World War II Europe. It encourages all of its clients, which number over 100, to implement policies that promote sustainable growth, health, education, social development programmes focusing on governance and poverty reduction mechanisms, the environment, private business and macroeconomic reform.

The World Bank Group is made up of five component organisations:

- International Bank for Reconstruction and Development (IBRD)
- International Development Association (IDA)
- International Finance Corporation (IFC)
- Multilateral Investment Guarantee Agency (MIGA)
- International Centre for Settlement of Investment Disputes (ICSID)

Functions of the World Bank

To Promote the Economic Development of the World's Poorer Countries

Eliminate poverty and provide assistance to the poor by offering loans, policy advice and technical assistance to those countries whose per capita GNP is less than $865 per year with special financial assistance through the International Development Association (IDA).

ENCOURAGE INVESTMENT FUNDS TO LDCs

Through its organisations, the World Bank obtains funds from the world's developed countries and uses these resources to provide loans to the least developed countries (LDCs) so that they can invest in infrastructure such as roads and schools. The International Finance Corporation (IFC) works to promote private sector investments by both foreign and local investors into LDCs. The Multilateral Investment Guarantee Agency (MIGA) supports direct foreign investment into a country by offering security against the investment in the event of political turmoil. The International Centre for Settlement of Investment Disputes (ICSID) facilitates and works towards a settlement in the event of a dispute between a foreign investor and a local country.

FINANCE CAPITAL PROJECTS IN MEMBER COUNTRIES

The World Bank gives loans and long-term financing to member states and private businesses in developing countries to assist with capital projects and programmes. It encourages private enterprises in developing countries through its affiliate, the International Finance Corporation (IFC). Examples in Ireland in the past have included building the original community schools by the Department of Education and Skills.

SUPERVISION OF DEVELOPMENT OF LDCs

The World Bank examines and develops support programmes to any endangerment to a country's livelihood (e.g. HIV/AIDS). It reduces the risk of projects by means of better appraisal and supervision mechanisms as well as a multidimensional approach to overall development. (This includes not only lending but also support for legal reform, educational programmes, environmental safety, anti-corruption measures and other types of social development.)

DEBT RELIEF FOR LDCs

The World Bank helps LDCs reduce their burden by extending the terms of loans and/or renegotiating interest rates. The International Development Association offers low (or even zero) interest rate loans to the world's poorest countries in order to help them reduce their burden. Many can receive accelerated debt relief through the Heavily Indebted Poor Countries Scheme, which reduces debt and debt service payments while encouraging social expenditure.

Achievements of the World Bank Group

- The largest source of finance in education.
- One of the largest financiers in the war against HIV/AIDS.
- Provides the most debt relief to the heavily indebted countries in the world.
- One of the prominent financiers of biodiversity projects.
- Helps in bringing basic amenities to the world's poorest people.
- Assists countries to be free from conflict.

Positive Economics

The European Investment Bank

The European Investment Bank (EIB), located in Luxembourg, is the European Union's financing institution. Its shareholders are the 27 member states of the Union, which have jointly subscribed its capital. The EIB's Board of Governors is composed of the Finance Ministers of these states. The EIB's role is to provide long-term finance in support of investment projects.

Inside the European Union, the EIB supports the EU's policy objectives in the following areas.

- **Small and medium-sized enterprises:** Stimulating investment by small businesses.
- **Cohesion and convergence:** Addressing economic and social imbalances in disadvantaged regions.
- **The fight against climate change:** Mitigating and adapting to the effects of global warming.
- **Environmental protection and sustainable communities:** Investing in a cleaner natural and urban environment.
- **Sustainable, competitive and secure energy:** Producing alternative energy and reducing dependence on imports.
- **The knowledge economy:** Promoting an economy that stimulates knowledge and creativity through investment in information and communication technologies as well as human and social capital.
- **Trans-European networks:** Constructing cross-border networks in transport, energy and communications.

Outside the EU, the EIB is active in over 150 countries (the pre-accession countries of South-East Europe, the Mediterranean partner countries, the African, Caribbean and Pacific countries, Asia and Latin America, Central Asia, Russia and other neighbours in the East). It works to implement the financial pillar of EU external co-operation and development policies in:

- Private sector development.
- Infrastructure development.
- Security of energy supply.
- Environmental sustainability.

The EIB, the largest international non-sovereign lender and borrower, raises the resources it needs to finance its lending activities by borrowing on the capital markets, mainly through public bond issues. Its AAA credit rating enables it to obtain the best terms on the market. As a not-for-profit institution, the EIB passes on this advantage in the terms it offers to the beneficiaries of its loans in both the public and private sectors.

The EIB works closely with the other EU institutions, especially the European Parliament, the European Council and the European Commission. The European Investment Fund is a subsidiary of the EIB.

The International Monetary Fund (IMF)

> The **IMF** is a co-operative intergovernmental institution that provides financial assistance and advice to member countries.

The IMF was established at the end of World War II, out of the Bretton Woods Conference in 1945. It was created out of a need to prevent economic crises like the Great Depression. With its sister organisation, the World Bank, the IMF is the largest public lender of funds in the world. It is a specialised agency of the United Nations and has 187 member countries. Membership is open to any country that conducts foreign policy and accepts the organisation's statutes. On joining the IMF, each member country is assigned a quota, based broadly on its relative size in the world economy. Members' quotas are a means of providing the IMF with the financial resources needed to lend to members in financial difficulty and are also a factor in determining members' representation on the Executive Board and their voting power in the IMF.

The International Monetary Fund © IMF

The IMF's Objectives

EXPANSION OF WORLD TRADE
The IMF promotes expansion in trade by encouraging member countries to adopt sound economic policies. It monitors economic and financial developments in member countries and gives advice to its members. In addition, it facilitates the growth of international trade, thus promoting job creation and economic growth and reducing poverty.

STRENGTHENING THE INTERNATIONAL MONETARY SYSTEM
The IMF is the central institution in the international monetary system. It serves as a forum for consultation and collaboration by members on international monetary and financial matters.

Promoting Exchange Rate Stability

The IMF promotes international monetary co-operation, supporting exchange rate stability and an open system of international payments. It provides a forum for consultation on international monetary problems. It tries to maintain orderly exchange relations among member countries and aims to avoid competitive devaluations.

Financing Temporary Balance of Payments Needs

The IMF lends to member countries that have balance of payments needs to provide temporary relief and enable countries to put in place orderly corrective measures and reform policies aimed at correcting underlying problems.

Combating Poverty in Low-income Countries

The IMF (with the World Bank) provides occasional loans to low-income member countries to help support these countries' efforts to eradicate poverty.

Operating a Multilateral System of Payments

The IMF operates this system in respect of current transactions between members and aims to eliminate foreign exchange restrictions that may hamper the growth of world trade. It supplements the currency reserves of its members through the allocation of SDRs (Special Drawing Rights).

Mobilising External Financing

IMF endorsement of a country's policies is an important catalyst for mobilising resources from bilateral and multilateral lenders and donors. They rely on IMF endorsement of a country's economic policies or might even require a formal IMF-supported economic programme before committing or disbursing their own resources to that country or granting debt relief. IMF policy assessments and recommendations also provide important signals to investors and financial markets regarding a country's economic future and impact on investor and market confidence in the economy.

Providing Technical Assistance and Training

Technical assistance and training are provided in the core areas of IMF expertise to help member countries design economic policies and improve economic management capabilities. For example, when the Soviet Union collapsed, the IMF stepped in and set up treasury systems for their central banks to help the transition from centrally planned to market-based economic systems.

Emergency Funds

The IMF also offers emergency funds to collapsed economies, as it did for Korea during the 1997 financial crisis in Asia. Emergency funds can also be loaned to countries that have faced economic crisis as a result of a natural disaster damaging devaluation.

Disseminating Information and Research

The IMF is a premier source of economic analysis of its member countries' economic policies and statistical information.

Ireland's Situation

The global financial crisis that erupted in 2008 brought to light the need for closer IMF surveillance of individual countries, for better analysis of the way in which economic shocks are transmitted across national borders and for deeper understanding between macroeconomic and financial sector developments.

It also highlighted the case for improvements in the range of lending instruments available, for an increase in the Fund's lending capacity and for institutional reform within the Fund.

The year 2010 saw a surge in IMF lending. The major arrangements put in place in 2010 were for Greece, Ireland, Mexico, Poland and Ukraine. The arrangements for Ireland (€19.3 billion in SDR) were provided through the Extended Fund Facility (EFF), a lending instrument that seeks to address medium-term needs. The IMF approved a three-year EFF arrangement for Ireland, under which the Fund will make €22.5 billion available. This is part of the overall financial package agreed under the Programme for Financial Assistance for Ireland with the Fund and European partners. The total funding being provided under the programme was €85 billion and was broken down as follows.

> **Task**
> Read the IMF's current analysis of Ireland at www.imf.org/external/country/irl/index.htm.

	Joint EU–IMF Programme for Financial Assistance for Ireland
€22.5 billion	European Financial Stability Mechanism (EFSM)
€17.7 billion	European Financial Stability Facility (EFSF)
€4.8 billion	Bilateral loans from the UK, Sweden and Denmark
€22.5 billion	IMF
€17.5 billion	State's contribution from the National Pensions Reserve Fund and other domestic cash resources

Positive Economics

EXAM ✓ Question 7(c), 2007 (20 marks)

The enlargement of the European Union (EU) continues with the addition of Bulgaria and Romania in January 2007. There are now 27 member states. Discuss **four** economic consequences for the Irish economy of the EU enlargement process.

Solution

Positive consequences	Negative consequences
Larger market: Resulting in increased sales opportunities for Irish firms. Irish consumers now have the opportunity to avail of a larger variety of goods and services.	**Lower costs of production:** Firms in the new member states have lower costs of production, making it difficult for Irish firms to compete with them.
Profitable investment opportunities: Irish firms may see that their profits could increase if they made investments in the new member countries.	**Increased competition:** Due to the higher cost base facing Irish firms, Irish consumers may travel to avail of cheaper services, resulting in reduced demand for Irish firms, e.g. dental/health services.
Source of labour/new skills: Irish firms may be able to meet their labour shortages by employing citizens from these countries/new skills may be available.	**Decline in funds for investment in Ireland:** Irish citizens may invest in the new member states, resulting in less funds being available for investment at home.
Wage demands moderate: If labour from these countries becomes available to Irish firms, this may ease the pressure on labour shortages and to a possible moderation in wage demands within Ireland.	**Agriculture:** As more EU funds will be needed in new states to develop their agriculture, this may result in less funds being available for Irish agriculture.
Educational opportunities: With new members, Irish third-level students now have the opportunity to pursue part of their studies in these countries – strengthening their opportunities for learning.	**Irish firms become more peripheral:** Ireland is one of the few EU member states not connected by land, so the transport costs involved in trade act as a further deterrent to trade.
	EU Structural Funds: The new members will require a greater proportion of these funds to develop their economies, thereby reducing the funds available for existing members, including Ireland. As the

29: The Global Economic System

Positive consequences	Negative consequences
• **Expansion of trade:** Enlargement means greater peace within the EU. This reduces uncertainty, which may encourage greater trade, resulting in economic growth and a growth in international trade.	EU requires greater finance, it may be necessary for Ireland to become a net contributor to the EU. • **Pressure on state's infrastructure:** Given that the new members have higher unemployment rates than Ireland, we can expect an increase in immigration. This may put increased pressure on the state's infrastructure, i.e. the health and education sectors.

EXAM ✓ Question 7(c), 2006 (25 marks)

Outline the economic role played by **two** of the following international banking organisations:

(i) The International Monetary Fund (IMF)

(ii) The World Bank

(iii) The European Central Bank (ECB)

Solution

(i) The International Monetary Fund (IMF)

- **Expansion of world trade:** The IMF encourages expansion in trade by encouraging member countries to adopt sound economic policies. It monitors economic and financial development in member countries and gives advice to its members.

- **Promote exchange rate stability:** The IMF promotes international monetary co-operation. It provides a forum for consultation on international monetary problems. It tries to maintain orderly exchange arrangements among countries and aims to avoid competitive devaluations.

- **Orderly correction of balance of payments problems:** The IMF lends to member countries with balance of payments problems to provide temporary finance and to support reform policies aimed at correcting the underlying problems.

- **Operation of a multilateral system of payments:** The IMF operates this system in respect of current transactions between members and aims to eliminate foreign exchange restrictions which may hamper the growth of world trade.

- **Provision of technical assistance and training:** Where a member needs help, the IMF will provide this assistance and training. When the Soviet Union collapsed, the IMF stepped in and set up treasury systems for their central banks to help the transition from centrally planned to marked-based economic systems.

(ii) The World Bank

- **Encourage investment funds to LDCs:** Obtains funds from the world's advanced countries and uses these resources to make loans available to LDCs so they can invest in roads, schools, etc.

- **Finance capital projects in member countries:** The World Bank gives loans to member states and to private businesses in these countries so as to assist with capital projects. Examples in Ireland in the past included the building of the original community schools by the DES.

- **Debt relief for LDCs:** The World Bank helps LDCs reduce their debt burden by extending the term of loans and/or renegotiating interest rates.

(iii) The European Central Bank (ECB)

- **Maintain price stability:** The key aim of the ECB is to maintain price stability. It does this by closely monitoring inflation in member countries and adjusting the base ECB interest rate so as to adjust spending.

- **Implements EU monetary policy:** Through its member central banks, the ECB monitors and advises on rates of interest, money supply and credit availability and it protects the value of the euro. Main measures are refinancing operations, standing facilities and minimum reserve requirements.

- **Holds and manages the official reserves of the euro area countries:** These are the EU's official holdings of gold, foreign currencies and other reserves held as security against the issue of the euro. The ECB manages these reserves on behalf of other countries.

- **Financial stability and supervision:** The member authorities must provide prudential supervision of credit institutions and ensure stability in the financial system.

- **Euro bank notes and coins:** The ECB has the exclusive right to authorise the issuance of banknotes within the euro area.

29: The Global Economic System

Questions

Short Questions

1. List the member states of the European Union.
2. List the objectives of the European Union.
3. What does CAP stand for?
4. What is the World Bank?
5. What is the IMF?

Long Questions

1. Outline the importance of membership of the European Union to Ireland.
2. Explain the role of the European Commission.
3. Explain the role of the European Parliament.
4. Discuss the role of the European Court of Auditors.
5. Evaluate the importance of the European Council of Ministers.
6. Discuss the role of the European Court of Justice.
7. Evaluate the Common Agricultural Policy.
8. Analyse the benefits of the Competition Policy.
9. Discuss the aspects of the Common Fisheries Policy.
10. Evaluate the benefits of the European Structural Policy for Ireland.
11. Explain the functions of the World Bank.
12. Explain the function of the European Investment Bank.
13. Discuss the objectives of the IMF.
14. Analyse the benefits the IMF provides to Ireland.

Chapter 30: Schools of Economic Thought

Schools of Economic Theory and Thought

The following are the main schools of economic theory and thought.

Mercantilists (1500–1780)
- They believed wealth consisted of gold and silver.
- They said countries should try to achieve a favourable balance of trade by increasing exports and lowering imports.
- They thought countries should acquire colonies to export to and thus acquire gold and silver.
- They believed a country should aim to be self-sufficient by pursuing protection policies.
- They held a view that the state should intervene to ensure a favourable balance of trade.

Physiocrats (1750–1800)
- They believed agriculture was the main source of a country's wealth.
- They promoted a laissez-faire economic system – state interference should be kept to a minimum.
- They believed the right to own private property was very important.
- They supported the idea of free competition.

Classical School (1780–1800)
- They supported the idea of a laissez-faire policy of no government interference in economic matters.

- They contributed to the labour theory of value.
- They believed that interest rates settled when savings equalled investment.
- They encouraged free international trade, i.e. no tariffs or other trade restrictions.
- They believed in the self-adjusting market mechanism, i.e. prices moved, bringing supply and demand into equilibrium.

Marxists
- They viewed history as a struggle between classes where workers would eventually control the means of production and redistribute wealth.
- They considered that labour produced a surplus value, which went to the capitalists in the form of profits.
- They believed socialism and later communism would replace capitalism, leading to a classless society with no need to struggle.

Neo-classical School
- They contributed towards the utility theory of value – the value of an item in the short run is determined by its utility and in the long run by its costs of production.
- They thought government intervention could prevent the growth of monopolies.
- They promoted the idea of quasi rent – short-term rent.
- They introduced the concept of elasticity.
- They advanced the MRP theory of wages, i.e. the price of labour is determined by what it contributes and an employer will stop employing workers when the contribution of the last worker equals the wage rate (MR = MC).
- Their main interest was on the household and firm and a focus on microeconomics began.

Keynesian School
- He thought that national income could be in equilibrium without reaching full employment.
- He opposed the classical view that in a recession with high unemployment, wages would fall, demand for labour would increase and a recovery would follow. Keynes thought that if wages fell, consumption would fall due to lower incomes and this would cause more unemployment.
- He favoured government intervention in the form of fiscal policy to stimulate demand.
- He introduced the multiplier.
- He developed the liquidity preference theory, i.e. interest rates determined by the demand for cash.
- He thought that the level of investment by entrepreneurs was influenced more by future business expectations rather than the rate of interest.

Positive Economics

Monetarists

- They believed in the use of monetary policy to control the economy and determine the level of economic activity.
- They contended that by reducing the money supply, firms and government would be unable to pay higher wages and there would be a reduction in demand pull inflation.
- They maintained that a fall in prices makes a country's exports more favourable, which should lead to increased exports and jobs.
- They believed stable prices would create a climate that encourages investment.
- They promoted the privatisation of state firms rather than government intervention in economic affairs.

Supply Siders

- They agreed with Say's law that supply creates its own demand and advocated an expansion of supply and not demand as a solution to economic problems.
- They maintained that government should introduce tax cuts to stimulate enterprise and create jobs. As a result, employment would rise and so would tax revenue.
- They promoted the deregulation of markets and the privatisation of state companies.

Economist	Main ideas
Thomas Mun	Encouraged trade surplus and self-sufficiency.
James Stuart	Government intervention.
François Quesnay	Agriculture – source of wealth. *Tableau Économique* – similar to the circular flow of income.
Jacques Turgot	Law of diminishing marginal returns as applied to agriculture. Non-government interference.
Adam Smith	Division of labour. Labour theory of value. Limited government interference. Canons of taxation.
Robert Thomas Malthus	Population grows faster than food supply. Iron law of wages.
David Ricardo	Law of comparative advantage. Theory of rent.
John Baptiste Say	Production created its own demand and therefore economic crises could not exist. Identified enterprise as the fourth factor of production.

30: Schools of Economic Thought

Economist	Main ideas
John Mill	Wages fund theory. Advocated free trade.
Karl Marx	Conflict between classes would lead to the replacement of capitalism by socialism.
Alfred Marshall	Marginal revenue productivity. Utility theory of value. Quasi rent. Elasticity, consumer surplus, long and short run.
James Bates Clark	Marginal productivity theory of wages. The accelerator principle.
John Maynard Keynes	Favoured government intervention in economic affairs through fiscal policy. Liquidity preference theory. National income could be in equilibrium at less than full employment. Multiplier.
Milton Friedman	Advocated the use of monetary policy. Control the money supply. Prices will stabilise, leading to an environment that encourages economic growth.

Three Main Economic Systems

Through their writings, the above economists have contributed significantly to the development of economic science. Their views have influenced how economic systems in countries are structured. The following are the three main systems that can be found in economies throughout the world.

Free Enterprise

A **FREE ENTERPRISE ECONOMY** is where private businesspeople make the decisions on the goods and services to be produced, e.g. the US. (This is sometimes known as a capitalist system.)

CHARACTERISTICS OF A FREE ENTERPRISE ECONOMY

- **The market mechanism:** Resources are allocated through the market/price mechanism – what the market (consumers) desire is what's produced.

- **Ownership of the factors of production:** Nearly all the factors of production are privately owned, e.g. Dunnes Stores is privately owned.

Positive Economics

St Stephen's Green, Dublin

- **Limited government interference:** The government exists to supply public goods, e.g. libraries and public parks, provide a legal framework within which markets can work, e.g. competition laws, and prevent the creation of monopolies (where one firm dominates the market).

- **Decentralised decision-making:** The allocation of scarce resources, the decisions on what to produce, how to produce and who gets the commodities are decided by the individuals/entrepreneurs.

- **Citizens are motivated by self-interest:** Consumers, producers and property owners are motivated by self-interest. Consumers aim to maximise utility (the satisfaction they get from consuming goods), producers aim to maximise profit and owners of factors of production aim to maximise their return.

Advantages of a Free Enterprise System

- **Improved choice:** Consumers with income have a wide choice of goods and services.

- **Greater efficiency:** Incentives exist for producers to be efficient. Those who are inefficient will be forced out by lower costs.

- **Continuous innovation:** Producers who are innovative will be rewarded through increased sales in the market.

- **Creates economic growth:** As all individuals are motivated by self-interest, each will strive towards their maximum efficiency and so aid economic growth.

- **Less bureaucracy:** As decisions are made by individuals within the society, the costs of a large administration to manage matters is significantly reduced.

Disadvantages of a Free Enterprise System

- **Distribution of income/wealth inequality:** Resources are allocated to those with spending power. Individuals who can't supply a factor of production have no income.

- **Lack of essential public services:** If an activity does not make a profit, it may not be available, e.g. education, health services – the government must provide these.

- **Vital services should not be in private hands:** It may be desirable to have certain services under government control and not in private hands, e.g. defence, judiciary, police.

Four Courts, Dublin

- **Growth of monopolies:** Some firms or groups of workers may try to gain control over individual markets, e.g. in some cases, large multinationals buy small companies so that they wouldn't grow large enough to threaten their market share.

- **Social costs of commodities are ignored:** Producers and consumers may pollute the environment and without government regulation, individuals would not pay additional costs to be more environmentally friendly. This may happen in economies where the principle of 'polluter pays' does not apply.

- **Unemployment/inflation:** If entrepreneurs choose the lowest cost of production or are pessimistic about profitability, then workers may become unemployed. If shortages occur, inflation may result.

Command/Centrally Planned Economy

CHARACTERISTICS OF A COMMAND/CENTRALLY PLANNED ECONOMY

> A **COMMAND/CENTRALLY PLANNED ECONOMY** is where the government makes the decisions on the goods and services to be produced, e.g. Cuba and North Korea. (This is sometimes known as a communist/socialist system.)

- **Planning mechanism:** Resources are allocated by the state through a planning mechanism, e.g. a government department is charged with this task.

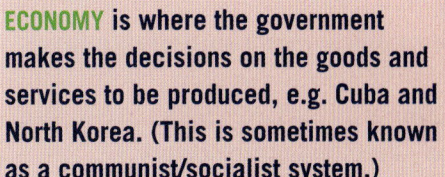

- **Ownership of factors of production:** All the factors of production are owned by the state apart from labour, though the use of labour can be directed by the state.

- **Motivated by the common good:** Consumers, workers and government are assumed to be selfless and co-operating together to work for the common good.

- **Maximum government interference:** Government exists to regulate all economic activity.

- **Centralised decision-making:** The allocation of resources, the decisions on what to produce, how to produce and who gets what commodities are decided by the state.

ADVANTAGES OF A COMMAND/CENTRALLY PLANNED ECONOMY

- **Reduced inequalities in society/more even distribution of wealth:** The government may place a great emphasis on providing all citizens with a minimum standard of living, e.g. subsidising essential food and housing.

- **Provision of essential services:** The state may provide services to citizens that it considers vital, such as health care, education and public infrastructure.

- **Economies of scale:** The large scale of production may mean that the government benefits from economies of scale (savings due to large-scale production). The government may be more efficient in the provision of commodities that require a large capital investment, e.g. energy generation, roads.

- **Full employment:** Historically, command/centrally planned economies were able to achieve full employment while those economies considered to be free enterprise suffered from unemployment.

Disadvantages of a Command/Centrally Planned Economy

- **Shortages in goods and services:** Because the state may limit prices, there may be excess demand and so shortages develop and the available goods may be allocated by a queuing system.

- **Restricted choice/freedom for individuals:** Workers may be allocated particular jobs or in certain areas and may be restricted in their ability to change jobs by state requirements. Consumers will have little say in what products and services are produced and the availability of some goods may be quite restricted.

- **Inefficiency:** Because there is little incentive for enterprise and innovation, individuals and firms are not encouraged to take risks, work harder or innovate.

- **Low economic growth:** As all individuals are not motivated by self-interest, this may result in reduced economic activity, in turn resulting in poor economic growth rates.

- **Bureaucracy/corruption/high taxes:** With so many decisions to be made, it may mean that the system becomes overly bureaucratic, further reducing incentives to work or be innovative. Taxes may have to rise to fund the administration involved. Corruption may develop within society.

Do you think that Ireland is moving towards a more free enterprise economic system or a more centrally planned economic system?

Ireland moving towards free enterprise:
- Privatisation of state companies, e.g. Eircom, Aer Lingus.
- Public Private Partnerships, e.g. building school, hospitals and toll roads.
- Deregulation of markets/allowing competition into the industry, e.g. deregulation of the taxi industry, allowing competitors into electricity generation and telecommunications networks.
- Encouraging entrepreneurship, e.g. County Enterprise Boards, changing curricula in schools, lowering PRSI and corporation tax.

Ireland moving towards a centrally planned economy:
- Increasing legislative framework, e.g. introduction of minimum wage rate, emergency legislation regarding VHI/Quinn health insurance.
- Appointment of regulators establishing tribunals of enquiry, e.g. regulator for aviation or financial services. Thousands of enquiries are currently examining the abuses of the free market system.
- Fear of the 'nanny state' – individuals may feel that much of our daily lives is controlled/interfered with by the state, e.g. smoking laws, planning laws.

Mixed Economy

A **MIXED ECONOMY** is an economy that incorporates elements of both central planning (government involvement) and private enterprise in its economic system.

ADVANTAGES OF A MIXED ECONOMY
- Efficiency is encouraged by free enterprise with regulation from the central government.
- Entrepreneurial talent is encouraged.
- Ensures a fairer distribution of wealth within the country rather than a totally free enterprise economy.
- Regulation by the government is essential to limit possible abuses of the market.
- Provision of essential services may be provided by the government.

DISADVANTAGES OF A MIXED ECONOMY
- The government may be forced to provide financial support to unsuccessful enterprises in the short term, which would cost the public in the long term.
- A large public sector and private sector may be politically divisive, which could affect how economic problems are solved.
- State intervention may result in higher taxes/bureaucracy/inefficiencies.

EXAM ✓ Question 4(b)(i), 2007 (15 marks)

'The Irish economy can be described as a **mixed economy**'. Outline **four** examples of economic activity in the Irish economy to support this view.

Solution

Any four of the following points would be an acceptable answer.

- **Existence of social partnership:** Allows for the involvement of the government and other social partners to set and achieve targets over a specified period of time.
- **Existence of semi-state bodies and private enterprises side by side:** Producing goods and services in industries that can be both profitable and unprofitable, including transport, energy and communications.

- **Government departments/various regulators:** Regulate economic activities through their actions, e.g. the financial services regulator.

- **Legislation:** Controls the activities of all individuals/firms, such as the various labour laws, e.g. minimum wage law, planning laws, Companies Acts.

- **Use of taxation/government expenditure:** The use of fiscal policy by the government affects economic activity and can alter market outcomes.

Questions

Short Questions

1. Define a mixed economy.
2. Define a centrally planned economy.
3. Define a free enterprise economy.
4. Which economist do you associate with the following?
   (a) Canons of taxation
   (b) Liquidity preference theory
   (c) The accelerator principle
   (d) Elasticity
   (e) The iron law of wages
   (f) Advocated monetary policy
   (g) View of society as a struggle between classes
   (h) Supply creates its own demand
   (i) The multiplier
5. What schools of economic thought do you associate with the following ideas?
   (a) Wealth consists of gold and silver
   (b) Quasi rent
   (c) Agriculture is the main source of wealth
   (d) Level of investment is influenced by business expectations
   (e) Self-adjusting market mechanism
   (f) Stable prices encourage investment
   (g) Socialism would replace capitalism
   (h) Promotes a laissez-faire economic system
   (i) Deregulation of markets and privatisation of state companies

30: Schools of Economic Thought

Long Questions

1. Do you consider the Irish economy to be moving more towards free enterprise or a centrally planned economy in recent years? Explain your answer with appropriate examples.
2. In relation to any one of the economic systems, outline two possible economic advantages and two possible economic disadvantages.
3. Write a note on the Keynesian school of economics.
4. Contrast the views of the Mercantalists and Physiocrats.
5. Explain three contributions of each of the following economists.
   (a) Keynes
   (b) Smith
   (c) Marshall
   (d) Friedman
   (e) Malthus
6. Is Malthus's theory on population relevant to today? Discuss.
7. Outline three contributions of the 'Supply Siders'.

Chapter 31: Exam Technique and Preparation

Introduction

A comprehensive knowledge of economics is not the only key to success in the Leaving Certificate examination. It is vital that you apply your knowledge and the material that you have studied to a strategy that will allow you to obtain a satisfactory result in your examination.

Revision Does Not Start Just Before Exams, But Well Before Exams!

Between your very first class of economics and the day you sit your Leaving Cert paper, you have hundreds of opportunities to make the process of revision as easy, effective and stress free as you want.

A revision timetable is a key element in your preparation. Take one topic at a time, study the content and memorise the key sections of that topic. Stick with your revision plan and practise questions on each topic from the exam papers. This will improve your ability to express your thoughts clearly.

Think smart and use your time wisely. For example, if a teacher brings up a definition as part of an explanation of a topic, try to remember it in your head. This is free revision time!

Use as Many Memory Hooks as You Can

For example:

- In the canons of taxation, there are two concepts that begin with 'c' and two with 'e'.
- Use **SPECS** when explaining equilibrium position in market structures.
- There are three steps to an inductive theory, so if you only have two points, there is something missing!

31: Exam Technique and Preparation

One-word Answers Are Unacceptable

A good writing style is very important. You must develop all answers: detailed and relevant points are required for answers, even for short questions. A good rule of thumb is to fill the space provided.

> **Example** **State one reason why prices of land for housing development have fallen in recent years.**
>
> **Answer** Credit crunch. (This answer gets you only half the marks at most.)
>
> **Answer** Credit crunch – difficulty in getting mortgages has resulted in a decline in demand for housing. (This answer will get you full marks as you have stated the reason and fully explained the answer.)

State and Explain

Candidates need to show presentation of work, i.e. you must **state and explain** in every answer – even short answers! Ensure your headings are clear (e.g. in red pen) with the explanation following (e.g. in blue/black pen). It is important to illustrate both a heading and explanation, as the method in which marks are allocated may be 2 marks for a heading and 3 marks for a clear and detailed explanation.

Use Bullet Point Answers

Students may prefer to write essay-style answers. Our advice – **DON'T!** Bullet point answers are preferred to ensure that you have a clear heading. This allows your explanation to be focused on one idea only and prevents you from duplicating points. Your answer should contain evidence of critical thinking and research.

Give Examples

Give examples, even if not required, as it will strengthen the answer. Make sure to **always** give examples when asked, as marks will be allocated for these examples.

> **Example** **Distinguish between fixed capital and social capital using relevant examples.**
>
> **Solution**
> - Fixed capital: This is the stock of fixed assets, e.g. plant, equipment and tools.
> - Social capital: This is the assets/wealth owned by the community/society in general, e.g. hospitals, parks, roads.

Label All Diagrams

Diagrams should be clear, large and properly labelled. Ensure each axis is labelled, e.g. P (price) and Q (quantity) on your demand/supply curves. Label each element clearly, e.g. MC, MR. With regard to demand and supply, if you are illustrating equilibrium, ensure that you clearly illustrate the equilibrium point, price and quantity. Double check that you have labelled **everything** on your diagrams.

Practise Explanations of the Diagrams Drawn

Pay particular attention to the explanations of the diagrams throughout the book. Learn the explanations to the diagrams for all market structures, e.g. perfect competition, imperfect competition, oligopoly, monopoly. Ensure you can also clearly illustrate and distinguish between short run and long run.

Where Applicable, Diagrams Must Be Graduated

Take the demand curve, for example – some years you may be required to have graduated curves, i.e. both the horizontal and vertical axis must be numbered in a logical and progressive sequence. As you can never be sure if this is required in the exam, to be safe, always draw a graduated curve where you see fit.

Ensure You Link Answers to the Question Asked

For example, if Ireland is stated in the question, then focus on it. It is important to always read the question carefully and relate your answer to the said question.

Example: Outline two measures the Irish government could take to increase consumer spending in the economy.

Solution:
- **Facilitate lending by the financial institution:** By assisting the financial institutions, the government may encourage them to give credit, which will lead to an increased supply of funds by borrowers/consumers.
- **Decrease direct taxes:** If the government decreases direct taxes, e.g. income tax, or increases the minimum wage, this would increase consumers' disposable incomes and so encourage spending.

Note:

The answer had to relate to the question, i.e. the answers had to relate to the government as well as to the Irish context. Always relate answers to what you are being asked.

Don't Wander Off the Point

For example, don't give deflation as an effect of something and continue to talk about deflation rather than the specific topic asked. You will only be awarded marks for relevant information and your time is precious. Stick to the question.

Identify the Outcome Verb

Before answering the question, identify and highlight the key outcome verb, e.g. analyse, compare, evaluate, discuss, outline, explain. Know exactly what the word means in the context of the question.

Keep Up to Date with Topics of Current Relevance

This could include such topics as price levels, exchange rates, interest rates, unemployment figures, economic growth figures (e.g. GDP, GNP), government budgetary position, etc. If you decide to do a question on the paper that requires any of the above current knowledge, it **must be current, exact and detailed**. The figures you should use in the exam should be the **latest** figures – you need your figures to correlate to the marking scheme. You can keep up to date with all this relevant information through www.edcodigital.ie.

Align Detail of Answer and Time to Available Marks

The general rule is that if there are 20 marks, give 4 points at 5 marks each (2 marks to state and 3 marks to explain for each point). This is generally true for 90% of the paper. However, there can be exceptions.

A safe rule to consider is to always give an extra point where possible. This covers you for all possibilities. It is impossible to know where on the paper this may occur, so give an extra point for good luck!

Apportion your time to marks allocated in order to give yourself sufficient time to answer all questions.

> **Example** **Discuss the characteristics of a good taxation system. (20 marks)**
> We would assume that this would be *4 points @ 5 marks each*. Not the case! Here, the examiner required **5 points @ 4 marks** each.

Know This Book Inside Out!

This book is a comprehensive toolkit for you to achieve the best possible result.

GOOD LUCK!

Glossary

accelerator principle An increase in demand for final goods results in a more than proportionate increase in demand for capital goods.

ad valorem tax A tax that increases with the value of the good.

aggregate demand The different quantities of a good that all consumers in the market are prepared to buy at each price. It is derived by adding together all the individual quantities demanded for the good at each price.

ageing population An ageing population is living longer, has an average life span that is increasing and has a growing percentage of the population who are in an older age bracket.

An Post A national organisation that provides a wide range of services that encompass postal, communication, retail and financial services.

average cost Total cost divided by quantity.

average propensity to consume The proportion of total income spent.

balance of payments A record of a country's monetary transactions with the rest of the world for a period of time (usually one year).

balance of trade The difference between the value of visible exports and visible imports.

balanced current budget One in which planned current government revenue equals planned current government expenditure.

barter The direct exchange of goods and services for other goods and services.

benefit-in-kind Non-monetary payment for providing a factor of production.

birth rate The average number of live births per 1,000 people per year.

black/shadow economy All economic activity that goes unrecorded in the national income accounts.

broaden the tax base Increase the number of people/areas on which the tax is levied/in the tax net.

building society An institution owned by its members as a mutual organisation.

capital Anything manmade that assists in the production of wealth.

capital account An account of a country's receipts and payments for capital items.

capital adequacy ratio The percentage of a bank's capital to its risk-weighted assets.

capital budget Outlines the government's planned expenditure and receipts on items not used up during the year, but which increase the productive capacity of the country.

capital deepening A scenario whereby the amount of capital increases, resulting in more capital per worker in the economy.

capital widening A scenario whereby the amount of capital per worker remains unchanged. An increase in the capital stock leaves the capital/labour ratio unchanged.

cartels/collusion Firms may enter into trade agreements with similar companies and divide up the market, thus ensuring limited or no competition exists.

census The official count of the nation's people and a compilation of economic, social and other data, used by the government in the formulation of development policies and plans. It occurs every four years.

Glossary

circular flow of income The flow of receipts and expenditure between companies and households.

closed economy An economy that does not engage in any international trade.

command/centrally planned economy An economy where the government makes the decisions on the goods and services to be produced.

commercial banks Institutions that provide deposit/lending services to personal consumers/businesses.

complementary goods Goods that are used jointly. The use of one involves the use of the other. An increase in the price of one good leads to a decrease in the quantity demanded for the other good.

composite demand When a commodity is required for a number of different uses.

constant tax price index A price index that keeps the indirect tax part of a price increase constant.

consumer An individual who makes the decision whether to buy goods or services.

consumer price index The official measure of inflation in Ireland. It measures the price changes of goods and services typically consumed by all consumers living in rural/urban areas, high/low income earners and from all age groups.

consumer surplus The benefit to consumers due to the difference between what consumers actually pay to consume a good and what they would have been willing to pay rather than go without the good.

cost push factors If a company experiences an increase in its cost of production, then it will probably pass on this increase by raising the selling price of the final good sold to the consumer.

credit union A group of people who save together and lend to each other.

cross elasticity of demand The proportionate/percentage change in the quantity demanded for one good caused by the proportionate/percentage change in the price of another good.

current budget The government's expected (planned) revenues and expenditures for day-to-day purposes for the forthcoming year.

current budget deficit One in which current planned government expenditure exceeds current planned government revenue.

current budget surplus One in which current planned government revenue exceeds current planned government expenditure.

current expenditure Is spent during the year on day-to-day items.

current revenue Money collected via direct and indirect taxes as well as other income during the year.

current transfers Subsidies and monies receivable from and taxes payable to the European Union.

cyclical unemployment Results from reduced demand for goods and services during an economic recession.

death rate The average number of deaths per 1,000 people per year.

debt securities Loans that can be bought or sold on a stock exchange.

deductive Examine a hypothesises, apply it to a situation and deduct a conclusion.

default Refers to not making good on a financial agreement.

deflationary budget One where revenue expenditure is decreasing or taxation is increasing. One in which more money is being leaked out of the economy than injected in and which contracts economic growth.

Positive Economics

demand   The number of units of goods a consumer will buy at various prices.

demand curve   A graph illustrating the demand for a good at various prices at any given time.

demand pull factors   If aggregate demand is greater than aggregate supply, prices will be forced upwards.

demand schedule   A table that shows the different quantities demanded for a good at various market prices at any given time.

demography   The statistical study of human population.

density of population   The average number of people per square kilometre.

dependency ratio   The ratio of the number of people aged under 15 and over 65 to the number of people aged between 15 and 65.

deposit facility   The facility to make overnight deposits with the ECB.

deregulation   A form of direct intervention that involves the government changing laws and practices which it deems to be detrimental to competition.

derived demand   When one commodity is an essential part of another commodity and it is demanded not for its own sake but because it is required to manufacture another good.

devaluation   The decrease in the value of one currency relative to that of other currencies.

direct investment   The net investment in buildings and machinery by foreign companies operating in a country.

direct tax   Tax on income and wealth.

dumping   This occurs when goods from a country are sold abroad at a lower price than the price charged for them at home.

duopoly   An oligopoly with just two participants.

economic development   An increase in GNP per head of population that is accompanied by a fundamental change in the structure of society.

economic good   A product or service that commands a price, gives utility and is transferable.

economic growth   An increase in GNP per head of population without any changes to the structure of society.

economic laws   Statements that under certain conditions, certain people will behave in a certain way.

economic rent   Any earnings of a factor of production above its supply price.

economic sustainability   Using resources to the maximum; responsible use so that the country would flourish into long-term prosperity.

economics   A social science that studies the allocation of scarce resources that have alternative uses.

effective demand   Consumers must be willing to buy *and* be capable of paying the price set by the supplier.

elasticity   A measure of responsiveness (sensitivity) of quantity demanded of a good to a change in some variable.

emigration   Irish citizens leaving Ireland and moving to live abroad.

enterprise   The factor of production that takes the initiative and bears the risk involved in setting up a business to produce goods.

equi-marginal utility   The principle of equi-marginal utility explains the behaviour of a consumer in distributing their limited income among various goods, taking into account the price and marginal utility of the goods.

equilibrium   If no interference in the market occurs (by the government or another agency), price will eventually settle at the level where quantity demanded equals quantity supplied. This position, where there is no tendency for prices to change, is called the market equilibrium.

euro interbank offered rate (Euribor) The interest rate at which banks offer to lend funds to other banks in the euro wholesale money market or interbank market.

European Investment Bank The European Union's financing institution.

European Regional Development Fund The promotion of economic and social cohesion within the European Union through the reduction of imbalances between regions or social groups.

European Social Fund The European Union's financial instrument for investing in people.

European Union An economic and political union that has as its main aim total co-operation among its members on all economic, political and monetary matters. The European Union is a free trade area where goods and services can freely move between member states. It imposes tariffs on imports from non-member countries (a customs union). There is also freedom of movement of labour and capital. Therefore, the European Union is a common market.

exchange rate Price of one currency in terms of another.

exchange rate policy This policy is directly controlled by the ECB and refers to the devaluation (making the currency worth less) and revaluation (making the currency worth more) of the euro in terms of other currencies.

exchequer balance The difference between (current and capital receipts) and (current and capital expenditure).

exchequer borrowing requirement Borrowing by the state to finance a current budget deficit and borrowing for capital purposes.

expenditure method The sum of all expenditure made by citizens.

explicit costs Costs incurred by a firm when it pays an amount of money for something.

exporting The production and sale of Irish goods and services to other countries.

external diseconomies of consumption An action taken by a consumer that imposes a cost on third parties for which they are not compensated.

external diseconomies of production A producer carries out an activity and imposes a cost on third parties for which they are not compensated.

external diseconomies of scale Forces outside a firm that cause the average/unit cost of that firm to increase as the industry grows in size.

external economies of consumption A consumer undertakes an action and it benefits third parties, for which the consumer is not compensated, e.g. a person volunteers the management skills they learned at work to co-ordinate a local youth club.

external economies of production Actions taken by producers that result in benefits to third parties for which the producer is not compensated.

external economies of scale Forces outside a firm that cause the average/unit cost of that firm to decline as the industry grows in size.

externalities Unintended costs or benefits to third parties.

factor costs The cost of the four factors of production (land, labour, capital and enterprise).

factor markets Markets on which the factors of production are bought and sold.

Positive Economics

factors affecting demand Price of the good, price of other goods, income of the consumer, expectations, tastes, unplanned factors and government regulations.

factors affecting elasticity of supply Firms' capacity, mobility of factors of production, time period, nature of the product, storage costs, cost conditions, products in joint supply, stock.

factors affecting price elasticity of demand Availability of close substitutes, complementary goods, luxury or necessity, proportion of income, durability, expectations of price change, length of time allowed for adjustment to price change, consumer purchasing habits/brand loyalty.

factors affecting supply of a good Price of the good, price of other goods, cost of production, unplanned factors, state of technology, taxation, objectives of the firm and number of firms in the industry.

fertility rate The number of live births in a geographic area in a year per 1,000 women of childbearing age.

fiduciary issue The proportion of a country's currency that is not backed by gold but by foreign currencies and securities. This is a concept based on trust.

final markets The buying and selling of finished goods takes place in final markets.

financial account This account deals with transactions in foreign financial assets and liabilities.

fiscal policy Actions taken by the government that influence the timing, magnitude and structure of current revenue (money in) and expenditure (money out).

fixed capital Stock of fixed assets such as plant, equipment and tools and private capital are assets owned by individuals.

fixed costs Costs that don't change as output changes.

fixed exchange rate An exchange rate regime whereby the values of currencies are agreed upon and each participating country undertakes to exchange the currency at that value.

floating An exchange rate regime whereby currencies fluctuate in value and the equilibrium rate is decided by the market forces of supply and demand.

free enterprise An economy where private businesspeople make the decisions on the goods and services to be produced.

free trade States that there are no barriers to the movement of goods and services between countries.

frictional unemployment A situation whereby there is a reduction in the demand for labour in a particular occupation, though jobs are available in other occupations and/or firms.

full employment A situation in which employment is available for all those prepared to work at existing wage levels. It occurs when everybody seeking work is employed at existing wage rates.

general government balance The net borrowing (surplus) of central and local government plus the net surplus of the Social Insurance Fund.

general government debt The general government debt includes the national debt as well as local government debt and some minor liabilities of government. In addition, the general government debt is a gross measure of debt and does not allow the netting of cash balances.

general government debt/GDP The general government debt includes the national debt as well as local government debt and some minor liabilities of government as a proportion of GDP.

general government deficit Combined deficit (or surplus) of central and local government.

general government deficit/GDP Combined deficit (or surplus) of central and local government as a proportion of GDP.

geographical mobility The ease with which a factor can move from one area to another.

Giffen goods Goods with a positive price effect, i.e. more is bought as the price rises and less is bought as the price falls.

Gold Standard A currency where notes were fully backed and redeemable in an equivalent amount of gold.

gross domestic product at factor cost The total value of input or expenditure within the country as a result of engaging in current economic activity in one year, valued at payments to factors of production. It is the output produced by the factors of production in the domestic economy irrespective of whether the factors are owned by Irish nationals or non-nationals, valued at payments to factors of production.

gross domestic product at market prices The total value of input or expenditure within the country as a result of engaging in current economic activity in one year, valued at current market prices **OR** the output produced by the factors of production in the domestic economy irrespective of whether the factors are owned by Irish nationals or non-nationals, valued at current market prices.

gross national income This is comprised of domestic and foreign income earned by the resident population of a country.

gross national product at factor cost The total value of output or expenditure valued at payments to factors of production, produced by Irish-owned factors of production, **OR** the value of the total goods and services produced in an economy over a specified period of time (e.g. a year) valued at payments to factors of production, produced by Irish-owned factors of production.

gross national product at market prices The total value of output or expenditure valued at today's market prices, produced by Irish-owned factors of production, before any adjustments are made for taxation, subsidies or depreciation **OR** the value of the total goods and services produced in an economy over a specified period of time (e.g. a year) valued at current/today's market prices, produced by Irish-owned factors of production.

Harmonised Index of Consumer Prices The HICP is the consumer price index but excludes mortgage interest, building materials, concrete blocks, union subscriptions, motor taxation and the non-service elements of motor and house insurance.

Human Development Index A summary composite index that measures a country's average achievements in three basic aspects of human development.

immigration Citizens of other countries entering Ireland to live.

imperfect competition Long run equilibrium occurs where MC = MR and AR = AC. Many producers supplying close but not perfect substitutes.

imperfect competition and monopoly MRP MPP × MR.

implicit costs Costs that do not involve the paying out of money.

importing The buying of foreign-produced goods and services.

Positive Economics

imposition/impact of taxation   The individual, firm, service or good on which the tax is levied.

incidence of taxation   The person who actually bears/pays the tax. Whether the impact and the incidence of taxation are the same depends on the relative price elasticity of demand and supply e.g. a good with an inelastic demand curve.

income   A flow of wealth that is received regularly for providing a factor of production.

income effect   The effect on the demand for a good arising from a change in the consumer's real income as a result of a change in the price of a good.

income elasticity of demand   YED measures the proportionate/percentage change in the demand for a good caused by the proportionate/percentage change in the income (Y) of consumers.

income method   The sum of income earned by the four factors of production (land, labour, capital and enterprise).

indirect tax   A tax on transactions.

individual demand   The quantities of a good that an individual consumer is prepared to buy at each price.

individual demand schedule   A list of the different quantities of a good that an individual consumer is prepared to buy at each price.

individual supply   The quantity of a good supplied by an individual firm at different prices.

individual supply curve   A graph illustrating the different quantities of a good made available for sale by an individual firm at various market prices at any given time.

individual supply schedule   A table illustrating the different quantities of a good made available for sale by an individual firm at various market prices at any given time.

inductive   Examine real situations and come up with generalisations.

industrial bank   An institution that specialises in providing instalment credit to personal borrowers and companies in the form of fixed-term loans and hire purchase facilities.

industry   All the firms in the marketplace selling the same product or service.

infant mortality   The number of children out of every 1,000 born alive who die on or before their first birthday.

inferior good   A good with a negative income effect. A rise in income causes less of these goods to be demanded, while a fall in income causes more of these goods to be demanded.

inflation   A steady and persistent increase in the general level of prices. Inflation is the rate at which your money loses its ability to buy things.

inflationary budget   One in which more money is being injected into the economy than is leaked and hence stimulates economic growth.

institutional unemployment   Arises because there are obstacles preventing the mobility of labour.

interbank market   Short-term money or foreign exchange markets that are only accessible to banks or financial institutions.

interest   Payment for capital.

intermediate markets   The buying and selling of partly finished goods takes place in this market.

internal diseconomies of scale   Forces within a firm that cause the average/unit cost of that firm to increase as it grows in size.

Glossary

internal economies of scale   Forces within a firm that cause the average/unit cost of that firm to decline as it grows in size.

International Monetary Fund   A co-operative intergovernmental institution that provides financial assistance and advice to member countries.

investment   The production of capital goods or any addition to capital stock in the economy.

invisible exports   Services sold to other countries.

invisible imports   Services that are bought from foreign countries.

joint demand   When the demand for one commodity is joined with the demand for another.

kinked demand curve   Two distinct demand curves crossing at the point where price is set.

labour   The human activity directed towards the production of wealth. Its payment is the wage rate.

labour hoarding   A firm may continue to employ labour, even though it is unprofitable to do so.

land   Anything provided by nature that helps in the production of wealth.

law of absolute advantage   States that each country should specialise in the production of that good in which it has an absolute advantage, i.e. if it can produce the good more efficiently/cheaply (at a lower cost) than other countries.

law of comparative advantage   Assuming there is free trade, a country should specialise in the production of those goods and services in which it is relatively most efficient and trade for the remainder of its requirements.

law of demand   An increase in price leads to a decrease in quantity demanded or a decrease in price leads to an increase in quantity demanded.

law of diminishing marginal return   As more and more of a variable factor is added to a fixed factor, at some stage the increase in output caused by the last unit of the variable factor will begin to decline.

law of diminishing marginal utility   As more units of a good are consumed, a point will eventually be reached where marginal (extra) utility begins to decline.

law of diminishing returns   As more labour is applied to the production process, at some stage the return from each additional worker will begin to decline.

least developed countries   Least developed countries (LDCs) represent the poorest and weakest segment of the international community.

legal tender   Money that must be accepted if offered as payment for a purchase or settlement of a debt.

life expectancy   The number of years, based on statistical averages, that a given person of a specific age, class or other demographic variable may be expected to live.

liquidity   A bank's need to have liquid assets in order to meet the demand for cash by its customers.

Live Register   A monthly count of all persons under 65 years of age who are claiming Jobseeker's Benefit, Jobseeker's Allowance and other registrants.

loanable funds theory of interest rates   The demand for funds was created by people who wanted assets now rather than in the future, i.e. people who wanted to invest, and the supply of funds was given by people who were prepared to forego present consumption, i.e. willing to save.

Positive Economics

long run A period of time during which all the factors of production are variable in quantity.

long run average cost curve The minimum point of each SAC curve joined together.

long run supply curve of a perfectly competitive firm The portion of its marginal cost curve which lies above the lowest point of its average cost curve.

loss of competitiveness A situation where our goods abroad are less attractive to foreign buyers.

lump sum tax A lump sum tax has the characteristic that the amount is not affected by the taxpayer's action. For example, people pay the same TV license irrespective of whether they have a 40-inch flat-screen TV or a 12-inch black and white TV.

M1 (narrow) currency supply Currency in circulation as well as current account balances.

M2 currency supply M1 as well as deposits with agreed maturity up to two years, deposits redeemable at notice up to three months and post office savings accounts.

M3 currency supply M2 as well as repo agreements, money market fund shares/ units and debt securities up to two years.

macroeconomics The study of aggregates (totals) in an economy.

marginal efficiency of capital Extra profit earned as a result of employing one extra unit of capital, i.e. the marginal revenue productivity of additional capital goods minus their cost.

marginal lending facility The facility to borrow money from the ECB against appropriate collateral.

marginal physical product The extra output produced when an additional unit of a factor of production is employed.

marginal propensity to consume The proportion of each additional unit of income which is spent.

marginal propensity to import Proportion of each additional unit of income which is spent on imports.

marginal propensity to save The proportion of each additional unit of income that is saved.

marginal propensity to tax The proportion of each additional unit of income that goes on tax.

marginal revenue The change in total revenue when an extra unit of output is sold.

marginal revenue productivity The MRP of a factor is the extra revenue earned when an additional unit of a factor of production is employed.

marginal utility The addition to total utility (TU)/the extra utility received, caused by the consumption of one extra unit of a good.

market/aggregate demand schedule A list of the different quantities of a good that all consumers in the market are prepared to buy at each price. It is derived by adding together all the individual demand schedules for the good.

market/aggregate supply The quantity of a good supplied by all the firms in the market at different prices.

market/aggregate supply curve A graph illustrating the total quantities of a good all the firms in the market are willing to make available for sale at various prices at any given time.

market/aggregate supply schedule A table illustrating the total quantities of a good that all the firms in the market are willing to make available for sale at various prices at any given time.

Glossary

market prices Prices consumers pay for goods and services.

Marshall-Lerner condition A condition in which a devaluation will improve a country's balance of trade if the sum of the elasticities of demand for exports and imports is greater than 1 (in absolute terms).

merchant bank An institution that deals with the commercial banking needs of international finance, long-term company loans and stock underwriting.

microeconomics The study of how an individual producer (one firm) and a consumer make decisions and attempt to solve their economic problems.

minimum reserve requirements The ECB requires credit institutions established in the euro area to hold deposits on accounts with their national central bank.

mixed economy An economy that incorporates elements of both central planning (government involvement) and private enterprise in its economic system.

monetary policy Actions by the ECB that influence the money supply, interest rates and the availability of credit.

money Anything that is generally accepted by people in exchange for goods and services or repayment of debt. Its functions include acting as a medium, a measure, a standard and a store.

money market securities Highly liquid, short-term loans.

monopoly The industry has only one seller.

movement along a demand curve Is caused by a change in the price of the good itself.

movement along a supply curve Is caused by a change in price of the good or service.

MRP curve The demand curve for any factor of production.

MRP of labour The demand curve for labour, which is downward sloping from left to right.

MRP theory of wages States that each worker is paid an amount equal to the additional revenue that is received from the employment of the last worker, i.e. the equivalent of the value that the last worker contributes.

multiplier The number of times an injection results in an increase in income.

multiplier formula A formula derived by John Maynard Keynes to show the precise relationship between an initial injection into the circular flow of income and the eventual total increase in national income resulting from the injection.

NAMA National Asset Management Agency.

national debt Includes domestic debt, which is money borrowed from individuals and financial institutions within the geographic borders of Ireland, e.g. post office savings, and external debt, which is money borrowed from individuals and institutions outside of Ireland, e.g. foreign bondholders.

national debt/GDP This is the total amount/accumulated total of outstanding borrowing by the government as a proportion of GDP.

national income The income accruing to the permanent residents of a country from current economic activity from supplying the factors of production during a specific period, which is usually one year. It is comprised of consumption (C) + investment (I) + government current expenditure (G) + exports (X) – imports (M).

net factor income from the rest of the world This is (income earned by Irish factors of production abroad and sent home (repatriated)) minus (income earned by foreign factors of production in Ireland and sent back (repatriated) to their own country).

Positive Economics

net migration The difference between outward migration (emigration) and inward migration (immigration) during a period of time.

net national product The total joint product of the resources of land, labour, capital and enterprise for a period of time, usually one year. It is the same as national income.

neutral budget Is neither inflationary nor deflationary.

nominal interest rate The interest rate unadjusted for inflation.

non-price competition Firms compete using methods other than changing their prices, e.g. giveaways, competitions, clubs.

normal good A good that obeys the law of demand and which has a positive income effect.

normal profits The minimum amount of profit an entrepreneur must receive if they are to stay in production in the long run. It is the supply price of the factor of production enterprise.

normative statement A statement that goes beyond facts and states what ought to happen.

NTMA The National Treasury Management Agency is the treasury of the government. It manages the assets and liabilities on behalf of the Irish government as well as the National Pension Reserve Fund, NAMA and the State Claims Agency and serves many other functions as well.

occupational mobility The ease with which a factor of production can move from one occupation to another.

oligopoly A market form in which the industry is dominated by a few/small number of sellers.

open economy An economy that does engage in international trade. Exists where there are no restrictions of any kind to the free movement of goods, services and the factors of production into and out of the economy.

open market operations Selling bonds and sucking up excess liquidity in the system.

opportunity cost Cost of foregone alternatives (choice).

optimum population When the average income per head is at its highest possible level under given economic resources.

overpopulation A country is overpopulated when an increase in population causes a decrease in the average income per head under given economic resources.

participation rate Percentage of the active population in the labour force.

perfect competition A firm engaged in perfect competition has a perfectly elastic demand curve. Average revenue is equal to marginal revenue, which is the same as price.

perfect competition MRP MPP multiplied by price equals MRP. This is always the case in perfect competition.

perfect/first degree price discrimination Occurs when the seller knows the maximum price that each consumer is willing to pay rather than do without the good/service and charges that exact price, i.e. eliminates consumer surplus.

perfectly elastic Any increase in the price of a good results in its quantity falling to zero.

perfectly inelastic The proportionate/percentage change in price of a good causes no change in the quantity demanded of that good.

portfolio investment The full list of investments that an individual or business holds.

positive statement A statement of what is or was and can be confirmed or denied by an analysis of the facts.

precautionary motive for holding money People hold money in liquid form in case of emergencies.

price competition Firms compete by changing their price points, etc.

price constancy There can be many MC curves cutting the discontinuous part of the MR without affecting price and quantity; this indicates that prices can be constant although costs increase slightly.

price discrimination When goods and services are sold to different consumers at varying ratios between marginal cost and price, i.e. P/MC is not constant.

price elasticity of demand Measures the percentage/proportionate change in the demand for a good caused by the percentage/proportionate change in the price of the good itself.

price elasticity of supply Measures the relationship between the proportionate/percentage change in quantity supplied and a proportionate/percentage change in price.

price taker A firm is a price taker if it accepts the price as it is set on the market and each firm supplies such a small fraction of the market that it cannot influence the market price.

primary liquidity ratio/liquidity coverage ratio The amount of money with respect to short-term deposits that the Central Bank requires commercial banks to keep in cash form.

primary sector This refers to the extraction of wealth from nature.

private cost The cost to the firm of making the good or providing the service.

privatisation The sale or transfer of public sector assets to the private sector.

producer surplus Difference between the lowest price a supplier is willing to accept for a good and the price they actually receive.

profitability The need for a bank to make as much profit as possible from its assets to appease its shareholders.

progressive taxation A taxation measure that takes proportionately more in tax as a person's income increases.

protectionism Efforts by a government to restrict free trade, particularly imports.

public sector borrowing requirement The exchequer borrowing requirement plus borrowing for semi-state/state-sponsored bodies and local authorities.

pull factors The factors that draw a person to another country (immigration).

push factors Factors that compel people to leave their own country (emigration).

quasi economic rent Economic rent of a temporary nature.

quota A physical limit placed by a government on the amount of a certain good allowed to enter the country.

real income The purchasing power (the amount of goods and services you can buy) of a person's money income.

real interest rate Nominal rate of interest minus the rate of inflation.

regional development Aimed at ensuring that all regions of a country share in the economic development of the country and are provided with the same opportunities.

regressive taxation A taxation measure that takes proportionately less in tax as a person's income increases.

relatively elastic The proportionate/percentage change in quantity demanded of a good is greater than the proportionate/percentage change in price of the good itself.

relatively inelastic The proportionate/percentage change in quantity demanded of a good is less than the proportionate/percentage change in price of that good.

repo agreements The sale and repurchase of securities in exchange for a fixed amount of cash.

reserve assets The currency or any other store of value that is primarily used by nations for their foreign reserves.

revenue buoyancy The actual taxation revenue collected during the year that is greater than that which had been planned for.

savings Savings is income not spent (consumed).

Say's law Supply creates its own demand.

seasonal unemployment Occurs when some members of the workforce are only in employment for a certain part of the year.

second degree price discrimination Occurs when the seller lowers their price because the purchaser is buying a large quantity.

secondary sector This refers to manufacturing industries.

shift along a supply curve Is caused by a change in any non-price determinant of supply – any other variable which influences quantity supplied.

shift in the demand curve Is caused by a change in any non-price determinant of demand.

short run A period of time during which at least one factor of production is fixed in supply.

short run supply curve of a firm in perfect competition The part of the MC curve which lies above the lowest point of the average variable cost curve.

skills mismatch A labour force is not equipped with the specific skills and experience that are required by firms offering employment.

social capital The assets/wealth owned by the community or society in general.

social cost A cost to society of an action or output/cost or price that society has to pay for the existence of a particular product/the price that society has to pay as a result of the production/consumption of a commodity.

social policy The provision of income and/or services for those who, for one reason or another, would find it difficult to provide for themselves if exposed to the full rigours of the market economy.

specific tax A specific tax is applied at a fixed rate per physical unit of the good taxed, regardless of its price. For example, car tax is levied on the size of the engine irrespective of whether the car is new or 20 years old.

speculative motive for holding money People demand money (wealth in liquid form) because the return from investment (rate of interest) is too low. If the return from investment is high (high interest rates), then the demand for money will be low.

statutory minimum wage The lowest wage that an employer must pay a member of staff.

stealth tax A stealth tax is applied so that it is largely unnoticed or not recognised as a tax, e.g. money that goes to the government from the National Lottery.

structural unemployment Refers to those who become unemployed because their skills are no longer in demand due to technical progress/competition.

subsistence wages theory/iron law of wages Any increase in wages above the subsistence level would cause an increase in population, which in turn would cause wage levels to fall.

Glossary

substitute goods Goods that satisfy the same needs and thus can be considered as alternatives to each other. If an increase in the price of one good leads to an increase in the demand for another good as an alternative, then the two goods are said to be substitutes.

substitution effect As the price of a good decreases, people are likely to purchase more of this good if they are to follow the equi-marginal principle.

supernormal profit A company covers its total costs (i.e. AR > AC) and is making extra profits.

supply curve A graph illustrating the number of units of a good made available for sale at various market prices at any given time. There is a positive relationship between price and quantity supplied. The supply curve is usually upward sloping from left to right.

supply (elastic) The proportionate change in quantity supplied is greater than the proportionate change in price.

supply (inelastic) A change in the price of the good causes less than a proportionate change in the demand for the good.

supply of labour The total number of hours worked in the economy during a specific period.

supply price The supply price of a factor of production is the minimum payment necessary to bring a factor into use and maintain it in that particular use.

supply schedule A table illustrating the different quantities of a good made available for sale at various market prices at any given time.

tariff A tax on imports.

tax avoidance Arranging one's affairs within the law so as to minimise tax liabilities.

tax evasion Reducing tax liabilities by making false returns or not making any returns at all.

tax harmonisation The aim of members of the European Union and other trading blocs to move all tax rates to the same rates, i.e. align with each member state/country.

taxation revenues Monies/incomes received by the government in the form of direct and indirect taxes and used in the running of the country.

terms of trade The ratio between the average price of exports and the average price of imports. It may be expressed as the index number showing the average price of exports divided by the average price of imports.

tertiary sector This refers to the supply of services.

theory of rent As population increased, it was necessary to use inferior land for crop production as all the fertile land was being used. This occurred because the fertile land was more productive and earns rent.

theory of surplus value Employers paid subsistence wages to employees, as the wages paid to workers were far lower than the value of goods produced.

third degree price discrimination Involves dividing up the market on the basis of price elasticity of demand.

tier 1 capital Comprised of profits (i.e. retained earnings) and certain types of shares. It relates to a bank's holding of capital, i.e. security against bank lending.

total fertility rate The average number of babies born to women during their reproductive years.

trade barrier A governmental policy that affects the flow of trade.

trade bloc A group of countries sharing free trade agreements with each other.

Positive Economics

trade cycle   Recurring patterns of expansion and contraction in the economy.

trade embargo   A complete ban on the import of a particular good or goods from a country or a total ban on all trade to and from a particular country.

transactions motive for holding money   Consumers require money for everyday purchases.

transfer earnings   The earnings of a factor in the next best alternative employment **OR** what a factor must receive to keep it in its present use and prevent it from transferring to another use.

transfer payments   Payments received for which no factor of production has been supplied or offered **OR** income people received for which they did not supply goods or services.

underemployment   A situation whereby a factor of production (e.g. labour), though not actually unemployed, is working below capacity.

underpopulation   A country is underpopulated when an increase in the population causes an increase in the average income per head under given economic resources.

unemployment   The state of an individual looking for a paying job but not having one.

unitary elastic   The proportionate/percentage change in the quantity demanded of a good is equal to the proportionate/percentage change in the price of that good.

utility   The amount of benefit or satisfaction derived from the consumption of a good or service.

utility theory   Demand was determined by the utility that a good possessed.

variable costs   Costs that vary as output changes.

visible exports   Goods sold to other countries.

visible imports   Goods that are bought from foreign countries.

wage fund theory   A certain amount of money is available for distribution and wages could not be increased unless savings increased (John Stuart Mill).

want   Anything in excess of needs that is not necessary for our survival.

wealth   Total value of all assets owned by an individual or group of people.

welfare   The overall condition of well-being of an individual or group of people.

William Baumol's model of sales maximisation   Managers may be more interested in maximising sales revenue than maximising profit.

working capital   All finished goods, work in progress goods and stocks of raw materials.

World Bank   An international organisation dedicated to providing financing, advice and research to developing nations to aid their economic advancement.

zero elasticity of supply   An increase in the selling price of the good does not result in any increase in supply.

zero income elasticity of demand   Goods that people purchase when their income is low. They do not purchase additional quantities of these goods when their income increases.

Index

Accelerator Principle, 288, 496
administrative barriers, 435
ad valorem tax, 496
Advantage, Law of Absolute, 420–1, 503
   assumptions of, 420
Advantage, Law of Comparative, 186
   sources of, 426
     for the Irish economy, 426
ageing population, 409–10, 496
aggregate demand, 289, 356, 390, 496, 504
An Post, 496
AR *See* revenue
Asia Pacific Economic Co-operation (APEC), 435, 438
average cost (ATC or AC), 97–100, 109, 112, 496
   fixed (AFC), 97–100, 112
   long run (LRAC), 102–3, 106
   short run curve (SAC), 101–2
   total (ATC), 97–100
   variable(AVC), 97–100, 112
average propensity to consume (APC), 275, 496
average revenue demand curve (AR), 132, 143

balance of autonomous transactions, 447
balance of invisible trade, 431
balance of payments, 445–64, 496
   on capital account, 446
     multinationals impact on, 449
   on current account, 445–6
   on financial account, 446
balance of trade, 430, 496
balanced current budget, 331, 496
banking, 229–53, 312
   collapse, 249
   ratios, 242, 243
   regulation, 250
banks
   objectives, 244–5
   types of, 236–42
barriers to trade, 434
barter, 230–1, 496
Baumol, William, 165–6, 510
benefit-in-kind, 259, 496
birth rate, 397, 414, 496
black economy, 320, 496
budget, 325–34

budgetary process, 328
building societies, 496
Buy Irish, 274

Camacho, Danica May, 413
canons of taxation, 347
capital, 205–20, 496
   account, 496
   adequacy ratio, 243, 496
   budget, 330, 496
   deepening, 209, 496
   expenditure, 330
   revenue, 328
   types of, 206
   widening, 209, 496
cartel, 496
cashless transactions, 235
Cassel, Gustav, 456
census, 410–1, 496
Central Bank of Ireland, 239–41, 328
Central Bank Reform Act, 239
central banks, intervention of, 218
Central Statistics Office (CSO), 255, 294
centrally planned economy, 9, 487–8, 497
Chamberlain, Edward, 130
circular flow of income, 272–4, 377, 497
Clark, John Bates, 289, 485
Classical School, 482
Classical Theory, 213–4
closed economy, 497
coinage, 231
collusion, 160, 163, 496
command system economy, 9, 487–8, 497
commercial banks, 241, 497
commodity system, 230–31
Common Agricultural Policy (CAP), 470
Common Fisheries Policy, (CFP), 469
communist system, 9, 321, 487–8
competition, 178, 202
competition, imperfect, 130–9, 501
   advantages and disadvantages of, 135–6
   assumptions/characteristics of, 130–2
   compared to monopoly, 144–5, 175
   compared to perfect competition, 136–7
   equilibrium, 133–5
competition, non-price, 137, 160
competition, perfect, 116–28, 130, 133, 347, 506
   and long run, 123–5
   and short run,120–3

assumptions/characteristics of, 118–9
benefits of, 125
compared to imperfect competition, 136–7
compared to monopoly, 144
disadvantages of, 126
competition, price, 137, 160
competition, pure, 117
Competition Act 2002, 146
Competition Authority, 146
Competition Policy, 470
competitiveness, 427
complementary goods, 497
composite demand, 497
composite price index, 295–6
conspicuous consumption, 35
constant tax price index (CTPI), 303–4, 497
consumer, 11–21, 497
   equilibrium, 15
   expectation, 31–2, 35
   surplus, 23, 178
   tastes, 32, 40
consumer behaviour, assumptions about, 12
consumer price index (CPI), 297–9, 305, 497
consumer surplus, 497
consumer trends, 299
cost
   average *See* average cost
   explicit, 224
   fixed, 94–5, 97–101
   implicit, 224, 501
   marginal(MC), 100, 109–13, 132
   private, 108
   overview of, 93
   total (TC), 95, 97–100, 110
   variable, 94–5, 98–100
cost curves, 101–3
cost of living index, 299
cost of production, 92
cost push factors, 497
Council of Ministers, 468
county enterprise board, 316
credit, 243–6
credit unions, 241, 497
cross elasticity of demand (CED), 81–3, 497
currency, 232
current budget, 331–4, 497
   deficit, 333, 348, 497
current expenditure, 330–1, 497
current revenue, 328, 497
cyclical unemployment, 497

death rate, 397, 400, 497
deductive research, 5, 6, 497
default, 337, 497
deflation, 303, 304, 313

deflationary budget, 497
demand, 22–41, 498
   composite, 496
   derived, 183
   effective, 498
   factors affecting, 28–34, 39, 40, 500
   law of, 23, 24, 70, 172, 503
      exceptions to, 35
   legislation affecting, 34
   perfectly inelastic, 74
   schedule, 23, 24
   types of, 23, 25
demand and price, 28, 92
demand curves, 24–34, 36, 38, 39, 40, 132–5, 138, 143–4, 155–6, 171, 183, 498
   in equilibrium, 59–65, 92, 193–4
   kinked, 161–3, 166, 503
      in equilibrium, 162–3
   movement along, 27, 38–9, 505
   shift in, 27–8, 38–9, 508
demand function, 28
demand pull factors, 310, 498
demand schedule, 498
demography, 396, 498
density of population, 403, 498
dependency ratio, 407, 498
deregulation, 147, 368, 498
derived demand, 169, 206, 498
devaluation, 457–60, 498
developing countries, 380–394
direct intervention, 367
direct investment, 446, 498
direct taxation, 341–3, 498
diseconomies of scale, 502
   external, 105–6
   internal, 105
dominant firm model, 164
drive to maturity, 383
dumping, 433, 498

economic
   aims of government, 355–79
   development, 380–94, 498
   goods, 12–13, 498
   growth, 287–8, 380–94
      stages of, 382–3, 498
   laws, 6, 7, 498
   planning, 368
   policy, 265
   rent, 186, 226, 498
   statements, 10
   sustainability, 344, 498
   systems, 9
   theories, 5
   vulnerability, 381

Index

Economic and Monetary Union (EMU), 453–5
Economic Table, 377
economics, 498
   branches, 10
   of population, 395–417
economies of scale, 103–7, 142
   external, 104–5, 499
   internal, 103–4, 503
economy
   closed, 274
   open, 274
   shocks to, 285
education, 34
elasticity, 69–90, 498
   cross, *See* cross elasticity of demand (CED)
   of income *See* income elasticity of demand (YED)
   of price *See* price elasticity of demand (PED)
   of supply *See* price elasticity of supply (PES)
   importance of understanding, 81
emigration, 498
   economic consequences of, 407–8
employment, 308–23
enterprise, 221–8, 498
Enterprise Ireland, 316
enterprises
   small scale, 106–7
entrepreneurs
   importance of, 225–6
entrepreneurs' profits, 226
Equi-marginal Utility Principle, 15–8, 498
equilibrium, 59–65, 92, 133–5, 143, 193, 272, 366, 498–9
Essay on the Principle of Population, 413
euro interbank borrowed rate (Euribor), 499
European Central Bank (ECB), 236, 367, 480
European Commission, 468
European Court of Auditors, 469
European Court of Justice, 469
European Currency Unit (ECU), 453
European Economic Community (EEC), 453
European Investment Bank (EIB), 474–5, 499
European Monetary System (EMS), 453
European Parliament, 468
European Regional Development Fund (ERDF), 446, 472, 499
   functions of, 237–9
European Social Fund, 472, 499
European Structural Funds, 471–2
European Structural Policy, 471
European Union, 435, 438, 453, 465–81, 499
   expansion of, 391–2
   importance of, 466–8
   institutions of, 468–9
   objectives of, 466

exam technique, 492–5
exchange rate, 304, 305, 451–3, 499
   factors affecting, 455–6
   policy, 367–72, 499
   types of, 460
expenditure, 272, 345, 348
expenditure categories, 297
expenditure method, 259–60, 499
explicit costs, 93, 499
exporting, 430, 499
exports
   benefits of to the economy, 431–2
   factors affecting, 277–8
   increase in, 448–9
   visible, 430
externalities, 108, 499

factor markets, 8, 168–79, 499
factors of production, 7, 92, 170, 178, 181, 223, 256
   demand for, 170
fertility rate, 398, 500
FETAC, 104
fiduciary issue, 232, 500
final markets, 8, 500
financial account, 446, 500
fiscal drag, 332
fiscal policy, 301, 326, 367–72, 451, 500
fixed costs, 94–5, 97–101, 500
fixed exchange rate, 460, 500
floating exchange rate, 460, 500
Foreign Direct Investment (FDI), 317
   deterrents to, 432
   and China, 436
foreign exchange, 267, 444–64
free enterprise system, 9, 485–6, 500
   in Ireland, 488
free trade, 347, 377, 433, 500
   agreements (FTAs), 435, 438
Friedman, Milton, 251, 485
full employment, 309–10, 356–8, 500
fundamental change, 384

general government deficit, 334, 501
Giffen goods, 35, 37, 501
global economic system, 465–81
Gold Standard, 232, 456, 501
   collapse of, 453
goods
   addictive, 35
   complementary, 29, 79, 82, 497
   demand for, 28–9
   elastic, 71
   inelastic, 73
   inferior, 31, 37

normal, 30, 37, 506
relatively elastic, 71
relatively inelastic, 73
substitute, 29, 40, 82, 509
unitary elastic, 71
government
  budget, 324–54
  current budget, 331–4
  debt, 334–8
  economic objectives, 355–79
    conflicts between, 372
  expenditure, 325–34, 361, 449
  finances, 324–54
  intervention, 164, 184–5, 289, 325–7
    and free trade, 433
  performance, 298
  policy, 192, 202, 265, 322
  regulations, 34
  revenue, 213, 226, 282, 309
  spending, 268, 274, 334
  strategies, 375–6
greying population, 409–10
gross domestic product (GDP), 261–4, 334, 501
gross national income (GNI), 263–4, 501
gross national product (GNP), 213, 262–4, 384, 501
growth, 380–94

Harmonised index of consumer prices (HICP), 304, 501
Heavily Indebted Poor Countries Scheme, 473
high mass consumption, 383
household budget inquiry, 297, 305
human development index (HDI), 385, 501
human vulnerability, 381

IBEC, 368
ICTU, 368
IFA, 368
immigration, 501
  economic consequences of, 408
implicit cost, 93
imperfect competition *See* competition
importing, 430, 501
imports
  benefits of to the economy, 431
  factors affecting, 278, 282, 304, 305
  visible, 430
income, 9, 40, 272, 502
income effect, 31, 36–7, 38, 502
income elasticity of demand (YED), 84–6, 502
income method, 256–9, 502

indirect taxation, 341–2, 502
individual demand, 502
individual supply, 502
inductive research, 5–6, 502
industrial banks, 241, 502
industry, 117, 502
inelastic demand, 73, 133
inferior goods, 31, 37, 85, 502
infinite credit, 245–6
inflation, 186, 282, 293–307, 298, 310, 364, 502
  calculating, 294
  causes of, 299–300
  measuring, 294–6
  problems of, 302–3
  remedies for, 301
infrastructure, 185, 203
injection, 273
Inquiry into the Nature and Causes of the Wealth of Nations, 347
institutional unemploymemt, 502
interest, 206, 502
  rate of 207–8
interest rates, 186, 214–9, 247–8, 276
intermediate markets, 8
International Bank for Reconstruction and Development (IBRD), 472
International Centre for Settlement of Investment Disputes, (ICSID), 472
International Development Association (IDA), 472
International Finance Corporation (IFC), 472
International Monetary Fund (IMF), 453, 475–7, 479–80, 503
International Rescue Committee, 401
international trade, 418–43
  importance of to Irish economy, 429–30
international trade and elasticity, 81
investment, 210–3, 273, 290, 446, 503
  factors affecting, 211–2, 277, 282
  importance of, 212–3
invisible trade, 445–7, 503
Irish national debt, 335–7
iron law of wages, 186, 413

job-sharing, 316–7
joint demand, 503

Keynes, John Maynard, 214, 272, 283, 289, 304, 305, 356, 485
Keynesian Presentation of National Income, 285–6
Keynesian School, 483
Keynesian Theory, 214–8
kinked demand curve, 161–3, 166

Index

labour, 189–204, 503
   demand for, 190
   efficiency of, 198–99
   elasticity of demand for, 197–8
   factors affecting demand for, 190–1
   hoarding, 171, 503
   mobility, 192, 196–7
   supply, 185, 191–2, 202
   supply curves, 192–6
labour theory of value, 321, 347
land, 180–8, 503
   as a factor of production, 182
   demand for, 183
   economic characteristics of, 182
   factors influencing price of, 184
   MRP of, 183
Law of Absolute Advantage, 420–1, 503
   Assumptions of, 420
Law of Comparative Advantage (LOCA), 186, 421–6, 503
   assumptions/limitations of, 426
Law of Demand, 23, 70, 172, 503
   exceptions to, 35
Law of Diminishing Marginal Utility, 13–5, 18, 503
Law of Diminishing (Marginal) Returns (LDMR), 96, 101, 172, 426, 503
Law of Equi-marginal Returns, 15–7
Laws of International Trade, 420–5
leakage, 273, 449
Least Developed Countries (LDCs), 380–394, 503
   benefits of economic development to, 390
   characteristics of, 386
   costs of economic development to, 390
   investment funds to, 473
legal tender, 235, 503
legislation, 34, 142
lender of last resort, 241
life expectancy, 403, 503
limit pricing, 164
liquidity, 503
liquidity coverage ratio, 242
liquidity preference theory, 214–8, 290
liquidity trap, 217–8
literacy, 387–8
Live Register, 311, 503
loanable funds theory of interest rates, 213–4, 503
location of industries, 185
long run average cost curve (LRAC), 102–3, 106, 504
long run period, 92–3, 178

M1, 242, 504
M2, 242, 504
M3, 242, 504
Maastricht Treaty, 243, 453
macroeconomy, 356
macroeconomics, 10, 504
Malthus, Thomas, 413, 484
marginal cost (MC), 100, 109–13, 132
marginal efficiency of capital (MEC), 208, 504
   factors influencing, 208–9
marginal physical product (MPP), 172–5, 199, 207, 504
marginal propensity to consume (MPC), 275–6, 280, 283, 504
marginal propensity to import (MPM), 278, 282–3, 504
marginal propensity to save (MPS), 280–1, 283, 504
marginal propensity to tax (MPT), 280, 283, 504
marginal revenue (MR), 108–13, 132, 504
marginal revenue curve, 132, 171
marginal revenue productivity (MRP), 170–5, 178, 207, 504, 505
   and wage setting, 199–200
   of land, 183
   of the worker, 190
marginal utility (MU), 13, 504
market equilibrium *See* equilibrium
market force of supply, 43
market structures, 117
market time periods
   long run period, 92–3, 178
   short run period, 92–3
      costs, 95
markets, 7, 8
Marshall, Alfred, 5, 177–8, 485
Marshall Lerner Condition, 459, 505
Marshall-Lerner Law, 81
Marx, Karl, 321, 485
Marxists, 483
Mercantilists, 438–9, 482
merchant banks, 241, 505
microeconomics, 10, 505
MR *See* revenue
migration, 405
Mill, John Stuart, 201, 485
minimum reserve requirements, 505
mixed economy, 9, 489–90, 505
mobility of labour, 196–7
Model of Sales Maximisation, 165–6, 510
Monetarists, 484
monetary policy, 231, 238–9, 301, 367–72, 505
money, 229–53, 505
   characteristics of, 234
   forms of, 235
   functions of, 232–33

history of, 230–1
representative, 232
monopolist, 154–6
monopoly, 130, 141–9, 175, 505
   advantages of, 145
   characteristics of, 141
   demand curves in, 143–4
   disadvantages of, 145–6
   equilibrium of, 143
   prevention of, 178
   regulation of, 146
   sources of, 142
monopoly and price discrimination, 152
'Monthly Economic Bulletin', 345
Multilateral Investment Guarantee Agency (MIGA), 472–73
multiplier, 278–80, 289, 505
multiplier formula, 283, 505
Mun, Thomas, 439, 484

NAMA, 248–9, 505
National Average Family Shopping Basket, 297, 305
National Development Plan, 368
national debt, 335–7, 505
national income, 254–70, 272, 290, 505
   determination of, 271–92
   methods of calculating, 255–61
   measuring, 255
   statistics, 264–5
      limitations of, 265
National Recovery Plan, 351
National Treasury Management Agency (NTMA), 336–7, 344, 506
nationalisation, 148, 374
   of banks, 377–8
needs, 4
negative income effect, 31
Neo-classical School, 483
net factor income, 256, 505
net migration, 405, 506
net national product (NNP), 264, 506
Nevic, Adnan, 413
normal good, 30, 37, 84, 506
normal profit, 97, 506
North American Free Trade Agreement (NAFTA), 435, 437

occupational mobility, 197, 506
oligopoly, 158–67, 506
   characteristics of, 159–60
   collusion in, 163–4
   definition, 159
   kinked demand curve in, 161–3, 166

One Market, One Money, 453
open economy, 419, 506
opportunity cost, 4–5, 93, 506
optimum population, 397, 506
overpopulation, 396, 412, 506

participation rate, 192, 506
partnership agreements, 301
perfect competition *See* competition
Physiocrats, 377, 482
population, 191, 395–417
portfolio investment, 446, 506
positive income effect, 30
post office, 242
precautionary motive, 215–6
price, 70, 92, 294–6
price discrimination, 151–7, 507
   conditions necessary for, 152
   degrees of, 153–4, 156
price effect, 36
price elasticity of demand (PED), 71–81, 132, 178, 507
   and devaluation, 459
   and total revenue, 74
   degree of, 71
   factors affecting, 79–81, 499
price elasticity of supply (PES), 86–8
   factors affecting, 88, 500
price inflation *See* inflation
price leadership, 164
price stability, 303
prices and incomes policy, 368
primary liquidity ratio, 242, 507
Principle of Equi-marginal Utility, 15–17
Principles of Political Economy and Taxation, The, 186
private enterprise, 9
privatisation, 148, 351–2, 374–5, 507
production
   cost of, 92
   four factors of, 7
   importance of, 212
production/output method, 260–1
profit, 221–8
   maximising conditions, 112
profits, 110
   importance of in a market economy, 224
   normal, 224
   supernormal, 224
property
   prices, 184
protectionism, 434, 507
public service charges, 345–6, 364–6
pull forces, 405, 507

Index

Purchasing Power Parity Theory, 456–7
push forces, 405, 507

quantitative easing, 304
Quarterly National Houseold Survey (QNHS), 312
quasi economic rent, 507
Quesnay, François, 377, 484
quotas, 434–5, 507

ratchet economy, 196
real income, 507
real interest rate, 507
recession, 203
rent
   economic, 176–9
   quasi economic, 176–8
rent of ability, 226
research methods, 5, 6
restricting entry, 195
retail banks, 241
returns to scale, 106
revaluation, 458
revenue, 325–34, 345, 348
   average (AR), 108–12
      demand curve, 132–39, 143–44
   marginal (MR), 108–13, 132
      curve, 132, 171
   total (TR), 95, 108–11
Ricardo, David, 186, 484
risk, 223–4
   insurable, 223
   non-insurable, 223
risk-takers, 222
Roosevelt, Theodore, 309
Rostow, Walt, 382, 384

savings, 273, 298
   increase in, 281
Say, Jean Baptiste, 54, 484
Say's Law, 54, 508
schools of economic thought, 482–91
science, 3
shadow economy, 320, 496
short run average cost curve (SAC), 101–2
short run period, 92–3
   costs, 95
shut down point, 95
simple price index, 294–5
Single European Market (SEM), 471
small and medium sized enterprise (SME), 446
small scale enterprises, 106–7
Smith, Adam, 117, 338, 347, 484

social benefits, 107
social capital, 508
social costs, 107, 508
social policy, 508
Social Insurance Fund, 331
social science, 4
social welfare payments, 203, 309, 313, 349, 449
socialist system, 9
SOLAS, 104
specialisation, 427, 439–41
speculative motive, 215–6
Stages of Economic Growth: A Non-Communist Manifesto, 382
state borrowings, 334–5
statements, economic, 10
statutory minimum wage, 319, 508
Stuart, James, 439, 484
subsidisation, 34
subsistence wages theory, 186, 413, 508
substitution effect, 36–7, 38, 509
substitution of products, 299
supernormal profits (SNP), 133–4, 143, 226, 509
supply, 43–57
   decrease in, 48, 50
   factors affecting, 45–53, 500
      cost of production, 50
      limited capacity, 46
      minimum market price, 45
      no. of sellers, 53
      objectives of the firm, 52
      price, 48, 92
      price of related goods, 49
      producer surplus, 54
      taxation, 52
      state of technology, 51
      subsidies, 52
      unforeseen, 50
   fixed (perfectly inelastic), 47
   increase in, 48, 50
   price, 176–9, 509
   restrictions on
      by fixed supply, 47
      by limited capacity, 46
      by minimum market price, 45
   types of, 43
supply curves, 44–53, 55, 509
   in equilibrium, 59–65, 92
   labour, 192–6
   movement along, 47, 505
   shift in, 47–8, 508
supply function, 48
Supply Siders, 484

sustainable economic growth, 358–61
Sweezy, Paul, 161

Tableau Économique, 377, 484
take-off, 382
tariffs, 434, 509
tax avoidance, 343, 509
tax evasion, 343, 509
tax harmonisation, 343, 509
taxation, 34, 81, 192, 203, 276, 298, 309, 313–4, 338–47, 366
   canons of, 338–9, 347
   functions of, 340
   principles of, 339
   progressive, 341, 507
   regressive, 341, 507
   types of, 341
terms of trade, 425, 439, 509
Theory of Monopolistic Competition, 130
theory of non-profit maximising behaviour, 165
theory of rent, 186, 509
theory of surplus value, 321, 509
tier 1 capital, 509
time periods, 92
TR *See* revenue
total costs (TC), 95, 97–100, 110
total fertility rate, 398, 509
total output, 439
total utility (TU), 13
Towards 2016, 368
trade barriers, 434, 509
trade cycles, 286–7, 510
trade embargo, 435
trade union, 195, 201
trading blocs, 435–8
traditional society, 382
transactions motive, 215–6
transitional stage, 382
transfer earnings, 176–9, 510
transfer payment, 257, 284, 326, 510
Turgot, Jacques, 377, 484

UN Committee for Development Policy, 381
underemployment, 317, 510
underpopulation, 396, 510
unemployment, 203, 289, 510
   causes of, 312
   impact of, 313
   Marx's view of, 321
   methods of measuring, 311–2
   rise in, 314
   strategies for reducing, 314–6
   types of, 310–1
UNESCO, 387
UNICEF, 401
unitary elastic demand, 73
utility 12–3, 23, 92, 510
   marginal (MU), 13
   total (TU), 13
   units of (utils), 13, 16
utility theory, 177–8, 510

variable cost, 94–5, 99, 510
visible trade, 445–7, 510

wage
   cuts, 289
   drift, 196
   levels, 191
   negotiations, 298
   rates, 190, 195, 200–1, 203, 213
wage fund theory, 201, 510
wants, 4
wealth, 9, 255, 510
weighted price index, 295–6
wholesale banks, 241
workers
   categories of, 200–1
World Bank, 472–3, 480, 510
World Bank Group (WBG), 472
World Trade Organization (WTO), 436–7

YED *See* income elasticity of demand